The Foreign Exchange and
Money Markets Guide

WILEY FINANCE EDITIONS

The Foreign Exchange and Money Markets Guide

A Wiley Finance Edition

Julian Walmsley

John Wiley & Sons, Inc.

New York • Chichester • Brisbane • Toronto • Singapore

Copyright © 1992, Julian Walmsley

Published by John Wiley & Sons, Inc.

All rights reserved. Published simultaneously in Canada.

Library of Congress Cataloging-in-Publication Data

Walmsley, Julian.
    The foreign exchange and money markets guide / Julian Walmsley.
       p.   cm.—(Wiley finance editions)
    Includes index.
    ISBN 0-471-53104-9
    1. Foreign exchange—Handbooks, manuals, etc. 2. Money market--Handbooks, manuals, etc. I. Title. II. Series.
HG3851.W386   1992
332.4'5—dc20   91-30370

Printed in the United States of America

10 9 8 7 6 5 4 3 2 1

Printed and bound by Malloy Lithographing, Inc.

Preface

With the boundaries of the world opening, this book provides a simple practical guide to professional dealing in the world's money and foreign exchange markets. This expanded and updated version of an earlier, more limited book is as free of jargon as possible. The rapid growth of derivatives—futures, swaps, options, FRAs, SAFEs—made it necessary to update and expand the earlier book. There is also an increased emphasis on technical and charting trading methods, which are more common now than in the early 1980s.

Part 1 sets out a brief background framework introducing the basic nature of money and foreign exchange markets, the Euromarkets, the international framework in which these markets operate, and a brief guide to the prediction of rate movements. Part 2 explains basic money market calculations before looking at concepts of net present value, forward rate agreements, CD and bond calculations. Part 3 contains detailed calculations used in the foreign exchange markets: spot and forward calculations and cross-rates, broken date forwards, forward-forwards, cross-currency interest arbitrage, holiday and withholding tax adjustment calculations, and currency unit calculations (ECU, SDR). Part 4 discusses derivatives: financial futures, interest rate and currency swaps, and options. The latter topic, because of its complexity, is broken into two parts: a basic explanation of the theory including Black-Scholes and binomial models and arbitrage-free interest rate lattices, and a second chapter covering applications such as caps and floors, butterflies, bull spreads, and the like. Part 5 steps back from the detailed calculation methods to consider overall questions of risk and exposure—interest rates and foreign exchange movements—as well as the vital, but often overlooked, issue of settlement risk and procedures. The Appendices cover a number of secondary technical matters such as detailed EMS divergence indicator calculations, Islamic value dates, CME and LIFFE margin calculations.

Acknowledgments

A book like this is always the outcome of help given by many people over the years and I must begin by thanking all those from different countries and institutions who have taught me about their local markets or specialized areas. I must particularly acknowledge help and guidance in the options area from Desmond Fitzgerald and Jacques Pezier at Mitsubishi Finance, and all the help given me over the years by many former colleagues, too numerous to name individually, in the various foreign exchange dealing operations of Barclays around the world. I must also thank the following for kindly supplying information: Steve Pearson at the Chicago Mercantile Exchange Statistical Department, the CBOE, the Banque de France, Banque Nationale Suisse, Danmarks Nationalbank, Norges Bank, Oesterreichische National-bank, Reserve Bank of Australia, Reserve Bank of New Zealand, and the Saudi Arabian Monetary Agency. I am also grateful to those who read and commented on all or part of the manuscript: Adrian Swan at Barclays Swaps, Mike Whittaker and John Tierney at Gerrard & National Intercommodities, David Blocker at Mitsubishi Finance, Professor Peter Pope of Strathclyde University, Robert Armstrong at KPMG Peat Marwick, Adam Parkes of Nomura, and Gerry Morgan at the Bank of England. Any remaining errors are of course my sole responsibility. I am also grateful to Susan Kirshner of Discount Corporation of New York Futures for kindly arranging permission for me to use the graphics from a package they have developed called *The Options Position Manager* for the evaluation of risk and reward in futures and options portfolios. Finally, I must again thank my wife Jane for her patience and forbearance in accepting yet more lost weekends and evenings.

Contents

2 Money Market Calculations

3 Foreign Exchange Calculations

4 Derivatives

5 Risk Issues

PART 1 Markets

1 Money Markets

There is much needless mystery about money and foreign exchange markets. But, in fact, the basics are very simple and can be summed up in two common phrases: "Time is money" and "Nothing ventured nothing gained." In jargon, the time value of money and the risk/reward balance. Net present value calculations, forward interest rate differentials, cross-currency interest rate swaps, binomial option trees—these notions sound complex, but can be boiled down to simple concepts. I have tried to avoid needless jargon when writing this book, but sometimes, for the sake of brevity, it helps to use the "correct" technical term.

Despite the minimal use of jargon, we will spend a lot of time on fairly detailed analysis. It is all needed for the various specialist operations we will discuss. But we should never lose sight of two principles: First, whatever we believe an instrument or position is worth, the fact is that *any financial instrument is only worth what someone else will pay for it*. This applies particularly to the more complex instruments such as options. Second, despite all the electronic hardware that has been brought to bear on global financial markets, the market is still only a collection of people. It will reflect their moods, their hopes, and their fears. Even the most exactly calculated arbitrage position could be blown out of the water because the rest of the market suddenly goes crazy.

For example, I was in a trading room in New York during the early course of the Falkland Islands conflict. The market was tense because no one knew how things might go. A great deal depended on the carrier *Hermes* (the chief British naval asset in the conflict). So when the chief foreign exchange dealer suddenly shouted "They've sunk the *Hermes,*" and began selling sterling heavily, the pound weakened sharply. The market assumed we had inside information. Then we saw the source of the dealer's fears. At the bottom of the Telerate quote screen, a message flashed "Carrier lost . . . Carrier lost . . . Carrier lost," to tell users that the line carrying Telerate's signal had been lost. We laughed . . . an expensive laugh.

Academics tell us that the market is efficient and rational: perhaps, but not always. It is made up of people, and they are not always rational or well-informed. So although much of this book is spent on fairly precise calculations, we should not forget the human element.

THE U.S. MONEY MARKET

Let's begin with domestic markets, in which a nation's money is traded internally. In this first discussion, we will concentrate on the United States, because the US$ is the world's most widely traded currency. But later in the chapter, we will bring in relevant comparisons to other countries where practices differ.

It sometimes helps to think of the money market as if it were a giant hydraulic machine stored under the floor. Sticking up through the floor boards are a series of glass tubes filled with varying levels of water. They are labeled "One month," "Three months," . . . and so on representing the interest rates for each of several periods. An outsider looking at this hypothetical marketplace would only see the water level in each glass tube. But underneath the floor, borrowers drain water from the pipes, and savers pour water in. If you were to lift up the floor boards, you can see an intricate criss-cross network of pipes sucking fluid out of the machine and pumping it back in again.

What are the sources of demand that drain money out of the system? From where does it come to be pumped back in again? One large suction device is the government. Payments of tax to the government drain money out of the market into the chests of the Treasury, until the Treasury pays the money back into the system through its purchase of goods and services. Thus money is drained out of the system every year at tax time, which tends to push interest rates up.

Also draining money from the system is the demand for funds by corporations. If they borrow heavily from banks, banks must in turn borrow from the market. The net effect then depends on what is done with the money. If all corporations reinvested the proceeds of their short-term borrowing in long-term Treasury Bonds, relative interest rates would change. Short rates would rise and long rates would fall, until the money reemerged from the black hole of the Treasury in the form of extra spending. That money would find its way back into the hands of individuals and corporations and would be deposited back into the banks, thus bringing shorter term interest rates down again. So money markets are in a constant state of flux, as they handle the ebbs and flows of payments through each nation's banking system.

Let's put that a bit more prosaically, and put the money market in its wider context, by looking at what is called a *flow of funds table* for the United States (Table 1.1). This includes the flow of funds through the whole of the U.S. financial system, not just the money market, because the statistics do not separate the money market alone.

Here we can see that private households during this quarter were net borrowers to the tune of $220.2 billion. Nonfinancial businesses were, as a sector, almost in balance, borrowing $294.2 billion and on-lending $290.9 (of which, according to the detailed Federal Reserve tables, the bulk—about $230 billion—was purchases of Treasury and corporate bonds, in this particular quarter). Mortgage pools were in balance because their activity consists of buying loans that are financed with matching bonds. In this quarter the main net supplier of credit to the system was the private financial sector (of which, according to the detail, $103 billion came from insurance and pension funds, and $144 billion from "other").

An important channel through which money market flows are influenced is the foreign exchange market. This is less apparent in the United States, where the domestic money market is large in relation to the international market. But it can clearly be seen in the case of a country such as Switzerland. Inflows from abroad into a small country can swamp the domestic money market with excess liquidity. During the late 1970s, for example, foreign demand for Swiss francs was very strong because of the weakness of the dollar. The flow of money into Swiss francs pushed the euro-Swiss franc

Table 1.1 Direct and Indirect Sources of Funds to U.S. Credit Markets, 1989/Q2

	Borrowing	Lending
U.S. government & Federal Reserve	70.9	−8.2
Foreign	4.2	11.8
State & local government (net)	27.7	*
Households (net)	220.2	*
Nonfinancial business	294.2	290.9
Sponsored credit agencies	12.7	45.6
Mortgage pools	93.3	93.3
Private financial firms	27.1	316.8
TOTAL	750.3	750.2

*Not shown separately

Source: Adapted from Federal Reserve Bulletin, December 1989.

deposit market into negative interest rates. One had to *pay* a Swiss bank for the privilege of placing money with it. Subsequently, the Swiss government imposed a 10% per quarter term commission tax, so that foreigners were receiving *minus* 40% per annum on Swiss franc deposits. Yet because the Swiss franc appreciated by 50% during one year, such an operation was still worthwhile.

Conversely, if a currency is seen to be under pressure, funds will flow out of that currency into others that are perceived to be stronger. In the case of those currencies where exchange controls restrict the free movement of funds, such movements can have a spectacular effect. Until exchange controls in the United Kingdom were lifted, pressure on sterling could produce overnight or very short-term euro sterling interest rates in excess of 100%. The author was present at one occasion when euro-French francs were lent out at a rate in excess of 5000% overnight. Here, speculators were borrowing a currency that was perceived to be about to devalue, and switching the proceeds into other currency. They hoped to repay the loan in devalued French francs.

A related effect arises when the central bank intervenes to support, or alternatively to lower, the value of its currency. If the central bank intervenes in *support* of its currency, it buys the domestic currency, and sells foreign exchange. Thus, the amount of domestic currency in circulation declines, which tends to push up domestic interest rates. Conversely, if it intervenes to *lower* the value of its currency, it supplies domestic currency to the market. Thus the supply of domestic currency in the hands of the market rises, tending to push down interest rates. Because the US$ is the most widely traded currency in the world (largely because professional foreign exchange traders usually trade the US$ as one side of their deal), the net effect on the U.S. money markets is that there is a constant swirl of funds into and out of the Federal Reserve and the dollar holdings of other central banks, resulting from the ebb and flow of foreign exchange transactions. (The technical effects of these transactions are analyzed in more detail in Chapter 3.)

Another set of effects on money market rates can be the flow into and out of other non-money-market participants. The Treasury has already been mentioned, but another example could be a major stock market issue. Again, this is less relevant to the United States. But in the United Kingdom, for example, large privatization issues such as British Telecom have led to significant money market effects on occasion. Investors subscribing to the issue wrote checks that then flowed though the clearing system to produce substantial short-term distortions in the marketplace. Likewise, there are seasonal effects on the money market for holidays such as Christmas, or Easter, when the public generally withdraws cash in the form of notes and coin from the banking system. This tends to drain funds from the money market, which then return after the holiday. Also, any interruption in the process of clearing checks for settlement can have money market effects. If the planes flying from Chicago to New York with checks for clearance are held up by fog, then the amount of *float* in the U.S. financial system briefly expands, until the checks are finally cleared. This tends to push interest rates down, in the absence of countervailing intervention by the Federal Reserve.

SUBMARKETS: FEDERAL FUNDS, REPOS, TREASURY BILLS, AND COMMERCIAL PAPER

So far, we have talked of the money market as if it were a single entity. This is not, in fact, the case. In most countries, the money market consists of a series of interconnected pools of money.

The most important submarket in the United States is that for *Federal funds* (Fed funds). By definition, Federal funds are balances held at the Federal Reserve. A bank that holds such a balance can settle a claim on it by another bank through same day transfer. It can arrange for that other bank's account to be credited with immediately available funds. Therefore, Fed funds play a central role in the U.S. money market. They are the final means by which banks settle debits and credits with each other.

Another reason why Fed funds are so important is that banks are required by the Federal Reserve to hold a minimum average balance in their reserve account at the Federal Reserve over the week—Wednesday to Wednesday. The minimum average balance is based on the total deposits held by the bank or depositary institution during the current settlement week.

Most federal fund transactions are for overnight maturity. This is done mainly because the amount of excess funds that a given lending bank holds varies daily in an unpredictable way. Transactions for longer periods also occur, although more rarely. Fed funds traded for periods other than overnight are referred to as *term Fed funds.*

Because of their central role in the financial system, the interest rate payable on Fed funds is a key indicator of U.S. financial policy. The market watches the Fed funds rate like a hawk, to see if there has been any change in official policy. A change in the Fed funds rate is generally regarded as signaling a change in Federal Reserve monetary policy (unless it is caused by technical factors beyond the Fed's control, such as unpredicted changes in bank reserves).

Another important submarket is the market for *repurchases.* This arises primarily from the financing requirements of bank and nonbank dealers who are trading in government bonds, CDs, and bankers acceptances. Much of their trading activity is financed by borrowing. The borrowings are secured by the assets purchased with the borrowed funds. The normal technique is as follows. The dealer finds a corporation, money market fund or other investor who has funds to invest overnight. The dealer sells them, say, $5 million of securities for roughly $5 million, which is paid in Federal funds to his or her bank by the investor's bank against delivery of the securities sold. At the same time, the dealer agrees to repurchase these securities the next day at a slightly higher price. Thus, the buyer of the securities is in effect making the dealer a one-day loan secured by the obligations sold to him. The difference between the purchase and sales prices on the repo transaction is the interest the investor earns on his loan. Alternatively, the purchase and sale prices in a repo transaction may be identical; in that case, the dealer pays the investor some explicit rate of interest.

The Federal Reserve is heavily involved in the repo market as part of its open market operations (discussed in the next section). The Fed buys Treasury bonds from the key market-makers—called *primary dealers*. The purchase is coupled with a commitment by the primary dealer to buy the bonds back tomorrow at a slightly higher price—the difference being effectively overnight interest. The repo is in fact a loan by the Federal Reserve to the primary dealer, but it is a loan secured on the Treasury bond. Thus it is considered a very safe investment, and the Federal Reserve arranges repos not only for itself but also for its "customers," which are other central banks whose currency reserves are held in U.S. dollars. (The use of repos as a tool of monetary policy is discussed next.) The Fed and the primary dealers are by no means the only players in the market, which is huge. Municipalities, banks, insurance companies, and corporations all use the market for short-term liquid investments. A survey by the Securities Investor Protection Corporation (SIPC) in November 1988 found a total of $755 billion outstanding (but of that an unknown amount would be double counting).

The Fed funds and repo markets are essentially for overnight money: longer-term Fed funds (term Feds) and repos (term repos) do exist but are much less common. For longer periods, investors use other instruments. The *primary market* consists of trading in newly issued instruments, and the *secondary market* consists of trading in the instruments after the primary market is ended. The distinction is more important in the bond market, but applies also to short-term money markets. The volume of secondary market activity varies from instrument to instrument. An indication of the level of trading in different instruments is given in Figure 1.1 and Table 1.2. It is confined to statistics reported by primary dealers, but gives a good overall indication of activity in the market as a whole.

As Table 1.2 shows, Treasury bills—bills issued by the U.S. government with a maturity of up to one year—are a very important part of the market. The very high quality of this "paper" (the general term for any tradeable debt) means that the market for it is very large and liquid: that is, large amounts can be traded in a single trade without difficulty. Blocks of $50 to 100 million in a single transaction present no problem. There is also a market for trading Treasury bills before they are actually issued—the *when issued* or *wi* market. The wi market trades bills once they have been auctioned but before settlement takes place. It is also possible to trade bills before the auction, sometimes called the *wiwi* market.

Treasury bonds and notes are issued for longer maturities—up to 30 years—and although they are closely linked to the money markets are really

US$bn. daily average trading volume

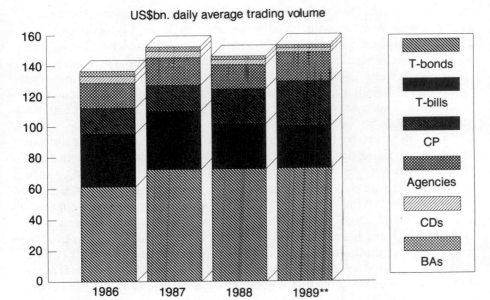

Figure 1.1   Primary dealers.

a separate market. Federal agency securities are bonds issued by agencies of the U.S. government such as the Government National Mortgage Association (GNMA) and again are part of the wider capital markets rather than the money markets as such.

A key part of the U.S. money market, which has grown enormously during the 1980s (partly because of the troubles of the American banking system) is *commercial paper* (CP). The CP market is now larger than that for Treasury bills in terms of outstanding volumes though, as Table 1.2 shows,

Table 1.2   U.S. Primary Dealers: Transactions (US$m Daily Average)

	1986	1987	1988	1989[†]
Treasury bills	34247	37924	29387	27667
Treasury bonds, etc.[††]	61197	72126	72236	72603
Federal agency securities	16747	18084	15903	19193
CDs	4355	4112	3369	2677
BAs	3272	2965	2316	2086
CP	16660	17135	22927	29145
Futures	10486	12196	12322	11441
Forwards*	9706	11319	10103	10730

*Forward transactions in U.S. Treasury and Federal agency securities.
[†]September.
[††]Excluding repos.
Source: Federal Reserve Bulletin, December 1989.

secondary market trading is about equal. Commercial paper consists of a short-term promissory note, usually maturing in 30 days or less, issued by a large corporation. Because of its short maturity, CP is widely regarded as a very safe investment for short-term funds. Commercial paper is generally issued on demand in response to the needs of investors, on a continuous basis. To sell commercial paper, a company must agree to be "rated" by a rating agency such as Moody's or Standard & Poor's who assess the credit quality and rate the CP accordingly.

This is an expensive and time-consuming process and for smaller sums of money many firms use the *bankers' acceptance* (BA) market. A firm shipping goods, say from the United States to Germany, might agree to take payment in the form of a bill drawn on the German importer. Once it has received the bill, it takes it to its U.S. banker who, in exchange for a commission, agrees to "accept" it: if the German firm does not pay, the bank will. Once the bill has been accepted by the bank, it becomes a high-quality instrument (assuming the bank's name is of high quality). The bill can be sold to investors. The BA is now backed by the German firm, the accepting bank, and in the last resort by the goods being shipped. Thus it is a very safe investment and BA's usually trade at interest rates below commercial paper, which is backed only by the promise to pay of the issuing firm. However, the BA market has stagnated while the CP market has grown: in 1984 the CP market totaled $237 billion against $78 billion of BAs, while in June 1989 the figures were $503 and $64 billion respectively. This is partly because the Federal Reserve rules restrict "eligible" BAs (those eligible for rediscount at the Fed) to transactions involving imports or exports, or the storage of goods. Commercial paper, by contrast, can be used to meet any financing needs.

An important short-term market is that for *certificates of deposit* (CDs). Certificates of deposit are issued by banks and are available in maturities ranging from as short as 14 days to as long as five or even seven years. The bulk of the market is usually under six months in maturity. In recent years, in the domestic U.S. market, the CD has been overtaken by the *deposit note,* an instrument resembling a corporate bond with a minimum maturity of 18 months (thus avoiding a reserve requirement) and usually paying a fixed rate. (If the bank wants to pay a floating rate, it will issue a floating rate deposit note, or it will do an *interest rate swap.* It commits itself to paying a floating rate to someone in exchange for that party paying it a fixed rate. The fixed rate income on the swap covers the fixed cost on the deposit note, leaving the bank paying a floating rate on the combined package of note and swap. Swaps are explained in detail in Chapter 15). A related instrument to the deposit note is the *medium term note,* which is really an extension of the commercial paper market to longer maturities.

While so far we have talked about trading assets and liabilities that will appear somewhere on a bank's or corporation's balance sheet, there is an important set of influences on trading in the money market that comes from trading in off-balance-sheet instruments, commonly known as derivatives

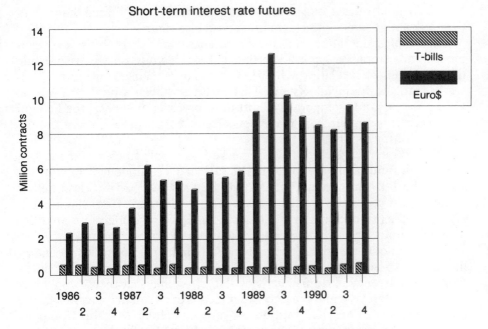

Figure 1.2 Chicago Mercantile Exchange turnover.

(discussed in Part 4). As well as interest rate swaps, these include financial futures and interest rate options. Trading in the financial futures markets, in particular, is of such volume that sometimes it will drive the "cash" or on-balance sheet markets. U.S. trading in money-market related futures is concentrated on the Chicago Mercantile Exchange, which has contracts based on Treasury bills and on Eurodollar deposits. As Figure 1.2 shows, the latter dominates trading (although in the early days it was the Treasury bill contract which was all-important):

The interest rate swap market (see Chapter 15) is closely linked both with the cash money market and the futures markets. When the range of Eurodollar futures contracts was extended out to three years from two years, the Exchange stated that this was partly at the request of the interest-rate-swap trading community. The market for forward rate agreements (see Chapter 6) is less important in the United States than in London but is another area linking the money markets to off-balance-sheet trading.

OPEN MARKET OPERATIONS

For many reasons, central banks sometimes want to adjust either the supply of money or the level of interest rates. They have available to them a number of techniques to do this. Different methods are used in different markets.

We will begin by describing those commonly used in the United States, and then talk about some of the techniques used elsewhere.

The simplest operation consists of a purchase of Treasury bills or government bonds from the banks. The banks' holdings of cash will rise, while their holdings of securities will fall. There is a permanent injection of reserves into the financial system. This might not always be desirable: the system may be only temporarily short of reserves. In that case, the Federal Reserve will use repurchase agreements (repos); and, in fact, repos are the main operating tool of the Fed.

The Fed intervenes on the "open market" to supply funds to the market, or to drain funds from the market. The primary technique by which this is done is the daily "go-around," at around 11:30 AM. The Fed decides whether it wants to supply funds to the market or to drain funds from the market. Having made this decision, it will do either a repurchase operation, in order to supply funds, or a reverse purchase, in order to drain.

The effect of these operations will depend on the reserve ratios on banks' liabilities. To see why this is so, consider an imaginary country called Home. Its currency is Home currency (HC). Assume that there is only one bank, call it Barclays, and the only other means of payment is cash. Suppose the government prints HC 1 million and pays it to Home Machine Company in exchange for machinery. HMC pays the cash into Barclays, whose balance sheet now becomes (assuming nil balances to start with):

	Liabilities	Assets
HMC deposit	HC 1 million	HC 1 million cash

Suppose that the government requires Barclays to hold 10% of its assets in cash. Then Barclays can lend the other HC 900,000 to General Motors Company (GM). They proceed to mark a credit limit for GM who draw this down, by taking out cash. Barclays' balance sheet is now:

Liabilities	Assets
HMC deposit HC 1 million	HC 100,000 cash
	HC 900,000 GM loan

GM hands the cash over to Shell in exchange for oil. Shell deposits the cash with Barclays:

Liabilities	Assets
HMC deposit HC 1 million	HC 1 million cash
Shell deposit HC 0.9 million	HC 0.9 million GM loan

Barclays can now lend 90% of HC 0.9 million, that is, HC 0.81 million to ICI. They will pay the money to Ford, who will deposit it with Barclays, and so on.

In fact, the system keeps expanding until the original HC 1 million in cash represents 10% of Barclays' total assets, which will total HC 10 million. At this point, Barclays won't lend any more money. If it did, the ratio of cash to assets would fall below 10%, and the government would object. In other words, the 10% ratio means that an extra HC 1 million of cash can support deposits of HC 10 million. The deposits created are 10 times the original cash. If the reserve ratio is R, the multiplier is $1 \div R$. In our example, $1 \div 0.1$ equals 10.

It follows that if we lower the reserve ratio to 5%, the multiplier rises from 10 to 20. The smaller the reserve ratio, the bigger the multiplier. Equally, a draining of reserves from the system will force it to shrink by the same ratio. So, open market operations can be a very powerful force by which the central bank can influence the level of the banking system's activity.

There is one important point about reserve requirements: Their effect on banking systems depends critically on how they are structured. The U.S. system has traditionally been to require 3% reserves to be held on transaction and time deposits (though this was relaxed in 1990 to help the U.S. banking system recover from its difficulties), which must be placed in an account with the Fed that pays no interest. This factor led to the growth of the huge Eurodollar market, which is exempt from reserve requirements.

An example may show the effects. Consider a bank with the alternative of taking a deposit in the United States or of booking the deposit through its London branch in the form of a Eurodollar deposit (see Chapter 2). Suppose that the domestic deposit attracts a 3% reserve requirement; suppose that the reserves must be held in the form of noninterest-bearing deposits at the Federal Reserve.

Assume the deposit is for $100. If the deposit is taken in the United States, only $97 is available for on-lending: the other $3 must be placed with the Federal Reserve, earning no interest. Suppose the bank pays 10% on the deposit. The $97 must be lent out at $10/.97 = 10.31\%$ to cover the extra costs of the sterilized reserve balance of $3: that is, if rates are at 10%, the reserves cost 0.31%. A bank that does not have to hold reserves can afford to bid, say, 1/8% better and lend 1/8% cheaper, beating the U.S. bank by 0.25%, and still have a profit margin of 0.06%. (See Figure 1.3.) This fact has spawned a multitrillion dollar market, the Euromarket, discussed in Chapter 2.

Open market operations, then, depend on reserve requirements for their effectiveness. But the interaction of reserve ratios and other controls can sometimes have unpredictable results because of the complexity and sophistication of today's financial markets. Accordingly, open market operations are not always as simple, nor as powerful, as the pure theoretical model would indicate.

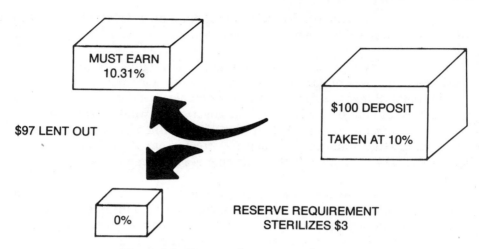

Figure 1.3   Impact of reserve requirements.

Still, they do give a flexible and effective way of steering the markets. Each day, the Fed enters the market to undertake these daily smoothing operations. Hence the common cry in the dealing room at 11:30 AM New York time or thereabouts, "Fed does repo" or "Fed does reverses." (A further refinement is that the Fed can operate in the market on behalf of its customers, or on behalf of the Federal Reserve System. The two are referred to as customer repo and system repo, respectively. The latter is thought to have policy significance whereas the former, which is an operation by the Fed on behalf of other central banks who want to invest their reserves in dollars, is not thought to have policy significance.)

OTHER TOOLS OF MONETARY POLICY

If the Fed wants to make a more permanent adjustment to the level of bank reserves, it can do so in one of two ways. It can offer to buy or sell Treasury bonds on an outright basis, rather than on a repurchase or resale basis where the operation will unwind; alternatively, and much more rarely, it may move to alter the level of its reserve requirements. The former operation is more common: usually, the Fed will signal to the market that it is willing to buy certain amounts of government bonds. (Often referred to in the market as a "coupon pass," meaning that the Fed is making a pass though the market to buy coupon-bearing government bonds. A similar operation on Treasury bills is referred to as a bills pass.)

Altering reserve requirements is a much more fundamental step, which the Fed takes only rarely. In 1980, for example, the Fed raised its "marginal reserve requirements" by 3%. Rises in bank borrowing were penalized by this method, which was an attempt to squeeze the domestic credit growth rate. Since that time, changes in reserve requirements have rarely been used as a element of monetary policy, since they have widespread and often distorting effects. In December 1990, however the Fed released its reserve requirements on time deposits to encourage banks to lend.

Another means by which the Federal Reserve supplies funds to the banking system is through its so-called *discount window.* This is the facility whereby the Fed, as *lender of last resort,* stands ready to supply funds to any member of the Federal Reserve System who needs them. A bank which is experiencing temporary financing difficulties, such as Continental Illinois in May 1984, may apply to the Federal Reserve for short-term assistance. Technically, the assistance is provided by a loan from the Fed against security of instruments that are eligible for rediscount at the Federal Reserve, such as eligible banker's acceptances, Treasury bills, or other high quality short-term monetary instruments. The discount window does not, however, form part of the normal routine monetary policy tools. This is because it is kept only for specific crisis requirements, and to a lesser extent for specific seasonal needs of certain agricultural or other banks.

In general, the senior management of most U.S. banks display a universal reluctance to borrow from the Fed unless they absolutely must. They prefer to keep a good record with the Fed, so that in time of trouble there will be no question of their being able to get help if they need it. Since borrowing at the discount window is a very cheap source of finance, there is some temptation to use the discount window as a cheap borrowing method: but the Fed regulates this strictly, and is not slow to indicate its displeasure if it feels that a bank is abusing the facility. In consequence, senior management are very wary of using the facility unless there is a very good reason.

Other central banks use similar tools to the Fed, but the balance of usage varies. (See the discussion of monetary policy in certain countries that follows.) The repurchase agreement is widely used, but nowhere is it so widely used as in the United States. Most central banks use repos on a longer term basis than daily. For example, since 1985 the Deutsche Bundesbank has regularly used repo agreements for 28- or 29-day periods. As an example, on October 9, 1990, the Bundesbank set a new tender for a 28-day security repurchase agreement, offering banks liquidity at variable bid rates. Banks had to make their bids on that day, with funds allocated to accounts the following day. Repurchase was fixed for November 7. The facility replaced an earlier facility totaling DM 23.1 billion, which had been fixed at rates of 7.95 to 8.10%.

Such agreements are normally offered weekly, and two-month repurchase tenders are executed also, usually at the beginning and middle of each month. To supplement repos, the Bundesbank also uses other open market techniques. One is the sale of very short-term Treasury bills at rates between its discount rate and the repo rate in order to prevent an excessive fall in day-to-day rates.

The Bank of Canada continuously uses repos with money market jobbers (the group of investment dealers authorized to enter into such agreements); they are called Purchase and Resale Agreements (PRAs). If the Bank wishes to offset unwarranted short-term pressure on rates, it may initiate Special PRAs in amounts and at rates of its choosing. If the Bank wants to drain funds, it will do Sale and Repurchase Agreements (SRAs).

The Bank of England, by contrast, tends not to use repurchases that often. It normally manages the money market by short-term operations though specialist firms (the "discount houses" and certain others) trading in short-term money market instruments to whom it will lend funds overnight, or to whom it sells Treasury bills to drain funds. Repurchase agreements are occasionally used on a medium-term basis for a month or more, if there is expected to be a unusual seasonal drain on liquidity, or some other special situation.

Open market operations in Japan tend to focus on purchases of bills by the Bank of Japan: for example on January 28, 1991, the Bank of Japan injected JPY 1.10 trillion into the market by buying a total of JPY 1.1 trillion of bills and recalling JPY 90 billion of outstanding loans. It offered to buy JPY 150 billion in Treasury bills under repurchase agreements starting January 30 and maturing March 6.

Activity in the Australian money market is similar to that in the United Kingdom, with a group called "authorized dealers" who function as the main conduit for the Reserve Bank of Australia's money market operations. The authorized dealers absorb the ebbs and flows or the banking system's fund needs. In turn they deal with the Reserve Bank in Treasury securities, or borrow money directly under the "lender of last resort" facility. The Reserve Bank of Australia and the Reserve Bank of New Zealand also use repurchases fairly regularly (they are often called sellbacks in Australia and New Zealand).

Elsewhere, for example in Sweden, on January 9, 1991, the Sveriges Riksbank used a SEK6 billion reverse repurchase offer to drain liquidity from the Swedish money market, after similar reverse repurchases from December 19 to 27 and December 27 to January 2. In Italy, an example might be the ITL 6.5 trillion tender for repurchases from January 25 to February 1, 1991.

Repurchase agreements depend for their functioning on banks holding sufficient quantities of eligible bonds. In Norway, for example, changes in reserve requirements in late 1986 meant that banks shed their holdings of Treasury bills and were compelled to hold certain volumes of government paper. As result, repurchase agreements have not been used as an instrument as liquidity control since 1987, their place being taken by fixed-rate loans by the central bank (F-loans), which are distributed by auction. In addition, liquidity is also managed by central bank purchases of certificates of deposit, foreign exchange swaps, and overnight loans (D-loans).

Foreign exchange swaps are an important means of liquidity management in a number of countries, particularly those where the foreign exchange market is large in relation to domestic money markets, such as Switzerland

and The Netherlands, but also in larger countries such as Germany. During 1989, for example, the Bundesbank conducted seven foreign exchange swap transactions equivalent to DM 2.2 billion with domestic banks in order to drain liquidity. The mechanics are laid out in Chapter 3.

Following this brief survey of central bank monetary policy tools, we turn to a short comparative survey of major money markets outside the United States.

THE UNITED KINGDOM

Traditionally, the core of the U.K. money market was the "discount market." This consisted of a group of discount houses, who were the only counterparties with whom the Bank of England would deal in its domestic money market operations. The bank would buy and sell Treasury bills, eligible bills issued by U.K. local authorities, and eligible bank bills with these firms. In turn, the discount houses absorbed the ebb and flow of commercial banks' funding needs. If they had surplus funds, the commercial banks could use them to increase their deposits with discount houses (usually "at call"), or buy money-market instruments from them. Likewise, where banks were short of funds, they could recall their call money loans from the discount houses, or sell paper to the houses. In exchange for their standing continuously ready to make markets in these instruments, the discount houses benefited from the privilege of access to the Bank as "lender of last resort."

After the "Big Bang" that reformed the London financial markets in 1986, the Bank of England in 1988 widened the discount market to include those commercial banks or other financial institutions who wished to take part in the market. Institutions accepted by the Bank as dealing counterparties were offered a direct dealing relationship with the Bank in eligible bills (bills eligible for rediscount at the Bank); borrowing facilities at the Bank; and facilities to borrow and lend gilt-edged stock. In exchange for these privileges, these firms undertook to offer callable deposit facilities and bids and offers of eligible bills to the market continuously, as well as to take part in the weekly underwriting of the Treasury bill tender.

The primary instruments of the Bank of England's money market policy are open market operations, conducted on a daily basis. The normal daily procedure is for the Bank to make a forecast of the money market's overall position, that is, whether it expects to have to inject or drain reserves—about 9:45 AM. The estimate is published on the news screens, for example, Reuters Monitor page RTCA—with a breakdown of the main contributory factors. If a very large shortage is forecast, the Bank may call for an early round of offers of eligible bills from the discount market and other institutions with which the Bank has agreed dealing facilities.

By convention, the banks have until noon to withdraw callable funds from the discount houses. By noon, the Bank is in a position to know the maximum probable shortage. A fresh forecast is made, and published if it is significantly different. At this point, the Bank will—if there is a shortage—normally call for offers of eligible bills. If there is a surplus, then, unless it is very large, the Bank waits until around 2:00 PM when it will invite bids for Treasury bills of appropriate maturities. If, after this, a discount house finds itself short of funds, it may borrow on a secured basis at 2:45 PM direct from the Bank. Interbank dealing continues until 3:00 PM when the Town Clearing (see Chapter 21) begins. If the Bank forces the discount houses to borrow for a minimum period rather than overnight, it is usually taken as a signal that it wishes to keep interest rates high.

There is a wide range of other participants in the London money market, particularly from overseas. The domestic sterling money market is in fact considerably smaller than the main money market in London, the Euro-market (see Chapter 2); thus the domestic market is very closely integrated into the international ebbs and flows of the currency markets, particularly since the abolition of exchange controls in 1979, and even more so since the entry of the United Kingdom into the exchange rate mechanism of the European Monetary System (see Chapter 4). The level of U.K. interest rates is therefore very strongly influenced by the strength or otherwise of sterling.

An interesting confirmation of this point and a glimpse into the type of trading on the London money markets came in the form of an article in the Bank of England Quarterly Bulletin in May 1990, on the role of money-market brokers in London. It reported the turnover of "listed brokers" (those approved by the Bank to do business in London) in their major markets, including sterling deposits (Table 1.3 and Figure 1.4). It is noticeable that the

Table 1.3   Listed Brokers' Turnover, 1988–1990 in £ Billion

	Foreign Exchange (1)	Foreign Currency Deposits (2)	Sterling Deposits (2)	FRAs, OTC Options, Interest Rate Currency Swaps (3)
1988 Q2	3142	1174	541	129
Q3	3274	1426	591	157
Q4	2957	1337	577	176
1989 Q1	3514	1460	586	299
Q2	4036	1595	565	377
Q3	4114	1612	631	352
Q4	4074	1746	656	392
1990 Q1	4820	1827	664	509

(1) includes spot, swaps, and outright forwards.
(2) includes turnover in commercial bills, certificates of deposit, commercial paper, U.K. local authority debt with an original maturity of up to five years, and other public sector debt with an original maturity of up to one year.
(3) broken down further in Figure 1.5.
Source: Adapted from Bank of England Quarterly Bulletin, May 1990.

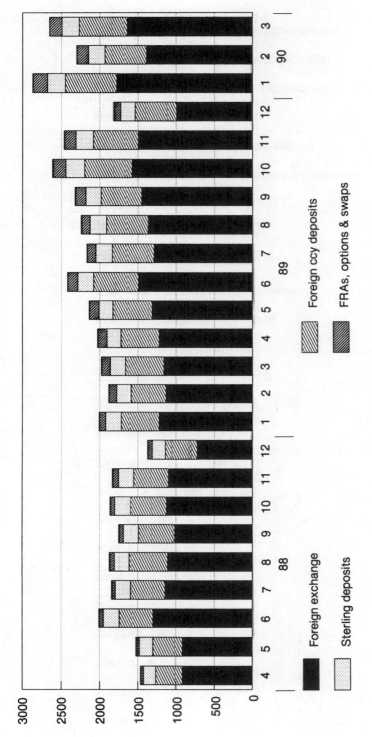

Figure 1.4 London markets listed brokers' turnover 1988–90.

Foreign exchange
Sterling deposits
Foreign ccy deposits
FRAs, options & swaps

19

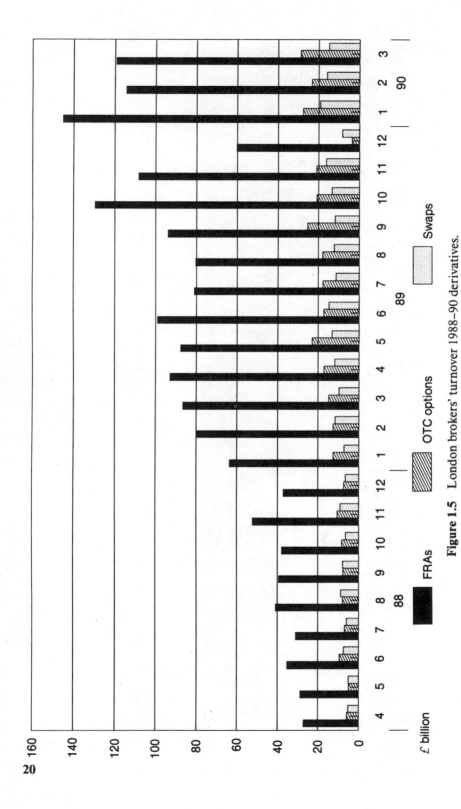

Figure 1.5 London brokers' turnover 1988–90 derivatives.

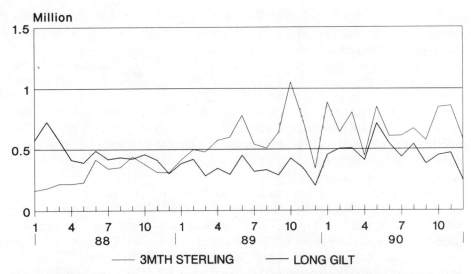

Figure 1.6   Sterling interest rate futures contract volume 1988–90.

volume of activity in foreign currency deposits is three times the volume of domestic sterling activity.

The same survey also provided an interesting insight into the growth of the derivatives markets (see Chapters 14 to 17) in London during this period; a major proportion of this activity is conducted in foreign currency, but forward rate agreements (FRAs), over-the-counter (OTC) options, in the form of caps, floors, and collars (see Chapter 17), and interest rate swaps all now play an integral part in the domestic sterling money market (Figure 1.5).

Finally, another important set of influences on the domestic U.K. money market is the market for financial futures (see Chapter 14). Financial futures contracts based on three-month sterling deposits were introduced in London in 1982; outside the ambit of the money market but closely linked there is also significant trading in a futures contract based on British government bonds (gilt-edged bonds). Figure 1.6 shows the level of recent activity in both contracts, and highlights the relative stagnation of the gilt contract, caused by a contraction in U.K. government debt outstanding.

GERMANY

In relation to the size of the economy, the German money market is fairly small and underdeveloped. It is predominantly an interbank market in which financial institutions trade central bank balances in a manner similar to the U.S. Fed funds market. Three main types of money-market paper are available in Germany: Treasury bills (Schatzwechsel), discount Treasury paper (Unverzinsliche Schatzanweisungen—USchatze), and prime acceptances. It was only in 1986 that the Bundesbank permitted the issuance of certificates of deposit by banks. The Bundesbank is directly involved as a counterparty in the vast majority of money-market transactions and thus directly controls rates on money-market paper.

The Bundesbank has kept tight control of the domestic financial situation, even after the 1985–1986 liberalization: it made CDs and short-term bank bonds subject to reserve requirements, and objected to the introduction of money-market mutual funds. Another inhibiting factor in the market was the turnover tax that stifled the growth in short-term money-market paper: this was lifted at the start of 1991, along with the legal restrictions inhibiting the development of commercial paper. The money market may now start to develop much more freely.

A second positive move in this area was the move, at the start of July 1990, to redefine Frankfurt Interbank Offered Rate (FIBOR). The traditional version of FIBOR was based on a 30/360 day year (see Chapter 6) and ran from today, while Deutschemark LIBOR was based on actual/360 and ran from the spot date, two business days ahead. When a major federal entity (Deutsche Bundesbahn) raised a floating rate note based on LIBOR rather than FIBOR, it was felt the time had come to bring FIBOR in line with international market practices.

The market for derivatives is also relatively limited, in that the Deutsche Termin Borse (the German financial futures market) only began operations in 1990 (although a lively market exists in London on LIFFE for the trading of futures and options on three-month DEM deposit rates and German government bonds). Again, however, the market should benefit from the creation of the DTB and other initiatives currently underway to foster its development.

Treasury money-market paper is issued by the federal government, federal railways, federal post office, and the *Lander* (provincial) governments after consultations with the Bundesbank. Such paper is called *financing paper* because its purpose is to finance the needs of the issuers. In contrast, *mobilization paper* is issued by the federal government at the request of the Bundesbank for the Bundesbank's open market purposes and is not dependent on the federal government's need for funds. If mobilization paper has been issued to its maximum limit the Bundesbank may request the government to issue *liquidity paper.*

The Bundesbank, which is legally independent of the German government and not obliged to follow the latter's instructions, has a very wide range of policy instruments with which to control domestic money markets. These include minimum reserve requirements, rediscount quotas, Lombard credit, open market securities operations and foreign exchange transactions. In addition, it can fix the level of discount and Lombard rates and repurchase rates.

Minimum reserve requirements are set by the Bundesbank on a long-term basis, that is, they are rarely changed. *Rediscount quotas* are also set on a long-term basis; they are the quotas fixing the amount of paper which the Bundesbank will rediscount for each individual bank. The global total is changed only rarely and usually in line with the perceived growth of the financial system as a whole; however, changes in the rediscount quota can sometimes signal a fundamental change in the Bundesbank's monetary policy.

Lombard credit represents loans granted by the Bundesbank to banks to overcome temporary liquidity squeezes. Technically it takes the form of a loan against specified collateral, as distinct from the rediscount facility where the Bundesbank buys paper from the bank. From time to time, the Bundesbank shuts off supply of credit via the Lombard facility or restricts access; it has also provided "special" Lombard credit (notably in 1973–1974 and 1981) where loans are made on restrictive terms. Normally, however, Lombard credit is not limited as to quantity, unlike the discount facility, which is restricted by rediscount quotas.

As we said earlier in the chapter, repurchase agreements form the Bundesbank's main technique for day-to-day liquidity management. They are in two forms: fixed rate (volume tender) and variable rate. In a fixed rate tender, the Bundesbank fixes the interest rate in advance and invites bids from banks. The banks say how much paper they want to sell to the Bundesbank at that rate.

The variable rate form comes in two types. Under the first approach, the Bundesbank specified a minimum acceptable rate. Banks then bid the amounts they would sell at various rates. The highest rate bids were filled first, down to a cut-off point: the "allotment rate." Successful bids were filled, not at the rate bid, but at the weighted average rate of accepted bids. This gave banks an incentive to bid aggressively, knowing they would not actually pay the rate they bid but something lower. Thus in 1988 the Bundesbank amended its approach: no minimum rate is set, and banks have actually to pay the rate they bid. The fixed-rate tender is sometimes used by the Bundesbank in fixed amounts at times of interest rate uncertainty to calm the market's nerves. Otherwise the variable rate tender is more common.

FRANCE

The money market in France was for many years heavily circumscribed by official controls. However, French financial markets generally were greatly liberalized during the 1980s and the money market has benefited in parallel. For example, until January 1986, only financial institutions and a small number of nonfinancial firms were allowed to hold French Treasury bills and notes in current accounts; there was a secondary market but its role was very limited. In January 1986, the authorities began issuing Treasury bills available to all investors; there is a weekly auction along the lines of the U.S. system.

Similarly, a group of firms resembling the U.S. primary dealer system (Specialistes en Valeurs du Tresor) was set up to help ensure liquidity in the market for government securities including Treasury bills. Settlements (see

Chapter 21) are through the SATURNE system, set up in September 1988. Secondary market liquidity in Treasury bills is still limited but improving. There is good liquidity in the "when-issued" market (marché décalé) whose trading volume is quite large relative to the normal secondary Treasury bill market—about 30% or so.

Other steps have been taken to improve the money market. They include reducing the personal income withholding tax rate for all money-market paper, introduced in 1990, and permitting mutual funds to treat this paper as securities so that if they wish they can hold 100% money-market paper instead of being obliged, as in the past, to also hold a minimum proportion in bonds.

The volume of other money-market paper, including CDs and commercial paper, has begun to grow rapidly (totaling FF700 billion compared with just under FF500 billion of Treasury bills) but the secondary market remains small. The CD market remains oriented to tailor-made issuance intended to be held to maturity rather than traded, and most money-market paper is very short—under 90 days to maturity at the time of issue, which does not encourage secondary market trading. However, the Banque de France recently introduced a facility for qualifying CDs to be settled through SATURNE and it is intended to introduce the same facility for commercial paper, so that secondary market activity will be easier to settle.

One area in which Paris has developed rapidly is in financial futures, where the MATIF (Marché à terme des Instruments Financiers) has proved a strong challenger to LIFFE as the center for European derivatives trading. In the first 9 months of 1990, 1,497,463 contracts were traded on PIBOR (Paris interbank offered rate) for a total nominal value of FF7,500 billion or about US$1,500 billion, compared with a nominal value of about $6,000 billion for its sterling counterpart and $26,000 billion for the Chicago Eurodollar contract.

In line with the liberalization of the markets, the tools of monetary policy in France have moved to a pattern more similar to that of the United States and United Kingdom. Where previously there was a fairly all-embracing system of credit controls that limited the growth of bank lending there is now a much more flexible set of policy tools which are primarily market-oriented. The Banque de France's open market operations on a day-to-day basis are reflected in its intervention rate, which determines the conditions on which it supplies funds to the market. At the same time, the authorities stepped up the role of reserve requirements to ensure that required reserve balances would be sufficiently important to act as a lever of monetary policy, as they do in the United Kingdom and United States. Reserve requirements were increased in July 1987, June 1988, and October 1989.

JAPAN

The Japanese money market was divided into two parts—the interbank market, restricted to financial institutions and in which the Bank of Japan executed policy, and the open market. The call money market, the US$ call market, and the bills market were part of the restricted interbank market, while others were open. The financial system in Japan has been steadily liberalized during the last decade. From being about 20% of the total, the open markets expanded to 40% in 1985 and are now estimated to be about 75%. Table 1.4 shows some key developments in recent years.

As Figure 1.7 shows, the results of this liberalization have been that the bond repurchase market (*gen-saki*), which was originally almost the only unregulated short-term money market, has stagnated while other markets have developed, notably the call money market that has now been greatly liberalized, and the market for CDs. The major gap is now the lack of a liquid Treasury bill market. Efforts have been made to develop this but there has been a difference of opinion between the Ministry of Finance and the Bank of Japan over the appropriate speed of development.

The unsecured overnight call money rate is now a key money-market rate. Traditionally, the call money market was divided into morning loans, which are settled before the bill clearing at 1:00 PM, afternoon loans which are settled by the close of business, and unconditional call money which settled the next day and is automatically extended from day-to-day unless called back. Until 1985, all unconditional call money was collateralized but in that year, unsecured call money was permitted; unsecured call money is normally overnight rather than extendable as in the case of secured unconditional call money.

Table 1.4   Key Japanese Financial Changes

1979	First yen CD issue permitted First gen-saki (bond sale/repurchase) with foreigners allowed
1980	Exchange control liberalized. Previously, what was not permitted was forbidden; now, what is not forbidden is permitted.
1981	Banks allowed to sell government bonds
1985	Euro-yen FRNs, zero coupons, dual currency and warrant bonds permitted. Creation of yen-denominated banker's acceptance market. Money market rate certificates permitted. Government bond futures market starts.
1986	Any borrower rated A or better permitted to tap Euro-yen bond market. Foreign commercial banks permitted to make Euro-yen issues. Japanese banks allowed to deal in yen-denominated foreign loans. Stock Exchange commissions reduced. Japan Offshore Market opened.
1987	Yen commercial paper permitted
1988	Bank of Japan shortens term of its bill operations to allow more flexibility; BoJ allows more flexibility in interbank rates particularly for unsecured call money
1989	JGB bond borrowing market permitted TIFFE futures on Euroyen created

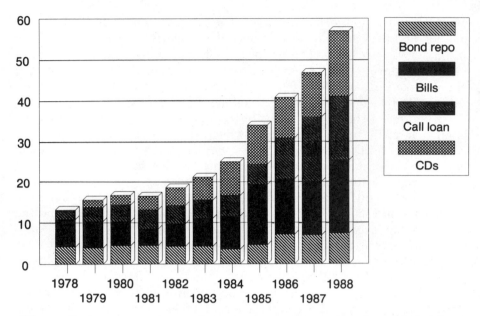

Figure 1.7   Japanese money market volumes year-end outstandings (JPY billion).

Part of the reason for the stagnation of the gen-saki market has been that it has been subject to the securities tax, unlike CDs. Figure 1.8 shows that the gen-saki market has recovered somewhat recently, in comparison to the over-all volume of bond trading; this is largely due to the development of tax-exempt gen-saki trading since 1986.

Although liberalization took time to come through, the development of the Japan Offshore Market (JOM) since 1986 was an important safety valve for the banks since it let them do much of the interbank trading that was restricted onshore; by August 1988, the JOMs volume had hit $395 billion (compared with $160 billion in New York's International Banking Facilities, created in 1981). The JOM has proved a reliable source of interbank funds when the domestic bill market dried up and thus gave the banks valuable flexibility. It is discussed at greater length in Chapter 2.

OTHER MARKETS

The domestic Swiss money market is fairly restricted, despite the interna-tional importance of the Swiss franc in the foreign exchanges and the Euromarket. The domestic market is almost exclusively a primary inter-bank market, because of a transfer tax which effectively eliminates sec-ondary market trading activity. Active participants in the domestic market number fewer than 40 banking institutions.

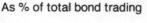

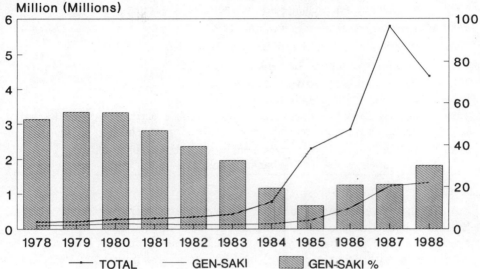

Figure 1.8 Gensaki trading (*Source:* Securities market in Japan 1990).

The Canadian money market is heavily influenced by its southern neighbor. There is a very large volume of "northbound" and "southbound" foreign exchange swaps (see Chapter 2 and Chapter 5 for influences on the market); but there are a number of institutional differences. One interesting feature of Canadian policy is the use of an official interest rate swap program (see Chapter 15) by the government of Canada: by end-1989, CAD 3 billion were outstanding, for terms ranging up to just under 15 years. The 1989 Bank of Canada Annual Report stated that "If the average spread between three-month bankers' acceptances and three-month Treasury bills continues to be just under 15 basis points . . . the government's effective floating rate cost of funds on its swaps will translate into about 72 basis points below the three-month Treasury bill rate."

The Australian money market was considerably liberalized during the 1980s, as Table 1.5 shows.

Though the liberalization ended in tears insofar as it encouraged the rapid growth of bank lending to entrepreneurs whose firms later proved to be unsound, it also laid the groundwork for a much more flexible and innovative financial system.

THE ECU MARKET

Finally, a new transnational money market is developing: that for the ECU. At present, there is still a relative shortage of money market instruments,

Table 1.5   Australian Money Market Liberalization

1979	Sydney Futures Exchange begins trading interest rate futures
1980	Bank deposit interest rate ceilings lifted
1981	Restrictions on overseas investment liberalized
1982	Quantitative controls on bank lending lifted
1983	Foreign banks allowed to set up in Australia Exchange controls abolished
1984	Reserve Bank introduces repos on government securities with authorized dealers; a group of "reporting bond dealers" is created
1985	Restrictions on foreign investment in Australian securities lifted Formation of new trading banks permitted.

but the currency's importance as the centerpiece of the European Monetary System is such that the market will almost certainly develop further. It is presently a pure Eurocurrency market (see Chapter 2) but it is included for comparison with other markets. The ECU itself is explained in detail in Chapter 4 and Chapter 13. Briefly, it is (at present) an artificial currency used in a number of European countries.

There is no domestic ECU market, since there is no country whose currency is the ECU. (As a result, there is no ECU lender of last resort, which at the moment poses potential problems to the ECU clearing system, which is described in Chapter 21.) There are two distinct ECUs, the private ECU and the official ECU. Their composition is identical; but private ECUs can be created by bundling together the appropriate amounts of currencies into a basket. Official ECUs can only be held by official institutions and are created as a result of swap arrangements between the European Monetary Cooperation Fund and members of the European Monetary System. Private and official ECUs are not exchangeable, or *fungible*, to use the technical term.

Private ECUs are traded like any other currency; in November 1988 the Bank of England reported forward ECU turnover of ECU 22.2 billion compared with ECU 8.5 billion in 1986. Major commercial banks provide continuous quotes for the ECU (normally they have computer systems for calculating the ECU value from the currency rates held in their systems) and these can be seen on the appropriate Reuters/Telerate screens. ECU lending by banks in the BIS reporting area grew from ECU 14 billion in 1983 to ECU 176 billion in 1991. An ECU clearing system is operated by the Bank for International Settlements in conjunction with the ECU Banking Association that has about 85 members worldwide; all ECU transactions are cleared daily through this system. London is now the main trading center.

Until recently, one problem with trading private ECUs was that the Deutsche Bundesbank defined the ECU as an index-linked unit of account, the use of which is banned in Germany (because of past inflationary excesses in the 1930s): the restrictions were revoked only in June 1987.

The EEC Commission is keen to develop the role of the ECU as a step towards creating a single monetary area in Europe; the first steps, therefore, have been for an exchange market, a clearing system, and bank deposits in the currency to develop. The next step has been to encourage the development of other financial markets. The first moves here were in the bond market: in April 1981, the Societe Financiere pour les Telecommunications et l'Electronique (SFTE) issued the first ECU bond. ECU bonds have now issued by a wide range of issuers, and in particular the governments of Italy and France have substantial bond issues outstanding that are quite liquid.

At the money-market end of the yield curve, there are good deposit markets but other instruments are a bit limited. The British government issues one-, three- and six-months discount Treasury bills. On September 14, 1988, the Bank of England announced the details of the terms of the ECU Treasury bills as well as a list of 29 institutions that had undertaken to make a secondary market in the paper and to participate in the first series of monthly tenders for new issues of ECU bills. The Bank also announced it would be prepared to make prices to buy back the bills from the market, at least until the secondary market was adequately established.

The bills are for one, three, and six months; they are issued at a discount; they are not subject to withholding tax. The main method of payment for and delivery of the bills is through the Euroclear and Cedel clearance systems, though the ECU Banking Association is studying the feasibility of a London-based clearing system.

The first issue was made on October 11, 1988, of ECU 900 million (split into ECU200 million of one month, ECU500 million of three-month, and ECU200 million of six-month paper). The tender was oversubscribed in all three maturities, by multiples between 3.5 and 4.6; bills were allotted at between 3/16% and 1/4% below ECU LIBID, allowing for immediate arbitrage by the Bank of England back into the banking system, had it felt so inclined. The program seems to be running successfully and provides a valuable addition to the range of ECU instruments. During January, February, and March 1990, for example, issues of ECU 300 m. each of one, three, and six months were made. In the following quarter, the monthly issue was raised from ECU 900m. to ECU 1 billion, in June applications for the paper amounted to ECU 1200m—a 20% oversubscription.

Other governments also issue "domestic" ECU paper: the Italian government's CTE issues, usually for five years, have played an important part in generating ECU swaps (see Chapter 15) because of tax considerations. It has also issued shorter term Treasury bills (BTE). The Spanish and French governments have ECU bonds outstanding: the French (OATs) are fairly liquid. In March 1991, the U.K. government issued a 10-year ECU Eurobond for ECU2.5 billion which is expected to provide a highly liquid benchmark for the market.

2 Euromarkets and Foreign Exchange

In Chapter 1, we discussed domestic money markets. In this chapter, we begin by discussing the Euromarket, which is a transnational money market, and then move on to its twin sister, the foreign exchange market.

THE EURODOLLAR MARKET

What is a Eurodollar? Briefly, it is a dollar deposit that is traded outside the United States. If Citibank in London places a U.S. dollar deposit with Midland Bank in London, that is a Eurodollar deposit transaction. The key feature of this operation is that it is not subject to Federal Reserve requirements. The Federal Reserve imposed a reserve requirement of 3% on deposits taken by U.S. banks until 1990. Therefore, for every US$100 deposited, only $97 could be lent out. If interest rates were 10%, the bank had to charge 10.31% to cover the cost of reserves. Therefore, a bank taking a U.S. dollar deposit in London could profitably undercut its domestic U.S. competitor.

This efficiency in reserve costs is the key reason for the spectacular growth of the Eurodollar deposit market, from its origins in the late 1950s to the multitrillion dollar market that it is today. Legend has it that the origin of the markets, however, was not because of this reserve efficiency, but political. During the 1950s, the Soviet Union was concerned that if it were to invest the dollars that it was earning from the sale of its oil abroad in the United States, it would face the possibility of a political decision to freeze its assets, since the Cold War was then at its height. (Jacques Attali, in his biography of Siegmund Warburg, states that the origins of the market go back even earlier, to the time of the Korean war, when the Chinese placed some deposits with Banque Commerciale pour l'Europe du Nord in the name of the National Bank of Hungary.)

In 1958, pressure on sterling led the Bank of England to ask British merchant banks to switch the financing of their third-country trade into U.S. dollars. British merchant bank demand met Russian supply, and the Eurodollar market was born. During the late 1960s, market growth was fueled by restrictions placed on it by President Johnson, as the Vietnam war placed a strain on the American balance of payment. A further kick to growth was given in the 1970s by the two successive oil crises, when Euro-banks were deeply involved in attempts to recycle the OPEC dollar earnings in the form of loans to less developed countries. Figure 2.1 shows the growth of the market over the years. It highlights how in recent years the pre-eminence of London has been challenged by the development of the International Banking Facilities in New York and the Japan Offshore Market in Tokyo.

Figure 2.2 shows the distribution of lending activity between the main centers—the United Kingdom remains market leader at $894 billion at end-1989 but is challenged by Japan's $830 billion and the $570 billion booked out of the United States. The high Luxembourg figure is misleading in that it should really be largely added to the German figure (because of Bundesbank reserve requirements German Euromarket activity is largely conducted from Luxembourg).

A significant difference between Euromarket and many domestic deposit markets is that the Euromarket is almost exclusively concerned with matched deposit dealing. That is, each deposit (liability) of an international bank will tend to be matched by an asset (usually a deposit in another bank) of the same currency and of similar maturity. Deliberate mismatches might be incurred with a view to making a profit, but the book of each bank as a whole will be matched within certain periods. Hence loans are typically made for a speci-fied period and funded by a deposit of a similar period. This is very different from a domestic market, where typically large amounts of lending are done on the basis of a prime (or base) rate, with these loans being funded day-to-day in the domestic overnight or short-date money market, or from retail deposits.

The Euromarket has two key roles:

1. It provides the links between different forward foreign exchange mar-kets. As we shall see in Chapters 9 and 10, forward foreign exchange rates are determined by relative interest differentials between Euro-currency deposits in the currency in question.
2. It provides a mechanism for the taking and placing of deposits free of domestic central bank restrictions. This has spawned a free-wheeling

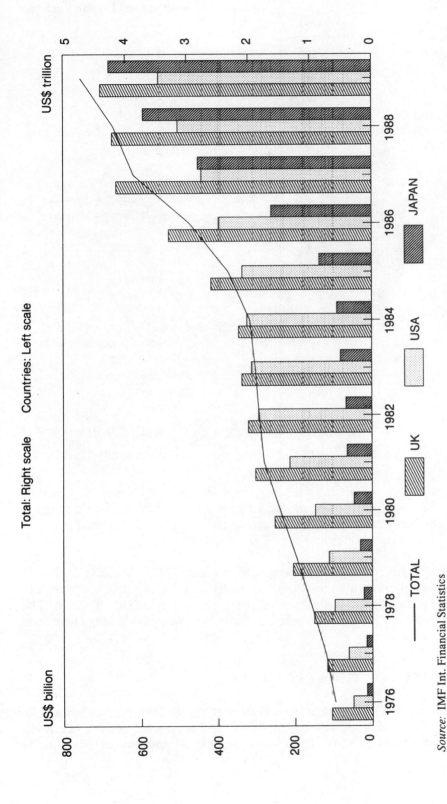

Figure 2.1 Cross-border interbank claims by country of lender (end year).

Source: IMF Int. Financial Statistics

33

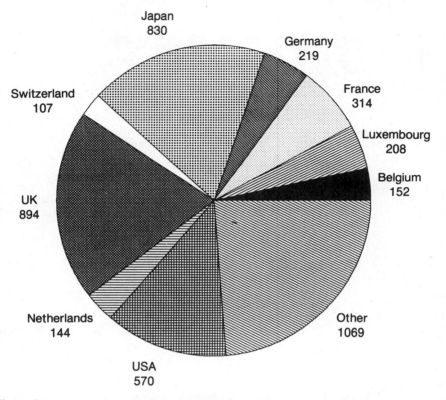

Figure 2.2   External assets of BIS reporting banks by country (US$ bn.) (*Source:* BIS Feb. 1990).

and innovative international banking system, where commercial banking and investment banking have blurred to produce a range of instruments from Eurocommercial paper, though syndicated Eurocredits to Eurobonds and even Euroequities.

The market is incidentally linked with a range of other markets, including those for interest rate and currency swaps, interest rate and currency options, financial futures, gold, and oil and other commodities. These will be discussed later in Part 4. Figure 2.3 shows the share of differing currencies in the market.

WORKINGS OF THE EUROMARKET

By its nature a professional, wholesale market, the Euromarket has a wide range of participants. The objectives of the Euromarket dealing operation vary from bank to bank. There are at least four central objectives usually

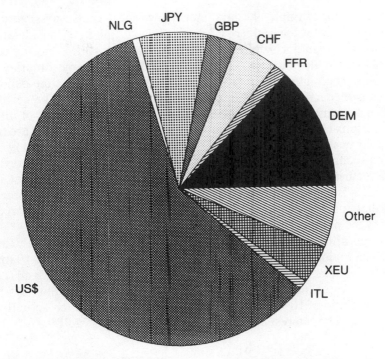

Figure 2.3 Euromarket currency distribution Sept. 89 liabilities of reporting banks $bn (*Source:* BIS).

present: to fund the bank's Eurocurrency loan book; to provide a service to depositing customers; to make profits from deliberate position taking; and to ensure that the bank is seen in the marketplace both as a taker and placer of funds, so that its name is kept in the market and is favorably received when it is necessary to raise funds.

By far the bulk of Euromarkets activity is concentrated in the time deposit market, that is, in the taking and placing of unsecured funds, without involving the purchase or sale of paper. This is different from the U.S. practice, where apart from the Federal funds market, banks typically lend to each other by means of repurchase agreements (involving, at least nominally, the repurchase and sale of securities), or by means of certificates of deposit. The great bulk of the market is of rather short maturity. A proportion of these deposits is on call, meaning they can be withdrawn without prior notice. However, since payment is normally effected by means of transfers in the currency's home country, the minimum practical period for delivery is usually two days. This payment convention corresponds to that in foreign exchange—two working days are required for delivery.

The great bulk of Eurodollar deposits carry a fixed maturity. Normally, the deposit will be effective two business days after the contract is put into effect, and mature, for example, 90 days later. However, it is also possible to deal "value today" or "value tomorrow," depending on time zone considerations.

Although the majority of Eurodollar deposits are time deposits, certificates of deposit also play an important part. By far the largest market is for Eurodollar negotiable CDs. These are large-denomination time-deposit liabilities evidenced by a written instrument or certificate. The certificate specifies the amount of the deposit, the maturity date, the rate of interest, and the terms under which the interest is calculated. While banks are free to offer their customers CDs in any size, the minimum denomination acceptable for secondary market trading—the buying and selling of previously issued securities—is usually $1 million. The term to maturity of newly issued CDs is based on negotiation between the bank and its customer, the individual instrument usually being tailored to fit the liquidity requirements of the purchaser.

The operation of the market is best understood by following a deal. For instance, a major corporation such as Exxon has a placement of $10 million in funds to make for three months. Exxon calls various banks and, on the basis of the rates quoted, decides to place the deposit with Barclays Bank. An interest rate of 10% is agreed on the 3-month deal (which actually runs for 91 days). The interest due is calculated as US$252,777.78:

$$\frac{10}{100} \times \frac{91 \times \$10m}{360} = \$252,777.78$$

An acceptance ticket is written, containing the basic facts of the deal. This ticket is then passed to the back-up operation of the bank, and a separate confirmation is sent out by the back-up office. On the start date of the deposit—the spot date—a CHIPS payment (see Chapter 21) is made by Exxon from, for example, Citibank to Barclays, for account of Barclays' Nassau branch. The funds never leave New York. They are simply credited to Barclays Nassau on a memorandum account at Barclays in New York. At maturity, Exxon decides that it wishes to roll the deposit over for a further three months. On checking the rates, it finds that Bank of America now pays a better rate than Barclays. Accordingly it instructs Barclays to transfer the principal and interest due by means of a CHIPS payment to Bank of America's London branch. Again the funds do not leave New York.

Euro-commercial paper existed in its own right before the arrival of underwritten facilities. Attempts were made in the early 1970s to develop a Euro-commercial paper market, which reached a peak of $2 billion in outstandings. But in 1974 the lifting of U.S. balance of payments controls cut back the market, as U.S. corporations found it cheaper to fund domestically. The growth of today's market began with underwritten facilities.

Underwritten note facilities began in 1978, with an issue by the New Zealand Shipping Corporation. But the instrument attracted little attention. None were issued in 1979, and the 1978 to 1983 period saw only a total of 86

Table 2.1   Euronote Market

	1987	1988	1989	Memo: Total Outstanding End-1989
Net new issues: ECP	19.4	19.9	5.3	58.5
Other Euronotes	1.8	−3.4	−2.4	11.1
Medium-term notes	2.2	3.0	4.0	9.6

Source: BIS Annual Report 1990.

facilities representing US $9 billion. The market began then to change its shape: during the early development of the market, the emphasis was mainly on underwritten facilities, but then the emphasis began to shift towards issues that are not underwritten—true Euro-commercial paper.

The reasons for this are partly the emphasis of central banks on capital weightings, and partly structural. Early underwritten facilities used the rather cumbersome device of the tender panel. (This was in part because a number of the issues were for Australian entities, and for Australian tax reasons a tender panel was desirable). However, many tender panel banks were not specialists in the placement of short-term securities and the paper traded weakly as a result. Many borrowers deserted the tender panel system for direct dealer relationships, which has become the system of choice. The market is now clearly maturing into an important short-term source of funds for global borrowers, but the rapid pace of growth has dropped back in view of the higher level shorter-term rates in 1989 and growing liberalization of domestic CP markets in countries such as Japan.

Another contributory factor was concern over corporate credit risk in the face of recession, which proved to be justified (Table 2.1). During 1989/1990 there were 11 defaults in the world's commercial paper markets, of which the largest were Polly Peck ($90m. of ECP), Drexel Burnham ($30m. of ECP), Mortgage and Realty Trust ($167m. of US CP) and Codec ($66m. of French CP).

LEGAL NATURE OF A EURODOLLAR

Finally, it is worth touching on an issue which was raised very briefly earlier. What is a Eurodollar? We said then that it was a dollar deposit which was traded outside the United States. Similarly, a Euro-Deutsche mark is a Deutsche-mark deposit traded outside Germany. We do need to make some refinements to this definition, however. For example, the International Banking Facilities in New York, and the Japan Offshore Market, allow effectively for the on-shore trading of Eurocurrencies. A dollar deposit placed with an IBF in New York is in fact a Eurodollar, because it is not subject to

Federal Reserve requirements. By contrast, a dollar deposit placed in Frank-furt is not a Eurodollar, because it is actually subject to Bundesbank reserve requirements. (Bundesbank reserve requirements do not operate by cur-rency, but by the location of the deposit-taker). Thus, the key determining factor in whether a currency deposit is or is not a Eurocurrency deposit is whether or not it is exempt from domestic reserve requirements.

A related issue is the legal question of jurisdiction over the Euromarkets. Traditionally, the Bank of England had jurisdiction over the Eurodollar and Eurocurrency activities of banks operating in London. It is the supervisory authority for these banks, and in London its word is (for practical purposes) law. But the taking and placing of U.S. dollar deposits (as was explained earlier) actually involves a transfer of U.S. dollar funds across the books of a bank in New York. Thus, Eurodollar activities are potentially subject to interference from the U.S. authorities. (See also Chapter 21 on the clearing and settlement issues.)

This apparently arcane point has been a vital issue on several occasions, notably the freeze imposed on Iranian assets by President Carter, the dispute between United States and Libya which led to the freezing of Libyan assets, and the multinational freeze on Iraqi assets after the Iraqi invasion of Kuwait. The whole issue hinges on the sensitive question of the extraterrito-rial application of one country's law (in this case, the United States) in the domestic activity of another country (in this case, the United Kingdom). In general, from the practical point of view, such questions are best left cloudy and unresolved, since otherwise politicians tend to become excited and do foolish things. However, there have been a number of legal cases that have shed light on related issues. They go back to the seizure of assets in Palestine in 1947 (Barclays Bank v Arab Bank), the case against Chase Manhattan regarding deposits in its branch in Saigon, the numerous cases arising out of the Iranian freeze, and perhaps most interesting the case of Libyan Arab Bank versus Bankers Trust.

The salient facts of the case are as follows. In 1973 Libyan Arab Foreign Bank (LAFB) opened a call deposit account at the London branch of Bankers Trust (BT). In 1980 a demand current account was opened in New York to give easy access to the New York clearing system (CHIPS). It was agreed between LAFB and BT that all day-to-day payments would be made out of LAFB's New York account but that any balance of over US$ 500,000 would be transferred to its London account in tranches of US$ 100,000, or the other way if there was a short-fall in New York, at the end of each day. It was further agreed that the New York account would be checked twice daily at 2:00 PM and 4:30 PM to check whether transfers should be made. President Reagan's freeze regulations came into effect at 4:10 PM Eastern Standard Time and within minutes the U.S. Treasury had informed U.S. banks of its effect. As a consequence, LAFB found its accounts in both New York and London frozen.

In the case, BT contended that Eurodollar denominated accounts were not repayable on demand in cash anywhere outside the United States, since they had to clear through the CHIPS system in New York. In September 1987, the High Court in London came to the view that the deposits were in London, subject to English law. The Presidential freeze of Libyan assets could affect the usual transfers via New York clearing, but this was not the only possible way to repay the money to the Libyans. Bankers Trust was obliged to use all methods open to it to discharge its obligation. It could pay cash (that is, bank notes) in dollars or in sterling, and it was obliged to pay not only the $131 million on the London deposit account but also an addition $161 million which should have been (but was not) transferred from the New York account to the London deposit account.

Other pertinent cases have involved Citibank and other banks operating in the Philippines at the time when Philippine banking assets were frozen. Clearly, each case will depend entirely on its circumstances. What the LAFB case does suggest, however, is that in general at least the British courts will tend to uphold the freedom of the Euro-markets from interference by other governments, unless the U.K. government also chooses to support this interference by making the actions of governments subject to legal enforcement in London. Naturally, the legal status of Eurocurrency deposits in other centers depends on the local legal arrangements.

THE FOREIGN EXCHANGE MARKET

What is the foreign exchange market? What is its role? It is the arena in which currencies of one country are exchanged for another, where settlement is made for international purchases and sales. Just as the domestic money market is the place where financial flows through a single economy are managed, so the foreign exchange market is where financial flows between countries are settled. Payments for imports and exports flow through the foreign exchange market; as do payments for international purchases and sales of assets. A Japanese investor buying IBM shares will go through the foreign exchange market to buy the U.S. dollars to pay the broker who has sold him the shares. Over the last decade, these international investment flows have played an increasingly important part in the foreign exchange market as securities markets have become more global. The foreign exchange market is also an arena for trading activities on a global scale by a range of participants. Their activities can drive currencies up and down depending on short-term views about the directions of important factors such as relevant interest rates, relevant inflation rates, and so on. (See Chapter 5.)

The foreign exchange market, therefore, is a turntable for the international flow of funds. Funds move into a country when its economic policies are seen as attractive or when firms within it are seen as being dynamic and well-managed, so that the stock market is attractive. Funds will flow out if there is political uncertainty, if interest rates are perceived as too low in relation to inflation, or if the country is perceived as running a chronic deficit on its balance of trade or payments, with no action forthcoming to rectify the problem. (These issues are discussed in more detail in Chapter 5.)

From time immemorial, governments and their central bankers have tried to influence the foreign exchange market. Typically, this has been done in two main ways: exchange controls and intervention. Exchange control regulations prevent the citizens of a country from doing certain things (such as sending money abroad) which are felt by the central bank to have a negative effect on the exchange rate.

Intervention can take two forms: either changing the level of interest rates on the currency so as to make it more or less attractive to foreigners, or else buying or selling the currency so as to raise or lower its market value. Sometimes a central bank can get away with merely looking as though it will do something: dealers will cry "the Bank of Japan is checking levels in the dollar," and that in itself may be enough to trigger a move in the dollar/yen rate. At other times, the central bank has to put its money where its mouth is, sometimes in ever larger and more desperate quantities. The Bank of England, for example, during the 1960s and 1970s often had to spend large amounts of money to support sterling. Those sums had to be borrowed from elsewhere—either from the Bank for International Settlements or the International Monetary Fund (see Chapter 4).

Although statistics have improved, nobody knows how big the world market for foreign exchange really is. All we do know is that it is huge. A recent estimate by the Bank for International Settlements (BIS) (Table 2.3) put the average daily turnover in the world market at $640 billion in April 1989 (net of double counting), which compares with an average daily turnover on the New York stock exchange of $8 billion for 1988. It also compares with the total foreign exchange reserves of industrial countries as reported by the International Monetary Fund at the end of 1989 of SDR344 billion (equivalent to $440 billion). In other words, the entire reserves of all industrial countries, if committed to foreign exchange intervention, could be swallowed up in two to three days' normal trading volume of the market. Turnover in the spot market alone, at an estimated $360 billion, is equivalent to 80% of world reserves. As the BIS points out, exchange rates are determined by the net demand for currencies rather than gross turnover, and also central bank intervention can have psychological effects. But the BIS concludes: "exchange market intervention on its own is bound to be of only limited significance over a longer period."

Figure 2.4 shows the growth of world foreign exchange reserves since the early 1960s and also shows the percentage change on an annual basis. Although the absolute figures have grown very rapidly during the 1980s, the speed of growth has never again attained the explosive 60% growth seen in 1971 when the pressure on the US dollar was at its height and all major governments were aggressively intervening to try and maintain the US dollar's link with gold. The BIS survey shows that on a comparable basis for the four countries that collected data for its previous 1986 survey (Canada, Japan, the

United States and the United Kingdom) turnover grew by 116% on average (Table 2.2).

In terms of which foreign exchange centers are most active, what hard evidence we have comes from central bank surveys of the market. The most recent of these was a survey conducted in April 1989 by some 20 central banks (Table 2.3). The same survey showed the currency composition of trading in major centers (Table 2.4).

A comparison of the three centers shows that the London market is more diversified than elsewhere: in Tokyo for example, 72% of turnover was contracted in $/Yen; in New York 85% of activity was between the dollar and the four major currencies (Deutsche marks, yen, sterling, and the Swiss franc) compared with 74% in London.

The London survey shows that 64% of foreign exchange business was for spot value. This is a sizeable fall from the 73% share in 1986, which is probably because of an increase in swaps business, and the development of other hedging instruments in the forward market. Within the forward market, of the 36% of total turnover, 24% was for maturities of under one month, 10% for forwards of maturity from one month to one year, and only 1% for forwards of maturity over one year. (The remaining 1% was accounted for by foreign currency options and futures. However, much currency and futures business is conducted by nonbank financial institutions not included in the survey.) The share of spot business varies from center to center: it is highest in the UK, followed by the United States (63%), Hong Kong (61%) and Australia (61%). In Canada and Japan, where swaps are the major market instrument, spot transactions account for only 40% of turnover.

Participants in the market consist of five main groups: central banks, commercial banks, other financial institutions, corporate customers, and brokers. By far the largest volume of trading is conducted by commercial banks, but the role of other financial institutions has grown considerably with the growth of global investment and also the growth of the derivatives markets in which the investment banks play an important role. In the corporate sector, the two largest trading groups have traditionally been the oil companies and commodity companies. This is because commodity markets generally trade on an international basis in a single currency (usually the

Table 2.2   Growth in Foreign Exchange Turnover 1986–1989 (%)

	Total Turnover	Customer Turnover	Spot Turnover
United Kingdom	108	221	81
United States	120	134	134
Japan	140	111	142
Canada	58	38	53

Source: "Survey of Foreign Exchange Market Activity," BIS, February 1990.

Table 2.3   Foreign Exchange Market Activity in April 1989 ($bn.)

United Kingdom	$187
United States	$129
Japan	$115
Switzerland	$57
Singapore	$55
Hong Kong	$49
Australia	$30
France	$26
Canada	$15
Netherlands	$13
Denmark	$13
Sweden	$13
Belgium	$10
Italy	$10
Other countries*	$22
TOTAL	$744
Adjustment for cross-border double counting:	$204
Total reported net turnover:	$540
Estimated gaps in reporting:	$100
Estimated global turnover:	$640

*Bahrain, Finland, Greece, Ireland, Norway, Portugal, and Spain

Source: "Survey of Foreign Exchange Market Activity," *Bank for International Settlements,* 14 February 1990.

dollar, but also sterling for certain commodities), but have sales denominated in the local market currency. The role of the central banks is generally passive, responding to events. But occasionally their policies can take on tremendous significance for the market players. Their role is discussed more fully next.

Of the counter-parties involved in the London market, 15% of turnover was done direct with customers. This compares with 11% in 1986 (9% with customers and 2% with other market participants who were included in the customer segment in 1989). The remaining 85% was interbank business, of which 38% was traded through the intermediation of a foreign exchange broker (see below). Thirteen percent was dealt direct between banks in London, and 34% direct between a bank in London and a bank overseas. (Of the 15% customer business, 9% was with financial institutions and 6% with nonfinancial institutions.)

These figures show a slight decline in the volume of interbank turnover compared with customer turnover as against 1986. By comparison with other

Table 2.4   Currency Composition

	London	Tokyo	New York
$/GBP	27	4	15
$/DEM	22	10	33
$/JPY	15	72	25
$/CHF	10	4	12
Other (including cross currency)	26	10	15

centers, London's figure is relatively high for interbank business and low for customer business: the share of customer business in Japan was reported at 30%, 27% in Canada, and 21% in Australia. Customer turnover was low in Hong Kong and Singapore (both 11%). The U.S. figure, at 15%, was the same as London's.

Though the customer turnover percentage may seem low, a single customer transaction can give rise to three or four interbank transactions in the normal course of events. The reasons are explained in Chapters 8 to 10, but as an example, a forward sterling/deutchmark transaction by a British bank in London with a British customer could give rise to a spot dollar sterling and a spot dollar/mark transaction, together with a dollar sterling swap (spot versus forward) and a dollar/mark swap.

The workings of the foreign exchange market differ a little in detail from center to center. In some countries, for example, particularly continental Europe, it is traditional for there to be a daily "fixing." In Germany, for example, it is customary for the banks to group together customer orders of a smaller amount and to present them as bids or offers at the daily fixing with the Bundesbank. The rate is moved until the balance of orders on either side is sufficient to clear the market, if necessary with some supplementary sales or purchases by the Bundesbank, and the daily "fixing rate" is then announced. The fixing rate is applied to certain routine transactions by the banks for their customers.

More and more, though, a worldwide pattern of foreign exchange trading is emerging that is common between the different centers. The major participants are the central banks, commercial banks, corporations, and foreign exchange brokers. Banks typically trade directly with other banks on the international markets, although sometimes they will trade through a broker if this is more convenient. In domestic markets, they will often also trade directly with one another but tend (perhaps more than internationally) also to use the services of a broker. Each of the two methods has its own advantages. In dealing directly, a bank can normally be sure of getting a price at which it can deal. The convention is that a bank which receives a call from another bank asking for a quotation will quote a "2-way" price at which it is prepared to buy or sell the currency. But this price may not be the best available in the market at the time, or it may only be good for a limited amount. On the other hand, it is the job of the broker to find his customer the best possible price in the market, by using his large communications network with many other banks in the market. Accordingly, on some occasions, a better price may be obtained through the broker: this, however, incurs a brokerage fee. At the same time, a bank contacted by a broker need not necessarily make a "2-way" price, so that the broker may not always be able to find the right side of the deal.

In some centers, brokers are allowed to service corporations in the foreign exchange market. It is quite common to see this in domestic money markets, but still unusual in the foreign exchange market. Banks dislike the practice, generally, because of the possible credit risk problem and the possible risk to customer relationships. In other centers, the practice is forbidden. Another restriction can be a ban on dealing with banks outside the country. When operating tight exchange controls, a central bank will often require all commercial deals to be done with an authorized bank in that country (since otherwise the controls are very hard to police).

Exchange controls are the earthworks that prevent the foreign exchange tide from flowing freely round the world. But the liberalization and globalization of the markets during the 1980s now means that most important countries have relatively free markets. As an example of what that has meant for previously restricted markets, the Deputy Governor of the Reserve Bank of Australia said in 1989 that before the 1983 liberalization of the Australian market, foreign exchange turnover was estimated at A\$1 billion daily; six years later, it was A\$35 billion daily.

Now all major countries are effectively free from exchange controls, and the world's communication networks are now so good that we can talk of a single world market for foreign exchange. It starts in New Zealand around 8:00 AM, just in time to catch the tail end of the previous night's U.S. market. Two or three hours later, Tokyo opens, followed an hour later by Hong Kong and Manila and then half an hour later by Singapore. By now, with the Far East market in full swing, the focus moves to the Near and Middle East. Bombay opens two hours after Singapore, followed after an hour and a half by Abu Dhabi, with Jeddah an hour behind, and Athens and Beirut an hour behind still. By this stage, trading in the Far and Middle East is usually thin and perhaps nervous as dealers wait to see how Europe will trade. Paris and Frankfurt open an hour ahead of London, and by this time Tokyo is starting to close down, so the European market can judge how the Japanese market has been trading by the way they deal to close out positions. By lunch time in London, New York is starting to open up, and as Europe closes down, so positions can be passed westward. During the afternoon in New York, trading tends to be quiet. The problem is there is nowhere to pass the position to. The San Francisco market, three hours behind, is effectively a satellite of the New York market. Positions can be passed on to New Zealand banks, but the market there is relatively limited. Increasingly, there has been a tendency for banks to open two or three shifts so as to run 24-hour dealing rooms, but the vast majority of the market still tends to work in daylight hours.

Like its trading, the influences on the foreign exchange market are world-wide. Not only domestic and international money markets, but a range of other markets also influence trading activity. Flows of funds into and out of the major stock markets, and the major bond markets, can have a significant impact. So, too, can sharp movements in either gold, oil, or some of the other major commodities. Activities in the futures markets can have an impact, as can flows arising out of the markets for interest rate or currency swaps, currency options, or other financial options markets. We will look at all of these markets in more detail. But before we do that, it may be useful to look at the history of these markets.

HISTORY OF THE FOREIGN EXCHANGE AND EURODOLLAR MARKETS

The history of foreign exchange market goes back a very long way: they were old when the Bible reports money changers being chased out of the Temple by Jesus Christ. The global market itself began to develop during the nineteenth century, as the term "cable" for sterling will attest. It derives from the rate for the cable transfer between London and New York.

By the 1920s, the markets were developed enough for Maynard Keynes to form a syndicate to speculate on the Deutschmark. But the economic chaos resulting from the Depression of the 1930s led to the so-called "beggar thy neighbor" policies of competitive depreciation whereby one country, in order to try to boost the level of its exports would depreciate its currency aggressively, only to be overtaken by another country intent on doing the same. This led to a reaction.

In 1944, the Allies met at Bretton Woods to lay down a post-war foundation for stable exchange rates. This took shape in the form of the International Monetary Fund (see Chapter 4). The object was to provide a system whereby exchange rates would be held stable and, if necessary, countries could be supplied with the finance to ensure that this took place.

The IMF's Articles of Agreement permitted adjustment of the currency's par value only if the country's balance of payments was in "fundamental disequilibrium." This was an imprecise concept, but it came to mean that exchange rates would be adjusted only as a last resort and only in conjunction with other policies to redress the disequilibrium.

The system worked well to begin with, since in the immediate post-war world financial flows were very tightly regulated by exchange controls in a number of countries. In 1958, however, the international convertibility of most major currencies was restored, and the international financial system began to experience regular exchange rate crises.

Early pressure on the US dollar led, in 1963, to the introduction of the Interest Equalization Tax. This was a tax on bond issues made in the United States by foreigners. It led to the growth of the Eurobond market and thus helped the growth of the Eurodollar market, which was also helped by the existence of the U.S. Regulation Q. This was a Federal Reserve regulation restricting the rate of interest that could be paid by U.S. banks on deposits to 5.25%. As U.S. interest rates rose with inflation, so much US$ deposit activity shifted to the Euromarket.

Once the pressure on the dollar eased, the next flash point was the pound sterling, which was widely perceived as over-valued given the United Kingdom's relatively high exchange rate, poor labor practices, and low productivity growth. The US dollar, however, also began to come under increasing pressure for similar reasons, exacerbated after 1965 by the impact of the Vietnam war on the U.S. balance of payments.

Sterling was the first to crack, in 1967, partly as a result of the Seven-Day War between Israel and Egypt, which triggered concern about sterling balances. These were balances held in sterling by foreign central banks and international investors as a result of the then key role played by sterling in the international financial system. The devaluation of sterling by 14.6% in November 1967 temporarily calmed the situation, but only briefly. The US dollar now stood exposed to the full force on international speculation, with sterling removed from the firing line.

In 1969, the fall of General De Gaulle resulted in strong upward pressure on the Deutschmark. The French franc was devalued by 11%, and the Deutschmark revalued by 9.3%. During 1970, the situation calmed down somewhat, but in 1971 the downward pressure on the dollar and the upward pressure on the Deutschmark was strongly renewed.

On May 28, 1971, U.S. Secretary of the Treasury John Connally announced that "we are not going to devalue. We are not going to change the price of gold." On August 15, President Nixon suspended convertibility of dollars into gold, and announced a domestic wage price freeze. In December, a meeting at the Smithsonian Institution in Washington agreed a realignment of currencies included a devaluation of the dollar.

Figure 2.4 puts in perspective the pressure on the international financial system during this period. As governments intervened to support the US dollar in ever larger amounts, world foreign exchange reserves exploded, growing by over 60% in 1971. (To see how intervention increases reserves, see Chapter 3.)

The Smithsonian agreement marked the beginning of the end for the gold-dollar link. The U.S. Treasury had sold, net, more than US$10 billion worth of gold between December 1958 and August 1971, cutting its gold stock in half. Sales to France and in the London gold market to stabilize the market price around the official price accounted for much of this total. In an effort to create an alternative international reserve asset, the United States pressed for the creation of a reserve asset whose supply could be

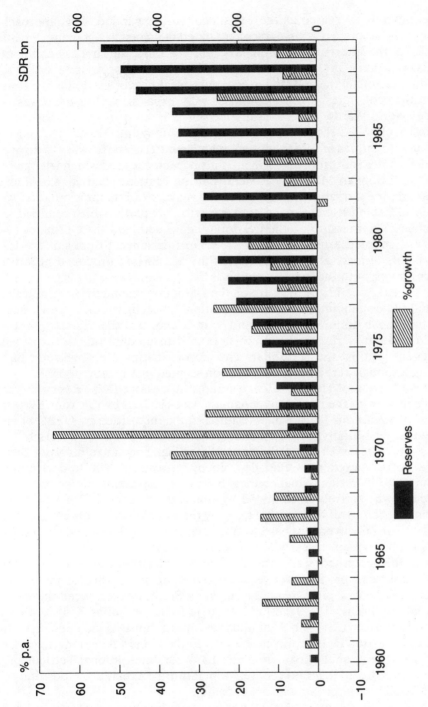

Figure 2.4 Growth in world reserves SDR bn & % growth (*Source:* IMF IFS yearbook 1990).

systematically increased as the world economy expanded. This approach eventually resulted in an agreement to create Special Drawing Rights (SDRs) of the International Monetary Fund in 1968; the first allocation of SDRs was made in January 1970. None of these efforts, however, were sufficient to offset the underlying economic weakness of the dollar at a time when the economies of other countries were expanding after the devastation of World War II.

In March, 1972 the European Economic Community (EEC) decided to fix narrow margins of 2.25% between member currencies, in order to form a "snake" in the Smithsonian "tunnel." This became the seed which later grew into the European Monetary System. During May, the United Kingdom, Denmark, Ireland, and Norway joined the snake; in June, the United Kingdom and Ireland left the snake, together with Denmark (which rejoined in October). The pressure on the US dollar continued, and the German government adopted exchange control measures designed to prevent the inflows from abroad; at about the same time, the Swiss introduced negative interest rates, with the same objective.

In February, 1973 the pressure on the US dollar became intense, and the United States announced a 10% devaluation. This triggered the announcement by Japan, followed by Italy and Switzerland, that their exchange rates would float; in March, the EEC ministers announced the joint float of snake currencies against the US dollar. The era of floating exchange rates had begun, although at the time, the situation seemed purely temporary.

The adoption of floating exchange rates turned out to be a very useful device in view of the imminent economic chaos caused by the Yom Kippur War in the Autumn 1973, which resulted in the imposition by OPEC of an oil embargo. Initially, the US dollar benefited as the oil producers redeposited their reserves in US dollars and sterling. The banks involved then proceeded to recycle the OPEC deposits by on-lending them to developing countries to help them finance their balance of payments problems. Such recycling was actively encouraged by major governments. But when the developing countries were unable to repay their borrowings, official support for the banks involved was hard to find, and the Less Developed Countries (LDC) debt crisis of the early 1980s began.

In both the United States and the United Kingdom, the failure of economic policy to produce the required reduction in balance of payments deficit led to severe pressure on the currency. Sterling experienced the crisis first, falling through $2.00 in March 1976; in June, the United Kingdom was forced to borrow US$5.3 billion under an international standby facility. In January 1977 the IMF approval of a loan to the United Kingdom, together with a further standby loan from the Bank for International Settlements allowed sterling to begin to recover, which in turn exposed the position of the US dollar to international attention.

The US dollar came under intense pressure during the summer and autumn, with other countries having to make desperate efforts to prevent outflows from the United States into their currency. In November, Japan imposed a 50% marginal reserve requirement on "free yen" balances, and in December the Bundesbank increased marginal reserve requirements on nonresident deposits to 100%. Negative interest rates in Switzerland reached −40% per annum.

In July 1979, Paul Volcker was appointed Chairman of the Federal Reserve, and in September and October he raised the U.S. discount rate from 10% to 12% imposing an 8% marginal reserve requirement, and announcing a "New Monetary Policy" that would focus henceforth on levels of bank reserves, rather than interest rates. Although this had the effect of temporarily stabilizing the situation, a further round of pressure began to develop in December 1979, when OPEC raised the oil price another 30% and the Soviet Union invaded Afghanistan. The price of gold moved from just under $400 per ounce at the end of September to $512 per ounce at the end of December, and $850 per ounce on January 25th.

In December 1981, the United States introduced International Banking Facilities (IBFs) which effectively allowed Euromarket activity in New York. IBFs are subject to restrictions aimed at stopping any leakage between IBFs and domestic banking. This was emulated in 1986 by the Japan Offshore Market.

Also in 1981, the new Reagan Administration decided to move away from what it judged to have been the heavy levels of foreign exchange intervention inherited from the previous administration. This reflected an ideological view that exchange rates were the product of economic policies, and that the "supply side" policies of the new administration would be sufficient to produce satisfactory market conditions. In reality, what happened was that a combination of short-sighted tax cuts, aggressive increases in defense spending, and a lack of administrative control produced a very rapid rise in the U.S. budget deficit, which was offset by very tight Federal Reserve monetary policy. This pushed the US dollar up sharply.

This in turn produced other repercussions, particularly for the LDCs, which had borrowed US dollars in order to finance the balance of payments deficit caused by previous oil price rises. The strength of the dollar and high dollar interest rates made their position increasingly difficult, and in August 1982 Mexico triggered the beginnings of an international LDC debt crisis by announcing that it could not meet its obligations. Partly as a response, and partly because U.S. inflation was showing signs of coming under control as a result of the strength of the dollar and the relative slow down of domestic demand, the Federal Reserve began to ease interest rates. This in turn triggered a strong bull market in U.S. dollar bonds and subsequently in U.S. equities.

By the summer of 1985, it was apparent that the ideologically based U.S. policy of "benign neglect" of the U.S. dollar appreciation (based in part on the simplistic view of President Reagan that "a strong dollar shows that the United States is strong") had led to massive distortions of international payments in balances. The U.S. external deficit was beginning to explode, as the United States was becoming increasingly uncompetitive: this in turn was leading to domestic U.S. demands for protection from foreign competition.

On September 22, at the Plaza Hotel in New York, the finance ministers of the Group of Five (United States, Japan, Germany, United Kingdom, France) met to try to deal with the situation. Behind the scenes, delicate negotiations on intervention strategy took place. A statement of intervention policy, dubbed the "non-paper" because of its sensitivity, was prepared but never made public. The non-paper looked for a 10/12% fall in the dollar, and intervention shares assigned as follows: United States, 25%; Germany, 25%; Japan, 25%; United Kingdom, 12.5%; France, 12.5%. The Europeans, however, objected feeling that the United States and Japan should share more of the burden. The United States offered a compromise; United States, 30%; Germany, 25%; Japan, 30%; United Kingdom, 5%; France, 10%.

The non-paper did not discuss interest rates and monetary policy, nor did the central bank governors attending the Plaza meeting discuss monetary policy or interest rates at the meeting. They considered the topic too sensitive to be discussed in the presence of politicians.

By January 1986, the United States was pressing other members of the Group of Five for a coordinated cut in interest rates, citing lower U.S. growth estimates for 1986 and also the collapse in oil prices as a justification. The Treasury secretary, James Baker warned that unless other countries cooperated, the dollar would fall further. The central bankers, however, resisted this pressure. It was against this background that in February 1987 officials of the Group of Seven met at the Louvre in Paris. They expressed concern that "further substantial exchange rate shifts could damage growth and adjustment prospects in their countries." Therefore, they agreed to open "cooperate closely to foster stability of exchange rates around current levels."

In fact, the commitments were much more precise: two specified midpoint rates were agreed: 1.8250 DM to the dollar and 153.50 yen to the dollar. Plus or minus 2.5% was determined as a first line of defense for mutual intervention on a voluntary basis, while at 5% consultation on policy adjustment was to be obligatory. Between these limits of 2.5% to 5%, intervention efforts were expected to intensify. Agreement was also reached on a total amount of US$4 billion of "war chest" for intervention purposes, with intervention totals assigned as roughly one third to the United States, one third to Japan, and one third to European countries.

However, the failure to follow through in terms of fiscal coordination undermined the success of the Louvre Accord. Tensions grew between the United States and other partners, particularly Germany. Veiled threats by the United States to force a further dollar depreciation unless Germany expanded its economy more rapidly unsettled the markets, triggering the crash of October 19th in the U.S. stock market. This, in turn, so terrified the U.S. administration that U.S. interest rates were pushed artificially low for too long. By the end of the year, the dollar's value had fallen 21% against the Yen and 14% against the Deustchmark from its levels at the time of the Louvre Accord in February. In these circumstances, the Group of Seven officials held a telephone conference in late December and in conjunction with the central banks operated a "bear trap" against dollar speculators. The U.S. dollar was forced up sharply at the start of January 1988.

By early 1989, the dollar was again rising strongly, until in early April the Group of Seven announced strong opposition to a further dollar rise, coupled with official dollar sales by the Bank of Japan (the first such intervention since late 1985). During 1989, the U.S. dollar continued its ascent: it benefited from the withholding tax fiasco in Germany, repeated government crises in Japan, and also the massacre in Tienanmen Square in China in June of 1989. In the latter quarter of the year, the dollar eased back, partly in response to the Group of Seven meeting on September 23, 1989 when the finance ministers and central bank governors publicly criticized the rise in the dollar as being inappropriate. Over the course of the year as a whole, net sales of dollars by 19 countries participating in the "consultation" of policy amounted to no less than $75 billion, with the United States and Japan contributing $40 billion, and the Bundesbank $4 billion.

Events in the international financial markets during 1990 could not help but be overshadowed by the dramatic developments on the geo-political scene: the collapse of the Berlin Wall in November 1989 and the subsequent rapid move towards German reunification transformed the prospects of the Deutschmark. A country with a strong external surplus, low inflation, and low interest rates was transformed into a much weaker economy with enormous capital requirements to refinance the crumbling infrastructure left by the failed communist regime. Long-term bond rates in Germany rose sharply over the course of the year, underpinning also a rise in Japanese interest rates, which over the course of the year triggered a collapse in the Japanese stock market. Stock markets around the world were further severely damaged by the invasion of Kuwait by Iraq in August 1990. This triggered a sharp rise in the price of oil from $18 to over US$40 at one point. The subsequent victory over Iraq provided a temporary boost to the dollar but the impact of recession offset this. Another factor was the growing debate within Europe about the European Monetary System, which culminated in December, 1991, in the historic agreement at Maastricht whereby a single European currency is to be in place by the end of this century.

3 Links Between Foreign Exchange and Money Markets

This chapter explores the links between foreign exchange and money markets. We start by seeing how the two link up at the level of a trader's position. Then we look at what this means for arbitrage. Then we look at how central banks intervene in the foreign exchange market, and in the domestic money market; and finally we discuss the effects that foreign exchange intervention can have in the domestic money market.

HANDLING AN EXPOSURE: FOREIGN EXCHANGE OR MONEY MARKET

We start with the point of view of a firm with foreign exchange exposure in a currency. As long as a currency has effective spot and forward exchange markets and money markets, and as long as exchange controls permit, an exposure can always be hedged in either market.

Suppose the treasurer of a British subsidiary of a U.S. company has a deutsche mark payment coming due in 90 days. He needs the funds now to send to the United States. He can borrow deutsche marks against his receivable and convert them into U.S. dollars now. Alternatively, he can sell the deutsche marks forward against U.S. dollar and borrow U.S. dollars against the foreign exchange. The choice between the two will depend on the rates involved (see Table 3.1).

Table 3.1   Financing a DEM Receivable: Money Market Route versus Foreign Exchange

| | Money Market Route | | Foreign Exchange Route | |
Day	Cash In	Cash Out	Cash In	Cash Out
DEM				
Day 1	DEM loan proceeds	Convert to US$		
Day 90	Receivable	Repayment of DEM loan	Receivable	Pay to bank to settle forward FX deal
US$				
Day 1	DEM loan proceeds	Remit to HQ	US$ loan proceeds against FX	Remit to HQ
Day 90				Repay US$ loan proceeds of forward

Step 1. Borrow DEM.	Step 1. Sell DEM forward against US$.
Step 2. Buy US$ and pay U.S. parent.	Step 2. Borrow US$ and pay United States.
Step 3. Receive DEM and repay loan.	Step 3. Receive DEM and settle forward deal.
	Step 4. Use proceeds of forward to repay loan.

A dealer in a bank has the option of handling his positions in the same way. If he received a CHF deposit for 90 days, and is lending sterling for 90 days, he will have the option of choosing the money market or the foreign exchange route. He can on-lend the Swiss francs or do a foreign exchange deal. He would buy sterling to on-lend and sell the sterling forward against CHF to repay his CHF deposit at maturity. Table 3.2 shows how his T-accounts would look.

ARBITRAGE

It follows from Tables 3.1 and 3.2 that there is a very close connection between the interest rate and the forward exchange rate. For example, suppose the Swiss franc is at a premium forward against sterling. In other words, the CHF is more expensive in the future than it is now. The dealer who is selling Swiss francs spot and buying them forward at a more expensive price in order to lend sterling will need to make more on his sterling lending than he would on his Swiss franc lending. Otherwise, it would not be worthwhile switching the funds into sterling. From this, we can derive some general rules. (The exact calculations are set out in Chapters 9 and 10.)

First, *the currency with the lower interest rate will sell at a premium in the forward market against the currency with the higher interest rate.* Suppose US$ three-month deposits yield 20% and DEM three-month deposits yield 10%. Then the deutsche mark must sell at a premium in the three-month forward market. Suppose it did not; suppose it sold at a discount. That

Table 3.2   Matching a Swiss Franc Liability and a Sterling Asset

Day	Money Market Route Cash In	Money Market Route Cash Out	Day	Foreign Exchange Route Cash In	Foreign Exchange Route Cash Out
CHF					
Day 1	CHF deposit	On-lent to market	Day 1	Receive deposit	Sell CHF for £STG
Day 90	Repay CHF	Market repays	Day 90	Receive CHF	Repay CHF deposit from forward
£STG					
Day 1	Borrow from market	Make £STG loan to customer	Day 1	Proceeds of CHF spot sale	Lend to customer
Day 90	Repay market	Customer repays	Day 90	Customer repays	Pay for forward CHF purchase

Step 1. Take CHF deposit; on-lend to market

Step 1. Take CHF deposit; swap it for £STG

Step 2. Lend £STG to customer, funding in market

Step 2. Lend £STG to customer

Step 3. Receive CHF repayment from market
Repay customer deposit

Step 3. Receive £STG repayment from customer
Settle forward CHF purchase

Step 4. Receive £STG repayment from customer
Repay market

---

means, conversely, that the dollar is at a premium against the deutsche mark. So a German investor could buy dollars spot and sell them forward at a profit. In addition, he picks up 10% interest differential. In a free market, this situation could never last. Investors would buy U.S. dollars spot and sell them forward until the weight of forward selling had driven the U.S. dollar to a discount. That is, the forward deutsche mark would show a premium.

The second rule is that this premium (on an annualized basis) will tend to equal the interest difference. Suppose, in our example again, it did not, and that it were only 5% per annum. Then it would cost a German investor only 5% per annum to buy spot dollars and sell them forward. Yet he would receive a 10% interest improvement, so there is still a net profit of 5%. Again, in a free market, this situation would not last. Funds would move out of DEM into dollars until there were no net profit in doing so; that is, until the forward margin (premium or discount) in annual terms equaled the interest differential.

Third, it follows from the equality of interest differentials and forward margins that if one changes for any reason, the other will move to offset it. In practice, the interest differential tends to be the dominant factor, because the vast bulk of activity in the forward exchange market is conducted inter-bank on a swap basis (see Chapter 2). This relationship can be summed up as: *If the interest differential moves in a currency's favor, the forward margin moves against it.* (See Figure 3.1.)

INTEREST
DIFFERENTIAL

FORWARD
MARGIN

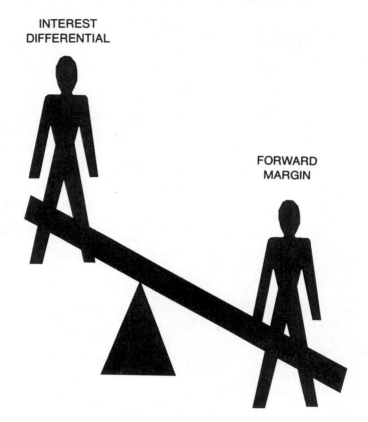

Figure 3.1   The forward margin moves to offset the interest differential.

To continue our example, suppose German interest rates rise from 10% to 15% while the U.S. dollar rate remains at 20%. Interest rates have moved in the deutsche mark's favor. So the forward premium on deutsche mark will *fall* from 10% to 5% per annum so that it equals the new interest differential of 5%. Conversely, suppose now that U.S. dollar rates also fall to 15%. The interest differential has moved *against* the US$, so the forward margins move in *favor* of the US$: the premium on deutsche marks (that is, discount on US$ against DEM) disappears entirely because both interest rates are now at 15% and the differential is zero.

It should be stressed that "interest differential" is very crude. To be strictly accurate, one should use something like "net accessible interest differential." In other words, the interest rate should apply to borrowing and lending that are accessible to the international market—unaffected by exchange controls. To take a classic case, during the period of heavy upward pressure on the Swiss franc in 1977 to 1979, interest rates on the domestic Swiss money market were running at around 2% to 3% per annum. But those interest rates were not available to nonresident holders of the Swiss francs. They were, on the contrary, charged a negative interest rate of—at its peak—10% per quarter, or rather more than minus 40% per annum. Domestic Swiss rates were not "accessible" to the market.

Secondly, the interest rate should be "net." It should be adjusted for any reserve requirement factors, interest withholding taxes, or other adjustments applicable to nonresidents. For example, before the introduction of International Banking Facilities in New York, a U.S. bank was able to pay a better interest rate on a dollar deposit with its branch in London, compared with the rate it could pay for a deposit with its head office in New York, because the latter was subject to the full range of Federal Reserve System reserve requirements.

Equally, if a nonresident were placing funds in a center where an interest withholding tax is levied on nonresidents, he would need to allow for this tax before comparing an interest rate on a deposit in another currency that does not attract withholding tax. It is possible that the withholding tax could be reclaimed under a double tax treaty between the depositor's country and the country in which the deposit is made. But against this must be set the extra cost and inconvenience of processing the claim, and so forth. Also, many of the countries that are Euromarket centers have a rather limited network of double tax treaties. If withholding tax has to be taken into account, the necessary adjustment formula is given in Chapter 12.

Finally, it should be mentioned that the relationship between the net interest differential and the swap market permits a bank's dealer to "create" a forward market if a deposit market is available. For example, if a dealer is asked to quote a forward price for a small amount of five-year Austrian schillings, he has a problem. The Austrian forward schilling market does not stretch that far forward and there is no real Euro-Austrian schilling deposit market. But if he can obtain deposit quotes for five years in the domestic Austrian market, and if he feels safe in assuming that these are in line with what would prevail in the Euroschilling market if there were one, he can manufacture a swap price using the formula given in Chapter 10. Naturally, this is a very rough and ready procedure. It would only be safe to do it for a small-sized deal and then only if adequate margin were taken.

In fact what happens is that if he has to sell forward schillings, he buys spot schillings now and places them on deposit, funding with borrowed dollars. The forward sale absorbs his foreign currency liquidity at maturity. Likewise, a forward purchase creates forward liquidity in the foreign currency. (See Figure 3.2.)

FOREIGN EXCHANGE INTERVENTION

Intervention by central banks in foreign exchange markets, in its "pure" form, consists of purchases/sales of foreign currency against domestic currency in the spot or forward markets. Other forms of intervention are

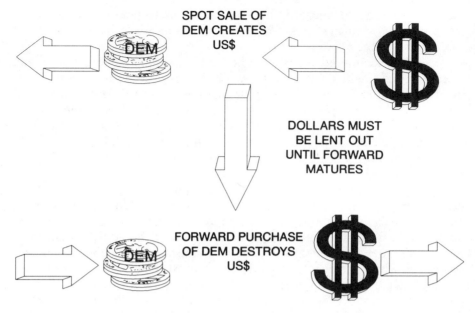

Figure 3.2   Creating US$ by selling & buying DEM.

indirect, such as money-market operations, charges in reserve requirements, and so on (see Chapter 1). In its "pure" form, then, intervention can
be divided into spot, swap, and outright forward operations.

A spot purchase or sale of foreign currency against domestic currency
tends to have an immediate effect on the spot exchange rate. If the deutsche
mark is rising, and the Bundesbank appears in the market to sell deutsche
marks and buy U.S. dollars, this will tend to depress the deutsche mark spot
rate. It will also increase the Bundesbank's foreign exchange reserves by the
amount of U.S. dollars bought. It may affect the German money supply,
depending on who buys the deutsche mark and whether he invests the
deutsche mark in bank deposits or government bonds or is forced (as in 1970)
to place the deutsche mark in a special deposit with the Bundesbank. In the
last two cases, the inflow is "sterilized" but in the first case it feeds through
into the money supply. (See a discussion of this problem later in the chapter.)

An outright forward purchase or sale of foreign currency against domestic currency tends to have an immediate effect on the margin between the
spot and forward rate. The effect on reserves does not show up until maturity, when it is the same as outlined in the last paragraph. The Bank of
England intervened in this way during 1964 through 1967. The aim was to
support the forward sterling rate and so reduce the discount on forward
sterling. This would cut the cost of forward cover on sterling assets and so
encourage investment in sterling assets. At the same time, operating on an
outright rather than a swap basis meant the Bank did not have to supply spot

Table 3.3   Bundesbank Use of Swaps to
Influence Money Markets (DM Billion)

Year	DM Billion
1984	3.3
1985	5.0
1986	24.0
1987	10.9
1988	3.0
1989	2.2

sterling to the market. But the devaluation of 1967 meant that these forward operations cost the Bank £350 million, and they were then abandoned.

A swap operation also alters the margin between the spot and the forward rate. But it has an immediate impact on the spot market as well. The counterparty receives funds on his account now. If the Bank of England had intervened in the swap instead of the outright market, it would have been selling sterling spot and buying it back forward. The counterparties would have been long of spot sterling, which they would probably have sold off. That was why the Bank dealt outright forward. But swaps have been used by some central banks to affect the cost of forward cover: a notable example is the Bundesbank which had amounts outstanding of up to $2.7 billion in 1958–1969 and 1971. However, experience tended to show that these swap interventions were misused by the combination of interest rate arbitrage and Bundesbank swap transactions to carry on "round-trip trades" that made it possible to obtain interest rate profits without using additional funds. The Bundesbank still deals in the swap market (Table 3.3). The aim of these

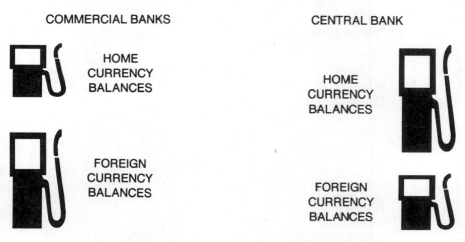

Figure 3.3   Stage one: Domestic liquidity shortage.

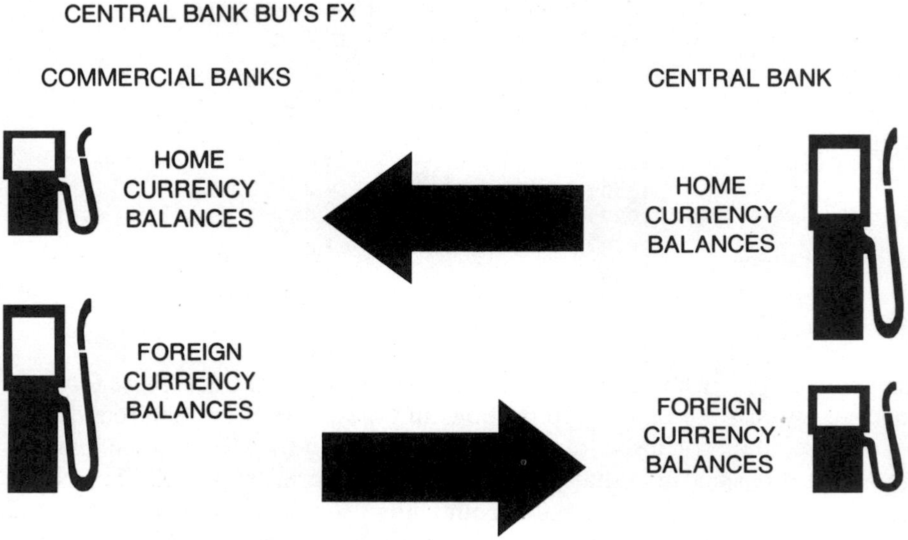

CENTRAL BANK BUYS FX

COMMERCIAL BANKS   CENTRAL BANK

HOME
CURRENCY
BALANCES

HOME
CURRENCY
BALANCES

FOREIGN
CURRENCY
BALANCES

FOREIGN
CURRENCY
BALANCES

Figure 3.4 Stage two: First leg of swap. Central bank provides Home balances in exchange for foreign currency balances.

swaps was not to cut the cost of forward cover, but liquidity management. This type of operation is common also in the Netherlands and Switzerland.

Figures 3.3 through 3.6 show how the Central Bank of an imaginary country called Home provides liquidity via a swap that runs over the domestic money-market reporting date.

Another example of the link between the foreign exchange and domestic money markets can be seen if we look at a drawing by the Federal Reserve Bank of New York on its swap network (see Chapter 4) to finance sales of

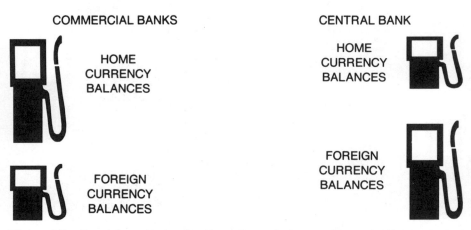

COMMERCIAL BANKS   CENTRAL BANK

HOME
CURRENCY
BALANCES

HOME
CURRENCY
BALANCES

FOREIGN
CURRENCY
BALANCES

FOREIGN
CURRENCY
BALANCES

Figure 3.5 Stage three: Reporting date. Home balances of commercial banks increased by swap.

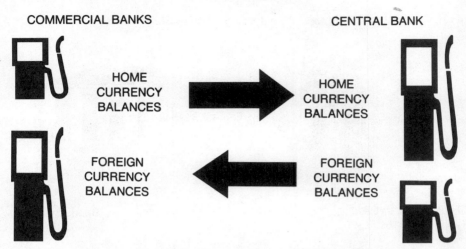

COMMERCIAL BANKS   CENTRAL BANK

HOME CURRENCY BALANCES   HOME CURRENCY BALANCES

FOREIGN CURRENCY BALANCES   FOREIGN CURRENCY BALANCES

Figure 3.6   Stage four: The swap unwinds. Commercial banks' Home balances fall again.

foreign currencies and stabilize the dollar. The drawing normally leads to two opposite and offsetting effects on bank reserves. First, the sale of a foreign currency for dollars by the Fed in the exchange market causes a fall in U.S. bank reserves. The U.S. bank receives foreign currency, paying over dollars to the Federal Reserve. This cuts its dollar reserves. Second, the reserves work their way back into the system. (See Figure 3.7.)

The way in which this happens will vary. It depends on the course of action taken by the securities trading desk at the Federal Reserve. Consider a swap with the Bundesbank. To start with, the swap drawing results in a credit of deutsche marks to the Federal Reserve's account at the Bundesbank. It also results in a credit of U.S. dollars to the account of the Bundesbank at the Federal Reserve. The latter account is then debited with these dollars that are invested in a special U.S. Treasury certificate of indebtedness. As a result, Treasury cash balances at the Reserve Bank increase. Under normal circumstances, the U.S. Treasury will then spend these dollars in the course of its operations, putting reserves back into the system, so the original reserve draining is offset. By comparison a direct intervention by the Federal Reserve in the foreign exchange markets to sell an existing balance of deutsche marks, that is, its own holding rather than the proceeds of a swap-drawing, will have an immediately draining effect on bank reserves, unless offset by other action. (See Figure 3.8.)

FOREIGN EXCHANGE INTERVENTION AND THE MONEY SUPPLY

At various points in this chapter we have touched on the links between foreign exchange and money markets and how these are used by participants

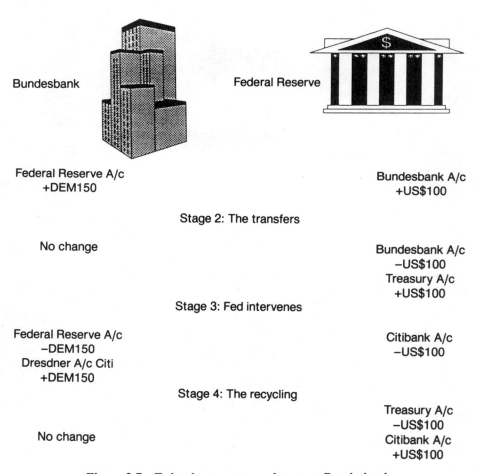

Figure 3.7   Federal reserve swap drawn on Bundesbank.

in the market, particularly by central banks when intervening. It is important to understand the wider effects of these links, because they affect the way in which central banks and governments operate their policies. For instance, a central bank that is committed to intervening in defense of a fixed exchange rate cannot control its money supply. If it does want to control money supply, it cannot intervene in unlimited amounts. To see why, we need to look at some examples of what happens when intervention takes place. The exact effects can be complex. They depend on our definitions of the money supply and the assumptions we make about how flows involved are financed. Very roughly, things work like this. If the authorities refuse to intervene in the foreign exchange market, an inflow of foreign

U.S.\$1 = DEM2

DEM	US\$
Federal Reserve A/C −200	−100 Citibank A/C
Dresdner Bank	
A/C Citibank +200	

Figure 3.8   Intervention Financed by Federal Reserve Balances.

currency will not change the country's foreign exchange reserves. Hence the inflow need not necessarily change the domestic money supply. But if the authorities intervene to buy the foreign currency, there will be an effect on the reserves. All other things being equal, this will affect the domestic money supply.

Perhaps the country which has had greatest experience of foreign currency inflows, and where these inflows have made most impact, is Switzerland. Because of Swiss support for a weakening dollar, Switzerland's reserves rose in December 1978 to 150% of average exports. That figure compares with 50% for the previous month. The change for the United States and for the United Kingdom during this period was negligible. As a result, the Swiss money supply, which had grown by less than 1% on average during 1977, grew by 19.8% during 1978.

It became clear to the Swiss authorities that this process could not be continued indefinitely. During 1979, the degree of dollar support was sharply reduced. That allowed a much more restrictive monetary policy. The money supply was actually reduced during 1979 by 1.2%. This was achieved at the price of a firm exchange rate. From an average of US\$ 1 = CHF 2.4035 during 1977, the Swiss franc strengthened to average 1.7880 during 1978 and 1.6627 during 1979. But a price was paid for this policy. The effects of the very rapid growth of money supply during 1978 and the subsequent weakening of the exchange rate during 1980 and 1981, were seen later in the consumer price index. This had risen by 0.8% on average during 1978, but rose 3.7% during 1979, 4.0% during 1980, and by March 1981 had risen by 6.4% compared with the same month of the previous year.

The detailed interrelationships are perhaps best understood by taking another case study. An interesting example occurred in the United Kingdom during 1977. The pound sterling was extremely firm during most of 1977. Sterling benefited from the arrangement of a medium-term standby facility for the Bank of England by the Bank for International Settlements in January 1977 and the decision by the Wilson government to raise medium-term external finance from the IMF. Until October of 1977, the Bank of England sold sterling to stop the pound from rising. As a result, the United Kingdom's external reserves rose. This tended to boost the money supply. To understand what actually went on, we will look again at our country called Home.

We start by making certain assumptions. First, all payments to Home residents from abroad are made in Home currency (HC). Second, the banks do not themselves hold foreign currency, nor do they lend HC abroad. Third, the public sector has no foreign currency transactions. Finally, we assume that nonresidents' HC deposits are excluded from the definition of the money supply.

We start with the way in which foreign exchange is taken into or paid out of the official reserves. The reserves are held by the Exchange Stabilization Fund (ESF). The ESF's working balances in HC are held in Treasury bills. When the ESF buys foreign currency it sells these Treasury bills back to the government. In exchange, it receives HC with which it can then pay the seller of foreign currency. In order to finance the payment to the ESF, the government is forced to borrow elsewhere. In effect, government securities are switched from the ESF to other holders.

Consider the case of a Home exporter who is owed HC 100 for an export delivery. Assume the overseas customer does not already hold Home currency. Then he will have to sell foreign currency for HC and pay the proceeds to the HC account of the exporter. Under our assumptions, the bank receiving the foreign currency will sell the currency immediately to the ESF. In order to buy the foreign currency from the bank, the ESF sells its Treasury bills to the government. This forces the latter to borrow elsewhere. In the absence of any other buyer, the government borrows from the banks. In effect, Home currency claims on the government are switched from the ESF to the banks. As there is a rise in the Home exporter's HC deposits, the money supply increases. The transactions associated with this change, as they affect the balance sheets of the banks and the ESF and the balance of payments are shown in Table 3.4.

An inflow may also take the form of a rise in Home currency bank deposits held by overseas residents. This will not affect the money supply. In this case,

Table 3.4   Effects of a Home Current Account Surplus

Sector	Liabilities	Assets
Home Banks		
Private sector HC deposits	+100	
HC claims on Treasury		+100
ESF		
Official reserves		+100
HC claims on Treasury		−100
Balance of Payments		
Current account: exports		+100
Capital account		
Change in reserves (increase, −)		−100

the overseas resident sells foreign currency to a Home bank and places the proceeds in an HC account. The bank again immediately sells the foreign currency to the ESF. The ESF sells Treasury bills back to the government, which borrows HC from the bank. So the bank has effectively taken an HC deposit from a nonresident in order to on-lend it immediately to the government. However, this time there is no increase in the money supply, as nonresidents' HC deposits are not included in the definition. The transactions are set out in Table 3.5. All of this has worked on the assumption that the ESF buys all foreign currency that is offered to it. Assume the ESF never intervenes, and assume still that neither Home banks nor the Home private sector hold foreign currency. Then it is clear that any foreign currency sold to Home residents is immediately sold back to nonresidents, because we have assumed that Home people never hold foreign currency. The exchange rate must move until nonresidents are willing to buy back the Home currency. It is the exchange rate which now takes the strain. The reserves do not change.

Let us now allow for residents' foreign currency holdings. They only affect the Home money supply when Home residents switch foreign currency into HC. To prove this, assume a Home current account surplus of HC 150 (see Table 3.6). Suppose that HC 50 of this is actually paid to the Home private sector in foreign currency. Suppose this foreign currency is deposited with the banks (who on-lend it to nonresidents). A further HC 60 worth is paid to Home residents in foreign currency and immediately sold for HC. The ESF finances its purchases of foreign currency by selling Treasury bills that are bought by the bank. The rest is financed by a fall in foreigners' HC bank deposits of HC 30 and a fall of HC 10 in overseas holdings of public sector HC debt. We assume this is sold to the banks. So bank lending to the government rises by the HC 10 of public sector debt, and HC 60 which the banks lend to the government to finance the increase in reserves. That makes a total of HC 70. This feeds straight through into Home money supply. So does the HC 30

Table 3.5   Effects of a Home Capital Account Surplus

Sector	Liabilities	Assets
Home Banks		
Nonresidents' HC deposits	+100	
HC claims on Treasury		+100
ESF		
Official reserves		+100
HC claims on Treasury		−100
Balance of Payments		
Current account		
Capital account		+100
Change in reserves (increase, −)		−100

Table 3.6   Effects of Home Current Account Surplus When Intervention Takes Place

Sector	Liabilities	Assets
HC deposits of private sector	+100	
HC deposits of nonresidents	− 30	
HC claims on public sector		+ 70
Foreign currency deposits of private sector	+ 50	
Foreign currency loans to nonresidents		+ 50
Balance of payments		
Private sector current account surplus which is used to finance:		+150
Foreign currency lending by Home banks (increase, −)		− 50
Overseas HC deposits with Home banks (increase, +)		− 30
Overseas lending to Home public sector (increase, +)		− 10
Change in reserves (increase, −)		− 60

fall in foreigners' HC bank deposits which are paid to U.K. residents. So there is a net rise in Home's money supply of HC 100. This is equal to the private sector current and capital account surplus on the balance of payments less the increase in Home private sector foreign currency holdings. In other words, the HC 50 paid to Home residents in foreign currency, which was not switched into HC, had no effect on Home's money supply.

Now, let's boil this down to what matters. Foreign currency inflows and outflows can affect a country's money supply. That can happen only if the Exchange Stabilization Fund, in our example, is intervening in the foreign exchange market on a net basis. That is, the ESF must not just buy and sell in the market to smooth exchange rate movements, but must be supplying foreign currency to the market or absorbing currency from the market. If intervention is taking place, the effect on the money supply need not be the same as the amount of intervention. As we saw, if the inflow produces a rise in nonresidents' deposits, the money supply need not be affected. Equally, the effect on the money supply depends on how the ESF finances its interventions. In our example, if the ESF's Treasury bill holdings could be refinanced from overseas, the effect on money supply would be offset. In other words, foreign currency flows will tend in general to affect the money supply—but not always; it depends on what else is happening. But, as a rule of thumb: *if Home central bank supports Home Currency, it drains funds from Home money; if it supports another currency, it adds funds to the Home market.*

4 The International Financial System

Now that we have looked at some of the major markets, it is time to see how they fit together. In this chapter, we see how individual domestic markets and the market for foreign exchange and international deposit markets mesh to form part of the international monetary systems. We look at some of the problems and ideas that have influenced the development of the system and we describe its components.

If one had to pick out three strands that weave the story together, they would probably be *international liquidity, adjustment,* and *choice of reserve asset.* We will look at each briefly. The word liquidity means having enough cash to meet day-to-day needs. For an individual, that means having enough cash in the bank, or readily saleable assets such as government bonds, to meet his or her regular monthly bills. For a country, it means having enough foreign currency to pay its monthly bills: the balance of imports, exports, and other cash flows, into and out of the country. It has to be in foreign currency because (with certain exceptions, such as U.S. dollars) other countries prefer to be paid in their own currency.

Liquidity and adjustment are in a sense opposites. If I do not have enough liquidity to meet my monthly bills, I have to cut my spending (or borrow). In other words, I have to adjust my behavior. It is the same for a country that is continually spending more abroad than it earns from abroad. In the end, it usually has to adjust its policies. The more liquidity it has, the less hurry there is about adjusting. The less liquidity it has, the more rapidly it must act. So liquidity and adjustment are a kind of trade off. Very often, countries have tried to put off adjusting their economies by using up liquidity, or by trying to get liquidity by borrowing. In most cases, they end up having to make adjustments—either to devalue their currency (to make their exports more competitive internationally and help the country earn more abroad) or cut back on spending on imports, often by painful domestic tax increases or interest rate rises. Over and over again the United Kingdom, Italy, Brazil, Mexico, and other countries have had to make the forced choice between adjustment and international liquidity. Much of the western world faced the same choice during the oil shocks of 1973/1975 and 1979/1980.

The third strand is choice of reserve asset. International liquidity consists of reserves of foreign currency, or gold, which is generally saleable for currencies, and certain other items. After the war, in 1945, international liquidity was held almost entirely in gold, U.S. dollars, and sterling. As confidence weakened in these two currencies, liquidity was switched into other currencies or gold. And the shock waves from these shifts of liquidity were seen in repeated currency crises (as we saw in the last chapter), which ended in sterling's 1967 devaluation and the 1971/73 devaluation of the U.S. dollar. Still today, as confidence in a currency fades or grows, international liquidity ebbs away from or flows into that currency.

INTERNATIONAL MONETARY FUND

The origins of today's international monetary system go back to 1944 when the Bretton Woods conference was held. At this conference, the International Monetary Fund (IMF) and the International Bank for Reconstruction and Development (IBRD, more commonly known as the World Bank) were established. The latter is mainly involved with development finance—a topic not covered here. The IMF aims to see that its members run their exchange rate and balance of payments policies in an orderly way. If need be, it helps them do so by lending them money. The funds to do this come from members' subscriptions (quotas), the IMF's borrowings, and other sources.

Under the original Articles of Agreement of the IMF, members agreed to make their currencies convertible; that is, not to restrict exchange of their currencies for others. They also agreed to fix par values for their currencies in terms of gold. This meant fixed exchange rates among currencies. It also meant (in theory) convertibility from currencies into gold. To help members meet these aims, the IMF would lend to them in proportion to their quotas.

The structure of the IMF is defined in its Articles of Agreement. It has a Board of Governors, which is its highest authority and meets once a year. But its day-to-day running is controlled by an Executive Board and the managing director. There are 21 executive directors. Of these, six are appointed by the countries with the largest quotas: United States, United Kingdom, Germany, France, Japan, and Saudi Arabia. The others are elected by the remaining members of the fund. The Executive Board selects the managing director, who is also chairman of the Executive Board.

The subscription, or quota, of a country depends on its national income, foreign currency reserves, and other factors. Quotas are normally reviewed at least every five years. The size of the quota decides two important things: how much a country can borrow from the IMF, and how much voting power it has. A country can borrow up to 100% of its quota, plus certain special facilities.

The borrowings are made in a series of slices or tranches. The more a country borrows, the more closely the IMF supervises its policies. For the first borrowing (the first credit tranche), the IMF requires a borrowing country to "make reasonable efforts" to overcome its problems. For second and higher tranches, the fund usually only lends on a standby basis. This means: (1) there are performance targets that the borrower must meet; (2) successive installments of the borrowing are only allowed if the targets are met.

The mechanics of the borrowing (drawing) are that a country uses its own currency to buy the currencies of other countries (or SDRs which are explained later). So a drawing on the IMF by a country raises the Fund's holdings of the country's currency, but reduces its holdings of the other currencies. The make-up of the fund's resources changes, but not the total. An example is shown in Table 4.1. The account of the IMF that holds these currencies is called the general account (as distinct from the SDR account).

Borrowings are made in tranches. The first of these is the reserve tranche: it is equivalent to drawing down a credit balance. For the reserve tranche, the country is lending its currency to Fund. Suppose the United Kingdom needs to borrow Deutschmarks. The United Kingdom buys Deutschmarks from the Fund and pays sterling. The Fund's Deutschmark holdings are now less than the amount Germany originally paid in: it is as if Germany had lent the Fund Deutschmarks to buy the United Kingdom's sterling. The difference between Germany's original quota and the Fund's present Deutschmark holdings is credited to Germany as its reserve tranche. A country has automatic access to the reserve tranche (since, after all, it lent the money to the Fund). After that, it can borrow four subsequent tranches, each equal to 25% of its quota, and, as we saw, subject to tighter and tighter control by the IMF.

In addition to its general balance of payments assistance, the Fund has a number of special facilities designed to address needs arising from specific factors. The first of these, established in 1963, was the *compensatory financing facility,* designed to help stabilize the earnings of countries exporting primary commodities. Countries experiencing balance of payments difficulties for reasons beyond their control, because of temporary short-falls in

Table 4.1   The United Kingdom Borrows DEM from the IMF General Account (£1 = DEM 3.00)

	UK Account with IMF (in £)	German Account with IMF (in DEM)
I. Before Drawing		
SDR holdings	100	100
Reserve tranche	0	0
Borrowings under		
First credit tranche	0	0
Second credit tranche	0	0
Third credit tranche	0	0
Fourth credit tranche	0	0
General Account holdings	£100 (U.K. original quota)	DEM 300 (German original quota)
II. U.K. Borrows DEM 300 and Pays in £100		
SDR holdings	100	100
Reserve tranche	0	300
Borrowings under		
First credit tranche	100	0
Second credit tranche	0	0
Third credit tranche	0	0
Fourth credit tranche	0	0
General Account holdings	£200	

export earnings, could borrow under this facility, if they cooperated with the Fund to find solutions to their problems. In 1988, the facility was broadened to become the *compensatory and contingency financing facility* (CCFF). This facility supersedes the compensatory financing facility, but keeps its essential features. It adds a mechanism for contingency financing of member countries that have entered into adjustment programs supported by the Fund. The compensatory financing facility's feature has been retained, but to it has been added a contingency mechanism, activated only in conjunction with Fund-supported programs of adjustment.

A second special facility, designed to smooth out fluctuations in the prices of primary commodities and so reduce variations in the export earnings of participating country, is the *buffer stock financing facility,* which was established in June 1969. Through this facility, the Fund can finance members' contributions to international schemes aimed at stabilizing commodity prices by building up a buffer stock.

During the 1970s, the IMF provided an *oil facility.* From 1974 to 1976, the Fund lent SDR 6.9 billion to 55 countries to help them overcome the impact of the oil price of 1973 and 1974.

In 1986, the *Structural Adjustment Facility* (SAF) was set up to provide low-cost financial assistance to low-income members facing serious balance of payment problems and needing to undertake programs of structural adjustment. In December 1987, the *Enhanced Structural Adjustment Facility* (ESAF) was set up to provide additional assistance to these countries. Countries eligible for SAF loans may borrow under the ESAF, but access under ESAF is considerably larger; it is normally expected to average about 150% of quota over a three-year program period, with provision for up to 350% in exceptional circumstances, compared with 70% under the SAF.

All this lending has to be financed. The main source of funds is the quotas subscribed to the IMF by member countries. Extra facilities have had to be arranged when the quotas were not enough. The first of these arrangements was known as the General Arrangements to Borrow (GAB). The GAB was set up in January 1962 in case the Fund had to make a large loan to the United States or the United Kingdom, the main reserve currency countries at the time. It was a four-year arrangement with 10 industrialized countries (the Group of Ten). Switzerland later took part as an associate (not directly, because Switzerland is not a member of IMF). The GAB continue in force, standing in 1989 at SDR17 billion. As well as from the GAB, the IMF has borrowed direct from certain countries in other ways. For example, in March 1981, the IMF borrowed two annual tranches of SDR 4 billion from the Saudi Arabian monetary authority. Other facilities have been arranged from time to time with other countries and through the Bank of International Settlements.

All of the Fund's lending and borrowing activities we have discussed so far are channeled through its General Resources Account. There is another account called the Special Drawing Rights (SDR) Account.

The SDR was created in July 1969 under the First Amendment to the IMF Articles Agreement. During the late 1960s, there were discussions of a possible shortage of international liquidity. It was feared that this might slow the growth of world trade. One way of increasing liquidity would have been an increase in the official price of gold. Legally this was tantamount to a devaluation of the dollar. The United States firmly opposed it. An alternative was to create a new form of international reserve asset through the IMF. The Special Drawing Right was called by this name to emphasize that it was a kind of borrowing, rather than a new currency. This was done to pacify France, which had argued for a revaluation of gold. The calculation and value of the SDR is fully explained in Chapter 13. For our purposes, what matters is that it represents an international reserve asset, which can be thought of as a currency issued by the IMF.

Members of the IMF can use SDRs to make international payments between themselves just as they could use U.S. dollars. When it was originally created, the possible uses of the SDR were very restricted. Over the years, they have been widened so that central banks can buy or sell SDRs among themselves, use SDRs to make loans or as security for loans, and deal in SDR swaps or forward SDRs.

In January 1981, the valuation of the SDR was very much simplified (see Chapter 13). In practical terms, the SDR is now equivalent to any other currency, with one major difference: private individuals cannot own it. SDRs can only be owned by member countries of the IMF and by 16 "prescribed holders" including the BIS, the Swiss National Bank, and various regional central banks (such as the Eastern Caribbean Central Bank) and development banks.

BANK FOR INTERNATIONAL SETTLEMENTS

The BIS is the central bankers' central bank. It is very discreet, and very influential. It was founded in 1930 to act as a trustee for the loans associated with the Young Plan for German reparations. The first members of the bank were the central banks of Belgium, France, Germany, Italy, Japan, and the United Kingdom, together with three private U.S. banks. The Federal Reserve Bank subsequently became a member along with all the major European central banks. Current membership consists of 30 central banks, of which 25 are European (including those of Eastern Europe except the U.S.S.R.) plus the United States, Canada, Japan, Australia, and South Africa. (The BIS was probably unique in having Albania and South Africa as co-members.) The board of directors is composed of the governors of the central banks of Belgium, France, Germany, Italy, and the United Kingdom, together with co-opted directors from among the governors of those member central banks that do not have an ex officio representative on the board. There are also five representatives of finance, industry, or commerce appointed by the governors of the permanent member central banks.

The BIS has three main functions. It acts as a bank, primarily as a central bankers' bank; it acts as a gathering place for central bankers, and a vehicle for international monetary cooperation; and it acts as trustee for various international loans. The BIS's role as an intermediary provides a number of advantages to other central banks. The first is anonymity: sometimes it is not convenient for a central bank to be seen to withdraw its funds from the market. The second is risk spreading: a deposit with the BIS is very safe since the bank is highly liquid. (Typically, three-quarters of the BIS's assets have maturities of under three months.) Finally, deposits placed with the BIS can usually be withdrawn at very short notice. The BIS uses the funds received from central banks primarily for lending to other central banks. Its lendings may be swaps against gold, covered credits secured by a pledge of gold or marketable short-term securities, unsecured credits, standby credits, and the like. It places the balance of its funds in short-term deposits with international banks.

The banking activities of the BIS are probably less vital than its role as a vehicle for international monetary cooperation. The most important part of this role is the least obtrusive: the monthly meetings of the BIS's board in

Basle. Before the foundation of the BIS, meetings of governors of central banks were usually attended with a blaze of publicity and speculation concerning a crisis. Routine meetings on a monthly basis have contributed much toward closer international monetary understandings. As a result, the BIS has been closely involved in almost every major international financial crisis since the war. The gold pool from 1961 to 1968 operated on the basis of directives issued in Basle by the governors of the central banks of the Group of Ten. Successive packages launched in defense of sterling were usually arrange at Basle. The network of swap arrangements maintained by the Federal Reserve Bank of New York developed originally from the swap arrangements undertaken at the first Basle agreement.

The BIS also plays a central role in the technical operations of the European Monetary System. Because of its original responsibility as a coordinator for international settlements in Europe, it has been closely involved in European payment arrangements since the war. During its lifetime, it has managed the Agreement on Multilateral Monetary Compensation set up in 1947 to handle postwar European clearing arrangements, the 1948 Intra-European Payments Agreement, the European Payments Union of 1950, its successor, the European Monetary Agreement of 1958, and most recently the European Monetary Cooperation Fund (EMCF) established in 1973, and the private interbank ECU clearing system.

The BIS also acts as agent for the European Monetary Fund, the successor to the EMCF, set up in 1979. That is, it handles the settlement of balances on behalf of the countries in the European Monetary System. It also runs the EC's system of short-term monetary support and manages the financial aspects of EC borrowings from overseas, and the private interbank ECU clearing system (see Chapter 21).

Finally, the BIS has an important research and coordination role in the Euromarkets. Its Annual Report and Quarterly Statistics are widely regarded as the most authoritative sources of information on developments on the Euromarkets. And the BIS also provides the secretariat for the Committee on Banking Regulations and Supervisory Practices set up in December 1974 by the central bank governors to coordinate bank supervision after the Herstatt crisis (see Chapter 2).

EUROPEAN MONETARY SYSTEM

With the evolution of the European Community toward a single market, it became necessary to help matters along by limiting exchange rate fluctuations between member states. The process was begun in 1972 by the creation of the "snake in the tunnel," a system where certain European currencies were fixed against each other but fluctuating within a "tunnel" against the U.S. dollar. The move to floating exchange rates derailed this and the system was relaunched in 1979 as the European Monetary System. Discussions are currently underway about enhancing the EMS and gradually moving toward a single currency for the European Community with a single European central bank (popularly dubbed the EuroFed). At Maastricht in December, 1991, member states committed themselves to a single currency before the year 2000. Britain insisted on being able to opt out. It remains to be seen whether EC members can achieve sufficient economic convergence to translate the dream into reality.

The European Monetary System (EMS) consists of three components: the Exchange Rate Mechanism (ERM), the European Monetary Cooperation Fund (EMCF), and the European Currency Unit. The ECU is explained in detail in Chapter 13. Briefly, it consists of an artificial currency unit that is made up from small amounts of the currencies of EMS members. The dollar equivalent of those currencies is added together to provide the value of the ECU.

The Exchange Rate Mechanism is a system under which those EMS members that take part are committed to keeping their currencies fixed against each other within certain bands. This is done by declaring a parity or *central rate* for each currency against the ECU. This implies a *parity grid*. The current parity grid is shown in Table 4.2.

At the time of writing, sterling and the peseta are allowed to fluctuate 6% either side of their central rates; other currencies have a 2.25% band. When a currency reaches the permitted limit it is said to be at the *intervention point*. When any two currencies reach their compulsory intervention rates against each other, the two central banks concerned are obliged to meet all bids/offers made to them at the relevant rate. This obligation is only binding, however, between the hours of 08:00 to 15:00 GMT. In some cases, this might mean a central bank selling a currency not held in its foreign exchange reserves or in an amount that exceeds its current holdings. Operationally this does not cause a problem, because the intervening central bank has the right to draw upon the very short-term financing facility (VSTF) of the EMCF, which is explained below. At the intervention point, access to the facility is automatic and the amount of credit available is unlimited. Since November 1987, however, the VSTF has also been available, in certain circumstances and in limited amounts, to finance intervention before a currency reaches a compulsory intervention point. However, such intervention may not be undertaken without the prior consent of a central bank whose currency is being used in the intervention.

There is an early warning system called the *divergence indicator* that measures the percentage of permitted fluctuation a currency has reached. When the divergence indicator is at 75% of the permitted maximum fluctuation, there is a presumption that the relevant central bank will intervene. But because the interactions of the parity grid are complex (see Appendix 1), in practice it is quite common for currencies to reach their compulsory intervention points before reaching or crossing their divergence threshold.

Table 4.2 Parity Grid

BILATERAL CENTRAL RATES AND SELLING AND BUYING RATES IN THE EMS FROM 9/10/90

		BEF100=	DKK100=	FRF100=	DEM100=	IEP1=	ITL1,000=	HFL100=	ESP100=	GBP1=
BELG/LUX	S		553.000	628.970	2109.50	56.5115	28.1930	1872.15	33.6930	64.6050
	C		540.723	614.977	2062.55	55.2545	27.5661	1830.54	31.7316	60.8451
BEF/LUF	B		528.700	601.295	2016.55	54.0250	26.9530	1789.85	29.8850	57.3035
DENMARK	S	18.9143		116.320	390.160	10.4511	5.21400	346.240	6.23100	11.9479
	C	18.4938		113.732	381.433	10.2186	5.09803	338.537	5.86837	11.2526
DKK	B	18.0831		111.200	373.000	9.9913	4.98500	331.020	5.52600	10.5976
FRANCE	S	16.6310	89.9250		343.050	9.18900	4.58450	304.440	5.47850	10.50550
	C	16.2608	87.9257		335.386	8.98480	4.48247	297.661	5.15981	9.89389
FRF	B	15.8990	85.9700		327.920	8.78500	4.38300	291.040	4.85950	9.31800
GERMANY	S	4.95900	26.8100	30.4950		2.74000	1.36700	90.7700	1.63300	3.13200
	C	4.84837	26.2162	29.8164		2.67894	1.33651	88.7526	1.53847	2.95000
DEM	B	4.74000	25.6300	29.1500		2.61900	1.30650	86.7800	1.44900	2.77800
IRELAND	S	1.85100	10.00870	11.3830	38.1825		0.510246	33.8868	0.609772	1.16920
	C	1.80981	9.78604	11.1299	37.3281		0.498895	33.1293	0.574281	1.10118
IEP	B	1.76950	9.56830	10.8825	36.4964		0.487799	32.3939	0.540858	1.03710
ITALY	S	3710.20	20062.0	22817.0	76540.0	2050.03		67912.0	1222.30	2343.62
	C	3627.64	19615.4	22309.1	74821.7	2004.43		66405.3	1151.11	2207.25
ITL	B	3546.90	19179.0	21813.0	73257.0	1959.84		64928.0	1084.10	2078.79
N-LANDS	S	5.58700	30.2100	34.3600	115.2350	3.08700	1.54000		1.84050	3.52950
	C	5.46286	29.5389	33.5953	112.6730	3.01848	1.50590		1.73345	3.32389
HFL	B	5.34150	28.8825	32.8475	110.1675	2.95100	1.47250		1.63250	3.13050
SPAIN	S	334.619	1809.40	2057.80	6901.70	184.892	92.2400	6125.30		203.600
	C	315.143	1704.05	1938.06	6500.00	174.131	86.8726	5768.83		191.750
ESP	B	296.802	1604.90	1825.30	6121.70	163.997	81.8200	5433.10		180.590
UK	S	1.74510	9.43610	10.7320	35.9970	0.964240	0.481050	31.9450	0.553740	
	C	1.64352	8.88687	10.1073	33.8984	0.908116	0.453053	30.0653	0.521514	
GBP	B	1.54790	8.36970	9.5190	31.9280	0.855260	0.426690	28.3340	0.491160	

S = Exchange rate at which the central bank of the country in the left-hand column will sell the currency identified in the row at the top of the level.
C = Bilateral selling rate
B = Exchange rate at which the central bank of the country in the left-hand column will buy the currency identified in the row at the top of the table.

The EMCF is important because of its short-term lending to EMS central banks when they are intervening in the foreign exchange markets. (It is often referred to as FECOM-Fonds Européen de Coopération Monetaire.) It is a rather shadowy institution, but one day it may prove to have been the seed from which grew the EuroFed. It runs the settlement and lending operations of the EMS. But it is itself run by the BIS; it is not like the International Monetary Fund in having a large independent staff. It evolved from the European Monetary Cooperation Fund. The EMCF was set up by the Council of Ministers of the European Economic Community in April 1973. They wanted it to aim at "(1) the progressive narrowing of the margins of fluctuation of the Community currencies against each other; (2) interventions in Community currencies on the exchange markets; and (3) settlements between central banks leading to a concerted policy on reserves."

The EMF has helped partially to achieve (1), and also partially (3), through the workings of the European Monetary System (EMS) (see Chapter 4). Progress on (2) has been limited, because a great deal of the time intervention has been caused by EEC currencies' movements against the U.S. dollar rather than among themselves. But a good deal of community intervention is now carried on in other EMS currencies.

The EMF's main job is to run a very-short term financing facility (VSTF) which finances intervention in EMS currencies. The VSTF allows unlimited credit among central banks involved in the EMS. The central bank that borrows from the EMF (say it is the Banca d'Italia) can extend the term of its borrowing by using the Short-Term Monetary Support facility (STMS). Otherwise it must repay within 45 days of the end of the month when it borrowed the money. (The maximum the Banca d'Italia can borrow under VSTF is 75 days.)

When it repays, the Banca d'Italia, in our example, must first use its holdings of the lender's currency. If it has borrowed from the Bundesbank it must repay as much as it can in DEM. But usually EMS central banks only hold working balances in other EMS members' currencies, so most of the debt has to be repaid in other currencies. Up to 50% of the remaining debt can be settled in ECUs. (The ECU is the European Currency Unit, a currency basket like the SDR, which is defined fully in Chapter 14. At this point we simply note that a part of the EMS central banks' reserves are held in ECUs.) After that, the Banca d'Italia can only use ECUs for repayment if the Bundesbank agrees. Otherwise, settlement must be made in proportion to the currencies in the borrower's reserves. Say 30% of Italy's reserves were in U.S. dollars: then 30% of its repayment would have to be in U.S. dollars.

If it did not want to repay immediately, the Banca d'Italia would turn to the STMS. The STMS lends to EMS central banks to finance temporary balance of payments deficits. Each country has a debtor quota, this amount being the maximum it is allowed to borrow, and a creditor quota, the amount it is committed to lend. On top of that there is the rallonge, which is a safety margin for the system as a whole. So a country can be asked to lend its creditor quota plus the total of the rallonge. Equally, it can borrow its debtor quota plus half of the rallonge. Take Germany as an example. The total it could borrow is ECU 1,740 million debtor quota plus ECU 4,400 million, half of the rallonge, for a total sum of ECU 6,140 million. It must lend, if asked to, ECU 3,480 million, its creditor quota, plus ECU 8,800 million, the rallonge, for a total of ECU 12,280 million. The lending amounts are twice the borrowing amounts. This gives a safety margin for the system as a whole. If a country needs to borrow, and all other countries in the system are also in deficit but one, the larger lending quotas plus the rallonge mean that the whole of the burden can be shifted to the country running a surplus.

The STMS can be used for a total of nine months. A country wanting to borrow for a longer period would apply to the EMF for medium-term financial assistance (MTFA). As a matter of fact, no one ever has, so the MTFA need not concern us much. We should note that lendings, if made, would be for two to five years and subject to economic policy conditions laid down by the EEC Council of Ministers. (This is probably why no one uses it: politically it is easier to be seen obeying the IMF, which is an impartial world body, than obeying other EEC members.)

As with all lendings, the EMF's credits have to be financed. The resources are provided by member central banks. They have each deposited 20% of their gold and dollar reserves with the EMF. Technically what happens is that they swap the gold and dollars for ECUs issued by the EMF. (See Chapter 13.) The swap is for three months. As each swap matures it is rolled over, but the amount involved is adjusted in line with the market value of gold and the dollar. The EMF's control over these reserves is very limited, though, since the central banks actually retain the dollars and gold involved, and they receive the interest earned on the dollars. However, the arrangement does represent a step toward the pooling of EC reserves.

ARAB MONETARY FUND

There is a regional Arab equivalent to the IMF, the Arab Monetary Fund, although it is neither large nor active. The AMF was set up by the Articles of Agreement of the Arab Monetary Fund concluded in April 1976 at Rabat in Morocco. The AMF was modeled closely on the IMF, and includes 20 Arab countries: Algeria, Bahrain, Egypt, Iraq, Jordan, Kuwait, Lebanon, Libya, Mauritania, Morocco, Oman, Qatar, Saudi Arabia, Somalia, Sudan, Syria, Tunisia, U.A.E., Yemen Arab Republic, and People's Democratic Republic of Yemen together with Palestine. Egypt's membership was suspended in April 1979. In the same month the AMF's paid-tip capital was increased to 124 million Arab Accounting Dinars (AAD 1 = SDR 3).

The major shareholders of the AMF are Saudi Arabia and Algeria. Its headquarters are in Abu Dhabi, and its primary work is to help member states with their balance of payments problems through short-term and medium-term loans (not exceeding seven years). It also gives guarantees designed to ease member borrowings from other sources. The AMF tries, too, to coordinate the monetary policies of member states and to extend technical assistance to their banking and monetary institutions.

Before the creation of the AMF, there were several Arab institutions which provided project finance, but none of them offered balance of payments support. This assistance was usually arranged on an ad hoc, bilateral basis through high-level political discussions with the leadership of the states concerned. The AMF represents an attempt to rationalize and institutionalize this function. On the other hand, with paid-in capital of only approximately US$ 400 million, it is a rather modest beginning. Furthermore, its development was held back by alleged embezzlement of large sums by a senior official.

CENTRAL BANK SWAP NETWORK

A foreign exchange swap is a spot purchase of a currency coupled with a forward sale. The calculations involved are discussed in Chapter 10. The effects on the timing of a bank's exposure, and how swaps are used by central banks to intervene in foreign exchange and money markets, are discussed in Chapter 3. This section discusses a rather special use of the swap by central banks: To borrow/lend foreign currency in exchange for domestic currency as a secured credit. The purpose is to lend the borrower foreign currency with which to intervene in the market.

The technique was first developed systematically by the U.S. Federal Reserve in the early 1960s. The first agreement was made by the Fed with the Banque de France in 1962. Between 1962 and 1967 the Fed negotiated agreements with other central banks and the BIS. Table 4.3 shows how the Federal Reserve swap network looked as of January 1989. Other countries have also put together swap arrangements, notably the United Kingdom in defense of sterling; and the Bank of Japan, for example, has a swap arrangement with the Swiss National Bank for 200 billion yen. The European Monetary Fund depends entirely on swaps for its resources.

We will look at the Federal Reserve network in detail since it is the most important. It consists of a set of standby credit agreements between the United States and other countries. Each arrangement provides for an exchange of currencies between the two countries with a commitment to reverse it in three months. At first, these swaps gave a full exchange risk guarantee to both central banks. After July 1973, the exchange risk on drawings by the Federal Reserve was shared evenly with the foreign central bank from which it was borrowing. Other central banks borrowing from the Federal Reserve had to take the full risk. Then in 1981, it was agreed that the earlier system would be restored.

To see how the swap network actually works, let's suppose the Federal Reserve wants to sell deutsche marks to support the U.S. dollar. Suppose it

**Table 4.3   Federal Reserve Swap Agreements as of
January 1, 1989 (in Millions of US$)**

Bank	Amount
Austrian National Bank	250
National Bank of Belgium	1,000
Bank of Canada	2,000
National Bank of Denmark	250
Bank of England	3,000
Banque de France	2,000
Deutsche Bundesbank	6,000
Banca d'Italia	3,000
Bank of Japan	5,000
Banco de Mexico	700
De Nederlandsche Bank	500
Bank of Norway	250
Bank of Sweden	300
Swiss National Bank	4,000
Bank for International Settlements:	
CHF/US$	600
Other European currencies/US$	1,250
	30,100

Source: Annual Report, Board of Governors of the Federal Reserve
System, 1989.

needs DEM 220 million (equivalent, say, to US$ 150 million) from the
Bundesbank. What actually happens is that it sells the Bundesbank US$ 150
million in exchange for DEM 220 million, with an agreed reversal in three
months' time at a fixed rate. The Bundesbank's reserves of foreign exchange
rise by US$ 150 million and those of the Federal Reserve rise by DEM 220
million. In other words, the swap has increased both central banks' reserves.
This apparent magic is caused by the fact that central banks report their
reserves as the total of the assets in foreign exchange, without deducting the
contingent liability on any forward exchange deals.

Central bank swaps, like any other swaps, can have an effect on the
domestic money market. We saw how this works in Chapter 3. But in general
the main reason central banks use them is to lay hands on foreign currency
with which to defend their own currency. The Federal Reserve for many
years did not hold foreign exchange reserves; hence its interest in developing
the swap technique in the early 1960s. Once the network was in place, the
Bank of England became an active user in the 1960s to defend sterling; the
Banque de France around the time of "the events of May" in 1968—and on
other occasions—also used the system, as have many other central banks.
During the period of "benign neglect" of the dollar, the swap network was
used only to give support to the Banco de Mexico; since the reversal of that
policy, the authorities would certainly use the swap network if they needed

to but in practice have not felt the requirement. During 1989, for example, the only use made of the network was a short-term drawing by Mexico.

THE FEDERAL RESERVE

In addition to the multinational institutions that we have described, there is a second set of key players in the international monetary system; the central banks of individual countries. Of these, the most important are the Federal Reserve, the Bank of Japan, the Bundesbank, the Bank of England, and the Banque de France.

Of the central banks we shall look at, the Federal Reserve is unique not only because of the central world role of the dollar but also because it is not one bank but twelve. It is a system rather than a bank. It was set up by Act of Congress much later than most other central banks—1913. The Federal Reserve Act divided the United States into 12 districts. It provided for the creation within each of a District Federal Reserve Bank. The system as a whole is controlled by the Federal Reserve's Board of Governors in Washington. The Board has 7 members appointed by the President and confirmed by the Senate. Members of the Board are appointed for 14-year terms, which limits the political control exercised by the President over the Board. The Chairman of the Board, who is named by the President, serves in that capacity for only 4 years although he can be reappointed. But his term does not start when the President's does, so an incoming President may have to wait until well into his term before appointing a new Chairman. Also, the Federal Reserve's independence is bolstered by the fact that it is a legally independent institution. The President and Executive arm of the U.S. government can exercise no direct control over it.

The Federal Reserve is subject to U.S. law, and so in the end comes under the authority of congress. The relevant law is the Full Employment Balanced Growth (Humphrey-Hawkins) Act of 1978. The act requires the Federal Reserve to present each year a report on monetary policy to Congress by February 20 and July 20. In the first of these, the Federal Reserve is required to set annual monetary policy targets. These have to be reviewed in the second report which also provisionally sets the next year's.

The way in which the Fed handles monetary policy is as follows. Although it is in principle a group of 12 banks, in practice the Fed works through two major bodies. The New York Fed handles the system's intervention in money and foreign exchange markets. Policy decisions on intervention are mainly controlled by the Federal Open Market Committee (FOMC). Members of the FOMC include all seven Governors of the system, together with the President of the New York Reserve Bank, and the Presidents of four of the other eleven district banks. Every member of the FOMC has one vote, but the Chairman of the Board of Governors has a decisive part in setting policy. He acts as chief spokesman for the system. It would be very unusual for a major policy action to be decided on by the FOMC if the Chairman of the Board of Governors had voted against: indeed, the news of a 4 to 3 vote against Paul Volcker in February 1986 was a major shock to the markets, even though the vote was subsequently reversed.

The FOMC normally meets about once a month. It reviews economic conditions, its goals, and current policy guidelines. At the end of the meeting, the FOMC issues a directive to the manager of the Open Market Account in New York. (The Open Market Account is the system's portfolio of U.S. Treasury and Federal Agency securities, and banker's acceptances, acquired in open market operations.) The directive sets a short-term target which the FOMC thinks is needed to meet its annual target. And it usually sets a limit on the movement in the Federal Funds interest rate. For example, the key parts of the August 1989 directive were:

> . . . (the FOMC) reaffirmed the ranges it had established in February for growth of M2 and M3 of 3–7% and 3.5–7.5% respectively, measured from the fourth quarter of 1988 to the fourth quarter of 1989 . . . the Committee seeks to maintain the existing degree of pressure on reserve positions . . . . slightly greater reserve restraint might or slightly lesser reserve restraint would be acceptable. . . . The Chairman may call for Committee consultation if it appears . . . that reserve conditions during the period before the next meeting are likely to be associated with a federal funds rate outside a range of 7–11%.

Note the difference of emphasis: tightening "might" be acceptable while easing "would" be. This directive was fairly evenly balanced; on other occasions, of course, the direction would be much more clear-cut.

The control of America's gold and foreign exchange reserves ultimately rests, not with the Fed, but with the U.S. Treasury. The Secretary of the Treasury is legally responsible for stabilizing the exchange value of the dollar, through the Exchange Stabilization Fund which is owned by the Treasury and which controls U.S. gold and foreign exchange reserves. The swap network was a way for the Fed to get hold of foreign exchange to use for intervention. But that is only temporary: it has to be repaid. The exchange stabilization fund owns the U.S. gold reserves and foreign exchange acquired from SDR sales and IMF drawings.

Policy on foreign exchange is controlled by the Treasury, whether the Fed likes it or not. Unfortunately, the Treasury is by its nature controlled by a politician. Thus, policy has swung back and forth over the years in line with changes in political complexion of the cabinet. During the 1960s, the Federal Reserve, with Treasury support, became very involved in international efforts to prop up fixed exchange rates. It developed a currency swap network; the Treasury issued Roosa bonds (U.S. Treasury bonds in foreign currency). By 1971, the U.S. Treasury Under Secretary John Connally had come to an "America first" view, which led to the dollar devaluation and the breaking of the gold-dollar link. For a few years, there was little intervention; "benign neglect" of the dollar was the policy. By 1977, this had led to unsustainable pressure on the dollar, and the swap network was reactivated. In 1981, under President Reagan, the pendulum swung back to another kind of benign neglect, based on the idea that intervention was wrong in principle. By 1985, this had led to unsupportable upward pressure on the dollar and was abandoned at the Plaza Agreement.

BANK OF ENGLAND

The Bank of England is the second oldest central bank (after the Sveriges Riksbank) in the world, and was founded in 1694. Until 1946, when it was nationalized, its shareholders remained private. So its evolution into the role of a central bank has been very gradual, in comparison with that of the Federal Reserve which was born as a full-fledged central bank. The Chancellor of the Exchequer controls the Bank, under the Bank of England Act of 1946. The Treasury has opened-ended power to give directives to the Bank on any subject except the affairs of a particular bank customer. Thus, unlike the Federal Reserve, the Bank of England is legally completely subordinate to the executive arm of the government. However, the Bank has traditionally exercised an independent influence of its own, largely because of its excellent working contacts with the City of London, from which the Treasury has traditionally been rather remote, and its network of overseas contacts with other central banks.

The Bank is controlled by its Court of Directors, which consists of the Governor, Deputy Governor, and 16 directors, all appointed by the Crown. The term of office of the Governor and the Deputy Governor is five years, that of the directors is four years. Four of the directors retire each year; they are eligible for reappointment.

The Bank of England is, with the Department of Trade to a minor degree, solely responsible for controlling what U.K. banks do. This centralization of control, together with the Bank's close working contacts with the banking system, has generally meant that its attitude toward regulation of city activities has been pragmatic and informal, in contrast to the bias towards regulation that we saw in the U.S. markets. This flexibility and informality helped the rapid development of the City of London's international financial activities during the 1960s and 1970s despite the weakness of sterling.

However, the United Kingdom's entry into the EEC forced the Bank to harmonize its attitudes with the more legalistic approach of its counterparts in Europe. For example, the Bank had to introduce, for the first time, a legal definition of a bank and banking activity, in the Banking Act of 1979. For the first time, also, this Act introduced a requirement that a bank should be recognized as such by the Bank of England in order to operate.

A more legalistic approach was also forced on the Bank as a result of the Financial Services Act of 1986, and the wider involvement of banks in the securities industry through the so-called "Big Bang" of around that time, under which the stock market was reformed and banks became heavily involved in the securities industry. Although the Bank of England had always been closely involved in the U.K. securities industry by virtue of its deep involvement in the City, the effects of "Big Bang" were to tie it even more closely into the securities markets. The Bank's role is thus wider, yet less clearly defined than that of the Federal Reserve.

As in the United States, the Treasury controls the United Kingdom's gold and foreign exchange reserves. But their day-to-day management is entrusted to the Bank of England, which was responsible for the country's reserves long before the Treasury was. Indeed, the low gold content of U.K. reserves can be traced back to the Bank's private sector origins. During the nineteenth century, its attitude was "maximum banking profits consistent with convertibility of sterling"; this meant low holdings of noninterest-bearing gold. More recent gold outflows were caused by the defense of sterling during the 1960s and 1970s. Since July 1979, 20% of the United Kingdom's reserves are on deposit, in exchange for ECUs with the European Monetary Fund.

DEUTSCHE BUNDESBANK

Unlike the Bank of England, the Bundesbank is legally independent of its government. Unlike the Federal Reserve's, that independence is not fettered by any equivalent of the Humphrey-Hawkins Act. Of the world's major central banks, the Bundesbank is probably the strongest: it has benefited from the German people's horror of inflation after their experiences of the 1930s. The Deutsche Bundesbank law of 1957 lays down in Article 12 that the Bundesbank "shall not be subject to instructions from the Federal Government." Of course, the Bundesbank must support government policy as far as it can without compromising its primary duty, the safety of the currency. And during the headlong rush to German monetary unification in 1989/90, the wishes of the Bundesbank were overridden by the political masters in Bonn, who were determined to achieve monetary unification on terms that would be acceptable in East Germany, even though the Bundesbank did not approve the details of the rate of exchange between the Deutschmark and the old Ostmark.

The Bundesbank is controlled by a central bank council, which usually meets every two weeks on a Thursday. (Sometimes these meetings are followed by a press conference, sometimes not. If it is announced that no press conference will be held, the market usually assumes there will be no change in policy). The council's members are appointed by the President of the Federal Republic, on the government's recommendation (which must follow consultation with the council). The members' terms are usually eight years. The Bundesbank controls 11 provincial central banks, each of which handles official business in its Land (province).

Unlike the United States, the United Kingdom, or France, but like Switzerland, Germany does not have any equivalent to the Exchange Stabilization Fund. The Bundesbank owns the country's reserves. Every change in the level of reserves alters the size of the Bundesbank's balance sheet and so the level of domestic currency (compare Chapter 3). The Bundesbank also owns Germany's gold reserves, which have remained fairly stable since 1971. Most of the gold holdings were acquired during 1951 to 1961, when the German "miracle" was taking place. In fact, in 1967, under U.S. pressure—exerted in the form of military leverage—Germany made a formal commitment that it would not try to convert its dollars into gold (compare other central banks' holdings, discussed next).

BANQUE DE FRANCE

The Banque de France dates back to Napoleon (it was founded in 1800) and, like Napoleon, has always been a strong believer in tight central control. More than any of the other central banks, it has traditionally had influence everywhere in its banking system. It has branches around the country, helping it to keep in close contact with credit conditions in each area. Its knowledge reaches down to the most minute details. For example, every bank, when approached to open a new account for a customer, had to contact the Banque. It must check whether or not any problems have ever been reported with this customer (and must report any problems as they occur). This gives the Banque credit information on every individual and company in the country.

Until 1946, the Banque de France, like the Bank of England, operated as a private company. Under the nationalization law, a reform of the Banque's statutes was provided for, but it did not in fact take place until 1973. The new statutes gave the Banque a much freer hand and laid down a new structure. Control of the Banque rests with the Governor, two Deputy Governors, and the General Council. The Governor and his deputies are appointed for an unlimited term by the President of the Republic. The council consists of 10 members, of whom one is elected by the staff of the Banque, and the rest are appointed by the Government. Counsellors serve for six years. The council normally meets once a week.

As a nationalized bank, the Banque de France does not have the independence of the Bundesbank of the Federal Reserve. But, as with the Bank of England, its prestige gave it authority (especially in the 1950s, when French governments rose and fell like a jack-in-the-box). More recently, however, the Banque's role has become less all embracing, as a result of the liberalization of the French financial markets during the 1980s. In particular, in 1985/86 the Banque abandoned its system of credit control. From December 1986, monetary policy has essentially been put into action by the Banque's fixing of its intervention rate on the interbank money market. At the same time, to offset the weakening of its direct control over credit, the Banque laid greater emphasis on reserve requirements. It widened the range of institutions subject to the reserve requirements, to include savings banks, municipal savings banks, and the major centralized savings institutions. Reserve requirements on sight deposits were lifted from 3% to 5%, raised to 5.5% in October 1989. Over the same period, other increases were made on term deposits, certificates of deposit and the like. The French financial system has been greatly liberalized compared with the tight controls imposed during the 1970s. The fundamental change has been the effective abolition of exchange control. This has opened the French financial system to external influences for the first time for 50 years. At the same time, however, strict internal fiscal discipline and the conquest of inflation by determined monetary policy has meant that the French Franc has been able to become much more closely linked to the Deutschmark in the European Monetary System (see next).

France's gold and foreign exchange reserves are owned by the Fonds de Stabilization des Changes (exchange stabilization fund) that is controlled by the Treasury but managed on a day-to-day basis by the Banque de France. For many years, France favored the role of gold as an international monetary asset. This emphasis flowed primarily from a political insistence that the financing of international trade and the source of international liquidity should not depend on any single national currency. Specifically, it should not depend on the dollar. The classic statement of this position was by General de Gaulle in 1965: "We hold as necessary that international exchange be established . . . on an indisputable monetary base that does not carry the mark of any particular country. What base? In truth, one does not see how in this respect it can have any criteria, any standard, other than gold . . . . which does not have any nationality, which is held eternally and universally . . . ."

From 1970 to 1980, whatever the original political reasons, this policy was extremely profitable for France, as gold went from US$ 35 per ounce to US$ 850. From 1980 to 1990, as gold moved from US$ 850 to US$ 390, however, that policy has been less attractive. In 1960, France held 46.89 million ounces of gold; in 1970, 100.91 (down from the peak of 149.54 in 1967: the "events of 1968" caused some drain). By 1980, the figure was 81.85 million ounces (but this total will have been affected by the swap made by all EMS members with the European Monetary Cooperation Fund, under which 20% of reserves were deposited in the exchange for Ecus). This figure held constant throughout the 1980s, as the price of gold collapsed in the early part of the decade, and remained low for the rest of the period.

A comparison of central bank gold holdings at this point may be of interest. (See Table 4.4.)

BANK OF JAPAN

Of the central banks we are considering, the Bank of Japan and the Swiss National Bank are the only ones still with private shareholders. Legally the bank is a special corporation under the Bank of Japan Law of 1942 (although

Table 4.4   1989 Holdings of Gold in Millions
of Ounces

United States	261.93
Germany	95.18
Switzerland	83.28
France	81.85
Italy	66.67
Netherlands	43.94
Belgium	30.23
Japan	24.23
Austria	20.66
United Kingdom	18.99
Canada	16.10

Source: International Monetary Fund, *International Financial Statistics Year Book 1990.*

it traces its origin to 1882) which is held 45% by the public and 55% by the government. In practice, the private shareholders have no say in running it. The Minister of Finance can give general directives to the bank, and can dismiss its officers. The usual Japanese "consensus" system, though, means that formal instructions almost never have to be given to the bank, but this does not mean that there are not often strong arguments between the two regarding policy.

The highest decision making body of the bank is its Policy Board, which is composed of the Governor, two representatives of the government (one representative each from the Ministry of Finance and the Economic Planning Agency), and four appointed representatives (one from the city banks, the regional banks, commerce and industry, and agriculture). Of these seven, the government representatives do not have voting power, so that decisions are taken by majority vote of the Governor and the appointed members. The appointed members are selected by the cabinet and approved by both houses of Diet for terms of four years, with reappointment possible. The Policy Board's decisions on discount rates and open market operations are independently made. However, discount rate changes would normally be subject to consultation with the Ministry of Finance. In the end, the Bank of Japan will normally have its way, but this may be preceded by a lengthy period of arguments with the Ministry.

Japan, like the United States, the United Kingdom, and France, has a separate foreign exchange fund. In fact it has a Foreign Exchange Funds Special Account and a Precious Metals Special Account for the gold reserves. The Foreign Exchange Funds Special Account raises its finance by borrowing from the Bank of Japan, by issuing short-term bills (Foreign Exchange Fund bills), and by selling surplus foreign currency balances to the Bank of Japan.

SWISS NATIONAL BANK

The Swiss National Bank, founded in 1905, has two headquarters. The legal and administrative headquarters are at Berne, but the bank's Directorate is at Zurich. It is a private corporation, but most of its shares have been held since the beginning by the Cantons and Cantonal banks. The SNB is controlled by a Bank Council consisting of 40 members. Detailed control of the bank is handled by a bank committee, chosen by the council. But for practical purposes, the body which matters is the Directorate, which fixes the discount rate and decides on monetary policy. It consists of the Governor and two Deputy Governors, appointed by the Federal Government for six years. It also has deputy members, are also appointed by the government for six years, and section directors, elected by the Bank Committee.

The SNB's international relationships are different from those of the other central banks we have looked at, because Switzerland has a strict policy of international neutrality. This has caused it to refuse to join the IMF and the World Bank. But the SNB works in parallel with other central banks, for instance in lending money to the IMF under the General Arrangements to Borrow and other IMF financings. The SNB is a shareholder in the BIS—not surprising, since the latter's headquarters is in Basle.

Like the Bundesbank, the Swiss National Bank owns the country's reserves, and they form part of its balance sheet. So any currency inflow immediately inflates the SNB's balance sheet. The bulk of the reserves are held in gold. The high level of gold holdings is partly due to the traditional legal requirement that 40% of the Swiss note circulation be backed by gold.

5 Forecasting the Markets

This chapter provides a brief account of how interest and exchange rates are forecast. For more detail, there are many excellent books on the subject, some of which are listed in the list of Further Reading at the end of this book. The purpose is not to recommend any single method since the correct method varies with the state of the market. Sometimes market psychology focuses on a particular factor, either because it is seen as critical in itself or because it is thought that the central bank or government of the country concerned thinks it is critical. At other times, news regarding that particular factor will be totally ignored. Sometimes, a particular technical theory (charting, oscillators, or some other technical measure) seems to perform particularly well, and gains adherents. Then its failure causes it to go out of fashion.

There are as many different ways of exchange rate forecasting as there are points of view. Broadly, though, one can class them into two kinds: fundamental and technical. We will start with fundamental methods then move on to technical methods. Finally, we will look at a longer-term, passive "optimization" approach.

THE FUNDAMENTAL APPROACH

The fundamental approach to interest and exchange rate forecasting focuses on the basic factors that shape the performance of an economy and hence the interest rates and exchange rate of the country concerned. Political or social factors vary widely and we will not attempt to describe them in this book. The economic factors that are relevant can be broadly classified into monetary, fiscal, and external policy.

But before discussing them, it is useful to make one basic point perhaps best summed up by Disraeli: "There are three kinds of lies: Lies, damned lies, and statistics." Most of our understanding of the economic situation comes from public statistics of one sort or another. Therefore, it is critical to interpret them properly. Many of the points I am going to make are obvious but easily get over looked in the heat of the moment (or in politicians' statements).

The first questions, as far as the markets go, are "Is this figure in line with what the market expected? How much is already discounted in the present price?" Next, "Is this number good or bad?" The answers to the last question get complicated, but we'll start with some general points.

First "Is the figure seasonally adjusted?" A lot of statistics, like money supply, exports and imports, industrial production, and so on are influenced by the season of the year. A bad unemployment figure in December does not mean much if the ground is frozen so all building workers are *temporarily* laid off. We should look to see if the figure is adjusted to take account of the season.

Then, too, all seasonal adjustment is guesswork. Most statistical series are adjusted by the so-called U.S. bureau of the Census X11 method. This relies on a long run of past data. The movements in the data are then split into four components: trend, cyclical, irregular, and seasonal. To do this effectively requires several years of data. So if the series is fairly new, the seasonal adjustment may not be very reliable.

Also look at the base date of the series. For example, just before an election, a politician may announce that inflation is running at x%. He does not say whether he took last month's increase and multiplied it by 12 to put in on an annual basis; the last three months multiplied by 4; or whatever. Likewise, different inflation numbers can be calculated: in the United Kingdom it is

Table 5.1 Lies, Damned Lies, and Statistics

Rising Statistics	Pessimistic View	Optimistic View
Consumer/wholesale prices	Inflationary: less competitive exports	Monetary policy will tighten and rates will rise
GDP, industrial production	Faster growth, higher inflation and higher imports	Economy performing well; interest rates may rise
Interest rates	The authorities aware of the currency's weakness	The authorities determined to bring inflation under control
Money supply	Inflationary	Interest rates will rise to correct the problem
Trade deficit	Trade deficit out of control; devaluation needed to restore balance	Deficit will be offset by capital inflows or is only cyclical
Inventories	Stockpiling due to fear of inflation; imports may rise	Unsold stocks mean economy is slowing; inflation will ease

quite common to exclude the effects of the mortgage interest rate; in the United States, the so-called "core" rate of inflation excludes food and energy prices on the grounds that these are volatile.

Yet another point is to check whether a figure is "real" or "nominal." That is, does it include inflation? Few people would think that the statement "GNP grew by 10% last quarter" meant much without knowing whether the price effects were included. But it is surprising how often monthly retail sale figures in nominal terms are taken to be in real terms, and vice versa.

Finally, there are always two ways of looking at a statistic. An optimist will say that a glass is half full of water, a pessimist that it is half empty. Similarly, the market will interpret a statistic one way or another depending on whether it is confident of the economic management of the country or not. For every optimistic interpretation, there is a pessimistic interpretation (see Table 5.1). Let's now look at some of the important parts of economic policy that move the markets. One of these is monetary policy.

MONETARY POLICY

During the late 1970s and early 1980s, there was a phase when "Monetarism" became a key component of economic policy in a number of countries, including the United States, the United Kingdom, and several others. The most notable experiment was by Paul Volcker in the United States, whose 1979

New Economic Policy was a form of strict monetarism that produced very sharp swings in interest rates. In recent years, an element of pragmatism has come back into most countries' monetary policy, as the realization has dawned that pure monetarism has many inherent problems. Nobody doubts that monetary policy means *something;* the question is exactly how much.

It would probably be fair to say that monetary policy only became a practical option when exchange rates were allowed to float in 1973. As we saw in Chapter 3, you can't have a completely fixed exchange rate and complete control of the money supply at the same time, unless you are very lucky. The intervention needed to stabilize the exchange rate will usually show up somewhere in the money supply. (It was this factor that determined Mrs Thatcher's resistance to the United Kingdom's entry into the Exchange Rate Mechanism of the European Monetary System. She argued that entry into the ERM meant that Britain would lose its monetary policy independence.)

In late 1974, Germany became the first country to announce a formal money supply target for the year ahead. In early 1975, the United States followed, along with Switzerland and Canada. In 1976, France and the United Kingdom announced targets. In many cases, these countries later adopted stricter versions, but then gradually came to relax the purity of their commitment to money supply targets.

The original ideas behind monetarism came from the *quantity theory of money.* This starts with a truism: The total money stock in a country circulates at a certain speed to finance the country's economic activity. To see what this means, imagine we are on an island with $500 in bills. The only product on the island is loaves of bread. Say 2000 loaves are produced, and paid for at 50 cents each. The annual value of production is $2000 \times \$0.50 = \$1000$. The turnover of the economy (its annual production value) equals the quantity of production (call it q) multiplied by its price (call it p). (See Figure 5.1.)

Every year the stock of money, $500, must turn over twice to pay for the turnover of the economy. If the islanders' children burn $250, there is only $250 in bills on the island. The money stock would have to circulate twice as fast (four times a year) to pay for the turnover. The number of times that money circulates in an economy is called its *velocity.* When the stock of money was $500, the annual velocity was two. Now it has had to rise to four.

The idea behind quantity theory was that velocity is usually fairly stable over time. A change in the quantity of money will show up in the price or quantity of output. Suppose our island prints another $250. The money stock is now $500 again. But suppose velocity now stays stable at four. Then our $500, turning over four times a year, is enough to finance annual turnover of $2000 but production of loaves is only 2000 (assume it cannot be increased). Then the extra supply of money can only end by bidding up prices until each loaf costs $1. When we assumed constant velocity, we assumed people are just

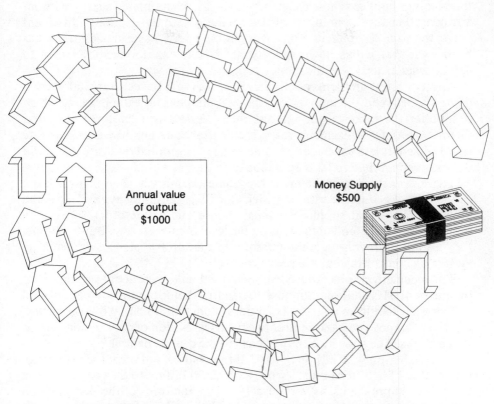

Figure 5.1 Money supply must circulate twice to finance production.

as inclined to spend money as before. If they get twice as much money, they will spend twice as much. If there is only the same number of loaves, the producers of loaves will be able to raise their prices.

The complications to this theory in real life mean it does not really work in this way. However, many traders, and many central banks, believe that controlling the money supply is important in controlling inflation. If the markets see that a central bank has the money supply under control, that makes the market more confident about that currency. As a result, monetary policy is important for a trader to understand.

Monetary Policy in Action

The first complication arises from deciding which money supply? Most countries have a range of financial instruments that could be considered money: notes and coin, demand deposits, balances on time deposit that can be used to make payments, certificates of deposit, and so on. Variations in the holdings between these can produce variations in money supply without any overall change in holdings of financial assets in the economy. In recent years, the pace of financial innovation in the major western economies has been such that it has been extraordinarily difficult for central banks to decide what exactly was the money supply.

Another set of problems comes from the fact that the central bank faces a dilemma between the amount of money it supplies and the price at which it supplies the money—the interest rate. We saw in Chapter 3 a similar dilemma with fixed exchange rates. If a central bank held the exchange rate rigidly fixed, it had to be ready to intervene in unlimited quantities. If it did not intervene, it had to let the rate move free.

There is a similar problem in the domestic market. The central bank cannot fix the interest rate at which it will supply money, and also the amount of money it supplies. It must choose one or the other. Normally, central banks have tended to focus on the level of interest rate. But to do this, they also often manipulate the quantity of money available in the banking system by controlling banking reserves.

The mechanism is as follows. Suppose the banking system as a whole has liabilities of $100 billion. Suppose the central bank requires banks to hold 10% of their liabilities in cash. Then the system will hold $10 billion in cash reserves. Suppose now the central bank sells $1 billion of government bonds to the banks. They pay $1 billion of cash to the central bank. Now the system as a whole has only $9 billion of cash. If the system is to meet the 10% ratio, the volume of liabilities must shrink from $100 billion to $90 billion. Since the money supply consists very largely of the liabilities of the banking system, the money supply must also shrink. That is why every day the Federal Reserve injects cash or drains it from the system: to control the growth rate of the money supply. The classic example of the extreme version of this policy was in the United States under Paul Volcker. In October 1979, the Federal Reserve decided to aim at very strict control of reserves in the banking system, regardless of the effect on interest rates. The effects can be seen in Figure 5.2.

Once a central bank has decided on its target, it must decide how it wants to implement it. To see what is involved, let's go back to our island. Now that the islanders have understood the link between money supply and inflation, they decide to appoint a central bank to deal with the problem. The central bank decides that for the year ahead that it can realistically expect production of loaves can grow by 10%, from 2000 to 2200. But because of the recent inflation, the baker's workmen have been getting restless and are demanding an increase in wages. So it seems likely that the island will probably have inflation of, say, 5%.

The central bank decides that velocity will probably remain stable, at four. It assumes that the price of a loaf will be 5% higher, namely $1.05. It assumes that production will be 2200. So it expects that the value of turnover on the island (gross national product) will be $2310 = 2200 × $1.05. So it knows the

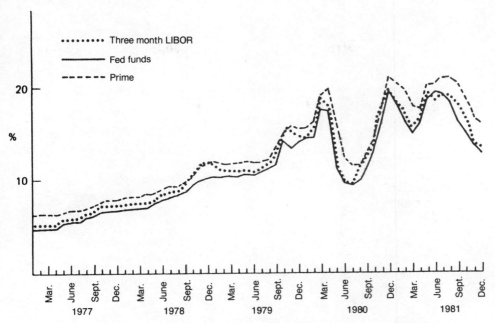

Figure 5.2 Prime, Fed. funds, and three-month LIBOR 1977–1981 (monthly averages in percent). *Source:* Data Resources, Inc.

money supply, circulating four times a year, must be enough to finance annual turnover of $2310. In other words, it concludes that the money supplied must equal $577.50, since if this amount turns over four times during the year, it equals $2310. In fact, the money supply must expand by just over 15%, to finance the 10% rise in production and 5% inflation.

Suppose, now, that the central bank decides that this is too high. It does not want inflation to be as high as 5%. Suppose it aims for 2.5%. Then it will expect the price of a loaf at the end of the year to be $1.025. It expects the growth in production in loaves to be unchanged, at 10%. This inflation figure implies a value of GNP = 2200 × $1.025 = $2255. If the velocity of circulation is still expected to be four, this means a supply of money of $563.75 will be sufficient. That is, the money supply must grow by just over 12.5%, financing a rise of 10% production and 2.5% inflation. (See Figure 5.3.)

When it decided to squeeze inflation by squeezing the money supply, the central bank made two big assumptions. First, it assumed that inflation could be cut from 5% to 2.5% without affecting production. But it might be that the baker's workmen, who we said were restless, might not be prepared to produce 10% more loaves without getting a larger increase in wages. They might go on strike, or they might not work as hard. In any event, production might not rise as fast as the central bank expects. In that case, its money supply target would be pitched too high, and inflation would rise higher than its intended 2.5%, while production would fall below target.

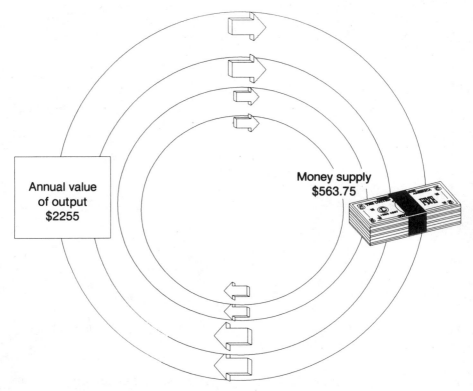

Figure 5.3   Now money supply must turn over four times to production.

The second big assumption that the central bank made was that velocity would stay stable at four. But suppose, for some reason, velocity fell to three. Then the projected money supply of $563.75 would only be enough to finance a GNP of $1691.25. If prices rose to $1.025, production would have to fall to 1650 loaves per annum. Conversely, for production to remain steady at 2200, the price per loaf would have to fall to 76.875 cents.

What has happened, has been a collapse in demand. As we said earlier, if you assume a stable velocity, that means you assume people are as likely to spend money as they did in the past. If velocity falls, that means people are no longer spending the money as quickly as they did. So when the central bank makes its forecast for the year ahead, it has to forecast not only inflation and production, but also how it thinks people's spending and saving habits are likely to move during the coming year. All this makes the process of fixing a monetary target quite complicated, and the process of achieving it even more complex.

Coming back from our island to reality, let's look at how some central banks look at these problems. In December 1989, the Bundesbank forecast a growth of real production potential in 1990 of 2.5%. The price level was assumed to rise at an average annual rate of 2%. In addition, 1/2% was allowed to take account of the slowdown in trend of the velocity of circulation of money. This yielded a growth rate of about 5% for the money stock M3. Because there was some uncertainty about the underlying calculations, the target was formulated in terms of a corridor of 4% to 6%.

Other central banks follow a rather similar process, but often much less formally than in Germany. The major complications in this approach arise from the instability of velocity of circulation of money. To quote from the 1989 Annual Report of the BIS:

> (Velocity) . . . was clearly affected last year by unpredictable disturbances or by structural financial change whose impact was difficult to foresee. An example of the former could be seen in Germany, where a sharp acceleration in the growth of currency in circulation, partly related to uncertainties associated with the planned introduction of a withholding tax on interest income, had to be accommodated. In France and Italy structural changes in the financial system contributed to strong rises in non-bank holdings of market instruments which are included in M3 but not in the targeted aggregates. In Switzerland, changes in the interbank clearing arrangements and the system of reserve requirements permitted banks to economize on the holding of balances at the National Bank to an exceptionally large extent. . . . Other large changes in velocity primarily reflected interest rate effects. (pp. 142–143)

Transmission of Monetary Policy

Once a central bank has decided on its monetary policy, we need to understand how a change in policy is transmitted through the financial system and affects money supply. There are two main ways of looking at this process. One side looks at the liabilities of the banking system, and the other looks at the assets.

Monetarists tend to look at the liability side. The view that focuses on the asset side has been described as the "European (and IMF) view of money creation." Both views must be true. The liabilities of the nation's banking system must always equal its assets. It is a question of which is primary. Just as some banks are inherent lenders, needing deposits with which to fund themselves, and other banks inherently deposit-takers, needing places to lend, one side or other of the national balance sheet can be seen as the driving force. And on your view of which side is primary, depends your view of the effectiveness of the individual policy tools involved.

Monetarists generally accept that interest rates are not very effective as a means of controlling the money supply. They therefore tend to argue for direct control on the liability side of the balance sheet. One way to do this is to control the supply of reserves available to the banking system. As we saw in Chapter 3, a change in the reserves of the banking system changes its liabilities in portion to a multiplier. So by controlling total reserves, the central bank can control total bank deposits.

Others would argue that when the authorities attempt to control any monetary total, the activities of the financial system in creating substitutes will change the demand for it. So its behavior will not reflect conditions accurately. This, again, fits in with the view referred to earlier as the European view of money creation. On this argument, controlling the supply of reserves to the banking system to stop it granting credit will mean that borrowers will look elsewhere (through the security markets for example). This is often called "disintermediation." Unless the central bank is always widening the network of its controls over lending, its money supply targets will became less and less useful. During the 1960s when the Bank of England tried to run direct controls on bank lending, all that happened was that nonbanks took up the slack demand for credit.

From the point of view of the market, it is my opinion that nobody really cares which targets are chosen, or which policy is adopted, as long as the markets are convinced that the authorities are really determined to keep the situation under control in the medium term. A classic example is the case of Switzerland, which was forced by inflows of foreign currency to entirely abandon money supply targets in 1979, without in any way affecting the market's belief in the long-term determination of the Swiss National Bank to hold down inflation.

FISCAL POLICY

We turn now to the other major area of policy which interacts with monetary policy: fiscal policy. This can be crudely defined as the government's tax and spending policy. Dealers need to understand two aspects of fiscal policy: first, its impact on the economy as a whole, and second, its effect on flows of tax payments through the markets.

The second effect is much simpler to understand than the first. As we said in Chapter 1, when money is withdrawn from bank accounts to pay taxes, liquidity flows from the private sector to the public sector. That is, tax payments tend to drain the money markets of liquidity. This is why the money markets became very tight over important tax payment dates, for example, April 15 every year in the United States. In the United Kingdom, January and February are traditionally tight months, because corporation tax becomes due and payable then.

The impact of fiscal policy on the economy as a whole is more complex. Many traders think of fiscal policy as being government deficit spending, and therefore almost automatically inflationary. To show why this need not be true, we must look at why governments started using fiscal policy to manage their economies after the war. During the worldwide slump of the 1930s, most people felt that fiscal policy was not a good way of boosting an economy out of a slump. Keynes showed that they were wrong. He argued that if the government spent an amount equal to the shortage of demand in an economy, it would create the extra demand without causing *excess* demand.

As long as the government did not spend more than the amount of the "deflationary gap," this need not cause inflation. On the contrary. The government was simply making use of slack sources in the economy. For some years after the war, this approach worked quite well in several countries. But the real world is very complex, and peoples' expectations tend to rise over time. So if the government is always seen to be supporting the economy like this, political pressure tends to build up to provide too much support, which tends to produce inflation.

More recently, people have argued that to add government spending to private spending is misleading. Private spending, they said, tends to be "crowded out" by government spending. So extra government spending does not change the volume of demand in an economy—only its composition. All these issues are still controversial and unresolved. For our purposes, we need to look at how the effects of fiscal policy are transmitted to the economy.

Suppose we have the following: the U.S. banking system in total has liabilities of $10,000 million and assets of cash $800 million; Treasury bills, $1000 million; and loans, $8200 million. Suppose in the next quarter the government runs a deficit of $280 million. That $280 million is paid to people who deposit it with the banks. Suppose that all of the deficit is financed by issuing Treasury bills. Suppose that the banks are the only buyers of Treasury bills. Then the $280 million extra in deposits that the banks receive is entirely invested in Treasury bills. So at the end of the quarter, we have a new balance sheet for the banking system of liabilities $10,280 million, and assets of cash $800 million; Treasury bills, $1280 million; and loans, $8200 million (Figure 5.4).

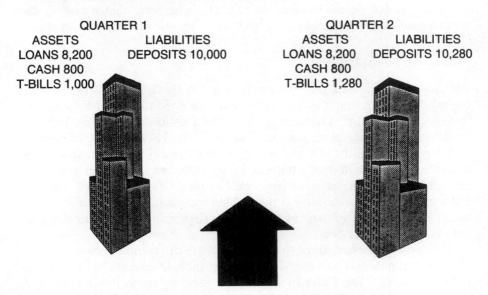

QUARTER 1

ASSETS	LIABILITIES
LOANS 8,200	DEPOSITS 10,000
CASH 800	
T-BILLS 1,000	

QUARTER 2

ASSETS	LIABILITIES
LOANS 8,200	DEPOSITS 10,280
CASH 800	
T-BILLS 1,280	

GOVERNMENT INJECTS $280 MILLION OF LIQUIDITY

Figure 5.4   Impact of injection of liquidity.

It looks as if nothing has changed, except that the balance sheet of the banking system has grown by $280 million on both sides. It is almost like a conjuring trick. What happens is that the government has spent more, the proceeds have come into the private sector's hands, which has lent the money to the banks, who have lent it back to the government. It is a more or less instant recycling. The key link is the fact that the government's "promise to pay" is regarded by the banks as being a completely safe investment. The circle can only be completed if the banks have confidence in the government's promise and invest all their extra deposits in Treasury bills.

Though it seems that nothing has changed, three things have in fact happened. First, the incomes of companies or individuals have risen by $280 million. So, other things being equal, their spending will tend to go up. This will push up someone else's income, and so on. Second, the public is now more liquid. It holds $280 million more bank deposits than it used to. If it has a planned ratio of bank deposits to total assets, the actual ratio will now be higher than planned. The public will start to shift assets out of bank deposits into other assets. Third, the banks hold more Treasury bills. If they have a planned ratio of Treasury bills to total lending, they will want to expand their lending.

So a rise in the government's deficit tends to expand the public's income, expand the public's holdings of bank deposits, and allow the banks to lend more. The effect of these changes on the rest of the economy depends on several things. If there is a great deal of unemployment, the effect will be different than if the economy is already fully stretched. Another question is the effect of the deficit on individuals' expectations about the future. If all other things are equal, though, we can say in general that a rise in the government's deficit tends to increase both economic activity and inflation.

Measuring Fiscal Policy

We have seen why fiscal policy is used in the way that it is, and why people in the markets think that it is important. Now we need to look at how we can measure exactly what is happening. The first question is what is included in fiscal policy. In federal nations, such as the United States and Germany, it may be right to split the fiscal effects of the central government and the social security system on the one hand from state and local governments on the other. In countries with important nationalized industries, such as France, we ought also to look at these. This is especially true if their investment, pricing, or employment policies are determined by political rather than commercial factors.

The next important thing to look at is the difference between policy changes and automatic changes. The former include changes in tax rates or public spending. The latter include social security commitments (such as unemployment benefits) which are automatically available to those who qualify. If unemployment rises, unemployment benefit payments will rise, so government spending rises, without any specific fiscal policy changes by the government. Often, people look at policy changes in a budget to assess its effect. But if the budget is certain to produce such a large change in unemployment that spending on social security drastically rises or falls, it might be right to take account of some of the budget's automatic effects as well as its policy changes.

Economists have dreamed up different ways to measure fiscal policy to take account of these complications. The simplest measure of all, of course, is the forecast change in the actual budget deficit or surplus. But as we saw, changes in unemployment will also affect the level of government spending. So some economists adjust the level of the actual budget balance on the basis of a fixed output or employment rate.

One approach is to measure what the budget deficit would be if the economy were at full employment. Another approach is to look at the long-term past average output level of the economy. This gives a cyclically adjusted budget balance, that is, what the budget balance would be if the economy were at the average output level of the past.

Another way of looking at budget deficits, which is often used, is to look at them as a percentage of the country's Gross National Product (GNP). A word of caution is in order: For each country, the comparison of the deficit as a percentage of GNP over time should be fairly consistent. But it is dangerous to compare the percentages of different countries, because the figure shows the operations of central government only. Regional governments' importance varies greatly among countries and ought to be taken into account.

BALANCE OF PAYMENTS

The balance of payments can be described as a record of a country's international economic accounts. That is, it records the goods and services that the economy has sold to and bought from the rest of the world, and the changes in the country's claims on and liabilities to the rest of the world. Because the balance of payments consists of double-entry bookkeeping, its components must necessarily balance, just like the accounts of a company. It is meaningless to say that a balance of payments is not in balance, just as it is meaningless to say that the accounts of a company do not balance.

When concern is expressed over a country's balance of payments, what is usually meant is that part of the balance—for example, the current account—is behaving in a way that puts strain on other parts of the balance that are needed to finance it. Hence the foreign exchange markets usually look at the behavior of the trade account or current account of a country to assess the likely pressure on a currency arising from the need to finance any deficit. But in theory, the behavior of any part of the balance of payments is irrelevant. Some other component in the balance will move to offset it.

For the sake of comparability, we shall concentrate on the presentation used by the IMF in its Balance of Payments Manual. The balance of payments breaks down into two main components: the current account, referring to goods, services, income, and transfers; and the capital account, covering financial assets and liabilities.

The current account itself can be broken down into the trade balance and other current items. The trade balance is the difference between exports and imports of goods. The other items in the current account include earnings from shipping and the like, spending on travel, income from investment (in the form of interest and dividends, or reinvested earnings which are left invested in the country where they were earned), and other goods and services. They also include transfers which can be either migrants' transfers or other transfers including official spending. The capital account can be split into four main sections: (1) direct investment: purchases of factories overseas and the like; (2) portfolio investment in shares or bonds; (3) other capital movements: borrowing and lending, changes in the credit terms given or taken by firms in international trade; and (4) movements in the country's official reserves.

These ideas can best be understood by looking at a specific case. Table 5.2 shows a simplified balance of payments for our old friend, Home Country. Home has earned a surplus on its trade accounts, because its exports at 190 were larger than its imports, at 165. So its trade balance shows a surplus of +25. It has had to pay interest and dividends to companies overseas that have invested in it, so there is a transfer on current account outwards, that is, −15. Quite a few workers from Home have gone abroad to work at better paying jobs, and they are sending money back to their families. So transfers from abroad back to Home show up a surplus of +40 in the balance of payments. Goods coming into Home tend to be shipped in foreign ships, so Home has to pay away 10 on shipping and transport account.

Table 5.2   Home Country Balance of Payments

Exports	190
Imports	165
Trade balance	+25
Interest and dividends	−15
Transfers	+40
Shipping, etc.	−10
Current account	+40
Capital account	
Direct investment	+200
Net lending	−100
Portfolio investment	−30
Change in reserves (− rise)	−110

When we add these three items to the trade balance, we find that Home has a current account surplus of +40. In a sense, that represents an inflow of cash. To show what happens to this cash, we look at the capital accounts. We see that firms from overseas are buying factories in Home, so that there is an inflow on direct investment account of 200. Home's banks have tended to prefer to lend abroad, so on net lending there is an outflow of 100, and similarly Home's investors tend to buy foreign stocks. So there is an outflow on portfolio investment of 30. If we add up what we have so far—current account +40, direct investment +200, net lending −100, portfolio −30—we come to a total of +110. (See Figure 5.5.)

The current account and the balance of capital accounts so far have meant a cash inflow of 110. The Home government adds these to its foreign currency reserves. To make the double-entry system balance, a rise in reserves has to be negative. (Any government's foreign exchange reserves are held, by definition, in foreign currency. Usually, these foreign currency reserves are held in Treasury bills or similar instruments overseas. In effect, the Home government is lending money to other governments by placing its reserves in these countries. So a rise in reserves has to be treated just the same as a net lending by Home's banks abroad.)

With the simple example in mind, we will look briefly at a more complicated case. We will look at the U.S. balance of payments for 1989 (Table 5.3). We can see that the trade deficit fell slightly in 1989, because exports (benefiting from the lagged effects of the dollar's depreciation in 1987–1989) improved faster than imports.

Therefore, the trade deficit improved from $127 billion to $114.8 billion. Investment income, for the first time in decades, turned negative in 1989: heavy U.S. borrowings from overseas caused large interest payments to the rest of the world. Other service income (e.g., insurance earnings, travel), however, helped to improve the current account for 1989 to $109.80. This

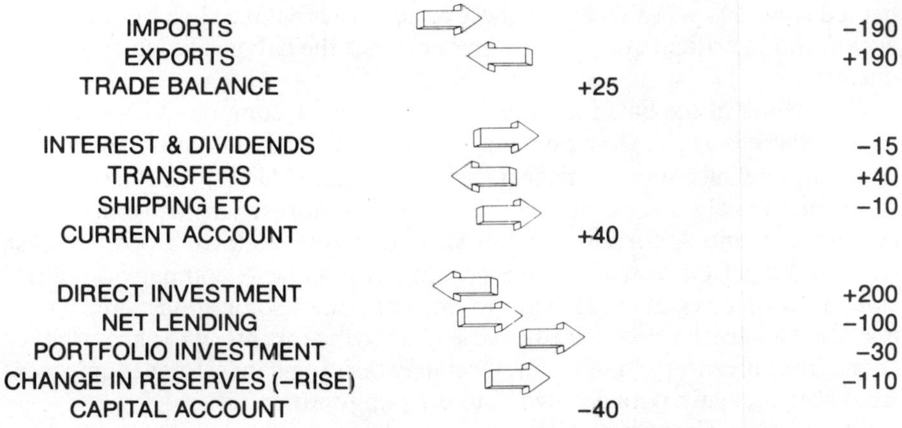

IMPORTS		−190
EXPORTS		+190
TRADE BALANCE	+25	
INTEREST & DIVIDENDS		−15
TRANSFERS		+40
SHIPPING ETC		−10
CURRENT ACCOUNT	+40	
DIRECT INVESTMENT		+200
NET LENDING		−100
PORTFOLIO INVESTMENT		−30
CHANGE IN RESERVES (−RISE)		−110
CAPITAL ACCOUNT	−40	

Figure 5.5 Home country balance of payments.

Table 5.3   U.S. Balance of Payments, 1988–1989 (in billion of US$)

	1988	1989
Exports	320.3	360.5
Imports	−447.3	−475.3
Trade balance	−127.0	−114.8
Military transactions	−5.5	−6.3
Investment income	1.6	−0.9
Other services	16.9	26.8
Remittances, etc	−14.9	−14.6
Current account	−128.9	−109.80
Net private capital flows	98.7	102.9
Net official asset flows	38.5	−15.4
Errors	−8.4	22.4

deficit was financed via the capital account: private U.S. entities borrowed $102.9 billion, which financed some official outflows.

The capital account is complex. First, there is a very large error element in the U.S. balance of payments accounts. Part of this comes from errors and omissions in the reporting of current account transactions. But people think that most of the error is from unrecorded flows of private capital. In 1989, this unrecorded inflow was very large. And it swung by $30 billion from the 1988 level. Other components of the capital account—short-term bank loans and portfolio investment, in particular—are very unstable, moving in response to perceived swings in confidence, interest rate levels, or corporate earnings prospects (in the case of equities).

Another very important source of capital flows can be changes in the terms of credit granted by firms in international trade. But the important point to realize is that the balance of payments consists of a whole new set of interconnected flows. As we said earlier, these must always balance just like any set of accounts; the critical question is whether or not the balance is achieved without strain.

If we think of the balance of payments as being a company's accounts, we can see there is a cash flow element—the current account—and there are the changes in balance sheet items that show up as capital flows. We can see that it is not necessarily a good or bad thing to be running a surplus or deficit on current account. A current account surplus is equivalent to a positive cash flow, and a deficit equivalent to a negative cash flow. A company (country) can be having a negative cash flow for many reasons, some good, some bad. It may have a negative cash flow because it is buying inventory so as to produce goods from inventory to sell later. Or it may be buying investment equipment from abroad, again with a view to building up production.

But, just like a company, a country cannot run a negative cash flow forever. It can only do it as long as other people are willing to lend to it. Hence, the foreign exchange market's concern about the current and trade accounts. These give a quick and easy indication of how the country's cash flow is doing. But it is also important to look at the balance sheet side, the capital flows.

Balance of Payments Policy

We now look at those government policies that affect the balance of payments. The most important of these are policy on the exchange rate, policy on borrowing from abroad, and trade policy. Exchange rate policy will be affected by many factors. But to put them in context, let us look at a simple case. Once again, we look at our Home Country. Home's exports per year are running at 100 widgets, while it is importing 200 widgets. The balance of widget trade, therefore, is in heavy deficit. Home's dictator is getting worried, so he orders a devaluation of the currency. In the past, Home's currency was set at HC2 = US$1. The dictator announces that henceforth the parity will be HC3 = US$1.

Since all Home's widget exports are priced in Home currency, buyers of Home's widgets find that they are cheaper. Suppose that in the past the widget was priced at HC2.0, so that the price to the foreign buyer was US$1. Suppose that Home's widget exporters keep their widget prices fixed in Home currency. Then, the foreign buyer finds that he or she has only to pay US$0.67 per widget that he buys from Home instead of US$1 as in the past. Home's exports are now one-third cheaper, and hence more competitive in international terms. Foreign buyers will buy more Home widgets, and less from elsewhere, so that Home's exports will rise.

Now let us look at Home's imports of widgets. Suppose that foreign sellers of widgets to Home priced their widgets in dollars. Suppose that they priced each widget at US$1. Then each widget was costing the Home importer HC2 to buy. But after the HC devaluation, assuming that foreign sellers of widget keep their prices fixed at US$1, the Home importer finds that each widget now costs him HC3. Clearly, he is going to tend to prefer to buy his widget domestically, rather than from the world market. So Home's imports should also fall.

The net result of all these changes should be an improvement in Home's trade balance. This is the classical argument for devaluation of a currency. Conversely, the classical argument for a revaluation is when the trade surplus is excessive. Revaluing the currency makes exports from the country more expensive, and imports into it cheaper, so it tends to reduce the trade surplus.

The real world is not so simple. The first point is that a devaluation of a currency usually increases domestic inflation. To see why, let's look again at Home's imports from abroad. We saw that the effect of the devaluation made imports more expensive. We assumed that this meant that Home people would cut back their imports of widgets. But part of Home's imports probably consist of essential raw materials, like oil or metals, which are used in the production of widgets.

So the effect of the devaluation will be to increase the costs of these essential imports and push up domestic widget production costs. The devaluation will also push up the price of imports of food and other consumption goods. That will probably lead Home's trade unions to ask for more wages. So a devaluation tends to be inflationary. In some countries where there is a very high level of essential imports from abroad, such as the United Kingdom, it has been suggested that the effect of a devaluation is washed out after a couple of years by the domestic inflation that results from it.

We should also notice the effect on domestic production. We saw that a devaluation of the Home currency made Home's exports more competitive in the world markets. We said this would lead to an increase in Home's exports of widgets. But if Home's producers of widget were already working flat out at full capacity, they would not produce more for exports. To be fully effective, a devaluation is best made when there is surplus domestic production capacity that is available to meet the extra world demand for exports that the devaluation creates.

Another complication is that very often exporters work on the basis of orders for some months or years ahead. So the effects of a devaluation or revaluation will not show up immediately in export or import volumes. What would happen to Home's balance of payment if the volumes of exports and imports did not change? Clearly, widget exports of 100 units now earn less in foreign currency, because their U.S. dollar price has fallen from $1 to $0.67.

So instead of earning $100 from abroad, Home only earns $67. Conversely, the import price of a widget is still fixed at US$1, so Home is still spending $200 a year to buy widgets from abroad. The first effect of a devaluation is perverse. It worsens the trade deficit. Earnings from exports fall; imports cost the same in dollar terms as they did before. This is often called the *J-curve effect*. The reason is that the trade balance looks like a J: to start with, it goes down the first part of the curve of the J, and then it goes up again later.

As to how long each stage lasts, economists and econometricians have been spending a long time trying to find out. The answer is, of course, that it varies a great deal among countries and over time. It depends on the average contract period for exports and imports; and it depends on the currency in which trade is invoiced.

Another complication in real life is that if an exporter is invoicing in foreign currency when his own currency is devalued, he has two choices: he can either cut his foreign currency price, in which his exports become more competitive and he sells more; or he can keep his price the same and sell the same volume but make more profit. If he keeps his foreign currency price unchanged, the effect of the devaluation simply feeds through to corporate profits. It does not produce any immediate improvement in the balance of payments (although, of course, because exporting is now more profitable, it will probably tend to increase the number of exporters over time).

Another area of balance of payments policy is trade policy. A government can discourage imports by tariffs, or by nontariff barriers. These latter are especially important in certain countries, such as Japan. Another way in which a country can try to reduce imports is by import deposits. These have often been used, for example, in Italy when the government wants to bring the balance of payments under control. An importer has to put down, say 50% of the value of the goods that he wants to import. The money has to be deposited, interest free, at the central bank.

After this basic outline of some of the fundamental factors that affect exchange rates, we turn now to technical methods for forecasting.

TECHNICAL METHODS OF FORECASTING: CHARTING

For many years, people active in markets such as the stock market and foreign exchange markets have argued that the best way to forecast future movements in rates is to analyze the patterns that can been seen in past movements. Collectively, the approaches used are often referred to as Technical or Chartist. The former, being the broader term, is the one that I shall use here.

The technical approach was first used in the equity and commodity markets. When exchange rates began floating, though, certain traders decided that they should look at a currency as just another commodity. The technical approach began to be applied to currencies. Chartists or technicians say that history repeats itself. They are more interested in the fact that a currency or interest rate breaks its historical support level than the reason for it. They look for unusual volumes of trading and breakouts, rather than the fundamental factors behind the market. In essence, technicians or chartists say that a price reflects the consensus of everyone in the market. They look at the movement of the herd, and believe in its statistical regularity. The chartist approach is the most widely known of the technical approaches, but there are others. They include the use of moving averages (and their more sophisticated variants, Box-Jenkins techniques), filters, price-volatility relationships, price momentum indices, and other techniques.

A very interesting analysis of the importance of these technical methods can be found in the Bank of England Quarterly Bulletin for November 1989, which reported a survey of chief foreign exchange dealers in the London market. The survey had a wide coverage, including over 200 responses. It assessed the way in which these dealers used technical methods. The survey found that about 90% of respondents used these methods for very short-term forecasting (intra-day to one week), with 60% judging them to be at least important as fundamentals. At longer forecast horizons, of one to three months or six months to one year, the weight given to fundamentals increased and for one year or over, 85% judged fundamentals to be more important than charts, with nearly 30% relying on pure fundamentals.

Therefore, even if you do not yourself believe in technical methods, it is important to understand how they work, because they clearly influence other people and how they behave in the short term, if not the medium term.

One approach, which can been seen either as simplistic or very sophisticated, is simply to argue that the forward exchange rate in the date in question is the best available forecast of the exchange rate. At the simplest level, it is a convenient expression of the market's views. The more sophisticated theorists would argue that the forward rate, because markets have efficiently priced all available information, represents the best possible forecast at any given time. Using the forward rate as a forecast has the major advantage that it is quick and cheap.

Empirical results on this were presented by C. Dunis and M. Feeny in *Exchange Rate Forecasting* (Woodhead-Faulkner/Simon and Schuster, 1989). In general, while the dollar was rising (January 1980–February 1985), the average forward premium was positive while the average exchange rate change was negative. This led to large forward rate prediction errors for the deutsche mark, Swiss franc, Dutch guilder, and four other currencies. In the weak-dollar period covering March 1985 to December 1988, the bias in the forward premium tended to have the opposite sign. Over the entire nine-year period, the average forward rate forecasting errors appear small and not significantly different from zero. Thus over the whole period, the forward could be viewed as unbiased predictor. But for periods of years on end, following the forward rate would have meant consistently getting it wrong in one direction or another.

The same book reports a series of studies on whether it is possible to outperform the forward rate. In some cases, technical strategies seemed to produce profits. However, there are two risks here. First, as more and more people follow the technical strategies, it will become more and more difficult to make money from them. Secondly, there is a selection problem: Which technical strategy?

Let's look at the possible technical methods in more detail. We begin with charting techniques. One of the most popular charting techniques is the bar chart (Figure 5.6). Generally, a bar chart records a price or rate daily, with a vertical line representing the daily price trading range. A small horizontal bar is often used to identify the closing price on a particular day. One studies the trend of these movements in an effort to find patterns. If a price repeatedly reaches a level without being able to break through it, that becomes the resistance area. If, later, the resistance area is penetrated upward, a significant price rise is expected. The signal is especially strong if the breakout happens when trading is active. Similarly, if a price seems to bounce off a floor price level. It is considered a sell signal if the price later falls through this level.

A second pattern which analysts look for is a trend line. By definition, a trend line requires a number of observations before it can be established. It is identified by successive daily levels which are continually higher or lower than the previous day's level. For example, a clear uptrend occurs when each day's low is reached at a higher level. When those are connected for an extended time, they form a trend line. Closing prices may occur at random above the line, but none should occur below the trend line. Equally, a downward trend is

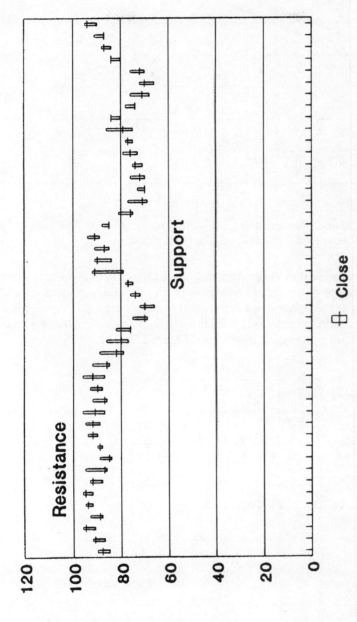

Figure 5.6 Basic bar chart formation (Adapted from E. W. Schwartz, *How to Use Interest Rate Futures*, Dow-Jones Irwin, Homewood, IL, 1979, p. 86).

109

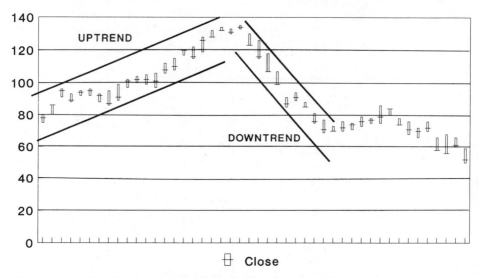

Figure 5.7 Channels (Adapted from E.W. Schwartz, *How to Use Interest Rate Futures,* Dow-Jones Irwin, Homewood, IL, 1979, p. 86).

seen from successive daily highs that are lower than previous ones. If the lines connecting the daily lows and those connecting the daily highs are parallel, this implies that the volatility of the market is not changing and a channel has been created. A breakout from a channel is considered a strong technical signal for a major uptrend or downtrend (Figure 5.7).

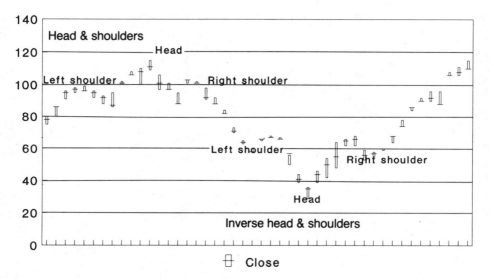

Figure 5.8 Head & shoulders formations (Adapted from E.W. Schwartz, *How to Use Interest Rate Futures,* Dow-Jones Irwin, Homewood, IL, 1979, p. 86).

Another important pattern is the head and shoulders formation (Figure 5.8). Essentially it consists of four distinct periods: the left shoulder, the head, the right shoulder, and an abrupt penetration through the level of the neck. If the neck level is not broken through, the formation is normally considered meaningless.

Another important formation is the double top. This usually signals the end of a rally. Often, the second top is sustained for a shorter period than the first one. Both the head and the double top formation may be reversed, in which case they are referred to as the inverted head and shoulders and the double bottom. In both cases, of course, the formations signal the reversal of a previous downward movement. (See Figure 5.9.)

Candle Charts

Candle charts are a Japanese invention. They developed in their present form in the Meiji period, based on early ideas of rice merchants. Generally, candle charts are produced in color, with price falls shown in black and rises in red. The chart is drawn just like any bar chart that shows the day's opening and closing prices. The difference lies in the portrayal of the space between open and close. In a candle chart, this space is drawn with a thicker line, red in color if the close was higher than the open, black if lower. Intra-day moves outside this range will show as a thin black line protruding above or below the body, given the appearance of a candle and its wick (Figure 5.10).

The Nippon Technical Analysts Association have produced a full treatment of the interpretation of candle charts (Y. Abe, et al. *Analysis of Stock*

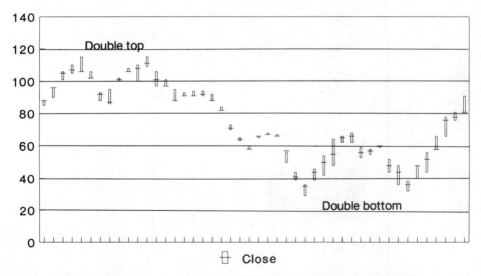

Figure 5.9 Double tops & bottoms (Adapted from E.W. Schwartz, *How to Use Interest Rate Futures,* Dow-Jones Irwin, Homewood, IL, 1979, p. 86).

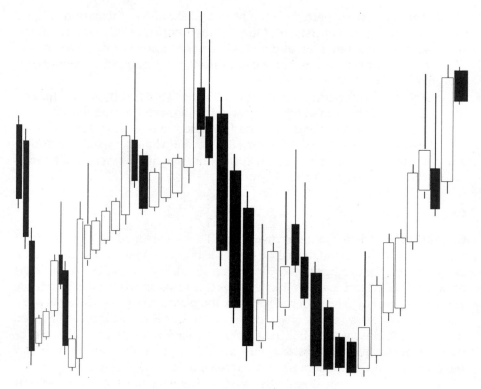

Figure 5.10 Sample candle chart.

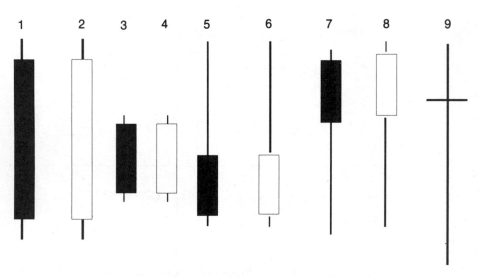

Figure 5.11 Typical candle patterns.

Prices in Japan). The analysis covers a wide range of patterns, of which a sample are shown in Figure 5.11.

The basic patterns are:

1. Major yin: Market closes near the low. Strongly bearish.
2. Major yang: Market closes near the high. Strongly bullish.
3. Minor yin: Market turning down.
4. Minor yang: Market turning up.
5. Yin with upper shadow: Market moved up from the opening, but could not hold the gain and closed below the opening. Rather bearish.
6. Yang with upper shadow: Rather bullish.
7. Yin with lower shadow: Bearish.
8. Yang with lower shadow: Bullish.
9. Jujisei (cross): Market closes at same price as it opened: A reversal is possible.

Channels

Several chartist concepts are used in another form by technical analysts who do not rely primarily on charts, but purely on the price series itself. For example, the *channel concept* can be used as part of a computer model.

We can define the ideas formally in this way. The highest and lowest closing price of the last N days are found. We get a sell signal if a price on day (N + 1) is lower than the lowest close of the N days. Stop orders are used to take action when the signals are given. Only one position can be signaled per day. We always have a position, be it long or short. We are never "square." When we get a new buy or sell signal, the old position is cut out at the same time. This method takes away any element of judgment. If the high and low of the day are equal, then we assume that the market is locked limit. Nothing is done on that day. The trade will done at the opening on the first day the market is not locked. This set of rules defines an intra-day closing price channel. A parallel definition can be made for inter-day closing price channel. In this case, we only get a buy signal if the close on day (N + 1) exceeds the highest close of the last N days. We then deal at the next's opening.

Filter Rule

Another technical method of analysis is the *filter rule*. This is independent of charting concepts. Investors following an x% filter rule take a long position in a currency that has risen x% from its most recent low point. They hold the position until the currency falls by x% from the highest level reached since the position was opened. Suppose we use a 2% rule. When a currency rises 2% from its recent low, we buy. When it falls 2%, we sell. The signal to sell is also a signal to go short. The short position is then until it is closed out on the next buy signal. Several studies have suggested it is possible to profit from filters. But one needs to allow for transactions and timing costs.

This point applies to all theoretical models. An interesting study in the equity market (A.F. Perold, "The implementation shortfall: Paper versus reality," *The Journal of Portfolio Management,* Spring 1988) showed how difficult it is to translate a wonderful model into real profits. The classic case is the Value Line Fund in the United States. Its actual 1965–1986 outperformance over the market was 2.5% per annum; the paper portfolio based on the Value Line rankings with weekly rebalancing has outperformed by almost 20% per annum. The difference is execution costs (higher in equities), delays in being able to implement, and failure to have orders executed at the theoretical price.

Cross-Over Method

Another technical method, more popular than the filter, is the cross-over method, sometimes called the *moving average method.* This also is completely independent of charting concepts. We work out two moving averages from the price. One is a short-term average, and one a long-term. If the short-term average is above the long-term average, one should be long, and if the short-term average is below the long-term average, one should be short. Actually this theory boils down to the "bandwagon" technique: Go long if the market has gone up, short if it has fallen.

The method works like this. The average of p days' closes and n days' close are calculated where p is less than n. The p index, then, is the shortterm index, and n the long-term. People often use 5, 10, 15, 20, or 200 days for the averages, for instance, a 5-day and a 15-day or a 10-day and 20-day average. The averages include today's close and use only business days. If the average of series p (the short-term) is above the average of series n, a buy order is placed on the opening the next day. Conversely, if below, a sell order is placed on the opening the next day. As before, the aim is always to hold a position, be it long or short. When we get a new buy or sell signal, the old position is cut out at the same time. If the high and low of the next day are equal, then, again we assume that the market is locked limit, and a trade cannot be made on that day. The trade will be done on the first day that the market is not locked.

Moving averages can be refined by using weights, so that the most recent data is given more importance. We can define the simple moving average as follows:

$$MA_t = \frac{1}{n}(S_t + S_{t-1} + \ldots + S_{t-n+1})$$

where S_t = exchange rate on day t, n = number of periods in average.

Using the same notation and calling a_i the series of decreasing weights we can write:

$$MA_t = \frac{a_1 S_t + a_2 S_{t-1} \ldots + a_n S_{t-n+1}}{a_1 + a_2 + \ldots a_n}$$

A particularly interesting and useful sort of weighted moving average is the exponential moving average. We can replace the weights we just used by a geometric progression $1, a, a^2 \ldots a^{n-1}$ and write:

$$MA_t = \frac{S_t + a S_{t-1} + a^2 S_{t-2} + \ldots a^{n-1} S_{t-n+1}}{1 + a + a^2 + \ldots + a^{n-1}}$$

The exponential moving average is widely used in currency trading systems, because it is simple to update and decreasing weight is given to older data. It can be shown* that we can write:

$$MA_{t+1} = (1 - a)S_{t+1} + aMA_t$$

and in particular if $a = 1/n$ where n is the number of periods in the moving average, we can write:

$$MA_{t+1} = \frac{(n - 1)S_{t+1} + MA_t}{n}$$

As a result, it is very simple to update an exponential moving average. Only the latest price and the previous period moving average need to be known. By comparison, to update a simple moving average requires deleting the oldest data in the previous period's moving average.

In practice, the above equation is often used with a reversal of the coefficient, in order to give avoid giving to much weight to the last data:

$$MA_{t+1} = \frac{(n - 1)MA_t + S_{t+1}}{n}$$

This formula is often used in updating several technical indicators, particularly the relative strength index (RSI).

When we are using a moving average model, we may well want to know the next cross-over point. (The treatment below follows that of Dunis and Feeny.) Finding in advance a possible cross-over implies predicting the exchange rate that would make both moving averages equal, just before the short-term average crosses above or below the long one. This can be done as

* See Dunis and Feeny, p. 168.

follows. Using our earlier notation and assuming n is greater than p, we can write that cross-overs occur when:

$$\frac{1}{p}\left(\sum_{j=1}^{p-1} S_{t-j+1} + S_{t+1}^*\right) = \frac{1}{n}\left(\sum_{i=1}^{n-1} S_{t-i+1} + S_{t+1}^*\right)$$

where $S_{t+1}^* =$ the rate that would trigger the stop.

After rearrangement, this can be written:

$$S_{t+1}^* = \frac{np}{n-p}\left(\frac{\sum_{i=1}^{n-1} S_{t-i+1}}{n} - \frac{\sum_{i=1}^{p-1} S_{t-j+1}}{p}\right)$$

We can substitute out the two moving averages prevailing at time T by rearranging the equation above:

$$S_{t+1}^* = \frac{np}{n-p}\left\{\left[\frac{n-1}{n}\right]\frac{\sum_{i=1}^{n-1} S_{t-i+1}}{n} - \left[\frac{p-1}{p}\right]\frac{\sum_{j=1}^{p-1} S_{t-j+1}}{p-1}\right\}$$

If we call $STMA_t$ the short term moving average prevailing at time t and $LTMA_t$ the long-term moving average at the same period, the cross-over level that would reverse the model in the following period is therefore:

$$S_{t+1}^* = \frac{np}{n-p}\left[\left(\frac{n-1}{n}\right) LTMA_t - \left(\frac{p-1}{p}\right) STMA_t\right]$$

The necessary information is readily available at time t, so here it is quite easy to place a timely stop order with a bank if one wishes to.

Momentum Models and Oscillators

Probably the best known variation on moving average cross-over strategies are the *Momentum models*. Although they operate exactly the same as cross-over models, their decision rule is based on either the difference between the faster and the slower moving average or on their ratio. With momentum models based on differences in moving averages, the momentum index will be positive in a rising market, when the faster moving average lies above the slower one. Conversely, it will be negative in a declining market, when the faster moving average lies below the slower one. The decision rule is to buy the currency whenever the momentum index crosses above the zero line into positive territory and to sell it when the momentum index crosses back below the zero line into negative territory (Figure 5.12).

Provided one uses the same pair of moving averages, the signals will be the same for this type of momentum model as for the double moving average

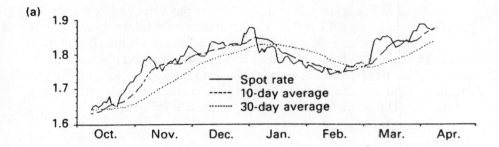

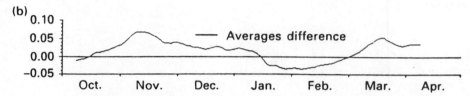

Figure 5.12 (a) GBP/USD rate from 8 October 1987 to 8 April 1988. (b) Momentum index showing the difference in the averages. (*Source:* Datastream. Reproduced from C. Dunis & M. Feeney, *Exchange Rate Forecasting,* Macmillan Press, London, 1989).

cross-over when constantly in the market. The same applies to the ratio momentum index, where the index will stand above one in a rising market when the faster moving average lies above the slow one. Conversely, it will be below one in a declining market. The decision rule is to buy when the index crosses above the one level and to sell when it moves back below.

What, then, is the point of momentum models rather than straight cross-over models? It is this: If we use the ratio form of the momentum model, to get rid of scale effects that might arise from a long-term trend in the currency, we can define levels beyond which the momentum index series very seldom varies. If we manage to identify these levels, we can than define them as over-bought or over-sold levels for a given exchange rate. One could use the reversal of the momentum index in the over-bought or over-sold area only as a signal to close out an existing position, rather than buying a new one. A new position will then be triggered only when the momentum index crosses back over the cross-over line. This would lead to the model not being constantly in the market and may sometimes be more profitable. If used in the ratio form so that they are free of scale effects, momentum models can help select from several exchange rates the one that is diverging most. Thus, momentum models allow comparisons between currencies.

Probably the most widely known oscillator is the *Relative Strength Index* (RSI). It measures the velocity of currency moves by dividing the average of up variations by the average of down variations over N events. The mathematical formula is such that the index is normalized between zero and one hundred. This has the advantage of making it comparable across different currencies so that we can identify those which are most strongly over bought or over-sold. The general formula for a N-event RSI is:

$$RSI_t^n = 100 - \frac{100}{1 + RS_t^n}$$

where:

$$RS_t^n = \frac{\left(\frac{1}{n}\right) \sum_{i=1}^{n} a_{it}}{\left(\frac{1}{n}\right) \sum_{i=1}^{n} b_{it}}$$

$$\text{and } a_{it} = S_{t-i+1} - S_{t-i} \text{ if } S_{t-i+1} > S_{t-1}$$

$$b_{it} = |S_{t-i+1} - S_{t-i}| \text{ if } S_{t-i+1} < S_{t-1}$$

Commonly used signals for over-bought and over-sold are 70 and 30, respectively. However, traders may wish to find this from their own experience.

A word of caution is merited: Over-bought and over-sold indicators seem to work better for closing out existing positions than for opening new ones. When a currency breaks out of its most recent range, the oscillator will rapidly move into the over-bought or over-sold area. A consolidation of the move may then occur, which will translate into what might prove only a temporary reversal of the oscillator. If one followed the oscillator to open a new position, one might open a new position that is contrary to the currency trend, which has been established by the new break out. In that sense, it may be better to use momentum indicators as a further decision rule in addition to the traditional cross-over.

WHY BOTHER? THE CASE FOR PASSIVE MANAGEMENT

There is a wide range of trading theories from which to choose, both fundamental and technical. How do we find the best method? If I knew for certain I wouldn't bother to write this book: I would have retired on the proceeds. But let's try to find a sensible way to operate. First, we have to set criteria for choosing the best theory. We need to know which theory is going to anticipate the future more accurately than the market will.

This raises the question of what the market's anticipation is, since the forward cannot strictly be taken as the market's anticipation, being dominated by interest differentials. However, there is no other clear-cut measure of expectations, short of conducting a regular sample poll. Also, the forward rate is relevant for the corporate treasurer or the investor, in that he or she has to decide whether or not to hedge a position. The current forward rate represents the alternative to taking an open position. So the forward rate is about the best option. But using the forward rate as a benchmark is only applicable if a method produces explicit forecasts. If, like most technical services, it simply produces a buy or a sell signal, another test is to work out the total return that would have been earned by slavishly following the service's signals.

The potential user should be clearly aware that track record itself is no guarantee of future performance. A second qualification which I would make from a personal point of view is that in committing oneself to a technical service, one must not be prepared merely to accept possibly long strings of losses but one must also be prepared to accept as an act of faith the technical method being used in the belief that is the best of all possible methods at this point in time. It is essential, therefore, that the trader or speculator who is following these services be prepared to accept a substantial commitment of capital even if there is a long series of losses, in the hope that the tide will turn eventually. Against this, however, it must be said of the fundamental services that the market's view of fundamentals changes unpredictably. A fundamentalist betting against the US$ from 1982 to 1985 would have been right, but would have lost money for three years.

It is by no means impossible to beat the forward rate. However, the profits from this are not risk free, so that the person aiming to beat the forward rate has to be prepared to assess the return on capital. Given the rapid reversals in exchange rates and the volatility in the market, it is not obvious that the profits are high relative to the risk involved: that is, equal or better returns might be obtained by employing the capital elsewhere.

This line of thinking has led many to consider another approach: the passive management of foreign exchange risk (some people call it "mean-variance optimization" or something similar). This approach is particularly applicable to longer-term investors or borrowers. The most basic argument is "it'll all come out in the wash." That is, over a long period of time, currencies tend to swing back and forth and there is no *a priori* reason for knowing where in the cycle we are at any given time. The U.S. dollar swung from DM1.67 in 1978 to DM3.46 in 1985 and to DM1.80 in 1989. If the investor is investing in a spread of international assets for the purpose of diversifying his risks, and has a long-term time horizon, then the impact of foreign exchange is itself a diversifying influence.

This argument assumes two things. First, that in the long run you cannot time the market consistently so as to make profits from foreign exchange. There are good reasons to believe this. Much analysis has been devoted to investors' ability to beat the stock market—and the bond markets—by market timing. In almost all cases, it has been shown that they fail to do so in the long run. Why should the foreign exchange markets be different? It is possible to do so for a year or two; but over 10 or 15 years is another matter. Banks can make money consistently in foreign exchange trading, but this is largely—in the very long run—because of the bid/offer spread. Position-taking in the market allows them to handle order flow, but there are very few banks able to point to consistent profitability from position-taking over 10 or 15 years—over and above the profit that might have been earned by taking the capital employed and investing it in the equity market. There is no reason to believe that the return on capital employed in foreign exchange market timing is any higher than that on equity or bond market timing. Why should foreign exchange be different from any other market?

There is a second major set of arguments in favor of passive management of foreign exchange risk for the long-term investor or borrower. This is that in the long run, hedged and unhedged international investments should offer the same returns. Suppose they did not. That would imply that foreign exchange markets continuously over- or under-priced the cost of hedging a given currency. The cost was always above or below the actual change in value that took place. For any given period, that might be true, since the hedging cost is technically driven by interest differentials. But in the very long run, there is no reason to believe this would happen. If it did, it would imply that an investor in one country would be consistently rewarded for taking foreign exchange risk and an investor in another would be consistently penalized. That seems contradictory.

If we accept the argument for passive management, then the next question is how to implement it, specifically the choice of neutral position. There are two extremes: always hedged or never hedged. The benchmark in the former case would be an unhedged index, and a hedged one in the latter instance.

The choice between the two depends on the investor's philosophy. One possible approach, used by many investors in managing their domestic portfolios, is that suggested by modern portfolio theory, that is, we opt for the choice that offers us least risk for the same return. Putting it another way, we look to choose a position on the efficient frontier.

Efficient Frontiers

Suppose you think that neither you nor anyone else has the gift of permanently timing the market right. Then the modern portfolio theorist argues that you should focus on setting up an "efficient" portfolio. You start by deciding how much risk you want to take. Risk is defined as variability of return. It is measured by the standard deviation of returns from an asset over time.

Suppose you are a U.S. investor considering whether to invest overseas. The Salomon Brothers High Grade Corporate Bond Index returned an annual 10.53% in the 10 years prior to 1988. Its annualized standard deviation was

15.4%. Over the same period, the Salomon Brothers Non-U.S. Bond Index returned 12.29% in US$ terms. Its annualized standard deviation was 16.34%. The non-U.S. bond index gave higher returns, at the price of higher risk.

The point of modern portfolio theory is that risk falls as you include different types of assets, as long as their returns are not perfectly correlated. Diversification pays. Say you hold both equities and bonds. They won't normally both perform badly in the same year. So the weak performance of one will be offset by the other. The portfolio as a whole will be more stable than either asset individually. Diversifying reduces your risk.

Let's look at a practical example. Suppose you think, after studying history and making your forecasts, that the following asset classes will produce a certain pattern of risks and returns. Let's say, over the next five years, you expect:

	U.S. Bonds	Non-U.S. Bonds
Return	8%	9.5%
Risk	9%	12%

And let's suppose you think the returns will have a correlation of 0.4, that is, U.S. bond returns will vary in line with non-U.S. bond returns 40% of the time.

To work out the risk of the combined portfolio, we need the covariance between the two assets, that is, the standard deviation of each asset (or pair of assets, if there were more than two) multiplied together and weighted by the correlation between the assets. So the covariance is $0.09 \times 0.12 \times 0.4 = 0.00432$. We'll also need the variances of the two assets, which is the square of the standard deviation (0.0081 and 0.0144, respectively).

Constructing a Frontier

Now we can find the risk and return of a portfolio combining these elements. Suppose we start by holding everything in U.S. bonds. Then we gradually push up the share of non-U.S. bonds to 100%. Finding the return is an easy calculation: a weighted average. The risk is a little more tricky.

Let's take the risk when we have 30% in non-U.S. bonds. The calculation is $0.0081 \times 0.49 + 0.0144 \times 0.09 + 2 \times 0.7 \times 0.3 \times 0.00432 = 0.0070794$. In other words: (U.S. bonds' variance × square of 70% weight + non-U.S. bonds' variance × square of 30% weight + 2 × 70% U.S. weight × 30% non-U.S. weight × covariance).

That is the variance of the combined portfolio: to find the standard deviation we take the square root, which comes out at 0.084139 or 8.41%. Now we do the sums for all the different weights and we get:

Combined Portfolio

US Fixed	Non-US	Risk	Return
100%	0%	9.00	8.0
90	10	8.65	8.1
80	20	8.45	8.2
70	30	8.41	8.3
60	40	8.54	8.4
50	50	8.82	8.5
etc.			

As you push up the share of non-U.S. bonds, the risk of the combined portfolio falls from 9.00% to 8.41% when you have 30% in non-U.S. bonds. While the risk is falling, though, the return is rising. You can get 30 basis points more return for less risk, if you push the share of non-U.S. bonds from 0% to 30%. The chart shows the same thing visually. If you're happy to take more risk in exchange for more return, you can push the non-U.S. bonds up to 50% or even beyond (Figure 5.13).

We can apply this approach to constructing a solution of our problem. Suppose we are a corporation with a given pattern of borrowing needs over say the next five years. We can say, well, we have no real idea of what the exchange rates will do over the next five years. But we would like to set up our borrowings in a manner that gets us close to the efficient frontier. That is, we want the pattern of our liabilities to get us the lowest cost for the least risk. This is the mirror image of the investor's problem, who wants the highest return for the

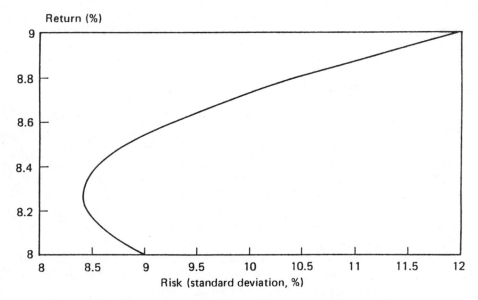

Figure 5.13   Risk and return: Effect of higher share of non-dollar bonds.

least risk. Suppose we want our borrowings to be five-year borrowings. Then we could take historical data and from it construct a frontier from the interest costs and exchange rate movements of the currencies in which we can borrow. We would set up our borrowing program in accordance with that efficient frontier. (In practice, things could get more complex: one might be looking at a three-dimensional version of the frontier to allow for different maturities.)

There are several caveats. First, what we have done is said: "We cannot forecast exchange rates. Instead, we will forecast that past returns, past variances, and past correlations can be projected into the future." It is by no means clear that this is right. Second, there are a good many practical issues, to which we now turn.

APPLYING THE MEAN-VARIANCE OPTIMIZATION APPROACH

Suppose we have constructed an efficient frontier which tells us as an investor (or as a borrower) what the possible combinations of risk and return are. Let's look at it from the point of view of an investor this time. An investor considering hedging foreign currency risk has three possible choices: forward foreign exchange, financial futures, or currency options (or, indeed, some of the so-called third generation hedging products that combine forward exchange and options). Let's suppose that we decide to keep things simple and stick to forward exchange.

The normal route, then, would be to sell forward currency against your equities or bonds, in the forward exchange market. Suppose you are a US$-based investor and you hold JPY150 million of 10-year Japanese government bonds, because you believe Japanese interest rates are about to fall. However, for the same reason, you expect a weakening in the yen. Then you would sell forward JPY150 million, for delivery in, say, three months' time.

The alternative is to sell forward to match the maturity of the bond, but this is much less attractive. Hedging a 10-year bond with a 10-year forward would be difficult, because the 10-year forward market is thin and illiquid. You would be conceding a substantial liquidity premium to the foreign exchange market for the privilege of executing the hedge. By the same token, unless you were willing to concede a second premium, you would be committed to holding the bond and its hedge to maturity.

If the forward sale is in US$, then you are in effect holding synthetic US$ Japanese bonds. Depending on the relative slope of the yield curves (which will affect the forward exchange premium or discount) this maneuver can produce attractive results. There is an implied exposure to the shape of the yield curve, but this is generally of much lesser impact than the effect of currency movements.

However, the costs of this operation need to be properly measured. Suppose you are running the position for a year, with three-month forward contracts. You will roll the hedges four times. Suppose you are hedging yen assets and today's spot is $1 = JPY150. On the Reuters screen today is a three-month forward price of 129/125 meaning a seller of yen forward would sell at 150–1.25 = 148.75. Suppose rates do not change at all in the next three months. At maturity of the forward, you buy back at 150 the yen you sold at 148.75 and you extend the contract at the same rate. You crystallize a cash flow difference (in this case a profit) and you pay the forward market spread each time you roll the contract.

Suppose the true interbank rate is 128/126: You are being charged a point each time you roll, say 4 points per annum. That costs 0.04/150 = 0.03% p.a. or three basis points. (For other, less liquid currencies, or for amounts smaller than standard inter-bank size, the cost would be higher; for a diversified portfolio perhaps 6 or 7 basis points would be a sensible average figure). More significant would be the cost of the odd cash flows thrown up by the rolling of forward contracts, particularly if losses require a sale of securities from elsewhere in the portfolio. Estimates of these costs vary but anywhere from 15 to 50 basis points, depending on size and frequency of cash-flows, would be appropriate. In addition, would be the costs of someone's time to handle the hedging program, or an outside manager's fees. Total costs would probably be a minimum of 1/4% and could range up to 3/4% per annum. Thought might also have to be given, in some cases, to the fact that the forward exchange gains or losses would be realized, while the gains or losses on the assets being hedged would generally be unrealized, with possible reporting/accounting implications.

SUMMARY

Looking back over this chapter as a whole, perhaps enough has been said to make it clear that there is no quick and simple solution to the problem of forecasting rates. There are as many different philosophies as there are people in the market. What suits you best will depend on your individual temperament and needs. But it is probably worth saying that since no one method is perfect it will usually pay to be pragmatic and cross-check using at least a couple of different methods. Finally, in summary, it is worth remembering a saying which I am told is in the Koran: "Those who claim to foretell the future are lying, even if they are later proven to be accurate."

PART **2** Money Market Calculations

6 Money Market Calculations

In this chapter, we discuss basic money market calculations as they relate to time deposits, including the calculation of forward forward deposit rates. Because the calculations are very closely related, this chapter also covers Forward Rate Agreements. We also look at net present value calculations and the zero-coupon curve, together with medium-term forward forward deposit rates. In Chapter 7, we discuss the relevant calculations as they apply to money-market paper such as certificates of deposit (CDs), Treasury bills and commercial paper, and some basic bond calculations.

For the sake of simplicity, we concentrate on Euromarket calculations. This allows us to focus on the transnational aspects of the market and avoids questions of reserve requirements or other features specific to particular markets. These issues are dealt with separately at the end of the chapter. Therefore, throughout this chapter, all comments relate (unless otherwise stated) to the Euromarket, that is, deposits traded outside the country of origin. Deposits traded in the country of origin are referred to as domestic.

CONVENTIONS

The Euromarkets use two bases for calculating interest. These are the 360-day year and the 365-day year. The 365-day year is used for sterling, the Irish pound, the Kuwaiti dinar, and the Belgian franc. All other currencies are dealt on a 360-day basis. The Belgian franc is also dealt on a 360-day basis if both parties to deal are non-Belgian. Sometimes the Canadian dollar is dealt on a 365-day basis with customers, but interbank Euro-Canadian is usually 360. Given mutual agreement, any basis can be used.

The method of calculation for 360-basis is as follows. Suppose the deal is for 91 days, the interest rate 10%, the principal amount US$1 million. Then the interest is calculated from:

$$\frac{10}{100} \times \frac{91}{360} \times 1,000,000 = 25,277.78$$

Because this method uses actual days elapsed and a 360-day year, it is sometimes called a 365/360 or actual/360 basis.

The calculation method for 365-day basis is similar. We replace 91/360 by 91/365:

$$\frac{10}{100} \times \frac{91}{365} \times 1,000,000 = 24,931.51$$

Note that for the same nominal interest rate of 10%, the 365-day basis produces a lower interest amount. Thus a 10% Eurodollar rate (360-day basis) is equivalent to a 10.13889% rate on a 365-day basis. Equally, a 9.863% Eurodollar rate, 360 basis, is equivalent to 10% on a 365-day basis. The 365-day method is sometimes called the 365/365 method, or actual/365.

Another method of calculating interest rates is used for Eurobonds and some domestic European deposits, and for U.S. corporate and municipal bonds. It can be described as the Continental, or 360/360 method compared with the Euromarket (365/360) or the sterling (365/365) method. The two latter methods compute interest on the actual day elapsed, whereas the Continental method treats the year as consisting of 12 30-day months. Thus, a deal running from December 5, 1980 to December 5, 1981 would be treated as a 360-day deal. A deal running from December 5, 1980 to May 12, 1981 would be treated as having 157 days ($5 \times 30 + 7$) instead of the actual 158 days. Note that the result of this method is to produce a lower effective rate, for a given nominal rate, than the 365/365-day sterling method, which in turn is lower than the 365/360 Euro- or U.S. method.

Euromarket practice is to pay interest at the maturity of the deal, except where periods of over one year are involved. In that case, interest is paid annually on the "anniversary" of the deal. Let's look at a two-year deal done on December 5, 1990. Interest would be paid on December 5, 1991.

Interest would be paid again, and the principal repaid, on December 5, 1992. A two-and-a-half year deal done on the same date would pay interest on the same dates, with a final interest payment (and repayment of principal) on June 5, 1993. If the anniversary is not a business day, the procedure adopted is the same as in the forward market (see Chapter 9); it will be rolled forward to the next business day, providing this does not take us into the next month.

The deposit market quotes two rates for a given period. The offered rate is the rate at which the dealer is prepared to lend money. The bid rate is the rate at which he is prepared to borrow. Normal U.S. practice is to quote the bid rate first. Normal London market practice is to quote the offered rate first. Hence $7^{1}/_4$–$^{1}/_2$ in the United States, $7^{1}/_2$–$^{1}/_4$ in London, both mean "I lend at $7^{1}/_2$%, borrow at $7^{1}/_4$%."

A large amount of Eurocurrency lending involves the London Interbank Offered Rate (LIBOR). It can be defined in two ways: (1) the rate at which funds are offered to a first-class bank in London for the maturity period in question; (2) the rate at which a first-class bank in London offers funds to another first-class bank in London. In either case, LIBOR attempts to measure the cost to a bank of raising new funds from the market in order to on-lend. It is the basis of almost all variable-rate lending in the Euromarkets. In view of its importance, it should be stressed that the LIBOR concept is purely judgmental. For example, three-month LIBOR for US$1000 million will very likely differ from three-month LIBOR for US$5 million. We are considering the dealer's judgement of what it would cost him to raise that amount for on-lending. It may well be that he judges that it would cost him more to raise the larger amount, because it will move the market against him. Hence, normal practice for any given loan is to calculate LIBOR as the average of the rates quoted by several "reference banks" selected for the purpose. The rates published in the financial press reflect a consensus of often diverse views. LIBOR is usually fixed at a time specified in the original loan agreements (normally 11:00 AM London time). It is quoted for deposits starting from the spot date (see below) for various periods, of which the most common are three- and six-months.

The LIBOR convention has spawned many variations. These include SIBOR (Saudi or Singapore Interbank Offered Rate), NIBOR or NYBOR (New York), KIBOR (Kuwait), PIBOR (Paris), FIBOR (Frankfurt), ADIBOR (Abu Dhabi), HKIBOR (Hong Kong), MIBOR (Madrid), and so on. In all cases, the concept attempts to measure a bank's funding costs for a loan, though the details vary from center to center. It is quite possible to apply the concept to other Eurodeposits or domestic deposits (for example, many domestic U.K. loans are linked to sterling LIBOR).

The spot convention for Euro-deposits is the same as for foreign exchange (see Chapter 8), that is, two working days. However, a difference may arise in the case of a holiday. Consider a situation where New York and Frankfurt were open, but London closed, on a given day. Then the foreign exchange market would normally deal US$/DEM for that day, but London would not normally deal Eurodeposits maturing on a day on which it was closed. It would be possible in theory to do so but would generally be inconvenient.

TYPES OF DEPOSIT

A call deposit is defined as a deposit which is repayable "at call." In practice, due to time zone considerations, and the need to transmit confirmations between countries, such deposits may be repayable at up to two days' notice, unless special arrangements have been made. The situation varies according to currency, and the ability to take call funds from a customer depends on the currency. In some currencies, there is not a well-developed call money market. This makes it difficult to lay off funds.

An overnight deposit is defined as a deposit made today that is repaid (or replaced) on the next business day. Overnight deposit trading is also complicated by time zone considerations. A Hong Kong bank can deal U.S. dollar deposits overnight without difficulty, since New York will normally be 13 hours behind, giving plenty of time for instructions to be processed in Hong Kong and acted on in New York. However, London cannot normally deal overnight deutsche mark deposits as deals have to be in the Frankfurt clearing by 8:00 AM. Effectively this means that processing and confirmation among the placing bank, the accepting bank, the placing bank's German correspondent, and the accepting bank's German correspondent would have to be completed by 8:00 AM on the same day as the deal, which is not really practical.

The time zone problem is less pressing for deposits starting tomorrow and maturing in the next business day, usually referred to as "tomorrow/next" or "tom/next." (It will be noticed that tom/next deals mature on the spot date.) It is possible to deal tom/next in most currencies that have a well-developed Eurocurrency market, but because of the time zone problem the market tends to dry up very early.

As in the foreign exchange market, the deposit market quotes spot/next (from spot to the next business day), spot/week, and so on.

A period deposit is defined as a deal starting on the spot date and maturing on some fixed and predetermined date. The phrase "the periods" usually refer to some or all of the "standard" periods of 1, 2, 3, 6, 9, or 12 months (see Chapter 9). Value date conventions for period deposits are the same as for foreign exchange, with the exception that it would be possible (though in practice unusual) to deal for a value date in which the dealing center was closed but the settlement center was open. For example, suppose that New York and Frankfurt were open, but London closed, on a given day. The foreign exchange market—and London—would deal US$/DEM for settlement on that day, but London would not normally deal Eurodollars or Euromark deposits for maturity on that day.

YIELD CURVE

A yield curve is a graph which plots interest rates against time. To make it meaningful, the different interest rates should be for comparable instruments. In this chapter, that means interest rates for a deposit with a bank. In other contexts, we might plot the interest rate for Treasury bills maturing, say, in one, three, six and twelve months and talk of a Treasury bill yield curve. Because of possible capital gains on a security (or CD) and the differing taxation treatment of interest earnings and capital gains, constructing a true yield curve for securities can be quite complex. But for "clean" deposits, the question of capital gain does not arise, so the yield curve concepts are quite simple.

Suppose we have the following set of rates: 1 week, 10%; 1 month, $10^1/2$%; 2 months, $10^1/2$%; 3 months, $10^3/4$%; 6 months, 11%; 9 months, $11^1/2$%; and 12 months, 12%. Then we can draw a simple yield curve as in Figure 6.1 (line AC). We can see that it slopes upward to the right. This is called a *normal upward-sloping,* or *positive yield curve.* It is normal, because under normal circumstances a lender requires a slightly higher rate to compensate him for locking away his funds for a longer period. Equally, a borrower will be prepared to pay slightly more for the benefit of insulating himself against interest rate movements for a longer time.

If the market thinks that rates are about to rise, the curve will rise more steeply; lenders will require extra compensation before they will lock in at today's rates. They believe that rates will soon be higher, and so they would be better off to wait until the rates rise before they lend. In this situation, it might be that the 3-month rate is 12%, 12 months, 13%. We could draw a yield curve like the dotted line ABDE in Figure 6.1.

Or it might be that the market expects rates to fall. In this case, lenders will be happy to lend for longer periods at rates below today's rates. They fear that if they wait before they lend, the rates they will receive will be lower still. In this case, the 12-month rate might be only 8%, with the 6-month rate 9%, and the 2-month rate $10^1/2$%. We could draw the dotted line ABFG in Figure 6.1.

Looking at a yield curve tells us a great deal about where the market thinks rates are going. If we look at Figure 6.1 we can see that, if today's yield curve is ABDE, the market expects rates to rise, but not for a couple of months, since AB is only sloping up gently in line with the normal pattern. If the yield curve were ABFG, the market is expecting rates to fall over a couple of months. Also, the slope of the curve suggests that between 2 and 6 months hence—BF on the curve—the market expects quite a sharp fall, which will steady off later; FG is flatter than BF. The yield curve is telling us visually about the implied forward forward rates (which are discussed later). We will come back to how the yield curve, the forward forward rates, and the implied zero-coupon rates are interlinked later in the chapter.

A technique used by many investors is called "riding the yield curve." Suppose in the shorter maturities the slope of the yield curve is positive (and is

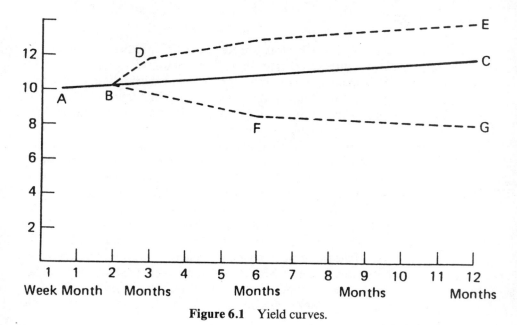

Figure 6.1 Yield curves.

expected to remain so). This means that, say, a 6-month CD yields more than a 3-month CD. If rates do not change drastically, an investor can pick up extra yield by buying the 6-month CD and selling it in 3-months to reinvest the proceeds in the 6-month CD. In effect, he is collecting the premium for staying long in a market where a premium is paid for staying long. Of course, if rates have risen sharply in the meantime—as has often happened in recent years—he has earned less than he could have by staying short.

MISMATCH (GAP)

This brings us to the question of mismatch (usually referred to as gap in the United States). Mismatch happens when a trader borrows or lends money for a longer or shorter period than would be needed to match his commitment. If a bank lends money for 6 months, and funds the lending initially with a 3-month deposit, it is mismatched. There are two kinds of mismatch: interest mismatch and funding mismatch (see Chapter 19). In our example, there is interest mismatch of 3 months. If after 6 months the loan is due for repayment, then the funding mismatch is also 3 months; if the 6-month loan is a roll-over loan whose final agreed maturity is, say, five years, then the funding mismatch is four years and nine months—the remaining period during which money must be raised to fund the loan.

Mismatching is the justification for a bank's existence. The origin of banking, after all, was in taking deposits, repayable at demand, and lending them out for a slightly longer period. It also carries risks; the control of these risks is discussed in Chapter 19. In proportion to the risk, it carries the chance of profits.

Suppose we have 1 month (30 days), 10 to $10\frac{1}{8}$%; 3 months, $10\frac{5}{8}$ to $\frac{3}{4}$%; and 6 months (180 days, $10\frac{5}{8}$ to $10\frac{3}{4}$%. The market expects a rise in rates in the next 3 months, followed by a leveling out. Suppose a customer borrows $10 million for 6 months from the bank, and the bank thinks the market has got it wrong, and rates will fall. Then it will fund itself, say, for 1 month at $10\frac{1}{8}$%. It earns $10,000,000 \times 10.75/100 \times 180/360 = \$537,500$ for the 6-month loan, paying $10,000,000 \times 10.125/100 \times 30/360 = \$84,375$ for the 1-month funds. Suppose in a month's time the rate for 5-month money (150 days) has fallen to 10%, costing $10,000,000 \times 10/100 \times 150/360 = \$416,666.67$ (ignoring interest on interest). Its total costs are $501,041.67 and its total earnings $537,500, leaving a profit of $36,458.33.

This compares with the $\frac{1}{8}$% that the bank would have earned if it had immediately been able to fund itself for 6 months at $10\frac{5}{8}$%, which would have shown a profit of only $6,250.00 if it had not run a deliberate mismatch. Of course, the $30,000 odd extra profit from this mismatch could just as easily have been a loss if the bank had misjudged rate movements. A number of the world's largest banks have lost tens of millions of dollars on mismatch positions; hence the need for tight controls.

BROKEN DATES

Suppose we need a period deposit rate for a date which is not a "standard" one; for instance, suppose we have the following Euro–deutsche mark rates:

1 month $12\frac{1}{8}$ to $12\frac{1}{4}$% 30 days
2 months $12\frac{3}{4}$ to $12\frac{7}{8}$% 62 days

We need a bid rate for one month and one week, that is, 37 days. The rough calculation is to take the bid rate for 30 days at $12\frac{1}{8}$%, and assume that the one week beyond the 30 days should be reckoned at the 2-month bid rate, namely $12\frac{3}{4}$%, so that all we have to do is average the two rates, weighting them by number of days involved:

$$\frac{30 \times 12.125 + 7 \times 12.75}{37} = \frac{363.75 + 89.25}{37} = \frac{453}{37} = 12.243\%$$

This method is the method used by most people in the market for a quick approximation of a broken date rate. Then they will make a quick mental adjustment to cover any special factors.

We need to think more carefully about the assumption that the seven days of the second month are "worth" 12¾%; this in fact is not so. To see why, let us look at an extreme example. Suppose we have US$ deposits:

1 month   (30 days) 10%
2 months (60 days) 20%

We need a 37-day rate again. Using our crude method we get:

$$\frac{30 \times 10 + 7 \times 20}{37} = \frac{440}{37} = 11.8919\%$$

Now we calculate a 50-day rate:

$$\frac{30 \times 10 + 20 \times 20}{50} = \frac{700}{50} = 14.9\%$$

Now a 59-day rate:

$$\frac{30 \times 10 + 29 \times 20}{59} = \frac{880}{59} = 14.9\%$$

But we know that our 60-day rate should be 20%; it seems improbable that the 59-day rate will only be 14.9% and the 60-day rate 20%, unless there are some very special factors (which, by assumption, there are not in our example).

What is happening is that the days in the second month are "worth" more than 20%. If you have earned an average return of 10% during the first 30 days, then in order to earn an average return of 20% over the whole 60 days, the second 30 days must be yielding more than 20%. Otherwise they cannot pull the average over the whole period up to the 20% required. In market jargon, the "forward forward rate for 60 days against 30 days" must be higher than 20%. In fact, it is 29.75196. If we now recalculate our 59-day rate, we find:

$$\frac{30 \times 10 + 29 \times 29.75196}{59} = \frac{1162.8068}{59} = 19.7086\%$$

which is clearly much more closely in line with what we should expect.

Notice that we have made a simplifying assumption about the second 30 days: that they can be treated all the same. We said that the forward forward rate for the whole of the second 30 days was about 29¾%. This might not be the case if there were special dates within the period. Suppose that in the middle of our second month (day 45) there was a special reporting date and as a result of balance sheet "window dressing" the market was prepared to bid 100% for money running from day 44 to day 46. (This happens regularly over year-end, for example.) Then we would have to refine our forward forward rate calculations. In practice, most dealers will simply make a mental adjustment for this factor rather than make elaborate calculations. It is important to be aware of how it might affect the rate calculation, though.

FORWARD FORWARD RATES

We turn now to the mechanics of calculating a forward forward rate. Although this might seem a rather specialized exercise, the forward forward rate is vital in at least two important areas: forward rate agreements (see below) and arbitrage between the deposit market and the financial futures market (see Chapter 14). For example, the rate on the 3-month Eurodollar futures contract is nothing but an implied forward forward rate. (Conversely, the deposit forward forward rates are often driven by the rates in the futures market.)

The simplest approach is to consider a specific case. A bank is lending for 60 days at 20% against a deposit for which it has paid 10% for 30 days. What is the breakeven rate on the second period—that is, how much can it afford to pay for a deposit starting on day 31 and maturing on day 60? We assume the deposit and loan are for US\$1 million and interest is paid on a 360-day basis. Then, the bank pays interest in the first period of

$$\frac{10}{100} \times \frac{30}{360} \times 1{,}000{,}000 = \$8{,}333.33$$

The bank earns interest over the lifetime of the loan of:

$$\frac{20}{100} \times \frac{60}{360} \times 1{,}000{,}000 = \$33{,}333.33$$

However, in accordance with Euromarket convention, interest earned on the 2-month loan is not paid to the bank until the end of the 2 months, whereas the bank must pay away interest on the 1-month deposit at maturity. So for the second period it not only has to fund its \$1 million principal amount but also the US\$8,333.33 which it has paid away in interest. So the amount to be funded in the second period is \$1,008,333.33.

Now we know that the bank has earnings of \$33,333.33 over the 2 months and costs (so far) of \$8,333.33. So there is a net \$25,000 which is available to pay the interest on our new principal of \$1,008,333.33. So to calculate our forward forward interest rate we work the \$25,000 as a percentage of the principal and annualize up from our 30-day period to a 360-day period:

$$\text{Forward rate} = 100 \times \frac{360}{30} \times \frac{25{,}000}{1008333.33} = 1200 \times 0.0247933 = 29.75196\%$$

In order to reduce this to a formula, we set up some definitions. The formula is set up in terms of middle market rates for simplicity.

$R1$ = rate for shorter, first period
$R2$ = rate for second period
$N1$ = number of days in first period
$N2$ = number of days in total second period, that is, including first
B = interest basis (usually 360)
P = principal amount
$I1$ = interest due in first period
$I2$ = interest due in second period
$I3$ = interest residual

Interest paid in the first period is:

$$I1 = \frac{R1}{100} \times \frac{N1}{B} \times P$$

Interest earned in total period is:

$$I2 = \frac{R2}{100} \times \frac{N2}{B} \times P$$

Hence interest available for the second period, $I3$ is:

$$I3 = I2 - I1 = R2 \times \frac{N2}{100} \times \frac{P}{B} - \frac{R1}{100} \times \frac{N1}{B} \times P = P\frac{(R2 \times N2 - R1 \times N1)}{100 \times B}$$

Our forward forward interest is calculated by working $I3$ back into an annual percentage of the principal (notice that the principal is now $P1 + I1$):

$$\text{Forward forward rate} = \frac{100 \times B \times I3}{(N2 - N1)(P + I1)} = \frac{P(R2 \times N2 - R1 \times N1)}{(N2 - N1)(P + I1)}$$

If we set the principal amount equal to \$1, or unity, the formula simplifies to:

$$\text{Forward forward rate} = \frac{R2 \times N2 - R1 \times N1}{\left[1 + \dfrac{R1 \times N1}{100 \times B}\right](N2 - N1)}$$

Putting that in words:

$$\text{Forward forward rate} = \frac{\left(\begin{array}{ccc}\text{Long} & & \text{Days in} \\ \text{period} & \times & \text{long} \\ \text{rate} & & \text{period}\end{array}\right) - \left(\begin{array}{ccc}\text{Short} & & \text{Days in} \\ \text{period} & \times & \text{short} \\ \text{rate} & & \text{period}\end{array}\right)}{\begin{array}{c}\text{Days left} \\ \text{in long} \\ \text{period}\end{array} \times \left[1 + \dfrac{\text{Short period rate} \times \text{Days in short period}}{100 \times \text{interest basis \{i.e. 360 or 365\}}}\right]}$$

Although we have worked throughout in terms of mid-market rates, the formula can be applied using actual bid and offer rates chosen appropriately. If we want the rate for forward forward lending, R2 will be the offered rate for the long period, R1 the bid rate for the short period. Conversely for the forward forward borrowing rate.

It is perhaps worth noting that this formula is widely used in the market, but expressed in different ways, some of which are superficially very different. For example, I have seen the following method:

1. Convert the rates into a yearly basis, that is, multiply the rate by the exact number of days and divide by 360.
2. Deduct the nearer factor from the further.
3. Divide the difference by the nearer factor plus 100.
4. Then multiply by 360 and divide by the number of days in the intervening period.
5. Multiply the result by 100.

This method is equivalent to that set out above, as we can see by following each step. Step 1 calculates $R2 \times N2/360$ and $R1 \times N1/360$. Steps 2 and 3 calculate

$$\frac{\dfrac{R2 \times N2 - R1 \times N1}{360}}{100 + \dfrac{R1 \times N1}{360}}$$

Steps 4 and 5 produce

$$\left[\frac{\dfrac{R2 \times N2 - R1 \times N1}{360}}{100 + \dfrac{R1 \times N1}{360}} \right] \times \frac{100 \times 360}{N2 - N1}$$

By canceling out the 360s in the numerator and dividing the bottom bracket by 100 to produce $1 + R3 \times N1/360 \times 100$, we can see that the two formulae are identical.

To show the application of the forward forward formula, consider the case of a corporate borrower who knows that in 3-months' time she will need to borrow $10 million for 3 months. Because the Treasurer of the company is conservative, she wishes to lock in the rate at which the borrowing is done now, and also to arrange the actual commitment of the loan. (In practice, the deal would probably be done through the Forward Rate Agreement market, but dealing in the forward forward market does actually lock up the funding.) The Treasurer approaches her bank and asks for a quotation on this basis.

Suppose the 3-month period has 90 days and the bid rate is 11%; the 6-month period is 182 days and the offered rate is 9%. In that case, the bank can raise funds for the longer period at 9%, laying them off temporarily at 11%, and so the forward forward rate is:

$$\frac{(9 \times 182) - (11 \times 90)}{92\left(1 + \dfrac{11 \times 90}{36000}\right)} = \frac{1,638 - 990}{92 \times 1.0275} = \frac{648}{94.53} = 6.855\%$$

and this is the rate at which the bank would be prepared to commit to lend to the corporation. (In practice, this would tie up both sides of the bank's balance sheet unnecessarily and the deal would be fixed through the Forward Rate Agreement market.)

COMPOUNDING AND INTEREST PAYMENT FREQUENCIES

The powerful effect of compounding of interest is well known. It is especially relevant in certain money market situations. We start by setting out the standard compounding formula in comparison with simple interest. On a simple interest basis, an investment of $1,000 at 10% on a 365-day basis for 365 days will yield $100 of interest. Suppose instead we place the funds in an investment account paying 10% but with interest compounded four times a year. Then the effective annual rate of interest (i*), given the simple rate (i), and the number of compounding periods (n), is given by:

$$i^* = \left(1 + \frac{i}{n}\right)^n - 1$$

Where the interest rates are in decimal form. So in our case, with $n = 4$ and $i = 0.10$, $i^* = 0.1038$ or 10.38% on an annual basis.

One of the commonest compounding conversions is from semi-annual to annual. There is a useful short-cut here. In this particular case, the formula produces $i + i^2/4$ and a simple rule of thumb is:

Convert semi-annual to annual: Additional basis points are found by squaring the interest rate and dividing by four.

For example, 12% squared and divided by four produces a 36 basis point adjustment to 12.36%.

The formula we have just laid out for finding the effective annual rate works well for annual calculations. But, going back to our investment account, suppose now that we know we will need the funds in 270 days' time. Then the number of compounding periods is not four, but three. And to compare the investment account with other 270-day investments (for example, a CD) we should allow for the fact that there will be less benefit from compounding. To do this, we should only compound as many periods as we will actually invest, and then gross up, to put the result back on an annual basis.

The formula we use for this is:

$$r = \left[\left(1 + \frac{i}{n}\right)^{n'} - 1\right] \times \frac{360}{t}$$

where r = the true periodic effective rate, n' = number of compounding periods until our investment horizon, and t = days in the investment horizon.

On this basis, the 10% investment account offers 10.25% over the period to the investment horizon. If the funds were left in the account for a year, we would get 10.38% p.a. The loss of a compounding date reduces the available yield; if we were offered a 270-day CD paying 10.3% over the period this would be a better bet than the account, even though the latter's effective annual rate is 10.38% because that effective rate relies on a compounding date from which we will never benefit.

Subject to this exception, the more compounding periods, the higher the effective annual yield. If an investment at 10% is compounded daily over 365 days, the effective annual rate is 10.52%. In fact, the effect tends to fall off with the number of compounding periods, as we can see from Table 6.1.

These compounding formulae only work if the interest rate remains constant. In our example, the investor was certain to get 10% on the investment account over the year. But usually we are not certain what we will earn when we come to invest the interest we receive. The only instrument on which the reinvestment rate on the interest is certain is one on which no interest is earned—a discount instrument that only pays interest at maturity. In the money market, this will typically be a Treasury bill, commercial paper, or a bankers' acceptance. In the bond market, it is the zero-coupon bond.

One final point: The formula used n' to denote the number of times interest was actually paid, which was appropriate because we were looking at an investment horizon that coincided with the date for payment of interest. It

Table 6.1   Effective Rate Changes

Number of Compounding Periods per Annum	Effective Rate
1	10
2	10.25
3	10.33
4	10.38
6	10.43
12	10.47
52	10.51
365	10.52

often happens that, in pricing a bond or an interest rate swap, we need a similar type of calculation for present value purposes (present value is explained in the next section). In those calculations, one is concerned also with valuing interest flows that may be accruing but not yet actually paid. In that case, we need to rewrite n' as nt/b where b is the interest basis to get the more general version of the formula. In our example above, n was 4, t was 270 and b was 360: so n' was $4 \times 270/360 = 3$. But suppose we were looking at a period of 295 days for our calculation: then we would have n' $= 4 \times 295/360 = 3.28$ and on that basis the interest applicable for the period would be 10.29%.

It may help to set the formula up from first principles. First we take the nominal periodic rate of interest, that is, 2.5% per quarter, and "decompound" this to a daily basis. Then we "recompound" back up over the appropriate fractional period. Our first step is to take the rate of interest down to a daily rate which we do by writing:

$$d = \left(1 + \frac{i}{n}\right)^{(1/360)}$$

where d = daily rate (bearing in mind that the market works on a 360-day year). So in this case we have d $= 1.025^{(1/360)} = 1.00006859$. Our next step is to recompound this up over the 295 days. So we must work out

$$d^* = d^t$$

where t = number of days to our investment horizon. We have $d^* = 1.00006859^{295} = 1.084302$.

Finally, to put the number back into an annual interest rate we gross up by the annual number of days:

$$r = \frac{(d^* - 1)*360}{295*100} = 10.28776$$

The net result is that a 10% annual rate decompounded over a 295-day period is equivalent to 10.29% annually. For those who prefer the entire process in one formula, it is as follows:

$$\text{Decompounded rate} = \left\{\left(\frac{1+i}{n}\right)^{(nt/360)} - 1\right\} \times \frac{360}{t \times 100}$$

It is very important to be aware of the impact of compounding. First, it is often a critical issue in swap market calculations (see Chapter 13) where one might be swapping against say a semi-annual or a quarterly rate: it is important to know the true annual rate implied. Second, in countries with high interest rates, the effects of interest on interest are significant. Countries such as Argentina have often had interest rates running at 200%–300% per annum.

With rates at these levels, the effect of compounding is significant. Consider the situation where you are offered the choice between a one-year deposit at 300% and the alternative of running an overnight funding position for the next 365 days at 200% p.a. (assuming you believe rates will not move). Which is the better bet? One might well be tempted to save 100% and run the overnight position, but if you apply the formula above, you will see that 200% compounded daily comes to a true annual rate of 634.88%, and if you really believe rates will stay steady, it would be far cheaper to raise one-year money at 300%. At higher rates, the impact is even more spectacular—300% compounded daily comes to 1884% p.a.

THE CONCEPT OF PRESENT VALUE

In the next chapter, we will use the concept of present value a lot. In this chapter, we need it to understand the relationship of forward forward rates to the zero-coupon curve and the pricing of forward rate agreements (see below) and so we will start with an explanation of present value.

The present value of a sum of money X due at some future date D is that sum of money which, if it were invested at the interest rate prevailing for deposits from today to D, would accumulate to X.

Let us take an example. You offer to buy my car, but you do not have enough money to pay me today. You offer to pay me $10,000 in one week's time. Since I need the car to go to work, I will have to replace the car today. If you do not pay me today, I will have to put up my own money to pay for the replacement car today. Since I have implicit faith in your ability to pay and in your trustworthiness, the only question in my mind is whether the present value of what you will pay me is more or less than what I will have to pay today for the replacement car.

Suppose I know that I can invest my money for one week at 8%. Then I know that if I invest $9,984.47 for 7 days on a 360-day basis I will have $9,984.47 \times (1 + [8/100 \times 7/360]) = \$10,000$. Putting that another way, I know that the present value of $10,000 in seven days' time is $9,984.47 using a discount rate of 8%. In fact, $9,984.47 = \$10,000/(1 + [8/100 \times 7/360])$. So if I can replace my car today for less than $9,984.47 it is worth my while to sell it for $10,000 due in one week's time. We can define a formula:

$$\text{Present value} = \frac{\text{Future value}}{1 + \dfrac{\text{Discount rate}}{100} \times \dfrac{\text{Days}}{360}}$$

Present Value over Several Periods

The formula we just defined is fine for what we were doing, namely discounting a single sum of money for a period of less than a year. To get the more general formula, it helps to start at the other end: a sum of money invested today. A sum with a present value of 100 invested today at an annual interest rate of r% will yield us $100(1 + r)$ at the end of year 1. (Note that r is a decimal: $10\% = 0.10$). At the end of year 2, we will have $100(1 + r)^2$ and at the end of year n we will have $100(1 + r)^n$. So we can say, Future value in year n = present value $\times (1 + r)^n$.

Therefore, turning the formula around:

$$\text{Present value} = \frac{\text{Future value in year n}}{(1 + r)^n}$$

Another way of saying this is that the present value is the future value discounted back to today at a rate of r. It is very important to realise that once we have discounted a sum of money back to today, it is valued in today's money. A sum of money, say $150, due in one year's time, discounted back to today, to produce say $135, is valued in today's money. Another sum, say $2000, due in five years' time, discounted back to today, to produce say $1750, is also valued in today's money. Because the two sums are valued in the same money, we can add them together.

Therefore, provided we discount each cash flow properly, we can discount every single cash flow in a stream of multiple cash flows back into a single sum of money. This is what happens when a bond dealer works out the price of a bond (see the next chapter). Each coupon payment on the bond is discounted back to today. The present value of each coupon, together with the present value of the bond's repayment amount, are added together. The total is the present value of all the cash flows of the bond. That total is what that stream of cash flows is worth today. Therefore, it will be the price that the dealer will be willing to bid for the bond.

Consider a stream of cash due at the end of each of the next five years: Year 1: $110; Year 2: $121; Year 3: $133.10; Year 4: $146.41; Year 5: $161.05.

Suppose we want to find the present value of this stream of cash flows. We can invest money for the five years at 10%, so that is the rate of discount we consider appropriate. What is the present value of the stream of flows?

We take our formula

$$\text{Present value} = \frac{\text{Future value in year n}}{(1 + r)^n}$$

and we apply it. The sum due at the end of Year 1 is to be discounted by $(1 + r)^1$, that is, 1.10; so $110 in a year's time is worth $100 today. Similarly, the sum due at the end of Year 2 is to be discounted by $(1 + r)^2$: that is, we work out $121/(1.10)^2$, which also turns out to be $100. Likewise, $133.1/(1.10)^3$ is worth $100; and if you check the others you will see they also are worth $100 today. So although the cash total of that stream of cash is

$671.56, the *total net present value* of the stream of cash is $500. We can write:

$$\begin{matrix} \text{Present value} \\ \text{of a stream} \\ \text{of cash flows} \end{matrix} = \frac{\begin{matrix}\text{Future value}\\\text{in year 1}\end{matrix}}{(1+r)^1} + \frac{\begin{matrix}\text{Future value}\\\text{in year 2}\end{matrix}}{(1+r)^2} + \ldots + \frac{\begin{matrix}\text{Future value}\\\text{in year n}\end{matrix}}{(1+r)^n}$$

Net Present Value of a Steady Cash Flow

If the stream of cash flows we are considering is a fixed amount, so that it is always the same like, for example, the coupon payment on a bond, there is a useful short cut we can use in our calculations. Suppose we have a regular stream of payments coming of $100 per annum. We can work out that the present value today of a stream of $100 per annum payable over the next five years, discounted at 10%, is ($90.91 + $82.64 + 75.13 + 68.30 + 62.09) or $379.07. That is to say,

$$\text{Net present value} = \$379.07 = \frac{\$100}{(1.10)} + \frac{\$100}{(1.10)^2} + \frac{\$100}{(1.10)^3} + \frac{\$100}{(1.10)^4} + \frac{\$100}{(1.10)^5}$$

We can let the payment of $100 be represented by c and the 10% discount rate by r. For convenience's sake, also, we can write $v = 1/(1+r)$. Then instead of having $100/(1.10) we have c times v and we can write the net present value of a regular cash flow c like this:

$$NPV = c(v + v^2 + v^3 + \ldots + v^n)$$

In our example, c was $100 and v was 1/1.10 or 0.9090909; v^2 would be 0.82645, and so on. (In other words, v is the "discount factor" applicable to each period).

We can simplify this some more. The expression in the brackets is often known as "an annuity certain." Mathematicians and actuaries tell us it can be simplified to $(1 - v^n)/r$ and so we have

$$NPV = \frac{c(1 - v^n)}{r}$$

which is a convenient formula because it can be calculated in one cell of a spreadsheet, no matter how many cash flows are involved, thereby saving a lot of machine memory!

YIELD CURVES, FORWARD RATES, ZERO-COUPON CURVES, AND MEDIUM-TERM FORWARD FORWARD RATES

Now that we have sorted out how to do present value calculations we can come back to the basic yield curve concept that we talked about earlier and dig a little deeper. The yield curve contains a lot of information embedded in it. First, the implied forward forward rates are indicated by the slope of the yield curve. If the slope between any two points is upward, the forward forward rate for the period between these points is above the current rates; if it is downward, it is below. So, embedded in the yield curve, is a second curve, of the forward forward rates. And there is also a third set of rates: the "zero-coupon" curve.

The zero-coupon rate for any given maturity is what the market would be prepared to pay on a deposit or bond which pays no interim interest payments, but only a lump sum at maturity. (Some people refer to the zero-coupon curve as the spot rate curve.) Although the zero-coupon curve may seem obscure, it can be important to interest rate swap dealers (see Chapter 13), because they can, if they choose, treat their interest rate positions as individual cash flows, which should be valued at the zero-coupon rate for that maturity.

We cannot observe the implied zero-coupon curve directly, and it has to be worked out step by step. A convenient way to do this is as follows. Let us look at the one-to-five year yield curve for Eurodollar deposits. Since interest payments, in line with Euromarket practice, are on an annual basis, the one-year deposit rate is in fact a zero-coupon rate: there are no interim interest payments. The two-year deposit rate is not, because there would normally be a payment of interest at the end of Year 1.

Suppose we are contemplating investing $1000 dollars. Suppose we have the following interest rates:

1 year	8%
2 years	9%
3 years	10%
4 years	11%
5 years	12%

Suppose we are interested in finding out what the two-year zero-coupon rate implied by these rates is. Suppose we deposit $1000 for two years at 9%. We know we will get two cash flows: a payment of $90 at the end of Year 1, and $1090 at the end of year 2. We will also receive a year's interest on the $90 coupon payment, but we do not know what that will be worth.

One way round this uncertainty is to take the following approach. I know the one-year zero-coupon rate is 8%. So I know that the present value today of that $90 is $83.33 (ignoring day-count questions and discounting on an annual basis). I would be indifferent between receiving $90 in a year's time and receiving $83.33 today by, say, assigning my right to the coupon to someone else. Suppose I do that. Then I now have a two-year zero-coupon deposit. I place $1000 − $83.33 = $916.67 today, and in two years I will receive $1090.

Now it is quite simple to work out the two-year zero-coupon rate: it is 9.045%. We can apply this technique step by step. The three-year deposit gives me cash flows of $100, $100, and $1100. I sell off the first two cash flows for $92.59 and $84.17, respectively. That makes my net investment today $823.24 which returns $1100 in three years' time, for an implied zero-coupon rate of 10.14%.

At the end of this process, I have the following yield curves:

	Deposit Yield Curve	Zero-Coupon Yield Curve
1 year	8	8.00
2 years	9	9.05
3 years	10	10.14
4 years	11	11.30
5 years	12	12.56

Now it is simple to find the medium-term forward forward rates. I know that I can earn 8% for one year on a zero-coupon basis; I can earn 9.05% for two years. The forward forward rate is that rate that will make me indifferent between the two. We find it by applying the forward forward formula we used earlier, except that we use years instead of days. So we have R1 = 8, R2 = 9.05, N1 = 1, N2 = 2, and the forward forward rate from Year 1 to Year 2 is:

$$F = \frac{9.05 \times 2 - 8 \times 1}{(2-1)\left(1 + \frac{8 \times 1}{100}\right)} = \frac{10.10}{1.08} = 9.35\%$$

FORWARD RATE AGREEMENTS

Forward forward rates are dealt through an active market in London and in certain other centers for Forward Rate Agreements (FRA). These are contracts between banks and their customers, or other banks, that allow for the forward hedging of interest rate movements: they are the money market equivalent of forward foreign exchange contracts. Another way of looking at them is to say they are single-period interest rate swaps.

They provide a very useful way to hedge against future movements in interest rates. Their prime advantage is that they allow this to be done without tying up large parts of the balance sheet. Until the FRA market was developed in the early 1980s, banks would trade their view of interest rates through forward forward deposits (see above). But this meant taking and placing deposits for the periods in question, which meant inflating both the asset and liability sides of the balance sheet. FRAs are a much more efficient method of handling the interest rate hedging required.

Let's define some terms. A Forward Rate Agreement is one where a notional borrower agrees with a notional lender the rate of interest which will be applied to a notional loan for some period in the future. Note the use of the word notional: there is no actual borrowing or lending involved. When the time comes to settle up, all that happens is an exchange of cash equal to the difference between the actual rate on the day and the rate agreed in the FRA.

The buyer of the FRA is the notional borrower—the party seeking protection against a rise in rates. The seller is the notional lender—the party seeking protection against a fall in rates. The contract amount (CA) is the notional sum on which the FRA is based. The contract rate (CR) is the rate of interest being hedged, usually LIBOR.

The contract period (CP) is the term from settlement date to maturity date, that is, the term of the notional deposit/loan. The settlement date is the date on which the settlement sum is payable. The maturity date is the date on which the notional loan/deposit matures. The settlement rate (SR) is the rate fixed on the fixing date as being that applicable to the settlement on the FRA. The fixing date is the date on which the settlement rate is fixed; for LIBOR that would normally be two business days ahead.

The settlement sum is the sum paid in settlement of the FRA. If paid at maturity it would be $(SR - CR) \times CP/360 \times CA/100$, assuming the currency in question is dealt on a 360-day year basis. However, in practice the custom in the FRA market is to pay the settlement sum on the settlement date. (The practical benefit is that this clears the deal off the books straight away and cuts down the credit exposure that would arise if one had to wait until the notional maturity date to be paid.)

Thus the settlement sum has to be discounted back from that which would be payable at maturity to its present value today. For this, we use the present value formula developed in the last section. Thus, for a sum paid on settlement date, the value would be

$$\frac{\left[(SR - CR) \times \dfrac{CP}{360} \times \dfrac{CA}{100}\right]}{\left(1 + \dfrac{SR \times CP}{36000}\right)}$$

Note that the numerator is the same as before; the denominator is the discount factor to bring the value back to today. The formula can be simplified to $(CR - SR) \times CP \times CA/(36000 + (SR \times CP))$.

Let's look at an example. I buy a 3×6 FRA for a contract amount (CA) of $10 million. The rate (CR) is 10.5%. The contract period (CP) is 90 days. When the contract comes to settle, the settlement rate (SR) is 12.25%. Then the settlement value of the FRA is $[(12.25 - 10.5) \times 90/360 \times 10,000,000/100]/(1 + [12.25 \times 90/36000])$. This gives us $43,750/1.030625 = $42,449.97. Had we been prepared to wait for settlement until the end of the contract period the sum payable would have been $43,750; the discount factor we apply to this to find its present value on the settlement date is 1.030625.

The way in which FRAs are priced is simple: if there is a financial futures market for a comparable instrument, pricing is taken from the futures market. If not, it is taken from the cash deposit yield curve. forward forward rates for the period in question are worked out and applied to FRAs. Thus, if I wanted to find the correct price for the 3×6 sterling FRA I could either look at the LIFFE 3-month sterling deposit future contract, or else look at the yield curve for 3-month and 6-month sterling deposits. From these I would work out the forward forward rate for 3 months against 6 months and this would give me the rate applicable for the FRA. Because the forward forward, FRA and futures markets are all closely integrated, arbitrage will keep the three markets in line.

One final point is to consider the way FRAs will trade as interest rates move. It follows from our forward forward formula, which drives the FRA price, that if the long rate (R2) moves, the FRA rate will move in the same direction by a factor of $N2/(N2 - N1)$. For example, consider a 3×6 FRA: 90 days $\times$ 180. The impact of a rise in the 6-month rate is $180/(180 - 90) \times 1\% = 2\%$.

Conversely, if the short rate, R1, moves, the FRA will move *in the opposite direction* by $N1(N2 - N1)$. For instance, in the same example a 1% rise in the short rate will push down the FRA rate by $-90/(180 - 90) \times 1\% = -1\%$. The shorter the contract period $(N2 - N1)$ and the further away the contract period is (i.e. the larger N1 is) the bigger the effect. For example, in a 9×12 FRA N1 is 270 and N2 is 360: the effect is $-270/(360 - 270) = -3\%$.

Therefore, *the pricing of the FRA is affected if the yield curve changes shape, even if the general level of rates does not change.* The size of the impact depends on the relative length of the period to settlement date compared with the contract period. Some general rules of thumb are:

- If all rates are going up, buy FRAs and buy the ones with the longest contract period to get maximum benefit. Conversely, if all rates are falling, sell the FRA with the longest contract period.
- If short rates are rising and long rates are unchanged, sell the FRA with the longest period to settlement date (for example, sell 9×12 rather than 3×12). Conversely, if short rates are falling with long rates unmoved, buy the longest-deferred settlement date FRA.

In the London market, it is normal practice to deal FRAs on *FRABBA terms*. These are the terms and conditions agreed for FRA dealing by the British Bankers' Association, and the practice has the obvious advantage that all parties in the market can take certain standard terms (for example, the convention for subsequent declaration of nonbusiness days) for granted.

FRABBA has also laid down the *British Bankers Association Interest Settlement Rate* (BBAISR) as the basis on which FRAs settle. The BBA

ISR is defined as the rate calculated by the information vendor (currently Telerate) from the rates quoted to it by eight BBA designated banks as being in their view the offered rate at which deposits in the contract currency are being quoted to prime banks in the London interbank market at 11 AM on the relevant fixing date for settlement date value. The calculation is done by eliminating the two highest (or in the event of equality, two of the highest) and the two lowest (or two of the lowest if equal). The average of the remaining four rates is then rounded up, if necessary, to five decimal places.

Similar arrangements exist in other markets such as Australia; there is an interesting technique also which has been developed in Australia: the FRACH contract. FRACH stands for FRA Clearing House. There is a 1-month and a 2-month contract. Trading takes place in minimum amounts of AUD 5 million and multiples thereof. The contract is based on the average daily 11 AM cash rate of each contract month. The contract is traded up to the last business day of the previous month and the rate is set for the contract month in arrears. For example, if the contract month was May, trading would occur up to and including April 30.

Bid and offer rates for the two traded contract months can be inserted by members on Reuters page YBCX; the best bid and offer is then displayed on page AFMZ. Each day a daily reference rate is set between the times of 10:30 AM and 11:00 AM each working day by Reuters using the information from AFMZ. The rate is the continuous average of the second highest bid and the second lowest offer. The monthly settlement rate is then calculated from the average of the daily rates.

Settlement on the contract is as follows:

$$\frac{\text{Settlement rate} - \text{Contract rate}}{100} \times \frac{\text{Days in contract month}}{365} \times \text{Contract amount}$$

For example, if Westpac borrowed AUD 25 million from ANZ at 16.50% for the May contract month, and the monthly settlement rate for May turned out to be 17.237%, we would have:

$$\frac{(17.237 - 16.5) \times 31 \times 25,000,000}{100 \times 365} = \text{AUD } 15,648.63$$

Westpac could either trade out of the position at any time up to and including April 30, by doing an offsetting contract, or it would hold on to the position, in which case it would settle on June 1. Settlement and clearing take place through Austraclear (see Chapter 21). Collectively, these arrangements make the FRACH a kind of hybrid between FRA and an over-the-counter financial future.

NEGATIVE INTEREST RATES

Many people raise their eyebrows at the idea of negative interest rates. But they do occur, and they can be highly profitable. It is very pleasant to be paid to borrow money. Negative rates generally happen in one of two ways: either there is intense upward pressure on a currency, or there is intense downward pressure which is expected to be only temporary.

Negative interest rates can be thrown up in the forward forward markets if a currency is under sufficiently intense pressure. During the spring of 1981, the French franc was extraordinarily weak, and the Banque de France was determined to support it by squeezing money market rates in the then thinly traded Euro-French franc deposit market. Overnight Euro-French francs at one point were lent out at over 5000% and one-week money was running at over 300%. Applying our forward forward formula above we can see that the forward rate for the remaining six days was −424%: by lending out at 5000% for a night, funded with one-week money, we could afford to lend for the remainder of the week at rates as low as −400% and still make money. Although this kind of situation can fairly be called an extreme case, fluctuations on this scale do occur in narrow money markets (e.g., also New Zealand where rates hit 1000% in 1984/5) and can be very profitable.

A good example of the effects of the opposite situation, currency inflows, is the Swiss franc in 1977/8. The inflow of hot money into Swiss francs was so great that the Swiss authorities imposed a commission on deposits with banks such that a foreign depositor in a Swiss bank account was paying 40% per annum for the privilege—a commission of 10% per quarter. Some people held on to their deposits, though, and watched the Swiss franc appreciate by 50%. A negative interest rate can be worthwhile if the currency is rising faster than the negative rate eats away your capital. Another example of this occurred in the late 1980s during a period of upward pressure on the Hong Kong dollar.

DOMESTIC MONEY MARKET CONSIDERATIONS

As a rule, Euromarket trading rooms tend to concentrate on clean deposits and CDs. Withholding tax, and other technical considerations tend to limit trading in other instruments. The discussion here will be very brief; for more detail see the Bibliography. We set the scene by looking at a general ranking of important markets (Table 6.2).

The U.S. Treasury bill market is the largest and most liquid in the world. A trade of $50 million presents no particular problem. This makes it an attractive short-term investment vehicle. Also, discount income on Treasury bills if under six-months' maturity is exempt from withholding tax. Interest payments on other Treasury securities, for example, notes and

Table 6.2   Global Money Market Size: Ranking by Instrument

	US$ Bn. Equivalent Outstanding
US$ Domestic commercial paper	420
US$ Treasury bills	397
US$ Euro-FRNs	130
JPY Domestic CDs	114
US$ Euro CDs	100
CAD Treasury bills	68
US$ Agency discount notes	65
US$ Domestic CDs	60
US$ Eurocommercial paper	60
JPY Gen-saki	60
GBP Certificates of deposit	59
AUD Bank bills of exchange	46
US$ Yankee bankers' acceptances	40
US$ Yankee commercial paper	35
CAD Bankers' acceptances	29
PTA Letras del Tesoro	28
FFR Bons a Taux Fixe (BTF)	25
US$ Domestic bankers' acceptances	25
GBP Euro-FRNs	17
CAD Commercial paper	16
CAD Provincial Treasury bills	16
GBP Eligible bank bills	16
US$ Yankee CDs	10
AUD Trading bank CDs	8
AUD Treasury notes	8
DEM Euro-FRNs	7
GBP Euro-commercial paper	6
GBP Treasury bills	5
Other*	26
Total	1,895

*Includes Euro-CDs and Euro-FRNs, ECU FRNs, AUD promissory notes, NZ$ bank-accepted bills and Treasury bills, ECU UK Treasury bills, AUD non-bank certificates of deposit, NZ$ Trading bank certificates of deposit, Irish Treasury bills, AUD Yankee FRNs and commercial paper, NZ$ Yankee FRNs and commercial paper, and ECU Yankee commercial paper.

Source: Merrill Lynch Guide to Global Money Market Instruments, Merrill Lynch
    Capital Markets, New York, 1988.

bonds, and discount on longer bills, attract withholding tax, although exemption can be obtained in certain cases. Treasury bills are issued in minimum denominations of $10,000. They are in book-entry form. That is, they are held in a computer; it is not possible to take physical delivery. Treasury bills are auctioned monthly. Prices are calculated on the basis of actual number of days and 30-day months over a 360-day year, on a discount basis (Chapter 7). As well as the cash market, the Treasury bill futures market is very large indeed (see Chapter 14).

After Treasury bills, commercial paper is the next important short-term market. Commercial paper (CP) is a promissory note, usually unsecured and issued by a corporation for up to 270 days. (This limitation ensures exemption from SEC registration procedures, though a rating is still needed from an agency.) Typically the maturity is 15 to 35 days. CP is usually issued in multiples of $100,000. Large issuers place their paper directly, using sales force if necessary. Others issue their paper through dealers. Either way, CP is normally the cheapest and most flexible method of short-term corporate financing. CP calculations, like Treasury bills, are on a discount basis. Euro-commercial paper (ECP) is an important outgrowth of the original U.S. commercial paper market. It is basically a very similar market except that the 270-day restriction does not apply, because the paper is not subject to SEC restrictions. Settlement in the ECP market is normally, like other Euromarket dealing, for spot value. Delivery of the paper is normally handled through the Eurobond clearing systems (Euroclear and Cedel). The relevant calculations are discussed in Chapter 7.

Bankers' acceptances are a smaller market in the United States, but acceptances have the major advantage that they do not require the lengthy and expensive rating agency assessment required of CP issuers (since the investor's credit risk in acceptances is the bank rather that the corporate borrower). A bankers' acceptance (BA) is a bill of exchange: an order by the drawee (accepting bank) to pay the payee a specific sum of money on a certain date. After the bank has accepted the bill it may hold it or, more typically, sell it in the market. BAs are discounted instruments, traded on an actual days/360-day-year basis (see Section 1). They are generally in bearer form and normally in any given maturity up to 180 days—usually about 90 days. The market trades in minimum lots of $1 million but more typically $5 million. BAs may be eligible for rediscount at the Fed, or ineligible. The distinction makes little practical difference except that the ineligible market may be a little less liquid, and may cost a little more because a bank selling then incurs a reserve required cost. The term Yankee BA is often used, by analogy with the Yankee bond market, to refer to an acceptance issued in the United States by a foreign issuer.

Repurchase agreements are another large market. There are several types of repurchase, depending on the market. We will begin with U.S. practice. A repurchase or repo deal is a sale of securities with a commitment to repurchase them at a set date. The rate is an ordinary interest rate (that is, add-on rather than discount) calculated an actual days/360-day year. So interest is calculated (assuming a discount security, and that sale and repurchase price are equal—the repo is "priced flat"):

$$\text{Interest due} = (\text{principal amount}) \times (\text{repo rate}) \times \frac{(\text{Days repo is outstanding})}{360}$$

The underlying securities are priced so as to give the lender (that is, the buyer of the security) a margin to protect himself. In some cases the pricing is not flat, but set in terms of a sales price and a repurchase price chosen to give an equivalent yield. In this case of course the RP rate is given by:

$$\text{RP rate} = \frac{(\text{Repurchase price} - \text{Sale price})}{\text{Sale price}} \times \frac{360}{\text{Days RP is outstanding}} \times 100$$

and the interest due is then calculated as before. Alternatively, given the repo rate, the repurchase price is found (by simple manipulation of the previous equation) as:

$$\text{Repurchase price} = \text{Sale price} \left[1 + \frac{\text{Repo rate} \times \text{Days outstanding}}{100 \times 360} \right]$$

This formula can be compared with the Japanese *gen-saki* formula below to see the impact of a securities sales tax.

If the security is not a discount one, but an interest-bearing one, things are more complex. Assume first that during the repurchase period no interest payment is made. Then all that happens is that both sales price and repurchase price have to be defined to include accrued interest. If, however, interest is paid during the life of the deal, street practice is to pay interest on the security price including accrued interest, until the next coupon date. Suppose we repo a bond at $102\frac{3}{8}$, which pays a coupon on day 11, which belongs to the seller. Then on day 12, the security is repriced to 100. Suppose the repo is done at 10% for 30 days; then the interest payable is given (if the principal amount were $100):

$$\frac{10 \times 102\frac{3}{8} \times 11}{100 \times 360} + \frac{10 \times 100 \times 19}{100 \times 360}$$

and then the repurchase price is:

$$102\frac{3}{8} + \frac{10 \times 102\frac{3}{8} \times 11}{100 \times 360} + \frac{10 \times 100 \times 19}{100 \times 360}$$

so the formula is

$$\begin{array}{c} \text{Repurchase} \\ \text{price} \end{array} = \begin{array}{c} \text{Sale} \\ \text{price} \end{array} + \frac{\begin{array}{c}\text{Repo}\\\text{rate}\end{array} \times \begin{array}{c}\text{Days till}\\\text{coupon}\end{array} \times \begin{array}{c}\text{Sale}\\\text{price}\end{array}}{100 \times 360} + \frac{\begin{array}{c}\text{Repo}\\\text{rate}\end{array} \times \begin{array}{c}\text{Days}\\\text{remaining}\end{array} \times 100}{100 \times 360}$$

Since the collapse in the United States in 1982 of Drysdale Securities which generated capital by building up accrued interest, attitudes to this type of deal have become a great deal more cautious. But in general, repurchase agreements are attractive because of their flexibility of term; repos can be done, in theory, for any maturity. In practice, the bulk is overnight. Typically the overnight repo rate is below the Fed funds rate, because corporations and other lenders who have no direct access to the Fed funds market are lenders in the overnight repo market. Also, the repo market is a secured market; Fed funds are unsecured.

Repos are also common in the international markets, both in domestic markets and in the Euromarket. The following description outlines Eurobond market practices. There are three principal types of transaction: U.S. style repo, sale/buyback, and security lending. The underlying securities are usually government bonds or high-quality Eurobonds. Security lending consists of the simple loan of the bonds against payment of a fee by the borrower. Rights to the underlying coupon remain with the lender. A sale/buyback differs from the U.S.-style repo in that the coupon on the bond accrues in favor of the buyer, rather than remaining with the seller as is U.S. practice; it is normally at a fixed rate for a fixed term of 1 week to 6 months. Settlement of the bonds is usually done through Euroclear or Cedel, the international bond depositories.

There is a comparable repo market in Japan, the gen-saki market. This is a repurchase market and the calculations are exactly the same as those for the U.S. repo market, with two modifications, one being a 365- rather than 360-day basis. The other is required if the investor pays the securities

Table 6.3 Domestic Money Market Interest Bases

Country	Calculation Basis
Australia	ACT/365
Austria	ACT/360
Belgium	ACT/365
Canada	ACT/365
Denmark	ACT/360
Eire	ACT/365
France	ACT/360
Germany	ACT/360
Japan	ACT/360
Netherlands	ACT/360 or 30E/360
New Zealand	ACT/365
Norway	30/360 (ACT/360 under 1 month; CDs ACT/365)
Saudi Arabia	ACT/360
Sweden	30E/360
Switzerland	ACT/360 or 30/360 (Federal Treasury bills)
United Kingdom	ACT/365
United States	ACT/360

transfer tax (which may be absorbed by his counterparty, but of course the rate will be adjusted to reflect this). The formula for a discount instrument is:

$$\text{Repurchase price} = \text{Sale price}\left[1 + \frac{\left(\dfrac{\text{Repo rate} \times \text{Days out}}{100 \times 360}\right)}{1 - \text{Tax rate}}\right]$$

That is, the price has to be grossed up to allow for the tax (currently 0.1% of face value, so the bottom line would be 0.9999). Similarly for the formula allowing for interest payments.

A problem when dealing in domestic markets—quite apart from settlement and tax issues—is the wide range of variations of interest calculation basis, compared with the common basis used in all Euromarket dealing (that is, actual days on a 360- or 365-day year). Table 6.3 attempts to give a summary of the interest calculation basis used in various domestic markets. Parallel information for bonds is given in the next chapter.

7 Money-Market Paper and Bond Calculations

In Chapter 6 we looked at time deposit calculations. Now we look at the calculations involved in trading money-market securities, or "paper." We also give a basic introduction to some bond calculations since they may be of help and are also relevant to the interest rate swap market (see Chapter 15).

There are two main differences between time deposit calculations and money-market securities trades. First, money-market paper can be, and often is, sold before maturity—there is secondary market trading. This is not normally the case with a time deposit, which is typically held to maturity. In looking at money-market paper, there is thus the possibility of a change in price of the instrument—the possibility of a capital gain or loss. Second, most deposits are dealt on an interest-bearing basis—I place $100 with you and get back, say, $105. But some money-market paper is dealt on a discount basis: I invest $92.75 with you and get back $100. That is, the face amount of the deal is the amount at maturity, not the amount at the start of the deal, as it is with interest-bearing deposits or interest-bearing instruments.

We will start with the more straight-forward money-market calculations for certificates of deposit and for discount securities, in each case considering short-term instruments with only one payment of interest. Then we cover the basic calculations involved in pricing a bond. These calculations are important not only for bond traders but also for those involved in medium-term interest rate swaps (see Chapter 15). Next we look at the very important concept of duration, which measures interest rate risk. We also touch briefly on convexity and immunization. We begin with the most ubiquitous inter-bank money-market instrument, the certificate of deposit.

CERTIFICATES OF DEPOSIT

Some years after the birth of the Eurodollar market, the certificate of deposit (CD) concept was introduced. The CD has since become an important source of funds for banks. The CD was first issued in the U.S. domestic market in 1961 and in the Euromarket in 1966. Essentially, a CD is an instrument (normally negotiable) evidencing a time deposit made with a bank at a fixed rate of interest for a fixed period. CDs bear interest and CD rates are in general quoted on an interest-bearing (rather than a discount) basis. Normally, interest on a US$ CD is calculated for actual days on a 360-day basis and paid at maturity. But for CDs issued with a maturity over one year, interest is normally paid annually.

Since its introduction, the concept of a CD has been introduced to most of the major money-markets. The speed at which this has happened has varied in accordance with the attitude of the domestic authorities of the currency concerned. For example, until 1986 the Bundesbank did not permit the issuance of deutschemark CDs. This was because, having suffered the effects on its currency of massive inflows from abroad during the 1970s, the Bundesbank was not anxious to encourage the growth of a money-market instrument that would allow foreigners to move into and out of the deutschemark market more easily. To this day, the Swiss authorities have not permitted the development of a Swiss franc CD market, for similar reasons.

Sterling CDs are dealt on a basis comparable to that of US$ CDs except that interest is calculated on a 365-day basis. Interest is paid annually on the anniversary of issue of CDs of maturity over one year. Japanese CDs are issued to a specific buyer and registered in his name, so that the transfer must be notarized and the issuing bank advised. They are also potentially subjected to withholding tax (depending on the relevant treaty.) Both features have limited their attractiveness internationally.

CDs are available in various types as well as various currencies. The first variation was the floating rate CD (FRCD). These were introduced in 1977. They have maturities, usually, of three to five years. Interest on FRCDs is normally payable semiannually and is usually linked to six-month LIBOR. Other FRCDs have been issued at different margins or at the "mean of bid and offer" (LIMEAN), or at the bid rate (LIBID).

Another variant is the discount CD. This was introduced early in 1981 in the U.S. domestic market and subsequently in London. Here the CD does not pay a stated rate of interest. Instead, the certificate bears a wording along the following lines: "XYZ Bank certifies that a sum has been deposited with this bank which together with interest solely in respect of the period to the maturity date will on the maturity date equal US$ X." The advantage of a discount CD is that its price can immediately be compared with other discount instruments such a Treasury bills. The disadvantage is that it cannot easily be compared with other CDs.

CD Calculations

Let's start by assuming that the life of the CD we are looking at is under one year, so that interest is due at maturity. Suppose we have a 15% CD for $1 million issued with 90 days to maturity. (As it is a US$ CD, it is dealt on a 360-day year basis.) What is the value at maturity? It is face value plus interest earned, calculated on a simple interest basis:

$$\text{Maturity value} = 1,000,000 + 1,000,000 \times \frac{15}{100} \times \frac{90}{360} = \$1,037,500$$

$$= \text{Principal} \left[1 + \frac{\text{Coupon}}{100} \times \frac{\text{Days from issue to maturity}}{360} \right]$$

At any point before maturity, this CD will have earned a certain amount of interest already—the "accrued interest." If we are buying a CD on a given day we will want to know the accrued interest, which is given by the following (suppose we buy the CD on day 30):

$$\text{Accrued interest} = 1,000,000 \times \frac{15}{100} \times \frac{30}{360} = \$12,500$$

$$= \text{Principal} \times \frac{\text{Coupon}}{100} \times \frac{\text{Days from issue to purchase}}{360}$$

We need to know what price we should be prepared to pay for this CD, assuming that the general level of interest rates is unchanged since it was issued. That is, a 60-day CD will currently also be issued at a coupon of 15%, so we have the choice between buying a new CD or the "secondary" CD which has been outstanding for some time, both yielding a coupon of 15%. We know, from our first formula above, that the new CD will at maturity be worth $1,000,000[1 + 15/100 \times 60/360] = \$1,025,000$. The amount we are prepared to pay for the old CD must be such as to produce an equal yield over the 60 days. That is, we must have:

$$\frac{1,037,500}{\text{Price for old CD}} = \frac{1,025,000}{1,000,000}$$

for the two yields to be equal. Hence,

$$\text{Price for old CD} = 1,000,000 \times \frac{1,037,500}{1,025,000} = 1,012,195.12$$

This price is a little below the face value plus accrued interest so far, which we know, from our first formula, to be $1,012,500. The reason is that although interest has accrued, it is not yet payable. The buyer must wait to receive it, and so will require a discount on the price he pays for accrued interest.

Suppose now that the general level of interest rates has changed so that a new 60-day CD pays 10%. Then we know, from our first formula, that its value per $1,000,000 at maturity will be $1,016,666.67. We want to know the price that we should pay for an old 90-day 15% CD with 60 days to run. As before, the value of the old CD at maturity is $1,037,500, and as before we calculate the price by dividing the values at maturity into each other:

Value of old CD at maturity = $1,037,500

$$\text{Price} = \frac{\text{Value of old CD at maturity}}{\text{Value of new CD at maturity}} \times \$1,000,000$$

$$= \frac{\$1,037,500}{\$1,016,666.67} \times \$1,000,000 = \$1,020,491.80$$

What we are doing is bidding up the price of the old CD to the point where the yield when we buy the old CD is equal to the 10% coupon available on a new CD. Because the value of the CD at maturity is a function of the coupon and the days from issue to maturity, as we saw earlier, we can calculate the price of the old CD in terms of interest rates:

$$\text{Price} = \frac{\text{Principal}}{\text{amount}} \times \left[\frac{1 + \dfrac{\text{Coupon on old CD}}{100} \times \dfrac{\text{Days from issue to maturity}}{360}}{1 + \dfrac{\text{Coupon on new CD}}{100} \times \dfrac{\text{Days from issue to maturity}}{360}} \right]$$

We can apply this to the case when we want to value a CD which we intend to buy in the market. To do this, we have to change the bottom line of the formula: instead of writing "coupon on new CD" we can put "current yield on CD" and instead of using the number of days from issue to maturity, we write the number of "days from purchase to maturity." This gives us:

$$\text{Price} = \frac{\text{Principal}}{\text{amount}} \times \left[\frac{1 + \dfrac{\text{Coupon on CD}}{100} \times \dfrac{\text{Days from issue to maturity}}{360}}{1 + \dfrac{\text{Yield on CD}}{100} \times \dfrac{\text{Days from purchase to maturity}}{360}} \right]$$

It follows from this formula that we can equally well calculate the yield on a CD if we know the price paid. By rewriting the formula, we can find that:

$$\text{Yield} = \frac{\text{Principal}}{\text{amount}} \times \left[\frac{1 + \dfrac{\text{Coupon on CD}}{100} \times \dfrac{\text{Days from issue to maturity}}{360}}{\text{Price}} \right] \times \frac{[360 \times 100]}{\text{Days from purchase to maturity}} - 1$$

This formula can be tested by seeing whether it works for the purchase of a CD on the issue date. In this case, the days from issue to maturity equal the days from purchase to maturity and the price equals the principal amount, so that the yield equals the coupon as one would expect.

Let's look now at the case of a trader who thinks that rates are going to come down and so buys a 90-day CD financing it with a 60-day deposit. The parallel case on the domestic U.S. market would be a CD financed by a term repo. The price at which we sell the CD after 60 days must be enough to pay our funding cost: so we know that we must have:

$$\text{Resale price} = \text{Principal}\left(1 + \frac{\text{Funding cost}}{100} \times \frac{\text{Days held}}{360} \right)$$

Suppose the CD is for $1 million and is funded at 12% for the 60 days that we hold it; then we must have:

$$\text{Price} = 1,000,000\left(1 + \frac{12}{100} \times \frac{60}{360} \right) = \$1,020,000$$

But we know from our yield formula above that we can find the yield on the CD if we know the price that is paid on it, which we have just found. So by using the price calculation above in the yield formula we can find the break-even yield at resale:

$$\text{Break-even yield} = \left[\frac{1 + \dfrac{\text{Coupon}}{100} \times \dfrac{\text{Days from issue to maturity}}{360}}{1 + \dfrac{\text{Funding cost}}{100} \times \dfrac{\text{Days held}}{360}} - 1 \right] \times \frac{[360 \times 100]}{\text{Days remaining from sale to maturity}}$$

Let's apply this formula to our 15% 90-day CD, assuming that we buy it on the issue date and we can finance it for 60 days at 12%. What yield can we afford to sell at and still break even? Our formula says:

$$\text{Break-even yield} = \left[\frac{1 + \frac{15}{100} \times \frac{90}{360}}{1 + \frac{12}{100} \times \frac{60}{360}}\right] \times \frac{[360 \times 100]}{30} = \frac{[1.0375]}{[1.02]} \times 1200 = 20.588\%$$

In other words, because we were making 3% profit for 60 days, we can afford to see rates move up a good deal in the secondary market before we take a loss.

If we are buying a CD in the secondary market rather than in the issue date, we have to use the yield at which we buy the CD rather than the coupon. The remaining life of the CD is no longer the period from issue to maturity, but the period from purchase to maturity. With these modifications the formula is now:

$$\text{Break-even yield} = \left[\frac{1 + \frac{\text{CD yield}}{100} \times \frac{\text{Days from purchase to maturity}}{360}}{1 + \frac{\text{Funding cost}}{100} \times \frac{\text{Days held}}{360}} - 1\right] \times \frac{[360 \times 100]}{\text{Days remaining from sale to maturity}}$$

We have looked at finding out what yield we can afford to sell at in order to break even. The opposite question is: If I know the yield at which I bought the CD, and the yield at which I sold, how much did I make during the holding period? The answer in general is that the holding period yield is (sale price − purchase price)/purchase price. It can be expressed as an annual interest rate by multiplying by 360/holding period. The most general case is going to be that in which we buy a CD in the secondary market then later resell it. The holding period yield on a CD bought at an issue is a special case of this general case where the yield at purchase equals the coupon. We can solve this general problem by taking the formula we have just worked out and turning it around. We are looking for the holding period yield, which must, if we are to break even, equal our funding cost. So we rewrite our formula and after some manipulation we get:

$$\text{Holding period yield} = \left[\frac{1 + \frac{\text{Yield when bought}}{100} \times \frac{\text{Days from purchase to maturity}}{360}}{\frac{\text{Yield when sold}}{100} \times \frac{\text{Days from sale to maturity}}{360}} - 1\right] \times \frac{[360 \times 100]}{\text{Holding period}}$$

So far, all our calculations have been for CDs whose maturity was less than one year. Calculations for CDs over one year are more complex because there are multiple interest payments. A computer or financial calculator is desirable. A problem is the variable number of days involved which can be affected by holidays. Also annual interest payments in CDs in the Euromarket are affected by leap years. Semiannual payments (for example, in the U.S. domestic market) are affected by the fact that the 365 days of the year are inherently impossible to divide equally into 182.5 days. The effect of holidays is also a complication.

However, the underlying principles are fairly straightforward. Let us assume that we are trading a CD with annual payments in a world with a 365-day year but no holidays and no leap years. Suppose it is a 5-year half-million-dollar CD paying 10% interest annually on January 1. Interest is $500,000 \times 10/100 \times 365/360 = \$50,694.44$. Suppose we hold the CD for 1 year and 37 days and wish to know the resale price if we sell at 9%. We proceed as follows: Today's price is the discounted value of future proceeds. We know that at the end of year 5 we will receive $500,000 plus interest of $50,694.44. We discount this sum back to the end of the fourth year at 9%:

$$\frac{550,694.44}{1 + \dfrac{9 \times 365}{100 \times 360}} = \$504,645.53$$

If the CD were sold on day 1 of year 5, we would receive this price plus the interest payable on that date. So we must now discount back to the end of year 4:

$$\frac{\$504,645.53 + \$50,694.44}{1 + \dfrac{9 \times 365}{100 \times 360}} = \frac{\$555,339.97}{1.09125} = \$508,902.61$$

To this discounted rate at the end of year 3 must be added the interest payable at that date, and the total must be discounted back to the end of year 2:

$$\frac{\$508,902.61 + \$50,694.44}{1 + \dfrac{9 \times 365}{100 \times 360}} = \frac{\$559,597.05}{1.09125} = \$512,803.71$$

We then take this price and add it to the interest due at that date, making a total of $563,498.15. We know that, as of day 37 in year 2 when we are selling the CD, this is the price we will receive if we hold the CD for another 328 days. So we discount this price over 328 days:

$$\frac{\$563,498.15}{1 + \dfrac{9 \times 328}{100 \times 360}} = \$520,793.11$$

Which is the price we need.

DISCOUNT SECURITIES

Treasury bills, commercial paper, bankers' acceptances, and various other instruments are dealt on a discount basis; and from time to time this applies also to CDs. In cases where local exchange control forbids forwards exchange cover on interest payable, it may also be convenient to deal clean deposits on a discount basis. We will set out the calculations as for a bill; they can of course be applied to the other instruments mentioned. We will look at the calculation for price given discount rate; discount rate given price; conversion of interest rate to discount and vice versa; holding period yield; and the forward-forward bill rate (bill parity).

Suppose we have a bill for $1 million which is being discounted at 10% for 90 days using a 360-day year. Then the discount amount is $10/100 \times 90/360 \times 1,000,000 = \$25,000$ or

$$\text{Discount amount} = \frac{\text{Discount rate}}{\dfrac{100 \times \text{Discount period}}{360 \times \text{Face value}}}$$

The price today is the face value less the discount amount, $975,000 or:

$$\text{Price} = \text{Face value}\left[1 - \frac{\text{Discount rate}}{100} \times \frac{\text{Discount period}}{360}\right]$$

To find the discount rate given the price or the discount amount, we manipulate this formula. If the discount amount is given we turn the first formula around to get:

$$\text{Discount rate} = \left[\frac{\text{Discount amount}}{\text{Face value}} \times \frac{360}{\text{Discount period}}\right]$$

Conversely, if we are given the price, we turn the second formula around to get:

$$\text{Discount rate} = \left[1 - \frac{\text{Price}}{\text{Face value}}\right] \times \frac{360}{\text{Discount period}}$$

We have been using a discount rate rather than an interest rate. The difference is that a discount rate is applied to the principal at the far end of the deal (the face value); an interest rate is applied to the principal at the near end. In our example, the face value is $1,000,000 and the principal at the near end is $975,000; so if we express the discount amount as a percentage of the near end we see that it is not 10% but 10.2564%. The formula for converting a discount rate to an interest rate is:

$$\text{Interest rate} = \frac{360 \times \dfrac{\text{Discount rate}}{100}}{360 - \dfrac{\text{Discount rate}}{100} \times \text{Discount period}}$$

where the interest rate is on a 360-day basis. To make it a 365-day basis we put 365 in the top line. Conversely, to get the discount rate from the interest rate we turn this formula around to get:

$$\text{Discount rate} = \frac{360 \times \dfrac{\text{Interest rate}}{100}}{360 + \dfrac{\text{Discount rate}}{100} \times \text{Discount period}}$$

Sometimes we need the holding period yield on a bill: the return earned by buying a bill and later selling it. The profit on the deal is sale price – purchase price, and in percentage terms is:

$$\frac{\text{Sale price} - \text{Purchase price}}{\text{Purchase price}} = \left[\frac{\text{Sale price}}{\text{Purchase price}} - 1 \right]$$

To gross this percentage up to a 365-day interest rate, we multiply by 365 divided by the holding period, so our final formula is:

$$\text{Holding period yield} = \left[\frac{\text{Sale price}}{\text{Purchase price}} - 1 \right] \times \frac{365}{\text{Holding period}}$$

To put this formula in terms of the yield at the time of sale and the yield at the time of purchase, we would work out the sale price and purchase price in terms of yield by using the formula for price. To put the holding period yield on a 360-day basis, we would "gross up" by 360 rather than 365 in the top line.

We sometimes need to decide between buying a long bill and buying a short bill. In these circumstances, we need the forward-forward (bill parity) rate. Say we can buy a 6-month bill or two 3-month ones. Given the rate on the 6-month bill and on the first 3-month bill, what must we earn on the second 3-month bill to make to two deals equal? We start by assuming that the same principal amount, $1 million, is invested in the 6-month bill and the 3-month bill. At the maturity of the longer bill, we will receive a certain amount (in fact, the face value of the long bill). To break even, this must equal the face value of the later, second short bill. That face value must be equal to the proceeds of the investment in the first short bill (the face value of the first short bill) plus the discount earned on the second short bill. Hence:

$$\begin{array}{ccc} \text{Discount on} \\ \text{second short bill} \end{array} = \begin{array}{c} \text{Face value of} \\ \text{long bill} \end{array} - \begin{array}{c} \text{Face value of} \\ \text{first short bill} \end{array}$$

To express this as a discount rate we express it as a percentage of the amount at the far end, that is, the face value of the long bill, and to express it as an annual rate we gross it up by 360 (or 365) divided by the length of the second short bill, over which the discount is earned. So we have:

$$\text{Break-even rate} = \frac{\text{Face value of long bill} - \text{Face value of first short bill}}{\text{Face value of long bill}} \times \frac{360}{\text{Days in second short bill}}$$

This formula can be rewritten in terms of discount rates, but then it becomes a little complicated to lay out in words.

EUROCOMMERCIAL PAPER CALCULATIONS

Eurocommercial paper (ECP) is issued on both a yield-bearing and a discount basis, though the latter is more common. The basis of ECP calculations is simply the standard discounting (or, if the ECP is interest-bearing, yield) calculations applicable to other short-term instruments.

Points to watch include:

1. Settlement basis: US commercial paper is same-day value, ECP can be same day but is more usually spot.
2. Days basis: 360 for US\$, 365 for sterling, and generally in line with Euro conventions for other currencies.

Otherwise the calculations are straightforward applications of the normal formulae. Thus, for interest-bearing paper,

$$\text{Settlement proceeds} = \text{Face amount} \times \left[\frac{1 + \dfrac{C \times D}{360 \times 100}}{1 + \dfrac{Y \times N}{360 \times 100}} \right]$$

where C = coupon, Y = yield, D = original maturity in days, N = days from settlement to maturity.

For discount paper, correspondingly, we have

$$\text{Settlement proceeds} = \left[\frac{\text{Face amount}}{1 + \dfrac{Y \times N}{360 \times 100}} \right]$$

Often the question arises, what is the all-in yield (or cost to the borrower) of ECP issued in one currency and swapped into another? Provided there are no particular value-date complications (that is, ECP settlement is done for spot value) the calculation of the all-in cost/yield is exactly the same as any other swapped borrowing.

For example, suppose we issue US$5 million of 30-day ECP for spot settlement. The paper is discount paper, and the rate is 7.5%. Then the proceeds on spot date are $4,968,944.10. Suppose spot DEM are 1.7150 per dollar, and the 30-day forward DEM premium is 50 basis points. Then the 30-day forward rate is 1.7100. So the DEM proceeds on spot date are DEM 8,521,739.13 and at maturity the DEM equivalent of the face amount is DEM 8,550,000. Then the implied interest rate is found from the following calculation:

$$\frac{8,550,000 - 8,521,739.13}{8,521,739.13} \times \frac{360}{30} \times 100 = \frac{28,260.87 \times 1200}{8,521,739.13} = 3.9796\%$$

$$\text{i.e., } \frac{F - P}{P} \times \frac{360}{D} \times 100$$

where F = face amount in foreign currency, P = proceeds at date of issue in foreign currency, and D = original maturity in days.

The issue becomes more complicated when the commercial paper value date is before the earliest possible foreign currency value date. Consider a German company issuing a banker's acceptance (BA) in New York. Settlement in the New York BA or commercial paper market is done on a same-day value basis. Unless the deal is done very early in the morning in New York, it is impossible to give good value in sterling for that day, because the cutoff for town clearing is 3:00 PM in London. And deutsche marks cannot be done at all, since the Frankfurt cutoff is 8:00 AM. Hence the dollar proceeds have to be invested overnight (and the German company must fund itself in deutsche marks overnight). If the paper is issued on a Friday, the delay is three days rather than overnight. In order to find the total cost, we need to go through the deal step by step.

Suppose on Tuesday the Germany company issues a BA for 30 days for $5 million. The discount rate is 14 1/8%. So the dollar proceeds received today are $4,941,145.83. These are invested overnight on the Fed funds market at 14 3/8%, so that proceeds plus interest the next day amount to $4,943,118.86. Today (Tuesday) we swap these anticipated proceeds into deutsche marks, value tomorrow, with the swap maturing after 29 days from the start (that is, 30 days from today) to coincide with the maturity of the acceptance. Deutsche marks value tomorrow can be bought, say at 2.3535 and the 29-day swap over tomorrow is a dollar discount/deutsche mark premium of 100 points, so the outright cost is 2.3435. So the deutsche mark value tomorrow, of the BA proceeds plus interest from the Fed funds investment, is 4,943,118.86 × 2.3535 = DMK 11,633,630.24. These funds will only be received tomorrow. To fund itself in the domestic market, the German corporation must borrow overnight deutsche marks. It can borrow up to that amount which with the interest cost will equal the sum available tomorrow from the acceptance deal. That is, the amount it can borrow today is equal to the deutsche mark proceeds of the acceptance, discounted back one day at the overnight deutsche mark rate (which is say, 9%). So the amount it borrows is equal to:

$$\frac{11,633,630.24}{1 + \dfrac{(1 \times 9)}{(360 \times 100)}}$$

We wrote $1 \times 9/100 \times 360$ to make it clear that this is an overnight deal. If the paper were issued on a Friday, the factor would be $3 \times 9/100 \times 360$.

This sum is the initial deutsche mark borrowing. The deutsche mark repayment value is the amount of deutsche marks required to repay the acceptance: that is, $5 million covered forward at 2.3435, making DMK 11,717,500. So the all-in deutsche mark borrowing, grossed up on a annual basis:

$$\frac{11,717,500 - 11,630,722.56}{11,630,722.56} \times \frac{360}{30} \times 100 = 8.9533\%$$

which can then be compared with the cost of raising deutsche marks directly.

BOND MARKET CALCULATIONS

The full range of bond market calculations is outside the scope of this book, but because bond markets are becoming increasingly interlinked through the foreign exchange and currency and interest rate swap markets, some knowledge of basic bond calculations is increasingly useful in any trading operation. This section lays out some of the basic calculations. (A full discussion can be had from *Yield Calculations,* by Paul Fage, Credit Suisse, First Boston, October 1986; see also my book on *Global Investing,* Macmillan/St. Martin's Press 1991.)

We start with simple bond calculations. It is a temptation to assume that one can just hit the buttons on the bond calculator but it is important to understand the principles on which they work at least.

The "classical" bond is an instrument bearing a fixed rate of interest, called its *coupon.* Valuing the classical bond is simple. Suppose we have a 10-year bond with a coupon of 5% per annum, which is paid once a year. Suppose it is issued in denominations with a face value of $100. The price at which it is issued is par, that is, a price of $100 per $100 face value. So the cash flows are that we invest $100 today and receive back $100 in 10 years' time, plus $5 per annum in interest in the meantime:

After 1 year	$5
After 2 years	$5
After 3 years	$5
•	
•	
•	
After 10 years	$105

The price of the bond is the value of these cash flows today. To find that present value, we use the NPV technique laid out in Chapter 6. So the price of the bond is the present value of all the cash flows given in our example, that is, we have:

$$P = \frac{5}{(1.05)} + \frac{5}{(1.05)^2} + \cdots \frac{+5}{(1.05)^{10}} + \frac{100}{(1.05)^{10}}$$

If we use the notation we used in Chapter 6, we can see that the present value of the last redemption amount of \$100 can be written $100v^n$. To it we can add the present value of the regular stream of coupon payments to get:

$$\text{Bond price} = P = \frac{c(1-v^n)}{r} + 100v^n$$

Using the formula we can see that our bond's price is:

$$\frac{5(1-.952380^{10})}{.05} + 100(.952380^{10}) = 100(1 - .952380^{10}) + 100(.952380^{10}) = 100$$

This is because we are discounting a 5% income stream at a discount rate of 5%. The coupon on the bond and its *yield to maturity* or *redemption yield* are the same: both 5%.

What do we mean by the yield to maturity? It is that rate of discount which makes the present value of the bond's cash flows equal to its market price. That is, given today's price, it tells us what the bond will yield over its life, allowing both for the income from the coupons and the change in price. If the bond's price in the market were 90, rather than the issue price of 100, there would be a capital gain of 10 points over the 10 years—a bit over 1% per annum—to be added to the coupon and so the yield would be a bit over 6% (actually 6.38%).

So, if the bond's yield to maturity (and hence the discount rate applied to its cash flows) were 7%, then the bond's price would be:

$$P = \frac{5(1-0.934579^{10})}{0.07} + 100(0.934579^{10}) = 85.95$$

The formula for yield to maturity given price cannot be given in the same way as that for price-given-yield since the result must be found by assuming a given yield, finding the implied price, comparing it with the market price, adjusting the yield to a closer estimate, finding the new price, and so on—a process of iteration.

Accrued Interest

The calculation we made above works for bond prices that are worked out for an exact number of periods to maturity. We were looking at a 10-year bond's cash flows, on the date the bond is issued.

What would the bond be worth, say, three months later? There are two parts to the answer. On the one hand, the bond will have a price that represents the future value of the cash-flows at the new market yield to maturity (say 11%). On the other, the seller of the bond has owned it for three months, with no interest being paid: the interest has accrued at a rate of 5% per annum.

To work out the accrued interest, we need to consider the exact number of days from the issue date of the bond to the date it is being sold. Suppose the bond was issued on March 1, 1992 and is being sold for delivery on June 7, 1992. How many days in this interval?

Suppose that the bond traded is a Eurobond and we want to calculate its accrued interest. To work this out, we must use the Eurobond interest calculation convention. This is laid down in the AIBD's rule no. 225 which says:

> With the exception of floating rate notes, accrued interest on a contract shall be calculated on a 360 days per year basis (each calendar month to be considered one-twelfth of 360 days, or 30 days, and each period from a date in one month to the same date in the next month to be considered 30 days) from and including the date of the last paid interest coupon or the date from which the interest is to accrue for a new issue, up to but excluding the value date of the transaction.

In our example the seller of the bond held it for March, April, and May—a total of 90 days. They have also held it for 6 days in June, excluding June 7, which is the value date of the sale. (See the next section for value date rules.) So there are 96 days of accrued interest to consider. Suppose the seller is selling $10 million worth of bonds. Then the accrued interest due is:

$$\frac{5}{100} \times \frac{96}{360} \times 10,000,000 = \$133,000$$

Bond Price Between Coupon Dates

In the previous section we worked out what the proper accrued interest should be on our bond—in this case, $133,000. Now we want to know what price should the bond itself be? The way we worked out its price before was (relatively) simple, because we were working out the price of the bond on the day of issue. There was no accrued interest to consider; and also, our discount factors were being applied to a round number of periods—10, in that case. Now, three months later, we have to consider a nine and three-quarter year bond.

Hence we have to calculate the price differently. The simplest way to proceed is to find what the bond would be worth on the next coupon date, that is, nine months from now, if today's rates were prevailing on that date. Then we discount that figure back to today's present value, using the appropriate discount rate.

Step one, then is to work out what this bond is worth on March 1, 1990 at a yield of 11%. We use our formula again:

$$P = \frac{c(1-v^n)}{r} + 100v^n$$

Here we have $v = 1/1.11 = .9009009$ and so

$$P = \frac{5(1-.9009009^9)}{.11} + 100\,(.9009009^9) = 27.69 + 39.09 = 66.78$$

To this should be added the coupon payable on that date—5—making a total value on that day of 71.78. Our next job is to discount that back to today, June 7, 1989. To do this, we have to use an odd period discount factor, using the procedure laid out in the previous chapter.

Here we have a discount rate of 11% p.a., using the previous chapter's method, this converts to 10.846%. So now we must discount the price of 66.78 that we worked out for value March 1, 1990, back to today, at the discount rate of 10.846%:

$$\frac{71.78}{\left(1 + \frac{.10846 \times 264}{360}\right)} = \frac{71.78}{1.079537333} = 66.49$$

We must bear in mind that this price of 66.49 includes accrued interest, which we have worked out at $133,000 per $10 million, that is, 1.33. So the "clean" price of the bond, excluding accrued interest, is 65.16.

VALUE DATES AND INTEREST BASIS

Value dates in bond markets differ according to local custom. The U.S. bond market, for example, will normally settle in one of three different ways: cash (delivery next day: normal for Treasury bonds); skip-day (delivery the second business day after the trade) or corporate (five business days after the trade—customary for corporate bonds). In the United Kingdom, gilt-edged normally settle cash (next day) and corporate debentures after two days. Eurobonds settle after seven calendar days. Likewise, the different markets have different interest calculation bases.

It is impossible to give all the possible interest calculations so always check with the counterparty regarding the value date if the market is unfamiliar to you. Table 7.1 may be of some general help.

Table 7.1   Common Interest Bases

U.K. money-markets	Annual actual/365
U.S. & Euro-money-markets	Annual actual/360
Treasury bonds (U.S. & U.K.)	Semi-annual, actual/365
Eurobonds (AIBD, Continental bonds)	Annual 30/360
Yankee bonds, federal agencies, U.S. corporate and municipal bonds	Semi-annual 30/360
U.S. commercial paper, bankers' acceptances	Discount basis, actual/360
U.K. bills of exchange, commercial paper	Discount basis, actual/365

Table 7.1 is a crude summary because the "days basis" varies from market to market. There are three main bases:

1. Actual: Take the number of days between the two dates. Used in U.S., U.K. and Japanese government bonds markets, U.K. and Japanese corporate and municipal bond markets (but not the U.S. corporate and municipal markets which use (2) below. Note Japan uses simple interest yields—see below). It is also used in France but, for domestic trades on government bonds, the normal value date is two business days after trade date and the accrued is calculated up to the calendar day after the trade date (that is, normally the day before value date).

2. 30-Day Month: Take the number of days between the two dates assuming 30-day months using the following method. The number of days between the dates D1/M1/Y1 and D2/M2/Y2 is given by:

   If D1 is 31 change to 30

   If D2 is 31 and D1 is 30 or 31 change D2 to 30, otherwise leave at 31.

   Then the number of days between dates is given by:

   $$(Y2 - Y1) \times 360 + (M2 - M1) \times 30 + (D2 - D1)$$

   This method is used in Switzerland and the U.S. federal agency, corporate, and Yankee bond markets.

3. Continental 30-day month: Take the number of days using the same formula but

   If D1 is 31 change to 30

   If D2 is 31 also change to 30

   This method is used in the Eurobond market, and in the domestic Austrian, Belgian, Dutch, German, and Swedish markets.

The next step is to determine the number of days in the year, because this also varies from market to market. Again there are three main methods:

1. Assume a 365 day year: Used in the French, U.K. and Japanese government bond markets as also their corporate and municipal markets.
2. Assume a year has n × days in current coupon period where n = coupon frequency: For example, if coupon is paid semi-annually the number of days in the period will range from 181 to 184 and the year from 362 to 368. Used in U.S. Treasury bond market.
3. Assume a year has 360 days: Used in Austrian, Belgian, Dutch, German, Swedish, Swiss, U.S. corporate and municipal markets and in the Eurobond market.

In general, actual/365 and 30/360 produce the same annual interest total, but if the payment is semi-annual there will be slight differences in the half-year coupon. To see the differences between 30/360 and actual/365, take a year in which the semi-annual coupon periods are divided into 181 and 184 days. Then on a $10 million borrowing priced at 10% semi-annual actual/365, the two coupon payments would be respectively $495,890.41 and $504,109.58, totalling $1 million. On the 30/360 basis, they would be $500,000 each. The annual total is the same, but there is a slight difference in the timing of the flows.

As mentioned, the U.S. Treasury bond market's day-count basis is not exactly actual/actual. Accrued interest on U.S. Treasury bonds follows the formula

$$\frac{N}{D} \times \frac{C}{F} \times FV$$

where N = number of days' accrual, D = number of days in coupon period, C = coupon/100, F = coupon payment frequency (normally 2), and FV = face value.

For example, $1 million of bonds traded for value July 2, 1989, coupon payable June 15 and December 15, coupon rate of 10%:

$$\frac{\frac{17}{183} \times 10}{200 \times 1,000,000} = 4,644.81$$

By comparison, the U.K. gilt accrued formula would be $N/365 \times C \times FV$. The effects of the different bases are summarized in Table 7.2.

Finally, interest calculations in Japan are radically different. Issues in the Japanese government bond market are quoted for dealing on a simple yield basis. Thus the price of a bond is found as follows:

Table 7.2   Interest Payments on Different Bases: Effective Annual Rate

Formula: Effective annual rate = $(1 + i/n)^n$			
Annual actual/365	10	Annual actual/360	10.14
Semi-annual actual/365	10.25	Semi-annual actual/360	10.40
Quarterly actual/365	10.38	Quarterly actual/360	10.53
Monthly actual/365	10.47	Monthly actual/360	10.62

$$P = 100 \times \left[\frac{(C \times Y + 100)}{(S \times Y + 100)} \right]$$

where C = coupon, P = price (excluding accrued), Y = exact number of years to maturity including fractions, and S = simple yield.

For example, government bond No. 89 has a coupon of 5.1% and matures on June 20, 1996. Purchasing on a simple yield of 4.77 for settlement on August 1, 1987 (so that the life is 8 years and 323 days or 8.884 years) would give a price of

$$100 \times \left[\frac{(5.1 \times 8.884) + 100}{(4.77 \times 8.884) + 100} \right] = 102.06$$

The relationship between simple yield and price is therefore:

$$S = 100 \times \frac{C}{P} + \left(\frac{100}{P - 1} \right) \times \frac{100}{Y}$$

and in our example the yield, given a price of 102.06, would be:

$$100 \times \frac{5.1}{102.06} + \left(\frac{100}{102.06 - 1} \right) \times \frac{100}{8.884} = 4.770$$

The total price payable for a purchase is equal to the sum of the price, as calculated above, accrued interest (coupon/100 × actual days in settlement period/365) and transfer tax, where applicable.

DURATION, CONVEXITY, AND REINVESTMENT RISK

We have looked at how to work out a bond's price. We should also think about how risky it is. Setting aside the question of whether the borrower might default, that is, its credit standing, there is the question of market risk: how volatile the bond will prove to be as interest rates vary. This depends on several factors: the coupon on the bond, its current yield in the market place, and the time to maturity: how "long" the bond is.

The traditional measure of "length" is the time to maturity, or if part of the principal is repaid before maturity, the weighted average life. But these measures are concerned only with principal: they ignore the fact that a coupon-bearing bond will also have interest payments before maturity. Duration is a measure of the bond's "length," and hence its riskiness, which takes the interim interest payments into account. Duration is the weighted average number of periods until cash flows occur, where the weights are the present value of the cash flow, expressed as a percentage of the price of the bond.

It may help to understand duration if we start with the simple case of a U.S. Treasury zero-coupon bond. This is a bond which pays no annual interest: the investor's return comes from buying the bond at a discount to its face value. Let's take a four-year zero-coupon bond that has a yield of 10%. What is its duration? In this case there is only cash flow, which occurs in time period 4, and only one weight, which on this occasion must be 1. So the duration of the zero-coupon bond is 4 years, and is equal to its maturity.

The next step is to look at a coupon-bearing bond. Let's start with a $100 bond that pays an annual coupon of 10% and has a two-year maturity. One way of looking at this bond is to argue that in fact it is a portfolio of two bonds. One, which matures in a year's time, is a zero-coupon bond worth $10. The second, which matures in two years' time, is a zero-coupon bond worth $110. Following the logic we just used on our four-year zero, the duration of the first bond is 1 and of the second is 2.

The combined duration of the "portfolio" is obtained by adding these together. But we need to allow for the fact that one "bond" is much smaller than the other. The way to do this is to weight them by their present values in cash terms. If we use a discount rate of 10% for the present value sums, then we see that the present value of $10 due in one year is $9.0909; the present value of $110 due in two years is $90.90909. Thus the present value (price) of the coupon bond is the total of the present value of its cash flows, $99.999999, say $100, and our weights are 0.0909 and 0.9090 respectively. Hence the duration is $1 \times 0.0909 + 2 \times 0.9090$ which comes to 1.9089, or 1.91 years.

Notice that the coupon bond's duration is shorter than its maturity. Duration is only equal to maturity for zero-coupon bonds. For all coupon-bearing bonds, duration will be less than the maturity. One other point to note is that, unlike the bond's maturity, its duration varies with the level of interest rates because of the changes in present value arising from a change in the discount rate. If we had used 11% as the discount factor in the present value calculation we just did, the duration would have come out to be about 1.88.

The full formula for duration is:

$$D = \frac{\sum\limits_{t=1}^{n} \dfrac{t.C_t}{(1+r)^t}}{\sum\limits_{t=1}^{n} \dfrac{C_t}{(1+r)^t}}$$

where t = period number, C_t = cash flow at time t, r = market yield on the bond.

We can rewrite this more simply: the bottom line is the price that we would pay for the bond today, call it P. We can define the individual weights on the top line as

$$W_t = \frac{\frac{C_t}{(1+r)^t}}{P}$$

Then we can write:

$$D = \sum_{t=1}^{n} t w_t$$

It can be shown (see Patrick Phillips, *Inside the New Gilt-edged Market,* Woodhead-Faulkner 1987) that we can rewrite this into a simple formula, suitable for a single cell of a spreadsheet:

$$D = \left(\frac{c}{2}\left[\frac{1-v^n}{(1-v)^2} - \frac{nv^n}{1-v}\right] + 100nv^{n-1}\right)\frac{v}{2P}$$

where c = coupon, $v = 1/(1+i)$, $i = y/200$, y = yield on the bond, and n = number of periods to maturity.

Some people may find it helpful to think about duration in more visual terms. A helpful way of looking at duration was given by R. W. Kopprasch in "Understanding Duration and Volatility" (Salomon Brothers, September 1985). Figure 7.1 shows the cash flows and present values of a 7-year 12% bond. The shaded area of each cash flow represents the present value of that cash flow. We can imagine that Figure 7.2 is a series of tins resting on a seesaw. The size of each tin is the cash flow due; the water in the tin is the present value of the cash flow. The distance between the centers of each cash flow container represents the amount of time between the cash flows. That is, each tin is one period apart.

If an investor were looking at this 7-year bond on a coupon date, the first tin would be one period away from the start. The second would be two periods away, and so on. The duration would be the distance from the investor to where we could put a fulcrum and balance the whole system (see Figure 7.2). It is the bond's "center of gravity."

Looking at duration in this way makes it clear that the duration of a zero-coupon bond equals its maturity. Because there is only one cash flow, the fulcrum must lie at that cash flow. For all other bonds, the duration is less than the maturity. For if there are intervening cash flows, the fulcrum cannot be at the end of the see-saw and still balance it.

The definition of duration that we have been using is sometimes called *Macaulay duration,* after the man who invented it. There is a related concept called *modified duration,* which is the Macaulay duration divided by $(1+r)$. (We need to be sure that r is correctly defined as the periodic yield. If r is 10% per annum we would write 1.10; if it were a semi-annual yield we

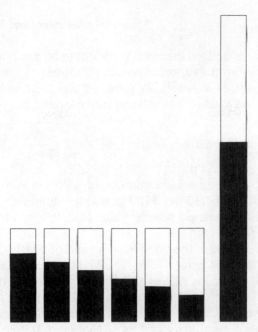

Figure 7.1 Cash flows and present values of 7-year 12% bond (Adapted from R.W. Kopprasch, *Understanding Duration and Volatility,* Salomon Brothers, New York, 1985).

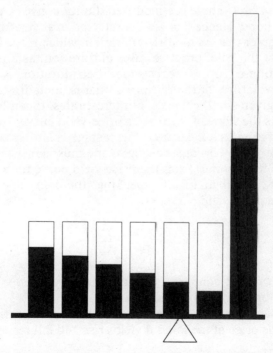

Figure 7.2 Cash flows and the duration fulcrum (Adapted from R.W. Kopprasch, *Understanding Duration and Volatility,* Salomon Brothers, New York, 1985).

would write 1.05.) Modified duration turns out to be a very good measure of the riskiness of the bond. It approximates very closely the percentage change in price as a result of a one basis point in yield. That is, it shows how vulnerable the bond's value is to interest rate movements.

$$\text{Modified duration, MD} = \sum_{t=1}^{n} \frac{tw_t}{(1+r)}$$

Let's go back to our 4-year zero coupon bond, yielding 10%. In that case, its current price will be $68.30 per $100 face value due in 4 years' time. That price is found by the standard present value calculation, which here is fairly simple: $PV = \$100/(1+r)^4$.

What would the price of the bond be at a yield of 10.01%? From the same formula we can find the price as $68.28. What is the percentage change in price for a one basis-point rise in yield? If we work out the prices of the bonds very precisely we will find that at 10% the price is $68.30135; at 10.01% the price is $68.27651 and the percentage difference, expressed as a percentage of the original price of $68.30135, is −0.036%. The percentage change in price is 3.6 times as large as the change in yield. The modified duration of this bond is $4/1.10 = 3.64$ years. In other words, *for a change in yield of 0.01%, the value of the bond changes by 0.01% × MD where MD is the modified duration.* Therefore modified duration gives a measure of the volatility of the bond. Hence it is usually referred to as volatility in the U.K. bond market, rather than as modified duration, which is the U.S. term.

This is one of the chief practical uses of duration: as a measure of the volatility of a bond. To be precise, modified duration is a measure of the percentage volatility of the full price (that is, including accrued interest) of a bond, given small changes in interest rates. It can be looked at in graphic terms as the slope of the bond's price-yield curve (Figure 7.3).

Modified duration as a measure of percentage volatility is only valid for small changes in yield. For larger changes, one must consider the security's convexity. (The term comes from the price-yield curve for a normal bond, which is convex.) Mathematically speaking, the convexity is the second derivative of the price-yield curve:

$$C = \frac{10000}{P} \times \frac{\delta^2 P}{\delta Y^2}$$

where P = dirty price of bond (i.e., including accrued interest), Y = periodic yield (e.g., semi-annual), and C = convexity.

A less formidable formula which is a practical approximation is to define Pp and Pm as the price of the bond if yields rise and fall respectively by one basis point. Then

$$C = \frac{10^3 \times (Pp + Pm - 2P)}{P}$$

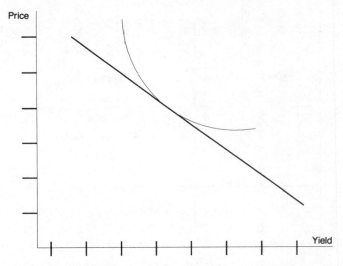

Figure 7.3 Duration and the slope of the price-yield curve.

DURATION AND IMMUNIZATION OF INTEREST RATE RISK

Suppose we have issued a fixed-rate zero-coupon bond due in January 1998. Suppose today is March 31, 1991. We want to be sure we have enough funds on hand to repay it. One way to do this would be to buy a zero-coupon bond of exactly the right amount maturing on exactly the right date. But suppose none is available. We can hedge this risk in another way, by seeking a coupon-bearing bond of the right duration. Suppose we can buy a 9% bond maturing in 10 years' time. Its duration is 6.79 years, near enough for our purposes.

Table 7.3 shows that by holding the bond to our time horizon we will lock in a return of 9%, no matter what happens to interest rates once we buy the bond. If rates rise, there will be a capital loss on the bond; but it will be offset by higher reinvestment income. The two offsetting forces of capital value and reinvestment earnings offset each other equally if the bond is held for the period of its duration. For example, if when we buy the bond interest rates rise to 11%, we show a capital loss of $112; if rates are at 11% when we come to sell it after 6.79 years, the capital loss will be $56, but it will be offset by $261 of accumulated interest on interest.

In other words, we can hedge a zero-coupon liability with a coupon-bearing bond, as long as we match the durations. Hence the importance of duration in interest risk hedging. As long as you can match the duration of your liabilities with the duration of your assets, you are relatively immune from interest rate risk. (I said relatively because the duration of a coupon-bearing bond drifts away from the duration of a zero-coupon bond as time passes and coupons are paid. Suppose I hedge a 3.5 year zero-coupon liability with a 4-year coupon bond which has a duration of 3.5. After 3.5 years, the zero-coupon will mature, but the other bond will now have a duration of about 0.5 years).

Table 7.3   Total Return on a 9 Percent Bond Due in 10 Years and Held through Various Holding Periods

Income Source	Interest Rate at Time of Reinvestment	Holding Period in Years					
		1	3	5	6.79*	9	10
Coupon income	5%	$ 90	$270	$450	$611	$ 810	$ 900
Capital gain or loss		287	234	175	100	39	-0-
Interest on interest		1	17	54	105	191	241
Total return and yield		$378 (37.0%)	$521 (15.0%)	$679 (11.0%)	$816 (9.0%)	$1,040 (8.5%)	$1,141 (8.2%)
Coupon income	7%	$ 90	$270	$450	$611	$ 810	$ 900
Capital gain or loss		132	109	83	56	19	-0-
Interest on interest		2	25	78	149	279	355
Total return (and yield)		$224 (22.0%)	$404 (12.0%)	$611 (10.0%)	$816 (9.0%)	$1,108 (8.6%)	$1,255 (8.5%)
Coupon income	9%	$ 90	$270	$450	$611	$ 810	$ 900
Capital gain or loss		0	0	0	0	0	0
Interest on interest		2	32	103	205	387	495
Total return (and yield)		$ 92 (9.0%)	$302 (9.0%)	$553 (9.0%)	$816 (9.0%)	$1,197 (9.0%)	$1,395 (9.0%)
Coupon income	11%	$ 90	$270	$450	$611	$ 810	$ 900
Capital gain or loss		-112	-95	-75	-56	-18	-0-
Interest on interest		2	40	129	261	502	647
Total return (and yield)		$ 20 (2.0%)	$215 (6.7%)	$504 (8.5%)	$816 (9.0%)	$1,294 (9.7%)	$1,547 (9.8%)

*Duration of a 9 percent bond bought at par and due in 10 years.

Source: P. E. Christensen et al., *Bond Portfolio Immunization in Securities,* Homewood, IL: Dow Jones Irwin, 1983.

PART 3 Foreign Exchange Calculations

8 Spot Deals

This chapter sets out the basics of a spot deal: where the settlement is made, when it is made, what the quotations mean, and how cross spot rates are worked out.

SETTLEMENT COUNTRY

A foreign exchange trade is an exchange of two currencies. When the deal has been agreed upon, the parties to the deal arrange settlement. This takes place in the two countries whose currencies are being used. For example, a deal exchanging U.S. dollars for deutsche marks is settled by a payment of U.S. dollars in the United States against a payment of deutsche marks in West Germany. In this book, the term *settlement country* will refer to the country where the actual transfer of funds is made.

Where the deal is made—the dealing center—need not be in one of the settlement countries. For example, it is possible to trade French francs against deutsche marks in New York. A company making a FFR/DEM deal with a bank in New York may think that its francs and deutsche marks are being transferred in New York. This will seem especially plausible if the bank is running accounts for the company in New York denominated in the two currencies. But the bank's own currency holdings which correspond to these accounts actually will be held in the settlement countries. Therefore, the

181

rules applying to such transactions—for instance, with respect to settlement dates—will be the same as for deals conducted in the normal way.

SPOT SETTLEMENT

A spot foreign exchange deal is one made for settlement in two working days' time. Thus under normal circumstances a spot deal done Monday is settled on Wednesday. A working day is defined as one in which both banks are open for business in both settlement countries; except that if the deal is done against the U.S. dollar, if the first of the two days is a holiday in the United States but not in the other settlement country, that day is also counted as a working day.

In the case of a US$/DEM deal, done on Monday, we would normally have settlement Wednesday. This would not be affected by a U.S. holiday on the Tuesday. But it would be affected by a German holiday on the Tuesday. In the latter case, the spot date would be postponed until Thursday, provided that both centers were open Thursday. If Tuesday were a normal day, but Wednesday were a holiday in either the United States or Germany, then the spot day would be Thursday (if both centers were open that day).

In the case of a US$/DEM deal done, say, in London, the occurrence of U.K. bank holidays during the spot period is entirely irrelevant since all bank account transfers are made in the settlement country rather that the dealing center. However, on the deposit market it would not be customary to deal for a date that was a holiday in the dealing center. In certain countries, such as the United States or Germany, bank holidays may affect only part of the country (depending on whether it is a local state holiday, or, if religious, whether the area is mainly Catholic or Protestant, etc.). In this case, the date for settlement could vary according to the regional location of the bank accounts involved. Except for this mention, this complication will be ignored in this book.

Settlement of both sides of a foreign exchange deal should be made on the same working day. Because of time zone differences, settlement on any given working day will take place earlier in the Far East, later in Europe, and later still in the United States.

This implies a risk. To continue the US$/DEM example, a bank selling deutsche marks may deliver them in Frankfurt before receiving the dollars in New York. If the recipient in Germany goes bankrupt before delivering the dollars (as happened in the case of Herstatt Bank), losses may arise. The principle that the two sides of the deal should be completed on the same day is referred to as the principle of *valeur compensee* or compensated value.

The only exception to the principle of compensated value arises for deals in Middle Eastern currencies for settlement on Friday. This is a holiday in most Middle Eastern countries. When this happens, the person buying the Middle Eastern currency (say Saudi riyals) makes payment (say in U.S.

dollars) on Friday. Delivery of the riyals takes place on Saturday, which is a normal business day in the relevant countries (see Appendix C).

QUOTED AND BASE CURRENCIES: DIRECT AND INDIRECT QUOTATION

The term *quoted currency* means the currency that is variable in an exchange rate quotation; the term *base currency* means the currency that is fixed. Thus if £1 = US$2.2550, sterling is the base currency and the U.S. dollar the quoted currency. For convenience, I shall write exchange rates as base/quoted (in this case £/US$).

Direct quotation takes the form of variable amounts of domestic currency against a fixed amount of foreign currency. The foreign currency is the base currency. A Swiss bank quoting 85.5 Swiss francs per 100 deutsche marks would be quoting direct; a variable amount of Swiss francs against a fixed deutsche mark amount. Many people say "normal" for direct currencies.

Indirect quotation, conversely, takes the form of fixed amounts of domestic currency against varying amounts of foreign currency. A British bank quoting £1 = DEM 4.1325 is quoting *indirect*. Many people in the market say "reciprocal" for indirect quotations.

In the United States, both types of quotations are used: for domestic business, U.S. terms are often used, that is, normal direct quotation (DEM1 = US$0.5525). For international business and increasingly for domestic business also, U.S. banks use European terms or reciprocal indirect quotation (US$1 = DEM1.81). The reason for this is the international market's habit of dealing against the U.S. dollar, using direct terms. U.S. banks have fallen into line with international market practice.

SELLING AND BUYING RATES

Where the currency's exchange control regulations permit, a bank will normally quote a "two way price" in the currency. So a bank might quote the exchange rate as US$1 = DEM2.2550/60. This conventional way of writing the rate shows that the bank will sell DEM2.2550 in exchange for US$1; it will buy deutsche marks at 2.2560. The lower rate is the selling rate for deutsche marks; the maxim is "sell low, buy high."

The reason for this apparent perversity is that the bank's "income" from a sale is fixed at $1; it tries to sell as few deutsche marks as possible in exchange for the $1. To test the maxim, suppose the bank sells DEM2.2550 million, receiving US$1 million. It then uses the US$1 million to buy DEM2.2560 million, netting a final profit of DEM1000. The narrower the spread between the selling and buying rates, the less the bank's profit.

The conventional quotation needs explaining when the "big figure" (of 2.23 in our example) is being straddled. Say we have a selling rate of 2.2495 and the buying rate is 2.2505. Normal market convention is to write this as 2.2495/05. The "big figure" on the left is 2.24; on the right side it is understood as being the next "big figure" up, 2.25.

CROSS-RATES

A cross-rate may be defined as an exchange rate that is calculated from two other rates. For example, the DEM/CHF rate can be derived as a cross-rate from the US$/CHF rate.

The practice in the world foreign exchange market at present is that currencies are mainly dealt against the U.S. dollar. If bank A asks bank B for its deutsche mark rate, that rate will be quoted against the U.S. dollar unless otherwise specified. Since the bulk of dealings are done against the U.S. dollar, it follows that the "market rate" for a currency at any moment is most accurately reflected in its exchange rate against the U.S. dollar. Thus a bank asked to quote £/DEM would normally calculate this rate from the £/US$ and US$/DEM rates, if an exact market rate is required. Increasingly, though, particularly within the European Monetary System, active markets also exist in trading these cross-rates directly (see below).

I will use the rule that an exchange rate between two currencies, neither of which is the U.S. dollar, will be referred to as a cross-rate. The term *exchange rate* will normally refer to the rate for a currency against the U.S. dollar, unless otherwise specified.

CALCULATION OF CROSS-RATE

There are three cases to consider; both exchange rates quoted direct or normal, both indirect or reciprocal, and the case where one is direct and the other indirect. Let's look first at the case where both are normal. For example, US$1 = DEM1.8110/20 and US$1 = CHF1.6230/40. The U.S. dollar is the base currency in both cases. We want to find the selling and buying rates for Swiss francs in terns of deutsche mark (the deutsche mark will be our base currency).

If we are selling Swiss francs, we must be buying deutsche marks. So we take the US$/CHF selling rate, 1.6230, and divide it by the buying rate for deutsche marks, 1.8120. (We divide by the currency that is to be the base, in this case the deutsche mark.) The selling cross-rate therefore is 89.56 CHF per 100 DEM after rounding in the bank's favor. Similarly, the buying rate is found by taking the CHF buying rate, 1.6240, and the DEM selling rate, 1.8110, to give 89.68. Again we round in favor of the bank—this time upwards.

A parallel procedure is followed when both currencies are reciprocal: the U.S. dollar is the quoted currency in both cases. For example, we have £1 = US$2.2530/40 and CAD 1 = US$0.8950/53. We want the cross-rates,

	Both Normal	Both Reciprocal	One Normal, One Reciprocal
Currency we want to show in the cross-rate as Quoted	US$ 1 = SFR 1.6230/40	CAN$ 1 = US$ 0.8950/53	£STG 1 = US$ 2.2530/40
	divide by	divide into	multiply by
Base	US$ 1 = DMK 1.8110/20	£STG 1 = US$ 2.2530/40	US$ 1 = DMK 1.8110/20

Figure 8.1 Calculating cross rates.

185

using sterling as the case currency. The rate at which we sell U.S. dollars against sterling (we buy sterling) is 2.2530. We buy US$ against CAD (we sell Canadian dollars) at 0.8953. Because we are dealing indirect currencies, we divide by the quoted currency. So we sell Canadian dollars against sterling at 2.5164.

When one rate is normal and the other reciprocal, the procedure is the same but we multiply (alternatively we may convert the reciprocal currency to normal by taking reciprocals and then dividing by the base currency). Suppose we have £1 = US$2.2530/40 and US$ = DEM1.8110/20. The rate at which we sell DEM against US$ is 1.8110; the rate at which we buy sterling against U.S. dollars (sell US$ against £STG) is 2.2530. Multiplying these gives a selling rate for DEM against £STG of 4.0801, and a buying rate of 4.0843. The calculations are summarized in Figure 8.1.

TRADING THE CROSSES

During the late 1970s and early 1980s, a very high proportion of interbank trading was done against the U.S. dollar. A few banks had someone who sometimes dealt sterling/mark direct occasionally, but cross trading was generally neglected. But the arrival of the European Monetary System (see Chapter 13) and the growth in importance of the JPY/DEM relationship has meant that more and more banks have begun trading the crosses in their own right.

The trader who is dealing the crosses has a harder job, because he or she has to watch three rates: the two rates against the US$, and the cross. Let's take an example. Today we have DEM1.8610/20 and JPY145.10/20 against the dollar. That implies a cross-rate of 77.92/03. The market sells JPY and buys DEM at 77.92 (145.10/1.8620); they buy JPY and sell DEM at 78.03 (145.20/1.8610). I shall refer to this as the implied cross rate.

Let's start with $10,000,000 and do the round trip. We buy JPY 1,451,000,000. Now we sell them for DEM at 78.03, producing DEM 18,595,412.02. We take these DEM and sell them for US$ at 1.8620, producing US$ 9,986,794.86. We have lost $13,000 and the reason is obvious: all the rates are in line, and we have paid three lots of bid/offer spread.

Now suppose that the cross-rate moves out of line. The implied cross is the same, but Heavy Hitter Bank has decided it wants to move the cross to 76.91/77.02. The cross trader can now buy JPY 1,451,000,000 as before. This time he buys the DEM cheaper, at 77.02, and so gets DEM 18,839,262.53 which can be sold at 1.8620 for $10,117,756.46. There is now a $117,000 profit because the actual cross was below the implied cross. DEM could be bought cheaply on the cross. So if the actual cross is below the implied, the DEM is cheap on the cross and the JPY is dear: buy JPY direct, sell them for DEM on the cross, and buy back US$ with DEM. Conversely, if the actual cross is above the implied, the DEM is dear on the cross: buy DEM direct, sell them for JPY on the cross, and buy back US$ with JPY.

9 Forward Contracts: Outrights

This chapter explains what a forward contract is, what premium and discount mean, and how to work out the cost of hedging, option forwards, cross and reciprocal forwards, and the value date for a forward contract.

WHAT IS A FORWARD?

A forward exchange contract is an agreement between a bank and another party to exchange one currency for another at some future date. The rate at which the exchange is to be made, the delivery date, and the amounts involved are fixed at the time of agreement.

Such a contract is to be distinguished from a foreign exchange futures contract. These are discussed in more detail in Chapter 14. However, for comparison, a futures foreign exchange contract is a contract between to parties for the exchange of a certain amount of foreign currency at a future date. The amount and the date are normally standard. For instance, in the case of the International Monetary Market of Chicago's sterling contract, the contract is for £62,500. Delivery is normally the third Wednesday of the contract month (March, June, September, or December). A futures contract need not involve a bank as counterparty. A forward contract is normally completed by delivery of all or part of the sum involved. This is unusual in the case of a futures contract which is usually closed by trading in the reverse direction before the maturity of the original futures contract.

PREMIUM AND DISCOUNT

Suppose a quoted currency is more expensive in the future than it is now in terms of the base currency. Then the quoted currency is said to stand at a premium in the forward market, relative to the base currency. Conversely, the base currency may be said to stand at a discount relative to the quoted currency.

Take the U.S. dollar as the base currency and the deutsche mark as the quoted currency. We may have a spot rate of US\$1 = DEM2.2500. The rate quoted by a bank today for delivery in 1 year's time (today's 1 year forward rate) may be US\$1 = DEM2.2150. In this example, the dollar buys fewer deutsche marks in a year's time than it does today. The dollar stands at a discount relative to the deutsche mark. Putting it in converse terms, the deutsche mark stands at a premium relative to the dollar.

The size of the dollar discount or deutsche mark premium is the difference between 2.2500 and 2.2150, that is, $3^{1}/_{2}$ pfennings. It would normally be quoted as 350 points. To arrive at the forward price, the deutsche mark premium or dollar discount must be *subtracted* from the spot. Conversely, a deutsche mark discount or dollar premium is added.

As in the spot market, banks in the forward market will normally quote a selling and a buying rate. The convention is that the selling rate for the quoted currency (the buying rate for the base currency) is quoted first. In our example, the spot rate might be quoted at 2.2500/10 and the one year forward discount for US\$ (or DEM premium) at 350/340. In other words, if the dealer is buying U.S. dollars forward he will charge a discount of 350 points, but if he is selling, he will give away only 340 points discount. In European terms, he will sell deutsche marks at a premium of 350, but only buy at a premium of 340.

There is an apparent inconsistency in the quotation. The spot is quoted at 2.2500/10, that is, low/high, and the deutsche mark premium/dollar discount at 350/340, that is, high/low. In both cases, the same convention is followed; that is, the selling rate for the quoted currency is given first. The apparent inconsistency flows simply from the fact that the deutsche mark premium/ dollar discount is to be *subtracted* from the spot rate. So the selling price for delivery in three months' time (often referred to as the outright three month price) is 2.2500 less 350 points, that is, 2.2150. Now the buying price is 2.2510 less 340 points, that is, 2.2170. So we can quote the 3-month outright as 2.2150/70 which matches the way in which the spot is quoted.

A price of 350/340 indicates a premium for the quoted currency in the forward market and a discount for the base currency; conversely, a price of 340/350 would indicate a discount for the quoted and a premium for the base.

This can be summed up (see Figure 9.1) as:

High/Low = Subtract

Low/High = Add

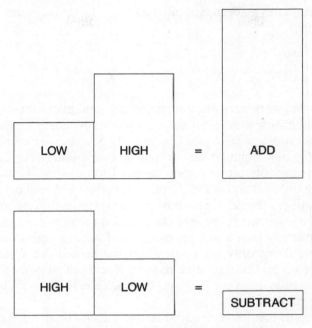

Figure 9.1   Treatment of forward margin.

In premium/discount terms in the United States:

High/Low = Discount for the dollar
Low/High = Premium for the dollar

Elsewhere the tag is reversed as the market there looks at rates in currency terms:

High/Low: Premium
Low/High: Discount

Occasionally on a Reuters Monitor or a table of rates the forward price may be quoted as "−5/+5" or "5P5." This indicates that the forward is "round par." This term means that the middle rate for a currency in the spot market is identical to the middle price available in the forward market; the forward price is at par with the spot. Thus the dealer will buy dollars against the currency at a discount and sell at a premium; in European terms he will charge a premium to sell the currency, and will only buy at a discount. It follows that a quotation of "−5/+5" or "5P5" applied to our spot rate example of 2.2500/10 would produce a forward price of 2.2495 selling rate and 2.2515 buying rate.

A quote of 20/00 (or 20/P) indicates a forward dollar discount or currency selling premium of 20, but that the bank only buy at par. A quote of 00/15 (or

P/15) indicates sales made at par, purchases at a dollar premium or currency discount of 15.

HEDGING COSTS

We often need to work out a percentage cost per annum of a forward contract. This varies according to whether our calculations are based on the spot price or the outright forward price (see Chapter 10). Views differ on this; my own view is that the choice should vary according to the underlying deal. If one is hedging a forward commitment, then the outright rate should be used. Thus a firm needing to buy forward DEM1 million against U.S. dollars for the purchase of machinery should use the outright rate. This is the important rate for its business; it determines the amount of dollars required. In other cases it may be more appropriate to use the spot rate. If we are considering an investment, we would probably want to express the hedging cost or profit as a percentage of our original investment, so we would probably use the spot rate. It is like the money market difference between a discount rate and an ordinary interest rate.

Suppose again that we have a spot rate of 2.2500/10 and a 3-months' forward rate of 350/340. Then, working on middle rates of 2.2505 and 345, we can calculate that the approximate hedging cost for 3 months is 0.0345 divided by 2.2505 or 0.0153. (We might prefer to use the market's selling rates of 2.2500 and 350) Multiplying by 100 to express this in percentage terms, we find this 1.53% for 3 months. We multiply this by four to gross it up to annual terms of 6.13%. (This is slightly inaccurate. If we really needed to be exact to six places of decimals or so, we would gross it up by compounding.)

The formula, therefore, is:

$$\text{Hedging cost} = \frac{\text{Forward premium}}{\text{Outright or spot}} \times \frac{12}{n} = \frac{F}{O} \times \frac{12}{n} \text{ or } \frac{S}{O} \times \frac{12}{n}$$

where n = number of months in forward contract.

OPTION FORWARDS

Under the normal forward contract discussed earlier, the exchange rate, the amount of currency involved, and the delivery date are all agreed upon when the deal is made. But the bank's customer may be uncertain exactly when he can deliver his funds. He may not know when his imports will arrive. In this case, he may take out an option forward.

An option forward contract is defined as a forward contract where the delivery date is at the customer's option. It is not like a currency option, where the customer is paying for the option to deal at a certain price. In a foreign exchange option forward contract, the deal is done, and the rate is fixed. The option applies only to the delivery date. Currency options are discussed in Chapters 15 and 16. Option forwards are a traditional instrument but are now less important.

As in a normal forward contract, the parties to an option contract agree at the time of the deal on the amount of currency and the exchange rate involved. The delivery date is fixed as being between two dates. So a contract may be "option from spot until December 6" or "option between 9 and 10 months."

In fixing the rate at which a deal is made, the bank will bear in mind the possibility that the customer may deliver at the worst possible time, and the rate will have to be quoted accordingly.

Suppose we have US$/DEM rates as follows:

Spot: 1.8100/10
3-Months: 300/290
6-Months: 590/580

The bank's customer wants to buy deutsche marks, option from spot until the 6-month date. Suppose the bank sells them at the spot price, and the customer does not take up delivery for 5 months. Then the customer has effectively avoided being charged the discount on his dollars, or paying the premium on deutsche marks, for a 6-month-forward purchase. So the bank assumes the worst, and charges the full 6 months' dollar discount/deutsche mark premium, making the outright 1.7510.

But suppose the bank were buying the deutsche marks from the customer, option from spot until the 6-months date. What if the bank gave the customer the full six months' dollar discount/deutsche mark premium, and the customer delivered on the spot date? Then the bank would find it had made an expensive purchase. It could buy deutsche marks for spot date value in the market at a better price. Accordingly, it takes the worst view and pays the customer only the spot price. In this case it would benefit the customer to try to narrow the option period say to "option between 3 and 6 months." Then the bank would give the customer 3-months' dollar discount/deutsche mark premium.

The general rule is that the bank gives the customer the worst rate ruling during the option period. So we have:

1. Dollar discount/currency premium
   (a) Bank sells currency, buys dollars; discount on dollar/currency premium is charged to the last date.
   (b) Bank buys currency, sells dollars; option from spot—no dollar discount/currency premium given. Option between two dates—dollar discount/currency premium given to first date.

2. Dollar premium/currency discount
   (a) Bank sells currency, buys dollars; option from spot—no dollar premium/currency discount given. Option between two dates—dollar premium/currency discount given to first date.
   (b) Bank buys currency, sells dollars; dollar premium/currency discount charged to the last date.
3. Currencies which move from premium to discount or vice versa
   (a) Banks sells currency, buys dollars: the highest dollar discount/currency premium during the period is charged.
   (b) Bank buys currency, sells dollars; the largest dollar premium/currency discount during the period is taken.

Here are some examples using the following rates:

	US$/DEM	US$/ITL	US$/DKK
Spot	1.8100/10	831.00/50	5.1920/30
3-Months	300/290	200/300	100/200
6-Months	590/580	400/600	150/50

The banks sells DEM option from spot to 3 months at $1.8100-0.03 = 1.7800$: buys DEM option from spot to 3 months at 1.8110; buys DEM option between 3 and 6 months at 1.7820; sells DEM option between 3 and 6 months at 1.7510. The bank sells ITL option from spot to 3 months at 831.00; buys ITL option from spot to 3 months at 834.50; sells ITL option between 3 and 6 months at 833.00. For DKK, where the 3 months is in currency discount/dollar premium, and the 6 months is in currency premium/dollar discount, the bank will sell DKK option spot to three months at 5.1920; buy DKK option from spot to 3 months at 5.2130; sell DKK option between 3 and 6 months at 5.1770, and buy DKK option between 3 and 6 months at 5.2130.

CROSS AND RECIPROCAL FORWARDS

A typical cross forward calculation arises when a customer needs a sterling/deutsche mark forward. For this to be exact, it should be worked out from the professional interbank prices, which are against the U.S. dollar. We have £STG/US$ spot 2.2500/10 and US$/DEM spot 1.8100/10. The 3-month £STG/US$ price is 350/340, while the 3-month US$/DEM price is 300/290.

We first find the outright 3-month £/US$ price, 2.2150/70, and the outright 3-month US$/DEM price, 1.7800/20. We then find the cross spot and 3-month outright prices along the lines of Chapter 8 (i.e., multiplying in this case). This gives us a 3-month outright price of 3.9427/3.9507 and a spot of 4.0725/4.0766.

The forward premium for deutsche marks against sterling is then found by subtracting the 3-month outright from the spot, giving us a premium of 1298/1259.

Let's take an example with a currency where the dollar is at a premium (the currency is at a discount). Suppose the French franc spot against the dollar is 4.2500/20 and the 3-month is 100/200, that is, dollar premium, franc discount. Then against sterling, using the same £/US$ rates we get a spot of 9.5625/9.5713, and a forward margin of 1266/1002; that is, the franc is at a premium against sterling although at a discount against the U.S. dollar (because sterling is at an even greater discount against the U.S. dollar).

Reciprocal forwards are sometimes needed when a currency is quoted both direct and indirect. An example is the Canadian dollar against the U.S. dollar, which can be quoted as either 91.22/25 or 1.0958/63; a forward quote may need to be turned around also. A similar case arises with the Irish pound, which is quoted in the market indirectly against sterling, for instance, IEP1 = £STG0.9625/35. If we want to turn around a forward quote for the Irish pound, for example, we go about it like this. Suppose we have a spot and three-month price using the Irish currency as the base and sterling as the quoted currency. Suppose the spot is IEP1 = £STG0.9410/20 and the 3-month margin is 150/120. We want to quote with sterling as the base.

First we find the three-month outright, with the Irish pound as base, that is, 0.9260/0.9300. Then we work out the reciprocals, obtaining 1.0615/1.0627 for the spot and 1.0752/1.0800 for the forward. (Note that the lower or selling price in Irish terms of 0.9410 produces the higher, or buying price in sterling terms of 1.0627.) The last step is to find the forward margins by subtracting the spot price from the three-month outright, yielding 137/173. Thus in Irish terms we have a spot of IEP1 = £0.9410/20 and sterling at a 3-month premium of 150/120; in sterling terms, a spot of £1 = IEP1.0615/27 and the Irish pound at a discount of 137/173.

Forwards Expressed as Outrights

The use of margins in forward quotations is convenient because the margins tend to move much less quickly than the spots, and because it is the margins that are relevant in the swap market. But certain currencies, such as the Venezuelan bolivar, have limited or nonexistent swap markets, so that the banks will often quote the forwards in outright form. Certain banks will often quote the forwards in outright form. Certain banks also quote other currencies, such as the South African rand or the Spanish peseta, in this form.

CALCULATION OF FORWARD VALUE DATES

The first step in finding the standard forward value dates for periods of one, two, three months, and so on, is to fix the spot date (see Chapter 8). The standard forward date will normally be the same date in the relevant month. So, if spot is October 3, 1 month is November 3, 2 months, December 3, and so on.

If the date so found is a holiday, then the date is rolled on to the next day in which banks are open for business in both centers. Say we are dealing US$/DEM for 1 month, November 3 is a weekend, or a holiday in New York or Frankfurt. We roll the date on to the 4th, if that day is a business day in both centers. If it is not, then we keep rolling the date on until such a day is reached.

Exceptions to this rule arise in the case of month-ends. A month-end date is the last day of a month where banks are open for business in the two settlement countries. In a US$/DEM deal, if November 30 is a U.S. holiday, then month-end would be November 29, provided that day is a business day in both centers.

There are two exceptions to the standard rule, both of which are concerned with month-ends. The first is the so-called "end-end" rule. This says that if the spot value date is a month-end, then all forward value dates are also month-ends. Suppose the October month-end is October 28, the 29th and 30th being a weekend and October 31 a public holiday. Suppose spot is October 28, that is, the month-end. Then the end-end rule makes the one-month date November 30 (if that is the November month-end), not November 28.

The second exception is that forward value dates must not be rolled on beyond the month-end. Suppose the one-month date would normally be March 31, but that date is a holiday. We do not roll the one-month date on to April 1, but instead roll it backward to March 30.

10 Forward Contracts: Swaps

In this chapter we look at swaps. After explaining how swaps are used to switch exposure between currencies and over time, we look at how they are used to "manufacture" interest rates. Then we look at how interest rates affect the swaps. Next we look at the use of medium-term swaps. Then we see how forward forward swaps work. Finally, we look at the use of swaps in extending contracts and in working out broken dates. It should be noted that this chapter is concerned only with swaps consisting of a combined spot and forward foreign exchange deal. Other swaps (interest rate and currency swaps) are discussed in Chapter 15.

WHAT IS A SWAP?

In general, a swap is an exchange of one currency for another on one day, matched by a reverse exchange on a later day. A typical swap trade might be the sale of £1 million against US$2.2 million for spot value, coupled with the purchase of £1 million for delivery in three months against US$2.17 million. We swapped £1 million into dollars: we sold £1 million and bought it back three months forward. The swap rate is the difference between the rates of exchange used in the two trades. In our example, where the spot trade is done at 2.2000 and the forward at 2.1700, the swap rate is 0.03 or 300 points.

In most swap deals, the two exchanges are made at the same time with the same counterparty. But this need not be the case. One could buy spot from one counterparty and sell outright forward to another. Such a trade may be called an "engineered" swap to distinguish it from the more usual or "pure" swap.

In the pure swap, the spot rate used is not very important. What matters is the swap rate: the premium or discount received for the forward sale of dollars which are bought spot. The market tends to use a spot rate that is close to the current market rate, but chosen so as to make calculation easy.

USING SWAPS

Swaps have two basic uses: (1) to switch a deal from one currency to another, and back again, on a hedged basis; and (2) to move a given currency deal forward or backward in time.

An example of the first kind of swap could be if a bank had to lend Eurolire. Because of Italian exchange controls and other problems, the "natural" market for Eurolire is very thin. So to provide Eurolire, a bank will normally borrow U.S. dollars, buy lire in the spot market, and sell them back in the forward market. It "manufactures" Eurolire from Eurodollars.

An example of the second type of deal is when a customer makes an outright forward sale of, say, DEM 5 million six-months forward to a bank. The bank will hedge this by a spot sale and a forward swap, rather than an outright deal. Interbank outright deals are very rare because they are regarded as too risky. It may be difficult to find a counterparty willing to take such a risk. So the bank will sell the DEM 5 million in the spot market. It will then do a swap, buying DEM 5 million spot and selling them forward. (The steps are set out in Figure 10.1.) The swap carries no exchange risk, and it is much easier to find a counterparty. So the swap market helps to bring a forward exposure nearer, so that it can be closed out more easily. Equally, it can be used to push an exposure away in time.

Suppose I am an exporter with a steady stream of French francs coming in. Suppose the franc is very weak, so that I am not inclined to sell my francs now, because I expect the currency to recover. Then I could, if the exchange control system in my country permits it, swap my francs for three or six months, let us say into sterling if I am based in the United Kingdom. I am still long of francs, but instead of switching out of francs I am effectively

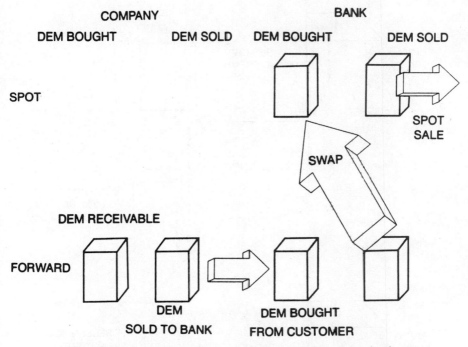

Figure 10.1 Using the swap to bring an exposure closer in time.

lending them and borrowing sterling against them. When the deal unwinds I receive my francs back again and can—I hope—sell them at a better rate. Figure 10.2. shows this in simple terms. Equally, a bank might want to run a basic long position in francs without showing it in the spot book. To do this it would swap the position out into the forward book. (We saw in Chapter 3 how a dealer would look at the foreign exchange and money market route to solve his problem. See also Chapter 11 on swapping out a position on the "short" dates.)

Another important use for swaps is as a straight trading operation. Swaps let us take a view on interest rates. Remember the rule of Chapter 3—if the interest differential moves in a currency's favor, the forward margin moves against it. So let's look at a situation where one-year US$ and £STG are both 10%. The forward margin will be near zero (if you are not sure why, read over Chapter 3). So a U.S. investor pays no premium for forward sterling. Suppose he thinks that in one month the 11-month interest rate for sterling will be below the 11-month US$ interest rate. That means that forward sterling will be at a premium. So it makes sense to buy forward sterling. And to do this without incurring an exchange risk, he can deal in the swap market. That is, he sells sterling spot and buys it 12 months forward, believing that in one month he can sell the sterling at a premium. The steps are set out in Figure 10.3.

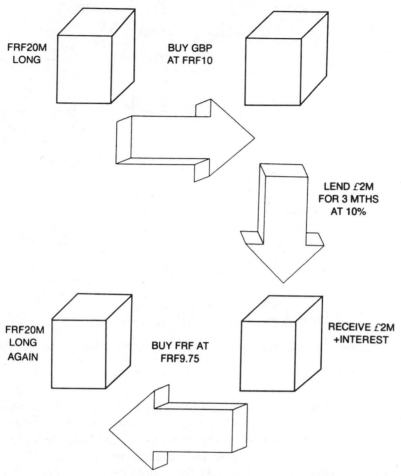

Figure 10.2   Pushing an exposure further away in time.

SWAP RATES IN PERCENTAGE TERMS

We often need to express the swap rate in percentage terms, usually to compare it with an interest differential. The choice of base—either the spot price or forward outright price—will depend on circumstances (see Chapter 9); in most professional deals, the relevant rate will be the outright forward rate. In our earlier example, with the spot at 2.20 and the forward at 2.17, the hedging cost for three months (90 days) would be 0.03/2.17 or 1.38%; if the spot is used as a base, the cost is 1.36%. These rates are normally annualized by multiplying by four (that is, number of days in a year—360—divided by number of days in a swap period—90). (The 360-day year is used to compare with Euro-rates. (See Chapter 6.) A 365-day basis could be used.)

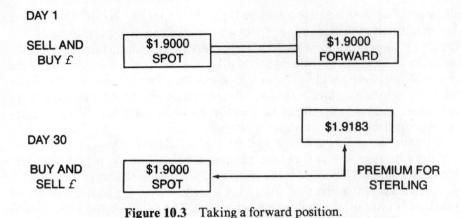

Figure 10.3 Taking a forward position.

This process can be summed up:

$$\text{Swap rate in \%} = \frac{\text{Swap rate in points}}{\text{Spot or outright in points}} \times \frac{360 \times 100}{\text{Number of days in swap}} = \frac{F}{\text{S or O}} \times \frac{360 \times 100}{N}$$

For a reciprocal currency like sterling, using the outright price gives higher swap costs if the hedged currency has a forward discount because then the outright is a smaller number that the spot. It works the other way around if it is at a premium. In our case, where the sterling was being sold spot and bought forward at a discount, the hedging cost rises from 1.36% using the spot rate for calculations, to 1.38% if the forward rate is used. Conversely, if forward sterling is at a premium, resulting in an outright forward rate of say, 2.23, then the hedging cost would fall to 1.35% (=0.03/2.23) on the outright basis.

FINDING INTEREST RATES FROM SWAP RATES—INTEREST UNHEDGED

We need the calculation of the swap yield if we must compare interest rates between currencies. Suppose we want to find the cheapest way to borrow Eurodeutschemarks. We can either borrow DEM directly or borrow another currency (typically Eurodollars) and swap into DEM. We have to find the cheapest rate at which a bank could lend DEM.

The quickest, crudest measure of the cost of the deal is like this. We take the Eurodollar interest rate and subtract the swap yield (be it positive or negative). Suppose we have a middle US$/DEM spot of 1.80 and that dollars are at a three-month discount (deutsche marks are at a premium) of 300 (middle). Suppose it cost us 10% to borrow three-month Eurodollars. We need the swap yield. As we saw above if F is the margin, S the spot and O the outright, the swap yield is F/S or F/O depending on circumstances. (When we work out the exact formula, we will see that the yield works out as F/S for normal or indirect currencies such as the deutsche mark and F/O for reciprocal or indirect currencies such as sterling.)

We take the swap yield here as 0.03/1.80 = 0.01667. This is 0.0667 if we multiply by four to put it out on an annual basis. Putting it in percentage terms, we have 6.67%. This is the swap profit. Because the bank is buying its forward dollars at a discount (receiving a premium on the forward deutsche marks it is selling), the swap yield is positive. The profit on the swap can be used to offset its Eurodollar costs. So the "manufactured" deutsche marks cost 10% less 6.67%, or 3.33%. We then compare this with the cost of raising Eurodeutschemarks directly (Figures 10.4. and 10.5).

If the currency being produced is at a discount in the forward market, F will be negative. Then R2 will be greater than R1. If the currency is at a premium, so F is positive, R2 will be less than R1. Effectively, R1 is the direct interest cost and F/S is the swap yield adjustment.

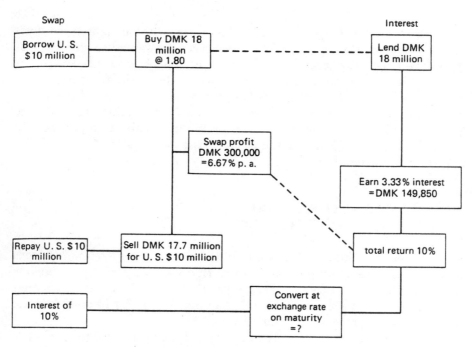

Figure 10.4 Arbitrage: Interest unhedged.

$$R2 = R1 - \left(\frac{F}{S} \times \frac{360}{N} \times 100\right)$$

where R1 = interest rate on currency borrowed
R2 = interest rate on currency lent
F = forward margin in points (treated as negative if the quoted currency
is at a discount—so that then R2 > R1)
S = spot rate in points
N = number of days

In words:

$$\frac{\text{Second currency}}{\text{interest rate}} = \frac{\text{First currency}}{\text{interest rate}} - \left(\frac{\text{Swap}}{\text{Spot}} \times \frac{360}{\text{days}} \times 100\right)$$

For an investor looking at the differential between the two currencies we would write:

$$\text{Interest differential} = \frac{\text{Swap}}{\text{Spot}} \times \frac{360}{\text{days}} \times 100$$

If the actual differential is bigger than the amount implied by the swap calculation, the switch is worth making.

© J. K. Walmsley, *The Foreign Exchange and Money Markets Guide,* John Wiley, New York, 1992.

Figure 10.5 Crude arbitrage formula.

FINDING INTEREST RATES FROM SWAP RATES—INTEREST HEDGED

This formula ignores the foreign exchange exposure on the interest payable on the deal. If there is a large swing in rates during the life of the deal, this could wipe out any profit. Suppose our rates are: spot DEM 2.35 one year 1141/1121, US$ deposits one year 14.75%. Then on the crude formula we have a deutsche mark yield of about 10%. But if at maturity the mark has weakened to 2.50, the realized yield is only 9%. (The deutsche mark interest earned is now worth less in dollar terms.) So the bank needs to have a formula that works on a fully hedged basis. This is set out in Figure 10.6.

To find it, we work through a deal step by step (Figure 10.7). We will use the rates from our first example, that is US$1 = DEM 1.8000 three-month forward dollar discount, DEM premium 300, and three-month Eurodollars (90 days) cost 10%. The bank borrows $10 million to swap into deutsche marks. It receives DEM 18 million spot and pays away DEM 17.7 million in three

The normal formula is used, for instance, when borrowing US\$ (first currency) and lending DEM (second currency):

Interest hedged formula: normal exchange rate

$$R2 = R1 \times \frac{B2}{B1} \frac{(S-F)}{S} + 100 \times \frac{B2}{N} \times \frac{F}{S}$$

In words:

$$\frac{\text{Second}}{\text{currency}} = \frac{\text{First}}{\text{currency}} \times \frac{\text{Second}}{\text{basis}} \times \frac{\text{Outright}}{\text{Spot}} + 100 \times \frac{\text{Second}}{\text{basis}} \times \frac{\text{Swap}}{\text{Spot}}$$
$$\text{interest rate} \quad \text{interest rate} \quad \text{First basis} \quad \quad \quad \text{Days}$$

This formula is exactly the same as the crude one except that the first currency's interest rate is multiplied by a factor to allow for the cost or benefit of selling the interest forward. The reciprocal formula is the same except that the adjustment factors change; it is used, for example, when borrowing US\$ (first currency) and lending £STG (second currency):

Interest hedged formula: reciprocal exchange rate

$$R2 = R1 \times \frac{B2}{B1} \times \frac{S}{S-F} + 100 \times \frac{B2}{N} \times \frac{F}{S+F}$$

In words:

$$\frac{\text{Second}}{\text{currency}} = \frac{\text{First}}{\text{currency}} \times \frac{\text{Second}}{\text{basis}} \times \frac{\text{Spot}}{\text{Outright}} + 100 \times \frac{\text{Second}}{\text{basis}} \times \frac{\text{Swap}}{\text{Outright}}$$
$$\text{interest rate} \quad \text{interest rate} \quad \text{First basis} \quad \quad \quad \text{Days}$$

The factor used to allow for the cost of hedging interest in inverted, and the swap yield is expressed as a percentage of the outright.

Note also that if we are going "backward"—that is, into dollars—the formula are reversed. If a normal currency is being borrowed to produce dollars we would use the "reciprocal" formula: if a reciprocal currency is borrowed, we use the "normal" formula.

Figure 10.6 Formula for fully hedged interest arbitrage.

months. The profit on the swap is DEM 300,000. Now we know that in 90 days the bank must pay interest of US$ 250,000. It will cover this interest by selling its deutsche mark earnings forward at 1.770. We know it will need DEM 442,500 (=250,000 × 1.77) in 90 days. It has made DEM 300,000 on the swap, so to break even, its DEM interest earnings must total DEM 142,500. These earnings are on a principal of DEM 18,000,000, therefore, over the three-month period, the interest rate is 142,500/18,000,000 = 0.79166%. Putting that on an annual basis, we multiply by four, getting 3.1666%

This compares with the 3.33% we worked out earlier. The reason that this rate is slightly lower is that the bank bought forward its dollar interest payable against its DEM interest earnings as well as swapping the DEM principal. Because the dollar was at a discount (the deutsche mark was at a premium) forward, it made an extra profit. This meant it could lower the deutsche mark interest rate at which it lent, and still break even. Conversely, if the dollar were at a premium and the currency were at a discount—for example, the Italian lira—its lending rate would have to be higher to compensate it for the extra cost of covering its ITL interest receivable.

To be absolutely accurate, our formula should take account of the spread in the spot rate, since the principal amount is swapped but the interest is sold forward outright (that is, using the other side of the spot). But the effect is very small. With the sort of rates we have used, a 10-point spot spread means 0.008% difference in the rate.

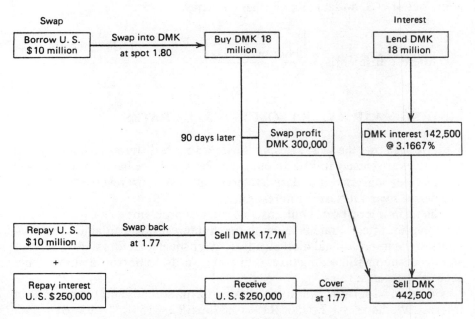

Figure 10.7   Fully hedged interest arbitrage.

The formula we have set up can be used to value a deal that is not hedged. To value the deal, we must predict the rate at which the interest earnings are sold off when they are received. To plug this assumed rate into the formula, we replace $(S - F)$—the rate at which we would sell off the interest if the deal were hedged—in the first term. So the normal formula is:

$$R2 = R1 \times \frac{B2}{B1} \times \frac{\text{Assumed rate}}{S} + 100 \times \frac{B2}{N} \times \frac{F}{S}$$

and the reciprocal formula is:

$$R2 = R1 \times \frac{B2}{B1} \times \frac{S}{\text{Assumed rate}} + 100 \times \frac{B2}{N} \times \frac{F}{(S - F)}$$

To revert to our example at the start of this section, if we plug in an assumed rate of 2.50, we see that to break even the bank must earn 10.99% rather than the 10.07% shown by the formula; in other words, if it lends at 10%, it ends up by losing nearly 1%. The calculation is:

$$R2 = 14.75 \times \frac{360}{360} \times \frac{2.50}{2.35} - 100 \times \frac{360}{365} \times \frac{0.1121}{2.35} = 15.915 - 4.7049 = 10.99$$

Several variations of the formula in Figure 10.6 exist, usually simplified to ignore the possibility of a 365-day basis and sometimes only applicable when going out of U.S. dollars into another currency. For example:

$$\text{Interest differential} = \frac{\left[\dfrac{360}{\text{Number of days}} + \dfrac{\text{US\$ cost}}{100}\right] \times [\text{Swap} \times 100]}{\text{Spot}}$$

FINDING SWAP RATES FROM INTEREST RATES

We have seen that the swap rate and the interest rate differential between two currencies are closely linked. In our examples so far, we have taken the swap rate as given and used it to derive interest rates. We now reverse the process and derive swap rates from interest rates.

The term interest rate contains a number of problems (see Chapter 6). In this chapter, interest rate is taken to mean interest rate available to participants in the international market, adjusted for special factors such as reserve asset costs and withholding taxes—in other words, to borrow a phrase, "net accessible interest rates."

We begin with the simplest formula, ignoring spreads and the hedging of interest. We have: $S = 2.0950$; $R1 = 10.875\%$; $R2 = 15\%$; $N = 92$; $B1 = 360$; $B2 = 365$ where S = middle spot rate: $R1$ = interest rate on dollars; $R2$ = interest rate on sterling; N = number of days in the deal; $B1$ = number of days in $ interest basis: and B2 = number of days in sterling interest basis.

Suppose we have £1 million to invest in either sterling or dollars: we want to know the forward margin which would make the two deals equivalent. We start by putting the interest rates on a common basis. For the sake of convenience, we shall put them on the 365-day basis, which means multiplying R1 by 365/360 to produce, say, 11%.

Now, if we swap into dollars, there is an interest loss of 4% for 92 days on $2,095,000, which must be compensated for by a profit on the swap. The exact loss is:

$$\frac{2,095,000 \times 4 \times 92}{360 \times 100} = \$21,415.55$$

We must therefore make at least $21,415.55 on our swap, so £1 million sold spot for $2,095,000 must cost only $2,095,000 − $21,415.55 = $2,073,584.45. Hence our break-even outright forward rate is 2.073584, say, 2.0736, making the break-even margin 214 points.

Notice that if our principal had been only £1, we would have had:

$$\frac{2.0950 \times 4 \times 92}{360 \times 100} = 0.0214$$

from which we can deduce a formula:

$$\text{Forward margin} = \frac{\text{Interest difference} \times \text{spot} \times \text{days}}{\text{Interest basis} \times 100}$$

$$F = \frac{S \times (R2 - R1) \times N}{B \times 100}$$

where we have S = spot in points; F = forward margin in points; N = number of days; and B = common interest basis.

This crude formula is convenient for quick calculations. To find the exact formula, we work through an example. The steps are set out in Figure 10.8. We have US$/DEM 1.9980/90, three-month (91-day) DEM interest rate is 12%, US$ interest rate is 18%. Suppose we have a principal amount of $1 million. If we place the US$ we have interest of $1,000,000 \times 18/100 \times 91/360 = \$45,500$. The DEM principal is DEM 1,998,000 earning DEM 60,606. The outright rate that we need is the one which equalizes principal and interest on both sides— $1,045,500 and DEM 2,058,606, that is, 2058606/1045500 = 1.9690. So the swap rate is 290.

To turn this into a formula, we write the interest rates as R1, R2, the spot as S, number of days as N, interest bases as B1, B2, principal amounts as P1, P2, and the outright as O. We have R1 = 18; R2 = 12; B1 = 360; B2 = 360; P1 = 1,000,000; P2 = 1,998,000 = P1 × S; S = 1.9980; and N = 91. Our dollar

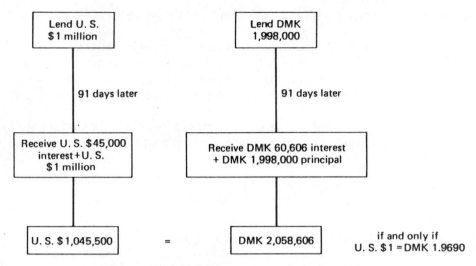

Figure 10.8   Finding a swap rate from interest rates.

interest is $1,000,000 \times 18/100 \times 91/360$ or $P1 \times R1/100 \times N/B1$. Our dollar total including principal is:

$$P1\left[1 + \frac{R1 \times N}{100 \times B1}\right] = 1,000,000\left[1 + \frac{18 \times 91}{36000}\right]$$

Similarly, our DEM total is:

$$1,998,000 \times \frac{12}{100} \times \frac{91}{360} \text{ or } P2\left[1 + \frac{R2 \times N}{100 \times B2}\right]$$

Because our DEM principal is $1,998,000 = 1,000,000 \times 1.9980$, that is, $(P2 = P1 \times S)$, we can write the second bracket as $P1 \times S$ $[1 + R2 \times N/(100 \times B2)]$. To get the outright we divide one into the other:

$$O = \frac{P1 \times S}{P1} \frac{\left[1 + \dfrac{R2 \times N}{100 \times B2}\right]}{\left[1 + \dfrac{R1 \times N}{100 \times B1}\right]}$$

Canceling out P1 we have:

$$O = \frac{S \times \left[1 + \dfrac{R2 \times N}{100 \times B2}\right]}{\left[1 + \dfrac{R1 \times N}{100 \times B1}\right]}$$

To get the swap rate, we subtract the spot rate from both sides. To test the formula we plug in our numbers:

$$O = \frac{1.9980\left[1 + \dfrac{12 \times 91}{100 \times 360}\right]}{\left[1 + \dfrac{18 \times 91}{100 \times 360}\right]} = 1.9980 \times \frac{1.03033}{1.0455} = 1.9690$$

The formula just given is for normal indirect currencies. Once again, it has to be amended for reciprocal (direct) currencies. Suppose we have the same dollar rates as before but we are looking at sterling. We have R2 = 16; B2 = 365; S = 2.3555; and P2 = P1/S = 424,538.31. As before, our dollar interest is:

$$P1 \times \frac{R1 \times N}{100 \times B1} = \$45,500$$

Our sterling interest is:

$$P2 \times \frac{R2 \times N}{100 \times B2} = \frac{P1}{S} \times \frac{R2 \times N}{100 \times B2} = \pounds16,935.01$$

Our sterling total is:

$$\frac{P1}{S}\left[1 \times \frac{R2 \times N}{100 \times B2}\right] = \pounds441,473.32$$

Because the exchange rate is quoted the other way up, we divide the dollar by the sterling amount to get 0:

$$O = \frac{P1\left[1 + \dfrac{R1 \times N}{100 \times B1}\right]}{\dfrac{P1}{S}\left[1 + \dfrac{R2 \times N}{100 \times B2}\right]} = S \times \frac{\left[1 + \dfrac{R1 \times N}{100 \times B1}\right]}{\left[1 + \dfrac{R2 \times N}{100 \times B2}\right]} = \frac{1,045,500}{441,473.32} = 2.3682$$

Giving a swap of 137 discount for dollars or 137 premium for sterling. The formula is identical, therefore, except that R1, B1 change places with R2, B2 (Figure 10.9). It is worth noting that if we go back now and apply this formula to the rates we used for the crude formula, the swap rate thrown up by the exact formula is 202 compared with 214 points—a difference of 12 points, which is proportionately quite large. It is well worth using the exact formula.

This formula produces a swap rate that is consistent with the fully hedged arbitrage formula. That is, if we take a US$ borrowing rate of 18%, DEM

Normal Formula:

$$F = S \left[\frac{1 + \dfrac{R2 \times N}{100 \times B2}}{1 + \dfrac{R1 \times N}{100 \times B1}} - 1 \right]$$

$$\text{Swap} = \text{Spot} \left[\frac{1 + \dfrac{\text{secondary currency rate} \times \text{days}}{100 \times \text{second interest basis}}}{1 + \dfrac{\text{first currency rate} \times \text{days}}{100 \times \text{first interest basis}}} - 1 \right]$$

Reciprocal formula:

$$F = S \left[\frac{1 + \dfrac{R1 \times N}{100 \times B1}}{1 + \dfrac{R2 \times N}{100 \times B2}} - 1 \right]$$

$$\text{Swap} = \text{Spot} \left[\frac{1 + \dfrac{\text{first currency interest rate} \times \text{days}}{100 \times \text{first interest basis}}}{1 + \dfrac{\text{second currency interest rate} \times \text{days}}{100 \times \text{second interest basis}}} - 1 \right]$$

where F = swap rate
S = spot
R1 = first currency interest rate
R2 = second currency interest rate
B1 = first currency interest basis
B2 = second currency interest basis
N = number of days

© J. K. Walmsley, *The Foreign Exchange & Money Markets Guide,* John Wiley & Sons, New York, 1992.

Figure 10.9   Calculation of swap from interest rates: formula.

spot of 1.998, and swap of 290, we can produce DEM on a fully hedged basis at 1% for 91 days. Go through the formula by hand to convince yourself of this.

MEDIUM-TERM CALCULATIONS

All our calculations so far have assumed that in each currency there is only one interest payment. That is, the forward foreign exchange transaction consisted of exchanging two zero-coupon cash flows. This is not the case if we are dealing for periods over one year. There are several ways to look at this problem. The cleanest is to convert both interest rates to zero coupon rates and then apply the formulas we have already developed.

We saw in Chapter 6 how we work out the zero coupon rate implied by a medium-term deposit. We took a one-to-five year yield curve for Eurodollar deposits:

Year 1	8%
Year 2	9%
Year 3	10%
Year 4	11%
Year 5	12%

We started by finding the two-year zero coupon rate implied by these rates. We started with a deposit of $1000 for two years at 9%. We took the present value today of the first interim interest payment of 9%, that is, $90. That turned out to be $83.33 when we discount it at the 8% rate applicable for the one-year period. We sold off our right to that interim coupon for $83.33. That reduced our initial net cash investment from $1000 to $916.67 today. In two years, we received $1090. The implied two-year zero coupon rate was 9.045%.

We applied this technique step by step. The three-year deposit gave cash flows of $100, $100, and $1100. We sold off the first two cash flows for $92.59 and $84.10, respectively. That made a net investment of $823.31 which returns $1100 in three years, for an implied zero coupon rate of 10.14%.

At the end of this process we had the following yield curves:

	Deposit Yield Curve	Zero Coupon Yield Curve
Year 1	8	8
Year 2	9	9.05
Year 3	10	10.14
Year 4	11	11.30
Year 5	12	12.56

We can duplicate this process for our other currency, say DEM. Suppose that here we have the following yield curve, and the following associated zero coupon curve:

	Deposit Yield Curve	Zero Coupon Yield Curve
Year 1	9	9
Year 2	8	7.96
Year 3	7	6.91
Year 4	6	5.85
Year 5	5	4.80

Notice that for the first year the DEM rate is above the US$ rate but that after that the pattern is reversed. Now all we do is take the formula we worked out earlier for calculating the forward rate from interest rates (Figure 10.9) and apply it. We can do this in two ways: the convenient and the accurate. The convenient is to simplify the formula by making N the number of years rather than the actual days in the period. On that basis our formula is: $F = S \times \{[1 + (R2 \times N/100)]/[1 + (R1 \times N/100)] - 1\}$ and we get the following results:

Year 1	0.0185
Year 2	− 0.0369
Year 3	− 0.1484
Year 4	− 0.3000
Year 5	− 0.4762

But the more accurate method is to use the actual number of days and the interest basis for each currency, in which case we use the identical formula to that of Figure 10.9 and we get (neglecting leap years of 366 days):

Year 1	0.0187
Year 2	− 0.0373
Year 3	− 0.1500
Year 4	− 0.3028
Year 5	− 0.4802

The error from neglecting the exact day-count is greater, the longer the deal. For the five-year forward rate, the convenient calculation shows 4762 points and the accurate one shows a price 40 points higher. (Even this is not completely accurate as we have not allowed for any 366-day years which would make a further couple of points difference.)

The converse question would arise if we had to work out a medium-term deposit rate from a set of interest rates and the forwards. Here we would use the formula quoted previously for the fully hedged calculation. Since we are dealing with normal currencies, the applicable formula is $R2 = R1 \times B2/B1 \times (S + F)/S + 100 \times B2/N \times F/S$. Taking the US$ rates as our starting point, we proceed to work out the two-year DEM interest rate that would apply, using the US$ zero coupon rates and the set of forwards that we have just worked out. Plugging the numbers into the formula gives us:

$$R2 = 9.05 \times 360/360 \times (1.9980 - 0.0373)/1.9980 + 100 \times 360/(2 \times 365) \times -.0373/1.9980$$

$$= 9.05 \times 1.9607/1.9980 - 100 \times 360/730 \times 0.018669$$

$$= 8.881 - .921$$

$$= 7.96$$

which matches the DEM zero coupon rate we started with. Thus the two formulae are consistent.

So far, we have worked a theoretically accurate way of working out what the rates should be. Often our problem is slightly different: we are confronted with a set of rates and want to know: Is it more attractive to deposit (or borrow) five-year Swiss francs at 8% or five-year U.S. dollars at 13%? Is there any kind of arbitrage profit possible in the rates we are facing? The answers here are a little more complex than the theoretical calculations because of the fact that we may not actually be able to deal at the theoretical zero coupon rates. We have to think about reinvestment risk.

We will begin by supposing that we have the choice of depositing Swiss francs at 8% for five years or U.S. dollars at 13%. Suppose our principal amount is $1 million and the spot rate is 1.8500. To begin with, we will make a simplifying assumption. We will assume that the Swiss franc interest receivable, and the dollar interest receivable, can both be reinvested on receipt, at the going rate (that is, 8% or 13%). We also assume that we as investors are willing to leave these intermediate interest payments in their respective currencies: that is, we are not eager to cover the Swiss franc interest receipts back into dollars, or vice versa.

On this basis, we ask: What five-year swap rate equalizes these two deals? Our assumptions mean that we can treat this deal exactly like the one in the previous section. That is, we calculate cumulative interest plus principal in the two currencies and divide one into the other to get the break-even outright rate. (See Table 10.1.)

But all this only applies on our original assumptions. Let's relax our assumption about the reinvestment rate. We can no longer guarantee that the Swiss Francs can be reinvested at 8% or the dollars at 13%. We see at

Table 10.1   Calculation of Medium-Term Swap from Deposit

	Amount	
Item	US$	CHF
Year 1 interest	131,805.56	150,055.56
Principal and interest at end or year 1	1,131,805.56	2,000,055.56
Year 2 interest	149,178.26	162,226.73
Principal and interest at end of year 2	1,280,983.82	2,162,282.28
Year 3 interest	168,840.78	175,385.12
Principal and interest at end of year 3	1,449,826.60	2,337,667.40
Year 4 interest	191,094.96	189,610.80
Principal and interest at end of year 4	1,640,919.54	2,527,278.20
Year 5 interest	216,282.31	204,990.34
Principal and interest at end of year 5	1,857,201.85	2,732,268.55

Note: The implied outright forward rate is given by the ratio of principal and interest at the end of year five, that is, 2,732,268.55/1,857,201.85 = approx. 1.4712. Remembering that the spot rate was 1.8500, this gives us a five-year swap rate of 3788 (Swiss franc premium, dollar discount). In fact we could apply this method to each of the intervening years, too. This would give us an annual swap rate of 828, 1620, 2376, 3098, and 3788.

once that we now have to make some assumptions about what reinvestment rates apply.

What difference does this make? For the sake of argument, suppose that all other rates are as before but we expect dollar reinvestment rates will be higher.

Say we expect 16%, 15½%, 14½%, 14% and 13%, respectively. The Swiss franc rates are 8% flat all the way through. Then we find swap rates of 1291, 2421, 3345, 4153, and 4795, respectively. We no longer have the fairly smooth progression we had earlier. The early swaps are proportionately much larger than the later, because the interest differential is higher.

This type of situation (or its converse) is much more common than our first assumption of unchanging rates. But if we relax that assumption, we find that the only way to solve our general problem is by trial and error (by iteration), unless we are given every single piece of information to begin with.

Let's look at a case where we are given all the information to begin with. We estimate that we can borrow five-year sterling at 14⅝%. We can lend five year dollars at 15³/₁₆%. We have the following spot and forward rates:

Spot $1,7800/10
Year 1   200/275
Year 2   300/400
Year 3   350/450
Year 4   400/500
Year 5   400/500

We start with a principal of £10 million. With this we buy $17.8 million. We know that our dollar interest receivable annually is $2,740,921.88 and our sterling interest payable is £1,462,500. We know that our dollar interest, sold forward for sterling at the market's buying rate for dollars (that is, the right hand side of the swap) will yield:

Year 1   £1,516,415.98
Year 2   £1,506,001.03
Year 3   £1,501,875.00
Year 4   £1,497,771.52
Year 5   £1,497,771.52

So our profit in sterling is:

Year 1   £53,915.98
Year 2   £43,501.03
Year 3   £39,375.00
Year 4   £35,271.52
Year 5   £35,271.52

and our profit in US$ terms is:

Year 1 $97,453.13
Year 2 $79,171.87
Year 3 $71,859.38
Year 4 $64,546.88
Year 5 $64,546.68

where the dollar equivalents are calculated at the relevant forward rates of 1.8075, 1.82, 1.825, 1.834, 1.83. (We use the left-hand side of the spot, because it is a swap deal rather than an outright.)

We assume (for simplicity) that these profits can also be lent out at the dollar lending rate of $15\,{}^{3}/_{16}\%$, from the date that they accrue until the maturity of the deal. This produces cumulative earnings from each year as follows:

Year 1 $171,560.45
Year 2 $121,000.45
Year 3 $ 95,344.17
Year 4 $ 74,349.93
Year 5 $ 64,546.87

The total over the five years is thus $526,801.87. On the other hand, we know that to hedge our principal amount of £10 million, we have to buy back £10 million five years hence at a sterling premium (dollar discount) of 500 points, which will cost us $500,000 at the far end. So the profit over the deal is $526,801.87 − 500,000 = $26,801.87. (Given the size of the principal amount, and the fact that lines are being tied up for five years, it is not a particularly attractive deal.)

Now we can explore the sensitivity of this deal to different assumptions. If we rework the figures in the assumption that accrued profits can be reinvested at only $14^{3}/16\%$ rather that $15^{3}/16\%$, for example, the total profit falls from nearly $27,000 to $15,500. But a 1% change in the sterling interest rate is much more powerful: if the dollar rate (and reinvestment rate) are held unchanged at $15^{3}/16\%$, but the sterling rate is raised to $15^{5}/8\%$, the deal swings from a profit of nearly $27,000 to a loss of over $1.2 million. The reason is that this interest rate is acting on the whole principal, rather than just the annual profits or losses as the reinvestment/refunding rate is. Equally, a rise of 100 points in the first year's swap rate cuts the profit from nearly $27,000 to about $1,000 whereas the same change in year 4 cuts the profit much less, to $10,000, because the dollar receivable is worth less in sterling terms in Year 1 and that cumulates over time. The impact in Year 4 is not cumulated over so long a time.

But the same rise of 100 points in Year 5 makes a difference of $100,000: because again it is applied to the whole principal, rather than the annual profits or losses which are much smaller. Summing up, then, the reinvestment rate and the intervening year's swap rates are not particularly critical compared with the five-year interest rates and the five-year swap rate. However, this does not mean they can be ignored. If the funding cost of the early losses in the deal were ignored, there would be an apparent profit of about $122,000 which does not exist.

FORWARD FORWARD SWAPS

A forward forward is a swap deal between two forward dates. It might be done to take a view on the swap rates (further ahead than we did earlier) or to offset other flows. For instance, the treasurer of Zum Beispiel GmbH might have DEM 5 million due in six months, but she might also have a DEM 5 million payment to make in one month. If she wants to lock in today's swap rates, she would do a forward forward deal.

Suppose we have:

DEM spot   2.1500 – 10
DEM one month   50/40
DEM six months   280/260

She knows that she must buy dollars for deutsche marks in six months, for which she will benefit from a dollar discount (receive a deutsche mark premium) of 260 points. She knows also that she must sell dollars for deutsche marks in one month for which she will pay a dollar discount (deutsche mark premium) of 50 points. The forward forward rate is the difference between the two: 210 points. If the deals were done as outrights, the one-month deal would be done at 2.1450 and the six-month at 2.1250 for a net benefit (dollar discount, deutsche mark premium) of only 200 points. Doing the deals separately is more expensive because it adds the cost of dealing on both sides of the spot rate.

A common use of forward forward rates is to take a view on interest rate movements. Suppose we have the following £STG/US$ rates:

Spot   1.8980/90
One month   20/10
Two months   30/20
Three months   40/30
Six months   40/30
Twelve months   30/20

This pattern happens when U.S. rates are slightly below U.K. rates for all periods, but rather less so at the far end. Suppose we think the market has got it wrong. We think that in the next six months U.K. rates will fall, but U.S. rates will not change very much. We think that in six months the six-month swap will be 100/200; that is, U.K. rates will be significantly below U.S. rates for the period. (Remember the rule of Chapter 3: When the interest differential goes against a currency, the swap goes in its favor.) So we decide to take a forward forward position "sixes against twelves."

We think sterling will go from discount to premium in this period (dollars will go from premium to discount). So we want to be long of sterling (short dollars) at the far end, vice versa at the near end. So we sell sterling at the near end for a discount of 40 and buy it back at the far end at a discount of 20. The whole operation costs us 20 points.

Suppose we get it right. In six months, the swap has moved to 100/200. We have to buy sterling at the near end and sell it at the far end. For this we get 100 points premium on our sterling at the far end against the 20 points discount we paid, netting 80 points in total. Of course, 80 points is small compared with the probable movement in the spot, but as a forward forward dealer, we are much less exposed than if we took an outright position. Our net exchange position will be only marginally affected by the spot rate's movements, but there will be a cash flow difference—there will be a profit/loss to be invested/funded over the period till the position unwinds.

Let's look at the arithmetic of the position.

Day 1:	Spot	1.8980/90
	6 months	40/30
	12 months	30/20
Day 180:	Spot	1.7500/10
	6 months	100/200

On day 1, we sell sterling and buy $5 million in the six-month period at 1.8940, making £2,639,915.52. We sell $5 million and buy £2,637,130.80 at 1.8960 in the one-year date. On day 180, we have to buy sterling at $1.7510, costing $4,622,492.08 and sell it forward at $1.7610, receiving $4,643,987.34. So we have a profit today of $377,507.92 the difference between our sale of $5 million for sterling and what we have to pay to cover it. On the far date, we sold $5 million and bought sterling but only receive $4,643,987.34 for the sterling we now sell back, giving us a loss at the far end of $356,012.66 and a net profit on the whole deal of $21,495.26

What would have happened if the forwards had moved the same way but the spot had gone the opposite way, to $2.0300/10? It costs us $5,361,668.30 to buy sterling at the near end—that is, spot. At the far end we get $5,382,383.96 for our sterling, giving us a profit on the whole deal of $20,715.66—about $1,000 less than before, but at the far end of the deal this time. The 28-cent movement in the spot hardly made any difference. But it does make a difference when we take into account the interest cost of funding the loss which we now have at the near end of the deal when we close it out.

Forward forward deals often crop up when a trader decides to cover a slightly different period from his natural interest. Let's look again at Zum Beispiel GmbH's treasurer, who has a South African rand receipt due in 13 months. She calls her bank late in the afternoon and is quoted:

Spot	2.5410/20
12 months	350/360
13 months	450/460

She asks why the 13-month dollar premium/rand discount is proportionately so high and is told that the South African prime rates have just risen after the close of business in Johannesburg (which is an hour ahead of Frankfurt). Since the interest differentials have gone in the rand's favor, the forwards move to offset this by going further into discount. She is told that the forwards are expected to rise again tomorrow and no one is eager to deal 13 months as it is an awkward period.

She decides to deal today but thinks it would not be worth paying the 100 points extra for the 13th month. She thinks that if she waits a month the situation will have settled. So she deals for 12 months which creates a forward forward position, "twelves against thirteens." She expects that if she waits a month her position—which will then be "elevens against twelves"— can be closed our for about 20 points.

If she is right, she has locked in her forward cover for the period at a total cost of 370 points instead of 450, because she avoided paying the extra cost of dealing into an "awkward" period.

SYNTHETIC AGREEMENTS FOR FORWARD EXCHANGE (SAFE)

A SAFE is the foreign exchange equivalent of a Forward Rate Agreement (see Chapter 6): a contract for differences that acts as a substitute for a forward/forward foreign exchange deal. It originated in proprietary products developed by certain commercial banks, and was developed into an instrument available to the London market as a whole under the aegis of the British Bankers' Association, who in April 1989 published the SAFEBBA Master Terms—analogous to the FRABBA terms for FRAs.

SAFEs come in two types: Exchange Rate Agreement (ERA) or Forward Exchange Agreement (FXA). The difference is that while the FXA is an agreement regarding changes in both forward spreads and spot rates, the ERA covers the forward spread only. The general settlement formula for both types of SAFE is as follows:

$$\left[A2 \times \left[\frac{(OER - SSR) + (CFS - SFS)}{1 + \left[\frac{L \times D}{100 \times B} \right]} \right] \right] - [(A1 \times (OER - SSR))]$$

where A1 = first contract amount

A2 = second contract amount (for ERAs A1 = A2)

CFS = contract forward spread

SFS = BBA Settlement forward spread

OER = outright exchange rate (set to zero for ERAs)

SSR = BBA Settlement spot rate (set to zero for ERAs)

L = BBA Interest Settlement Rate for the secondary currency (expressed as a number, not as a decimal)

D = number of calendar days in the swap period

B = 360 or 365

In this context, the primary currency is defined as that in which the contract amounts are expressed and the other currency is referred to as the secondary currency. The first contract amount is the amount of currency that would notionally be exchanged on the settlement date (which is actually the starting date for the SAFE) and the second contract amount is the amount that would notionally have been exchanged on the maturity date. These two amounts can be different in the case of an FXA but not for an ERA.

In essence, the SAFE cuts down the settlement risk—and thus the credit exposure—on a forward forward foreign exchange contract. Suppose today one month against four-month forward forward dollar sterling swaps were trading at 55/51. Today is May 6, 1992 with spot May 10 and the one-month date June 10, the four-months date September 12.

Suppose I buy sterling forward forward at 51. (That is, I contract to sell it on June 10 and buy it back on September 12.) Suppose on June 10 when the deal then comes to settle, the forward margin for that period is 60. Then I can close out at a profit of 9 points. But that profit would in theory only be due in September. To cut down the settlement risk, we can settle the difference today, just like we did in the Forward Rate Agreement in Chapter 6. As with the FRA, we will use the relevant BBA interest settlement rate to discount the sums involved.

So far we have ignored any movements in the spot rate during the life of the deal. Suppose now we allow for this; say the spot rate in May is $1.8600 and it has moved to $1.9000 when the deal comes to settle. Suppose I deal an FXA of £10 million (i.e., the first and second contract amounts in this case are equal). Then, bearing in mind there will be 93 days from June 10 to September 12 and assuming a BBA interest settlement rate of 7.5%, the settlement amount would be:

$$
\left[(1.9000 - 1.8600) + \frac{(1.8600 - .0051) - (1.9000 - .0060)}{\left(1 + 93 \times \frac{7.5}{36000} \right)} \right]
$$

$$
\times \ 10,000,000 = \$16,431.64
$$

This SAFE exactly corresponds to a matched pair of swaps. Under the first, forward forward swap done on May 6, I buy £10 million at $1.8600 value June 10 and sell £10 million at $1.8549 value September 12; this is closed off with a second swap on June 8 where I sell £10 million at $1.9000 value June 10 and buy back £10 million at $1.8940 value September 12. The key difference is that under the SAFE, I am not contractually obliged to make or take payments in the amount of £10 million: I am only obliged to settle the difference amount, which as we see is a very small sum compared with the principal amounts. Thus, like a forward rate agreement and an interest rate swap, and for the same reasons (it is driven by interest differentials), the SAFE incurs a credit exposure that is only a fraction of the amount of the notional underlying principal, provided the two contract amounts are within 10% of each other.

EXTENDING MATURING CONTRACTS

A further common use of a swap is where a forward sale of, for example, deutsche marks has been made to cover an export receivable. As maturity approaches, it is found that the funds will not be received in time. A swap has to be done to adjust the maturity date.

At this point, we must allow for accumulated profit or loss. Suppose we use the original contract's spot rate as the "spot" rate on which the new swap is based. For example, suppose the corporation originally sold the bank deutsche marks two months forward against U.S. dollars; suppose the deal was done off a spot rate of 1.8000 and a DEM premium/dollars discount of 200, making an outright of 1.7800. Assume we now have to extend for a further two months owing to payment delays, and that the two-month DEM premium is now 220. If we use the original outright rate of 1.7800 as the "spot" for our new extension, the new outright rate will be 1.7580. But suppose in the meantime the deutsche mark has strengthened to 1.7000. The firm has made a loss—or less profit than it might have—by selling forward when it did.

Hence, if the bank lets the old deal mature, and does a new deal based on today's rates, the customer will be delivering deutsche marks sold to the bank at 1.7800. But he will have to buy them from the bank in order to

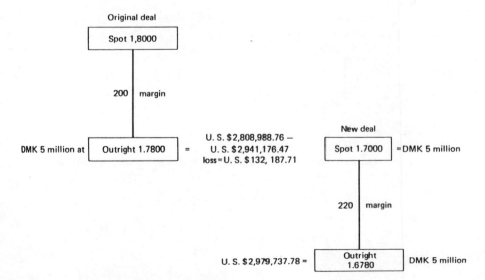

Figure 10.10 Extension of a contract at current rate.

deliver them, and must pay 1.7000 for them. Then he will sell them back to the bank at $1.7000 - 0.0220 = 1.6780$. The steps are set out in Figure 10.10. Suppose his original sale had been DEM 5 million. At the original rate, this would have produced $2,808,988.76. But to buy in DEM 5 million for the extension at 1.7000 will cost him $2,941,176.47—crystallizing a loss of $132,187.71. The deutsche marks are now sold forward at the current outright rate of 1.6780, yielding $2,979,737.78 at the new maturity. If at this postponed maturity date it were necessary again to extend the deal, and the spot had moved back up to 1.8000, the extension would now crystallize a profit; and so on.

On the other hand, if the deal is extended at the original rate, the extension would not throw up any cash difference. (See Figure 10.11.) But there would be a hidden loss which could continue to accumulate indefinitely. This is an inherently undesirable possibility for both sides; the bank is providing an unsecured loan, and the corporation's books are not reflecting its true position. Hence it is generally recommended that all extensions of forwards be made at current market rates. The drawback for a firm whose business requires many changes in delivery dates—such as a commodity trader—is that this method continually throws up a string of small profits or losses which have to be taken into or out of the normal cash flow of the business. So the choice of the correct rate on which to base the extensions to be made at current market rates: cash flow simplicity requires that they be carried out at the original rates.

If a forward contract is extended at the historic rate, then the bank should adjust for the fact that it is lending the customer his loss (or taking his profit as a deposit). This has to be worked back into the swap rate. We look at how this is done next.

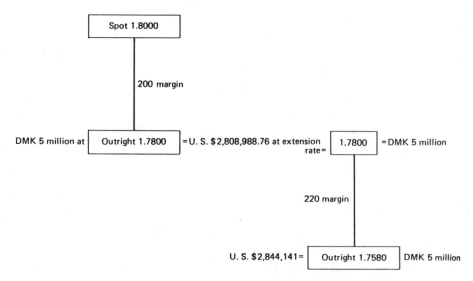

Figure 10.11   Extension at original rate.

EXTENSIONS AT HISTORIC RATES

Using current rates, the calculation of how to extend a maturing contract is straightforward; we saw it in the previous section. DEM5 million sold forward at an outright rate of 1.7800 were extended at the new forward rate of 1.6780. The old forward was closed out by a spot purchase of DEM 5 million at 1.7000. This threw up a loss of $132,187.71.

But suppose for some reason the contract is extended off the historic rate. (It should be stressed that the practice of extensions at historic rates is generally discouraged by the authorities. The reason is that the technique has in the past been used by speculative operators to conceal bad positions; there is a serious danger of loss of control. However, there can sometimes be valid operational reasons for permitting the practice, providing it is properly controlled). In this case, the customer buys DEM 5 million to close out the old contract as before. But he does it at 1.7800, so his cash loss does not show up. It only shows up in a smaller dollar inflow at the maturity of the new contract. The bank has lent him his loss until the new maturity. How do we adjust for this?

We start by realizing that this is a special case of the formula on page 208. That is, we have to get a swap adjustment from the interest the bank will charge its customer for lending it the loss (or taking the profit on deposit). It is a special case of the formula for swap rates from interest rates: one of the interest rates is zero. There is a loan of U.S. dollars to the customer but no deutsche mark deposit by the customer. So we take the formula

$$F = S \left[\frac{1 + \dfrac{R2 \times N}{B2 \times 100}}{1 + \dfrac{R1 \times N}{B1 \times 100}} - 1 \right]$$

We see that the denominator is 1, because $R1 = 0$. So now we have:

$$F = S \left[\frac{R2 \times N}{B \times 100} \right]$$

where F = adjustment needed; S = current spot rate; $R2$ = dollar interest rate; N = days in new contract; and $B = 360$.

Using the rates we had earlier, and assuming the dollar rate is 10%, we can write :

$$F = 1.7000 \left[\frac{10 \times 60}{360 \times 100} \right] = 0.0283 = 283 \text{ points}$$

This would be the adjustment if the bank lent the whole of the principal amount to the customer. But of course it is only lending the loss, so the adjustment has to be weighted accordingly. To find the dollar amount of the loss, we take the difference between the new rate (1.7000) and the old (1.7800) as a percentage of the new rate, and apply this to the dollar amount of the old forward contract (being the dollar equivalent at maturity of the old forward). In our example:

$$\frac{1.7000 - 1.7800}{1.7000} \times 2{,}808{,}988.76 = 132{,}187.71$$

To generalize this into a formula, we say that the dollar amount at the maturity of the original contract was $1. Then the dollar loss is given by:

$$\frac{\$1 \times 1.7000 - 1.7800}{1.7000} = \frac{\text{new rate} - \text{old rate}}{\text{new rate}}$$

If we designate the new spot rate Sn and the old So we can write this as

$$\frac{Sn - So}{Sn}$$

and the whole formula is:

$$F = \frac{Sn - So}{Sn} \times Sn \left[\frac{R \times N}{B \times 100} \right] = \frac{(Sn - So) \times R \times N}{B \times 100}$$

where F = adjustment to forward; So = old contract rate; Sn = new contract rate; R = interest rate on currency being received by customer at maturity (here, dollars); B = interest basis for interest rate; and N = number of days in new contract.

When we use the numbers from our example, we have:

$$F = \frac{(1.7000 - 1.7800) \times 10 \times 60}{360 \times 100} = -0.0013 = 13 \text{ points against customer}$$

So instead of showing 220 points in the customer's favor in the new forward, the bank will show only 207. If the rates had moved in the customer's favor, F would be positive and the swap would be adjusted in the customer's favor.

BROKEN DATES

A forward (or a deposit) transaction which is not for certain standard dates—normally 1, 2, 3, 6, or 12 months, and in some cases 1, 2, 3, 4, 5, 6, 7, 8, 9, 10, 11, or 12 months—is referred to as a "broken" or "odd" date. Calculation of the outright forward price for such a date is made by using the swap rates. Suppose that we are buying deutsche marks against sterling, the spot rate is

DEM 3.0, and the two-month premium is 300 while the three-month premium is 450. Suppose that we are dealing on April 3 (spot 5th) for June 15 for a date which is two months and 10 days ahead. A convenient method of calculation is as follows.

The third month—between June 5 and July 5—has 30 days in it; so we take 10/30ths, or 1/3rd, of the third month's premium (which is 450 less 300, that is 150 points), totaling 50 points. This is added to the two-month premium of 300, to produce a total of 350; so our outright rate for June 15 would be 3.000 − 0.0350 = 2.9650.

This "pro rata" method of calculation is acceptable for normal maturities where no special factors (for example, days of peak interest rates) are involved (see Chapter 12, Adjustments). The pro rata method is not always acceptable for shorter maturities, however. These are discussed in Chapter 11.

11 Short Dates

In this chapter, we look at the special features of deals done for value before spot. In particular we explain why the swap rate is reversed for outright deals before spot.

A short date forward or deposit rate is normally defined as one which is for a maturity shorter than one month. A stricter definition would be one week; and an even stricter definition would include only rates before spot. However, the normal use is for rates up to one month.

We saw (Chapter 8) that under normal circumstances the spot date for exchange and deposit deals is two working days forward. This allows some dealing for value before spot; that is, value today or value tomorrow. These deals are normally tightly constrained by time factors. Deals done value today are only really possible for currencies whose time zone is substantially behind that in which the deal is being struck. For example, it is possible to deal dollar/sterling in London for value today, because the five- or six-hour delay between London and New York gives time to get the instructions processed in New York. But dollar/yen in New York cannot really be dealt value today because there will be no chance to get the deal processed in Tokyo, which has closed by the time New York opens for business.

Subject to these constraints, therefore, it is possible to deal for value before spot only for certain currencies in certain countries. Given that normally there are two days between today and spot, this gives us two margins: that from today until tomorrow (overnight or O/N) and that from tomorrow until the next business day (tomorrow/next, tom/next, or T/N). These margins parallel the deposit rates for the same period.

The tom/next swap is the rate at which a currency can be bought or sold against the next business day, which is also the spot date. If a deal were maturing value tomorrow, and it had to be rolled over to the next day, the tom/next adjustment would be used to calculate the new rate. The tom/next market is, as is the deposit market, a bit less affected by time zone constraints than the overnight market. But it still tends to dry up during the course of the morning. Its importance lies in the fact that it is used to roll over a spot position (hence in the United States it is often referred to as the roll-over) since it is the last business day before spot.

USING SHORT DATE SWAPS

Short date swaps work just like any other swaps. The only difference comes when we use them to calculate outright rates before spot. Suppose we have a US$/DEM spot rate of DEM 2.2535/40. Suppose we have a swap rate from Wednesday to Thursday of 11/5. Suppose spot is Wednesday and we want Thursday's rate. This is a perfectly normal forward, so we have spot DEM 2.2535/40 and forward 11/5, making Thursday's rate DEM 2.2524/35 (remembering high/low = subtract). Notice that the spread has gone up from 5 points to 11 points. The spread on the outright equals the spread on the spot plus the spread on the forward.

But suppose now that our spot rate of DEM 2.2535/40 is actually for Thursday. We want Wednesday's rate—a rate before spot. Our forward margins have to be worked *backward* in time to a date before spot. To go from Wednesday to Thursday, we subtracted 11/5. So to come back from Thursday to Wednesday should we *add* 11/5? What happens if we do? We get DEM 2.2546/45. Our spread has gone negative; our selling rate is higher than our buying. Something is wrong.

Let's look at this another way. We know that the forward margin of 5 points from Wednesday to Thursday is the bank's—and the market's—rate for buying DEM and selling US$. Suppose on Wednesday we want to buy DEM for value Wednesday and sell them for value Thursday. We have to sell DEM to the market at the market's *buying* rate for DEMs, that is, 5 points. Since the deutsche mark is at a premium, the dollar at a discount, we will earn 5 points. If we deal the opposite way around, sell DEM for value Wednesday and buy them for value Thursday, it will cost us 11 points.

Now let's look again at our spot for Thursday, which is DEM 2.2535/40. The market sells DEM value Thursday at 2.2535. At what rate will a bank sell value Wednesday? It has to cover its Wednesday position by buying DEM for value Wednesday (so that it can sell them to its customer). As always in a forward, it will deal value spot and then swap to its desired date—in this case Wednesday. It buys DEM value Thursday at 2.2535 from the market. Then in the swap market it buys DEM for value Wednesday, selling them off again on Thursday to square up its spot position. But we saw just now that it earns 5 points by doing this. So it can sell DEM value Wednesday at 5 points better than value Thursday; that is, 2.2540. Conversely, we saw that if it dealt the opposite way round, that is, bought DEMs value Wednesday, it would cost the bank 11 points to do the swap.

So it has to add this to Thursday's buying rate of 2.2540, making 2.2551 its buying rate for Wednesday.

In other words, when dealing outright before spot, the margin must be turned around. To go from Thursday's DEM 2.2535/40 to Wednesday we don't add 11/5—we add 5/11, to get Wednesday's DEM 2.2540/51. If you stop to think about it, it does make sense, because this is a "backward" margin, not a "forward." We are going backward in time from the spot rate. The rule is: *Overnight and tom/next go backward, not forward, so you must turn them around to get the outright.* But once again, *this applies only to outrights.* It is only then that you work backward from spot. If you are swapping from tomorrow to the next day, you are going forward, so you don't turn the rates around. It's only when you want to use the tom/next to bring a rate back from spot to tomorrow that you turn it around. Not when you are doing a swap from tomorrow to spot. The latter case is a perfectly ordinary forward.

Let's now look at a short date cross-rate. Suppose we need a £/DEM tom/next margin. We have the following rates:

Spot US$/DEM	2.0510/15	Spot £/US$	2.2513/18
Tom/next	5/4		3/2

We reverse the two margins and apply them to the spot rates to get outright value tomorrow:

US$/DEM	2.0514/20	£/US$	2.2515/21

We then calculate the relevant cross-rates:

Value tomorrow:	4.6187/4.6213
Spot:	4.6172/94

This gives a margin from tomorrow to spot (that is, tom/next) of 15/19, which must be reversed again to 19/15. Inspection confirms that this is correct, since 19/15 shows that the DEM spot is at a premium over tomorrow. This is true, since the selling rate value tomorrow at 4.6187 is higher than the spot of 4.6172, and similarly on the buying side. In fact, the mechanics of the calculation are exactly the same as those for any other cross-forward calculation. The only difference is the need to reverse the margins before starting the calculation, and then to reverse them back again after completion.

OTHER SHORT DATES

Another short date rate which is commonly quoted is the spot/next rate. This is used for swapping from spot value to the next business day. It is often needed in working out cross rate adjustments; see Chapter 12. Like other short date rates for value *after* spot there is no question of turning the spot/next margin round in calculations. It is an ordinary forward.

Other short dates often quoted include the one-week, two-week, and less frequently, three-week swap rates. (For all short dates after spot, there is no question of reversing the swap.) For rates between these dates, one tends to calculate a rate on a pro rata basis. We take the rates for the standard periods before and after the date in question, and work out the daily average margin between these two dates. But short date rates are very heavily affected by special factors, most notably month-end dates, reserve asset "makeup dates," tax payment dates, or other days when reporting requirements or liquidity factors have a distorting impact. The rate has to be worked out exactly from interest rates (see Chapter 10). For example, since the end-of-year US$ deposit market is not uncommonly bid 40% or more for a day or two, it would be wrong to work out a swap rate on a pro rata basis if it included the year-end (see Chapters 10 and 12).

SWAPPING OUT A POSITION IN THE SHORT DATES

The short date market is widely used for swapping out a position. Let's look at an example. We believe that the deutsche mark will be weaker in three months than today. We could sell outright forward DEMs in the three months' date. But we feel this is too risky. Accordingly, we do a swap; we buy spot deutsche marks (say DEM1 million) and simultaneously sell the same amount forward in the three-month period. We are now overbought for value spot, and oversold for value three months hence. Unless further action is taken, the DEM1 million that are due to arrive on our account two days hence, on spot date, will remain there, earning no interest, until the forward sale matures, when they will be paid away to our counterparty.

Hence we have two alternative courses of action. We can either lend the money out from the spot date to the three-month date, or we can ensure that the money does not arrive on our account on the spot date, by selling it off in the short date market. In other words, we buy and sell in the tom/next market (hence the tom/next is often called the roll-over in the United States). The sequence of actions looks like this:

	Sell	Buy
Tomorrow		DEM1 million
Spot	DEM1 million	DEM1 million
Three months	DEM1 million	

This operation amounts to lending the deutsche marks out day-to-day through the swap. We are undertaking a long-term forward liability and

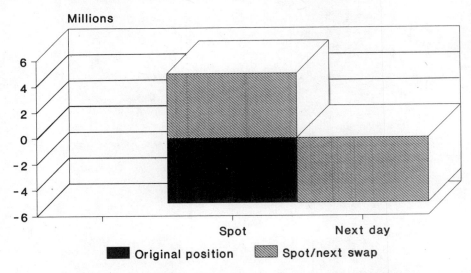

Figure 11.1 Swapping out a position using the spot/next rollover.

covering it on a day-to-day basis in the tom/next market. By contrast, an outright forward sale in the three-month period would be completely uncovered. We have now shifted our position nearer in time so that it is less risky. If we want to go oversold on an outright basis, we can now sell off our DEM1 million that are due to arrive on the account tomorrow, knowing that funds will come into the account from our tom/next swap, which itself has squared off our three-month swap. The risk is much closer and more easily controllable. On the other hand, swapping a position out day-to-day means writing a lot of tickets if we run the position for a while, so there is an extra cost. The compounding factor also has to be considered. In this case, it would work in our favor, but if we were selling a discount currency it would work against us.

Figure 11.1 shows how if we are short £5 million for value spot, we can use the spot/next swap to buy spot and sell the next day. Our spot position is now square, and the position has been rolled forward to the next day—i.e. off the balance sheet.

12 Adjustments

In this chapter, we explain how to adjust forward quotes for a nonstandard date. Then we show how to adjust cross prices for the effects of a holiday in one country. Next we show how to allow for payment today, and how to adjust a deposit quote for withholding tax and reserve requirements. Finally, we show how to price the negotiation of a check.

NONSTANDARD RUNS

A helpful way of approaching this topic is to break the swap margin down into individual days. Suppose today is April 8, spot 10th, and we are looking at a one-month US$/DEM swap from April 10 to May 10—a 30-day period. Suppose the swap is 105/90. Then we can say, crudely, that "the days are running at 3$^{1}/_{2}$/3"—that is, the daily average margin is the total margin in the period divided by the number of days. In order to get a swap from April 10 to May 9—a run of 29 days—we would reduce the swap by 3$^{1}/_{2}$/3, making it 101$^{1}/_{2}$/87.

Equally, we might want to adjust this run by bringing its start date forward a day as well, to April 9. Suppose that the tom/next (see Chapter 11) is also running at 3$^{1}/_{2}$/3; then we would add this on to the margin to bring it back to 105/90. On the other hand, if the short date market were very tight, for instance, by reason of the U.S. Federal funds rate being very high, the tom/next rate might be 10/7, in which case we would adjust the run of April

10/May 9 at 101^1/$_2$/87 by adding on 10/7 to make the run April 9/May 9 a total of 111^1/$_2$/94.

This case shows that the forward margin need not be the total of a uniform daily average rate of 3^1/$_2$/3 as we started by assuming. It might be that our original one-month swap of 105/90 concealed the fact that each week the Wednesday/Thursday swap premium was typically lower than other days. Suppose there were a weekly reporting procedure in Germany which induced banks to bid for deutsche marks value Wednesday to sell back Thursday. (This doesn't happen, but parallel examples do occur. And the classic example of this used to be Thursday/Friday dollars because of the New York Clearing House funds system.) Then our weekly swap might look like this:

Monday/Tuesday	3/2^1/$_2$	
Tuesday/Wednesday	3/2^1/$_2$	
Wednesday/Thursday	5/6	
Thursday/Friday	3/2^1/$_2$	
Friday/Monday	9/7^1/$_2$	(that is, three "normal" days: Friday/Saturday, Saturday/Sunday, Sunday/Monday)

The way to adjust a standard forward run to a nonstandard one is to find the number of days' adjustment required at the start and end of the standard run, then find the daily swap rate for those days (making allowance for special factors). Finally, add or subtract those individual margins from the standard rate.

NONSTANDARD FORWARD RUNS—EXAMPLES

The following example is essentially a forward forward transaction (see Chapter 10), and applies in a sense to any calculation where we seek forward margins over a date different from spot.

A customer has a forward contract maturing with a bank for value the day after spot. He wants to extend it, say for a month. Suppose that last month he sold the bank NLG for July 18; today is July 15, spot the 17th. He wants to extend to August 17 (today's one-month date). We have the following rates:

NLG/US$	2.3220/30	(Value July 17)
Spot/next	5/3	(July 17/18)
One month	85/75	(July 17–August 17)

Assuming that we are renewing the contract at current market rates (see Chapter 10), the bank sells the NLG back to the customer at 2.3215

(2.3220–0.0005) for value July 18. The bank now needs to know the swap from July 18 to August 17. To do this, it deducts the spot/next (July 17/18) from the one month (July 17/August 17) to give a margin of 80/72. So the bank pays the customer a further premium of 72 points for the swap from July 18 to August 17.

Let's look now at the case where a customer has sold deutsche marks forward to his bank for value March 31 at 2.0120. Today is March 11, spot is March 13. His accounts people say that the deutsche marks will not be paid to him until April 17. As he prefers always to hedge his deutsche mark receivables immediately, he wants to change the maturity date of the existing contract at once. He therefore asks the bank to quote him a rate to adjust the maturity from March 31 to April 17.

Suppose the rates are as follows:

Spot	2.0230/40	(March 13)
One month	110/100	(April 13)
Two months	200/180	(May 13)

We find the swap from March 13 to 31 on a pro rata basis (18 days out of 31) as 64/58; and we work out the swap from March 13 to April 17 as 122/110. We do this interpolating between the one- and two-month swap margins on a pro rata basis, to get 12/10 as the swap from April 13 to April 17 (4/30ths of 200 – 110 and 180 – 100) and adding the result to the one-month margin (see Chapter 10). So the swap margin from March 31 to April 17 is 58/52 (that is, 122/110 minus 64/58). As the bank has already bought these deutsche marks from the customer, it will make a new swap over March 31 (the choice of spot rate on which the contract is to be based being determined according to Chapter 10); it will sell back value March 31, and buy forward value April 17, paying a further premium of 52 points to the customer.

A very common case is when we want a set of standard periods over spot and over tomorrow. We have the following rates for the French franc:

FRF/US$		
	5.0510/20 spot	(September 23)
	5/par tom/next	(September 22/23)
	130/120 one month	(September 23–October 23)
	5/2	(October 22/23)
	270/250 two months	(September 23–November 23)
	6/3	(November 22/23)

We need to find one and two months over tomorrow. Our quote for value tomorrow is 5.0510/25 (remembering that we reverse the tom/next). Our one-month quotation is 130/120 less the adjustment at the far end, of 5/2, plus the adjustment at the near end of 5/par, making 130/118. Our two-month quotation is 270/250 less the far end adjustment of 6/3, plus the near end 5/par, making 269/247. So we have:

FRF/US$ value	September 22	5.0510/25
One month	Sep. 22–Oct. 22	130/118
Two months	Sep. 22–Nov. 22	269/247

HOLIDAYS

These principles have to be used when the effect of holidays has to be taken into account in cross-rates. Suppose we are looking at a FRF/DEM cross-rate calculation. Today is April 6, and the US$/FRF rate is being quoted spot April 8. But the US$/DEM rate is being quoted spot the 9th, as the 8th is a holiday in Germany. We see from the rules of Chapter 8, that the FRF/DEM spot date will be the 9th. So we must adjust the US$/FRF rate, in order to make it appropriate for the 9th, before working out the cross-rate. We therefore have to find the rate for the US$/FRF swap for the 8th against the 9th—which is of course the spot/next swap rate—and apply it to the FRF spot. Suppose we have the following rates:

FRF/US$	spot (8th): 5.0210/20
	spot/next (8th/9th): 15/10
DEM/US$	spot (9th): 2.0815/25

We calculate the outright rate for FRF/US$ value the 9th as 5.0195/5.0210 (5.0210 − 0.0015:5.0220 − 0.0010). We then find the cross-rate for value April 9 by dividing 5.0195 by 2.0825 to get a selling rate for FRF/DEM of 2.4103; Similarly we have 5.0210 divided by 2.0815 for a buying rate of 2.4122 FRF per DEM, value April 9.

Equally, if in the above case it had been France which had been on holiday on the 8th, the DEM/US$ rate would have required adjustment. The rule, therefore, is: *Adjust the currency of the country which is not on holiday, until we get to the first date when both countries are working.*

A parallel procedure has to be applied in the case of the forward margins. Suppose we are again considering FRF/DEM rates, and this time today is May 7, spot May 9 for both currencies. We are considering a one-month deal, which would normally be June 9, but for the fact that France is on holiday that day. We therefore have:

FRF/US$	5.0335/45(value May 9)
	120/100(May 9–June 10)

DEM/US$ 2.0780/90(value May 9)
                300/290(May 9/June 9)
                10/9(June 9/June 10)

We adjust the DEM forward by adding on 10/9 to give us 310/299 for the period May 9 to June 10, giving us a cross of 2.4211/2.4228 and forward margins of 295/318.

The following situation would require some care. We are dealing £/Y and today is February 25:

GBP/US$ 1.7070/80   (February 28)
                30/40   (February 28–March 31)

JPY/US$ 211.50/60   (February 27)
                100/90   (February 27–March 27)

The United Kingdom is on holiday on February 27, and Japan is on holiday March 31. Notice that because the United Kingdom's spot is dealing for the end of the month, the forward rate is also (see Chapter 9). However, the Japanese forward is not: and because Japan is on holiday on March 31, the cross forward should theoretically be rolled into April—but this would contradict the over-month-end rule of Chapter 9. So the cross forward must be dealt for March 30, which means the sterling/dollar forward must be brought backward to March 30 by adjusting for the rate for March 30/31. And the yen must be rolled forward from March 27 by adjusting by the rate for March 27/30. Also, we must adjust the spot yen to February 28. Thus, we have:

GBP/US$ 1.7070/80   (February 28)
                30/40   (February 28–March 31)
                2/3   (March 30–31)

JPY/US$ 211.50/60   (February 27)
                10/5   (February 27–28)
                100/90   (February 27–March 27)
                5/4   (March 27–30)

We proceed first to sort out the spot calculation, for February 28. This is a matter of adjusting the yen rate to 211.40/55 for value February 28. Next we find forward margins for the two currencies for the period February 28 to March 30. We start by adjusting the sterling rate to end on March 30 by removing the rate for the 30th to the 31st of March; thus the sterling forward margin becomes 28/37 for the period February 28–March 30.

Turning now to the yen, we need a forward for the period February 28–March 30. Notice that the original margin was February 27–March 27. We start therefore by adjusting this to run over February 28 by removing the rate for February 27/28, that is, 10/5. This gives us a rate of 90/85 for February 28–March 27. We must then add in the rate at the far end, to extend the margin from March 27 to March 30: adding in the 5/4 quoted for that period gives us a forward rate of 95/89 for the period of February 28–March 30, so we now have:

GBP/US$	1.7070/80	(February 28)
	28/37	(February 28–March 30)
JPY/US$	211.40/55	(February 28)
	95/89	(February 28–March 30)

Bearing in mind that the pound is quoted indirect so that we multiply (see Chapter 8), we have:

GBP/JPY   360.85/361.33 value February 28
              103/74 margin for March 30 over February 28

Fortunately we don't often have to deal with such complex cases. The complexity, though, arises simply from the number of adjustments required—and, in the instance given, the need to be on the alert for the value-date rules—rather than any intrinsic difficulty in the calculation.

The formula required may be set out as follows:

M = cross margin required to be calculated
$S1$ = spot rate for first currency, unadjusted
$S2$ = spot rate for second currency, unadjusted
$F1$ = forward rate for first currency, unadjusted
$F2$ = forward rate for second currency, unadjusted
A = spot adjustment for first currency ⎤
B = spot adjustment for second currency ⎥ any or all
C = forward adjustment for first currency ⎥ of which may
D = forward adjustment for second currency ⎦ be zero

$$M = [(S1 - A) \times (S2 - B)] - [((S1 - A) - (F1 - A + C)) \times ((S2 - B) - (F2 - B + D))]$$

or in words

$$\text{Margin} = \frac{\text{Adjusted spot}}{\text{for first}} \times \frac{\text{Adjusted second}}{\text{spot}}$$

$$- \left[\frac{\text{Adjusted first}}{\text{spot}} - \frac{\text{Adjusted first}}{\text{margin}}\right]$$

$$\times \left[\frac{\text{Adjusted second}}{\text{spot}} - \frac{\text{Adjusted second}}{\text{margin}}\right]$$

This formula is set out in full to match the steps just taken. (For two direct currencies, we would divide rather than multiply.) However, there is a short-cut possible on the right-hand side.

Where we are calculating the cross outright forward, the spot adjustments are made both to the spot rate and to the forward rate. So they cancel each other out. This is equivalent to saying that we could have proceeded as follows: Calculate adjusted spot cross sterling/yen as before; adjust sterling forward as before; take unadjusted spot yen, and apply to it the forward margin adjusted only for the period March 27–30; that is, instead of apply-ing a margin of 95/89 to 211.40/55 we apply 105/94 to 211.50/60. The end result is the same, and this shortcut method is perfectly acceptable, provid-ing we understand why it is correct: The spot adjustment "washes out" because it is applied to both the spot and, in the opposite direction, the forward. Hence the shortcut formula is:

$$\text{Margin} = \frac{\text{Adjusted first}}{\text{spot}} \times \frac{\text{Adjusted second}}{\text{spot}}$$

$$- \left[\frac{\text{Unadjusted first}}{\text{outright}} - \frac{\text{First forward}}{\text{adjustment}} \right]$$

$$\times \left[\frac{\text{Unadjusted second}}{\text{outright}} - \frac{\text{Second forward}}{\text{adjustment}} \right]$$

$$M = [(S1 - A) \times (S2 - B)] - [(S1 - F1 - C) \times (S2 - F2 - D)]$$

PAYMENT TODAY

Depending on time zone, it is sometimes possible to deal for value today, with good value being given on both sides of the deal today. For instance, if at 11:00 AM. London time, a company sells a bank in London U.S. dollars, against payment of sterling, it is possible for both these payments to be made for value that day, as the London clearing does not close until 2:30 and there is a five-hour delay permitting the payment of U.S. dollars on the same day. However, if the same company sold the bank deutsche marks, good value in deutsche marks could not be given for value that day, as the Frankfurt clearing closes at 8:00 AM for value that day. The bank would be able to pay its customer sterling, but would not receive the deutsche marks until the next day.

The practice in these circumstances would be for the bank to allow for the fact that it is "out of funds" overnight, until the deutsche marks arrive on its account in Frankfurt. Because it is left short of sterling, the bank will charge its sterling lending rate; the lending rate will be worked back into its DEM/£ rate to reflect its costs. This is a special case of the formula we worked out in Chapter 10 for working out swaps from two deposit rates. In this case, the deutsche mark rate overnight is zero, because the bank does not have the use of the money. So our original formula:

$$F = S \left[\frac{1 + \dfrac{R2 \times N}{B2 \times 100}}{1 + \dfrac{R1 \times N}{B1 \times 100}} - 1 \right]$$

simplifies to:

$$F = S \left[\frac{R2 \times N}{B2 \times 100} \right]$$

because the bottom line simplifies to one, as $R1 = 0$. The rate to which the "forward" adjustment F is being applied is not the spot rate S, but the rate for tomorrow, call it T. So we can write:

$$\text{Adjustment} = T \times \frac{N}{365} \times \frac{R}{100}$$

where T = rate for value tomorrow; N = number of days that the bank is "out of funds" normally one, but three at weekends, and so on; and R = lending rate for sterling overnight (or three days, etc.).

EFFECT OF WITHHOLDING TAX AND RESERVE REQUIREMENTS

The bulk of this book which is concerned with rates, arbitrage calculations, and the like assumes that the interest rates used are "net accessible interest rates." The word "net" implies "net of all withholding tax and other tax adjustments, and net of all reserve requirement costs"; while the word "accessible" means "generally available to the international market," that is, taking into account the effects if any of exchange control regulations. Sometimes we must adjust for these factors.

The impact of a withholding tax can be summarized in the following formula:

$$\text{Adjustment} = 100 \times \frac{a}{100} \times \frac{b}{100} \times \frac{c}{12} \times \frac{d}{100}$$

where a = interest rate charged on the loan made by the bank to the borrower whose country imposes withholding tax; b = rate of withholding tax; c = number of months between deduction of withholding tax by the borrower's country and the date tax is repaid to the bank; and d = bank's domestic currency interest rate for the period.

As an example, suppose a U.K. bank lends at 10% for one year in June 1991 to a Swiss borrower who is required to deduct withholding tax on the loan at 35%. Swiss withholding tax is repaid at the end of the calendar year for which it is deducted, so the bank is out of funds on the withheld portion for six months (from June 1992 when the interest is paid and tax deducted till January 1993 when the tax is repaid). Suppose that the interest rate (forward forward) for June 1992 to December 1992 is today 13%. Then the adjustment needed is:

$$100 \times \frac{10}{100} \times \frac{35}{100} \times \frac{6}{12} \times \frac{13}{100} = 0.2275\%$$

Another adjustment is needed in domestic dealing to allow for the cost of reserve requirements. In the United States, for instance, loans tend to be made at prime which allows for reserve costs: but on the bid side, when taking funds by the issue of CDs, it may be necessary to adjust the bid rate for reserve costs. In the United Kingdom, domestic sterling loans to a nonbank are often made at LIBOR plus a margin plus reserve asset cost. The formula is complicated by the fact that there may be several kinds of reserve assets, some of which yield interest while others do not. The general formula is:

$$\text{Adjustment} = \frac{A1R1 + A2(R1 - R2) + A3(R1 - R3) \ldots + AN(R1 - RN)}{100 - (A1 + A2 \ldots + AN)}$$

where A1 = amount required to be held interest free (if not permitted to be netted against liabilities); A2 = amount required to be held at first rate of interest; A3 = amount required to be held at second rate of interest; AN = amount required to be held at Nth.MDBR/ rate of interest; R1 = interest rate the bank can earn on liquid assets (say, three-month deposit rate); R2 = rate received on A2; and RN = rate received on AN.

In the U.S. case, the formula simplifies to A1 R1/(100 − A1) since there is only one class of reserve asset, namely balances at the Federal Reserve. Often dealers quote the all-in rate which of course is:

$$R1 = \frac{A1\,R1}{1 - A1} = \frac{R1 - A1\,R1 + A1\,R1}{1 - A1} = \frac{R1}{1 - A1}$$

Hence if a bank issues a CD at 12% with a 3% reserve requirement, the adjustment is 0.371; the all-in-cost is 12.371%. In the United Kingdom and other countries, there are several classes of reserve asset, some of which bear interest. A suitable U.K. formula for reserve asset costs might be:

$$\text{Adjustment} = \frac{A1\,R1 + A2(R1 - R2) + A3(R1 - R3)}{100 - (A1 + A3)}$$

where A1 = interest-free balances held at Bank of England; A2 = secured deposits required to be held with the discount market; A3 = amount of special deposits (if any) called for by the Bank of England R1 = three-month sterling interbank offered rate (that is, the rate on lendings forgone); R2 = interest earned on deposits with the discount market; and R3 = interest earned on special deposits.

Suppose A1 = 0.5%, A2 = 6%, and A3 = 2%, R1 = 12%, R2 = 10%, and R3 = 8%. Then:

$$\text{Adjustment} = \frac{0.5 \times 12 + 6(12 - 10) + 2(12 - 8)}{100 - (6 + 2)} = \frac{6 + 12 + 8}{92} = 0.28\%$$

Notice that in the denominator of this formula, A2 is not included. The reason is that reserve assets are required by the Bank of England to be held against net eligible liabilities. Secured deposits with the discount market are allowed to be netted off before calculating eligible liabilities, which does not apply to interest-free balances or Special Deposits at the Bank. If we think for a moment we see that the bottom line of the formula measures the total amount of assets the bank can use to earn enough to cover the cost of its reserves. If required interest-free balances at the Bank rise, say, to 2½% from ½%, the bank has 2% fewer interest-earning assets. But if the secured deposits requirement rises by 2% to 8%, the bank can raise 2% more eligible liabilities and lend them out in the market, because it can net off the extra 2% of discount market deposits before working out its required reserves. So the general formula has to be applied carefully as regards netting of reserve assets against liabilities.

NEGOTIATION

A bank will often buy, or negotiate, a foreign currency check from one of its customers. The check will then be sent to the country in which it is payable for clearance. For example, a bookseller may sell books by post to a Japanese customer, and receive in return a check drawn on a bank in Tokyo, expressed in Japanese yen. He will sell the check to his bank in exchange for his domestic currency, say dollars; the bank will then send the check to its Tokyo branch or correspondent, who will present it to the Japanese bank for payment.

The bank's foreign exchange rate for this transaction has to reflect-as in the similar case of payment today—the fact that it pays away funds to its domestic customer before being credited with the Japanese yen. The length of time involved in such a transaction depends both on the distance between the bank and the overseas center—Tokyo in this case—and on the efficiency of the domestic clearing system in the overseas center. Hence the foreign exchange rate applied to the transaction must reflect the cost to the bank of being out of funds for the relevant period of time; the adjustment will depend on prevailing interest rates and on the number of days involved. The formula to be applied is that used in Section 4.

13 Artificial Currency Units

In this chapter we explain what an artificial currency unit is. We look at the two most important, the SDR and the ECU, and some other units. Then we look at the EC's green currencies, and at the concept of a trade-weighted exchange rate.

Artificial currency units can be split into three main types. These are standardized units used in international monetary cooperation; units of account used in multinational agreements; and "currency cocktails" consisting of units created out of a number of national currencies.

Standardized units with the aim of helping international transfers have included the gold franc of the Latin Monetary Union which nominally existed among Belgium, France, Greece, Italy, and Switzerland between 1865 and 1921, and the CFA franc of the Communaute Financière Africaine. However, they have been rare.

Units of account have been widely adopted for the purpose of international agreements. Examples include the accounts of the BIS which have been kept in "Swiss gold francs" since 1930; the Telecommunication Convention of 1932 (which adopted the gold franc of the Latin Union as its unit of account); the Convention for the Unification of Certain Rules Regarding Air Transport, 1929 (which adopted the so-called Poincare gold franc); and the EC unit of account (which was defined as equal to the then gold equivalent of one U.S. dollar). The EC unit has now been phased out in favor of the ECU. The chief aim of the artificial currency has been to help the bookkeeping of a multinational organization such as the BIS or EC or (as in the case of the air transport convention) to lay down international standards of value for payments.

Currency cocktails have had a slightly different purpose, namely to protect borrowers or lenders from the effects of currency fluctuations. Hence, they are primarily a post-1945 phenomenon. The first such cocktail was the European Unit of Account which was launched in 1961 with a bond issue for SACOR of Portugal. However, this original version of the EUA was essentially a currency option; the investor had the option of taking payment in one of the 17 currencies of members of the European Payments Union.

Currency baskets consist of an average of a number of currencies. The first basket was the Eurco, but the concept was effectively launched by the International Monetary Fund (IMF) when in June 1974 it revalued its Special Drawing Rights by setting one SDR equal to the sum of specified amounts of selected currencies. As these currencies fluctuated, so the value of the SDR fluctuated. In 1975, the EC followed suit by setting up a new European Unit of Account, which in 1979 was superseded by the European Currency Unit.

SPECIAL DRAWING RIGHTS

The nature of the SDR is twofold: It constitutes an international reserve asset and also an international unit of account. The SDR was created by the First Amendment to the IMF's Articles of Association. This created a Special Drawing Account (SDA) at the IMF. Member states were issued with Special Drawing Rights, permitting them to obtain convertible currencies from the SDA under certain circumstances. Only member states, and certain designated official institutions, may at present legally hold SDRs. During 1970, the first tranche of SDR allocations was made, in three annual installments, totaling SDR 9,500 million approximately; allocations were made according to member states' quotas at the IMF. The valuation of the SDR at this time was defined in terms of the gold value of one U.S. dollar.

However, in 1971 the U.S. dollar was devalued. The SDR did not devalue, and its value was set at SDR 1 = US$ 1.08571. Following the second dollar devaluation of February 1973, its value was set at SDR 1 = US$ 1.20835. The IMF recognized the arrival of a floating exchange rate system and on July 1, 1974 introduced a new SDR, consisting of 16 units of currency, whose values were added together to produce the value of one SDR. This was the so-called standard basket. (See Appendix C for a discussion of the mathematics of currency baskets.) The amounts were chosen to reflect the relative importance in world trade of the currencies involved, and were set so that the value on July 1, 1974 of the new and the old SDR was US$ 1.20835. The method used was to determine the percentage share of the basket to be held by each currency. These percentages are converted into units of currency on the base date. These then constitute the basket.

The composition of the SDR basket was revised effective July 1, 1978. It was announced that this basket would be revised at five-year intervals.

However, effective January 1,1981 the IMF announced a new, simplified basket for the SDR consisting of:

Currency	Amount
US$	0.54
DEM	0.46
£STG	0.0710
FFR	0.74
Y	34

The valuation method for the SDR may be illustrated as follows. We will calculate the value of the SDR against the US$ for convenience; then, to express the SDR against any other currency, we would simply take the exchange rate in the market for that currency against the US$ and calculate the cross rate against the SDR as if it were a normal exchange rate. We assume that there are no holiday complications.

The calculation is as follows: suppose we have the following exchange rates: DEM 2.0950/60 per US$; FFR 5.0750/60; Y 211.20/30; £STG 1 = US$ 2.1540/50. Then our calculation is (using middle rates for convenience):

$$\text{SDR } 1 = \text{US\$ } 0.54 + \frac{.46}{2.0955} + 0.0710 \times 2.1545 + \frac{.74}{5.0755} + \frac{34}{211.25} = \text{US\$ } 1.2192$$

In other words, the SDR is the total dollar value of the "bits" of national currency in the basket. To find the interest rate we would take a weighted average. Suppose we have US$, one month, 11%; DEMs, 6.5%; FFR, 12.5%; Y, 6.5% and STG, 12%. Then we take the weights, which are each currency as a percentage of the US$ value of the SDR; so the dollar's weight is $0.54/1.2192 = 44.3\%$ and the DEM's weight is $0.46/2.0955 \times 1/1.2192 = 18.0\%$, and so on, to get SDR rate $= 0.54/1.2192 \times 11 + 0.46/ 2.0955 \times 1/1.2192 \times 6.5 + 0.0710 \times 2.1545/1.2192 \times 12 + 0.74/5.0755 \times 1/ 1.2192 \times 12.5 + 34/211.25 \times 1/1.2192 \times 6.5 = 9.90\%$.

As we said earlier, private institutions may not legally hold SDRs, although they may deal in instruments linked to the value of the SDR. IMF member states, and certain designated official institutions, include the BIS, the Swiss National Bank, the World Bank, the International Development Association, the Andean Reserve Fund, the Arab Monetary Fund, the East Caribbean Currency Authority, the International Fund for Agricultural Development, and the Nordic Investment Bank are allowed to hold SDRs. The BIS itself has taken deposits denominated in SDRs from the IMF: these represented part of the profits derived from the sale of the IMF's gold, and were deposited pending their disbursement as loans to low-income developing countries. Official holders of SDRs are also permitted to use SDRs to obtain convertible currencies via the fund's Special Drawing Account and to transfer SDRs among themselves in settlement of financial obligations. They may use SDRs in loans, and in the provision of security for the performance of financial obligations, by means of either a pledge of SDRs or an agreement for transfer and retransfer of SDRs. In 1979, they were allowed to make SDR swaps among themselves and to trade in forward SDRs. The IMF must be notified of such deals as it handles the bookkeeping for the transaction.

These changes have been introduced by the IMF as part of its plans to make the SDR more widely used in international finance; the simplification of the basket to five currencies was also a part of this process. Accordingly, private institutions have become more involved in the SDR market (although in point of fact, this should be referred to as "the market for currency instruments index-linked to the SDR" since the banks cannot legally own SDRs). For example, since 1975, and particularly since the introduction of the simplified basket in 1981, a market in deposits linked to the SDR has existed.

The mechanics are as follows: A company wanting to make an SDR-linked deposit would deposit, say, US$ with a bank. These would be valued in terms of SDRs at a specified exchange rate, either a rate quoted by the bank, or the official IMF rate. On maturity of the deposit, the US$ equivalent of the SDR deposit would be calculated and repaid to the customer together with interest.

Suppose the customer asks the bank for a three-month SDR price for SDR 1 million; payment to be made in US$. The bank has the following rates:

US$/DEM	2.2525/35	US$	three-month bid 14¼
JPY	226.50/60	DEM	three-month bid 9½
FRF	5.9810/30	JPY	three-month bid 6⅛
£STG	1.8110/20	FRF	three-month bid 15½
		£STG	three-month bid 13½

First, using the method set out above, the bank works out the spot rate for SDRs, that is, SDR 1 = US$ 1.1467. Then it works out the interest rate by taking a weighted average to get 12.398%, say, 12⅜%. An alternative method is to work out the three-month forward SDR (in the same way as the spot, but using outrights). Then the forward margin can be used, combined with the US$ rate, to "manufacture" the SDR rate just as for any currency, by using the formula of Figure 10.6. Many banks quote the SDR rate as:

$$\text{SDR rate} = \left[\left(1 + \left(\frac{E \times D}{360} + 100 \right) \right) \times \frac{S}{F} - 1 \right] \times \frac{360}{D}$$

where D = number of days; E = Eurodollar offered rate; S = spot SDR; and F = forward SDR. This equates to the formula of Figure 10.6.

The company wishes to deposit SDR 1 million; it pays US$1,146,700 to the bank, which records that it owes the customer the US$ equivalent of SDR 1 million. The term of the deposit is three months (90 days) and the rate of interest 12⅜%. The SDR (and the ECU) are dealt on a 360-day basis.

Then the interest rate due is the dollar equivalent of SDR30,937.50, and at maturity the bank must repay the dollar equivalent of SDR1,030,937.50; if the exchange rate at maturity is SDR1 = US$1.2565/75, the dollar amount will be US$1,295,372.97. From the customer's point of view the operation is exactly the same as that of buying any other currency; instead of making a DEM deposit, he is making one in SDRs. The advantage to him is simply that the SDR being a composite of five currencies, will probably be more stable than any one individual currency. Movements in its components will probably tend to offset one another. However, the story is not quite so simple for the bank, as it has to hedge its SDR risk and is unable to do so directly, unless it can find a borrower of SDRs. It will have to swap the dollars it receives into the component currencies of the SDR; so each SDR deal involves at least four exchange swap and deposit deals.

Another fairly long-standing SDR-based market has been in the Eurobond market, where certain borrowers, particularly from Scandinavia, have on occasion issued bonds whose repayment value is linked to the SDR. The first such issue was made by Alusuisse in 1975. The first Eurocurrency credit with a tranche denominated in SDRs was made on behalf of the Kingdom of Sweden in 1981. These markets, however, are beyond our scope.

The first CD denominated in SDRs was issued by Chemical Bank in June 1980, and in January 1981 a group of seven banks in London announced that they would issue and trade in secondary SDR CDs.

A clearing system for SDR-linked deposits has been established by Morgan Guaranty's Brussels branch, along the lines of the Euroclear bond clearing organization managed by the same firm. The accounts involved are maintained in Brussels on a memorandum basis only, and have their counterpart in deposits in any one of the countries where a component currency of the SDR is the lawful currency. Thus they are subject in principle to Belgian law and to the law of the country where the counterpart deposit is located.

This arrangement shows some of the problems that may arise from SDR-linked deposits. Another problem is the possibility of a change in the composition of the SDR; this has already happened three times in seven years. Normal arrangements in the SDR market are that if this happens, existing deposits would be valued on maturity on the basis of the SDR composition existing when the deposit was placed. Subsequent renewals would take place on the basis of the new basket.

The SDR-linked market is still developing, and conditions are not so standardized as in other markets; accordingly they may vary widely as a result of negotiation between the parties.

EUROPEAN CURRENCY UNIT

The European Currency Unit (ECU) has its origin in the European Communities (EC) unit of account (u.a.). The Treaty of Rome created the u.a. as a unit of account for EC institutions. It was then defined as equal to 0.88867088 grams of 0.9 fine gold, the official par value of the U.S. dollar. Following successive devaluations of the U.S. dollar, the emergence of floating currencies, and the creation of the SDR basket concept, the EC decided to introduce a basket unit of account for its own accounting. This was known as the European Unit of Account (EUA) (not to be confused with the earlier, private European Unit of Account). It was defined as equal to the sum of the following amounts: FBC 3.66 + LuxFr 0.14 + HFL 0.286 + DKK 0.217 + DEM 0.828 + ITL 109 + FRF 1.15 + £STG 0.0885 + IEP 0.00759. The EUA was introduced first in 1975 in respect of the Lome Convention on development aid, and the European Investment Bank's balance sheet. It was subsequently introduced in respect of the European Coal and Steel Community's operational budget (1976), the General Budget of the European Communities (1978), and customs matters (1979).

The European Currency Unit was created in 1978 with a value identical to that of the European Unit of Account, and an identical composition (but with a revision clause permitting changes, unlike the EUA). It took over all the existing functions of the EUA and was also introduced as the unit of account for the European Monetary System (see Chapter 4), where it took over from the European Monetary Unit of Account, a slightly different unit of account used for the bookkeeping of the European Monetary Cooperation Fund previously. Under the European Monetary System, EC members' currencies are linked to a central rate defined in terms of the ECU. (See Appendix 3 on the mathematics of currency basket parities.)

The ECU as an official currency was born on December 18th, 1978, as part of the setting up of the European Monetary System (EMS) of linked exchange rates by members of the European Communities (EC). The EC regulation which created it defines the ECU as a "basket of members' currencies," that is the sum of fixed amounts of each of the members' currency. The first definition of the amounts fixed the makeup of the ECU from its beginnings to the first revision, which took place on September 17, 1984, when the Greek drachma was included, Greece having joined the EC in the interim. In September 1989, the basket was revised again to accommodate two new members, Spain and Portugal. Table 13.1 below shows the effect of the changes.

Revision of the amounts of currency in the basket usually takes place every 5 years, so the next revision will be due in September 1994, subject to the outcome of any discussions regarding economic and monetary union. Between revision dates, changes can be made if the weight of one of the currencies has changed by more than 25%.

The value of the ECU in U.S. dollars is found by taking the dollar value of 0.828 deutsche marks, adding to it the value of 0.0885 pounds sterling, and so on. The EEC provides an official value each day using central-bank-provided exchange rates at 2:30 PM; the result is quoted on Reuters Monitor page FXEZ. As well as being the official unit of account for all EEC transactions, the ECU also plays a key role in the European Monetary System (EMS), since EMS

Table 13.1   ECU Composition

	1979–84	1984–89	Since 1989
Deutsche mark	0.82800	0.71900	0.6242
£ Sterling	0.08850	0.08780	0.08784
French franc	1.15000	1.31000	1.332
Italian lira	109.00000	140.00000	151.8
Dutch guilder	0.28600	0.25600	0.2198
Belgian franc	3.66000	3.71000	3.301
Luxembourg franc	0.14000	0.14000	0.13
Danish Krone	0.27700	0.21900	0.1976
Irish punt	0.00759	0.00871	0.00855
Greek drachma	0	1.15000	1.44
Spanish peseta	0	0	6.885
Portuguese escudo	0	0	1.393

members' exchange rates are defined in terms of a "central rate" fixing their currency in terms of ECU (see Chapter 4).

Official ECUs can only be held by the central banks of the EEC and other central banks who have been given permission. Private ECUs are traded like any other currency; in the Bank of England's 1986 foreign exchange survey, ECU trading was reported at around $900 million daily. Major commercial banks provide continuous quotes for the ECU (normally they have computer systems for calculating the ECU value from the currency rates held in their systems) and these can be seen on the appropriate Reuters/Telerate screens. ECU lending by banks in the BIS reporting area grew from ECU 14 billion in 1983 to ECU 90 billion in 1988. ECU certificates of deposit have also been issued and there is an active and important ECU bond market. The British government, for example, issued ECU 2.5 billion of gilts (gilt-edged bonds, so-called because of their high quality) in February 1991 and the French government also issues regularly in the ECU market as do Italy.

An ECU clearing system (see Chapter 21) is operated by the Bank for International Settlements in conjunction with the ECU Banking Association which has about 85 members worldwide; all ECU transactions are cleared daily through this system. ECU certificates of deposit have also been issued.

Until recently, one problem with trading private ECUs was that the Deutsche Bundesbank defined the ECU as an index-linked unit of account, the use of which is banned in Germany (because of past inflationary excesses in the 1930s): the restrictions were revoked only in June 1987.

OTHER CURRENCY UNITS

A wide range of other currency units have been devised on various occasions for various purposes. They include: Arab dinar, Arcru, Asian Monetary Unit,

Barclays B-Unit, Eurco, European Currency Unit (private, non-EEC version also known as the European Monetary Unit), European Unit of Account, Gold francs, and Islamic dinars.

The Arab Accounting Dinar is used in the accounts of the Arab Monetary Fund. The Arcru is a privately developed currency unit (Arcru stands for Arab Currency Related Unit) which is no longer widely used. The Asian Monetary Unit is used in the Asian Clearing Union that settles payments imbalances among Bangladesh, Burma, India, Iran, Nepal, Pakistan, and Sri Lanka. The Barclays B-Unit was developed by Barclays Bank International to facilitate international trade. It is not now used.

The Eurco or European Composite Unit was introduced in 1973 in a loan to the European Investment Bank. It was defined as the sum of DEM 0.9, FRF 1.2, HFL 0.35, FBC 4.5, DKK 0.2, ITL 80, IEP 0.005, STG 0.075, and LuxFr 0.5. In this issue, interest was payable in the currency chosen by the borrower, while principal was repayable in the currency chosen by the lender. The ECU in its private form was introduced in 1970. It sets up fixed exchange rates among the currencies of the six member states of the EEC at that time (ECU 1 = DEM 3.2225). Thus, it set up a currency option arrangement rather than a true unit of account. Since the investor could ask for repayment of principal in the strongest of the six currencies, the concept was very attractive to lenders, but less so to borrowers. It was also used under the title European Monetary Unit.

The European Monetary Unit of Account was used in the bookkeeping of the European Monetary Cooperation Fund before the introduction of the European Currency Unit. One EMUA was defined as equal to DEM 3.21978, FBC 48.6572, DKK 7.57831, FRF 5.55419, and HFL 3.35507. It was designed to guarantee the exchange value of outstanding balances in the fund.

The European Unit of Account, in its private version, was introduced in 1963 for a bond issue by the Portuguese company SACOR. The initial formula (which was changed subsequently in various ways for various issues) was that the EUA was set equal to the then gold value of the U.S. dollar, 0.88867088 grams of fine gold. The bond contract defined 17 reference currencies (those of the members of the then European Payments Union), whose currencies in turn had gold par values. Thus the cross rates among the 17 reference currencies were determined by their gold par values. The EUA's gold value would only change if (1) all reference currencies had changed in the same direction; and (2) at least two-thirds had changed in the same direction. These complex rules ensured that no change in the EUA's gold value took place between 1961 and 1971 when the U.S. dollar devalued against gold. The EUA was then linked to the EMUA (see above) and then, following the launch of the European Currency Unit, to the latter unit. The EUA was set equal to ECU 1.1972258. This value of the EUA in terms of the ECU will remain constant until (1) all currencies of the ECU which are in the EMS (at the time of writing, all the EC currencies other than the Portuguese escudo and the Greek drachma) change their central rates (par values) against the ECU; and

(2) a majority of such changes are in one direction. If both these conditions are satisfied, the value of the EUA to the ECU will be changed in the same direction as the majority have changed, to the extent of the smallest percentage change of this majority group. Detailed provisions have also been made in bond issues using the EUA in the event of reference currencies not having clearly defined values and so forth.

Gold francs have been used as units of account for many years, and a number of different varieties exist. Perhaps the first was that of the Latin Monetary Union which linked certain European countries between 1865 and 1921. This gold franc was subsequently adopted as the basis for the Telecommunication Convention of 1932. Its value was defined as 10/31 of a gram of gold 0.900 fine. A second gold franc, known also as the Poincare franc, was used in the Convention for the Unification of Certain Rules Regarding Air Transport of 1929 and related conventions; it was defined as equal to 65 1/2 milligrams of gold 0.900 fine. (This was replaced by the SDR under the Montreal Protocol of 1975.) The statutes of the Bank for International Settlements provide that the authorized capital of the bank shall be 500 million Swiss gold francs, equivalent to 145,161,280.32 grams fine gold; and the annual accounts of the BIS are maintained in these gold francs.

GREEN CURRENCIES

Reference is occasionally made to "green" currencies. These are the notional rates of exchange used by the EEC in the management of its Common Agricultural Policy. As such, they cannot be dealt in directly. However, they do impinge on the foreign exchange operations of corporations involved in EEC agriculture.

In 1962, the EEC issued its Regulation 129/62 setting up a unit of account for agricultural purposes. Its value was declared equal to 0.88867088 grams of fine gold-equivalent to US$1 at the time. This gave rates of exchange (Green rates) of u.a.1 = DEM 4.0 = FRF 4.93706, for example. Hence, when the EEC set a price of u.a. 212.30 per ton for white sugar, this was equivalent to DEM 849.20 and FRF 1048.14.

However, in 1969, the French franc devalued, changing its parity against gold so that its value against the unit of account moved to FRF 5.55419. This would have resulted in a rise in the price of white sugar to $212.30 \times 5.55419 = 1179.15$, a rise of 12.6% which would have been paralleled in all other agricultural commodities. The inflationary effects of this were unacceptable to the French government, which arranged to postpone the devaluation of the Green rate.

This meant, however, that white sugar sold in France still for FRF 1048.14: if exported to Germany, the French exporter would receive DEM 849.20, for which his bank would give him FFR 1179.15. It was necessary to prevent cheap French exports from swamping the German market. The EEC decided to place a tax on French exports to the rest of the EEC, and to subsidize French imports from the EEC. These taxes and subsidies were referred to as Monetary Compensatory Amounts, or MCAs.

The move to floating exchange rates during 1971 through 1973 forced the EEC to move toward a corresponding system of floating MCAs to offset exchange rate movements. This came in a series of regulations of which the most notable were 974/71, providing for variable MCAs, and 509/73, providing for a weekly variation in MCAs to cope with the floating of sterling. By this stage, telegrams from the EEC Commission to member states, setting out new MCAs, averaged 40 to 50 feet in length.

In order to simplify matters, a new system was devised in June 1973 (Regulation 1463/74). The unit of account on which the system depended was no longer linked to the U.S. dollar but to the central rates of the "joint float" currencies of the EEC. This meant that for member currencies, MCAs were fixed provided central rates were unchanged, even if the joint float varied against the dollar. For nonmember currencies, such as sterling, variable MCAs continued in force.

Following the entry into force of the European Monetary System (see Chapter 4) on March 12, 1979, the unit of account laid down for calculating agricultural prices was the ECU. The EEC wanted to maintain the common level of prices. So it was decided that the price levels in old units of account would be multiplied by an adjustment coefficient. This factor came to 1.208953.

Summing up simply, we can say that

Green rate of exchange + MCA = Market rate of exchange

It follows that since firms actually trade in market rates of exchange on a daily basis, and MCAs are (at present) fixed on the basis of average rates of exchange during the previous week, there is some scope for profitable activity by firms able to forecast the likely level of the MCA.

CALCULATION OF TRADE-WEIGHTED EXCHANGE RATES (EFFECTIVE EXCHANGE RATES)

While not strictly an artificial currency unit, the calculation of a trade-weighted index for a currency is related to the concept and so is included here. Before the advent of floating rates, a devaluation or revaluation of a currency occurred against all other currencies simultaneously. A 5% revaluation of the deutsche mark against the U.S. dollar implied a 5% revaluation against the French franc, and so on. With the advent of floating rates, however, the impact of a 5% revaluation against the U.S. dollar coupled with a 2½% devaluation against the Swiss franc is not clear-cut. Hence attempts were made to take account of the average change of a currency against all others.

A 20% depreciation of the Argentine Austral against the deutsche mark is less important to Germany than a 10% depreciation of the French franc, since France is a much more important trading partner for Germany than Argentina. So the various currencies' changes need to be weighted by taking account of the share of a country's trade held by a partner currency.

Such a trade-weighted index may be called a "simple average" trade weighted index. Suppose we have four countries, A, B, C, and D. Suppose we are constructing a trade-weighted index for A and that A's exports and imports are conducted with B, C, and D in the following proportions: B, 50%; C, 30%; D, 20%. Suppose in Period 1 we have the following exchange rates for one unit of A's currency against the others: A1 = B2 = C2.5 = D3. Suppose in Period 2 A revalues against B by 10%, devalues against C by 20%, and revalues against D by 15%. Then we can weight the percentage changes and add them: +10% × 0.5 − 20% × 0.3 + 15% × 0.2. The weighted change is 2%: so if we express the index for Period 1 as 100, that for Period 2 is 102.

However, this simple index takes no account of the effects of the exchange rate on changes in third-country trade. Thus, because A has devalued against C by 20%, it is now able to encroach on C's trade with B, and so on. To take full account of these effects requires a matrix of cross-elasticities in international trade, and this is the approach adopted by the IMF in its Multilateral Exchange Rate Model and by the U.K. Treasury in its index for sterling.

The exact method of calculation is complex and varies from country to country. A widely used index is that calculated by Morgan Guaranty Trust Co. of New York which is a geometric index of exchange rates weighted by proportions of trade. Morgan also calculates a "real" effective exchange rate. This makes an adjustment to take account of inflation to attain the "real" effective exchange rate. Suppose that taking 1977 as a base, the U.S. dollar has appreciated in effective terms from 100 to 107.5. Suppose that inflation over this period has been 22.5%: the "inflation-adjusted" or "real" effective index will total 130. The Japanese yen may have appreciated in effective terms over the same period by 12%, but if inflation in Japan over that period has been only 15%, the real effective exchange rate index will have risen only to 127. A difficulty in interpretation here is the choice of correct index to apply: export prices, domestic retail prices, or wholesale prices, for example. The inflation-adjusted index produced by Morgan Guaranty uses wholesale prices of non-food manufacturers.

PART 4 Derivatives

14 Financial Futures

THE MARKETS

In this section of the book, we will look at the *derivative markets*. Derivatives is a term which is usually applied to futures, options, and interest rate and currency swaps. These are markets that were "derived" from other markets: the first financial futures contracts were derived from the foreign exchange market, interest rate swaps were derived from the Eurobond market, and so on. In general, the derivatives markets have shown very rapid growth during the 1980s. For example, in 1980 the annual trading volume of interest rate futures contracts was 12 million. By 1989, that had grown to over 200 million. In 1980, the share of futures activity accounted for by the United States

257

was 100%: by 1989, the figure was 60%, as the market had begun to move to a global footing. Interest rate and currency swaps also grew during the decade, from a volume of perhaps $1 to 2 billion of currency swaps outstanding in 1980 (when interest rate swaps did not exist) to over $1000 billion in 1989. Options, particularly options traded over-the-counter (that is, outside organized exchanges) also grew strongly and by 1989 the BIS estimated daily foreign exchange option trading at $22 billion, of which 80% was OTC; during that year, as a whole, 40 million contracts for interest rate options or options on interest rate futures were traded on organized exchanges.

Of these markets, the first to develop was that for financial futures, which now make up a very important segment of the worldwide financial markets. Futures contracts are standardized agreements to buy or sell a specific commodity at a specific time and place in the future, at a price established through open outcry in a central, regulated marketplace. The two key components of a futures contract are that the agreement is standardized and that price is the only variable. The origins of such contracts go back to Chicago in the nineteenth century, when futures contracts on grain were first developed. (Some would argue they go back to the Dutch tulip mania of 1634).

A financial futures contract is a contract to deliver, or take delivery of, a financial instrument at a future date. For example, a Treasury bill futures contract is a contract to deliver, or take delivery of, a Treasury bill on a specified date. In some cases, where delivery is difficult, the contract may be settled by a cash payment, for example, Eurodollar futures contracts.

Let us take a simple example. I want to invest $100,000 in a U.S. Treasury bond for delivery in June. I can wait until June—taking the risk that the price might move against me—or I can buy a futures contract. I go to the futures market and see that the price for June 15 delivery is 92: if I were to settle today, I would have to pay $92,000. I buy one contract. I do not pay for the bonds today. Instead, I put up a margin deposit.

The amount of this margin is fixed by the Exchange at $4500 per contract. So I put up $4500 on deposit with my futures broker. The deposit is evidence of my good faith that I will fulfill my obligation to take delivery of the bonds in June. As bond prices vary, the value of my futures contract varies. I have a profit or loss on my purchase. If losses erode the value of my margin, my broker will call on me to put up extra margin. Conversely, if I earn profits, I will get back some margin. The aim is to keep the margin stable in line with the value of my obligation.

When the contract comes to settlement, suppose I decide to take delivery of the bonds. A settlement price for the bonds is fixed. Say that price is 105. Then I must pay $105,000 for my bonds; but on that settlement day, my futures contract is also worth $105,000. So I have a $13,000 profit on the futures contract which offsets the rise in price of the bonds. The futures contract has served to fix my bond purchase price.

The main attraction of futures in risk management is their leverage, or gearing in U.K. terminology. Suppose a trader deliberately takes a position, either as a straightforward speculation, or as an arbitrage. The simplest case is the trader who wants to back his judgment on the outlook for interest rates or currencies. The essential difference between doing this in the futures market and doing it in the "cash market" is that in the futures market, one can trade on margin. This gives a high degree of leverage. This leverage lets the speculator make large profits compared with the amount of margin money committed.

Suppose on December 1, 1991, a trader thinks interest rates will rise in the next few months, causing bond prices to fall. He deposits the required margin (say, $4500 per contract) with his broker. He sells two Treasury bond futures contracts at 67-00. Two weeks later, interest rates have risen. Prices for Treasury bond futures contracts have dropped to 66-08. The trader closes his position by buying two bond futures contracts. He makes a profit of $750 on each contract. The $1500 profit on the $8000 margin is a return of over 18% during the two weeks, before deducting commission and exchange fees. Leverage has increased his returns.

This leverage works both ways, making it possible to lose more money than originally invested. Because of this, prices are marked to market on a daily basis by the exchanges. Settlement is made daily through the clearing corporation. Thus, if prices move against an investor, his account is debited.

If the debits reduce the money in the margin account below the prescribed "maintenance" level, additional margin ("variation margin") must be posted to bring it back up to the initial margin level. Hence the investor quickly feels the effect of any weakening in his position, through margin calls. It is this margin call system which has generally protected the exchanges and their member firms from losses via investor default: although investors are highly leveraged, the margin maintenance system quickly brings to light any potential problems.

Another attractive feature for those who wish to trade in the major futures markets for its own sake is that they are very liquid. Average daily trading volume on the Chicago Board of Trade Treasury bond futures contract in 1990 was over 300,000 contracts for a face value of $30 billion. One could shift a significant volume in this market without making a major impact. In other instruments, this is less true. Many futures contracts have not proved successful, and daily volume is negligible. In this case, if one wishes to trade in a particular instrument which is not readily available, one is reduced to trading in a proxy instrument, and making allowances by means of appropriate weighting factors, considered next.

Table 14.1 gives the date of introduction of major contracts, Table 14.2 shows the main activity in 1990. As will be seen, the development of financial futures is recent. The International Monetary Market in Chicago opened futures trading in seven foreign currencies in May 1972. The first interest rate futures contract was introduced in October 1975, but the first really successful interest rates futures contract was the 91-day Treasury Bill contract introduced by the IMM in January 1976, followed in August 1977 by the Chicago Board of Trade (CBOT) futures contracts on U.S. Treasury Bonds.

Table 14.1   Date of Introduction of Some of the Major Futures Contracts

1972	IMM:	Foreign exchange
1974	IMM,Comex:	Gold
1975	CBOT:	GNMA
1976	IMM:	Treasury bill
1977	CBOT:	Treasury bond
	CBOT:	90-day commercial paper
1978	Sydney:	Gold futures
1979	Sydney:	Bank bill futures
	CBOT:	US Treasury notes
1980	IMM:	CD
	Sydney:	A$ futures
1981	IMM:	Eurodollar
1982	LIFFE:	£, DM, SFR, Yen
	LIFFE:	Euro$, Long gilt, 3-month sterling deposits
	CME:	S&P 500
1983	Sydney:	All Ordinaries Share Price Index
1984	LIFFE:	FT-SE 100, UST-bonds
	Sydney:	Australian Treasury bonds
1985	Tokyo SE:	JGB futures
1986	MATIF:	French government bonds
	SIMEX:	Nikkei-DJ futures
1988	Tokyo SE:	TOPIX futures
	Osaka SE:	Nikkei-225 futures
	LIFFE:	Bund future
1989	TIFFE:	Euroyen, yen/$
	LIFFE:	Bund option, Euro-DM LIBOR future
1990	DTB:	Bund future, DAX future, DAX options
1991	LIFFE:	Italian government bond futures
	MATIF:	Italian government bond futures

In September 1982, the London International Financial Futures Exchanges (LIFFE) opened for business. It started with two contracts, for Eurodollars and the pound sterling, but by early December the initial complement of seven contracts had all been introduced: short sterling interest rates; long gilt edged government securities; Swiss franc, Japanese yen, and deutsch mark futures. More recently LIFFE has introduced a successful futures contract based on German government bonds (Bunds), following this up in April 1989 with a future based on DEM LIBOR and an option on the Bund future. By June 1989, DEM-denominated contracts accounted for 21% of LIFFE's volume, with almost 490,000 contracts changing hands during the month. Indeed, in the first half of 1989, over 40% of LIFFE's volume was

Table 14.2   Top Futures Contracts 1990

	Million Contracts Traded	Exchange
U.S. T-bond	75.5	CBOT
Euro$	34.7	CME
Euroyen	20.8	TIFFE
JGB	16.3	TSE
Notionnel	16.0	MATIF
Nikkei225	13.6	Osaka
S&P500	12.1	CME
Bund	9.6	LIFFE
DEM	9.2	CME
3 mo. Sterling	8.4	LIFFE
JPY	7.4	CME
CHF	6.5	CME
U.S. T-note	6.0	CBOT
Long gilt	5.6	LIFFE
90-day bank bills	5.0	Sydney

Top Futures Exchanges 1990 (m. contracts)

CBOT	154.2
CME	103.0
NYMEX	42.5
LIFFE	34.2
MATIF	28.6
OSAKA	22.8
TSE	22.7
TIFFE	20.9
COMEX	18.3
TOCOM	14.8

Source: Futures & Options World, February 1991.

non-sterling based, emphasizing the international nature of the London futures market. In July 1989 LIFFE underwent a reorganization whereby a
holding company—LIFFE (Holdings) PLC—was set up to take on functions
that are not part of LIFFE's statutory activity as a recognized exchange. Seats
on the Exchange were traded for shares in the new holding company, to which
are attached trading permits in the exchange (see Table 14.3).

The Tokyo futures market was established in October 1985. But in an
astonishing explosion of trading, volume in the Japanese government bond
futures contract on the Tokyo futures exchange after only 10 months
exceeded that in the U.S. Treasury Bond contract. Daily trading in the
Japanese contract reached an average of $32.8 billion in August 1986, com-
pared with $19.7 billion in U.S. Bond contracts. The market is housed in the

Table 14.3   LIFFE Trading Volumes

	Futures	Options
1982	240,150	–
1983	1,365,630	–
1984	2,581,579	–
1985	3,372,915	169,950
1986	6,426,718	479,789
1987	12,426,718	1,174,031
1988	13,868,743	1,781,198
1989	21,660,610	2,178,453
1990	29,798,671	4,371,292

Source: LIFFE.

Tokyo stock exchange building and is open from 9 to 11 AM and from 1 to 3 PM. As always, Japan is unique. There is no pit on the floor of an exchange, no crowd of jostling traders. Most of the people in the room are seated at computer terminals. The futures exchange at its foundation had to blend with the existing methods of the Tokyo market. This meant that there must be a continuing role for Saitori (brown-jacket men). The Saitori match buy and sell orders. They do not take positions themselves. Thus, futures brokers placing orders, or wishing to trade their own book, must telephone the Saitori allotted to them to place the order via the terminal, and wait word of execution from the Saitori.

In September 1988, the Tokyo Stock Exchange introduced futures based on its TOPIX equity index, and its Osaka counterpart introduced a contract on the Nikkei 225 equity index. In June 1989, the Tokyo International Financial Futures Exchange (TIFFE) opened for business, trading euroyen and eurodollar deposit contracts as well as a yen/dollar contract. The former has been successful—for example, on January 18 1990 78,712 contracts changed hands—but the yen/dollar future's volume has been negligible.

The next important financial futures exchange to open after Tokyo was in France, where in February 1986 the Marché à terme des instruments financiers (MATIF) was opened. Initially an average of 350, perhaps 400 contracts per day was expected for its inaugural contract, a 10-year government long bond. But within the first week, the daily trading average was 3400 contracts. The MATIF has gone on to establish itself as a serious challenger to LIFFE as a center for derivatives trading in Europe, though it has suffered the odd problem, such as the FFR250 million lost by the state-owned nuclear fuels company, Cogema, on the MATIF and in related options trading. A contract on French Treasury bills was introduced in 1986, which developed poorly, owing to the lack of liquidity in the secondary cash market, but in September 1988 the MATIF successfully introduced a contract on PIBOR (Paris Inter-Bank Offered Rate) and, in the spring of 1989, a deutsche mark deposit contract to compete with LIFFE.

Other important financial futures exchanges operate in Toronto, Singapore, Hong Kong, and Sydney. A futures and options exchange in Denmark opened in September 1988. In November 1990, after many delays caused by regulatory issues and the general conservatism of German financial circles, the Deutsche Terminborse (DTB) opened for business to trade DAX futures and a Bund future (as well as options on selected German equities).

Global expansion of the futures and options markets seems likely to continue. Futures and options markets have spread as far afield as Brazil and also Chile where a futures contract on the peso has been put in place. (For countries with limited foreign exchange reserves, a futures contract on the currency which can be cash-settled in domestic currency provides a useful method of hedging exchange rate risk without draining foreign exchange reserves).

A key issue is the battle between traditional "open outcry" (whereby prices are set by an auction in a "pit" where traders shout bids and offers) and the new technology. The latter is represented by Globex, a joint venture between Reuters, the Chicago Mercantile Exchange, the Chicago Board of Trade and MATIF, and also by LIFFE's screen-based trading system. This is the Automated Pit Trading System (APT), which aims to emulate the features of open outcry pit trading. LIFFE, the CBOT and the CME are exploring links between the three electronic systems, though the scale and complexity of the Globex project has delayed its implementation.

Originally developed for use outside the Exchange's normal working hours, the APT system is also being used during trading hours for the re-launched LIFFE contract on Japanese Government Bonds (JGBs). The APT system has been successful, trading just under 1 million contracts in the first year of operation; it traded over 31,000 contracts in October 1990 when sterling entered the ERM after normal pit trading hours. The DTB also has a screen trading system which appears to work quite well.

ORGANIZATION OF THE MARKETS

Before discussing the financial futures contracts in more detail, let's review the organization of the markets. Since the major markets today are generally floor-traded rather than computer-traded, the discussion will tend to concentrate on the traditional style of futures market.

The following description, in outline, applies to the CBOT, the IMM, and other similar institutions. Essentially, the membership of the market can be divided into two categories: brokers and locals. Brokers trade for nonmember customers and for other members. Locals trade for themselves. The locals are essential for the liquidity of the market. They are usually involved in three types of trading.

1. *Position traders.* They will take a position, sometimes very large, and keep it until something causes them to change their mind. Position

traders are relatively long-term traders, particularly compared to scalpers.

2. *Scalpers.* These are floor traders who are constantly buying and selling. Often, scalpers keep positions for only a matter of minutes or seconds. Their contribution to the market is continuous moment-by-moment liquidity.

3. *Spreaders.* They concern themselves with the relative value of one contract month against another. They are arbitraging one period against another. Their contribution to the market is to give liquidity to the more distant periods.

The other main source of liquidity is the very large number of small, individual speculators who trade on the exchange through the brokers. Although each may trade only one or two contracts, there are many thousands trading on the exchange, who again contribute to liquidity.

Trading takes place in the pits during specific hours. There is a separate trading area for each contract, so there is a bond pit, a Eurodollar pit, and so on. Orders are received on the trading floor by telephone or telex, and passed to the broker in the pit. Traders shout out the quantity and the price at which they want to buy or sell. They also use standard hand signals, especially when trading is noisy. The process is shown in Figure 14.1.

By the close of each day's trading, every member submits a trade confirmation record for every deal done on behalf of the firm or its customers. Every one of these trades must be "cleared," that is, verified and guaranteed, by the clearing-house. The clearing-house settles the account of each member firm at the end of the trading day. It matches each of the day's purchases and sales. It collects all losses and pays all profits. Its contribution to the safety of the market is to be the buyer from every seller and the seller to every buyer. A sale of Treasury bill contracts by A to B becomes a sale (by A) to the clearing-house and a purchase (by B) from the clearing-house.

This is a key safeguard for users of the exchanges. There is no need to worry who has taken the other side of the trade. The exchange clearing-house itself guarantees the performance of every trade because it is the exchange itself which takes the opposite side to every contract. However, the exchange will not deal directly with public customers, but only with its clearing members.

In effect, the exchange does business only with its clearing members and the clearing members do business with all others. For example, the exchange sets margins for its clearing members and its clearing members in turn set margins for their customers. Thus, customer margins flow directly to the clearing member who, in turn, must settle with the exchange at the close of business each day. Each day the exchange requires a cash settlement from the clearing member based on the day's market positions and activity. This is regardless of the status of the member's customer margin money. A clearing member might let a customer be short of margin for a period of time, but

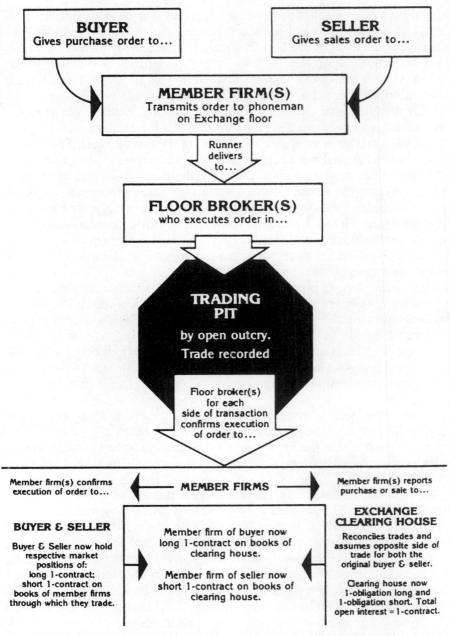

Figure 14.1 Order execution process (Adapted from "Trading in Tomorrows," IMM, Chicago, p. 11).

this would have to be funded at its own expense. The clearing-house would not allow a clearing member to be undermargined overnight. Also, the exchange will supervise the financial status of its clearing members. So far, these arrangements appear to have been successful in preventing major problems; both the CBOT and the IMM state that there has never been a financial loss due to default on a futures contract on their exchanges.

With the growth of electronic trading, it may be useful to compare the traditional trading system described above with the electronic markets. A floor-traded market is a pure auction from the open to the close. Trades take place when the highest bid meets the lowest offer. In theory, when two orders at the same price come to market, the first order to reach the pit gets priority. But in practice, the human element sometimes takes priority. Say a mild-mannered trader comes into the pit 10 seconds before an aggressive one with the same order. Although the quiet trader has priority, the noisy, aggressive one will probably get his order filled first. The human element also produces "out-trades"—disputed trades where traders disagree whether they bought or sold, or the amount done.

The market that is probably the largest electronic market today is the Japanese equity index futures market. Only members of the Osaka Securities Exchange have access to the terminals for trading Nikkei futures. It costs millions of dollars to join the Exchange and it will not rent terminals to nonmembers. Thus the private individual is excluded from being a "local." This is not true of a floor trading exchange such as Chicago. Out-trades in Tokyo are not the result of disagreement: they can only arise from keyboard input errors.

All buy and sell orders are displayed on the screen along with their quantities. Orders can be placed at a limit above or below the market, at the bid or offer, or at the market. However, buyers and sellers remain anonymous. This puts all market participants on an equal footing, unlike the Chicago market.

A special feature of the Japanese market is the role of the Saitori, mentioned earlier. Their role is to keep an orderly market by maintaining an "indication price" which is their best estimate of the "right" price for the market. Usually, this is the last traded price. But if the Saitori feels that the price has moved since the last trade, he will raise or lower the indication price.

This is important when there is an imbalance in the market. Imbalances often occur in Tokyo because all market orders must clear for a trade to take place. If there are 1000 buy contracts and 500 sell contracts, all to be done "at market," no trade will take place. This rule also applies to market openings and closings. For this reason, it can take as much as an hour or more to open the futures market if there is an imbalance. The Saitori tries to remedy order imbalances by moving the indication price. However, he can only change the indication price by a limited amount at a time. And he must wait a defined period before making another change. This is intended to "slow down the market." But if the real market price is moving faster than the

Saitori can move, no trades can ever take place until the market reaches "limit up" or "limit down."

The German system, on the DTB, is different because it does not have any human intervention. Price limits do not exist and imbalances do not lock the market—orders can be partially filled. The first order entered into the system is filled, then, the next, until all possible trades are completed. Thus market continuity should be better than in Japan.

A useful comparison of the Japanese electronic and U.S. "human" systems under stress came in August 1990 when Iraq invaded Kuwait. A calculation by Goldman Sachs of the average daily time that the Nikkei and S&P futures contracts were not available for trading during August was 2.7 minutes for the S&P and 60.2 for the Nikkei. That is, during the month, the Nikkei was locked and untradeable for an average of an hour a day. Furthermore, the S&P averaged 2,500 trades per day in an average amount of 19 contracts for a daily trading volume of 45,500 contracts. The Nikkei averaged 374 trades per day for 161 contracts for an average volume of 60,400. That is, the Nikkei traded more sporadically but in larger size. Trading was concentrated into shorter intervals. And the median tick move—the change in market level—was twice as large for the Nikkei than the S&P 500.

A one-month test under very unusual circumstances is by no means conclusive. But the results do suggest that the Japanese system, which excludes individual locals and locks out imbalanced markets, provided a less continuous market than the free-for-all S&P 500. However, it is not a true test of electronic trading vs floor trading, since the DTB and LIFFE systems operated differently. Neither, however, was trading a major contract electronically during this period so it is not possible to compare them. Electronic systems do have many advantages: fairer order priority, anonymity, fewer errors, and faster dissemination of information. Provided they do not exclude individual "local" traders as the Japanese system does, good electronic systems may in the long run prove the better system, assuming they are allowed to operate continuously by partially filling orders.

It is because of these problems that LIFFE's APT system has tried to create "electronic open outcry." The key difference is that APT is not an order matching system under which bids and offers are stored until they can be filled. APT bids and offers, as in the pits on the trading floor, are only valid "for as long as the breath is warm." To achieve this, there is a price: the APT terminal has to be a high-powered workstation capable of 12 million calculations per second.

EURODOLLAR FUTURES

There is now a wide range of instruments traded in the financial futures markets, from the simplest, (the Eurodollar or Treasury bill contract) to the more complex (Treasury bonds, stock index futures) to the exotic (DIFFS—

contracts developed in Chicago for trading on interest rate differentials between two currencies). An exhaustive survey would probably also exhaust the reader's patience, since the differences between many of these, for example, a contract on three-month US$ deposits and a contract on three-month sterling deposits are relatively minor and confined to clearing and settlement issues rather than any major differences in concept. Therefore this chapter discusses only four kinds of contract: a short-term interest rate contract, a short-term discount rate contract (Treasury bills), a bond contract, and a foreign exchange contract. With variations applicable to local clearing and settlement conditions, the principles explained should be applicable to futures markets on foreign exchange and money markets worldwide.

Eurodollar Future Contracts

We will start with what is perhaps the simplest futures contract, the Eurodollar future. It is also probably the most important short-term interest rate futures contract on a worldwide basis. To give an idea of the scale of the IMM's liquidity in this contract, in normal times 500 lots and often 1000 lots can change hands without changing the price. That is, up to $1 billion can be done in a single trade.

The Eurodollar contract is traded in substantially similar form in Chicago, on the IMM, in London, on LIFFE, and in Singapore on SIMEX. SIMEX and the IMM have a "mutual offset" arrangement whereby positions taken in Singapore can be closed in Chicago and vice versa.

The IMM contract is for a $1 million face value Eurodollar time deposit with three-months' maturity. Last trading day is the second London business day before the third Wednesday of the delivery month. Delivery months are March, June, September, December, and the spot (current) month. A specific feature of this contract is that it is cash-settled. That is, unlike the Treasury bill or Treasury bond contracts, physical delivery of the underlying instrument does not take place. The primary reason for this is that there would be an implied credit risk on the bank whose Eurodollar deposit was delivered. Since the Eurodollar futures market now stretches out almost to four years in maturity, predicting the credit quality risk would be difficult.

The cash settlement has been an important element in the success of the contract. The domestic U.S. CD contract (which settled by actual delivery of CDs) was introduced in 1981. The Mexican crisis of 1982 and Continental Illinois' collapse in 1984 quickly meant that the traditional CD "run" (whereby the top ten U.S. banks' paper was traded interchangeably) disintegrated. Traders delivered the weakest CDs into the futures contract; buyers of CD futures found themselves "wearing" weak paper. This process destroyed the contract. Cash settlement means there is no risk of this happening.

The size of the Eurodollar contract is $1 million face amount. The price is quoted in terms of the IMM index, that is, the difference between the deposit rate and 100. Thus, a Eurodollar deposit rate of 9% is quoted in index form as 91.00. Prices are quoted in multiples of 0.01 (thus the minimum possible change in the value of the contract—the *tick value*—is US$25: 0.01/100 × 90/ 360 × $1,000,000).

The settlement mechanics are that on the last trading day the IMM clearing-house contacts 12 major London "reference" banks for their perception of the LIBOR rate at which prime banks can raise three-month deposits, both at the end of trading and at a random time in the last 90 minutes of trading. After eliminating the two highest and the two lowest quotes, the average of the remaining eight is taken as the LIBOR rate. Suppose this works out at 8.5%. Then the "settlement price" which is used to work out the payments due to and due from holders of outstanding futures contracts will be $100 - 8.5 = 91.5$. That is: on the settlement date, the interest rate implied by the futures contract must be equal to the cash three month deposit rate prevailing at that time. So in fact looking at futures prices gives a quick forecast of where the market sees the three-month Eurodollar rate going.

Suppose today is June 13, 1991. The September Eurodollar futures contract is trading at 93.5. That means that the market is saying that in September Eurodollar rates will be at 6.5%. (Remember the contract prices as $100 - $ Eurodollar rate). I believe that by the time we get to September 15, the rate will have risen sharply to 9%. That would imply that on its settlement date the Eurodollar future will trade at 91. The market expects rates to fall, I expect rates to rise. I sell 50 September Eurodollar contracts at 93.5. If I am right, then in September, the futures contract will settle at 91. I sold at 93.5; I close out the position by buying back at 91. I will make a profit of 2.5, or 250 ticks. Since we know the value of a tick is $25 , that means my profit will be $6,250 per contract, or $312,500 in total.

Here I simply traded on my view of rates. But another way of looking at this is to argue that by dealing today at 93.5 I have effectively "locked in" a deposit rate of 6.5% in September. That ability to lock in future rates is what makes the Eurodollar futures market so attractive to banks, since it allows them not only to trade speculative interest rate views but also to offer hedges to their corporate customers who are borrowing (see the section on hedging below) and also to arbitrage against other markets, notably the rate for forward rate agreements (see Chapter 6) and interest rate swaps (see Chapter 15 and the section Futures and FRAs).

TREASURY BILL FUTURES

The IMM Treasury bill future was the first successful interest rate futures contract and, though it has lost ground to the Eurodollar contract, it remains an important instrument in its own right as well as being used in "TED spread" trading (see below). The main reasons for its decline are firstly that the Euro contract, introduced in 1982, was soon traded on other exchanges worldwide, while a position in the IMM Treasury bills contract can only be traded during Chicago hours. Secondly, trading in the secondary Treasury bill market can be affected by the amount of paper locked away. In the spring of 1989, for example, of $7 billion of 3-month bills auctioned, $4.4 billion were bought by "non-competitive" buyers intending to hold the bills as investments to maturity. Thus of that bill only $2.6 billion was available; an aggressive investment bank, working perhaps with one or two other institutions, could easily establish a sizable enough position in the cash market to squeeze the futures market. A few squeezes of this type were enough to discourage some trading in the futures market, which in turn made the market easier to squeeze.

The standard contract is for 13-week U.S. Treasury bills having a face value at maturity of US$1 million. The delivery unit on the IMM is Treasury bills maturing 90 days hence. At the seller's option, he can deliver 91- or 92-day maturity bills. (In point of fact, the vast majority of deliveries are made in 91-day bills.) The price is quoted in terms of the IMM index, that is, the difference between the actual rate and 100. (It should be borne in mind that Treasury bill rates are quoted on a discount basis and not a yield basis, see Chapter 7). Prices are quoted in multiples of 0.01 (thus the tick value is US$25, as for the Eurodollar contract).

Contracts for the 90-day Treasury bill are traded for March, June, September, and December. Trading in the contract normally ends on the second business day after the 13-week Treasury bill auction of the third week of the delivery month (that is, usually the Wednesday following the third Monday of the month). Delivery takes place the following day (the Thursday).

Unlike the Eurodollar contract, the Treasury bill contract settles by delivery of a Treasury bill. So the pricing of the Treasury bill future is primarily driven by its relationship to the cash market for Treasury bills. The link between the two markets is called the *implied repo rate*. The basic idea behind the implied repo rate can be explained as follows. Suppose I buy a Treasury bill which is deliverable into the futures contract. At the same time I sell a Treasury bill future, with the intent of delivering the cash bill as settlement of my futures position. This position will have a revenue and a cost. The revenue will be the profit (if any) on the sale price of the future in excess of the cost of the cash bill. The cost will be the cost of financing my holding of the cash bill until I deliver it in the futures settlement. The implied repo rate is the rate that I can afford to pay as a cost of finance, and still break even.

The implied repo rate measures the interest expense saved by a leveraged buyer who chooses a futures contract instead of a cash settlement purchase. It measures the time value of money for the time period between cash and futures settlement dates. *If the implied repo rate is above the actual financing rate for the period, futures are expensive relative to the underlying instrument.* We should buy cash and sell futures. Conversely, *if the implied repo rate is below the actual rate, futures are cheap relative to the instrument.* We should buy futures and sell cash.

In practice, of course, these rules cannot be automatically followed because of the fact that the trader is uncertain about the amount of variation margin that will have to be paid or received in the interval from now to maturity, nor is he always able to arrange finance for the period from now to maturity at a single fixed rate.

CALCULATING THE IMPLIED REPO RATE

Suppose today, August 3, 1994, I can sell September bill futures at 89.14 (that is, a rate of 10.86%). Since delivery will be due on Thursday, September 22, the December 22 bill is the deliverable bill to the September contract. Assume that today I can buy the cash Treasury bill maturing December 22 at a discount of 10.52%. Is it profitable to buy the cash bill and sell it into the September future?

The purchase price (see Chapter 7) of the cash bill is found as follows:

$$P = 100 - \left(\frac{R \times N}{360}\right)$$

where P = bill price; R = discount rate; N = days to bill maturity.

In this case, R = 10.52% and N = 140 (delivery is August 4th). Therefore, P = 100 − (10.52 × 140/360) = 95.909. The selling price in September, via the futures contract, is found from the same formula, with R = 10.86% and N = 91. Therefore, P = 100 − (10.86 × 91/360) = 97.255.

From these two prices, we can now find out the implied repo rate. It is the annualized rate of return which is earned by buying the bill at 95.909 and selling it 49 days later at 97.255. We will be able to afford to pay a financing cost which is no higher than that return. The calculation is the same as for any other annualized return:

$$\text{Implied repo} = \left(\frac{97.255}{95.909} - 1\right) \times \frac{360}{49} = .1031 \text{ or } 10.31\%$$

If we do this trade, we will earn a return of 10.31%. Provided we can finance our Treasury bill holding for less than that, we will make a profit. However, it is unlikely that we would lock up our finance for the whole period in advance, because a more common use of this trade, if there is an arbitrage opportunity, is to put the trade on and hold it until the arbitrage disappears. At that point, we unwind our financing and sell the position. Thus our financing would normally be the overnight repo rate (hence the origin of the term). So then the position would be subject to financing risk. If overnight repo rates jumped sharply, we would have to cut the position, probably at a loss.

Generalizing from the above, the *general formula for the implied repo rate* is as follows:

$$\text{Implied repo rate} = 100 \times \left(\frac{Pf}{Pc} - 1\right) \times \frac{360}{N}$$

where Pf = futures price and Pc = cash price.

For the Treasury bill calculation, if we want to express the formula in terms of interest rates, it is:

$$IRP = \left[\frac{100 - Rf \times \dfrac{91}{360}}{100 - Rc \times \dfrac{Dc}{360}} - 1 \right] \times \frac{360}{Dc\text{-}91}$$

where Rf = futures bill discount rate; Rc = cash deliverable bill discount rate; and Dc = number of days to cash bill maturity.

BOND FUTURES

In the arena of bond contracts, the U.S. Treasury bond contract is probably the most important on a worldwide basis, although trading volume has been eclipsed by the JGB contract in Tokyo. The main center for trading the contract is Chicago; LIFFE introduced a U.S. Treasury bond contract but it has not performed particularly well. Trading volume on the Chicago Board of Trade bond contracts has grown as shown in Table 14.4.

The chief contract is the 20-year bond contract, so that is the one we will discuss. Quotations on the bond contracts, to make them comparable with the cash market, are in terms of the price of the notional underlying Treasury bond (which is a 20-year bond with an 8% coupon) and they are quoted not in decimals but in 1/32nds. Thus, a price of 98-16 means 98 and 16/32nds or 98.50 in decimal terms. (In this book, when referring to bond contracts, I shall write 98-16 to show a price in 1/32nds and 98.50 if the price is converted to decimals.) The notional face amount of the bond is $100,000. Delivery may be made on any day during the last month of the contract's life. The party who is short the contract may decide when to deliver. When he does so, the CBOT notifies the holder of a long position that he must take delivery.

Table 14.4   Trading Volume in U.S. Treasury Bond and Note Contracts (millions)

	20-Year Bonds	10-Year Notes	5-Year Notes	Total
1985	40.45	2.86		43.31
1986	52.60	4.43		57.03
1987	66.84	5.25		72.10
1988	70.31	5.20	0.51	76.02
1989	70.30	6.11	1.78	78.19
1990	75.50	6.05	2.53	84.09

Source: Chicago Board of Trade.

The long position chosen is that which was put on at the earliest date of all the long positions still outstanding. The following day, the short delivers to the long, against cash payment in Fed funds.

The bond delivered must be of "deliverable grade." That is, it must be a standard coupon-bearing U.S. Treasury bond maturing at least 15 years from the first day of the delivery month. The price of the cash bond which is implied by the futures contract is converted, by means of a "conversion factor" supplied by the Exchange, to an equivalent price comparable to that of the deliverable bond. Suppose the future is trading at 101.50 in decimal terms and there is a deliverable, 18-year bond with a coupon of 11.25%. Suppose the exchange's conversion factor for this bond is 0.954. Then the adjusted futures price for this bond is $101.50 \times 0.954 = 96.831$.

Looking at that the other way round, suppose I own this 11.25% bond. Then I know I can sell it into the futures market for 96.831. Suppose the actual cash price in the market is 96.55. In both cases, for simplicity, we ignore accrued interest. Suppose the first delivery date for the futures contract is in 10 days' time. Suppose I can borrow ten-day money for 8% and there is no coupon due on the cash bond between now and the futures delivery date. Then if I borrow the price of the bond, buy the cash bond, sell it into the futures market, and hold it until the time comes for delivery into the futures settlement process, I can make a profit.

I work this out as follows. Work out the discount factor which gives the present value today of 96.831 in ten days' time at 8%. This, using a 360-day year, is $(1 + 8/100 \times 10/360) = 1.002222$. Discount the adjusted futures price back to today: this is $96.831/1.002222 = 96.616$. So the present value today of the adjusted futures price of this bond, at which I can sell it, is 96.616; but I can buy the bond for 96.55. So I can buy the cash bond today, sell it for future delivery, and finance it until delivery date at 8%, to show a profit overall. Such a trade is called a *cash-and-carry*. This type of arbitrage means that the *fair value* of the future is determined by the price of cash Treasury bonds and by short-term financing costs.

In this example, we have ignored the coupon payable on the cash bond. While I hold the bond, the coupon is accruing in my favor. Suppose we are looking at the 8.75% bonds of November 2008 and they are currently trading in the market at 68-26 or 68.8125 in decimal terms. Suppose today the accrued interest outstanding on that bond is 2.12 in decimal terms, then the total price of the cash bond today is 70.9325, say 70.93. Today is August 11, and the September contract price is 64-03 or 64.09375. Assume I deliver on the first possible date, September 1. Thus I will hold the bond for 20 days, financing it at 8%. My total cost, therefore, will be $70.93 \times (1 + 8/100 \times 20/360) = 70.93 \times 1.004444 = 71.25$.

On September 1, the accrued interest on the cash bond, for which I will be paid by the buyer, will be 2.60. Suppose the conversion factor for this particular cash bond is 1.0757. Then the adjusted futures price is $64.09375 \times 1.0757 = 68.95$. Including accrued, the total price will be 71.55.

There is a difference between the all-in adjusted futures price (71.55) and the all-in cash price allowing for financing cost to delivery (71.25) of 0.30 which would be my profit on the trade.

Comparing the yield on the bond we buy with the financing cost shows us the *cost of carry.* Suppose we buy a bond yielding 12% and finance it at 8%. Carrying this position earns us 4% per annum. There is *positive carry.* Conversely if short rates are above long rates, so that financing cost is more than the yield on the bond.

A related concept is that of "basis" to which we return in more detail below. *Basis* is defined as *the cash price less the futures price:* the difference between the two. As the delivery month on the futures contract approaches, the cash and futures prices tend to converge. The basis approaches zero. This is because the influences on the price of both the cash commodity and the expiring futures contract are identical at the time of delivery. If there were a difference between the two prices, there would be an opportunity for arbitrage. If the Treasury bond futures contract sold at a higher price than cash Treasury bonds, traders could sell the futures contract, buy Treasury bonds in the cash market, and make delivery on the futures contract to cover their futures sale, realizing an arbitrage profit.

There is a similarity to the forward foreign exchange margin. The forward margin also tends to get smaller as the period of the forward contract shortens. It reaches zero when the forward price is for spot. And just as the forward margin is influenced by the relative interest rates of the two currencies involved, so the basis is influenced by interest rates, although in a different way. Basis is positive or negative, depending on whether the cash price is higher or lower than the futures price.

If short-term interest rates are below long-term rates, dealers who hold bonds are earning coupon income which is more than the cost of financing them. They can afford to quote lower prices on deferred sales. That leads to discounts on distant contracts. In this situation, basis is positive (basis = cash − futures = +). Putting it in another way, the dealer is earning "positive carry"—coupon income exceeds financing costs. *Positive carry means a positive basis, and a positive yield curve* (see Chapter 6). If the yield curve has a negative slope, so that long-term rates are below short-term rates, dealers face financing costs which are more than their coupon income. So they must charge higher prices on deferred sales to compensate for holding the bonds. They face negative carry, and the futures market will show a negative basis. *Negative yield curve, therefore, means negative carry and negative basis.*

One final point on cash and carry: the calculations depend on whether carry is positive or negative. As the short, in the example above, I have the choice of delivery date. Normally, for a cash-and-carry, one would calculate carry to the last *rational* delivery date. Thus, if carry is positive, I will deliver on the last possible day; if negative, on the first.

CHEAPEST TO DELIVER

How do we know which bond will be delivered into the futures contract? The answer is, that bond which it is cheapest to deliver for the trader who is short. Let's take an example. Suppose the futures contract is at a price of 79-05. Suppose also that the cash market has just three issues available for delivery against that contract. These are the $8\frac{3}{4}$% 2008 at 85-28 (yielding 10.30%), the $9\frac{1}{8}$% 2009 at 88-29(10.34%), and the $10\frac{3}{8}$% 2009 at 99-27(10.39%). Comparing yields, the $10\frac{3}{8}$% is the highest; while in terms of price, the $8\frac{3}{4}$% is the lowest. Intuitively, therefore, it would seem that one of these two bonds is the "cheapest" in the futures market.

However, if the T-bond futures conversion factors are 1.0790, 1.1194, and 1.254 respectively (these were the actual factors on the day in question), then the price of the $8\frac{1}{4}$% bond would have to be 85.41 (in decimal terms) while it is actually 85.88 in the market. The $9\frac{1}{8}$% would have to be 88.61 (against an actual 88.91) and the $10\frac{3}{8}$% 99.26 (actual 99.84).

Comparing the theoretical and actual prices, we can see that if the short is buying in the market, he will make a loss of 0.47 points on the $8\frac{3}{4}$%, and 0.58 on the $10\frac{3}{8}$%, while he will show a loss of only 0.30 on the $9\frac{1}{8}$%. Therefore, of these three issues, the $9\frac{1}{8}$% is the "cheapest" for the short to buy. The $10\frac{3}{8}$%, which in yield to maturity terms was "cheapest" or best value, represents the greatest loss in terms of delivery to the futures market.

This comparison was done on the day of delivery. If we are considering, before delivery, which bond is the cheapest to deliver, then what we do is take the adjusted futures price and compare it with the cash prices of the different bonds in the market—the reverse of the exercise we did in the last section. There, we started with the cash price, worked out the all-in cost allowing for financing, and compared it with the futures price to see if we could make a profit. Here, we are effectively working out the break-even financing rate: the implied repo rate. *The bond that is the cheapest to deliver is that which has the highest implied repo rate.* The long pays the financing cost; the short earns it. So the short looks for the highest implied repo rate.

In general, if bond yields are above 8%, then the lower the coupon and the longer the maturity, the cheaper it will be to deliver. If yields are below 8%, then the shorter the maturity and the higher the coupon, the cheaper the bond is to deliver. (Remember, the notional bond in the futures contract has an 8% coupon).

FOREIGN EXCHANGE FUTURES

Foreign exchange futures are not so important in their own right as interest rate futures contracts, since the liquid interbank forward foreign exchange market has always provided tough competition for the futures. But there is an important market for arbitraging between the futures and forward markets and so it is important to understand the mechanics.

We will take as an example the Chicago Mercantile Exchange contract for sterling. This is for an amount of £62,500, with contracts for March, June, September, and December. Delivery date is the third Wednesday of the contract month, and delivery is made by payment of sterling against dollars paid by the buyer of the contract.

The operation of the market is very simple. Today is January 11, 1993. The March futures contract settles on the third Wednesday: on March 17, 1993. The future is trading at $1.9217. I know that in the interbank forward market the $/£ rate for that date is $1.9212. I buy interbank forward £625,000 and sell ten futures contracts to make a five-point profit per contract.

Because this type of arbitrage is so easy, many banks specialize in "trading the IMM dates." Therefore, the futures market price is in practice fixed by the cash market price for that day, which is worked out in the usual manner (see Chapters 9 and 10).

There are two complications to this simplicity. The first is that traditionally U.S. foreign exchange quotations were reciprocal, that is, DEM1 = 0.6579 rather than US$1 = DEM 1.5200. Thus in comparing with the normal interbank forward quotations, one has to invert the futures price.

The second complication applies when dealing crosses. It flows from the fact that the standard amounts of the contracts are expressed in the foreign currency. Thus the yen contract is for Y12,500,000; the DEM contract is for DEM 125,000. Unless the YEN/DEM cross is at 100, one of these two contracts will be "heavier" than the other. Suppose the actual YEN/DEM cross is DEM 1 = YEN 90. Then the yen contract is worth DEM 138,888.89 while the DEM contract is worth DEM 125,000. Therefore in trading the crosses on the futures market one would need to weight the size of one's position. The weight is the current cross rate as a proportion of the cross-rate implied by the contracts. In this case the number of yen contracts would be 90% of the number of DEM contracts, for example, one might sell 180 yen contracts and buy 200 DEM ones.

HEDGING

To hedge is to reduce risk. When an investor faces the risk of a change in interest or exchange rates which he does not want to bear, he may use financial futures to offset the risk. If the risk is of a fall in interest rates, he buys futures and if the risk is of a rise, he sells futures. To be precise, one may say that in such circumstances a hedger transfers risk by temporarily offsetting a position in a cash market with a related position in a futures market.

Let's look first at a short hedge. Suppose that a corporation has agreed to borrow Eurodollars on a three-month roll over basis. It fears that interest rates are about to rise. It wants to lock in current interest rate levels on its borrowings. It will then sell Eurodollar futures contracts to the amount required. This is a "short" hedge. The mechanics are as follows.

Suppose today is March 14, 1992. Three-month Eurodollar LIBOR is 8%. Three-month Eurodollar futures for delivery June 16 are 92 (8%) but the firm fears that by June three-month LIBOR on its $10 million borrowing could be 10%. That would mean that the spot contract in June would be 90. So the firm sells 10 June contracts at 92. If its fears are correct, and the June contracts do go to 90, it buys back the contracts on June 14 (last trading day for the contract) at 90 and makes a profit of 2.00 per contract, that is, 200 basis points. Each basis point on a $1 million contract is worth $25, so its profit is $25 × 200 × 10 = $50,000.

It now borrows for three months (say 90 days) at 10%, costing: 10/100 × 10 million × 90/360 = $250,000. From this can be deducted the profit on the futures, making a total cost of $200,000, producing an effective rate of 8% which the borrower has locked in today for three months hence. In other words, it has locked in today's futures rate for its borrowing.

What would have happened if the interest rate had gone the other way, say, to 6%? Then the Euro contracts would have traded at around 94. Closing them out would have cost 2.00 per contract, so the loss would be $50,000. The cost of the cash borrowing would now be 6/100 × 10 million × 90/360 = $150,000, and the all in cost would again be $200,000. In other words, the cost is insensitive to interest rate movements.

What we have just said is broadly true. But the hedge will not actually be perfect for several reasons. First, there would be an impact from changes in the pattern of variation margin during the interval to the futures delivery date. In practice, we are hedging a future cash flow with an instrument where profits and losses hit our books today. A related point is whether one should hedge not the nominal amount of the borrowing, but today's present value of that amount. (For a slightly more detailed analysis see the section Futures and FRAs.)

Second, there will be basis risk: the futures market may not move exactly in line with the cash market. Particularly if rates turn out to be fairly stable, there can be a bigger profit and loss impact from basis risk than from interest rate movements.

Third, there can be an impact from variations in the LIBOR period. Suppose that the LIBOR period over June 16 is not 90 days as we assumed but 92 days, all other figures being unchanged. Then if the LIBOR rate has fallen to 12% our total cost works out at 15.16%, around 1/16% lower than before. Conversely, if LIBOR had risen to 18%, our all-in cost would be 15.29%, just under 1/15% the other way. The effect of the longer cash market period has been to alter the relative weighting of the cash interest cost

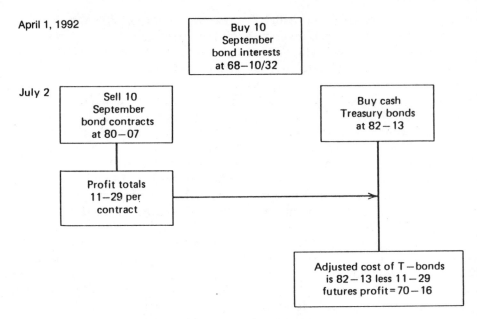

Figure 14.2   Hedging a bond holding.

against the futures hedge. (That is, the durations of the cash and futures are now slightly different, see Chapter 7.)

Let's look now at a "long" hedge: hedging assets rather than liabilities. Consider an institutional investor in U.S. Treasury bonds (see Figure 14.2). On April 1, 1992, she expects that in three months she will receive US$1 million, which she plans to invest in Treasury bonds. The investor suspects that rates are at or near their peak. At this point, 20-year 8¼% Treasury bonds are yielding 9%. Their "cash" price is 93-03.

The investor wants to lock in today's yield level, in case it falls in the course of the next three months, before she receives her funds. Her first step is to buy 10 September futures contracts. Each futures contract for U.S. Treasury bonds has a face value of US$100,000, so her total purchase is equal in value to the amount that she plans to invest in July. She buys them at the current futures price of 91-30 (91.9375).

By July 2, suppose that interest rates have dropped as she expected, and, accordingly, the price of bonds has risen. She sells her 10 futures contracts at the new price of 107-04 (107.125). This gives her a profit of $15,187.50 per contract, for a total profit of $151,875 for the 10 contracts. She has now received her US$1 million which she proceeds to invest in Treasury bonds. The price of cash Treasury bonds as distinct from futures has risen from 93-03 (93.09375) to 107-20 (107.625).

If she had been able to invest in April, she would have made a profit of $145,312.5. This is in effect an opportunity loss for the portfolio. But it is offset by the gain in the futures market. In fact, while the investor pays $1,076,250 for bonds with a face value of $1 million, her net cost is only $924,375 after we allow for $151,875 futures profit. In effect, by dealing in April in the futures market, the investor has protected her July investment, and established, in advance, a yield higher than that available at the time of the deal in July.

In this example, the opportunity loss was $145,312.50 and the futures gain was $151,875. That is, the futures market was not a perfect hedge. The reason for this is that the futures market price and the "cash" market price do not move exactly in parallel. The cash price in April was 93-03 (93.09375) while the future price for September was 91-30 (91.9375). The cash price rose 14-17 (14.53125) while the futures price rose 15-06 (15.1875). In the futures market, this is referred to as a change in the basis.

MANAGING THE HEDGE PROGRAM

Financial futures are very attractive instruments with which to hedge interest rate exposure. However, it is important that any hedge program be properly managed. The process of hedging with futures is dynamic. A hedge, once started, must be actively managed and continually evaluated and monitored. It is unwise simply to put a hedge in place and then forget about it. This is because, with very few exceptions, hedges are rarely "perfect." The hedging process usually involves making a judgment about the appropriate instrument to use as a hedge vehicle, and the current market conditions in the hedge instrument. (This point is touched on from a different viewpoint—that of FAS80—in Chapter 18.)

A crucial point in any hedge program is for the hedger and his management to have clear in their minds the aims of the program. It sometimes happens that the hedge program shows a loss; this loss offsets an unexpected profit in the underlying cash position. It has happened that management have been concerned by these losses: yet they should not be worried, since the underlying position has netted out. What is really happening is that they wish now that they had never entered into the hedge, but had run an open position. Yet this was not the original intention, and 20/20 hindsight should not be used to criticize the performance of the hedge.

By definition, the hedger is willing to forego opportunity to reduce the risk of adverse movement. But he may have limits as to how much opportunity he is willing to give up. For example, an investor may set a specific target, such as a minimum rate of 8% for Treasury bill investments over the next six months. But if rates rise, futures losses will offset the opportunity gain of rolling over the Treasury bills at a higher rate. Just how much opportunity will be willingly foregone; that is, what is the hedger's "zone of tolerance"?

Assume the answer is a rise in rates of 200 basis points. Then Figure 14.3 shows one way of setting these parameters. Between January to March, the hedger is within the zone of tolerance, and hedges are left on. From March to mid-May rates are within the range or above the target, therefore the hedges would be lifted. In mid-May, when rates fall again, the hedges would be reinstated.

This strategy merits a word of caution. There is a fine line between managing and trading a hedge. Without the explicit parameters set in the preceding example, lifting the hedge to avoid opportunity loss would be speculative. Furthermore, risk would be increased because if the hedge was no longer in place and rates dropped sharply, the investor would be hit twice or "whipsawed."

The potential hedger should be aware that hedging is only one alternative in the management of interest rate risk. It is not always the best solution. The sequence of steps outlined below allows the potential hedger to choose other alternatives.

1. Identify the interest rate risk.
2. Specify and evaluate nonhedging strategies.
3. Evaluate hedging as a strategy.
4. Select the most appropriate hedging strategy.

The first step is to correctly identify the risk. For example, floating rate liabilities appear to imply a risk if rates rise, but if the other side of the

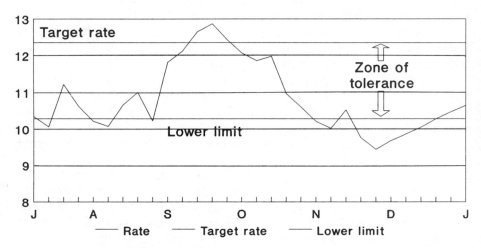

Figure 14.3   Hedge parameters: setting a zone of tolerance (Adapted from N. Roth-stein & J. Little (eds.), *Financial Futures Handbook,* Dow-Jones Irwin).

balance sheet consists of floating rate assets, or other short-term assets being rolled over, then there is a natural hedge. Similarly, futures hedging is right if the risk is symmetric—that is, if rate movements in one direction produce an advantage, or rate movements in the other produce a disadvantage.

Consider, however, an insurance company that offers investors a fixed return, say 8%, for 5 years on funds invested today, but allows investors to withdraw their funds if yields rise in the first year. If rates rise, investors will withdraw their funds, but if rates fall, the funds will be left until maturity. In this case the insurance company's risk is not symmetric, but has a pattern similar to that of an option. The investor in this example holds a put—the right to sell a 4-year instrument to the insurance company at a fixed price. The appropriate hedge would not be a futures contract but an option.

CROSS AND WEIGHTED HEDGES

Hedging a risk in one instrument by a futures contract for a different, but related, instrument is called a *cross hedge*. Our investor in Treasury bonds was able to trade in a contract which exactly matched the instrument she wanted to buy. This would not always be the case. Instead of buying Treasury bonds, she might have been planning to buy corporate bonds. There is, at present, no futures market for corporate bonds. But she might still have wished to protect her interest rate earnings. She might have decided that a hedge in the U.S. Treasury bond market was better than no hedge at all.

Let's look at a pension fund manager with a portfolio of corporate bonds with a face value of $10 million, an average maturity of 20 years, and a current market value of $7,346,875 on January 2. The pension fund manager wants to protect the value of the portfolio from a possible rise in interest rates. He sells 100 June Treasury bond futures at 81-20 in a U.S. Treasury bond futures market.

By March 14, interest rates have risen and the manager decides to sell the corporate bonds. He sells the bonds at $6,440,625 for a $906,250 loss. He buys back 100 U.S. Treasury bond futures at 69-20 and gains $1,200,000. The extra profit here was because the price of the Treasury bond contracts fell over the period by 14.7%, compared with a fall of only 12.34% in the average price of his corporate bonds. The cross hedge was not "perfect." Equally, he could have a loss if the average price of the corporate bonds had fallen faster than the price of the Treasury bonds. The spread might have moved against him rather than in his favor.

So far we have looked at two types of operation: hedging a cash position in U.S. Treasury bonds with a futures position, and hedging a cash position in corporate bonds with a Treasury bond futures position. In the second case, we took the risk of a change in the relationship, or basis, between the two types of bonds. In the first case, we implicitly assumed that the U.S. Treasury bonds held were the same coupon and maturity as those traded in the futures contract. In general, this will not be true.

In this situation, a third type of hedge, the "weighted hedge," is needed to cope with two factors: differences in maturity and differences in coupon. The simpler case is differences in maturity. The value of one basis point yield changes $50 for a $1 million 6-month discounted instrument, as against $25 for a $1 million 3-month discounted instrument:

90 days: $0.01/100 \times 1$ million $\times 90/360$ = $25
180 days: $0.01/100 \times 1$ million $\times 180/360$ = $50

To see this in practice, let's assume that we need to invest $15 million in a 6-month (180-day) CD on August 28, 1987. Today is July 31, 1987, and the rate today on a 180-day CD is 7.5%. To save complications about different coupons (which we look at in our next example), assume that the yield curve is completely flat; that is, a 90-day CD also yields 7.5% today. If today's rates prevailed on August 28, we would earn $562,500 in interest on our 180-day CD. To protect these earnings, we buy 90-day Eurodollar futures. Suppose we did not weight our hedge to compensate for the fact that the futures maturity is half what we need. We would buy $15 million worth, that is 15 contracts, at 92.5 (100 minus 7.5%).

Suppose on August 28 the rate for a 180-day CD (and a 90-day CD) has fallen to 5%. Then when we buy our $15 million CD we will only earn $375,000 instead of the $562,500 we had hoped for, a loss of $187,500. But our futures contracts are now priced at 95 (100 minus 5%) so we have picked up 250 basis points on 15 contracts. We know that on a 90-day Eurodollar futures contract, 1 basis point in dollar terms is worth $25, so we have made a profit of $250 \times 15 \times \$25 = \$93,750$. But this is only half our interest loss on the CD. So in fact, we needed 30 contracts to be properly hedged. The diagram in Figure 14.4 illustrates the effect.

This technique of weighting the hedge is also often used in another situation: where the longer dated contracts have too little liquidity. In that case, traders will often "stack" their hedges in the near contract. In our example, if we were an insurance company with known inflows of premium income over the next five years that we wanted to hedge now, the futures market would not stretch far enough out, nor would it necessarily have enough liquidity in the further contracts. We might load more of the hedge into the nearer contracts. The risk, of course, is of a change in the pattern, rather than the level, of rates. In that case, the near contracts might not move parallel to the far contracts and the hedge would be very imperfect.

In more complex situations, the hedge weighting calculations are often based on duration, which is covered in Chapter 7. So far as futures themselves are concerned, the duration of a futures contract cannot be determined using the standard calculation. There are no definable cash flows associated with a futures contract.

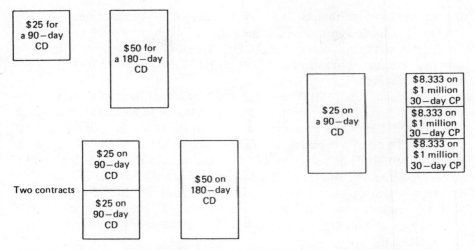

Figure 14.4   Effect of maturity on value of a basis point on face value $1 million.

But a practical approach is to argue that the duration of the futures contract is similar to that of the underlying security on which the futures contract is based. Thus, if we are looking at a Treasury bond future, and the duration of the underlying notional Treasury bond is say 9.4 years, we could argue that the future will respond to rate movements "as if" it had a duration of 9.4 years (allowing for the effect of carry). This duration can be added to portfolio duration for a long position or subtracted for a short position, and the net result will be net portfolio duration. Thus, it is not necessary to have an actual duration value of the futures contract, yet the effect on portfolio duration can be found.

STRADDLES AND SPREADS

It's possible to have a position which looks exactly like the cross hedges we just looked at, but for a totally different reason. We might go into a trade like that with a deliberate intent to profit from a change in the relationship: rather than hoping that the relationship will remain stable so that our hedge will work. The operation might look like a cross hedge, but would in fact be a speculative position. It is usually called a spread position (or sometimes a straddle).

An active spread market is the so-called *TED spread* (Treasury/Eurodollar spread). Since the Eurodollar and Treasury bill contracts trade for the same periods, it is possible to trade the spread between them. The TED spread is calculated by taking the Treasury bill futures price minus the Eurodollar futures price. The primary reason for trading the TED spread is to take a view on investors' perception of the relative credit quality of the U.S. Treasury and the top international banks. In times of crisis for the international banking system (and indeed in times of crisis generally) investors tend to withdraw funds from banks and invest them in U.S. Treasury bills: there is a "flight to quality." Treasury bill rates will fall relative to Eurodollar deposits: the TED spread will widen.

Suppose the March 1993 Treasury bill future is trading at 95.05 (reflecting an implied Treasury bill rate of 4.95%—on a discount basis) and the March 1993 Eurodollar future is trading at 94.12 (reflecting a Eurodollar deposit rate of 5.88% on a yield basis) the TED spread would be $95.05 - 94.12 = 0.93$. It would be quoted as being "at 93." Suppose we feel the gap will widen to, say, 113. We would "buy the TED spread." We would buy the Treasury bill futures—which we expect to outperform—and sell the Eurodollar futures, which we expect to underperform. (Figure 14.5). Conversely, if we thought tension was unwinding, we would sell the spread: sell Treasuries and buy Eurodollars.

There are other influences on the TED spread, notably changes in the direction of short term interest rates. Suppose the spread is at 93 and we feel this is "normal." Suppose rates are at 6%. What should happen to the spread if rates went to 12%? If we look at the spread as a fairly constant percentage of yields, then we would expect the TED spread to widen as rates rise, and conversely. Similarly, changes in the flows of funds in the short term market, such as a halt in issuance of Treasury bills because of Congressional difficulties in adapting the Treasury debt ceiling, or the impact of a very large syndicated Eurodollar credit rollover, can affect the TED spread.

A third operation of this type is to take a position in the same instrument but in different periods, one against the other. This is usually called a *spread,* but some people call it a *straddle.* Suppose interest rates are rising. On March 14, 1992, a trader sees that the December 1992 Treasury bond

Day 1	Sell 10 March Eurodollar contracts at 94.12
	Buy 10 March T-bill contracts at 95.05
	Spread = 93 basis points.
Day 15	Buy 10 March Eurodollar contracts at 93.72
	Sell 10 March T-bill contracts at 94.85
	Spread = 113 basis Points.
Profit:	40 basis points × $25 × 10 contracts = $10,000
Loss:	20 basis points × $25 × 10 contracts = $5,000
	Net profit = $5,000

Figure 14.5   Buying the TED Spread.

contract is trading at a discount to the March 1993 contract (that is, December interest rates are above those for March). The trader thinks the yield curve will change shape. Interest rates will peak soon and begin to fall. When they do, the December contract will yield a lower interest rate compared with the March contract. That is, the spread between the two contracts will shift from negative to positive. The trader decides to gamble on this by buying a December 1992 T-bond contract at 69-26 and selling a March 1983 contract at 70-18. (The price spread between the two contracts is a negative one of 24/32.)

Three months later, on June 14, the yield curve has shifted from negative to positive. The spread between the two contracts has become more positive-it has strengthened. The December contract at 81-22 is now trading at a premium to the March 1993 contract at 81-15. This is a positive spread of 7/32 compared with the previous negative 24/32. Prices for both contracts moved up but at different rates. So the trader's losses on the short March position were more than offset by the gain on the long December position. The loss on the March contract was 10-29(10.90625 points), while the gain on the December contract was 11-28(11.875). The net gain was 31/32. Since each point or 1/32 is worth \$31.25 on the Treasury bond contract, the net gain was \$968.75.

Two typical spreads are the bear spread and the bull spread. The bear spread is based on the idea that, generally, during a falling market, the nearby month will fall faster than the further month. The trader will go short of the nearby month and go long of the further month. This is equivalent, in money market terms, to borrowing the nearby month and lending the further month because we expect short rates to rise faster than long rates. In futures market terms, the operation is called selling the spread. The bull spread is called buying the spread-buying (going long or lending) the nearby month and selling (shorting or borrowing) the further month. Again, the assumption is that the nearby month is likely to move faster than the further month.

FUTURES AND FRAs

Eurodollar futures are closely linked to the market for FRAs (see Chapter 6) and—since FRAs are a kind of single-period swap—the interest rate swap market by "swaps against the strip" (see the next section and Chapter 15). Suppose today is March 13, 1992, and the three- and six-month Eurodollar deposits, value March 15, are trading at 8.25% and 8.5%, respectively. Suppose the days in each period are 90 and 180, respectively. We know from our forward forward formula (see Chapter 6) that the FRA rate should be $(8.5 \times 180 - 8.25 \times 90)/([180 - 90] \times [1 + \{8.25 \times 90/36000\}]) = (1{,}530 - 742.50)/(90 \times 1.020625) = 787.5/91.85625 = 8.57\%$.

That would imply a futures price for June (the price for a 90-day Eurodollar deposit running from June 15 to September 15) of 91.43. Suppose in fact that the future were trading at 91.25, implying a forward rate of 8.75. Then it would be possible to buy the future (hedging against a fall in rates) and also to buy the FRA (hedging against a rise in rates). The future would lock in a lending rate of 8.75% and the FRA would lock in a borrowing rate of 8.57% for a spread of 18 basis points. In other words *if the FRA rate is below the rate given by the future, buy the future and buy the FRA.* Conversely, *if the FRA rate is above the future, sell the FRA and sell the future.*

The hedge will not be quite so perfect as it looks, because of the time value of money on the variation margin. Consider a company with a $10 million floating rate loan linked to six-month LIBOR. It fears rates will rise, and so buys a 6×12 FRA from its bank. Suppose we have the following conditions: value March 19, 1991 we have:

LIBOR		FUTURE	
3 months	8.50%	Jun	91.28
6 months	8.70%	Sep	91.17
9 months	8.88%	Dec	91.02
1 year	9.05%		

For convenience we take the year as having 360 days and six months as having 180. Thus the forward rate is $(9.05 \times 360 - 8.7 \times 180)/(180 \times [1 + (8.7 \times 180/36000)]) = 9.01\%$. Suppose the bank loads its quote to 9.10%. Having done the deal it wants to hedge using the futures market. It sells 10 September contracts (at an implied rate of 8.83%) and 10 December contracts at an implied rate of 8.98%.

The implied total cost over the six months period that is locked in by the futures contracts is worked out by compounding the near contract (at 8.83%) up over the second period at the second rate of 8.98%: $(1 + 8.83 \times 90/36000) \times (1 + 8.98 \times 90/36000) = 1.022075 \times 1.02245 = 1.045020584 = 4.502\%$ per six months which equates to just over 9% annually.

It looks as if the bank has locked a 10 basis point profit over six months on $10 million—say $5000.But now suppose, the day after the deal is done, that cash Eurodollar rates fall 1% and stay fixed at that level until the September futures date. We would have the following rates:

LIBOR		FUTURE	
3 months	7.50%		
6 months	7.70%	Sep	92.07
9 months	7.88%	Dec	91.92
1 year	8.05%		

The September futures contract we sold has risen by 90 ticks, and the December by 90 ticks. Bearing in mind that the tick on this contract (see above) is worth $25 and we did 10 contracts in each maturity, our loss totals $2 \times 10 \times 90 \times 25 = \$45,000$. Since we have assumed that rates now remain rigidly fixed to the September delivery date, there are no further changes in our position and no variation margin movements; we have to fund this loss till delivery date. Say we do this at the six-month rate of 7.7%, then our funding cost is $1,732.50 ($45,000 at 7.7% for half a year)—one-third of our apparent profit disappears.

The problem is that the value of a future settlement amount under the FRA is being hedged with an instrument which throws up changes in value *today*. One way round this would be to *hedge not the settlement amount but the present value of the settlement amount*. (This is called "tailing the hedge.") With the passage of time, that present value rises, so that one would gradually increase the size of the hedge as we get closer to the settlement date, if we want to be perfectly hedged. (But by that time, we might be happy to leave the balance of the position open).

THE STRIP YIELD CURVE

A very important application of Eurodollar futures lies in their use to create synthetic Eurodollar deposits either for a hedge or for an arbitrage. To understand this, we begin with the idea of the strip.

For any financial instrument for which there is a futures market, we can create a synthetic longer term instrument using the underlying cash instrument plus a series, or strip, of futures contracts. For example, suppose it is March 15, and I buy a three-month Treasury bill maturing June 15. I could also buy June, September, December, and March Treasury bill futures so that I can fix the rate at which I roll over the cash three-month bill when it expires. In fact, I have created a synthetic 15-month Treasury bill.

We can take the same approach with Eurodollar futures. The combination of a three-month deposit with three subsequent Eurodollar futures contracts can create a synthetic one-year deposit. This can be arbitraged against the actual one-year deposit. But in terms of balance sheet usage, it is more effective to arbitrage against the one-year interest rate swap market (see Chapter 15). To do this trade, we need to know how work out the one-year rate from the futures strip.

We know the formula for the forward forward deposit rate as calculated from two deposits (see Chapter 6). But here we have to work out backwards: because the futures rate is the equivalent of the forward forward deposit rate. We want to find the long period deposit rate from the short period rate and the forward forward rate. So we have:

$$\begin{array}{c} \text{Long} \\ \text{period} \\ \text{rate} \end{array} = \cfrac{360}{\begin{array}{c} \text{long} \\ \text{period} \\ \text{days} \end{array}} \left[\cfrac{\begin{array}{c} \text{Futures rate} \times \\ \text{(difference between} \\ \text{long and short period days)} \end{array}}{360} + 1 \right] \left[\cfrac{1 + \cfrac{\text{Short}}{\text{rate}} \times \cfrac{\text{Short}}{\text{days}}}{360} - 1 \right]$$

$$R2 = \frac{360}{N2} \left(\frac{R'(N2 - N1)}{360} + 1 \right)\left(\frac{1 + R1N1}{360} - 1 \right)$$

where R1 = short period deposit rate; R' = rate implied by futures contract; N1 = short period days; N2 = long period days; and R2 = long period rate.

To work out the strip, we start by working out the six month rate from the three-month rate and the nearby futures contract, then the nine-month rate from the resulting six-month rate and the next futures contract, and then the twelve-month rate from the resulting nine-month rate and the next futures contract.

Let's take an example. Today is March 15. We know what the 90-day Eurodollar rate is in the ordinary, or "cash," market. We know the 90-day Eurodollar prices on the IMM for June, September, and December. What we want to know is what, in the ordinary Eurodollar market, the rates for 180-day, 270-day, and 360-day Eurodollars would have to be to match the prices implied by the futures market. Suppose we have:

90-day Eurodollar	14.40%
IMM June Eurodollar	84.88 = 15.12%
September	84.96 = 15.04%
December	85.16 = 14.84%

We take the cash Eurodollar rate and the June futures Eurodollar rates for 90 and 180 days, respectively. Putting them into the formula, we get:

$$R2 = \frac{360}{180} \left(\frac{0.1512(180 - 90)}{360} + 1 \right)\left(\frac{1 + 0.1440 \times 90}{360} - 1 \right)$$

$$= 2 \left[(0.0378 + 1)(1 + 0.036) - 1 \right]$$

$$= 0.1503216$$

$$= 15.03\%$$

A 180-day Eurodollar should fetch 15.03% to match the combined 90-day Eurodollar plus June futures contract. The next step is to work out a 270-day Eurodollar, using the 180-day rate we have just calculated as the cash rate, R1, in our formula. The result of combining the 15.03% "synthetic" 180-day Eurodollar with the 15.04% on the September futures contract comes out at 15.4%. We then take this "synthetic" 270-day rate and combine it with the December futures contract rate to produce a "synthetic" 360-day Eurodollar at 15.696%.

These successive steps have produced a strip yield curve that looks like this, compared with the actual (or cash market) yield curve:

	Strip Yield Curve	Cash Market Yield Curve
90-day "cash" Eurodollar	14.40%	14.40
Synthetic 180-day Eurodollar	15.03%	14.40
Synthetic 270-day Eurodollar	15.41	14.30
Synthetic 360-day Eurodollar	15.696	14.30

The strip yield curve calculated from these formulas differs from the implied forward rates in the "cash" markets. There are two reasons: First, the participants in the futures markets may not entirely share the view of participants in the cash markets. Second, the two markets may be imperfectly linked. The Eurodollar cash and futures markets are very tightly bound together, but there are times when they can move out of line, if only briefly; and in the cash markets there are credit exposure considerations that do not affect futures trading. The spread here has been exaggerated to make the point.

RAW BASIS AND ADJUSTED BASIS

At various stages, we have touched on basis. Basis is defined as the arithmetic difference between the cash price and the futures price (basis equals cash minus futures). If the futures contract and the cash contract are for the same instrument, the basis risk purely reflects the difference between the two markets for the same underlying security. If, however, the futures contract is for a different instrument, then the basis also contains the risk that the relationship between the underlying instrument and the futures contract may change. For simplicity, we will look at the basis where the futures instrument and the cash instrument are the same.

When looking at basis, it is important to split off the carry cost component from the "raw" basis. For example, suppose one wishes to make an investment over a one-year period. A natural response would be to consider a one-year Treasury bill. Let us suppose that this Treasury bill yields 7%. On the other hand, suppose that one can buy a (strictly hypothetical) futures contract on a one-year bill with three months to run, for delivery in nine months' time. Suppose that this contract is priced at 92. At first sight, this looks like a good deal. We can earn 8%, and yet we do not have to put up our funds until 9 months hence. There is a raw basis of 1 point (Figure 14.6).

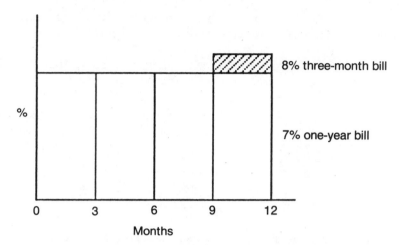

Figure 14.6 Alternatives: 7% one-year treasury bill; 8% three-month treasury bill in nine months' time.

But this is not the end of the story. To make a true comparison, we have to consider the first nine months. Supposing that we can invest nine month money at 5%. Then we lose 2% per annum over a nine month period, i.e., 1.5% in total (Figure 14.7). Strictly speaking, we should add this 1.5 to the cost of the futures contract, making it 93.5 for an implied forward yield of 6.5% (ignoring compounding) (Figure 14.8). So although at first blush it looks attractive, the futures price is in fact expensive. On the other hand, if there were an inverted yield curve, so that the nine-month rate were 9%, then the futures price ought to be adjusted to 90.5. The carry basis of 1.5 should be subtracted from the futures price to give a total basis of 2.5 points.

The total basis, therefore, can be split into two parts: the carry basis, and a residual that could be called the "true basis value." That is, the "raw" basis needs to be adjusted for the carry basis to arrive at the true value of the basis. It is only after making this adjustment for carry that one can see whether or not the futures contract is "rich" or "cheap" to the cash market.

Therefore, in working out the implied futures break-even yield—the yield at which one is indifferent between holding cash and investing it until the futures delivery date, or buying a cash instrument today—there are three distinct components to be worked out. They are (1) the cash security we could buy today, (2) the rate we would earn by investing until delivery date, and (3) the futures contract. Any two of these elements can be used to find a break-even level (price or yield) for the third element.

These considerations are important when analyzing the impact of yield curve changes. Suppose that we have a parallel shift in the yield curve, so that all rates rise by 1%. The price of the one-year bill will respond in accordance with its one year maturity; hence its price volatility will be

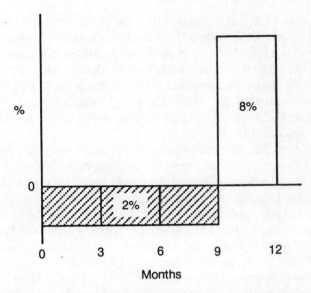

Figure 14.7 All-in yield allowing for nine-month give-up of 2%.

"Raw" futures price:

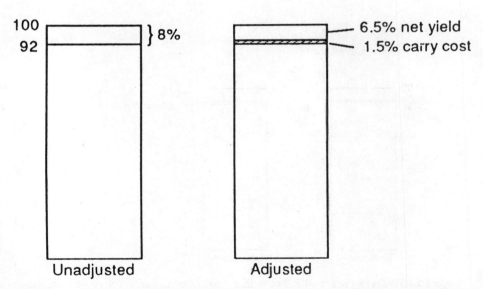

Figure 14.8 Futures price and implied yield adjusted for nine-month yield give-up ("carry cost").

greater than that of a three-month bill. The price basis between the two securities will change, even when the yield basis remains constant.

More importantly, since parallel shifts are relatively rare, any changes in shape of the yield curve will generally lead to changes in the carry spread. Suppose we look again at our original example, when the one-year rate is 7%, and the nine-month rate 5%. Then the "true" futures price is 93.5, rather than the apparent 92 implied by the 8% yield on the three months bill to be delivered in nine months.

However, if the yield curve now inverts so that the nine-month rate snaps up to 9%, but the one-year rate remains unchanged at 7%, then the "true" futures price falls to 90.5. Although the yield on a three-month bill to be delivered in nine months has remained unchanged at 8%, and the one-year bill rate has remained unchanged at 7%, the change in the nine-month cash yield has meant that the basis has altered (Figure 14.9). If the futures price remains at 92, investors will buy the futures contract, and invest the first nine-months' cash at 9%, for an enhanced all in yield.

Thus, the futures contract has volatility of a different kind than a cash security. A cash security is related to a particular maturity point in a yield curve and will be directly sensitive to changes at that particular point. But the futures contract is affected by yield curve changes along other points of the yield curve. So *changes in the shape of the yield curve will change the value of the futures contract.* This underscores the danger in viewing a futures contract as being directly equivalent to an investment in the cash security. The diagram (Figure 14.10) shows this in graphic form.

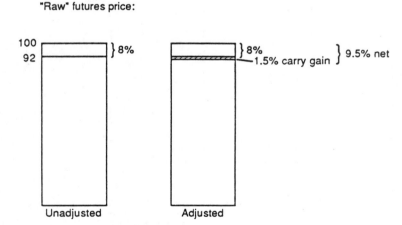

Figure 14.9 As in Figure 14.8, but with a 1.5% gain on carry. Carry gain improves net yield.

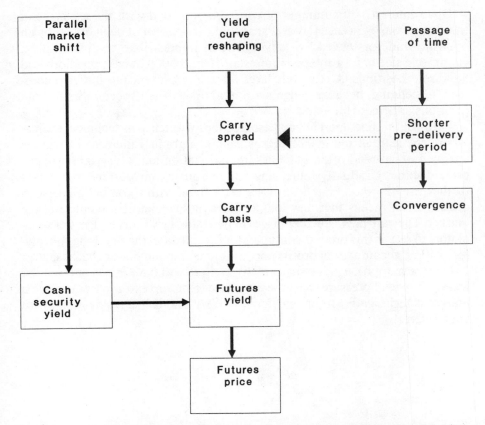

Figure 14.10 Carry basis response patterns (Adapted from N. Rothstein & J. Little (eds.), *Financial Futures Handbook,* Dow-Jones Irwin).

OPEN INTEREST AND VOLUME

Any trader in the futures markets needs to know the liquidity and depth of his markets. The two most general measurements of liquidity and depth for any futures market are trading volume and open interest. Trading volume is the number of contracts traded during a period of time; open interest is the number of open contract units at a point in time.

Futures trading volume is reported as one side only. In other words, a daily volume of 12,000 means 12,000 contracts bought and 12,000 contracts sold. Buys and sells are not added together. The number of contracts bought always equals the number sold since there must be a buyer for every seller. A large volume of trading is a good indication of a liquid market. Liquidity can be gauged by the ability of market participants to execute commercial-size orders quickly at a price close to the price of the last transaction.

Open interest is the number of contracts recorded with the exchange at the close of business each day as transactions that have not been off-set by an opposite trade or settled by delivery. Open interest, like trading volume, counts one side only—an open interest of 5000 is 5000 bought positions and 5000 sold positions. A relatively large open interest tends to indicate commercial hedging, because hedgers are more likely than speculators to hold positions as prices fluctuate.

Both volume and open interest are frequently watched as technical indicators of the state of the market. For example, a gradual increase in volume during a downtrend often indicates a continuation and acceleration of the price decline. Gradually increasing volume during an uptrend suggests a further rise in prices. Equally, a rising price trend with a gradual increase in open interest means that new long hedgers or speculators are entering the market. They are paying higher prices to persuade new short hedgers or speculators to sell. If this process continues for several days, the new long speculators will be accumulating profits and additional buying power (because they have extra margin). The new speculative sellers will have losses and will be feeling financial pressure (because they have to put up extra margin). Such a market is technically strong, particularly if volume is increasing along with open interest.

15 Swaps

The swaps discussed in this chapter are different from those discussed earlier in the context of the forward exchange market. Like those deals, they involve the exchange of one thing for another, hence the common name. But these deals are generally longer term (though there is a thriving one-year interest rate swap market). Often they are conducted by the capital markets arm of a bank, rather than the money and foreign exchange trading operations. On the other hand, many banks group all these activities together, on the grounds that all these markets are interlinked, which is the reason for including them in this book.

ORIGINS OF THE SWAP MARKET

Swaps, as defined above, took off during the 1980s. From perhaps $2 billion outstanding in 1980 the interest rate and currency swap market has now grown to the point where an estimated $1,000 billion of contracts are now outstanding. The first swaps to emerge were currency swaps, which began in the mid-1960s. But the market remained a fairly small one during the 1970s. The emergence of the interest rate swap, in 1980/81, together with the decision by the World Bank to embark on an ambitious currency swap program, transformed the situation.

The market now has a huge range of counterparties, using swaps for a range of different reasons. Banks use swaps for asset and liability management; corporations use them for similar purposes and also to raise finance through the bond market, notably the Eurobond market, at rates which are better than those their bankers can offer. This flexibility has led to a huge growth in the market. In 1980, the market size for currency swaps was perhaps $2 billion; interest rate swaps did not exist. The International Swap Dealers' Association (which covers a large part, but by no means all, of the market) has published the figures in Table 15.1 for market volume in 1989.

Figure 15.1 shows the volume of new swaps dealt in some of the key market sectors during 1987-90, and their maturity structure is shown in Figure 15.2.

Swaps have had a great impact on the international bond market. Earlier issuers of new Eurobonds were relatively tied down. If they issued, say, a Deutschmark bond, the extent to which they could hedge the long term exchange risk of the bond was rather limited. The growth of the currency swap market meant that for the first time, issuers could tap the currency market where they could raise the cheapest funds. A company such as BMW could issue a bond denominated in New Zealand dollars and then do a currency swap to transform its liability into Deutschmarks. Equally, the growth of the interest rate swap market meant a similar liberation in the choice between

Table 15.1   Swap Market Volume, 1989

US$bn.	Interest Rate Swaps	Currency Swaps
US$	993.7	354.2
JPY	128.0	201.1
GBP	100.4	33.5
DEM	84.6	53.8
AUD	67.6	61.8
FFR	42.0	8.4
CAD	29.2	32.6
CHF	28.6	64.8
XEU	18.9	39.9
NLG	6.0	10.1
HKD	2.1	0.6
BEF	0.8	3.0
NZD	0.4	5.8

Source: ISDA, reported in *"International Banking and Financial Market Developments,* Bank for International Settlements, November 1990.

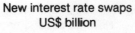

New interest rate swaps
US$ billion

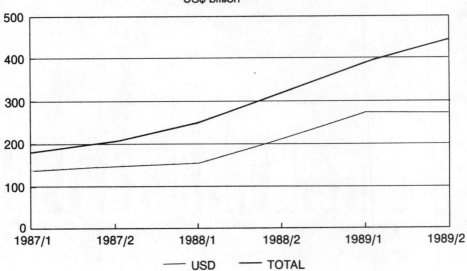

Source: ISDA/BIS

New non$ interest rate swaps by currency
US$ billion

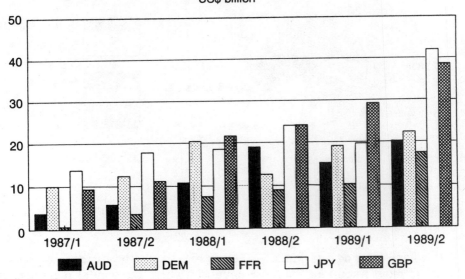

Source: ISDA/BIS

Figure 15.1 Interest rate swaps: growth and currency distribution.

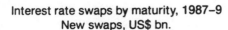

Interest rate swaps by maturity, 1987-9
New swaps, US$ bn.

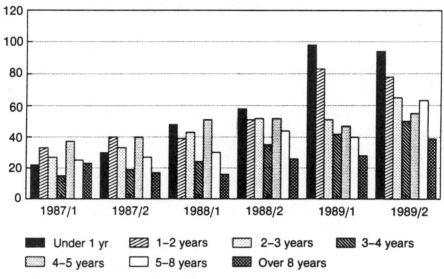

Source: ISDA/BIS

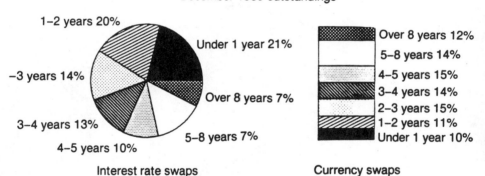

Swaps by maturity
December 1989 outstandings

Interest rate swaps   Currency swaps

Source: ISDA/BIS

Figure 15.2 Swap market growth and structure.

fixed and floating rate bonds. As Figure 15.3 shows, the currency swap market is more important for those countries where the capital market is an
important international source of funds, for example Switzerland, whereas
the interest rate swap market tends to be more active in those currencies
where domestic financial markets are relatively active.

Once the swap technique had been invented, of course, people found many
other ways of using it. The market has even been used by governments: the

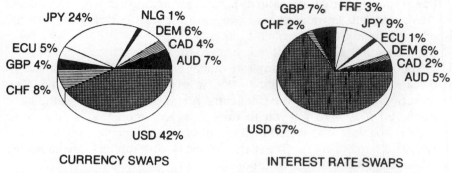

Figure 15.3 Swap market: end–1989 amounts outstanding, US$m.

governments of France and Canada have both done interest rate swaps. In the longer run it is conceivable that the market may be used by central banks for yield curve management, just as in the past they have used forward exchange markets.

Interest rate swaps have been used to switch from floating rate to fixed, from fixed to floating, from fixed-rate to zero coupon, from zero coupon to floating, from zero coupon to semi annual fixed, and so on. Essentially, the combination of interest rate and currency swaps now means that any stream of cash flows can be transformed into virtually any other stream: annual AIBD basis Japanese yen payments can be transformed into quarterly US dollar, amortizing lease type payments, if desired, at a price.

Despite early worries about the credit risk implied in swaps, an International Swaps Dealers Association survey showed total write-offs of US$33 million on portfolios aggregating over $250 billion, a default rate of 0.01%—considerably better than traditional banking default rates. (Although a government veto on swap payments due from the London borough of Hammersmith and Fulham caused problems: partly for political reasons the municipality had used swaps and options to generate revenue from speculative transactions. The legal ability of the municipality to undertake such activity was later overturned by the House of Lords, on the grounds that they were *ultra vires*).

INTEREST RATE SWAPS

An interest rate swap lets an institution manage its liabilities: whether they be fixed rate, or floating rate. Many people find the concept confusing. It may help to think of a fixed-floating interest rate swap as issuing a fixed rate bond to refinance a floating rate note, or vice versa.

The only difference is that in the swap there is no actual borrowing or lending (this is where the market differs from that for currency swaps, where the principal amounts of the swap are actually exchanged under normal circumstances, at least at maturity). Another analogy is with the foreign exchange market: an interest rate swap is a forward contract to exchange interest payments. An example may help.

Suppose it is 1 December 1988; you are the corporate treasurer of XYZ Ltd. You have borrowed floating-rate money from a syndicate of banks, for five years at six-month US$ Libor + 1/2%, in an amount of $10 million. Your corporation does not have the financial strength to access the public bond markets. So it is hard for you to raise five year money at a fixed rate. However, you fear that interest rates will rise. You decide to enter into a swap with a bank to fix for five years the cost of your interest rate liabilities, which would otherwise rise as Libor rises.

Suppose the bank quotes you a fixed rate of 9.5%, payable semi-annually on a 30/360 basis against six-month Libor. Payment on both sides is in arrears. Then you are committed to the cash flows in Table 15.2.

On the other side will be the floating rate income. The bank pays you six month Libor. Consider two possibilities: Libor rises by 1/4% every six months over the period from a starting level of 8%, and Libor falls by 1/4%. Then we will have (assuming for simplicity the Libor is paid also on a 30/360 basis— normally it is on actual/360 for US$ swaps) (see Table 15.3).

The payments by the bank to you will exactly match your Libor payments to your banking syndicate, except for the latter's 1/2% margin. So the Libor payments always net to zero, and your cost is fixed at the 91/2% swap rate plus the 1/2% syndicate margin, for an all-in cost of 10%.

The origins of the interest rate swap technique were in the Eurobond market where fixed rate issuers wished to raise floating rate money. A typical example in the early days would be a Japanese bank. Because most banks typically lend money on a floating rate basis, Japanese banks were not in the habit of issuing fixed-rate Eurobonds. They did not need fixed-rate funds. Therefore, their paper was relatively scarce in the fixed-rate bond market, and commanded attractive premiums. Thus, they were able to issue cheaply and then to swap into floating rate funds.

Table 15.2 Interest Rate Swap Cash Flows

1 Jun 1989	$475,000
1 Dec	$475,000
1 Jun 1990	$475,000
1 Dec	$475,000
1 Jun 1991	$475,000
1 Dec	$475,000
1 Jun 1992	$475,000
1 Dec	$475,000
1 Jun 1993	$475,000
1 Dec	$475,000

Table 15.3   Swap Flows if Rates Rise/Fall

| | FIXED PAYMENT | INCOME | |
		CASE I Libor Rises	CASE II Libor Falls
1 Jun 1989	$475,000	$400,000	$400,000
1 Dec	$475,000	$412,500	$387,500
1 Jun 1990	$475,000	$425,000	$375,000
1 Dec	$475,000	$437,500	$362,500
1 Jun 1991	$475,000	$450,000	$350,000
1 Dec	$475,000	$462,500	$337,500
1 Jun 1992	$475,000	$475,000	$325,000
1 Dec	$475,000	$487,500	$312,500
1 Jun 1993	$475,000	$500,000	$300,000
1 Dec	$475,000	$512,500	$287,500

An example would be as follows: a strong borrower, AAA, would pay Libor + $1/8$% for a seven-year revolving credit from its banks, if it chose to arrange one. For a seven-year bond issue, it would pay 11%. Conversely, a weaker borrower, BBB, must pay 12% for a seven-year bond issue or Libor + $1/2$% for seven year money from his bank.

The difference between the two borrowers in the bank credit market is only $3/8$%; in the bond market it is 1%: a "credit differential" of $5/8$%. The first swaps used this differential to arbitrage. AAA issued a bond and entered into a swap with BBB. Both borrowers were able to save money: here, the $5/8$% is split as to $3/8$% for AAA and $1/4$% for BBB (see Figure 15.4).

PRICING AN INTEREST RATE SWAP

Suppose today is March 3, 1991. You are pricing a swap for your corporation which is interested in swapping out of 6-month US$ Libor and paying a fixed US$ rate. On consulting a Reuters swap screen (such as SWAP or HIRS) you see the following:

Treasury	Swap Spread	Swap Cost
2 Year 7.64	T + 47/54	8.11/18
3 Year 7.75	T + 65/70	8.40/45
4 Year 7.78	T + 68/76	8.46/54
5 Year 7.90	T + 70/78	8.60/68

To interpret this data, one needs to know that swap rates are priced off the corresponding U.S. Treasury bond. Thus, if the company were to pay fixed

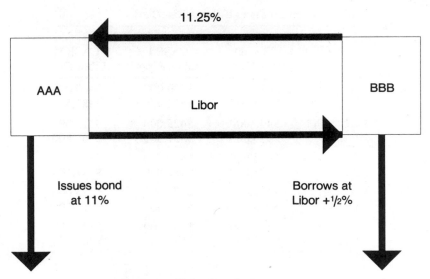

Figure 15.4   Classical swap.

for two years, the swap cost would be the Treasury rate, 7.64%, plus the swap spread of 54 basis points, for an all-in total of 8.18%, plus the credit spread (if any) being charged by the intermediary bank for providing the swap. If the company wanted to deal in the opposite direction, i.e. receive a fixed rate, the spread would be 47 basis points for an all-in cost of 8.11%, which is what it would be paid by the market, less any credit spread charged by the bank.

It is important to be aware that the rate is quoted on a "Treasury bond basis," that is, a semi-annual actual/365 rate. To convert this to a 360-day rate we multiply by 360/365 to convert 8.18% to 8.07% (note the 11 basis point difference). To convert this to an annual rate (to make it comparable to, say, a Eurodollar money market line) we need to use the following formula:

$$r = \left(\frac{1+i}{n}\right)^n$$

where r = annual rate; i = semi-annual rate; and n = number of periods per annum (2 in this case).

In this case we have

$$r = (1 + .0807/2)^2$$

$$= 8.23\%$$

(or we could use the short-cut of Chapter 6: square the rate and divide by 4 to find an adjustment of 16 basis points). In summary, to convert a Treasury bond rate to an annual money market rate: (a) Multiply by 360/365—reducing the nominal rate (by 11 points in this case) and (b) compound up to annual—raising the nominal rate (by 16 points in this case). If the company borrows on a Eurodollar money market basis but is charged interest semi-annually rather than annually then the current swap rate for comparison purposes would be 8.07%.

Armed with this information, you quote a rate of say 8.27% to the company's Chief Financial Officer who replies "It's an excellent rate and I would like to take it, but I won't be drawing down on my revolver for another two weeks, so can we please start the swap for that date?" It is possible to do such a swap with a forward start date, but the price must be adjusted.

The reason is that the price quoted by the market to us will change. When such a deal is done, our counterpart in the market will hedge its position by taking a short position in Treasury bonds (effectively committing to pay the Treasury rate of 7.64% and earn the reverse repo rate of 6%, say). Running this position will cost them 1.64% per annum for a two week period, say 6 basis points ($1.64 \times 2/52$ approximately), which is spread over the life of the deal—in this case two years—for a cost of 3 basis points per annum, making the adjusted cost to the company 8.30% rather than 8.27%.

Another peculiarity in US$ interest rate swap pricing that arises from the fact that they price in relation to Treasuries is that the calculation of Treasury bond yields can be influenced by whether the bond being used for pricing purposes has a long or short first coupon. The points involved are technical and can usually be ignored as long as one is satisfied that the Treasury bond yield has been correctly calculated.

WHAT DETERMINES SWAP SPREADS?

The answer to this question depends on which segment of the market we are discussing. (See Figure 15.5.) The short end of the US$ interest rate swap curve, for example, tends to be much more volatile, because it is much more influenced by the futures market, against which arbitrages tend to be run for short swaps. The supply and demand factors in the US$ interst rate swap market overall include:

1. Volume of bond issues available to be swapped, that is, the condition of the US$ bond market, both Euro and domestic; the former being heavily influenced also by currency considerations and the number of issuers requiring floating rather than fixed; which is influenced also by expectations about the course of rates.
2. Volume of other fixed-rate instruments being placed and available to be swapped out of; for example, deals are often driven by medium-term deposits and certainly there are swaps out of CD issues. Similarly, the domestic U.S. private placement market is often a source of

Swaps & Spreads

Dollar Spreads Still Higher

Dollar spreads (in the 5-year area) reached their lowpoint late last summer at around 45 points (measured relative to US T-bond yields). Since then, they have moved up to near 75 points. A similar rise has occurred for longer maturity swap spreads.

One factor in the rise has been an increased liquidity premium on US T-bonds, meaning that the spread between yields on these and all other fixed rates (even prime euro-dollar bond yields) has tended to rise. Amidst the highly uncertain economic and political climate, investors have been understandably reluctant to enter into commitments (or assets) out of which there is not cheap and easy exist.

5-Year $ Swap Rate v. A & AA Corporate Yields

A second factor has been the increased quality spread which is typical of recession. For example, in the US domestic corporate bond market, A-rated yields have risen relative to AA-rated yields, and the latter relative to AAA benchmark yields. Thus corporations who face raised yield spreads in the public bond market can see advantage from switching to bank loans combined with a swap (away from fixed-rate debt issues) as a way of obtaining fixed rate finance.

It is true that margins on bank finance are also rising – but by less than the spreads in bond markets. Moreover, some corporations previously able to raise funds in the fixed rate bond market are effectively cut off from that source, as minimum credit standards there increase, and their own rating perhaps declines below investment grade.

Over the coming quarter, the factor mentioned will most likely continue to operate and some further upward pressure

on swap spreads is expected. An added factor in the same direction would be a growing perception that long-term fixed rates are near a lowpoint, triggering a substantial increase in borrowers' target proportion for fixed-rate dollar liabilities.

10-Year Yield Spreads: AAA Euro $ v. US T-Bonds & AA US Corporates

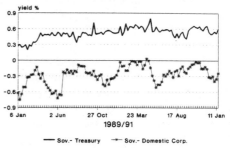

DM Swap Spreads – Hardly Visible

DM swap spreads, measured relative to Bund yields, are still very low by historical comparison, even if they have risen slightly from their end year lows. Behind the narrow spread lies in part the huge increase in public sector borrowing – meaning a relative scarcity for non-government fixed rate assets. Thus the yield spread, for example, of euro-DM paper over Bund yields is abnormally low (excluding 1987-8, when yield comparisons were distorted by withholding tax considerations). Also would-be fixed-rate payers have been in scarce supply at the present high absolute level of DM yields. And international borrowers have been unusually reluctant to

DM Swap Spreads: 5 & 10 Years (Relative to Bund Yields)

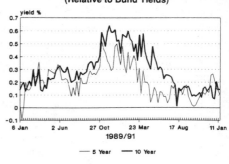

Figure 15.5   Reprinted with permission from "Market Perspectives" Mitsubishi Finance International, London.

take on fixed-rate DM liabilities, given the likelihood of DM appreciation and their increased interest cost.

Over the quarter ahead. DM swap spreads could rise somewhat. Foreign borrowers will most likely see diminished exchange risk in taking on DM liabilities. And if short-maturity fixed-rates do indeed fall as suggested here, some borrowers could decide to increase the proportion of their DM liabilities in fixed-rate form.

Yield Spreads: AAA Euro-DM v. Bund

Other European Swap Spreads

Elsewhere in Europe, Swiss franc swap rates in absolute terms have tended to fall slightly vis-à-vis DM swap rates. Unlike in the DM sector. there has been continuing supply (into the swap market of could-be fixed-rate receivers) from the international bond new issue market (in this case denominated in Swiss francs). A slight decline in Swiss franc swap rates is expected over the coming quarter, in line with franc bond yields.

5-Year Swap Rates: DM & SF

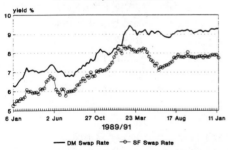

In the ECU sector, swap rates have been far above prime ECU yields for short and medium-term maturities. Yet little asset-swap business appears to have been unleashed in the form of switching out of ECU fixed-rate bonds into ECU deposits or FRNs coupled with a position in a swap as a

fixed-rate receiver. ECU swap rates appear to be underpinned by end-commercial demand in the "high coupn" European countries. In the 5-year area. ECU swap rates are slightly below French franc rates – making them attractive to French borrowers.

5-Year ECU & FF Swap Rates

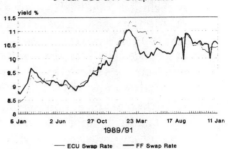

In the British pound sector there has been some increase recently in swap spreads (measured relative to gilt-edged yields) from the exceptionally low level of late last year. The big fall in the absolute level of rates since last summer together with the still high level of money market rates appears to be triggering some switch of corporate liabilities from floating rate to fixed (the transformation happening via the swap market).

5-Year $ & £ Swap Spreads
(Relative to Govt. Yields)

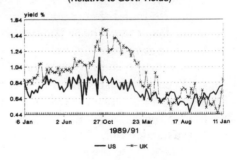

Figure 15.5 (*Continued*)

supply. When U.S. insurance companies have excess cash flow they often give attractive fixed rate loans which are then swapped into floating.

3. At the shorter end of the market, swappers are often hedging the other side with futures contracts or FRAs, so if the futures are trading rich against the cash markets, it can be profitable to be a fixed rate receiver on a swap and sell a strip of futures contracts.

4. A technical point is that swap market-makers will often hold their positions hedged against Treasury bonds. Normally, if they are payers, say, in the three-year swap, they will be long of three-year Treasuries as a hedge. The Treasuries will be financed in the "repo" market. If the repo rate rises above the Treasury rate, there will be a cost of carry and they will want to sell off the position, driving down the swap spread.

5. A further technical point is that when a new Treasury bond issue in a given maturity appears, swaps start to price against the "when-issued" Treasury, which generally yields a little less; swap spreads tend to kick up to compensate around the time of the changeover. This factor should wash out over time but often does not for a while.

Demand factors include:

1. The major influence is the corporate sector's general view of rates. If there is a consensus that rates will fall, swap spreads tend to fall, and vice versa. However, if the Treasury bond market traders are more bullish than the corporate sector, spreads tend to widen (as Treasuries fall faster than the swap rates) and vice versa.

2. When swap rates are below those on domestic U.S. private placements, medium-term borrowers switch into the swap market.

3. When swap rates are above those available on the bond market for comparable issuers, demand switches to the public bond market.

4. At times banks—particularly domestic U.S. banks—are willing to make unmatched fixed rate loans, especially when rates are falling. This tends to push swap spreads down by reducing demand for swaps by fixed-rate borrowers. Conversely, a pull-out by banks switches corporate demand to the swap market.

Other influences include the fact that the swap market is dominated by banking counterparties: corporate to corporate deals are less common than when the market started. So when there is concern about the banking system, spreads rise against Treasuries. At the time of the Continental Illinois crisis in 1984, spreads at the shorter end—two and three years—jumped around 40 to 50 basis points very quickly. Seasonal factors are also relevant: the market is relatively young to show a true seasonal pattern but certainly towards the end of the tax year it is quite common to see a clearing-out of positions, sometimes on the basis of up-front cash payments in exchange for off-market coupons.

SWAPS AGAINST THE STRIP

An important use of interest rate swaps by money market operations is in arbitrage against financial futures. This type of swap is structured slightly differently from the medium-term market, in that a one-year interest rate swap is done with a single fixed payment at maturity on the fixed-rate side, with four payments of three-month LIBOR on the other. The three-month LIBOR rolls can be hedged with futures.

Suppose today is December 13, and we contract to pay a fixed rate in a one-year interest rate swap of 7.9375%. The swap is for $10 million and is dealt for value spot, that is, December 15, with LIBOR rolls on March 15, June 15, and September 15. We agree with our counterparty that the first fix is 7.6%. Suppose that in the futures market the June Eurodollar contract, settling June 15, is trading at 92.25, while the September 15 and December 15 contracts are trading at 92.05 and 91.10.

We have paid fixed and will receive floating: our risk is that rates may fall. To hedge against this we buy the futures contracts: 10 contracts each for March, June and September. Suppose now that rates do in fact fall, and then rise again: LIBOR in March turns out to be 5%, in June it is 6%, and in September it is 7%. What happens to our deal? (See Table 15.4.)

The futures settle at 95, 94 and 93 in June, September and December respectively. The first LIBOR payment is determined by the fact that the initial fix was at 7.6%. (For the sake of simplicity we have assumed each quarter has 90 days.) Subsequent LIBOR payments vary with the market: but these variations are offset by changes in the value of the futures position. We can see this if we look at what might happen if rates move in the opposite direction: 11% in March, 12% in June, and 13% in September (see Table 15.5).

The net cash-flows are identical, though here the futures positions turn in a loss which offsets the rising stream of income from the LIBOR side of the swap. (In reality, one would need to allow, in analyzing the deal, for the interest element gained by having the initial net cash inflows compared with

Table 15.4 One-Year Interest Rate Swap Cash-Flows: Falling Rates

	LIBOR Income	Futures P&L	Fixed Payment	Net
March 15	190,000	0	0	190,000
June 15	125,000	68,750	0	193,750
Sept. 15	150,000	48,750	0	198,750
Dec. 15	175,000	47,500	793,750	−571,250
TOTAL				11,250

Table 15.5   One-Year Interest Rate Swap Cash-Flows: Rising Rates

	LIBOR Income	Futures P&L	Fixed Payment	Net
March 15	190,000	0	0	190,000
June 15	275,000	− 81,250	0	193,750
Sept. 15	300,000	−101,250	0	198,750
Dec. 15	325,000	−102,500	793,750	−571,250
TOTAL				11,250

the final net cash outflow; and changes in interest rates will affect the pattern of variation margin on the futures position favorably or unfavorably).

ASSET SWAPS

An important investment application for swaps is in the so-called "asset swap" market. Asset swaps are a way to shift paper from one market to another. Bonds have been issued consisting of floating rate notes swapped into fixed rates. An example would be the BECS issue in 1985, in which $100 million of U.K. government U.S. dollar floating rate notes were swapped into fixed-rate dollar bonds, producing "synthetic US dollar gilt edged bonds." More often, a fixed-rate bond is coupled with an interest rate (and perhaps a currency) swap, to produce a synthetic floating rate note.

It was not long before investment banks realized the value of the asset swap technique. Put bluntly, a failed fixed-rate bond could be transformed into a floating rate note and placed with banks, who are well accustomed to buying floating rate instruments. A particularly widespread use of the technique has been in the Japanese equity warrant bond market.

At its height, bonds in this market were being issued with coupons as low as 1% or 2%. This was because the attractions of the warrant were so great, that the bond to which the warrant was attached could be relatively lowly valued. Thus, immediately after the bond was issued, and the warrants were stripped away from it, the straight bond would fall to a sharp discount: a price of $70 or even $60 per $100 nominal. Traditionally, many investors are not interested in buying deep discount, low coupon bonds, for accounting and other reasons. Thus, while the warrant was a roaring success, the bonds would languish.

It was not long before the asset swappers perceived the opportunity. They would move in to buy the unwanted bonds, couple them with an interest rate swap, and sell them to the banks. These bonds, however, were operationally a great deal more complex to swap, because of the deep discount nature of the cash flows.

Asset swap activity has had both positive and negative effects. On the positive side, for every new issue, there is now generally a floor point below which the bond cannot fall. At some point it becomes "swappable": the bond's spread over Treasuries is above the spread which the swap market requires to swap

Table 15.6   Low Coupon Swap Cash Flows

	Pay to Swap Market	Receive 2% Coupon from X	Pay 30 bp Spread to X	Net
13/12/89	9,550,000	2,000,000	300,000	7,850,000
13/12/90	9,550,000	2,000,000	300,000	7,850,000
13/12/91	9,550,000	2,000,000	300,000	7,850,000
13/12/92	9,550,000	2,000,000	300,000	7,850,000
13/12/93	9,550,000	2,000,000	300,000	7,850,000

into floating rate. At that point, the bond can be redistributed into the floating rate market. This provides a natural floor price for the bond in the fixed rate market.

An example of an asset swap at work may be of interest. A low-coupon ex-warrant Japanese bond is swapped into floating rate: Today is December 13, 1988. We own a $100,000,000 five-year ex-warrant bond issue bearing a coupon of 2%. The price of the bonds is 69.73 for a yield (AIBD basis) of 9.98%. It is proposed to sell the bonds to X Bank who will buy the bonds at par and in exchange pay us the 2% coupon annually. In exchange, we will pay 12-month Libor (12-month Libor is used here for simplicity) + 30 basis points. To cover ourselves, we do a swap in the market at 9.55% (AIBD basis, against 12-month Libor). Our cash flows are shown in Table 15.6.

The key to valuing this deal is the net present value of the swap flows. If we revalue at 9.98%, which is the yield on the low-coupon bonds, on the grounds that in theory we can invest funds at that rate, the NPV of the stream of swap losses is $29,772,886.53. On the bond side, we buy the bonds at 69.73 and sell them at par, for a cash gain of $30,270,000. The difference is $497,113.47 which when spread back out over five years at a rate of 9.98% per annum is equivalent to an annual payment of $131,070 or roughly 13 basis points.

What has happened is that there was a profit margin of 43 basis points between the underlying yield on the bond and the swap rate paid to switch into a floating rate. That margin has been split as to 30 basis points to X Bank and 13 basis points for ourselves.

The example is simplified by ignoring interim six-monthly payments which would normally occur as the market tends to use six-month Libor; and if any other interest rate is used for the net present value calculations—the swap rate—then the symmetry of the deal disappears.

AN ISSUE-DRIVEN INTEREST RATE SWAP

A $100,000,000 five-year bond is being launched on August 1, 1989, for payment on August 15. It bears a 9.75% coupon and is being launched at 101.25, with fees of 1.25%. The five-year swap from August 1, 1989 to August 15, 1994 (that is, a slightly long five-year swap) is at 10% (annual 30/360) versus six-month Libor. The swap group is asked to price the swap after adjusting for the present value of the short first payment (see below).

The bond cash flows and the swap cash flows (allowing for a short first period—"stub period"—of August 1–15, 1989, on which we assume the Libor is fixed at, say, 7.25%), will be as shown in Table 15.7.

We need to find the net present value of the stub payment of $106,944.44. This is going to be earned by the swap group; it can be spread back out over time to push up the swap rate paid to the issuer.

To find the present value of the stub payment we must use the correct discount rate. This is the swap rate, but it is decompounded to turn it into a rate applicable to a 14-day period. The decompounding formula is (1) Convert rate to an annual effective rate (2) Take down to a daily rate (3) Compound back up over the number of days involved (4) Deduct 1, then gross up by 365/number of days to a percentage rate. Here we have the swap rate already at an annual effective rate of 10%. We take it down to a daily rate: $1.10^{(1/365)} = 1.0002611579$. There are 14 days involved: $1.0002611579^{14} = 1.003662423266$. So we now deduct 1 and we have $.003662423266 \times 365/14 = 9.54846\%$.

That is, a 10% rate decompounded down to a 14-day period is equivalent to a 9.54846% over that period. We now use this rate to discount our stub payment of $106,944.44 over 14 days. This discounts back to $106,554.19, that is, about 10.6 basis points on the principal amount. These 10.6 basis points need to be spread out over the five-years, making due allowance for the time value of money.

This is done by using the PMT function on an HP12C or Lotus spreadsheet to answer the question, what annual payment over five years at 10% extinguishes a loan of $106,554.19? The answer turns out to be $28,108.72 if we spread the lump sum over five years (to be truly exact it should be over five years and 14 days but the computations then would be rather tedious). That is, the swap rate of 10% can be adjusted up to 10.028%, say 10.03%. It may seem a lot of work for three basis points—but on a deal of that size it is worth the extra effort.

Table 15.7   Issue-Driven Interest Rate Swap

15 Aug 1989	$100,000,000*	$106,944.44
15 Aug 1990	$9,750,000	$10,000,000
15 Aug 1991	$9,750,000	$10,000,000
15 Aug 1992	$9,750,000	$10,000,000
15 Aug 1993	$9,750,000	$10,000,000
15 Aug 1994	$109,750,000	$10,000,000

*Net of fees.

CURRENCY SWAPS

The currency swap market is thought to have begun in the United Kingdom during the 1960s. The reason was the existence of U.K. exchange controls at that time which prevented U.K. firms wishing to invest abroad from simply selling sterling to buy foreign currency. The Bank of England wanted to prevent outflows of sterling, and so required British firms to borrow overseas to finance overseas investments. This had the drawback that their overseas subsidiaries were often quite weak credits compared with the U.K. parent; yet the U.K. parent often could not guarantee the overseas subsidiary because of exchange controls. So bankers came up with the idea of a swap between the U.K. parent and an overseas counterparty. The use of the swap meant that the Bank of England could be sure that an outflow of sterling today would be offset by an inflow at a later date when the swap unwound.

It may be helpful to start with a brief outline of how a currency swap works. Suppose that ICI needs US$ for its operations in the United States, and DuPont needs sterling for its U.K. operations. A solution to their need is for ICI to sell its sterling to Du Pont for dollars. To cut out the risk of exchange rate movements, they contract to reverse the deal in, say, five years. Say ICI sells £10 million to DuPont in exchange for $18 million (see Figure 15.6).

Effectively, ICI is lending sterling to DuPont, who are lending dollars to ICI. (Though the legal structure does not involve any assets on the balance sheet nor is the deal documented as a loan: it is an exchange of currencies).

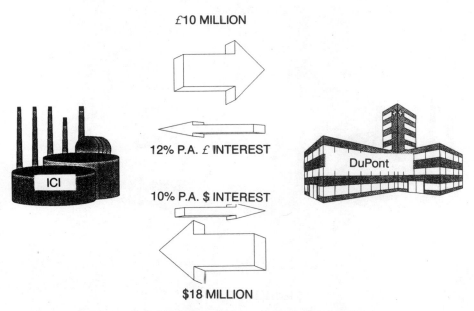

£10 MILLION

12% P.A. £ INTEREST

ICI

DuPont

10% P.A. $ INTEREST

$18 MILLION

Figure 15.6   ICI sells £10m. to Dupont for $18 m.

So during the life of the deal, ICI pay the rate for five-year dollar loans—say 10%—and DuPont pay the rate for five-year sterling loans—say 12%. At the end of the deal, ICI and DuPont re-exchange. (In some countries, such as the United Kingdom, it is desirable to interpose a bank between the two parties, because tax law would otherwise require the interest payments to be made net of tax. Interposing a bank also has the advantage of insulating the two parties from the credit risk of the other.) (See Figure 15.7.)

The cash flows are set out in the table from ICI's point of view, assuming that ICI borrowed the £10 million to lend to DuPont, also at 12%. At the start of the deal there is an inflow of £10 million from the original funding. This is paid across to DuPont at the start of the swap. In exchange, there is an inflow of $18 million from DuPont. The net effect is an inflow of $18 million.

For each of the next five years, ICI pays its lending bankers £1.2 million in interest on the original funding, and receives a corresponding payment from DuPont of £1.2 million, while paying out $1.8 million to DuPont. (Where practical, these payments are netted off.) The last payment includes redemption of the principal amounts. The net result is that a sterling stream of cashflows is transformed into a dollar stream (see Table 15.8).

Let us look at an issuer who wants to raise five-year money in U.S. dollars. Suppose his advisers tell him that the cheapest course would be to raise five-year deutsche marks, and swap them into U.S. dollars. How will this work?

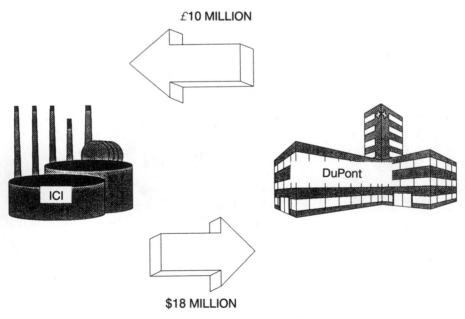

£10 MILLION

$18 MILLION

Figure 15.7   The swap unwinds.

Table 15.8   Sterling Currency Swap

	Swap US$	Cashflows £	Original Funding	Net
Day 1	$18m.	(£10m.)	£10m.	$18m.
Year 1	($ 1.8m.)	£ 1.2m.	(£ 1.2m.)	($ 1.8m.)
Year 2	($ 1.8m.)	£ 1.2m.	(£ 1.2m.)	($ 1.8m.)
Year 3	($ 1.8m.)	£ 1.2m.	(£ 1.2m.)	($ 1.8m.)
Year 4	($ 1.8m.)	£ 1.2m.	(£ 1.2m.)	($ 1.8m.)
Year 5	($19.8m.)	£11.2m.	(£11.2m.)	($19.8m.)

Suppose the rate (ignoring fees) for five-year DEM Eurobonds is 7% and the bond is issued at par for DEM200 million. Suppose today's spot US$/DEM rate is $1 = DEM2.00. Suppose that an American corporation wants five-year DEM financing at a rate of 8%, in exchange for being paid 10% on the US$ equivalent financing it will provide. We assume that the deal can be structured so that all interim flows, and the principal being re-exchanged at maturity, can be exchanged at a rate of $1 = DEM2.00 (see Table 15.9).

Here the issuer's bond cost is 7%, but he earns 8% on the swap, so there is a net additional 1% saving, making a total US$ cost of 9% per annum. What has happened is that the issuer, perhaps because it is a better known credit in the Euromarket, is able to raise five-year money cheaper than its swap counterpart: in exchange for passing on the cheap DEM, it is able to borrow cheap dollars.

Notice that the final cash flow includes exchange of principal amounts, unlike the interest rate swap deal; thus, the credit exposure (see below) on a currency swap will usually be much larger than under an interest rate swap. (In fact, in a currency swap, it is theoretically possible to lose more than 100% of the principal amount). It is theoretically possible to do a currency swap without exchanging principal at the end of the deal (it is quite common to do so without the initial exchange, which can be done in the spot market) but in that case the terms would normally include a "floating principal amount" which is recalculated for each interest payment date.

Table 15.9   Deutsche Mark Currency Swap

	Swap US$	Cashflows DEM	Original Funding	Net
Day 1	$100m.	(DEM200m.)	DEM200m.	$100m.
Year 1	($ 10m.)	DEM 16m.	(DEM 14m.)	($ 9m.)
Year 2	($ 10m.)	DEM 16m.	(DEM 14m.)	($ 9m.)
Year 3	($ 10m.)	DEM 16m.	(DEM 14m.)	($ 9m.)
Year 4	($ 10m.)	DEM 16m.	(DEM 14m.)	($ 9m.)
Year 5	($110m.)	DEM216m.	(DEM214m.)	($109m.)

The IBM/World Bank Swap

A more detailed real-life example may be of interest. In 1981 IBM and the World Bank entered into a currency swap: the World Bank, which had issued comparatively little US$ paper, could raise funds at an attractive rate in the U.S. market. It wanted CHF and DEM, but had issued a lot of bonds in Switzerland and Germany. IBM wanted to crystallize its foreign exchange gains on some existing CHF and DEM bonds outstanding. The solution benefitting both was for the World Bank to issue a US$ bond and swap the proceeds with IBM. Details of the transaction have never been published in full; the following outline draws on D. R. Bock's description (*Swap Finance*, B. Antl, ed., Euromoney Publications, London 1986, pp 218–223).

The bond issue was launched on August 11, 1981, settling August 25, which became the settlement date for the swap. The first annual exchange under the swap, however, was to be on March 30, the next coupon date on IBM's bonds—215 days (rather than 360 days) from the start date.

The first step was to calculate the value of the CHF and DEM flows which were (say) at 8% and 11% p.a. respectively. The initial 215-day period meant that the discount factors were $215/360 = 0.597222$, 1.597222, 2.597222 and so on. Applying the Swiss franc rate of 8%, then, the discount factors were $1/(1.08)^{0.597222} = 0.95507746$, $1/(1.08)^{1.597222} = 0.88433099$ etc. (See Table 15.10.)

The final terms of the swap were agreed on August 11, two weeks before the settlement date. So the World Bank bought the CHF and DEM NPV amounts worked out above, using two-week forward foreign exchange contracts. Supposing that these contracts were at CHF2.18 and DEM2.56 per US$, the dollar amounts needed by the World Bank were $87,783,247 to buy the CHF and $117,701,753 for the DEM, totalling $205,485,000.

It was then necessary to work out the dollar amount of the bond to be issued. Supposing the issue to be at a coupon of 16% with fees of 2.15% (i.e. net proceeds of 97.85%) the dollar amount of the bond issue had to be $205,485,000/0.9785 = $210,000,000$. So the final results of the deal are shown in Table 15.11.

Table 15.10   IBM/World Bank Swap Cash Flows

Exchange Date	CHF Flows	CHF Discount Factor	DEM Flows	DEM Discount Factor
3/30/82	12,375,000	0.95507746	30,000,000	0.93957644
3/30/83	12,375,000	0.88433099	30,000,000	0.84646526
3/30/84	12,375,000	0.81882499	30,000,000	0.76258132
3/30/85	12,375,000	0.75818128	30,000,000	0.68701020
3/30/86	212,375,000	0.70201045	330,000,000	0.61892811
NPV	CHF191,367,478		DEM301,315,273	

Table 15.11   IBM/World Bank Swap: Final Outcome

Exchange Date	CHF Flows	DEM Flows	US$ Flows
30 March 1982	12,375,000	30,000,000	20,066,667*
30 March 1983	12,375,000	30,000,000	33,600,000
30 March 1984	12,375,000	30,000,000	33,600,000
30 March 1985	12,375,000	30,000,000	33,600,000
30 March 1986	212,375,000	330,000,000	243,600,000
Discount rate	8%	11%	16.8%[†]
NPV	CHF191,367,478	DEM301,315,273	$205,485,000
FX forward	CHF2.18/$	DEM2.56/$	—
US$ NPV	$87,783,247	$117,701,753	$205,485,000

*The first $ amount is less because of the partial first period on the bond issue.
[†]The yield to maturity on a 16% bond, due 30 March 1986 and bought on 25 August 1981 is 16.61%.

SWAP CREDIT RISK

An important aspect of swaps is a question of credit risk. The credit risk on an interest rate swap falls into two parts. First, the risk that the counterparty fails. Second, the risk that interest rates have moved in the wrong direction. Thus, if interest rates move in the wrong direction but the counterparty does not fail, there is no loss: equally, if the counterparty fails but interest rates have moved favorably, the bank doing the original swap may find that the bankruptcy of its counterpart crystallizes a profit, rather than a loss. It should be noted, therefore, that the credit risk here is in fact two-way: the bank has a credit risk on its counterparty, but if rates move the other way, the counterparty will have a credit risk on it.

To illustrate the credit risk, let us suppose that a bank enters into a swap deal with a corporation which agrees to pay 14% for five years against 6-month LIBOR. Interest rates fall sharply, but after two years, the corporation goes bankrupt. There are three years remaining in the life of the swap, and at this time, the three-year rate is 10%. Accordingly, the bank undertakes a new swap with another counterparty, which agrees to pay the bank 10% for the next three years. Assuming that the bank had covered its original contract, let us say with another bank, its original obligation to pay 14% to the other bank is still in force for the next three years.

Hence, on the one hand, it is receiving 10% and, on the other, paying 14%, and it has crystallized a loss for three years. In the converse case, in the event that rates had risen sharply after the contract was concluded, the bank would crystallize a profit: on the other hand, it is quite probable that the trustee in bankruptcy would elect to continue the contract, since it is favorable to the firm, rather than default. The whole subject of credit risk for swaps and other off-balance sheet instruments is dealt with more fully in Chapter 21.

UNWINDING AN INTEREST RATE SWAP

Once an interest rate swap has been entered into, its parties normally expect it to run to maturity. But there may be times when we need to reverse or cancel the swap because circumstances have changed and the swap is no longer required; or one party may want to crystallise a profit made on the swap; or it may be necessary to value the swap for "mark-to-market" purposes. In all these cases, a valuation of the swap needs to be made.

To do this we begin by recognising that for valuation purposes a swap can be treated as if it were a combination of a fixed-rate bond and a floating-rate note. Suppose we have done the following swap:

Coupon:	8%
Start date:	30 October, 1986
Maturity:	30 October, 1991
First LIBOR:	$5^7/8$%
Fixed rate basis:	Semi-annual, actual/365
Floating rate:	Six-month Libor, payable semi-annually, actual/360
Notional amount:	$10 million
Counterparty:	ABC Bank

It is just over two weeks later, November 14, and the swap rate has risen to 9%. We originally contracted to pay the fixed rate: now we want to lock our profit. So we approach ABC Bank and ask for a price for a swap against six-month Libor maturing October 30, 1991, with Libor roll dates on April 30 and October 30 (i.e. there is a short, "stub" period to the first coupon payment—it would normally be May 14 for a November 14 start). ABC Bank is willing to pay 9%. We then ask ABC Bank to quote a price for canceling the original swap: that is, ABC Bank will pay us a lump sum in exchange for terminating its original deal with us.

ABC's valuation of the swap will proceed as follows. Suppose the Libor fixing agreed for the period November 14, 1986—April 30, 1987 is $6^1/16$%. Then on the next coupon date, April 30, ABC Bank would expect to receive $6^1/16$% × $10 million × 167/360 (since there are 167 days from November 14 to April 30, and the Libor side of the deal is on an actual/360 basis). This totals $281,232.63. Similarly, on the first swap, it was due to pay $5^7/8$% × $10 million × 182/360 or a total of $297,013.88. So on the first period LIBOR payments, ABC Bank is due to pay us the net difference between these two sums, namely $297,013.88 − $281,232.63 = $15,781.25.

We come now to consider the fixed payments. Here we have an initial stream of payments which we committed to pay ABC Bank at 8%. Since they are on an actual/365 day basis, the payments due vary slightly according to the number of days in the period (183 or 182 days); they are shown in Table 15.12.

Now we need to find the net present value of these flows. The calculation is complicated by the fact that we have a short first "stub" period. The simplest way is to work out the NPV on the next coupon date, i.e. April 30, 1987. We value the stream of flows using the new swap rate of 9%, and on that basis the NPV of the stream of flows from October 30, 1987–April 30, 1991 is $300,089 approximately.

The next step is to consider the discount factor for the odd first period. We have a total of 167 days in this period. Our first step is work that out as a fraction of the year: 167/365 is 0.4575. Then we apply this fractional compounding period to our discount rate of 9%, after we have converted the 9% to a true annual rate i.e. 9.2025%. That is, we have $1.092025^{0.4575} = 1.0411$ as our discount factor. We apply this factor to the total income stream due on April 30, 1987, that is, the NPV of the future coupons plus the "stub" period payment, which is $12,102.33. This produces ($300,089 + $12,102)/1.0411 = $299,866 as the NPV of the fixed income stream from the pair of swaps.

On the other side, we have worked out that the Libor differences amount to $15,781 in our favor: however, this income is not due till the first coupon date, so we need to discount it back to today, using the odd period discount factor again. So $15,781/1.0411 = $15,158. Adding these two together gives us $299,866 + $15,158 = $315,024 as the NPV of the pair of swaps: i.e. that is what ABC Bank should be willing to pay us in exchange for canceling the deal.

A shorter method, once one understands what is happening, is to apply the normal present value formula using fractional exponents. In this case, then, all of the flows would have been discounted with discount factors having exponents of 1.0411, 2.0411, 3.0411 etc.

Table 15.12   Fixed Payments

	We Pay	ABC Pays	Net to Us
30 April 1987	$398,904.11	$411,006.44	$12,102.33
30 October	$401,095.89	$451,232.88	$50,136.99
30 April 1988	$401,095.89	$451,232.88	$50,136.99
30 October	$401,095.89	$451,232.88	$50,136.99
30 April 1989	$398,904.11	$448,767.12	$49,863.01
30 October	$401,095.89	$451,232.88	$50,136.99
30 April 1990	$398,904.11	$448,767.12	$49,863.01
30 October	$401,095.89	$451,232.88	$50,136.99
30 April 1991	$398,904.11	$448,767.12	$49,863.01
30 October	$401,095.89	$451,232.88	$50,136.01

To repeat, then, the value of the swap is the net present value of the stream of fixed payments that would result from matching it off against a new swap at today's rates, net of the Libor payments due on the floating side. This valuation method would be applied in marking a swap to market or in valuing a swap for unwinding purposes.

SWAPS VALUATION AND ACCOUNTING

The subject of valuing and accounting for swaps has been bedevilled by debates between proponents of various views and by the fact that swaps are applied in so many different financial contexts. The key debate has been between accrual accounting and market-to-market. Proponents of accrual accounting argue that the value of the swap should not be fully taken to income until it has expired because until maturity there remains a credit risk, which means there is a risk that the income is not in fact earned. The parallel is with the interest earned on a loan.

Proponents of mark-to-market point out that the net present value of the income stream from a swap will vary in line with market rates of interest. For example, take the case of a firm which has entered into an asset swap whereby they hold a bond and an interest rate swap as a combined package. The bond must be marked to market under existing accounting rules: if the interest rate swap is not, there will not be a true picture of the value of the position.

On the other hand, where a swap has been booked against a bank loan, perhaps to make it into a fixed rate, since the loan is not marked to market, it would be inconsistent to mark the swap to market. The difficulty arises from the fact that swaps are used both by operations who customarily mark to market—bond traders for example—and those who do not—e.g. bank lending departments.

Essentially the appropriate treatment must depend on (a) the treatment given to the asset or liability which the swap is hedging; (b) the intent of the original swap—was it taken on as a trading position or to hedge an exposure?; (c) local applicable regulations.

COMMODITY SWAPS

An important extension of the swap technique has been to the commodity markets—an interesting example of history moving full circle, since it was the commodity markets which developed futures, without which swaps would not have grown to the scale they have done. The most widely used commodity swap market is that for oil and related products, but the technique has been used in gold and copper markets also and in principle could be applied to the market for any commodity where there is a standardized, traded commodity—though preferably one where there are futures contracts which allow for the laying off of short-term risk.

An example of how the commodity swap technique can fit into the wider framework of international finance was a deal done with a Mexican copper firm. This deal opened the way to voluntary new bank lending to a Mexican borrower at a time when the country was not seen as a good risk. The Mexican firm borrowed about $200 million from a banking syndicate, with repayments coming from the sale of copper to a Belgian company. The sale price is fixed at the average market price at time of delivery—so clearly the Mexican firm would be exposed to a fall in the copper price over the three-year term of the loan. The solution was a three-year copper swap with Paribas, a French bank, under which the bank contracted to pay a fixed price for the Mexican firm's copper, in exchange for receiving the floating, market price. To eliminate its risk, it is understood, the French bank entered into a matching, opposite swap with a copper user which wished to hedge against a rise in copper prices.

These applications are part of a wider trend of integrating commodity and financial markets. For example, the gold market has developed significant activity in gold borrowing and lending; gold loans have been made to gold producers, and the banks involved in the loans are active borrowers of gold from gold holders, so that there is now a gold LIBOR just as there is a $ LIBOR or a yen LIBOR. Another related move has been the introduction of Forward Rate Agreements (see Chapter 6) on gold. These allow gold borrowers and lenders to hedge short-term movements in the gold LIBOR rate.

The whole financial markets technology—swaps, options, caps, floors, collars and so on—can in principle be applied to any commodity. However, the practical restrictions are that there has to be a sufficiently widely traded benchmark and preferably a decent futures market for hedging. In fact, the question of liquidity in these markets becomes of key importance for bank intermediaries such as Paribas, because of the question of counterparty risk.

If a swap counterparty fails, banks will normally seek to find another counterparty to step into the swap so that the bank's position is still matched. But whereas it is fairly straightforward to assess the counterparty risk on a five year interest rate swap against three month Libor—there will always be someone who is prepared to replace a defaulted swap at a price because so many firms are exposed to Libor—this does not apply to, say, a five-year copper swap.

In the copper swap discussed above, the French bank faces two risks: (a) the copper price movement—which could be positive or negative; (b) the risk that they are left with an open swap position which cannot be closed out at any price. As these markets develop they will raise interesting questions for the regulators regarding the capital adequacy rules that have been put in place for swaps. (See Chapter 18 on capital adequacy.)

The role of the regulators will clearly be important: in the United States, commodity swaps were inhibited by regulatory uncertainty, with the Commodity Futures Trading Commission (CFTC) trying to exercise its sway over the swaps market until July 1989, when it announced that it would not seek to exert its authority over commoodity swaps, provided (1) commodity swaps must not be marketed to the public; (2) they must be "negotiated by the parties as to their material terms, based upon individualized credit determinations, and documented by the parties in an agreement or series of agreements that is not fully standardized"; (3) they "must create obligations that are terminable, absent default, only with the consent of the counterparty"; (4) they must "not [be] supported by the credit of a clearing organization . . [or] . . . primarily or routinely supported by a mark-to-market margin and variation settlement system designed to eliminate individualized credit risk"; (5) they must be "undertaken in conjunction with the parties' line of business."

These conditions represent bureaucratic interference at its worst, since (2) is not just pointless but harmful—the more standardized the better, since it helps market liquidity. The CFTC is busily trying to prevent the development of "readily transferred" swaps—a positively retrograde step since it tends to discourage participants from unwinding positions and clearing them off their books.

16 Options Principles

Options are a very useful tool in money and foreign exchange markets. They allow us the luxury of a one-way bet. We can bet that a rate will go up and make a profit from that; but if it comes down, we don't lose. They are particularly useful for hedging cash flows when we feel rather uncertain about the future. They have a second use: They can be used to take leveraged, or geared, positions. These attractions have led to very rapid growth in the options markets in recent years. There are options on "cash" markets for foreign exchange, deposits, bonds, bills, equities, and commodities; there are options on swaps, and on equity indices; and there are options on a range of futures contracts. This chapter covers the principles of options, and Chapter 17 covers some applications.

THE ROLE OF OPTIONS

People think options are complex. This is only partly true. The basic fact
about an option is that it is a one-way bet. You pay a price for the privilege of
the one-way bet. Deciding on whether that price is worth it to you is very
simple. It has very little to do with the market's calculation of fair value—
where all the complexity lies. The golden rule is to use your common sense
and assess the value to you. It is like buying a house. The vendor may tell you
how much he or she spent on the plumbing and wiring, how many years they
have spent redecorating. But your only decision is: Either the house is worth
it to you at that price or it isn't.

A long time ago, Adam Smith drew this same distinction between price in
the market and value to the owner: "Nothing is more useful than water: but
it will purchase scarce anything; scarce anything can be had in exchange for
it. A diamond, on the contrary, has scarce any value in use; but a very great
quantity of other goods may frequently be had in exchange for it."

It is the same with buying an option. Either the option meets your business
or investment needs at a price that you think is worth it, or not. If you are
buying an option, the value to you may be much more—or much less—than
the market is charging. Conversely, if you are selling (or writing) an option, no
matter what you think the fair value of the option is, its price will be what the
market will pay for it. All those elaborate computer models mean nothing if
no one wants to buy the option. Although there are some quite complicated
theories of options pricing, the final decision is the same as any other financial decision: Is the value of this thing, to me, more or less than the price in the
market? Having said all that, we still need to know how the market values
options. That is what we look at in the next two chapters. We start by looking
at the role of options in the marketplace today.

Options serve the needs of a number of users—investors, hedgers and speculators. For the investor, and for the hedger, the main attraction of options is
that they give him or her a one-way bet. A pension fund may own shares in
IBM; the option allows them to protect themselves (insure themselves) against
the risk of a fall in the stock while allowing them to gain from a rise. Or take a
corporation borrowing at six-month Libor. Financial markets have been
volatile; the Treasurer is very uncertain about the direction of the next move
in rates, but the company is heavily borrowed and can ill afford a sharp rise in
rates. By buying an interest rate cap (a type of option) the Treasurer can
protect the company against a rise in rates while leaving the company posi-
tioned to benefit from any possible fall.

The cost of the option needs to be factored into the calculation. Sometimes, if uncertainty in the financial markets is very widespread, the cost of
the option will be excessive in relation to the company's risk. Often, however, this is not the case. Historically, it has quite often been possible to buy
interest rate insurance at relatively low cost (as Chemical Bank proved in

1989 when its profit and loss figures were hit by a revaluation of its interest rate options book: they had been priced too cheaply).

For the speculator, one of the main attractions of options is that they give the speculator a great deal of gearing or leverage. One can make large percentage profits from only a small change in the price of the underlying currency. And the risk is limited to a fixed dollar amount—the price originally paid for the option. Suppose for example we have sterling trading at $2.00 and a six-month option to buy sterling at $2.20 costs us $0.025, that is 2.5 cents. Suppose sterling jumps now to $2.10. For reasons we will explain below, the option's price would not move exactly in proportion, so the option's price may rise from $0.025 to $0.035. Sterling rose by 5%: but the price of the option rose by 40%.

Options are also important because they bring an extra dimension to financial instruments. First, the development of options markets has meant it is possible to trade volatility. That is, one can take a view not on the direction of a price change, but on how volatile it will be. An example would be the "straddle" trade discussed next. The trader takes no view on the direction of the market but bets that it will be more volatile than today. Secondly, many of the new financial instruments, particularly those seen in the bond markets (see J. K. Walmsley, *The New Financial Instruments,* John Wiley, New York, 1988) have "embedded" in them a form of option: either an interest rate option, or a currency option. Thus, analysis of these instruments depends on option pricing.

THE OPTIONS MARKET

Though they have only recently taken off in volume worldwide, options have been around a long time. "Traditional" options on equities (effectively an over-the-counter option written by a market-maker) developed on the London stock market in the nineteenth century. But until 1973, it was possible to buy an option, but it was not really possible to trade it. Exchange traded options were introduced in 1973 by the Chicago Board Options Exchange (CBOE). The single most important CBOE innovation was to set up standard option prices and expiry dates. This allowed development of a secondary market. That brought liquidity into options trading.

Both the options and futures industry have been experiencing a period of worldwide growth. The over-the-counter market has grown explosively, but its growth is difficult to measure in the absence of reliable statistics. The growth of exchange-listed options has been rapid. The CBOE was followed by the American Stock Exchange, the Philadelphia Stock Exchange, the Midwest Stock Exchange, and the Pacific Stock Exchange. Until 1982, growth in the United States was held back by the struggles between the various regulatory bodies. From 1982 to 1985, the dominant feature was the explosion of new contracts in the United States as the various exchanges struggled for successful market products. 1985/6 began to see this spread of futures and options abroad.

Early players were the European Options Exchange in Amsterdam and the London Stock Exchange, and the London International Financial Futures Exchange (LIFFE, set up in 1982, merged with the Stock Exchange's London Traded Options Market in 1991 to form the London Derivatives Exchange). In Sweden, the Optionsmaklarna (OM) has become an international player, setting up its operations in London and other centers also. In France, the Monep is active and the Deutsche Terminborse has options on equities. Table 16.1 shows the major contracts worldwide.

The debate on over-the-counter versus exchange traded options has been ongoing. The merits of exchange trading are transparency—the last price at which the contract traded is always known—and (usually) liquidity—a traded option that we have bought can be sold again. This is not so easy for an over-the-counter option. Proponents of over-the-counter options point to their flexibility—an option can be tailored to suit the user's needs and in particular can be written for a longer term; most exchange-traded options have a maximum maturity of one year and the vast bulk are for three or six months. Liquidity in certain options markets—notably currency and some interest rate options—is also sometimes better in the over-the-counter market than on the exchanges. In stock market options, the reverse is generally true, at least for options on individual stocks, although a number of market-makers in London and elsewhere will write over-the-counter options in size on equity indexes.

Another issue that arises in comparing OTC versus exchange-traded options is the legal and tax position. In many cases, the tax treatment of an option varies depending on whether or not it is traded on a recognized exchange. Likewise the legal position regarding OTC options can be tricky (as in the recent case in the United Kingdom where the local authority,

Table 16.1   The Top 10 Financial Options Contracts (M. Contracts) 1990

S&P 100	CBOE	68.8
Treasury bond	CBOT	27.3
S&P 500	CBOE	12.1
Nikkei 225	Osaka	9.2
Notionnel	MATIF	7.4
Eurodollar	CME	6.8
XMI (MMI)	Amex	5.6
OMX	OM	5.2
DEM	PHLX	4.9
SMI	Soffex	4.7

Source: Futures & Options World, February 1991.

Hammersmith & Fulham, was found not to have the legal power to write OTC option contracts).

By contrast, when dealing on an exchange, one's counterparty is the clearing house. For practical purposes, in normal circumstances, the question of credit risk does not arise. The Options Clearing Corporation in the United States, which is owned by its members, has substantial protection in place against possible default; in London, options contracts clear through the International Commodities Clearing House (ICCH) which is owned by several major banks (Barclays, Lloyds, National Westminster, Midland, Royal Bank of Scotland, and Standard Chartered Bank), who between them represent an extremely strong credit.

Traded *options on debt instruments* were introduced later than on stocks. The first was in October 1982, when the CBOT introduced an options contract on Treasury bond futures. In subsequent years, they have become quite widely spread. There is an option on the Treasury note future (CBOT), an option on Eurodollar futures (IMM), options on specific Treasury bonds (CBOE) and Treasury notes (CBOE), together with options on 10-year Treasury notes (AMEX), and options on 13-week Treasury bills (AMEX). In addition, in Montreal, options on Government of Canada long-term bonds are traded, while in Europe, the LIFFE offers options on gilt-edged and the European Options Exchange offers options on Dutch State loans. In addition, many banks will write over-the-counter options on specific interest rates or securities. One of the most widely used is the area of caps and floors which is dealt with in Chapter 17.

The over-the-counter market in *currency options* began to develop in the early 1980s, but the first listed currency options were those on the Philadelphia Stock Exchange, which were introduced in December 1982. Options are also traded on the IMM, which introduced an option on the Deutsche mark in 1983, and the Chicago Board Options Exchange, which has options on Deutsche marks, Swiss francs, French francs, Canadian dollars, Sterling, and Japanese yen. Options have also been introduced on the London International Financial Futures Exchange (LIFFE). In general, exchange-traded options extend up to 9 months only, though the over-the-counter market offers longer-term options. It is also possible to indirectly buy long-term currency options by buying securities with embedded currency options.

Options on futures are also widely available. An option on a futures contract differs from the more traditional options in only one essential way: the underlying security is not a cash security, but a futures contract on the security. So if an option buyer exercises his call, he acquires a long position in futures instead of a long position in the cash security. The resulting long and short futures positions are like any other future positions and are subject to daily marking to market.

Although an option on a futures contract may seem complicated, in many ways it is simpler to analyze and trade than an option on a cash instrument. This is because the impact of the cash flows of the security is already taken into account in the price of the futures contract. Hence, it need not be considered in pricing the option. Futures do not pay coupons. As a result, the highest volume of trading in debt options on the exchanges has been in options on futures contracts. These contracts include options on Treasury bond futures, options on Treasury note futures, and options on Eurodollar time deposit rate futures.

The mechanics of taking delivery are that the futures position is established at the strike price, then immediately marked to market. The difference between the strike price and the current futures price is paid to the call option holder, if the mark to market shows up a loss.

Finally we should mention *warrants,* a kind of sister market to the options market. A warrant is an option; the basic difference is that a warrant is usually listed on a stock exchange rather than traded on an options exchange. Also, a warrant usually has a longer life—warrants exist with maturities of 10 or 15 years. A number of banks have issued currency and interest rate warrants (see J. K. Walmsley, *New Financial Instruments,* John Wiley, New York, 1988), and there is a large market for equity warrants (particularly on Japanese stocks).

BASICS OF AN OPTION CONTRACT

An option is an agreement between two parties. One party grants the other the right to buy or sell an instrument under certain conditions. The instrument may be a stock, bond, futures contract, interest rate, or foreign currency. The counterparty pays a *premium* for the privilege of being able to buy or sell the instrument, without committing to do so. There two basic types of options: puts and calls. A *call* option gives the buyer the right to buy or "call away" a specified amount of the underlying instrument at the specified price, during a specified period. The price at which the instrument may be bought is the *exercise price* or the *strike price.* The last date on which the option may be exercised is called the *expiry date,* or the maturity date. A *put* option gives the buyer the right to sell or put to the writer a specified amount of the underlying instrument at the strike price until the expiry date.

The period during which the option can be exercised depends on its type— American, or European. Under an American option, the holder of the option has the right to exercise at any time before maturity. Under a European option, the holder may only exercise it at the time of expiration, or for a short period beforehand.

A call option is best described by a simple example. Suppose Bank A sells us a three-month European call option on the DEM at a strike of DM2.00, in an amount of DM10,000,000. This means that we have the right, in three months, to pay $5 million to buy DM 10 million. Clearly, if the DEM strengthens to, say, DM1.90 per dollar (so that it would cost us $5,263,157 to buy DM10,000,000 in the market) the option will have substantial value to us.

Conversely, if, at the maturity of the option, the spot rate is DM2.20, the option will have no value.

Let's put together some basic building blocks for analyzing options. Let's look at an option on sterling at $2.00 per £1: a call option, American style. Let's see how the option would behave on the last day of its life. When spot sterling is trading in the market at say $2.20, it would be possible to buy the option, exercise it at $2.00, and sell at $2.20. So the option will be worth at least $0.20—the difference between $2.00 and $2.20. If the option costs less, one could buy, exercise, and sell for a net profit. And it will be worth no more than $0.20—if it were worth more, anyone buying the option would take a loss (assuming we are trading in the final few minutes of the option's life). Conversely, if sterling were trading at $2.10 at this time, the option would be worth $0.10. If the pound were below $2.00, the option would be worthless— you could buy sterling cheaper directly in the market than by exercising the right to buy at $2.00.

We said that if sterling were trading at $2.10 at the maturity of the option it would be worth $0.10. This difference between the currency price and the exercise price of the call option is often called its *intrinsic value*. Thus, when sterling is at $2.10, the option has an intrinsic value of $0.10: at $2.30, an intrinsic value of $0.30. The only thing that affects intrinsic value is the gap between price of the underlying instrument (in this case sterling) and the strike price. Any excess premium over the intrinsic value of the option is called the *time value*, which is discussed more fully below.

If the sterling is above the strike price, then the option will have intrinsic value, and is said to be "in the money." If the sterling's value equals the strike price, then the intrinsic value is zero. The option is said to be "at the money." If sterling is trading below the strike price, then the option is said to be "out of the money."

OPTION PAY-OFF DIAGRAMS

It is possible to draw a diagram showing the outcomes for different exchange rates at maturity—an option pay-off diagram. Table 16.2 and Figure 16.1 show the results. This is the basic payoff profile of a call option, to which we will often return. At this stage, the key point to note is that there is unlimited profit potential as the pound rises, and limited loss as it falls. (There will be a loss, not shown in the table: the loss is the amount of premium spent in buying an option which turned out to be worthless at expiry).

We can do the same exercise for a put on the pound at $2.00, see Table 16.3. Again, we can draw the profile of the put in the last few minutes of its life (Figure 16.2). There is unlimited profit potential, this time as sterling falls, and limited risk of loss—the maximum loss will be the premium paid out.

Let's look at the position that would arise if instead of buying a call we had sold, or written, a call. When we bought a call, we had the right but not

Table 16.2   Call Option Payoff Profile—Strike $2.00

Market Rate at Maturity	Intrinsic Value of the Option
$2.40	.40
2.30	.30
2.20	.20
2.10	.10
2.00	0
1.90	0
1.80	0
1.70	0
1.60	0

the obligation, to buy sterling at $2.00. But now we have sold the call. We have the obligation, but not the right, to sell the pound at $2.00. If sterling rises above $2.00, we must sell it to the party who bought the option, instead of selling in the marketplace. So we will make a loss. The loss is unlimited: for example, if sterling rises to $3.00 our loss will be $1.00 per pound. If sterling, at the expiry of the option, closes below $2.00, we will make a profit. Our profit will be the premium we charged for selling the option. Our profit is limited to the premium. So the writer of a call has unlimited risk, with a limited profit potential. We can see this in the diagram (Figure 16.3). The same applies if we were to write a put (Figure 16.4). Why would anyone be

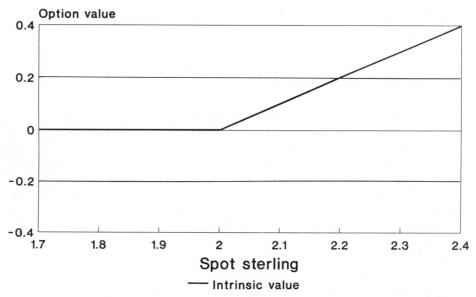

Figure 16.1   Call option profile.

Table 16.3 Put Option Payoff Profile—Strike $2.00

Market Rate	Intrinsic Value
$2.40	0
2.30	0
2.20	0
2.10	0
2.00	0
1.90	.10
1.80	.20
1.70	.30
1.60	.40

crazy enough to write options, then? Well, writing an open (or "naked") options position can be very risky: but it can be well rewarded, in the shape of a substantial premium. After all, that is how insurance companies make money. They take risks in exchange for premium income. Also, there are hedging techniques which can reduce the risk.

Finally, because we will be needing to combine positions later, it will be helpful if we show a similar payoff diagram for the straightforward long and short positions. Figure 16.5 shows the payoff if we are long sterling at, say, $2.00—our profit rises as sterling rises, as sterling falls we start to make a loss. Likewise we can draw the payoff from being short (see Figure 16.6).

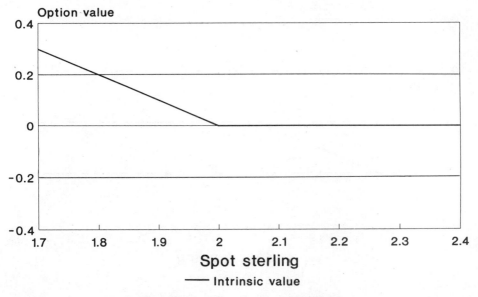

Figure 16.2 Put option payoff profile.

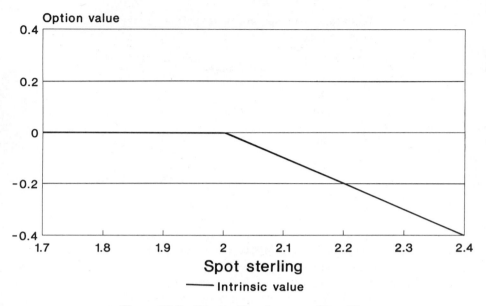

Figure 16.3 Short call option: payoff profile.

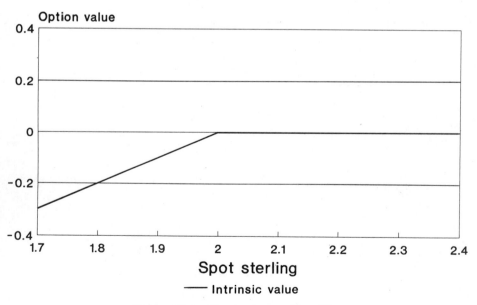

Figure 16.4 Short put: payoff profile.

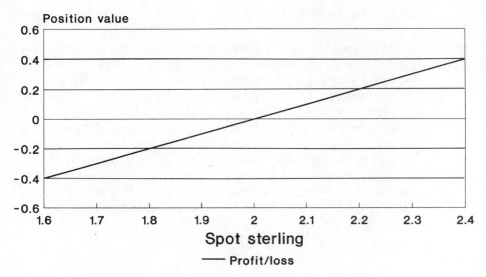

Figure 16.5 Long asset position payoff profile.

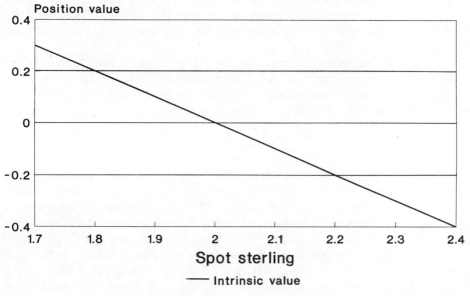

Figure 16.6 Short asset: payoff profile.

COMBINED POSITIONS

More complex options strategies can be employed (and are discussed in the next chapter). The first one we will introduce is a very important one because it shows the relationship of puts and calls to the underlying asset. If you look at the diagram for being long an asset, you will see a line sloping up from left to right. If you look at the diagram for being long a call, you will see a line sloping up from left to right in the top right corner of the diagram. If you look at the diagram for being short on a put, you will see a diagram sloping up from left to right again, but this time in the bottom left corner. This suggests that being short a put, and long a call at the same strike, will produce the same payoff profile as being long the asset. This is in fact right: it will always be true that, for any given strike level for a put and call, we can write:

$$+ \text{asset} = + \text{call} - \text{put}$$

where + means we are long, − means we are short. Thus being long of a call and short a put on a given asset is equivalent in profit terms to being long of the asset. Conversely, to be short the asset is the same as being long a put and short the call. More formally, we could write C for the price of the call, P for the price of the put, A for the price of the asset and S for the strike price:

$$A - S = C - P$$

That is, the intrinsic value of the option (the difference between asset price and the strike of the option) will be equal to the difference between the price of the call and the price of the put. This is known in the jargon as "put call parity."

Note that the above statement of put-call parity is strictly true only for American options—those allowing exercise at any time. If the two options involved were European options allowing only for exercise at maturity, we would have to allow for the time value of money:

$$PV(A - S) = C - P$$

where PV means the present value. Also, we can rearrange the original equation. We could write, for example, + asset + put = + call or + asset − call = − put. So if we owned the asset and a put on the asset, it would be the same as owning a call on the asset; if we owned the asset and had sold a call on it, it would be the same as being short a put on the asset. This put-call parity is often useful when we want to construct a *synthetic* position—either to create a put, for example, if we cannot buy a put directly in the market, or even to create the asset from the put and the call—a synthetic asset. These positions are set out in the next chapter.

Table 16.4 Option straddle

	Put Option Strike $2.00	Call Option Strike $2.00	
Market Rate	Put Intrinsic Value	Call Intrinsic Value	Combined Intrinsic Value
$1.60	0.4	0	0.4
1.70	0.3	0	0.3
1.80	0.2	0	0.2
1.90	0.1	0	0.1
2.00	0	0	0
2.10	0	0.1	0.1
2.20	0	0.2	0.2
2.30	0	0.3	0.3
2.40	0	0.4	0.4

The next two basic combinations of option positions are the straddle and the strangle. The *straddle* is when we buy a put and a call at the same strike price. Although we pay out two lots of premium, we will make money if the market becomes volatile. Either the put or the call will pay off. We lose out if the market stays stable. Let's combine the put and call on sterling at $2.00 that we looked at. We would get the pay-off pattern as shown in Table 16.4, Figure 16.7.

The *strangle* is a similar strategy, but the put and call have different exercise prices. Normally one or both of the options bought are out of the

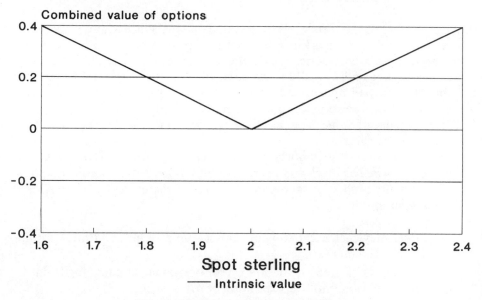

Figure 16.7 Straddle payoff profile.

Table 16.5   Option Strangle

Market Rate	Put Option Strike $2.00 Put Intrinsic Value	Call Option Strike $2.10 Call Intrinsic Value	Combined Intrinsic Value
$M1.60	0.4	0	0.4
1.70	0.3	0	0.3
1.80	0.2	0	0.2
1.90	0.1	0	0.1
2.00	0	0	0
2.10	0	0	0
2.20	0	0.1	0.1
2.30	0	0.2	0.2
2.40	0	0.3	0.3

money, so that the cost of the strangle is less than the straddle. The price paid is that the strangle needs a larger market move to pay off than the straddle. Suppose we do the same as before but with a call strike price of $2.10 (Table 16.5, Figure 16.8).

In the next chapter, we will see how more complex option combinations can be created to meet specific needs.

OPTION VALUATION

We come now to the theory of how to value options. Once again, it should be stressed that this is a black art. It is not a science. A classic example of this came when the large American bank, Bankers Trust, was forced by the Federal Reserve to take an $80 million charge to earnings because the Fed felt that Bankers Trust had not properly valued their option book. As we shall see, there will always be room for doubt about the value of an individual option. This is because its value depends on an *estimate* of the future volatility of the underlying instrument.

The first, and most important, model used in options pricing was that developed by Fisher Black and Myron Scholes in 1973. We will discuss some of the variants to this model below. The Black-Scholes model made several critical assumptions:

1. Prices may change rapidly but cannot "jump." One can trade continuously in the market.
2. There is a risk-free rate of interest for borrowing and lending from the current period until the expiration of the option.
3. Transactions costs and taxes are ignored.

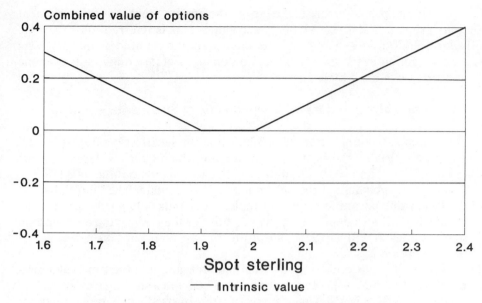

Figure 16.8   Strangle payoff profile.

4. The continuously compounded rate of return of the asset has a normal distribution—that is, the asset price is log-normally distributed.

Given these assumptions, Black & Scholes showed that the price of the option would be determined by

1. The current price of the underlying instrument.
2. The exercise price of the option.
3. The remaining life of the option.
4. The level of interest rates.
5. The projected volatility of the underlying instrument.

Of these, all but (5) are known at the time the option is priced: thus *volatility is the key to options pricing.*

In looking at the option's value, the first two factors are primary. This is clear if we look at the option on the day that it expires. On that day, only the currency price and the striking price of the option determine the option's value. The other factors have no bearing. Look at our earlier example of a $2.00 call on sterling. We said that if sterling were trading at $2.10 at the maturity of the option it would be worth $0.10. When sterling is at $2.10, the option has an intrinsic value of $0.10: at $2.30, an intrinsic value of $0.30. The only thing that affects intrinsic value is the gap between price of the underlying instrument (in this case sterling) and the strike price.

But in the period before the expiry of the option, there is another element in its price, in addition to its intrinsic value. This is referred to as the *time value* premium. In general, the time value premium is found by the following formula for an in the money call option on an asset (sterling in our example above):

Call time value premium = Call option price + Strike price – Asset price

For example, sterling is trading at $2.05, and the sterling October $2.00 call is priced at $0.08. The in the money amount (the intrinsic value) is 5 cents ($2.05 – $2.00) and so the time value (price less intrinsic value) is 3 (8 – 5).

The intrinsic value of the option is easy to calculate. The "fair value" of the time value premium is not so simple. It depends only partly on the time to maturity. It also depends on the volatility of the underlying asset and on interest rates. It will vary, too, according to how far in- or out-of-the-money the call option is.

If the call is out of the money, then the premium and the time value premium are the same. Let's say sterling is at $2.05 and a sterling October $2.10 call sells at $.04. The call has no intrinsic value by itself when the currency (at $2.05) is below the striking price ($2.10). So both the premium and the time value premium of the call are 4 points.

The option's time value premium decays much more rapidly in the last few weeks of its life than it does in the first few weeks. In fact, for reasons we will see later, the rate of decay is related to the square root of the time remaining. To illustrate this we can draw a graph of the effect of time on an option's premium. The chart (Figure 16.9) shows the effect of holding everything else constant. As the option comes closer to expiry, it loses value more and more quickly.

Another important point about time value is that it is always greatest for an option which is at-the-money. If the option is deep in or out of the money its time value is very low. We can see why this is if we think of the deal from the point of view of the option writer. Suppose we are quoting to write an option to sell sterling at $2.10. Once the option is written, then as we get closer to expiry, if sterling is near $2.10, we will need to be thinking about buying some sterling. We need to buy to cover our commitment to deliver sterling at $2.10. Now suppose there are 30 days to go on this option and sterling is now at $1.80. Then the risk of our having to deliver on this option is quite small—sterling is not very likely to rise 30 cents in 30 days. Equally, as one day passes and there are now 29 days to run, our risk will decline, but not by very much, since the risk was already small. So the fall in the premium we will charge will not be large. The effect of time value on the premium is small in these circumstances.

Conversely, suppose we are quoting the same option and sterling is trading today at $2.40. The option is virtually certain to be exercised. We will buy sterling now to cover our position since we will almost certainly have to

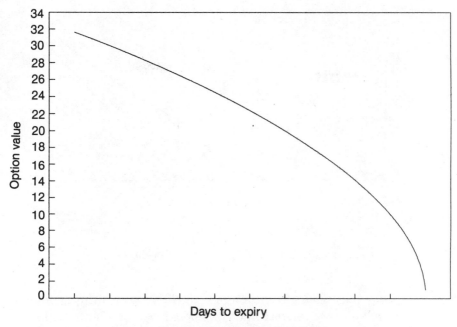

Figure 16.9 Option value over time.

deliver. Again, if the maturity of the option which we are quoting were to be shortened by a day, our risk will not be much less. So the premium we charge will not fall much. Time value of a deep in-the-money option is low.

It is when the option is at the money that our uncertainty is greatest. If we are quoting a $2.10 option for sterling and sterling is trading at $2.10 then the market could go either way from now till maturity. In these circumstances, an extra day's life on the option really does have an effect on our risk. Time value is at its greatest when the option is at the money.

We can illustrate this (Figure 16.10). The figure shows the value of the option premium at maturity and 30 days before maturity. The shaded area between the two lines is the time value of the option and as can be seen the gap between the two lines is at its widest when the option is at the money.

VOLATILITY

A key factor in option pricing is volatility. The more volatile an instrument, the higher the associated option price. Volatility is a measure of how the price of the underlying instrument varies. It is defined as the *standard deviation* in price returns of the instrument underlying the option.

What is the standard deviation? To find the standard deviation of a series of numbers we work as follows. Suppose we measure an overnight interest

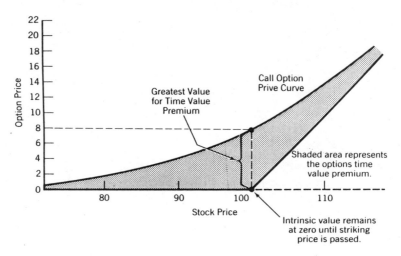

Figure 16.10   Time valve out-, at- and in-the-money.

rate over two weeks, giving us 10 observations. We want to measure how variable, or volatile, the interest rate is. Suppose we observe the following interest rates, in percent: 6, 12, 11, 14, 7, 9, 11, 3, 12, 8. The first step is to work out the average or mean interest rate over the period: this is 9.30%. Then we measure how much each rate varies from the mean. We want to average that variation, allowing for negative variations as well as positive. The easiest way to do this is to calculate the differences—14 – 9.30—and square them. Thus in this case we have $-4.7^2 = 22.09$. This makes sure we have positive numbers. We add up the squared totals and average them (Strictly speaking we divide by n – 1, where n is the number of observations). The result is called the variance. In this case, it is 11.12 (working to two decimal places). But because the variance is the result of squaring the percentage rates it is more meaningful to take the square root, which in this case is 3.33. The square root of the variance is called the standard deviation. We have a series of interest rates with an average, or mean, of 9.30% and a standard deviation of 3.33%. The standard deviation gives us a measure of how likely the interest rate is to stray away from its mean. Of course, this is a historical number: next month's standard deviation could be quite different. Volatility itself can be volatile.

Measuring the volatility of an instrument in terms of its standard deviation gives us an idea of its likely trading range, all other things being equal. For example, if a currency priced at $1.00 has an annualized volatility of 20%, then the most likely range of prices (i.e. within one standard deviation) by the end of the year is $0.85 and $1.20 ($1.00 divided by 1.2 and multiplied by 1.2, respectively). To be precise, the definition of annual historic volatility normally used in the options markets is:

$$\text{Volatility} = \sqrt{\text{Variance}\left[\log\left(\frac{p_t}{P_{t-1}}\right)\right]} \times 250$$

where $t = 1 \ldots n$; n is the number of trading days over which volatility is measured (We assume 250 trading days per annum, others use calendar days, i.e., 365).

Let's take a call option on sterling with a strike price of $2.10, when the currency is at $2.00. If the expected volatility of sterling is 20%, there is a greater chance that the price will be above $2.10 at the expiry of the option than if expected volatility is only 10%. The fact that there is a higher probability of large price falls is of no concern to the holder of a call option because his loss is limited to the premium paid. So he will be prepared to pay more for an option on a currency which has an expected volatility of 20%, than he would for an option on a currency with an expected volatility of 10%. Equally, the writer of the call option faces a greater risk on the more volatile currency, and therefore will charge a higher premium to write it.

Estimating the future volatility of the underlying instrument is perhaps the hardest task in pricing an option. It is the only variable affecting the option premium that is not directly observable in the market when the option is priced. All we know at that point is what its volatility has been in the past. Conversely, once the option is priced (for example, an exchange-trade option where we can see the price at which the option last traded) we can work out what volatility is implied in the price, assuming we know the options pricing formula that was used.

THE BINOMIAL MODEL

Different writers of options in the market will price their options differently because they have differing views on future volatility. It is this that makes option pricing a bit of a black art. To add to the confusion, there are a number of different options pricing models. The most widely known is that of Black and Scholes. The Black model is a variant of Black-Scholes suitable for options on futures. Other popular models are the Garman-Kohlhagen modification of Black-Scholes (widely used for currency options) and the Cox-Ross-Rubinstein model, or binomial model, which overcomes the problems the Black-Scholes model has in handling dividend payments on underlying equities. The binomial and Black Scholes models converge when trading is assumed to be continuous. In practice, bigger errors are likely to result from wrong forecasts of volatility than minor variations in the underlying theoretical models. Of the models mentioned, the binomial is one of the most commonly used. It is also rather easier to explain intuitively, so we will start with it before moving on to the Black-Scholes model.

Let's start with an American call on sterling at $2.00. Spot sterling today is trading at $2.05. We'll call the exercise price of $2.00 E, and the spot price S. Then $S - E = \$0.05$. That is, if we buy the option and exercise today, the option will pay us 5 cents. So the call will be worth *at least* $0.05 and probably more if there is any time to expiry. If we write the value of the call as C we know we must have $C \geq S - E$. Also, since we know we can choose to walk away from the option, its value can never be negative: we can never be harmed by owning it. So we know the value of a call will always be $C \geq 0$. In fact, we can write $C \geq$ [Maximum of 0, S – E].

Can we make this more exact? One way to proceed is to start with the concept of a riskless hedge: a hedge that eliminates all risk.

The assumptions behind most riskless hedge valuation models are as follows:

1. Prices may change rapidly but cannot "jump."
2. There is a risk-free rate of interest for borrowing and lending from the current period until the expiration of the option.
3. Transactions costs and taxes are ignored.

What we will do is set out a "binomial tree" showing the possible outcomes of the movement in sterling over time. At any point, sterling can move up or down. At each point along the branches of the tree we will work out the fair price of an option on sterling, working back from the future to today. The approach was initiated by William Sharpe and developed further by Cox, Ross, and Rubinstein.

We assume a starting price for sterling of $2.00. Then we assume the price of sterling in each period can rise or fall by $.01: it is equally likely to rise or fall. A three period example is shown in Figure 16.11. At the start of the first period, we want to value a European call option. It has a strike of $1.99. It expires after two periods, i.e. at the start of the third period. How do we set about this?

To start with, we know the value of the option at expiry. On expiry, sterling can be either $1.98, $2.00, or $2.02. And the option will be worth

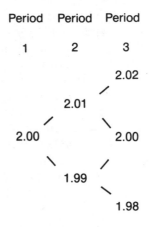

Figure 16.11   Sterling binomial tree.

$.03 if sterling's price is \$2.02, \$.01 if it is \$2.00, and nothing if it is \$1.98. Next, to get back from period 3 to period 2, we use the riskless hedge.

Let us assume sterling's price is \$2.01 at the start of period 2. We want to find the option price. We do this by imagining a portfolio. It is long one pound sterling, and short one call option on sterling with a strike of \$1.99. At the start of the next period (period 3), the price of sterling could rise from \$2.01 to \$2.02 or fall to \$2.00. The option writer must deliver sterling at the strike price of \$1.99. So, at \$2.02, he will lose \$.03. Likewise, if sterling falls to \$2.00, he will lose \$.01.

So at the start of period 3, whether the price moves up or down, the value of the portfolio will be \$1.99 (\$2.02 − \$.03 or \$2.00 − \$.01). So there is no risk in this portfolio. It can earn no more than the risk free rate. (If it did, arbitragers would borrow to invest in it and would drive down the return). Likewise, it cannot earn less (there would be arbitrage in the opposite direction). So the rate of return on the risk free portfolio must equal the risk free rate. Let us assume that the risk free rate is 0.02% per period. (If our periods were days, that would compound up to about 7.5% on a 360-day year.) Then the return on the portfolio will also be 0.02% per period.

We can now find a price for the option at the start of the second period, given the sterling price of \$2.01 we assumed above. We know the portfolio earns the risk free rate. And we know it ends up worth \$1.99. So the starting value, or cost, of the portfolio must be \$1.99 discounted back over one period. That is, \$1.99/1.0002 or \$1.9896. But we also know that the cost of buying the portfolio is \$2.01 (the price of the underlying sterling) less any premium earned on the option written.

Therefore, the option must earn \$2.01 − \$1.9896 = \$0.0204. If it did not, the portfolio would not be worth exactly \$1.9801. Any other option cost would mean the risk-free portfolio does not earn the risk-free rate. So, if the price of sterling at the start of period 2 is \$2.01, then the value of the option must be \$0.0204.

We can now use the same method to solve for a different price. What is the option price, if the price of sterling at the start of period 2 is \$1.99? In this case, we set up another portfolio. It has one pound sterling, plus, now, two short calls.

We chose the number of calls to be two by asking: how many calls are needed to make the portfolio riskless (that is, the same value whatever happens to sterling's price, whether it rises from \$1.99 to \$2.00 or falls to \$1.98)? To find this, say K is the number of \$1.99 calls written. We know that if the price rises to \$2.00, we must deliver at \$1.99, and so each call will lose \$0.01. If the price falls to \$1.98, there is no loss. So we want K such that $\$2.00 − K \times \$.01 = \$1.98 − K \times \$0$. So $\$2.00 − \$1.98 = K \times \$.01 − K \times \$0 = K \times \$.01$ and so $\$.02 = K \times \$.01$. Solving for K shows that we need two short calls to make the portfolio riskless. (Before, we had $\$2.02 − K \times \$.03 = \$2.00 − K \times \$.01$ and so $\$.02 = \$.02 \times K$ and hence K = 1.)

Now the price at the start of period 3 can go from our assumed $1.99 to either $2.00 or $1.98. At $2.00, the option has a $.01 loss for a total loss of $.02 on the two options. At $1.98, the option expires worthless. Thus, the portfolio next period will be worth $1.98, regardless of whether the price goes up to $2.00 or down to $1.98 ($2.00 – $.02 or $1.98 – $0). So its initial cost must be $1.98/1.0002, that is, $1.9796. Sterling costs $1.99. The two options, then, must earn $1.99 – 1.9796 = $.0104, by the same reasoning as before. *So, each option must be worth $0.0052.* We now know the option's value for the two possible prices of period 2 (Figure 16.12).

There is one last step. We must work back to today. Suppose we set up a portfolio that is long one pound sterling, and short 1.32 call options. (To find that number we use the same approach as before. We say we must have $2.01 – $0.0204K = $1.99 – $0.0052K so $.02 = ($0.0204 – $0.0052)K so K = $.02/$.0152 = 1.32.) In Table 16.6, we show that if the price of sterling goes up to $2.01, the value of the portfolio will be $1.9831. It will still be worth that if the price of sterling falls to $1.99. Therefore, the cost of the portfolio today must be $1.9831/1.0002, or $1.9827. But that cost must also equal $2.00, the value of our holding of sterling today, minus the revenue from selling 1.32 calls. *So each call must sell for ($2.00 – 1.9827)/1.32 = $0.0131.*

We have at last worked back to answer our question. We have found the fair price for the option today if sterling is selling for $2.00. Given the risk-free rate of interest and the set of possible future prices, $0.0131 is the only possible answer. To solve for the fair value of longer term options, all we need is a bigger set of possible prices. Then we can use the same method to find the current fair price of the option.

All this may seem far from the real world. After all, prices move all the time, not just once per period. Even worse, they can move to any one of many new values, not just two, as we have assumed. But if the reader is

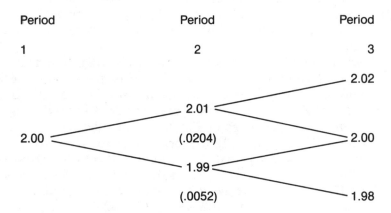

Figure 16.12 Sterling binomial tree: period 2 prices.

Table 16.6   Portfolio Values
(Portfolio = 1 Pound Sterling (Long) + 1.32 Calls (Short))

Case	Price of £	Short Call Position Value	Portfolio Value
Price rises to $2.01	2.01	1.32×0.0204	$2.01 - .0269 = 1.9831$
Price falls to $1.99	1.99	1.32×0.0052	$1.99 - 0.0069 = 1.9831$

willing to accept our basic assumptions, his objections can be overcome by suitably changing the binomial model.

Our model worked over three periods. If we divide these into infinitely short periods, we move towards continuous price changes. Now we have a very large number of observations. In these circumstances, we can generalize the model to become the Black-Scholes model. But before we do that we will look at the normal distribution.

NORMAL DISTRIBUTION

The normal distribution is well known in statistical theory: it is bell-shaped (Figure 16.13).

The normal distribution is important is because it is quite a realistic representation of the distribution of a number of common occurrences. The reason for this is the *Central Limit Theorem*—once described as "one of the most remarkable in all mathematics." It says that no matter what the nature of the

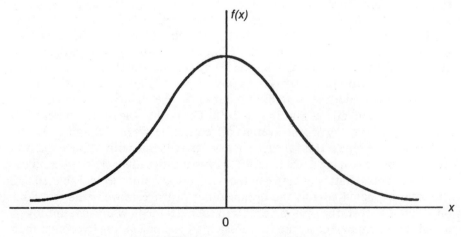

Figure 16.13   Normal distribution.

underlying distribution, provided it has a finite variance, it will approximate to the normal distribution for large samples. Since most statistical distributions that are likely to apply in the real world have finite variances, that means that we can argue that *for sufficiently large samples* we are justified in assuming that the underlying distribution of changes in the exchange rate (or whatever else we are writing an option on) is normal. More exactly, the standardized, continuously compounded rate of return of the asset (sterling in our example) tends to approximate a normal distribution. Hence, the relative change in price (S*/S) has a normal distribution, where S* is the new price and S the old. (So in fact the exchange rate itself will have what is called a "log-normal" distribution: its logarithm is normally distributed.)

Suppose we write an option on a currency whose price is 100. We know the price movements of the exchange rate over the last six months. These suggest its probability distribution is quite like a normal distribution. Over the last six months the currency price's mean, or average, is 100. Its standard deviation, or variability, is 12.

How do we find the probability that the currency's price on maturity of the option is a given distance from the mean? We use the area underneath the curve between the mean and the price at maturity. How do we measure this area? The easiest way is by looking up a table for the "standardized normal" distribution. (That is, the distribution of a normal variable with mean 0 and standard deviation of 1).

So the "standardized normal" distribution has to be applied to our currency. We do this by taking all the possible exchange rates. We subtract from them the mean of 100, and then divide the result by 12, the standard deviation. We have now "standardized" our exchange rate distribution. In mathematician's terms, we apply the transformation (x minus mean/standard deviation). An example will illustrate this.

Let's take the probability of the exchange rate being, say, 0 to 3% higher than the original price. That is, between 100 and 103. We take x = 100 and x = 103 and write (x − mean)/standard deviation, or (100 − 100)/12 = 0 and (103 − 100)/12 = 0.25. We then find the probability that x is between 0 and 0.25 in the standard normal distribution, by looking it up in the statistical tables for the normal distribution. Here it is shown by the area under the curve marked with the letter A in Figure 16.14. The area A is roughly 10% of the total area under the distribution curve. So the chance of the price being between 100 and 103 at maturity is 10%. The cost to the option seller of this event will average $1\frac{1}{2}$% (the average difference between 100 and 103).

Suppose we repeat this for each slice of 3 percentage points above the strike price. Then we will get a whole series of probabilities for each event. And each event has a cost, half way between the percentage points, as in Table 16.7. So the total expected cost to the option seller of price movements is 4.802%. So given this cost, the option seller will then decide how uncertain they feel about this estimated cost, and if necessary add some loading to protect themselves, and then price the option accordingly.

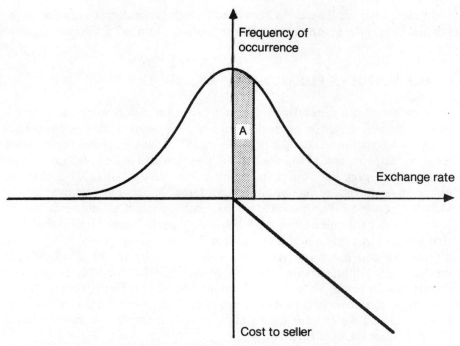

Figure 16.14 Possible prices at maturity—standardized normal distribution.

Table 16.7 Exchange Rate Charges: Normal Curve

Percentage Range above Srike Price	Average Value of Range (A)	Probability of Occurrence (the Area Under the Normal Distribution Curve) (B)	Expected Cost to Option Seller (A × B)
0–3	1.5	0.0987	0.1480
3–6	4.5	0.0928	0.4176
6–9	7.5	0.0823	0.6172
9–12	10.5	0.0675	0.7087
12–15	13.5	0.0531	0.7168
15–18	16.5	0.0388	0.6402
18–21	19.5	0.0267	0.5206
21–24	22.5	0.0173	0.3892
24–27	25.5	0.0106	0.2703
27–30	28.5	0.0060	0.1710
30–33	31.5	0.0032	0.1008
33–36	34.5	0.0016	0.0552
36–39	37.5	0.0008	0.0300
39–42	40.5	0.0004	0.0162
TOTALS		0.5	4.8018

In fact, what we have done here is add up the cumulative area under the normal curve: the technical term for this is the cumulative normal density.

BLACK-SCHOLES FORMULA

We have seen, in a general way, how the binomial model works, and how it can be argued that, for large numbers of independent observations over time, the logarithm of changes in price, $\log(S^*/S)$, has a normal distribution (that is, the price has a "log-normal distribution"). The assumption of normality does agree with common sense: it says that small relative changes, either up or down, are very common, but large changes become proportionately less common. The normal distribution has a mean, μ, and variance, σ^2. If we consider the behavior of $\log(S^*/S)$ over T periods we will find that over that time it has a mean μ and variance $\sigma^2 T$.

Now we can move on from the binomial model to the Black-Scholes model. Black-Scholes assumes that the price is log-normal, which as we have seen is usually reasonable—though not for bonds, which we discuss below— and this assumption gets us away from specifying a binomial-type path for prices. Instead we can set up a (fairly) simple formula. We can write the Black-Scholes formula like this:

$$C = N(d1)S - e^{-rT} N(d2)E$$

where $N(.)$ refers to the cumulative normal density. (We saw how to use $N(.)$ earlier when we explained the normal density.)

What this formula says is that the value of the call is equal to the expected value of what we will get from the call, minus the expected cost. We can say that $N(d1)S$ is the expected value of the asset we will acquire under the call: we will get an asset with a value of S. That asset is weighted by a probability: $N(d1)$ is the probability we will exercise. (We will see later that $N(d1)$ is also the "delta" of the option). And $e^{-rT}N(d2)E$ is the expected cost, in present value terms, of having to exercise the option. And the call is worth the net difference between what we expect to get and what we expect to have to pay for it.

What are d1 and d2? We define d1 as $[\ln(S/E) + (r + \sigma^2/2)T]/\sigma\sqrt{T}]$. What does this unwieldy beast mean? It's difficult to give an intuitive interpretation, but one way of going about it is to look at it like this. The standard deviation of the distribution over the life of the option, T, is given by $\sigma\sqrt{T}$. We could write out d1 and d2 like this:

$$d1 = (\ln(S/E) + rT + \sigma^2 T/2)/\sigma\sqrt{T}$$
$$d2 = d1 - \sigma\sqrt{T} = (\ln(S/E) + rT - \sigma^2 T/2)/\sigma\sqrt{T}$$

So we can write:

$$d1 = V + \sigma\sqrt{T} \text{ and } d2 = V - \sigma\sqrt{T}$$

where

$$V = \frac{\ln(S/E) + rT}{\sigma\sqrt{T}}$$

What is V? We can think of it as the value of the option pay-off, measured in terms of standard deviations. That is, dividing all through by $\sigma\sqrt{T}$ is as if we were changing the units of measurement into the numbers of standard deviations. The Black-Scholes model is summarized in Figure 16.15.

Variants to the Black-Scholes Formula

Given its assumptions, the Black-Scholes method is powerful and consistent, but the assumptions are heroic. The biggest leap of faith is when we assume the distribution of price changes is normal. As we said, this is fine, provided we have a large number of observations *from a stable underlying distribution.* If there is structural change going on, or if central bank intervention or monetary policies change, we do not necessarily satisfy that condition. Over the very long run, it may be true that there is a normal distribution at work: but it may be around an underlying trend. If you had been short sterling from 1948 to 1976 you would have made a ton of money because sterling went from $4.80 to $1.50: there was a trend in the United Kingdom's external position. The exchange rate itself did not have a stable mean, which is a precondition for a normal distribution to exist. A related point is the *fat tails argument:* the "tails" are the extreme left and right hand portions of the bell-shaped curve of the normal distribution. There is some empirical evidence to suggest that in practice these tails are "fatter" than predicted by the normal distribution. In other words, we seem to get extreme swings in rates more often than would be predicted by the normal distribution. Argument continues on this point.

The second great leap of faith is when we assume that future price behavior can be predicted from past prices. We assume the standard deviation of the stock's price movements will remain the same. In other words, that volatility will remain stable. Another problem is that we must assume the market in the underlying instrument is continuous and perfect. As traders well know, particularly in options-related markets, this is by no means the case.

There are also some specific technical problems with the Black-Scholes model: interest rate options have to be looked at separately because it will not always be true that the price of the asset is independent of the risk-free rate of interest. The model needs to be modified to handle assets deliverable

$$C = S\,N(d1) - Xe^{-rT}\,N(d2)$$

Where

$$d1 = \frac{\ln\left(\dfrac{S}{E}\right) + \left(\dfrac{r + \sigma^2}{2}\right)T}{\sqrt{T}}$$

$$d2 = d1 - \sigma\sqrt{T}$$

C   = call option premium
S   = current asset price
E   = exercise price
T   = time to expiration
σ   = standard deviation of the asset price (volatility)
ln   = natural logarithm
N(.) = cumulative normal distribution function
r   = riskless rate of interest

By way of reference, we set out here some concepts to be discussed later.

Delta $\dfrac{\delta C}{\delta E} = N(d1)$

Gamma $\dfrac{\delta}{\delta S} = \dfrac{n(d1)}{S\sigma\sqrt{T}}$

Theta $\dfrac{\delta C}{\delta T} = \dfrac{S\sigma}{2\sqrt{T}}\,n(d1) + rEe^{-rt}\,(N(d2))$

Kappa* $\dfrac{\delta c}{\delta \sigma} = S\sqrt{T}n(d1)$

where n(d1) = standard normal density and N(d1) = cumulative normal
*also known as epsilon, vega, or zeta

Figure 16.15   The Black-Scholes formula.

in the future (for example, for options on futures contracts): this variation gives the *Black model*. The Black-Scholes model is not well adapted for situations where dividends or other cash flows are earned on the underlying asset: there is the possibility of early exercise (see next section). In these situations, the binomial model discussed earlier would normally be used.

MEASURES OF OPTION RISK AND SENSITIVITY: THE GREEK ALPHABET

In managing an options book, dealers pay attention to a number of risk measures. The most important are referred to as delta, gamma, kappa (or vega), and theta. Other measures sometimes referred to are rho and lambda. (The phrase, "It's all Greek to me" takes on a new meaning in the world of options.)

The *delta* of an option is the change in the price of the option that results from a change of one dollar in the price of the underlying asset. Delta varies between 0 and 1 (or 0% and 100% depending how you want to express it). Figure 16.16 shows how delta rises from very low values when the option is out of the money to 1 when the option is deep in the money. At that point the option is certain to be exercised, has no time value, and behaves like the asset itself.

We defined delta as the change in the option price for a change in asset price. That means that delta can be defined as the slope of the tangent to the option's price curve. It measures the sensitivity of the option's price to the underlying asset. The more in-the-money the option is, the more sensitive its price is to that of the asset. Conversely, for a deep out-of-the-money option, even quite a large change in the asset price will have no effect. The question is sometimes asked: why does delta change if volatility changes? The answer is: because a change in volatility changes the shape of the premium/asset price curve, hence the slope of the curve (delta) changes.

Another way of looking at delta is to say that it measures the probability that the option will be exercised. When the option is deep out of the money, there is little chance that it will be exercised, and delta is zero. When the

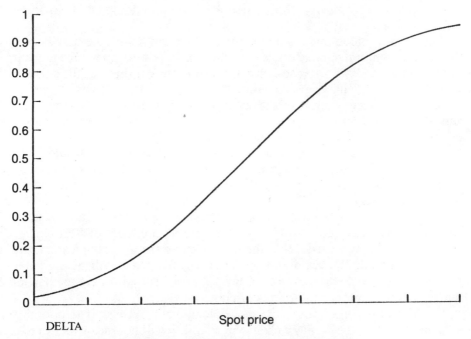

Figure 16.16 Delta curve rises with spot price.

option is deep in the money, the option is almost 100% certain to be exercised, and delta will be one. When the option is at-the-money, the chances are 50/50 and delta will be around 0.5. The implication of this is that delta can be used as a measure of the exposure implied by an option position. Suppose we have written a call on $100 million Eurodollar futures at 90.5 (an implied interest rate of 9.5%). Suppose the delta of the position is currently 0.25: that is, a 25% chance the option can be exercised against us. On a probability-weighted basis, therefore, our exposure is equivalent to being short $25 million worth of Eurodollar futures at 90.5. Therefore, to hedge our position, we could buy $25 million of futures. This is the concept of *delta-weighted hedging* discussed in Chapter 17.

The next important measure of option sensitivity is *gamma*. This measures the sensitivity of delta to changes in the asset price. Thus *gamma is a measure of the stability of delta*. The higher gamma is, the more rapidly delta changes as the price of the asset changes. If we look again at Figure 16.16, we can see that delta does not change much as the asset price changes if the option is deep out of the money. Thus gamma is low. Nor does delta respond much to changes in asset price when the option is deep in the money. Again, gamma is low. Gamma is highest when the option is at the money. It is then that delta is moving most quickly. For the delta-weighted hedger, it is important to measure gamma. A high gamma means the hedge must be adjusted much more often: delta hedging a high-gamma position tends to be much more expensive. (See Chapter 17.) Gamma is highest when the option is at-the-money and when it is short-dated. It is lowest for long-dated out of the money options.

Another way of looking at gamma is to say that it measures the curviness of the option premium curve. Just as the delta measures the slope of the tangent to the curve at today's price, so gamma measures the curviness of the curve at that point. (In the language of calculus, delta is the first derivative and gamma the second derivative). You might say that delta is the speed of change, and gamma is the acceleration. Figure 16.17 shows the effect of gamma for different asset price levels and days to maturity.

Offsets to gamma—ways of hedging our gamma exposure—would be to sell short-dated at-the-money options if we are long, and buy if we are short; we can avoid building up exposure to gamma by dealing in out-of-the-money far dated options.

The next measure we must look at is called *kappa* (or vega or zeta or epsilon). This measures the impact on the option's premium of a 1% change in volatility. We said earlier that the more volatile the underlying asset, the more the valuable the option on the asset will be. There will be a greater chance the option could move in our favor during its lifetime. Kappa particularly affects longer-dated options pricing.

Kappa is at its largest for at-the-money long-dated options. If an option is deep in- or out-of-the money a change in volatility will not mean very much, whereas it could have a significant effect if the option is at-the-money.

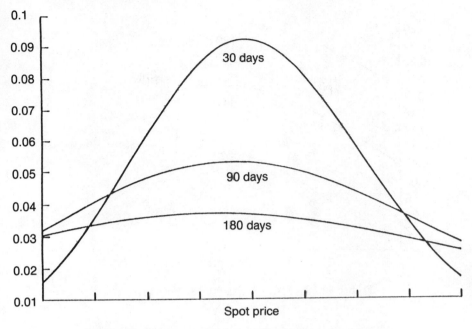

Figure 16.17 GAMMA: 30, 90, 180 days to expiry.

Likewise, kappa is more important for a long-dated option since the longer time allows a greater chance for the option to move in the buyer's favor. Figure 16.18 shows the effect of kappa for different asset price levels and days to maturity. Offsets to kappa are to write options if we are long of kappa, buy options if short; and if we do not want to build up kappa we should tend to deal in out-of-the-money options.

The fourth important measure of options sensitivity is *theta*. Theta measures the impact of time on an option's fair value. More exactly, it measures the effect of a shortening of 1 day in the option's life to maturity on the option premium. We said earlier that early in an option's life the effect of time decay is not very large. It increases as the option's life shortens, and the reason for this is fairly clear. The percentage impact on the option's value of a 1-day shortening in its life is small if the option has 90 days to run, but much larger if it has only 1 day left. Also, theta has a bigger impact on at-the-money options. We saw earlier that time value for deep in/out-of-the-money options is small. Figure 16.19 shows how theta behaves for different periods to maturity and asset price levels. Figure 16.20 shows the effect of theta on an at-the-money option compared with in/out-of-the-money options.

Finally, two other measures which are sometimes used are *rho* and *lambda*. Rho measures the sensitivity of the option's price to interest rates. It can be defined as the dollar change in the option's price for a 1% change in the rate of

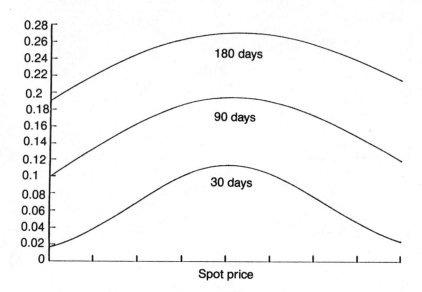

Figure 16.18 KAPPA: 30, 90, 180 days to expiry.

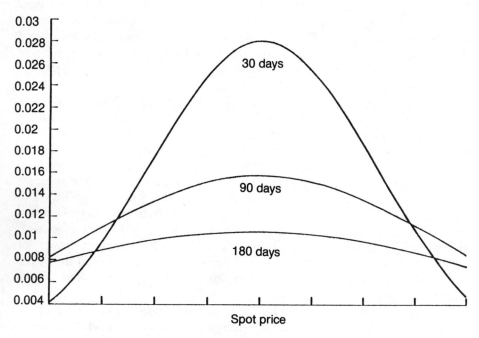

Figure 16.19 THETA: 30, 90, 180 days to expiry.

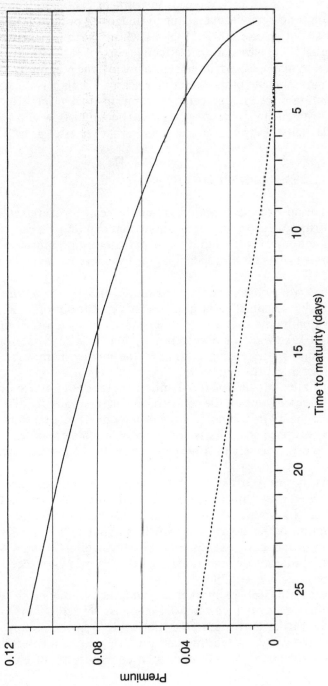

Figure 16.20 Time decay.

interest. Rho can be divided into two effects. The first is the effect of interest rate changes on the price of the asset, which will be important if the option is on a bond or on a currency for forward delivery. The second reflects the fact that an option is a geared, or leveraged, instrument. The option gives the holder a claim on the asset, without having to finance its purchase. For example, I could buy an option on 1,000 IBM shares, whose worth is $100,000; if the option costs me $2,500, I have obtained effective control of $100,000 of assets for $2,500. My alternative would have been to borrow the remaining $97,500 to finance outright purchase of the underlying shares. Lambda is the percentage change in option price for a percentage change in stock price; effectively, it is the delta restated into percentage terms. (Economists would say that lambda is the elasticity of the option price with respect to asset price.)

AMERICAN VS. EUROPEAN OPTIONS

We have said that an American option is one that can be exercised at any time until maturity. A European option is one that can only be exercised at maturity. Common sense tells us that the American option must always be worth at least as much as the European: it conveys more rights and so must be worth more.

The question is *how much* more. The answer depends on the nature of the underlying asset. For instance, if the asset underlying the option is an equity which pays dividends, there can be circumstances in which it is optimal to exercise early. Likewise, for a currency option on a high interest rate currency—sterling—if the option is deep in the money, it may be worth exercising in order to get the high yield.

This will normally only be true if the option's price does not itself reflect the value of the dividend due on the equity or the interest rate payable on the currency: that is, the market is not pricing efficiently. It can be shown that the right of early exercise is not in itself normally worth a great deal. It will almost always be better to sell an American option in the marketplace than to exercise it.

The reason is that until it expires the American option will have some time value. In an efficient market, someone will always be willing to pay something for that time value. There are three exceptions to this rule: (1) for an American option on an instrument which is about to pay a cash flow: under certain conditions early exercise may be worthwhile; (2) when dealing costs in the options market are high; and (3) when the option is so deep in the money that time value is negligible.

If dealing costs in the options market are high, then it may be cheaper to exercise the option than to incur the dealing cost by selling the option. Likewise, we saw earlier that when an option is deep in-the-money it will have almost no time value, and in this case exercise will be the best choice. Suppose spot sterling is $1.50; we own a three-month $1.40 call worth

$0.10, that is, the call has no time value. Suppose three-month forward sterling is trading at $1.45. Then we can exercise the option at $1.40, and sell in the spot market at $1.50, for a profit of $0.10. If we still need sterling, we can buy forward at $1.45. Alternatively, we can sell the option for $0.10, and buy forward at $1.45. In either case the net cost of forward sterling to us is $1.35.

There is one exception to this: the holder of an in-the-money option on a futures position who is hedging a futures position may find it optimal to exercise, because of the difference between the marginining procedures: the futures position is tying up variation margin, but the option position is not giving the benefit (unless the Exchange is using the SPAN system—see Appendix E). This does not apply on the CME or LIFFE, where the two positions can be linked together.

OPTIONS ON INTEREST RATES: YIELD LATTICES

There is a variety of options which are traded on interest rates. These include exchange-traded options on Treasury bonds, Eurodollar futures, short-term sterling rates, gilt-edged bonds, OATs, and so on. But in terms of trading volume, probably the larger market is in OTC options, particularly caps and floors. A specific example of a cap is discussed from the customer's point of view in Chapter 17; here we will concentrate on some of the theoretical issues that arise in pricing interest rate options.

Options on interest rates raise a number of special problems. First, there is the problem of early exercise which can arise for American options on instruments where there are underlying cash flows. But even for European options, there are complications which mean that Black-Scholes models are not right for many options on interest rates. In general, for options on short-term interest rates—an option on the three-month Eurodollar future—Black-Scholes models are reasonably acceptable. But for longer-term interest rate options— such as options on bonds—there are some fairly serious problems:

1. The underlying yield on the bond is likely to be correlated with the risk-free rate—not independent as Black-Scholes would need.
2. Since bonds have a maturity, their price volatility falls towards zero as they approach maturity—Black-Scholes assume volatility remains constant.
3. An assumed log-normal distribution of bond prices under Black-Scholes allows the possibility that the price of the bond could go high enough to imply a negative yield.

Getting round these problems means that we have to abandon the classical form of the Black-Scholes model. One solution is to go to a model based not on the bond's price but on its yield. If yields follow a lognormal pattern, their minimum will be zero, so we get round the negative yield problem. Using a yield distribution also gets round the fall in price volatility as we move towards maturity.

We still have other problems: Should we assume a constant volatility across the yield curve? Can we assume the yield curve always shifts in parallel? A possible approach to resolving all these various problems is to try to build a binomial model of yields. (The approach outlined here follows L. J. Dyer & D. P. Jacob, "A Practitioner's Guide to Fixed-Income Option Models," *The Journal of International Securities Markets,* Spring 1989.)

The arbitrage-free binomial models are based on a "lattice" of interest rates. This is designed to satisfy conditions that prevent changes in the yield curve that would permit arbitrage opportunities. Most of these models assume a multiplicative binomial process. This approximates a lognormal yield distribution. We start with an initial set of forward short-term rates and the noarbitrage condition is used to adjust it. We adjust so that the prices of bonds with different maturities correspond to those obtained from today's yield curve and so that no arbitrage among bonds is possible along the yield curve.

A yield lattice is designed so that the period between lattice points corresponds to a short-term rate. The "distance" between the lattice points (that is, the maturity of the short-term rates chosen) affects how accurate the model will be, and how long it takes to run. The shorter the distance, the more points there will be in the lattice and the more accurate it will be, but the longer the model will take to produce an answer. One way is to test if the value of the option changes much when we increase the number of points in the lattice. If not, then we have chosen a lattice of about the right size. Once we have tested that, we can use the lattice to price other similar options with reasonable confidence.

Let's look at a specific example. Suppose one-, two-, and three-period zero-coupon bonds yield 8%, 9%, and 9.5% respectively. Assume that the logarithm of the one-period rate follows a binomial process. It has unknown mean K and a 10% volatility. From today, the rate can go up to the next point (or "node") on the lattice, or down. Then the short-term rate at the up node is $r^u_{t+1} = r_t e^{(K+0.10)}$ and the rate for the down node is $r^d_{t+1} = r_t e^{(K-0.10)}$. Assuming that the probability of a rise or fall in the rate is equal, then the mean of $\ln(r_{t+1}/r_t)$ is equal to K and the standard deviation of the yield changes is 10%. Figure 16.21 shows the outcome if we assume K is zero.

The next step is to adjust K so that the prices of zero-coupon bonds as fixed by the lattice are actually the same as the prices implied by today's yield curve. For a two-period bond, given our starting yield of 9%, the price is $84.17 (100/1.09^2). What price is implied by the lattice in Figure 16.21? What we do is take the principal at maturity, $100, and discount it back to today going along each path in the lattice. We average all the resulting prices. We take $100 and discount it back using the up path of 8% and 8.84%, and using the down path of 8% and 7.24%. The average of these prices is $85.71, which is the expected price of the bond today.

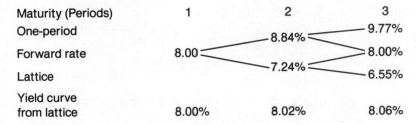

Maturity (Periods)	1	2	3
One-period			9.77%
		8.84%	
Forward rate	8.00		8.00%
		7.24%	
Lattice			6.55%
Yield curve from lattice	8.00%	8.02%	8.06%

Figure 16.21 Binomial lattice of one-period forward rates based on the initial 8% one-period rate and 10% yield volatility.

This differs from the actual price today of $84.17. So we must adjust the lattice. We do this by adjusting K; if we adjust K, we adjust the yields but not their volatility. In this example, if we set K equal to 0.22 in the first period, the expected discounted price of the two-period zero-coupon bond becomes $84.17 that matches the current market price. For a three-period bond, we set K equal to 0.0455 to make the expected discounted value of the three-period zero-coupon bond on the lattice match its value today of $76.17 ($100/1.095^3$). We can see the results of this process in Figure 16.22.

The next step is to find the option values. We can find the value of a two-year European put and call with a strike price of $90 on the three-year bond as follows (see Figure 16.23). Given the rates at the start of period 3 (8.54%, 10.44% or 12.75%) then the bond will have a price of either $92.13 ($100/1.0854), $90.56 or $88.70. At that point, we know the payoffs on a $90 strike call option will be either $2.13, $0.56, or zero. We can discount these payoffs back to today, using the short-term rates in Figure 16.22. We find that the expected value of the call is $0.69, and finding the put by the same process we see it is $0.27 (Figure 16.23).

If our lattice model is free of arbitrage—that is, it is consistent—then the put-call parity will hold. The difference between the value of the call and the put will equal the difference between the value of the underlying bond and the discounted value of the strike price. The value of the three-period zero-coupon bond today is $76.17. The strike price of $90, discounted back

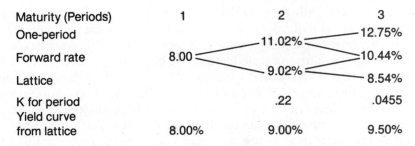

Maturity (Periods)	1	2	3
One-period			12.75%
		11.02%	
Forward rate	8.00		10.44%
		9.02%	
Lattice			8.54%
K for period		.22	.0455
Yield curve from lattice	8.00%	9.00%	9.50%

Figure 16.22 Lattice adjusted to provide the initial yield curve.

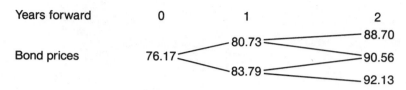

VALUE OF A TWO-YEAR CALL ON THE THREE-YEAR
BOND STRUCK AT 90

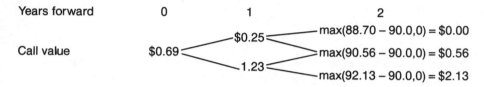

VALUE OF A TWO-YEAR PUT ON THE THREE-YEAR
BOND STRUCK AT 90

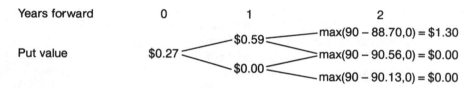

Figure 16.23   Arbitrage-free option prices.

two years at the two year rate of 9%, is $75.75. The difference between these two is $0.42: which is equal the to the difference between the call and the put. Put-call parity is satisfied.

It is worth making a few points about this procedure. We assumed equal probability of rates rising or falling. That can be changed: we could have said there is a 60% chance of rates rising and 40% of a fall. That would mean changing the values of K that we need to make sure no arbitrage is possible, but the procedure otherwise is unchanged. It is in theory possible to use a different value of K for each node in a given time period, but if we do that, then the lattice is not connected up any more. That would mean the cash flows along every path through the lattice are different. That dramatically increases the amount of calculation needed. For a connected lattice, we have to solve $n(n + 1)/2$ equations. So for a 20-period lattice we must solve 210 equations, but for a disconnected lattice, we have to solve 2^n equations. For a 20-period lattice, we would have to solve 1,048,576 equations. Which would take a little longer. To handle this type of lattice, people normally use sampling procedures or else turn to Monte Carlo simulations (which are discussed in the context of swap credit risk in Chapter 21).

One of the attractions of this approach is that for a given volatility and yield curve only one lattice needs to be created. Once this is done, all securities regardless of any uncertainty about their payoff, can be priced with the same lattice. The main weakness of this approach is that it is not very useful for instruments where the pay-off depends not just on the interest rates at the time of the pay-off but also on the entire path of interest rates from today until the pay-off. In those circumstances, the lattice is disconnected and we have the practical computation problem mentioned. In those circumstances, Monte Carlo simulations might be used, but the Monte Carlo technique has some difficulty in handling American options. Finally, the point should be made that all the yield curve models we have discussed here are driven by the short-term rates alone. A truly theoretically robust model would be to build a multifactor model, but there comes a point where one has to balance theoretical purity against practicality!

CURRENCY OPTIONS

We come now to currency options. One simple point should be made at the outset: Up to now it has been quite clear when we talk about an option, what it is the option is on. But now we have scope for confusion. Is a DEM/US$ call a call on the DEM and a put on the US$, or a call on the US$ and a put on the DEM? For exchange-traded options, this is not generally a real problem but when quoting OTC options it is very important for all parties to be clear precisely what is meant.

Consider the following example:

1. Buy a June 15 DEM call struck at DEM 1.50 for 2%.
2. Buy a June 15 DEM call struck at DEM 1.50 for $0.0133.
3. Buy a June 15 DEM call struck at $0.67 for $0.0133.
4. Buy a June 15 US$ put struck at DEM 1.50 for DEM 0.026.

All of these are quotations for precisely the same deal. The method used in (1) or (2) might be used in the OTC market in London or New York; method (4) might be used by a Continental bank in the OTC market; method (3) is that used in the exchange traded market. It is a question first of which is the base currency and which the quoted; second whether the currency is quoted in indirect or direct terms (that is, DEM 1.50 per dollar or $0.67 per DEM); and third whether the premium is quoted as an amount of currency or, as is common in the wholesale interbank market, as a percentage.

To get around some of these problems, the British Bankers' Association (BBA) in 1985 introduced the so-called LICOM terms: This stipulates the following definitions (amongst others):

- **Call:** An Option by which the Grantor grants the Purchaser the right to buy the Underlying Currency.

- **Counter Currency:** The currency to be exchanged for the Underlying Currency being (1) in respect of US$ related Options, the US$ with the non-US$ currency as the Underlying Currency and (2) in respect of non-US$ related Options, the currency stipulated at the time of quotation with the Underlying Currency also stipulated at the same time.
- **Settlement Price:** The exchange rate between the Underlying Currency and the Counter Currency ruling at 1500 hours London time on the Exercise date, determined [by an information vendor—Telerate—who will take the 8 most recent currency prices for the currency available within its system and average the middle 4 of these prices] as published by the information vendor for the time being designated by the BBA.
- **Underlying Currency:** The currency in which the Option is granted which means (1) in respect of US$ related Options, the non-US$ currency with the US$ as the Counter Currency and (2) in respect of non-US$ related Options, the currency stipulated at the time of quotation with the Counter Currency also stipulated at the same time.

Note, incidentally, that the LICOM terms provide for net cash settlement for options (that is, a cash difference is paid rather than there being a commitment to do a spot foreign exchange deal at the time of settlement. This reduces counterparty credit risk considerably).

Options pricing for currency options follows the same basic principle as for other options pricing. But there are several differences, of which the most important arise from the fact that we now have two sets of interest rates to consider, one in each currency (see Figure 16.24). We know, therefore, that

---

- For an American option, the intrinsic value is the greater of the difference between the spot and the strike, or the forward and the strike
- For a European option, the intrinsic value is the difference between the forward and the strike

This means that for a high-interest rate currency (e.g., ITL, GBP):

American call premium > European
American put premium = European

For a low interest rate currency (e.g., DEM, CHF):

American put premium > European
American call premium = European

Figure 16.24   Effects of interest rates on currency options.

Higher interest rate currency (e.g., ITL, GBP):

At-the-money calls struck at spot rate

At-the-money puts struck at forward rate

Low interest rate currency (e.g., JPY, CHF)

At-the-money calls struck at forward rate

At-the-money puts struck at spot rate

Figure 16.25 Currency option strike conventions.

the forward exchange rate will be different from the spot rate. There are two sets of effects to consider:

1. The effect of the interest differential.
2. The effect of changes in the interest differential.

Let us look first at a situation where spot sterling is trading at $2.00 and three-month forward sterling is trading at $1.95. Let us look at a three-month American call on sterling with a strike of $1.95: the option is in-the-money, because I can exercise at $1.95 and sell at $2.00. So the American call is worth at least its intrinsic value of $0.05. But suppose the option were a European option: I can only exercise at expiry. The value, S, of the optioned asset is not the spot price but the forward price. In other words, *the American call includes the forward points; the European call does not.*

To allow for this, the conventions in Figure 16.25 tend to be used.

GARMAN-KOHLHAGEN CURRENCY OPTIONS MODEL

In discussing the Black-Scholes model earlier, we glossed over an important fact: in a foreign currency option, there are two rates of interest involved, the domestic and the foreign rate of interest. In 1983, Garman and Kohlhagen modified the Black-Scholes model to handle foreign currency options by allowing for this. Using the same notation that we had before, the Garman-Kohlhagen model for a European call is:

$$C = e^{-r_f T} SN(d1) - Ee^{-r_d T} N(d2)$$

where r_f is the foreign interest rate and r_d the domestic interest rate to the expiry date of the option. The first term reflects the fact that the spot rate is not the true price of the asset because we are dealing with a European call:

the spot has to be converted into the equivalent of a forward rate. The definitions of the other terms are as before, except that d1 is rewritten:

$$d1 = \frac{\ln(S/E) + \left(r_d - r_f + \frac{\sigma^2}{2}\right)T}{\sigma\sqrt{T}}$$

By comparison, the original Black-Scholes formula was:

$$C = SN(d1) - Ee^{-rT}N(d2)$$

We can if we choose rewrite the Garman-Kohlhagen formula in terms of forwards:

$$C = [FN(D1) - EN(D2)]e^{-r_dT}$$

where

$$D1 = \frac{\ln\left(\frac{F}{E}\right) + \left(\frac{\sigma^2}{2}\right)T}{\sigma\sqrt{T}}$$

and

$$D2 = D1 - \sigma\sqrt{T}$$

Using this, rather simpler notation, we can also write the formula for a European put as follows:

$$P = [F[N(D1) - 1] - E[N(D2) - 1]]e^{-r_dT}$$

An alternative approach is to modify the binomial model to allow for two rates of interest.[1] As with the single currency binomial, in the limit the binomial model tends towards the Black-Scholes/Garman-Kohlhagen model.

Another point where currency options differ from other options is that in the foreign exchange market, unlike most interest rate markets, there is a widely traded and liquid forward market. This means that the buyer or seller of an option has always the choice of comparing the option with the price available in the forward market: it also allows for the possibility of combining the two. These are the so-called "third generation" products, which are discussed in the next chapter.

[1] Bodurtha, J. N. & Courtadon, G. R., *The Pricing of Foreign Currency Options*, Monograph Series in Finance & Economics, Monograph 1987–4/5, New York University, 1988.

17 Options Applications

In Chapter 16, we looked at some of the concepts underlying options, their pricing, and the risks associated with options. In this chapter, we look at some of the practical applications of options strategies and trading. We begin with a specific application of options to the money markets—caps and floors. We look at them not just from the point of view of the seller, but also the buyer's break-even analysis. We look at various options strategies and then move on to the practicalities of managing exposure.

CAPS AND FLOORS

The market for caps and floors is an extension of the over-the-counter market in fixed-income options, discussed in Chapter 16. The interest rate cap sets a maximum level, or cap, on a short-term rate index. The buyer of the cap is compensated if the index goes above the strike level. Similarly, a floor provides a minimum rate on some index. The cap can be thought of as a series of single-period options. For example, a cap on three-month LIBOR for four years can be looked at as 12 options of differing maturities on LIBOR. Thus the pricing is handled by the methods outlined in Chapter 16. Once we have priced the cap or floor, there is a question of whether anyone would want to buy it. Our pricing arrives at a value that is consistent with a theoretical model. But in the real world, the borrower or investor has the alternative of borrowing or lending at a fixed rate. They will analyze the cap or floor in that context.

Before doing the analysis, we will explore the nature of caps and floors in more detail. A cap or floor contract is specified by the following:

1. *Underlying index.* Caps and floors can be created on many indexes. For example, caps can be bought on one-, three-, or six-month LIBOR. Caps and floors have been set on the following indices: LIBOR, commercial paper, prime, Treasury bills, certificates of deposit, and on certain tax-exempt rates.

2. *Maturity.* This has ranged from three months to twelve years.

3. *Frequency.* This covers the reset dates, on which the level of rates is compared with the strike level to find what payment needs to be made—monthly, quarterly, and semi-annual are most common. Similarly, frequency refers to the payment dates.

4. *Strike level.* Usually, one fixed level applies to the entire program, although the level can change over time in a predetermined way.

5. *Notional principal amount.* Like the strike level, the amount underlying the contract can be constant or it can change over time.

A typical cap agreement could have the following terms:

Underlying index: three-month LIBOR (as per Reuters LIBO screen)
Term of cap   : 3 years
Rate fixing   : quarterly
Strike level   : 8%
Payment   : quarterly, in arrears (actual/360 calculation basis)
Notional amount : $30 million
Up front fee   : 1.12% of par ($336 thousand)

In this agreement, the writer of the cap would pay the owner of the cap in any quarter when three-month LIBOR was over the 8% cap level on the fixing date. If LIBOR were quoted at 9% on the fixing date, the payment would be:

$$\frac{9}{100} \times \frac{92}{360} \times \$30 \text{ million} - \frac{8}{100} \times \frac{92}{360} \times \$30 \text{ million} = \$76{,}666.67.$$

In this case, the writer would pay the holder of the interest rate cap $76,666.67. On the other hand, if LIBOR were at or below 8%, no payment would be made.

When considering whether to buy a cap, a corporate Treasurer may well consider its cost over the life of the cap deal, given a particular interest rate outlook. Table 17.1 shows one such analysis, of a quarterly cap on three-month LIBOR.

Table 17.1 Sample Cap Deal Structure

Cap strike rate	8.50%	Payments p.a.		4
Cap fee	1.12%	Amortized cap cost		0.11
Fixed funding	8.00%	IRR (semi-annual bond eqvt)		8.90%
Term in years	3			

Quarter	LIBOR Rate	Liability Cash Flow	Cap Payoff	Capped Cash Flow at 8%	Cap Cost Amortized	Net Cash Flow
0		−100				−100
1	6.00%	1.52	0	1.52	0.11	1.63
2	10.00%	2.53	−0.38	2.15	0.11	2.26
3	10.00%	2.53	−0.38	2.15	0.11	2.26
4	10.00%	2.53	−0.38	2.15	0.11	2.26
5	10.00%	2.53	−0.38	2.15	0.11	2.26
6	10.00%	2.53	−0.38	2.15	0.11	2.26
7	10.00%	2.53	−0.38	2.15	0.11	2.26
8	10.00%	2.53	−0.38	2.15	0.11	2.26
9	10.00%	2.53	−0.38	2.15	0.11	2.26
10	10.00%	2.53	−0.38	2.15	0.11	2.26
11	10.00%	2.53	−0.38	2.15	0.11	2.26
12	10.00%	102.53	−0.38	102.15	0.11	102.26

Here we have a $100 million borrowing at LIBOR repaid after 3 years, plus a cap with a strike rate of 8.5%, costing 1.12%, for 3 years, on an amount of $100 million. The alternative is fixed-rate funding for 3 years at 8%. Our first step is to amortize the cost of the cap over the deal's life. At 8%, this amortized cap cost comes to 0.11% per quarter. That is, if we borrowed at 8% enough to pay to the cost of the cap, and repaid it quarterly, principal and interest payments on the loan would equate to 0.11% per quarter.

Suppose that for the first period, three-month LIBOR is fixed at 6%. Then our borrowing cost is $1.52 million, and there is no payment under the cap. Hence our all-in cost for the period is $1.63 million. Now suppose that LIBOR jumps to 10%, and remains there for the life of the deal. Our borrowing cost jumps to $2.53 million per quarter, and we receive a payoff from the writer of the cap of $0.38 million, making our net cost $2.15 million plus the amortized cost of the cap, or $2.26 million.

We can price the true cost of funds under this outlook as the internal rate of return of the column headed "Net Cash Flow": this comes to 8.9% on a semi-annual bond basis. Therefore, we would have been better off to have fixed in the first place at 8% than to pay the cap premium, because rates did not remain low for long enough to allow us to pay off the cost of the cap.

Table 17.2 shows that in this situation, LIBOR would have to remain at 6% for five quarters, 15 months, for the cap to be a better alternative. Table 17.3 highlights a point that may not be immediately obvious: As far as the

Table 17.2 Cap Break-Even Analysis

Cap strike rate	8.50%	Payments p.a.	4
Cap fee	1.12%	Amort. cap cost	0.11
Fixed funding	8.00%	IRR (s/a bond eqvt)	7.99%
Term in years	3		

Quarter	LIBOR Rate	Liability Cash Flow	Cap Payoff	Capped Cash Flow at 8%	Cap Cost Amortized	Net Cash Flow
0		−100		−100		
1	6.00%	1.52	0	1.52	0.11	1.63
2	6.00%	1.52	0.00	1.52	0.11	1.63
3	6.00%	1.52	0.00	1.52	0.11	1.63
4	6.00%	1.52	0.00	1.52	0.11	1.63
5	6.00%	1.52	0.00	1.52	0.11	1.63
6	10.00%	2.53	−0.38	2.15	0.11	2.26
7	10.00%	2.53	−0.38	2.15	0.11	2.26
8	10.00%	2.53	−0.38	2.15	0.11	2.26
9	10.00%	2.53	−0.38	2.15	0.11	2.26
10	10.00%	2.53	−0.38	2.15	0.11	2.26
11	10.00%	2.53	−0.38	2.15	0.11	2.26
12	10.00%	102.53	−0.38	102.15	0.11	102.26

Table 17.3 Cap Analysis: Smaller Rise in LIBOR

Cap strike rate	8.50%	Payments p.a.	4
Cap fee	1.12%	Amort. cap cost	0.11
Fixed funding	8.00%	IRR (s/a bond eqvt)	7.99%
Term in years	3		

Quarter	LIBOR Rate	Liability Cash Flow	Cap Payoff	Capped Cash Flow at 8%	Cap Cost Amortized	Net Cash Flow
0		−100		−100		
1	6.00%	1.52	0	1.52	0.11	1.63
2	6.00%	1.52	0.00	1.52	0.11	1.63
3	6.00%	1.52	0.00	1.52	0.11	1.63
4	6.00%	1.52	0.00	1.52	0.11	1.63
5	6.00%	1.52	0.00	1.52	0.11	1.63
6	8.75%	2.22	−0.06	2.15	0.11	2.26
7	8.75%	2.22	−0.06	2.15	0.11	2.26
8	8.75%	2.22	−0.06	2.15	0.11	2.26
9	8.75%	2.22	−0.06	2.15	0.11	2.26
10	8.75%	2.22	−0.06	2.15	0.11	2.26
11	8.75%	2.22	−0.06	2.15	0.11	2.26
12	8.75%	102.22	−0.06	102.15	0.11	102.26

borrower is concerned, it does not matter how high rates go, once they go through the cap strike level. If, instead of going to 10%, they go to only 8.75%, his smaller pay off is balanced by a smaller borrowing cost, so that the IRR of the entire deal is still 7.99%. All that matters is that LIBOR should go through the strike level; after that, it does not matter how high rates go. This is due to the cap's being an option, and thus a one-way bet. The converse is true for the writer of the cap.

Another way of looking at the break-even is to ask the question: given that the LIBOR for the first period is fixed at 6%, what rate can be reached in period two and remain thereafter, so that we break even. As Table 17.4 shows, the answer is 7.49%. If rates go above 7.49%, and remain there, then we would have been better off taking fixed-rate funding. A quick and dirty approximation, to this break-even rate can be found by taking the annual cap cost (0.44%) and deducting it from the fixed funding rate of 8%. The resulting figure is 7.56%, not far from the true rate.

By the same token, one might ask what the break-even rate would be for the writer of a cap. Given the same initial rate as in Table 17.4, Table 17.5 shows that thereafter the rate must rise to 8.96% for the writer of the cap to break even. In this context, cap earnings are defined as the initial cap fee of 1.12%, less the net present value—at the fixed funding rate of 8%—of the stream of cap payoffs of 0.12 per period.

Table 17.4   Cap Analysis: Break-Even Rate

Cap strike rate	8.50%	Payments p.a.	4
Cap fee	1.12%	Amort. cap cost	0.11
Fixed funding	8.00%	IRR (s/a bond eqvt)	8.00%
Term in years	3		

Quarter	LIBOR Rate	Liability Cash Flow	Cap Payoff	Capped Cash Flow at 8%	Cap Cost Amortized	Net Cash Flow
0		−100		−100		
1	6.50%	1.65	0	1.52	0.11	1.63
2	7.49%	1.90	0.00	1.52	0.11	1.63
3	7.49%	1.90	0.00	1.52	0.11	1.63
4	7.49%	1.90	0.00	1.52	0.11	1.63
5	7.49%	1.90	0.00	1.52	0.11	1.63
6	7.49%	1.90	−0.06	2.15	0.11	2.26
7	7.49%	1.90	−0.06	2.15	0.11	2.26
8	7.49%	1.90	−0.06	2.15	0.11	2.26
9	7.49%	1.90	−0.06	2.15	0.11	2.26
10	7.49%	1.90	−0.06	2.15	0.11	2.26
11	7.49%	1.90	−0.06	2.15	0.11	2.26
12	7.49%	101.90	−0.06	102.15	0.11	102.26

Table 17.5   Cap Analysis: Break-Even for Writer

Cap strike rate	8.50%	Payments p.a.	4
Cap fee	1.12%	Amort. cap cost	0.11
Fixed funding	8.00%	IRR (s/a bond eqvt)	8.95%
Term in years	3	Net cap earnings	.00%

Quarter	LIBOR Rate	Liability Cash Flow	Cap Payoff	Capped Cash Flow at 8%	Cap Cost Amortized	Net Cash Flow
0		−100		−100		
1	6.50%	1.65	0	1.65	0.11	1.76
2	8.96%	2.27	0.12	2.15	0.11	2.26
3	8.96%	2.27	0.12	2.15	0.11	2.26
4	8.96%	2.27	0.12	2.15	0.11	2.26
5	8.96%	2.27	0.12	2.15	0.11	2.26
6	8.96%	2.27	0.12	2.15	0.11	2.26
7	8.96%	2.27	0.12	2.15	0.11	2.26
8	8.96%	2.27	0.12	2.15	0.11	2.26
9	8.96%	2.27	0.12	2.15	0.11	2.26
10	8.96%	2.27	0.12	2.15	0.11	2.26
11	8.96%	2.27	0.12	2.15	0.11	2.26
12	8.96%	102.27	0.12	102.15	0.11	102.26

Looking at it another way, the writer of the cap must pay away 0.12 per period, which is more or less offset by the amortized cap earnings of 0.11 per period. We can also look at the borrower's break-even cost in this way. Here the break-even rate against which we are comparing is not the cap strike rate of 8.5%, but the alternative rate for the borrower, the fixed funding rate of 8%.

Our first step is to express this as a quarterly rate, to make it comparable with the amortized cost of the cap of 0.11 per period per period. 8% semi-annually equates to 8.16 per annum, which equates to 1.98% per period. From this we deduct the 0.11% per period cost of the cap amortized, plus one basis point to allow for the fact that the initial 0.11% was essentially thrown away, to arrive at a net rate per period of 1.86%. This compounds up to 7.65% per annum, or 7.51% semi-annually, about the same as our break-even calculation.

As we saw in Chapter 16, puts and calls are related to each other through the price of the underlying security. In the case of caps and floors, the common denominator is the interest rate swap. Let us assume a flat yield curve. Three month LIBOR and a 5-year interest rate swap are both at 8%. In this case, a 5-year cap is equivalent to a 5-year floor plus a commitment to pay the 5-year swap rate of 8%. This holds true when both the cap and the floor are struck at the swap rate and if the fixed rate is paid on the same basis as the floating rate. It can be shown that these positions will produce the same cash flows under any interest rate movement.

For a rate above the cap level, say 10%, the holder of the cap will be paid the difference between LIBOR and 8%, or 2%. The floor and swap combination produce the same cash flow. Since rates are above 8%, the floor by itself produces no income, while the swap entitles the holder to the difference between the 8% fixed outflow and the 10% LIBOR—2% again. For rates below the cap level, say 6%, the cap holder receives no payment. The holder of the floor plus the swap also has no net cash flow. The floor generates a positive cash flow equal to the difference between 8% and LIBOR, 2%, which is just enough to cover the shortfall on the interest rate swap between the fixed payment outflow of 8% and the floating payment received, 6%. At exactly 8%, none of the instruments produces cash flows.

OPTION STRATEGIES

In this section we discuss some of the different combinations of puts and calls that options traders use. We will display the profit payoff diagram for each strategy and look at some of the basic risk/reward issues. Throughout this section we will, for brevity, use the following abbreviations:

+	means long
−	means short
C	means call
P	means put
@E1, @E2,	means at exercise price 1, at exercise price 2, E1 being the lowest, E2 a higher price, and E3 the next higher, and so on
T1	means the nearest maturity date, T2 the next, and so on

We start with the two simplest cases: where we buy a call option or a put option. (See Figures 17.1 and 17.2.)

Long a call option: +C @E1

Outlook:	Bullish
Profit potential:	Unlimited
Loss potential:	Limited
Time decay:	Against the buyer. Worst at-the-money

The buyer of a call option on sterling at $2.00 thinks sterling will rise above that level. As it does so his profit is unlimited. The risk is that sterling is below $2.00 at maturity. If so, the option buyer's loss is limited to the premium paid. Because the seller charges a time value element in the price of the option, the buyer of a call option suffers the effects of time decay. The time premium is largest for an at-the-money option, so time decay is worst for the buyer of such an option.

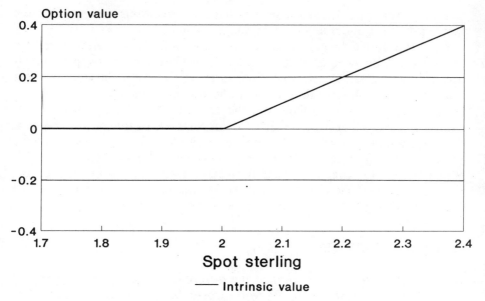

Figure 17.1   Call option profile.

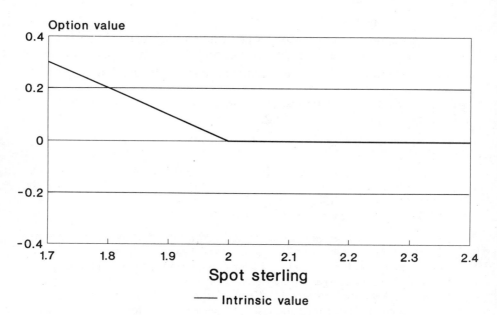

Figure 17.2   Put option payoff profile.

Long a put option +P @E1

Outlook:	Bearish
Profit potential:	Unlimited
Loss potential:	Limited
Time decay:	Against the buyer. Worst at-the-money

The buyer of a put option on sterling at $2.00 believes sterling will fall below that level. As it does so his profit is unlimited. The risk of loss is that sterling settles above $2.00 at maturity. In that case the option buyer's loss is limited to the premium paid. The buyer of the option pays time value to the seller and so time decay works against him. Time value is highest for an at-the-money option and so time decay is most negative for an at-the-money put.

Now we will consider various combinations of options. We will see a range of different combinations, but they can usually be broken down into three types:

1. *Vertical spreads:* Options with same expiry date, but a different strike price.
2. *Horizontal spreads:* Options at the same strike price, but a different expiry date. Sometimes referred to as calendar spreads.
3. *Diagonal spreads:* Combinations of vertical and horizontal spreads.

Depending on where the strike prices of the options composing them are fixed, spreads can cost a net premium or earn a net premium. In the former case, they are referred to as debit spreads; in the latter as credit spreads. We begin with vertical spreads since they do not have the complications of time built in. The first of these is the bull spread (see Figure 17.3).

Bull spread + C @E1 – C @E2; or: +P @E1 – P @E2

Outlook:	Bullish, but not overwhelmingly
Profit potential:	Limited
Loss potential:	Limited
Time decay:	Fairly neutral (depending where the option strikes are set)

The buyer of a bull spread on sterling between, say $2.00 and $2.20 buys a call on sterling at $2.00 and sells a call at $2.20. The sale of the call at the higher exercise price brings in premium which helps offset the cost of the $2.00 call. This is cheaper than buying a $2.00 call outright. But the saving is at the cost of giving up any profit beyond $2.20. So this deal would be done if one were bullish on sterling but unconvinced it would go to $2.20.

The strategy can be exercised by doing puts at the same level. Here the $2.20 put pays off below $2.00; its cost is paid for by selling a put at $2.20 which cuts the total premium paid, but costs money if sterling goes above $2.20. The basic view is that sterling will trade between $2.00 and $2.20.

In both cases time decay on the option sold helps offset the decay on the option bought: the net effect depends on how close the two strike prices are.

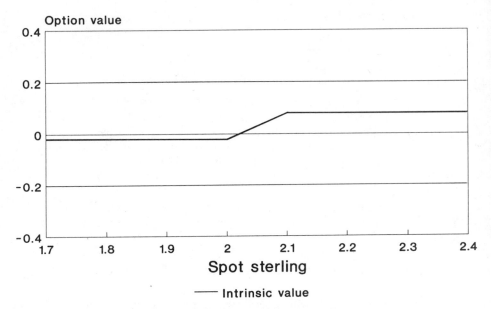

Figure 17.3   Bull spread payoff profile.

A popular strategy, particularly for corporations hedging their exchange risk, is the cylinder. (Or the fence, or the tunnel—the strategy has been given many different names by the marketing teams of different banks anxious to convince their customers that they invented the idea.) Here protection is bought below a certain level, at the price of giving away profit if the rate goes above a certain level (or vice versa if the strategy is dealt in the opposite direction). Cylinders can be structured so they are net debit spreads, net credit spreads, or so that the net premium is zero. This will be done by adjusting the strike prices. *The fact that a zero cost is charged does not mean the customer is getting a free ride,* since the strikes may have been set so that on the other side the bank can sell off the two component positions at a handsome profit. It is however the zero up-front cost which is the feature that has traditionally made it attractive to corporate customers. This is attractive to corporate treasurers who do not want to have to explain to their Board of Directors why they are paying out good money to get protection against an exchange rate move that may never happen. (A traditional problem in a number of companies who for some reason do not accept the analogy with insurance on physical property: a fire insurance premium is good money paid out to protect you against something which may never happen). (See Figure 17.4.)

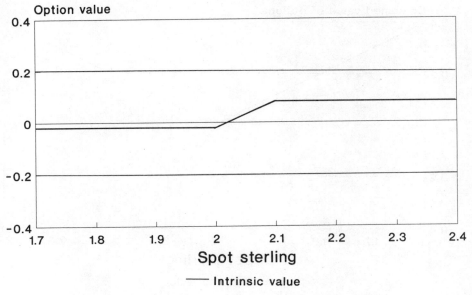

Figure 17.4   Cylinder.

Cylinder + P@E1 – C@E2 or +C@E1 – P@E2

Outlook: Bearish but wanting cheap protection
Profit potential: Limited
Loss potential: Limited
Time decay: Neutral depending on strikes

The next strategy is the straddle. This is unique to the options market. Up to now all the strategies we have looked at have involved a view on the direction of the market. Such a view could be traded in the cash market without difficulty. But the straddle allows to take a position on the volatility of the market without committing ourselves to a view on its direction. If we think the volatility of the market will rise, we can buy a straddle; if we think it will fall, we can sell a straddle. (See Figure 17.5)

Straddle + C@E1 + P@E1

Outlook: Market volatility will rise. Neutral on market direction.
Profit potential: Unlimited
Loss potential: Limited to premium
Time decay: Doubly negative (both legs of the trade decay against you)

Above the strike, the call pays off; below the strike, the put pays off. Whichever way the market moves, you make money. But it has to move enough to pay for the double premium paid out to get into the deal, and it has to move fairly quickly because time decay is working against you twice as hard.

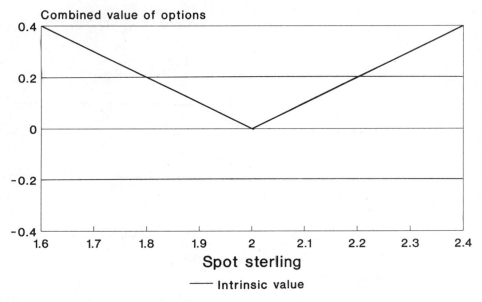

Figure 17.5   Straddle payoff profile.

A strangle is essentially a straddle but with the two options at a different strike. The buyer of a strangle has the same volatility view as the buyer of a straddle, but looks for a different payoff pattern. The strangle loses money over a wider range than the straddle, but loses less if the market does not move at all. Thus it is essentially a less aggressive bet than the straddle. The short seller of the strangle takes the opposite view: he or she is a seller of volatility. (See Figure 17.6.)

Strangle + C@E1 + P@E2

Outlook:	Market volatility will rise. Neutral on market direction.
Profit potential:	Unlimited
Loss potential:	Limited
Time decay:	Doubly negative

The butterfly consists of the sale of a straddle combined with purchase of call options below and above the straddle's strike. It is a straddle with stop-loss protection. It is a position loved by options brokers since it involves four separate contracts and thus four sets of commission. Options traders need to consider the transactions costs involved. But it can be a good, limited-risk method of profiting from the sale of volatility. The short butterfly position is sometimes called a sandwich spread—the dealer hopes to sandwich the price movement within the spread. (See Figure 17.7)

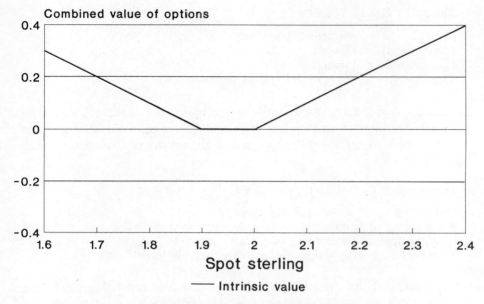

Figure 17.6 Strangle payoff profile.

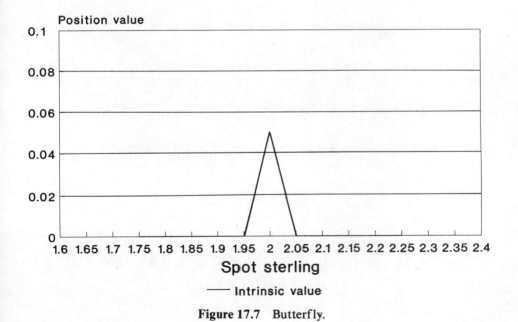

Figure 17.7 Butterfly.

Butterfly + C@E1 – 2C@E2 + C@E3

Outlook: Market will stay stable.
Profit potential: Limited
Loss potential: Limited
Time decay: Fairly neutral (depending on strikes)

The condor is to the strangle what the butterfly is to the straddle. That is, the condor is a strangle with stop-loss. The dealer buys calls outside the range of the strangle to cut down the risk of a large movement against him. (See Figure 17.8.)

Condor + C@E1 – C@E2 – C@E3 + C@E4

Outlook: Market will stay stable
Profit potential: Limited (but over wider range than butterfly)
Loss potential: Limited (but more than butterfly)
Time decay: Fairly neutral (depending on strike levels)

Up to now all the positions we have looked at have been balanced, in the sense that options sold and bought have generally matched. Ratio spreads are spread trades where the puts and calls bought or sold are in a ratio to each other. Thus the call ratio spread consists of buying a call at one strike and selling several calls at another. (See Figure 17.9.)

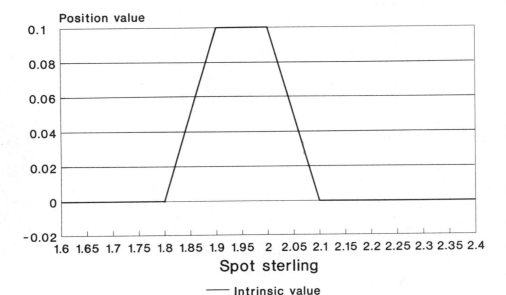

Figure 17.8   Condor.

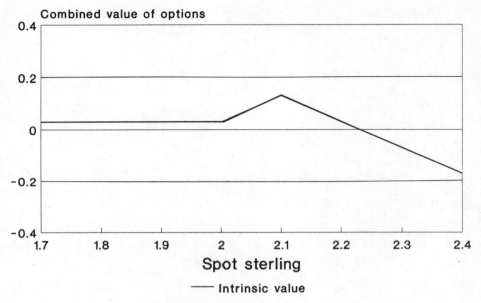

Figure 17.9 Ratio call spread.

Call ratio spread + C@E1 – nC@E2 (where n is usually from 2 to 5)

Outlook:	Bearish but not aggressively so
Profit potential:	Limited
Loss potential:	Unlimited
Time decay:	In our favor (how much depends how many calls sold)

The same approach can be taken with a put ratio spread. (See Figure 17.10.)

Put ratio spread + P@E2 – nP@E1 (n usually from 2 to 5)

Outlook:	Bullish but not aggressively so
Profit potential:	Limited
Loss potential:	Unlimited
Time decay:	In our favor (how much depends how many puts sold)

The call ratio backspread is another name for the sale of a call ratio spread: we sell a call at the lower strike and buy several calls at the higher strike. (See Figure 17.11.)

Call ratio backspread – C@E1 + nC@E2 (where n is usually from 2 to 5)

Outlook:	Bullish, we believe volatility will also rise
Profit potential:	Unlimited
Loss potential:	Limited
Time decay:	Works against us (how much depends how many calls we buy)

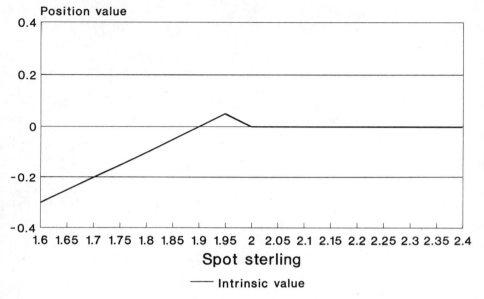

Figure 17.10   Put ratio spread.

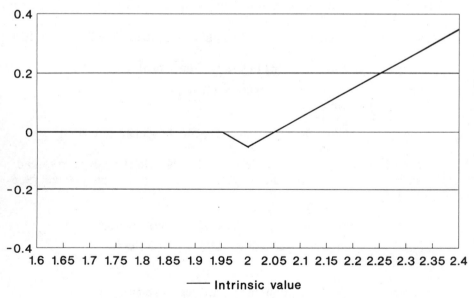

Figure 17.11   Call ratio backspread.

378

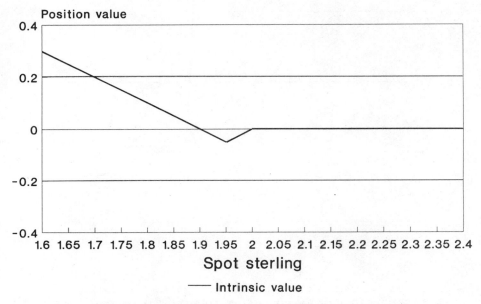

Figure 17.12   Put ratio backspread.

Similarly, the put ratio backspread is the sale of a put ratio spread: sell a put at the lower strike and buy several puts at the higher strike. (See Figure 17.12.)

Put ratio backspread – P@E2; + nP@E1 (n from 2 to 5)

Outlook:	Bearish, expecting the market to be volatile
Profit potential:	Unlimited
Loss potential:	Limited
Time decay:	Works against us (depending how many puts we buy)

So far, all the strategies we have considered are option combinations which expire on the same day. Collectively, these spreads are called *vertical* spreads. Now we come to consider the effect of time: we allow the options to mature on different dates. Options strategies with different maturities involved are often called *horizontal* or *calendar* spreads. One could in principle have many of the above spreads with different maturity dates for different components of the spread, but this would reduce the risk protection given and in most cases break up the logic of the spreads. The most widely used calendar spread is the simple sale of a call for one maturity coupled with the purchase of a call for a further maturity. (See Figure 17.13.)

Calendar spread – C@T1 + C@T2

Outlook:	Neutral on market direction, long volatility, short time decay

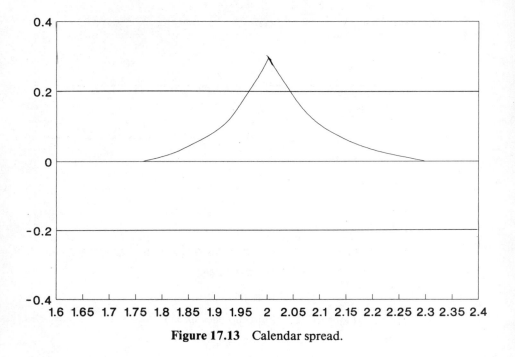

Figure 17.13 Calendar spread.

Net value of position predetermined as soon as trade is done

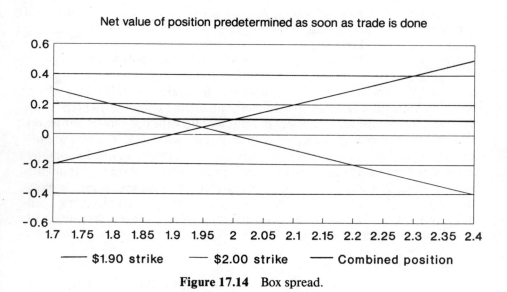

——— $1.90 strike   —— $2.00 strike   ——— Combined position

Figure 17.14 Box spread.

Profit potential:	Limited. Maximum potential if the asset price is near the strike when the first option matures. At that point, we would close out the far option.
Loss potential:	Limited. Losses on the near short should in part be offset by the long position for the far date; though this may not always happen.
Time decay:	Works in our favor (the near option decays faster than the further option)

Finally, we look at an option trade where everything is known from the start: the entire position is locked up from day 1. This is called a box spread. It relies on the put-call parity (see Chapter 16) to buy and sell two artificial assets established at different effective prices. We buy a call and sell a put at E1 and sell a call and buy a put at E2. In effect, it is a bet on the funding cost/interest earned between doing the trade and its maturity. (See Figure 17.14.)

Box spread + C@E1 – P@E1 – C@E2 + P@E2

Outlook:	Neutral on market. Aims to lock up an interest rate
Profit potential:	Limited
Loss potential:	Limited

STRATEGIES COMBINING OPTIONS AND ASSETS

Up to now we have looked only at options positions where the options are traded on their own, or in combination with other options. Now we look at combining options positions with underlying assets.

The first such application would arise in the simple case where we hold a position and would like to protect it through options. Imagine we have bought £1,000,000 at $1.80 and sterling is now trading at $1.95. We have a profit but we feel sterling will move up further. On the other hand, we would like some protection in case it falls unexpectedly. Suppose the $1.90 put is trading at 3 cents. We decide to cover ourselves on the Philadelphia Exchange by buying 16 contracts (of £62,500 each). This costs us $0.03 × 62,500 × 16 = $30,000. At the worst, where sterling falls sharply, we will sell at $1.90 – .03 = $1.87. So our minimum profit is $(1.87 – 1.80) × 1,000,000 = $70,000. The payoff profile is shown in Figure 17.15.

As we mentioned in Chapter 16, this position can be looked at as a synthetic call on sterling. That can be seen from the fact that an alternative way to trade here would have been to sell out the existing position to lock in profits, and then buy a call on sterling. Which of these two routes we take will depend on the relative pricing of the puts and calls. Likewise, if no puts are available, it would be possible to create a put by selling the underlying asset short and buying a call.

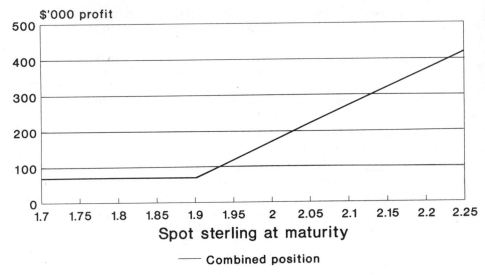

$'000 profit

Spot sterling at maturity

——— Combined position

Figure 17.15   Asset + put position equates to a call.

Another trade combining the underlying asset with options is the conversion (and its opposite the reversal). The conversion is the sale of an artificial asset covered by the purchase of the asset. The sale of the artificial asset is done by selling a call and buying a put, which is equivalent to a short sale of the asset.

An example would be options on the December Eurodollar futures. Suppose the future is trading at 92.00. Let the December 91.00 call on the future be trading at 1.50 and the put at 0.20. We buy the put for 0.20 and sell the call for 1.50 for a net credit of 1.30. Effectively, we are short the future. To close our position we buy the future at 92.00. What will happen at expiry? Suppose the future settles at 90.00 when the December expiry arrives. Then the 91.00 put will be worth 1.00 and the call will have no value. Our options positions give a profit of 1 point.

But we are long the future at 92.00 which we now close out at 90.00 for a loss of 2 points. Thus our net position is a loss of 1 point at expiry. We made 1.50 on the initial position so the net profit on the deal as a whole is 50 basis points. (Slightly more if we allow for the interest we could earn on the initial profit.) There is a similar outcome if the future settles at maturity at, say, 94.00. Now, the 91.00 call loses us 3 points, the put expires worthless, and the future makes a profit of 2 points, for a net loss once again of 1 point.

The reversal is the opposite trade: buy the artificial asset and sell short the actual asset. That is, buy a call and sell a put, covering with a short sale of the asset.

An important trading strategy involving the underlying asset and the related options is the *covered write*. Here, we own the underlying asset and write a call option against it. Our risk is covered by our ownership of the underlying asset—that is, if the call is exercised against us, we own the asset that must be delivered already. Our risk is thus limited to the fact that we will sell the asset at a price which may be less than we could otherwise get for it if the market really improves. On the other hand, we will have earned option premium income to compensate us for this risk.

Suppose we have bought $10 million worth of Eurodollar March futures at 89.5. We think that rates will not improve that much: we expect rates at that date to be trading at 10%. We might write a call option for $10 million at 91.00 for a premium of say 0.50. That means that the net cost of our position is effectively the 89.5 we paid for the futures less the 0.5 of premium earned, or 89.00. Suppose we are right, and rates are at 10% when the delivery date comes. Then no-one will exercise the call against us, since they can buy in the market at 90 rather than the 91 they would pay via the call option. We have earned 1 point profit. Now suppose that we were wrong. Rates collapsed. The future traded at 93 on the settlement date. The call is exercised against us and we must sell at 91. But our net cost was 89 so we have earned 2 points profit. If we had not written the call, we would have made a 4-point profit. We have limited our gain. But if the market remains stable, the call option premium is an enhancement to income. (See Figure 17.16.)

Covered call writing is a very popular strategy in the stock market. Investors use it to earn a supplementary income. Applied consistently over time, it can be a money-spinner. One is effectively writing insurance policies: and

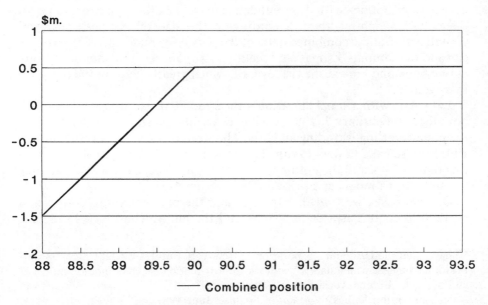

Figure 17.16 Eurodollar future covered call.

insurance companies, over time, tend to prosper provided they are prudently managed. It is common to write shorter-dated options, to take advantage of the fact that time value works more rapidly in the writer's favor.

Simple covered call writing has some weaknesses. If the market falls sharply, the option written loses value very quickly and its time value will disappear. Conversely, a sharp rise in the market will have a similar effect on time value. *Dynamic covered call writing* is an attempt to get around this problem by making sure that the option written always has large time decay. As the market rises, we "roll up" the strike (buy back the outstanding option and sell a new one with a higher strike). Conversely, we roll down if the market falls. This approach itself has two problems: the obvious one is higher transactions costs. Second, it increases the risk of being "whipsawed." The market rises sharply: we buy back the old option, write a new one at a higher strike, incurring a dealing spread. The market now falls sharply: we reverse the process, incurring more dealing costs, and so on.

MANAGING OPTIONS EXPOSURES

We come now to the practicalities of running an options book. That includes the measurement of exposure for the book as a whole, including worst-case analysis; and once the exposure is measured, deciding what to do about it: hedging and managing the position.

Before doing that, it is worth pointing out one very important property of the risk measures that we introduced earlier: they are *additive.* That is, if we have a set of options with different deltas in our position, we can add up all the deltas (weighting them according to the size of the positions) and we will arrive at the combined delta of the portfolio as a whole. Similarly, we can add the gammas, kappas, and thetas. So we can treat our combined book as one book and look at the risk overall, which greatly helps in the practical management.

Let's start with a simple position—the straddle on sterling at $2.00. Suppose that on February 7, 1991, we buy a straddle on sterling at $2.00 when the pound sterling is trading at $2.00. The straddle expires on September 6, 1991, and so has 212 days to run. The underlying risk-free rate of interest to that date is 13%, and the option is priced at a volatility of 22%. We can plug this data into a model and price up the position.*

On this basis, we find that the call and the put option are both worth $0.1270; the call has a delta of 0.51 and the put a delta of −0.45. So the

---

* I have used the Discount Corporation of New York Futures model called Options Position Manager which uses a quadratic approximation for the binomial model as laid out in G. Barone-Adesi & R. E. Whaley, "Efficient Analytic Approximation of American Option Values," *Journal of Finance,* June 1987; but other models would show results which are not dissimilar.

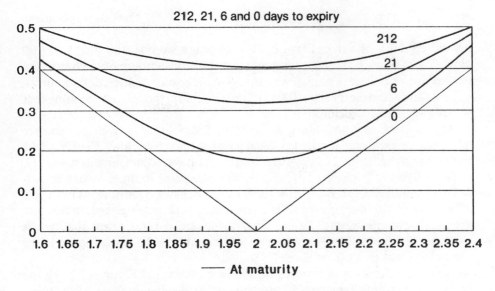

At maturity

Figure 17.17 Straddle: Payoff over time.

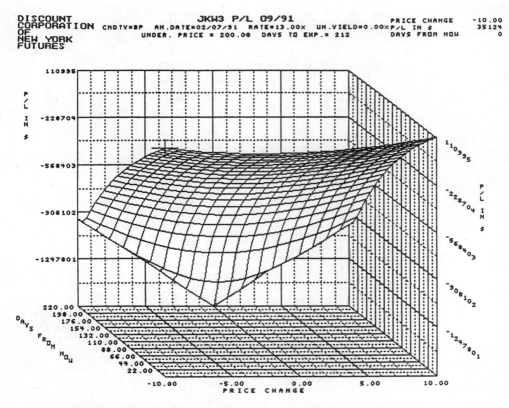

Figure 17.18 Straddle payoff in three dimensions: Seen from below.

combined delta of our position is .064. Suppose we buy 100 puts and 100 calls. Then, since the futures contract is for the same amount of sterling as the underlying option, we could, if we wanted to make our position delta-neutral, sell 6 futures contracts (100×0.064). For simplicity, though, let's assume that we simply hold the options position.

At maturity, our position will look like Figure 16.7: a V-shape. But we have not yet reached maturity. What does it look like now? Figure 17.17 shows our straddle for 212 days to maturity, 21 days, 6 days, and at maturity.

In fact, each of these curves is a snapshot at a point in time: we can draw a 3-dimensional chart showing how the position behaves over time, as in Figure 17.18 and 17.19. Interpreting a 3D chart takes a little getting used to: what we are looking at in Figure 17.18 is a long, downward-curving arrow that comes to a point on the last day; it is shown from the underside, while Figure 17.19 shows the same thing from above.

How does the delta of this position behave over time? Figure 17.20 shows that delta starts off today as a fairly straight line sloping up from left to right,

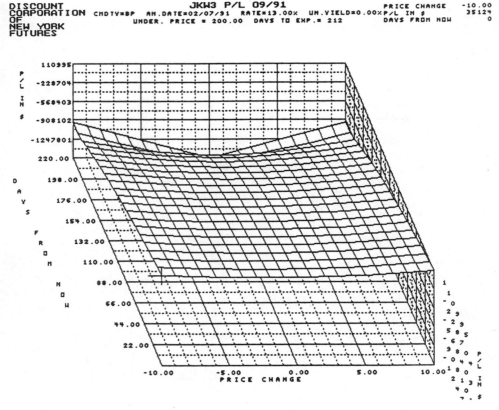

Figure 17.19   Payoff of Figure 17.18 seen from above.

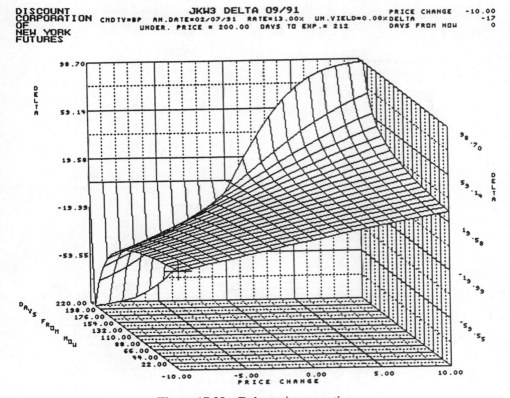

DISCOUNT
CORPORATION   JKW3 DELTA 09/91   PRICE CHANGE -10.00
OF   CMDTY=BP AN.DATE=02/07/91 RATE=13.00% UN.YIELD=0.00%DELTA   -17
NEW YORK   UNDER. PRICE = 200.00 DAYS TO EXP.= 212   DAYS FROM NOW   0
FUTURES

Figure 17.20   Delta twists over time.

with a relatively mild slope. As we get closer to maturity, the line becomes much steeper and more curved. This is another way of saying gamma is rising, which is rather dramatically clear when we look at Figure 17.21. From a low level, gamma rises strongly until on the last day of the option it becomes relatively large. Conversely, the effect of kappa (or zeta as Discount Corporation call it) declines (Figure 17.22) as does theta, though here we see how the dramatic rise in gamma on the last day is offset by an equally dramatic collapse in theta. (Figure 17.23).

Let's move on six months in the life of the option to August 17, 1991, assuming that rates have not moved at all. We now look at the same charts again: Figure 17.24 shows us that in terms of overall profitability we are well down the slippery slope already, and from here on in life gets much tougher. Moral: it pays to bale out of long options positions reasonably early unless things are going your way. Figure 17.25 shows how the slope of the delta line has begun to steepen sharply and it is beginning to curve (gamma, the measure of curvature of delta, is starting to rise). This is confirmed by Figure 17.26 which shows us that gamma is about to become a fairly serious problem for us;

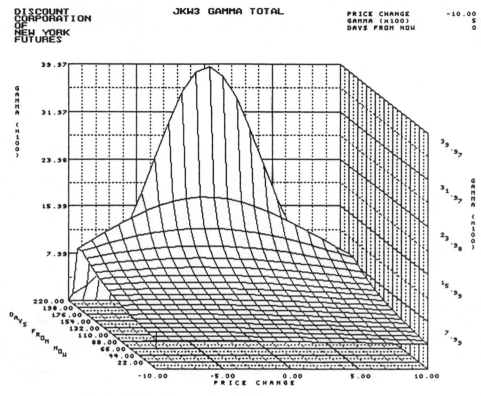

Figure 17.21   Gamma: impact increases as maturity nears.

Figure 17.27 shows how kappa (zeta) is eroding, and Figure 17.28 shows how sharply theta is about to begin to work against us, though at this point the curve is still fairly flat.

The construction of these graphs assumed that options values were constructed at a constant volatility of 22%. Experience shows that volatilities for options away-from-the-money (that is, in or out) tend to be rather higher than at-the-money volatilities. Some people in the market describe this as the "volatility smile" (Figure 17.29) or volatility "skew."

We could redraw these graphs using a volatility smile: we assume that spot sterling is at $2.00 and the $2.00 options are priced at 22% volatility. For each 2.5 cents away from the money we assume a 2% rise in volatility. (For example, a $1.95 option is priced at 26%; a $2.10 option at 30%.) As Figure 17.30 shows, when compared with Figure 17.18, the effect is to turn what was a gentle curve today into a V-shape (though the effect at maturity is much less, since kappa is less). Now a price change today can have a much greater profit and loss impact than in Figure 17.18, where the P&L impact of quite wide swings was fairly minor.

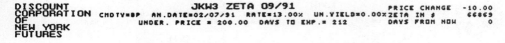

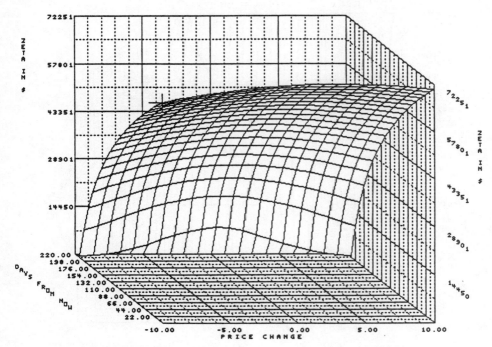

Figure 17.22   Declining effect of kappa (zeta) as we near maturity.

Figures 17.31 to 17.34 show the effects on our four main measures of option sensitivity. The main effects are to somewhat soften the impact of gamma and theta, respectively. The charts we have looked at show how important the effect of the passage of time is on the option position. These are emphatically not positions you can simply put on and forget about (unless they perfectly match some other position).

DELTA-WEIGHTED HEDGING

Delta-weighted hedging, or variants of it, is crucial to the workings of the over-the-counter options market, particularly where options are being written on instruments without an exchange-traded option market. For example, the hedging of interest rate caps, floors, and collars must be done by some kind of delta-weighted or other hedging strategy since there are no exchange-traded caps, floors, or collars.

To see how this works, think back to what delta is. We saw in the last chapter that one way of looking at delta is to think of it as the probability

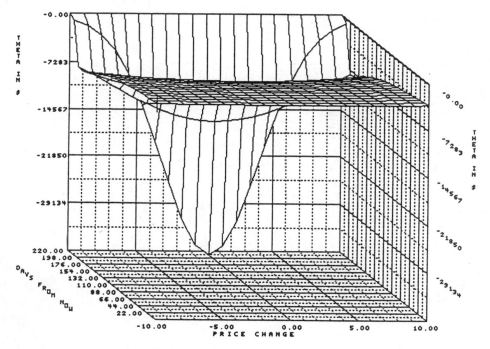

Figure 17.23   Theta is sharply negative close to expiring.

that the option will be exercised. Suppose I have sold an option on the equity of IBM at a strike price of $110 per share. The shares are trading today at $80. Suppose the delta of this call option today is measured as 0.01. There is very little probability, if the stock is at $80, that anyone is going to exercise a $110 call against me. So I will not bother to hedge my position.

Suppose now the stock jumps to $105. Delta rises to say 0.45. There is a 45% chance the option will be exercised against me. I will hedge about 45% of my position. Now the stock jumps to $200. Delta is at 0.999. It is virtually certain that the option will be exercised against me and I will buy the full amount of the position so as to be able to deliver on the option. So delta-weighted hedging is a hedging approach based on the probability that the option will be exercised against me.

Let's take the case of a company that wants to buy a European call option on £100 million for three months. The strike is fixed at $2.00. The bank which has sold the call does not want to buy a matching option, either over-the-counter or on an exchange, because it feels the options are over-priced. However, it wants to hedge its risk. It would probably use a delta-weighted approach. Suppose sterling today is trading at $1.80 and the delta

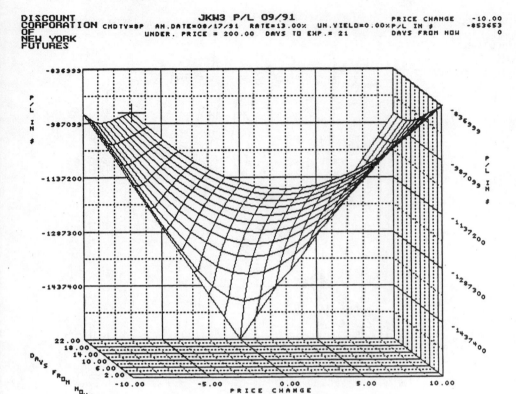

DISCOUNT   JKW3 P/L 09/91   PRICE CHANGE   -10.00
CORPORATION CMDTV=BP AM.DATE=08/17/91 RATE=13.00% UM.VIELD=0.00%P/L IM $ -853653
OF   UNDER. PRICE = 200.00 DAVS TO EXP.= 21   DAVS FROM NOW   0
NEW YORK
FUTURES

Figure 17.24 Time has worked against the straddle.

on this option is assessed by the bank as being 0.05. There is a 5% chance that the option might be exercised against it. Then it would buy £5 million to hedge its position. As a matter of normal dealing practice (see Chapter 10), it would probably buy the sterling in the spot market to lock the exchange risk and then separately do a forward three-month swap to shift the position into the three-month maturity. So the £5 million is bought spot. Now sterling jumps to $1.90 and the delta rises to say 0.15: there is a 15% chance of exercise. The bank will buy another £10 million to bring its total holdings to £15 million.

Suppose sterling falls back to $1.85 and the delta drops to 0.10. The bank will sell £5 million of the £10 million it bought at $1.90. It will take a loss. Now suppose the same thing happens again: sterling rises to $1.90 and then falls back to $1.85. The bank will take another loss. The more sterling rises and falls—the more volatile sterling is—the bigger the bank's loss. Thus successful delta hedging depends critically on getting the right estimate of volatility. The premium charged for the option must be big enough to cover the expected stream of losses that will be generated by the delta hedge as sterling moves up and down.

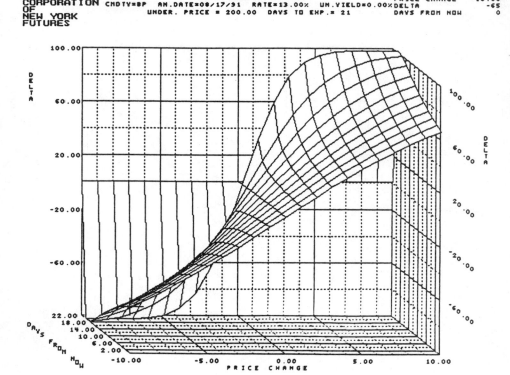

Figure 17.25   Delta is beginning to steepen.

Many market users ask: "why delta hedge? Why employ a hedging technique which is expected to generate a stream of losses?" The answer is that although delta hedging is certainly not very attractive, it is often the least bad alternative. If a matching option cannot be bought to cover the position, or is too expensive, then delta hedging may be the only way to control the option writer's risk.

A second important point about delta hedging is the role of gamma. As we saw in the last chapter, a high gamma means that the option premium curve is very "curvy." So this option's delta will move more quickly, for a given change in sterling, if the option's gamma is high. The more quickly delta moves, the more often a delta hedger must adjust his hedge. That means higher transactions costs. So a high gamma option will tend to be more expensive to hedge than one with a lower gamma. Gamma is highest for short-dated, at-the-money options. These will therefore tend to be the most expensive to hedge by delta hedging. On the other hand, we saw in Chapter 16 that theta is highest for short-dated, at-the-money options, and theta works in favor of the option writer. Time decay works in his or her favor. So theta will be a partial offset to high gamma.

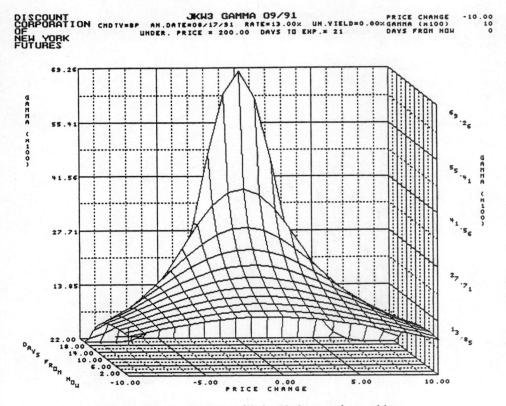

Figure 17.26 Gamma will shortly be a major problem.

Market participants have developed a number of related strategies for options replication in addition to delta-weighted hedging. There are simpler variants of dynamic hedging strategies—"hedge an additional x% of the remaining exposure for each y% move in the market," and so on. Equally, if one has a view of the basic underlying trend in the market, one would not follow pure delta hedging. All of these techniques are not without risk. The most obvious example comes from the stock market, where this kind of hedging was glorified with the name of portfolio insurance.

The crash of 1987 illustrated the problems:

- The dynamic hedger is selling into a falling market and buying into a rising one. If the position is large, then there could be liquidity problems.
- In a volatile market the underlying asset's price can jump up or down by a significant amount before the dynamic hedger can act to adjust the balance of the hedge. The position could become over- or under-hedged as the market "gaps" up or down.

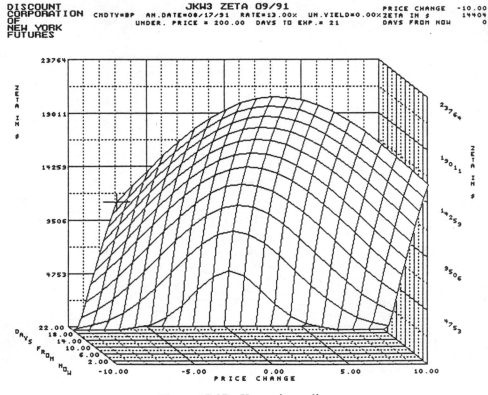

Figure 17.27   Kappa is eroding.

The Brady report on the U.S. stock market crash in 1987 stated that portfolio insurers "approached Monday 19 October with a huge amount of selling already dictated by their models. With the market already down 10%, their models dictated that, at a minimum, $12 billion of equities should already have been sold. Less than $4 billion had in fact been sold."

So delta hedging is by no means without risk. The risk is a good deal less in the foreign exchange and money markets than in the stock market, since the underlying liquidity in the major markets is far greater than even the biggest stock market. But for large positions, or in secondary currencies, the liquidity risk is very relevant.

VOLATILITY CONES

Given the critical importance of the volatility estimate in pricing an option, it may be worth spending some time thinking about how we should make that estimate. Often traders use gut feel, or pricing in line with implied

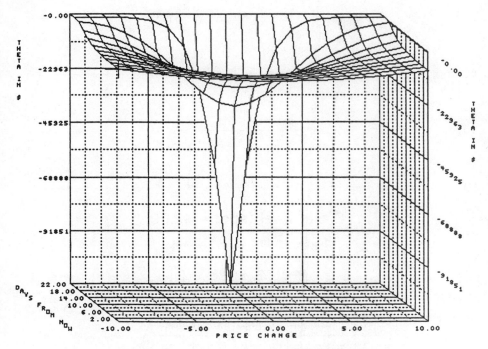

Figure 17.28   Theta is about to sharpen against us.

volatilities seen in the market. This may be satisfactory. The evidence in other markets is that spending huge sums of money or large amounts of time in building sophisticated forecasting models does not necessarily achieve performance improvements in proportion to the effort. One recent study concluded: "on a time-varying ex ante basis, the simpler the model, the better it performs . . . evidence from this study strongly supports the 'keep it simple' approach to forecasting."* The same study recommended exponential smoothing or regression analysis as likely techniques for volatility forecasting.

A way of looking at volatility which I find quite helpful is the so-called *volatility cone* (Figure 17.35). This starts by considering the *term structure of volatility*. The smoothly curved lines represent upper and lower bounds of historical volatilities for trading horizons ranging from 1 month to 1 year. The data is drawn from the two previous years.

* E. Dimson & P. Marsh, "Volatility forecasting without data-snooping," *Journal of Banking and Finance* 1990.

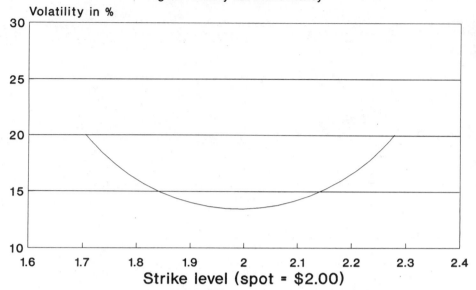

Figure 17.29 Volatility smile.

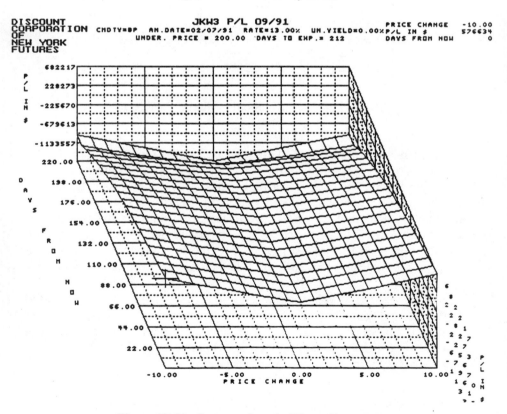

Figure 17.30 Impact of a volatility smile on P/L.

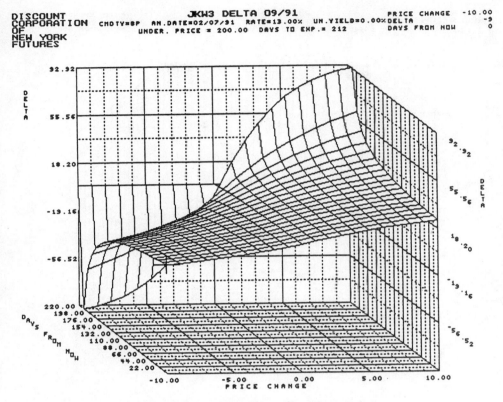

Figure 17.31   Volatility smile softens delta.

The resulting volatility cones show that short-term historical volatilities are substantially more variable than longer-term historical volatilities. This can be seen in the greater distance between the maximum and minimum 30-day historical volatilities (shown toward the left of the chart) and the maximum and minimum 180-day historical volatilities (shown in the middle of the chart). The chart also shows the recent history of implied volatilities for the nearest contract (the lead contract) it shows the past quarter's behavior of the current lead option. The left-most point of the line is the value of implied volatility for the contract on the last trading day of the most recent quarter.

THIRD GENERATION PRODUCTS

In recent years, a number of hedging concepts have been developed that collectively have been called "third generation" techniques. The idea is that forward exchange and futures were the first generation, options the second generation. The third generation combines the two. In practice, most of these products were developed in order to allow corporate treasurers or

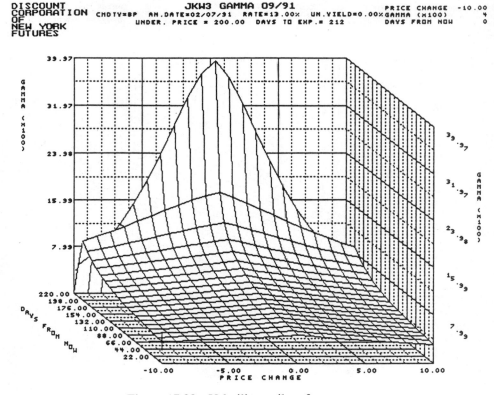

Figure 17.32   Volatility smile softens gamma.

fund managers to use options without appearing to do so. This avoided the
need for lengthy explanations to a board or to trustees whose grasp of the
advantages of options might be rather limited. In some cases, banks also
used these products in order to conceal from their customers the true costs
of the product they were buying. In most cases it is usually cheapest for the
customer to buy the component parts separately. However, where there are
regulatory or tax advantages the third generation products may be useful.
For example, in the United Kingdom, the Inland Revenue took the view
that an option was a wasting asset, therefore losses on options purchased
were not tax deductible. A loss on a forward exchange contract, however,
was allowable. Thus combining the forward and the option allowed for
better tax treatment.

We will look at three kinds of third generation product. They are the
break forward, the range forward, and the participating contract. (Unfortunately the marketing departments of many banks, in an effort to make the
bank's product seem different, have dreamed up many different names for
these products. Thus break forwards have been called a Boston option, a
FOX [forward with optional exit] and so on.)

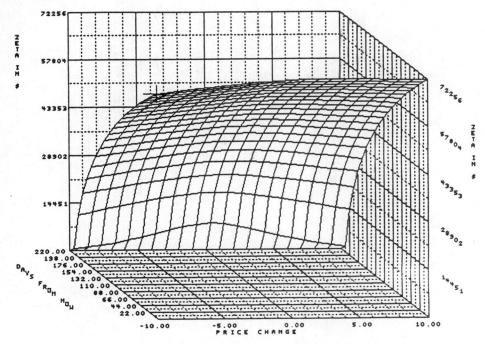

Figure 17.33   Kappa is flattened.

The *break forward* is a forward contract combined with a call or put. For example, a corporate customer requires to buy forward sterling value June 15. Today is March 15; the interest rate to June 15 is 10%. The forward rate is $1.65 for June 15, and the $1.60 June 15 put costs $0.036. The bank will offer to sell forward to the customer at a certain rate, with a "free" put at $1.60. How is that forward rate determined? The bank will protect itself by buying forward sterling to sell to the customer and by buying the $1.60 puts. It will fund the cost of the premium paid today on those puts at 10%. So the funded put costs $0.036 × (1 + 10% × 91/365) = $.0009 + $.036 = $.0369. The bank offers to sell forward at 1.65 + .0369 = $1.6869 (instead of the $1.6500 available in the market) with a "free" put at $1.60. The corporate customer buys forward at $1.6869. If sterling is below $1.60 at maturity, the customer exercises the put. Say sterling were at $1.55: then the customer will exercise the put (crystallizing a loss of $1.6869 − $1.6000 of $0.0869) and will buy in the market at $1.55. The next total cost to the customer will be $1.6369 ($1.5500 + $0.0869). But that will still be less than the $1.6500 that the customer would have paid if it had simply covered forward.

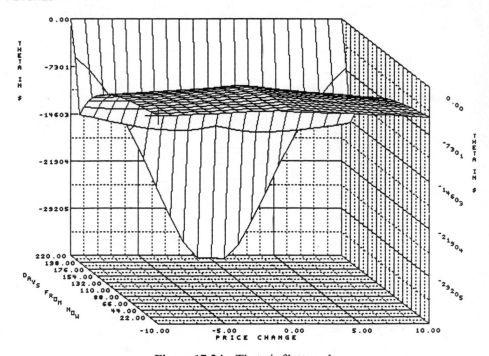

DISCOUNT
CORPORATION
OF
NEW YORK
FUTURES

JKW3 THETA 09/91

CMDTV=BP AN.DATE=02/07/91 RATE=13.00% UN.YIELD=0.00% THETA IN $
UNDER. PRICE = 200.00 DAYS TO EXP.= 212

PRICE CHANGE -10.00
                  -4412
DAYS FROM NOW   0

Figure 17.34 Theta is flattened.

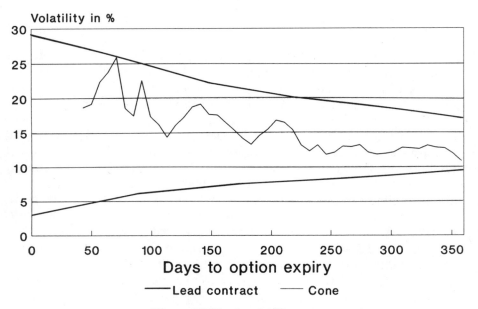

Figure 17.35 A volatility cone

The *range forward* is an extension of the break forward to give an upper and a lower limit. Outside the range of those limits, the customer is protected. Inside the range, the customer is exposed. Suppose again our corporate customer wants to buy forward sterling value June 15. As before, today is March 15; the interest rate to June 15 is 10% and the forward rate is $1.65 for June 15. As before, the $1.60 June 15 put costs $0.036; the $1.90 June 15 call costs $0.042. The bank offers to sell to its customer at whatever the June 15 spot rate turns out to be. The offer is subject to a maximum of $1.90 and minimum of $1.60, and the trade will be adjusted by a set amount representing the bank's fee for the deal. The customer knows it will not have to pay more than $1.90 (plus fee). In exchange, it gives up the hope of profiting below $1.60.

What is happening is that the bank effectively sells a call to the customer and buys a put from the customer. It sells the call for $0.042, buying the put for $0.036, for a net cost to the customer of $0.006. This cost is funded for 91 days at 10% for an all-in cost at maturity of $0.0062. So the final deal includes a fee of $0.0062 added to whatever rate the contract is traded at. A variant of this approach is to adjust the strike prices of the upper and lower limits so that the net premium payable is zero.

Participating contracts are an interesting variation. In the two previous deals, the cost to the customer is varied by changing the strike levels of the option. Another way to do this is set a particular strike and then to vary the cost by varying the proportion of the deal's size. Once again, our corporate requires to buy forward sterling value June 15; today is March 15; the interest rate to June 15 is 10% and the forward rate is $1.65 for June 15. The $1.70 June 15 put costs $0.08 and the $1.70 June 15 call costs $.05. The bank offers to sell forward to customer at $1.70—an above market rate—but will share 37.5% of its profits on the deal with its customer.

How is that share arrived at? In fact, it's fixed by the ratio of the costs of the call to that of the put: 37.5% is given back because the call costs 62.5% of the put (.05 versus .08). Suppose the deal is for £62,500,000 and the exchange-traded puts and calls that the bank uses to hedge its position are for £62,500 each. The bank will hedge its upside risk by buying 1,000 calls, and will fund this by selling 625 puts, for no net outlay of premium. If sterling falls, it has sold at $1.70 to the customer, but will profit from the fact that it has sold only 625 puts; this profit is available to be passed on to the customer. (Obviously in real life the percentage will be adjusted to allow the bank a profit.)

The range forward uses puts and calls with different strikes to arrive at a premium of zero, or close to it; the participating contract uses the same strikes but adjusts the amount of the deal on one side to achieve the same result.

OTHER OPTION PRODUCTS

There are a number of other types of option available. One of the most common is the *tender-to-contract option*. This is a scheme designed to help corporations bidding for contracts overseas. They know that if they win the contract they will have foreign currency exposure that they will need to hedge; on the other hand, if the contract is not won they will have no exposure.

Schemes have been devised to meet this kind of situation: one choice is to write an option on an option: an option contract giving the right to buy an option at some future date on certain terms. Another choice is to charge the full premium for the underlying option on day one, subject to a partial refund of the premium if the tender fails to win the contract. In exchange for the right to obtain the partial refund, the option buyer gives up the right to exercise the option independently of their success in the underlying tender. That is, if the tender fails, then the option cannot be exercised.

Another type of option is the *Asian option* (by contrast with the American and European options described earlier). The Asian option is an average rate option. It cash settles on the expiry date according to the difference between the strike rate and the average exchange rate over the option's life. Average rate options are a valuable hedging tool for many corporates whose risk is not on large cash-flows on particular dates, but on smaller cashflows on a regular basis. Also, the premium will normally be substantially less than for a European or American option, and this is another attraction to the corporate hedger.

The *look-back option* gives the buyer the right to "look back" over the period of the option and deal at the best possible rate during that period: for which, of course, they are charged a sizeable premium. Consider a 3-month sterling lookback call, traded with spot initially at $1.9500. If sterling falls continuously over the three months to, say, $1.9000, the option will be at-the-money on expiry. If sterling rises continuously, the option will behave as a $1.9500 call. If sterling is volatile, falling to, say $1.8500 before returning to $1.9500 at expiry, the option behaves as a $1.8500 call. Since the look-back option will always expire in-or at-the-money, the premium will always be greater than for the at-the-money spot European option.

The *down-and-out* option expires prematurely if the exchange rate falls below a certain level during the life of the option. Thus a $1.9500 call with a down-and-out feature at $1.8500 (the "out-strike") will become valueless if the rate at any time falls below $1.8500. Down-and-out options may be attractive to option sellers; and since conventional options involve no risk of premature expiry for the buyer, down-and-out options are always cheaper than the corresponding European option. *Up-and-away* options are the converse: they expire prematurely if rates ever exceed a specified level.

Inside trading range options expire prematurely if rates ever move outside a specified range. A $1.9500 call with a trading range of $1.85/2.05 will expire valueless if sterling falls below $1.8500 or rises above $2.0500. Conversely, *outside trading range* options expire valueless unless rates have been both sides of a specified range. A $1.9500 call with an outside trading range of $1.85/2.05 is valueless at maturity unless rates have been both below $1.8500 and above $2.0500 during the life of the option.

These option types are rather obscure but there is an arbitrage relationship between them: if you buy the $1.9500 call down-and-out at $1.8500, and the $1.9500 call up-and-away at $2.0500, as well as buying the $1.9500 call with outside trading range $1.85/2.05, you have created the same position as if you bought the conventional European $1.9500 call together with the $1.9500 call with inside trading range $1.85/2.05.

Another option type is the *money back* option, under which the premium is returned if the option is not exercised (the premium is set at a high enough level that the interest earned on it is sufficient to pay the true option cost).

PART 5 Risk Issues

18 Risk

GENERAL CONTROL OF RISK

Everything in this book, in one way or another, is about taking risk to earn a return. But uncontrolled risk can be disastrous. The next three chapters are about measuring and controlling various risks. This chapter discusses some of the general concepts involved. There are many possible ways to classify risk. One way, is to split risk into name, liquidity, credit, control, and market. Market risk can be subdivided into forced sale risk, interest risk, exchange risk, basis risk, volatility risk, and risk of change in shape of the yield curve (see Figure 18.1).

An important general point needs to be made at the start. Traditional risk controls consisted largely of fixed limits. For example, a forward exchange dealer might be told "You must not have an exposure greater than $15m. in the one-year maturity and $10 million in the two-year maturity." The introduction of the BIS controls (see Chapter 21) means that, increasingly, exposures are being "marked to market" as part of the risk control process. A second general trend is that firms are harnessing the power of the computer

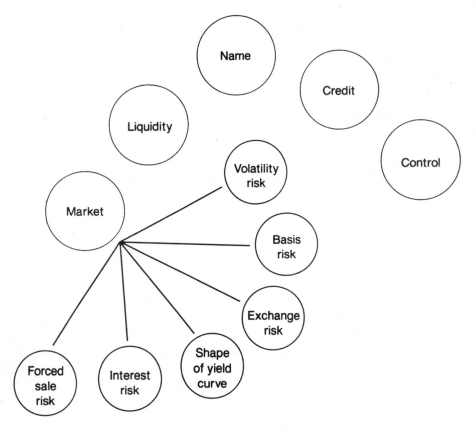

Figure 18.1   Types of risk.

to provide a sensitivity analysis of positions: "What if rates move by 5%?" At the extreme, some banks are using Monte Carlo simulation techniques to generate literally millions of "what-if" scenarios.

But before getting into the details, we start by pointing out that a very large part of risk control has nothing to do with systems or procedures but with basic common sense. This means looking through the procedures to think about the real world, and recognizing that that world has imperfections.

Sophisticated tools are useless unless the basics are right. The golden rule is that rigid rules are no substitute for a good relationship with the dealing and backup teams. But there are obvious basics. The first is separation between the dealing room and the back office. This should prevent unauthorized dealing from being concealed by inadequate back office procedures. The risk is that (as in the Lloyds Bank Lugano affair in 1976) an unauthorized position loses money and is "doubled up" in the hope of turning around.

In this context, a truism that bears repeating is that the test of a dealer is not how much profit he or she makes but the ability to take losses early rather than hang on until too late. Certain banks set traders profit targets; they are then given incentives, or pressurized, to meet or exceed them. There is a risk that this policy can lead to overtrading. Another sensitive area is the question of requests to deal at rates which are "away from the market." This may sometimes be needed to help a broker. The broker is then expected to repay the "points" (away from the market price) he has "borrowed" later. But it can also be a sign that a dealer is beginning to try to conceal a position that is going sour. It is also important to make sure that too much business is not directed toward one broker or bank.

There are many other ways in which Murphy's law can apply (Murphy's law: "What can go wrong, will go wrong). The past has lessons to teach, after all. Many banks came to appreciate foreign exchange settlement risk more clearly after the 1974 collapse of ID Herstatt, a German private bank which thought it was a good idea to sell short more sterling than most banks ever see (it was a good idea, but a year too soon). The Bundesbank made the mistake of closing Herstatt's doors at 4:30 PM in Frankfurt while New York was still open, so that the DEM side of trades settled, but not the US$ side. In foreign exchange, time zone considerations matter.

Another basic lesson, making sure that there is an independent check on dealers' activity by ensuring separate confirmations to an independent back office, was neglected by Volkswagen AG (VW) which in its 1986 results made provisions for DEM382 million of foreign exchange losses. The foreign exchange manager and at least one other employee entered into fake foreign exchange contracts with the National Bank of Hungary in cooperation with an external currency broker. The fraud came to light when the Hungarian National Bank said documents which VW thought covered forward foreign exchange deals were false. On at least one occasion, the deals were done at a rate 26 pfennigs off the current market rate, which itself should have been a red flag.

An unthinking application of formal rules led to considerable embarrassment at County NatWest in 1987. A Scotsman (whose previous claim to fame had been as a successful worm farmer), became involved in option trading when his son was hired by National Westminster Bank's investment banking subsidiary, County NatWest, as an equity salesman. During the first nine months of 1987 all went well. The father's option turnover during that period exceeded £8 million, generating commissions for County NatWest of over £100,000 and an income for the worm breeder of £250,000, much of which had been generated by writing put options on the U.K. stock market index (the FTSE index contract). By mid-October 1987, he had written about 50% of the outstanding January 1988 puts on the FTSE index. On October 19, 1987, to use *Variety's* immortal words, Wall St. laid an egg. The puts shot up in price and the loss incurred by County NatWest in respect of margin calls which could not be met was over £3 million. The worrying point is that before the crash, County NatWest's compliance department had questioned their employee regarding his trading activities with his father, and gave him a clean bill of health. No-one looked beyond the legal issues to consider the market risk implicit in a private individual's controlling 50% of an option series.

A deeper risk exists when dealing with apparently highly respectable counterparts: governments. The International Tin Council was set up by 22 tin-producing and consuming governments (including Japan, Germany, and the United Kingdom). They signed the treaty that created the Council, and gave it their support: bankers doing business with the ITC were assured that it had the backing of these governments. In October 1985, the ITC defaulted on debts of £900 million. For a long time, it had been buying up tin in the market in an attempt to stabilize the price: but the selling pressure became too great.

Brokers who bought tin on the London Metal Exchange on behalf of the ITC were left with a metal that lost almost half its value. Banks lost money as the value of ITC loan collateral fell. But when the governments were asked to step up to support the organization, the only reply was the sound of hands being washed. The creditors sued, and the British Court of Appeal held that the governments were not liable for the ITC's debts. The moral is that a government's verbal assurance isn't worth the paper it's written on. Entities which seem to have government backing may not in fact do so.

Another recent painful example, from the swaps market, was the U.K. local authorities (municipalities), who were able to walk away from losing positions by claiming that they should never have been able to take them on in the first place because they were illegal (*ultra vires*). In general, dealing with any political entity is fraught with inherent risk. The Biblical saying sums it up: "Put not thy trust in princes."

NAME RISK

Because so many things can go wrong, outsiders when they assess another institution think first in a general way about that institution's standing and reputation: the "quality of the name." Risk to the firm's name is the most important, though the most nebulous, risk. Any institution that hopes to do business must have a good reputation. Once that is lost, confidence of counterparties will no longer be available, and it will find it impossible to deal in the markets.

We can break down the risk further: moral hazard, and over-exposure. If an institution's employees engage in criminal or immoral activities, the reputation of the institution will be at risk. An isolated instance of such conduct, however, as at Volkswagen, can be a great deal less damaging than the other type of main risk, namely over-exposure in the market. If an institution is thought to be overtrading, counterparties will become much more careful about the degree of credit they are willing to grant it. Thus, most banks and other corporations active in financial markets will normally have controls on the extent of trading activity that are expressed not merely in terms of position risk but also of total transaction volume or "name in the market."

In the foreign exchange market, for example, a limit on the total foreign exchange book is normally set. It is necessary to have some control on the volume of activity to prevent overtrading and to keep total exposure under reasonable control. Normally the aggregate book would be defined as all outstanding foreign currency contracts (purchases plus sales, spots plus forwards) with customers, banks, branches, and subsidiaries. Interest arbitrage spot and forward contracts with counterparties should be included, but if interest arbitrage transactions are generated internally within a dealing room (say, between subsections of the room), these ought to be excluded. They do not put the bank at risk in the outside world. A similar limit would apply to the total outstanding volume of the Eurocurrency and domestic currency book. At the same time, these limits cannot be too small: a bank will need a certain reputation in the market-place. If the firm has not dealt in the market for the last 7 years, it cannot expect an instant response from the market when it telephones for a price.

LIQUIDITY RISK

Liquidity risk flows from the basic fact that any business may be profitable, but can still go bankrupt because it does not have enough cash on hand to pay its immediate bills. Most banks which collapse do so because of liquidity problems, rather than solvency problems. The collapse of Continental Illinois in 1984, for example, followed revelations of severe losses on its energy lending portfolio. But that in itself was not enough to push the bank into difficulties. What really caused the problems was that news about the losses caused counterparty banks in the Eurodollar market (Continental's prime funding source) to cut back on their interbank lines of credit. It was the drying up of liquidity, rather than the solvency problem, which caused Continental to get into difficulties. The two are often related: but an instructive comparison can be made with Bank of America, which also experienced heavy losses during the 1980s. Unlike Continental, it also had a very large retail deposit base which was much more stable than the international wholesale market on which Continental depended for its funding. Thus, it remained liquid throughout its crisis, and was able to survive.

Banks will normally control liquidity risk by monitoring their funding ladders (see Chapter 19) which track the maturity of liabilities against maturity of assets. Corporate treasurers similarly seek to ensure that they have at a minimum sufficient committed lines of credit from their banks for sufficient maturity to overcome any short-term funding pressures.

CREDIT RISK

Credit risk is an obvious and fundamental risk for any bank. Lending will mostly be controlled by a set of counterparty limits fixed in relation to the counterparty's perceived credit worthiness. But other activities—notably forward commitments such as forward foreign exchange, forward rate agreements and swaps—also imply credit exposure. There is a need to assess the overall picture.

Extensive discussions in this area led up to the issue in December 1987 of a proposal by the Bank for International Settlement representing the first initiative aimed at regulating bank capital adequacy on a global basis. The BIS proposal is focused primarily on credit risk, since it laid down a two-tiered capital standard measured against risk-weighted assets. The risk weightings were defined in terms of credit risk equivalent.

The BIS Ratio agreement was left to be implemented by national authorities. In the United States, the Federal Reserve in cooperation with the Comptroller of the Currency and the Federal Deposit Insurance Corporation developed capital adequacy guidelines, and similar guidelines were implemented by the Bank of Japan. The European Community in December 1989 published a solvency ratio directive, laying down general principles which are then implemented by the national central banks. There are differences between the implementations in detail, for example, the treatment of holdings of subordinated debt in Japan and the United States is less restrictive than that applied by the Bank of England, and the Japanese definition of Tier Two includes elements of unrealized gains on equity holdings. The broad outlines of the principles are consistent. They are discussed in more detail in Chapter 21 on credit and related risks.

There is a fundamental point to be made: Strong ratios need not mean strong banks. The collapse of the British bank, Johnson Matthey, was a case in point. To quote the British Bankers Association: "like many of the fringe banks before it, it boasted ample capital ratios and would have passed the statistical tests of most prescriptive systems with flying colours. Its problems stemmed from loan concentration, poor loan quality and gravely inadequate management systems." The U.S. thrift industry provides a raft of similar examples.

In the foreign exchange and money market area, a number of subsidiary questions arise in that the credit risk on some of these instruments is not always clear. Credit risks in foreign exchange occur in two areas. The first type of risk is on outstanding forward contracts. Suppose a customer went bankrupt after doing a forward sale of deutsche marks to a bank. The bank would have to buy forward deutsche marks to replace those it would have been receiving from the customer. It is at risk because the rates might have moved against it. The risk is marginal rather than total. The amount at risk is determined by the possible exchange rate movement. This type of risk is controlled by an aggregate limit on outstanding forwards. The second area of risk is often called the settlement risk, or credit risk. It is best seen in the failure of Herstatt Bank, referred to earlier. Banks which had delivered DEM to Herstatt against US$ found that they did not receive the US$ although they had paid for DEM to Herstatt. So banks will normally set a limit on the total value they will allow for settlement on any one day. A refinement would be to include in this amount a part of outstanding forwards, say over one year.

The trend in the market-place today is to move beyond setting a fixed cash limit exposure, and towards recognizing that on any given day the exposure will vary in line with market conditions. This trend has been explicitly recognized by the Bank for International Settlements risk weightings (see below), which require a deal with a customer to be "marked to market" on a regular basis and an allowance made for future exposure of 3 to 5% (See Chapter 21). Captial weightings are then applied to the resulting exposure.

A typical example might be that Bank A will set a limit for Company X in the following terms: maximum settlement risk, $20 million; maximum exposure up to 1 year, $10 million; maximum aggregate exposure on "BIS formula basis" (see Chapter 21), $40 million.

As well as these limits, a bank will set credit limits on the money market side. First, there will be limits on its total lendings to any single counterparty. These will be set just like any other lending limit. A refinement would be to set sub-limits, smaller in size, for medium-term lending. A less obvious credit risk is incurred when taking deposits. First, when accepting an overnight deposit in a currency in a distant center (for example, a London bank taking ovenight Eurodollars), a bank can find itself repaying the deposit before it is sent the initial confirmation that the deposit was made. It may be repaying a nonexistent deposit. Second, a bank which takes a very large amount of deposits from a single customer may become vulnerable to sudden withdrawals. This latter risk is not so much a credit risk as a liquidity risk.

Measuring the bank's true exposure in some of these markets—particularly options markets—is extremely difficult. There is no magic formula which can be simply applied. The BIS formula is essentially arbitrary, although it reflects the best judgment of a group of experienced central bankers. The measurement of risk in these areas has a large element of judgment. Indeed, some banks have resorted to Monte Carlo simulation techniques to estimate their risks: by throwing the dice often enough you try to see the pattern of risk. These issues are discussed in Chapter 21.

CONTROL RISKS

The next set of risks can be called control risks. They can be broadly subdivided into systems risks and settlement risks. Systems risks are best illustrated by the plight of the Bank of New York in 1985. The bank is one of the largest clearing banks for trading in U.S. Treasury bonds. In the process of installing a sophisticated new system, it failed to test the system adequately in advance. The result was that the system broke down during its early operations. The bank thus acquired the unfortunate distinction of having to arrange probably the largest single overnight borrowing facility in history: $24 billion from the Federal Reserve. It goes without saying that such an occasion can be both expensive and embarrassing. The same occasion highlights the potential possible scale of risk arising from a snarl-up in settlements.

Another example of the problem, from a related market, was the settlements problem that emerged in the London securities markets during and immediately after the reforms of 1986—the so-called "Big Bang." What began as small problems accumulated owing to the rising volume of trading and the shortage of experienced settlement staff in the London market. The main trading firms found themselves funding a massive back-log of unsettled transactions. Bills of several million pounds to finance unsettled trades, were common. Other settlement risks can be even more painful: the attempted fraud on Hill Samuel, under which the criminals had successfully penetrated the EUCLID system for transferring Eurobonds, but were fortunately detected before completing their transfer, is an illustration of the risks that can arise from the settlements process.

MARKET RISK

Market risk will be discussed in detail in the next chapters, covering interest rate risk and foreign exchange risk. As a general comment, however, it is worth saying that there are four basic components of market exposure: (1) the level of rates; (2) the shape of the yield curve (or in forward foreign exchange, the relative shape of two yield curves); (3) volatility exposure, for options; and (4) basis risk between different markets.

Measurement of the scale of risk varies from institution to institution. Some institutions run "scenario analysis" showing what happen to them under various market assumptions. Others break down risk into predefined categories and allocate risk limits to each category which then remain fixed.

The Bank of England, in its risk assessment of London institutions, includes a separate category of market risk: "forced-sale risk." This aims to assess the extra risk arising from being a forced seller when seeking to close a position and will depend on the degree of market liquidity.

The derivatives markets pose their own special set of risks. Some of these are traditional risks transferred to another context: for example, the leverage effect of futures. Once the exposure is correctly identified as being not merely the margin, but the amount of underlying assets controlled through the futures market, the measurement of risk is fairly straightforward. It is like the risk on the underlying instrument on which the futures contract is based. Similarly, the risks in the interest rate and currency swap markets are generally similar to those in the underlying interest rate and foreign exchange markets.

Risks in the options market, however, are somewhat more complex. The first and primary risk is the difficulty of valuing the contracts properly. In general, this is fairly limited for exchange-traded options, since the current price in the market can be generally be taken as a good guide. (Although this need not apply if the market is not very liquid.)

It is for the over-the-counter (OTC) options markets that the real difficulty arises. The complexity of the valuation models can be such that only a very few people in the institution understand them. There can be room for argument about the assumptions applied. The classic example was the disclosure some years ago that Bankers Trust was forced by the Federal Reserve to take a charge to its fourth-quarter earnings of $80m. This arose out of a disagreement between the Federal Reserve and the bank over the proper valuation of Bankers Trust's options book. If two institutions of the experience and standing of Bankers Trust and the Federal Reserve cannot agree about valuation of the options book, then clearly there is considerable scope for distortion of true positions.

A related issue is that even if the position has been correctly valued, the complexity of some of these markets means that the number of institutions involved is extremely small. Therefore, the forced-sale risk is much greater. That is, if there are only four or five institutions in the whole world who understand the transaction, your ability to trade out of it in times of serious difficult is greatly reduced compared with your ability to trade out of a spot foreign exchange position.

VOLATILITY AND BASIS RISK

In the next two chapters we will discuss interest and foreign exchange risk in detail. The chapter on interest risk will also cover the question of exposure to changes in the shape of the yield curve. But there are other important forms of market risk which require discussion here—volatility risk and basis risk.

Volatility risk is exposure to changes in volatility levels. The risk arises mainly in the case of options. There are at least two levels of risk. First is the straightforward risk that the options book—be it in interest rates, foreign exchange, or any other market—has been wrongly priced. That is, the assumed volatility built into the pricing has been incorrectly estimated. Chemical Bank some years ago reported a substantial hit to its quarterly earnings from its mispriced interest rate cap book: volatility had been systematically underestimated. Some people refer to this as "the black box" risk: Members of staff may rely blindly on some computer program which does not in fact properly price a specific risk.

A more subtle type of volatility risk is gamma risk in a delta-weighted hedging operation (see Chapter 16). If gamma is high, then small changes in underlying prices will produce large changes in delta, and therefore will mean large rebalancing of hedges, crystallizing large hedging losses and incurring high transactions costs.

Basis risk raises the whole question of the efficacy or otherwise of hedging. A cautionary tale in this regard is that of Franklin Savings. This was a U.S. savings and loan institution, but it was not run into the ground by irresponsible or obviously fraudulent management as were so many other U.S. thrifts.

Its demise came about because of a dispute between itself and the U.S. regulators over the effectiveness or otherwise of its hedging program.

At the root of the dispute was FAS80, the U.S. financial accounting standard covering hedge accounting. Briefly, FAS80 laid down that gains and losses from a hedging program could be deferred if the firm could demonstrate two factors: correlation and offset. Correlation means that hedges and the underlying liabilities or assets must have some connexion. Offset simply means that hedges and things being hedged should move in opposite directions and not the same way. But FAS80 did not define these terms precisely.

Franklin's policy was to test for correlation at the start of the hedge and then again after six months, arguing that the hedge needed time to stabilize. The U.S. authorities argued for the net-offset approach, which essentially tests hedges on a cumulative basis over a rolling 12-month period. Franklin argued that this approach was flawed when interest rates were volatile: hedges that passed on a month-to-month basis failed when tested cumulatively. When the matter went to court, the evidence of expert witnesses conflicted; and in 1989 the FASB taskforce tried to reach a consensus on correlation testing and failed. The matter was dropped without resolution. The outcome, therefore, was that the U.S. authorities in effect threw up their hands and said "We do not really know what constitutes a hedge."

Enough has been said to indicate that evaluating the effectiveness of a hedging program is by no means simple. The degree of basis risk can vary according to differing market conditions, and when measured over different periods of time. As a final general observation on market risk it is worth repeating the comment of RGL Liesching: "Losses migrate into portfolios that are not marked to market (corporate liabilities, investment portfolios, pension funds, and so on). Similarly, the losses which occur in risk management come from those areas of the management process which are not focused on—which are not marked to market."

CONTROL BY THE AUTHORITIES

Analysis of the way in which the BIS ratios and other risk controls are applied is complicated by the fact that different countries apply the detail of their rules in different ways. However, the principles involved are generally common ground, so that one example can usefully stand for all. The following is drawn from the so-called "Grey paper" published in April 1988 by the Bank of England: "The Regulation of the Wholesale Markets in Sterling, Foreign Exchange and Bullion." It is of wider interest because London allows banks to combine commercial and investment banking in a way in which Tokyo and New York (at the time of writing) do not.

The Bank believes in a three-fold approach to capital adequacy testing for wholesale market principals. First, since the major risks faced by such firms relate typically to position risk, the test concentrates on establishing marginal capital requirements against these positions in relation to a maximum risk-to-capital ratio normally set at 100%. Where open positions are run, more capital will be needed than where they are hedged by offsetting positions and other instruments. The hedging rules are adopted by the Bank are closer to those in place in the United Kingdom for gilt-edged market makers, and for those used in the United States by the Fed for the supervision of specialist government securities dealers, than to the simpler rules used by the SEC. Nevertheless, the resulting weights are very close to the SEC's.

Second, the Bank applies a small additional requirement to all nonbank principals' unsettled transactions to allow for the risk of loss due to counterparty failure before settlement. Third, the Bank will set a further capital requirement to capture credit or default risk in all its forms, including that created by off-balance-sheet transactions such as forwards and swaps.

In terms of the scale of protection afforded by the test, the Bank has decided that it is prudent for firms to have resources sufficient to absorb the loss resulting from an adverse 3% movement in yields on a 1-month Treasury bill (equivalent to a quarter percent movement in price), but from a rather lower ($1^1/2$%) movement in yield on sovereign paper of 1-year maturity. Positions are to be monitored by daily mark-to-market. Higher weights will also be applied to concentrated positions, to provide additional protection against default against any one issuer or counterparty.

The 100% risk-to-capital guideline is a maximum upper limit. If it is breached, the Bank will wish to examine the reasons for itimmediately with the institution involved. Unless the Bank is satisfied, the institution involved will be required to take immediate action. "Failure to do so will call into question its listed status." The risk-to-capital ratio is required to be observed continuously. Reporting is fortnightly, but the Bank reserves the right to call for additional returns at any time.

Capital adequacy arrangements for brokers are different. In the traditional wholesale markets, brokers are simply "name-passers." Deals are arranged, and when arranged, the names of the principals are exchanged. In other markets, such as the U.S. Treasuries market, a "blind broking" system is used, in which the broker is actually acting as a principal, but only on a matched bases. More stringent capital requirements will apply to matched principal brokers than to name-passing brokers.

HEDGED POSITIONS

Off-setting positions will in certain circumstances be regarded by the Bank as fully hedged, that is, giving rise to no interest rate risk. For positions to qualify for this treatment, they should be of equal size and essentially the same instrument (for example, foreign exchange or gold/silver forwards; or identical securities) and the interest payments should be determined—where applicable—by reference to the same interest rate. In addition, the

Table 18.1   Allowance for Hedging

Short Positions	Long Positions									
	<1 Month	1–3 Months	3–6 Months	6–12 Months	1–2 Years	2–5 Years	5–10 Years	10–20 Years	Over 20 Years	Undated
1 month or less	1	1	1	—	—	—	—	—	—	—
1–3 months	1	1	1	1	—	—	—	—	—	—
3–6 months	1	1	.5	.5	1	—	—	—	—	—
6–12 months	—	1	.5	.4	.5	1	—	—	—	—
1–2 years	—	—	1	.5	.35	.4	1	—	—	—
2–5 years	—	—	—	1	.4	.33	.35	1	—	—
5–10 years	—	—	—	—	1	.35	.32	.35	1	1
10–20 years	—	—	—	—	—	1	.35	.3	.3	1
Over 20 years	—	—	—	—	—	—	1	.3	.25	1
Undated	—	—	—	—	—	—	1	1	1	.33

Source: Bank of England/SIB.

next interest fixing date and/or residual maturity should correspond within the following limits: less than 1 month hence, same day; between 1 month and 1 year hence, within 7 days; over 1 year hence, within 30 days.

For other hedges, risk will be assessed as a proportion of the basic risk inherent in the long and short positions concerned. In general, no off-set will be allowed to that part of the risk weight which represents factors other than interest rate changes; no off-set will be allowed between positions in different currencies or between index-linked and conventional instruments (equities too will be assessed separately); but considerable credit will be given for hedging even across maturity bands.

A hedge will be considered to exist between positions of equal interest-risk-weighted value, and the risk of such a hedged "pair" will be taken as the risk as one of those positions multiplied by the appropriate factor shown in Table 18.1. Thus, a long position of £40m in 3-year gilts (risk weight 3) would be weighted at £480,000 (1.2%) if matched by a short position of £60m in an 18-month sterling fixed interest security (risk weight 2) and the risk of the latter would effectively be ignored. Thus the risk assessed would be only one fifth of that which the two positions would otherwise attract.

TREATMENT OF OFF-BALANCE-SHEET INSTRUMENTS

All off-balance-sheet items are included by the Bank in the assessment of risk exposure, being assessed on the basis of position and, where relevant, credit risk. The maturity of positions in futures, forwards, and FRAs will be taken as equivalent to the period until delivery or exercise of the contract, plus (where applicable) the life of the underlying security. Thus a long position in the June Eurodollar contract taken in April will be weighted on the same basis as a long position in a marketable instrument with a maturity of five months and a short position with a maturity of two months. Where the deliverable instrument under a futures contract can fall into more than one maturity band (for example, a bond futures contract with varying maturities deliverable), it would be treated as a position in the shorter of the bands.

Other forms of forward commitment, such as sale and repurchase, will also be included. In general, such commitments are treated as giving rise to an exposure in the same way as if the position itself was held on the balance sheet.

Options are treated slightly differently. They are delta-weighted. That is, options are treated as if they were positions in the delta times the amount of the underlying instrument to which the option gives an entitlement. The deltas used should be those of the exchange concerned; or for OTC options, those calculated by the firm itself in its own measurement of the position risk involved, subject to the Bank's acceptance that the model underlying the measurement is reasonable. In addition to this measurement of position risk, the Bank will also require, that the credit risk inherent in OTC bought options be recognised and an appropriate capital charge assessed.

The treatment of swaps for interest rate risk purposes is the same as for on-balance-sheet instruments. An interest rate swap under which a firm receives floating rate interest and pays fixed will be weighted as if it is a long position in a floating rate instrument of maturity equivalent to the period until the next interest fixing and a short position in a fixed rate instrument of maturity equivalent to the maturity of the swap. In many cases, however, the swap will be hedged by on-balance-sheet positions or by other swaps and the full or partial hedging rules will apply.

EXPOSURES TO INDIVIDUAL COUNTERPARTIES

The Bank will ask for reports of all exposures to individual counterparties or issuers which are greater than 10% of capital base. Some of these exposures may attract nil credit risk, either because of the status of the counterparty concerned or because the exposure is fully secured or collateralised in a way that does not itself give rise to credit risk. For all other large exposures, an additional weight of 1% will be applied to the excess over 10%, rising to 5% for any excess above 25% of capital base. For exposures which are substantially higher than 25% of capital base, the Bank will consider whether higher additional weights should be set, and where the exposure is in the form of a nonmarketable asset, it may decide to deduct any excess over 25% of capital base in full from the firm's capital base.

Where the risk is in the form of a claim on a counterparty in a transaction awaiting settlement, the exposure will be taken as the replacement cost of the contract; in other words, the sum will normally be much less than the principal involved.

A bank that has many trades outstanding with one counterparty in a single instrument can greatly reduce its exposure if it can net them off. That is to say, if bank A has sold £10m to bank B, and bought £8m back from the same bank for value the same day, is it legally entitled to offset the proceeds of one contract against the other for a net exposure of only £2m?

NETTING SYSTEMS

The BIS ratios permit, where recognized by the relevant supervisory authority, the netting of interbank positions. The legal status of netting will vary from country to country. Accordingly, what is said here can only be general in nature.

Movement towards netting on a cross-border basis and multi currency netting systems has been encouraged by the Bank for International Settlements. In February 1989, the BIS produced a Report on Netting Schemes (sometimes referred to as the Angell Report). In November 1990, this was followed up by the Report of the Committee on Interbank Netting Schemes. The report recommended further pursuit of multilateral netting schemes, on the grounds that "by reducing the number and overall value of payments between financial institutions, netting can enhance the efficiency of domestic payment systems and reduce the settlement costs associated with the growing volume of foreign exchange market activity. Netting can also reduce the size of credit and liquidity exposures incurred by market participants and thereby contribute to the containment of systemic risk." The report laid down perceived minimum standards for multilateral netting schemes, principally that they should have a well-founded legal basis under all relevant jurisdictions, clearly defined procedures for the management of credit and liquidity risks, fair and open access to admission, and operational reliability of technical systems and back-up facilities. The committee suggested a presumption that the "host country" central bank in whose market the netting system is located or operating will undertake supervision. The committee did, however, address potential problems:

> The application of communications and computer technologies to banking services has made possible the geographic dispersion of the functions of netting or clearing, on the one hand, and the ultimate settlements in a given currency, on the other. Although multilateral netting systems directly link the credit and liquidity risks and risk management of banks in different countries, there is no one central bank or supervisory authority in a natural position to consider the overall soundness and prudential adequacy of these systems.

Bilateral netting arrangements are in place between a number of participants in the foreign exchange markets. More recently, attempts have been made to develop a multilateral netting system. As an example, the ECHO netting project (for Exchange Clearing House Organisation) aims to set up a common Clearing House which becomes the common counterparty for all deals arranged among the members. The principles are, of course, precisely the same as those for a domestic clearing house, such as that which handles the settlement of bank checks. Thus, a bank which does 3000 deals a day, involving 24 currencies, with its main interbank counterparties will have to make 3000 payments and receive 3000 payments, a total of 6000 entries over its nostro account. If all the counterparties were members of the clearing house, then the bank would make or receive a maximum of only 24 items in total. The reduction in cost and risk are very significant.

The issue does not apply only to the foreign exchange market, for the International Swap Dealers Association has also been actively seeking to promote world-wide swap netting agreements. It successfully lobbied for a change to the U.S. bankruptcy law to allow for netting out of swaps to prevent "cherry-picking" (the practice whereby a liquidator of a firm would acknowledge only those contracts that were favorable and dispute the rest).

The *International Financing Review* (November 17, 1990) reported that the U.S. law firm of Cravath, Swaine and Moore took opinions from a number of countries to see if the terms of the ISDA Master Swap Agreements would be adhered to under local laws as far as netting was concerned. The following is a quotation from that report, but it should be stressed that it is merely a summary of complex opinions, and in no way necessarily represents the full legal position in the country concerned.

Canada. Canadian law will generally uphold the automatic transactions and netting provisions of the Swap Agreements. Canadian insolvency law may affect the rights of the parties to a Swap Agreement if the insolvent party is incorporated under Canadian law, or has assets or carries on business in Canada, if proceedings are taken in Canada.

UK. Automatic termination provisions should apply. There is some doubt over netting, because of the precedent of the British Eagle case. This led to section 107 of the Insolvency Act 1986, which provides that the property of the bankrupt be applied *pari passu,* without preferring one creditor over another. However, the UK lawyers Linklaters and Paines are quoted as believing that the British Eagle case does not put swap netting at great risk.

France. In general, a French court sitting in bankruptcy will abide by the governing law chosen by the parties, unless there is a direct conflict with French public policy. In that case, the court will probably apply French law. A French court, according to the legal opinion, would not allow a bankruptcy trustee to "cherry-pick." Netting could proceed. French bankruptcy law provides that foreign currency denominated claims be converted into French francs. This overrides the swap agreement.

Germany. There is no problem with termination or netting. As with French law, foreign currency claims must be converted into the local currency, overriding the terms of the swap agreement.

Italy. Automatic termination provisions apply. An Italian court would apply the governing law selected in the swap agreement unless contrary to Italian public policy. Cherry-picking would not be allowed. There would be no obstacle to netting, but foreign currency claims would be converted to Italian lira, again overriding the swap agreement.

Japan. A Japanese court might not uphold the termination provisions but, if it did decide to terminate, it would probably terminate the whole swaps contract, using the governing law chosen in the swap agreement. Set-off of netting provisions is likely to be upheld.

19 Money Market Risk

Money market risk is fundamental to the operations of a bank. It consists of two parts: funding risk and interest risk. Funding risk, or liquidity risk, arises from the danger of lending long and borrowing short. Interest risk arises from the effect on profit or loss of changes in interest rates.

LIQUIDITY

In setting up liquidity policy, a bank—or any firm—needs to think first of the times when it might need cash, and its reliance on marketable assets and liquid claims of others. It will have to look at their safety if there is a general market crisis. Second, it has to make sure it can finance any immediate or expected need for cash.

As far as protection against crisis, the usual policy is for banks to buy government securities or prime certificates of deposit of first-class banks to give a "cushion" of assets that are readily marketable. They can then be sold for cash if the bank has an urgent need for them. This assumes that these are institutions whose credit standing will be untouched in a crisis. Therefore, the bank will be able to sell the assets without incurring a great loss. This is, of course, only an assumption; but it is the only practical one that can be made. If Armageddon comes, there will be little that even the most farsighted treasurer could do to protect his or her bank.

The second line of defense will be stand-by arrangements made between banks. If one of the parties to the stand-by arrangement falls into difficulties, the counterparty will provide funds to help. The third line of defense is the "lender of last resort:" the central bank of the country in which the headquarters of the bank are located. The Basle Concordat of 1975 among the major central banks of the world began to lay the foundations for supervision of international banking operations. At the same time, there was to some extent an implicit acceptance of a lender-of-last-resort function for international banks' operations. However, the Banco Ambrosiano affair in 1985, when Italy and Luxembourg disagreed, and the BCCI affair in 1991, showed that there are limits to certain central banks' willingness or ability to interpret the Concordat in a broad way.

Liquidity or funding risks are caused by a mismatch in final maturity dates. A lending with a final maturity date of one year, funded by a 1-month deposit, causes a liquidity risk for the remaining 11 months. The bank cannot be certain of laying its hands on the money for the next 11 months. In an extreme case, if a bank becomes so illiquid that it cannot fund itself from day to day, it must close down.

Funding risk and interest risk are closely connected, but quite distinct (Figure 19.1). Suppose a lending has a maturity of 1 year, but is based on a 3-month roll-over. If it is funded by a 3-month deposit, the funding risk remains for the last nine months. The interest rate risk is nil for the current

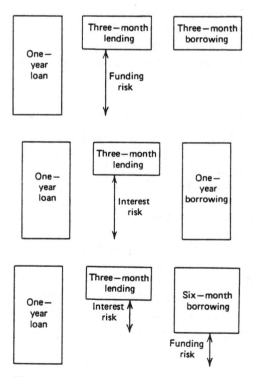

Figure 19.1   Interest versus funding risk.

three months. And it is cut out in future each time the bank funds the 3-month roll-over with a 3-month deposit. But if the 3-month roll-over lending is financed by a 6-month deposit, there is not only a liquidity risk but also an interest risk. The interest rate that the bank might earn for the last three months before the next roll-over date is uncertain (since the rate will only be set at maturity of the first 3-month lending). These two different risks can only be measured on separate ladders, since the same item can put the bank at risk in two different periods. A 5-year loan funded by a 3-month borrowing would cause a 5-year funding risk, but the interest risk will be covered every three months. If roll-over business is an important part of a bank's total book, it may need a separate interest rate ladder.

Problems can arise even when the bank's book is totally matched. Suppose a trader borrows one year funds at, say, 14% in the expectation that rates will rise, but instead they fall sharply, soon afterwards. He decides to minimize further loss by covering the position at 13%. As far as liquidity and interest mismatch are concerned, he is exactly matched: but there is a built-in loss in his position that needs to be detected.

MONEY MARKET MATURITY LADDER

A deposit maturity mismatch ladder will normally be essential. The methods used will depend on the business of the bank. An example might be as follows. Separate ladders are made up for local currency liabilities and assets, and foreign currency liabilities and assets, by currency. Maturities are split into time bands, on the basis of time left to maturity (not the original life of the deal, nor the next roll-over date). The time band used is (1) the first date at which call or notice deposits can be required to be repaid; (2) the due dates of bills of exchange, promissory notes, or CDs; (3) the last repayment date of a government stock or similar security; (4) the agreed repayment dates for time deposits; or (5) the agreed repayment date for each installment of a medium-term loan. Table 19.1 shows what the effect of this might be.

We see that call assets in local currency exceed liabilities. The opposite situation occurs in the foreign currency book. So the net final mismatch is negative at 4,733 in accounting currency terms. In both local and foreign currency, this mismatch is slightly increased by a net borrowing in the one-to-seven-day period, while in the eight-day-to-one-month period the position is dominated by a large overlent position in the foreign currency book. This brings the cumulative final mismatch to an overlent position. This runs up to the 3- to 6-month period, from when on the bank is overborrowed up to the 3-year period.

The maturity mismatch ladder will need to be supplemented by various items of other information. For example, the treatment of overdrafts (if any) will be influenced by the extent to which some of them are "hard core," that is, being used as a permanent borrowing. In setting up Table 19.1, we

Table 19.1 Deposit Mismatch Ladder

Period	Local Currency Mismatch				Foreign Currency Mismatch				Final Mismatch	
	Liabilities (1)	Assets (2)	-P (3)	-C (4)	Liabilities (5)	Assets (6)	-P (7)	-C (8)	-P (9)	-C (10)
Call and Savings	(2,322)	6,460	4,138	4,093	(8,982)	111	(8,871)	(9,624)	(4,733)	(5,531)
One-seven days	(4,045)	4,000	(45)	4,112	(6,998)	6,245	(753)	(3,566)	798	546
Eight days-one month	(14,743)	14,762	19	4,332	(3,159)	9,217	6,058	1,024	6,077	5,356
One-two months	—	220	220	7,425	—	4,590	4,590	9,468	4,810	16,893
Two-three months	—	3,093	3,093	5,472	—	8,444	8,444		11,537	(2,726)
Three-six months	(22,281)	20,328	(1,953)	3,198	(36,314)	18,648	(17,666)	(8,198)	(19,619)	(10,699)
Six-nine months	(4,713)	2,439	(2,274)	4,293	(7,498)	1,799	(5,699)	(13,897)	(7,973)	(10,831)
Nine-twelve months	(2,345)	3,440	1,095	4,317	(6,119)	4,892	(1,227)	(15,124)	132	(9,082)
Overdraft[a]	—	24	24	6,707	—	1,725	1,725	(13,399)	1,749	(4,918)
One-two years	(5,005)	7,395	2,390	7,293	(3,847)	5,621	1,774	(11,625)	4,164	(4,164)
Two-three years	(654)	1,240	586	9,597	(320)	488	168	(11,457)	754	168
Three-four years	(3,760)	6,064	2,304	9,597	(92)	2,120	2,028	(9,429)	4,332	7,838
Four-five years	(698)	8,368	7,670	17,267	—	—	—	(9,429)	7,670	15,813
Longer	—	7,975	7,975	25,242	—	—	—	(9,429)	7,975	
Capital and infrastructure	(20,316)	4,503	(15,813)	9,429	—	—	—	(9,429)		
Totals	(80,882)	90,311	9,429	—	(73,329)	63,900	(9,429)	—	(15,813)	nil

Note: P = this period, C = cumulative.
[a] Treated as 12-month loans.

assumed that anyway, in practice, overdrafts are not repayable on demand, but need to be treated as 12-month assets. Hardcore overdrafts ought properly to be treated as even longer. It is also important to include information on other commitments. If we do, we can see the bank's exposure if customers were to use all existing facilities in a crisis. Undrawn money market lines or overdraft facilities can cause large potential extra exposure. Contingent liabilities under standby arrangements, documentary credits or acceptances also need to be measured.

Also we cannot judge the bank's overall position without knowing what mismatch the local central bank will accept. And we need to know from the ordinary interest income and expense accounting procedure whether the book is currently profitable. We need also to know how much the book is vulnerable to sudden shifts in interest rates; the interest rate risk.

INTEREST MISMATCH LADDER

For this purpose, an interest rate mismatch ladder will be needed. This classifies balances by the time for which the interest rate is fixed rather than by their final maturity. So a loan repayable after 5 years and rolled over at a 6-month rate would be shown in a 5-year band in the deposit maturity mismatch ladder, and in the 6-month band in the interest mismatch ladder. Table 19.2 shows an interest mismatch ladder in its simplest form.

Table 19.2 shows where the bank is most at risk from sudden interest rate movements. In this case, for example, the bank is overlent in the Euromarket in all periods beyond three months. As a result, a sudden rise in certain interest rates would make much of the longer-term book unprofitable until the fixed rate assets had run off.

Table 19.2   Interest Mismatch Ladder

Interest Rate Period	Euro		Local Currency		Net
	Liabilities	Assets	Liabilities	Assets	
Non-interest bearing	1,100	—	22,795	12,171	−11,724
At variable rates (notice up to seven days)	4,255	300	2,000	24	−5,931
Fixed rates up to three months	19,846	13,421	22,958	20,688	−8,695
Three-twelve months	31,422	35,347	31,174	36,775	+9,526
One-two years	6,111	8,481	6,455	7,227	+3,142
Two-three years	3,980	5,054	640	1,625	+2,059
Three-four years	377	1,905	3,680	4,049	+1,897
Four-five years	849	1,150	680	2,520	+2,141
Five years plus	79	148	—	6,232	+6,301
	68,019	65,806	90,382	91,311	−1,284

Table 19.3   Weighted Average Rate per Block

Contract	Amount		Days		Product 1	Rate	Product
1)	2	×	5	=	10	× 12	120
2)	3	×	10	=	30	× 11.5	345
3)	5	×	28	=	140	× 11	1540
					180		2005

Note: Weighted average rate for time block = 2005/180 = 11.14%.

A more refined interest rate mismatch ladder would take into account the interest rates at which the deals were originally done. We can find the weighted averages for outstanding contracts on the ladders for placings (assets) and raisings (liabilities) by time blocks. We will take into account the amount, number of days from report date to maturity date, and the rate. For example, suppose the placings maturing in a given 1-month time block on a ladder at report date were US$2 million maturing in 5 days at 12%, US$3 million maturing in 10 days at 11½%, and US$5 million maturing in 28 days at 11%. Then the weighted average for the placings in that time block could be

Table 19.4   Domestic Money Position

	Over-night	Call and Notice	One Week	One Month	Two Months	Three Months	Four Months	Five Months	Six Months
Raisings									
Banks	87	31	66	222	102	37	6	8	24
Commercials	15	130	39	31	53	21	16	3	4
CDs	—	—	5	28	35	24	12	15	29
Branches and subsidiaries	18	16	17	28	36	7	3	2	4
Subtotal	120	177	127	309	226	89	37	28	61
Average cost	11.63	11.60	12.07	12.21	12.49	12.56	12.50	12.66	12.64
Lendings									
Reserves	110	—	—	—	—	—	—	—	—
CDs	—	—	—	—	17	18	14	6	11
Banks	34	4	40	51	51	55	86	26	26
Commercials	10	—	74	41	41	38	5	—	—
Branches and subsidiaries	4	—	16	57	57	11	7	5	16
Other lendings	—	—	10	—	—	9	—	—	—
Subtotal	158	4	140	149	166	131	112	37	53
Average yield	11.87	11.4	11.85	12.67	12.99	12.59	13.42	13.12	14.19
Period mismatch	38	−173	13	−160	−60	42	75	9	−8
Cumulative mismatch	24	−14	159	146	306	366	324	249	240

calculated as shown in Table 19.3. We can see from this example that the effect of the US$5-million deal at the lower rate of 11% has tended to pull down the weighted average rate for the time block.

An example of this technique can be seen in Table 19.4. This is a simplified balance sheet of a domestic money market dealing room. Short-term operations are broken down into overnight, call and notice, 1-week, and 1-month. Thereafter monthly time blocks are used up to the 1-year period, after which the division is into years. We can see that the overnight operations are running at a profit, but the call and notice and 1-week periods are both generating a loss. Apart from these, though, and the 7-month, 10-month, and 3-year operations, all the other time blocks are showing a profit. Notice that the row labeled "cumulative mismatch" is cumulated from the furthest date and not the nearest date on the ladder. The reason for this is to prevent long-term problems from being hidden by short-term cosmetics. Suppose the bank were heavily overlent in the longer periods, such as the 2-, 3-, or 4-year, but were very much overborrowed in the shorter periods. Cumulating from the near end to the far end might give the idea that the bank is overfunded for most of the earlier part of its book, and that the overlending in the far periods was adequately financed.

Seven Months	Eight Months	Nine Months	Ten Months	Eleven Months	Twelve Months	Two Years	Three Years	Four Years	Five Years	Five Years
1	8	1	20	1	1	1	4	—	—	—
3	13	—	1	—	—	3	—	—	—	—
2	2	12	11	1	2	—	5	—	—	—
13	2	3	2	1	1	—	5	24	—	—
19	25	16	34	3	4	4	14	24	—	—
13.64	12.40	13.50	12.24	12.01	12.50	13.35	13.33	12.04	—	—
—	—	—	—	—	—	—	—	—	—	—
14	19	26	15	7	11	20	1	5	1	2
9	14	15	27	6	16	—	9	28	—	2
—	—	11	—	—	—	4	—	2	—	—
4	10	1	3	1	—	—	—	1	—	—
—	7	—	—	—	14	28	37	14	7	—
27	50	53	45	14	41	52	47	50	8	4
13.55	13.12	13.57	11.98	12.85	13.17	13.41	13.11	13.71	14.07	13.30
8	25	37	11	11	37	48	33	26	8	4
248	240	215	178	167	156	119	71	38	12	4

MORE SOPHISTICATED TECHNIQUES

Looking at this position becomes more complex when we consider derivatives. We need to add in the exposure that might arise from futures, options, and swaps. Conceptually, swaps are identical to a combined purchase or sale of a fixed rate asset coupled with a sale or purchase of a floating rate asset (putting that another way, a fixed rate lending funded by a floating rate borrowing, or vice versa). They raise no new issues of principle in reporting terms once they are properly identified.

Futures positions likewise are fairly straightforward: the crucial point is to ensure that positions are properly reported to include not only the margin amounts but the underlying exposures. Once this is done, the underlying exposure is again conceptually identical to a position in the underlying asset for the total underlying amount and can be treated accordingly. (Some complications arise from the question of basis risk and for deliverable instruments the question of properly identifying the cheapest to deliver, but broadly the risk is fairly clearcut.)

Options raise other issues. Up to now, revaluing our positions was fairly simple: we took an assumed level of interest rates, and by applying them to the book, reached a figure for profit and loss. We can do this also, of course, for the options positions. But that does not capture all the dimensions of risk. There are at least three dimensions to options risk: market movements, changes in volatility, and time. Changes in each of these variables can impact our profit and loss. People seek to handle this extra complexity in different ways, but probably the most common approach is to try and undertake some form of "sensitivity analysis" which shows the impact of changes in the different variables on profits and losses.

The methods set so far for measuring interest rate risk are those which would be applicable for a bank with straightforward money market deposit operations. However, in recent years, banks have also become much more active in medium-term interest rate risk through the development of the interest rate swap market. The measurement of interest rate sensitivity in the medium-term market poses different questions.

All through this chapter, we have implicitly ignored the fact that a dollar receivable in 5 years time is worth less in practice than a dollar receivable today. The time value of money is critical to measuring the interest rate risk of a bank's medium-term swap book, and also its securities trading activity. The duration of the bank's exposures is also critical. (These concepts were defined in Chapter 6.)

It will be desirable to have some sense of the duration and convexity of the firm's overall interest-sensitive positions, although as a general rule it would probably make more sense to focus on specific "books" than the bank's balance sheet as a whole, since there will be so many complex internal offsets that the balance sheet as a whole may have little meaning in terms of interest rate exposure. In addition, single measures such as duration have very little meaning at this broad level of aggregation. Providing adequate computer systems are available (and if they are not some other risk control questions arise rather quickly) it would be desirable to construct interest risk scenarios showing the impact of a change in the level of rates; a change in the slope of the yield curve (particularly important for forward positions such as forward rate agreements, forward-forward deposits, and interest rate futures); changes in the volatility of interest rates (which would affect the valuation of interest rate options, caps, collars and floors); and changes in basis risk (for example, the impact of a change in the spread relationship between LIBOR and U.S. Treasury bills, or between U.S. Treasury bonds and Eurobonds).

In this context it may be worth referring to the controls applied by the authorities as regards exposures. Table 19.5 sets out the weights applied by the Bank of England to unhedged long positions held by principals. The weights are related not only to the inherent price volatility of each group of assets, but also reflect an assessment of the risk that a borrower might default on its obligations: that is, the combined market risk and credit risk. Thus, the rows of the matrix classified positions by issuer (and thereby reflect credit, and to some extent forced sale, risk) while the columns refer to maturity (an important element in position risk).

Table 19.6 shows the breakdown of these weights into the various components that are identified above, which are assessed separately in the detailed reporting forms. In producing the figure for total risk exposure, positions will be weighted as indicated in table 19.6 and then summed regardless of sign. All positions must be valued on the basis of current market prices on a daily basis.

Finally, it is worth mentioning that some institutions have begun to apply Monte Carlo simulation techniques to their interest rate exposure; the Monte Carlo technique is discussed in more detail in Chapter 21 where we see how it can be used to assess swap exposure.

INTERNAL PRICING

The treasurer of a bank will have to cope with widely varying regulations from country to country. In addition, he or she has many internal control problems to contend with. One of the most widespread of these is the so-called "transfer pricing" issue. The question here is intimately related to the whole question of centralization versus decentralization. Since, in general, most banks centralize their treasury functions, it is a fairly widespread problem. It comes up both in foreign exchange and in deposit business. The issue is most clearly seen in foreign exchange. In the event that a customer calls for a price, he will very often be routed either through a branch or through a "corporate desk." The branch or corporate desk will then get a market price from the professional market foreign exchange dealers. The issue is whether the customer desk or the branch should be given a "turn" or "loading" and so be able to show a profit for

Table 19.5   Risk Weights for Unhedged Long Positions—%

	Residual Maturity									
	1 Month or Less	1–3 Months	3–6 Months	6–12 Months	1–2 Years	2–5 Years	5–10 Years	10–20 Years	Over 20 Years	Undated
Marketable paper issued by a government in its domestic market	0.25	0.5	1	1.5	2	3	4	5	6	6
Other marketable public sector paper	0.5	0.75	1.25	2	2.5	4	5	6.5	7.5	8
Non-marketable public sector loans etc.	0.5	1.75	4	6.5	7.5	8.5	10	11.5	12.5	n/a
Banks, building societies etc:										
marketable	0.75	1	1.5	2.25	3	4.25	5.5	7	8	9
nonmarketable	0.75	2.5	4.5	7	9	11	13	15	18	n/a
Commercial paper, eurobonds, equities etc.	1	1.25	1.75	2.75	3.25	4.5	5.75	7.5	8.5	10
Nonmarketable nonbank private sector	4	7	9.5	11.5	13	16	18	20	22	n/a

Table 19.6 Components of Risk Weights—%

					Residual Maturity					
	1 Month or Less	1–3 Months	3–6 Months	6–12 Months	1–2 Years	2–5 Years	5–10 Years	10–20 Years	Over 20 Years	Undated
(a) Interest rate risk[1]										
All positions	0.25	0.5	1	1.5	2	3	4	5	6	6
(b) Forced sale risk[2]										
Government[3]	Nil	Nil	Nil	Nil	Nil	Nil	Nil	Nil	Nil	Nil
Other public sector	0.25	0.25	0.25	0.25	0.25	0.75	0.75	1.25	1.25	1.75
Banks etc.	0.25	0.25	0.25	0.5	0.75	0.75	1.0	1.5	1.5	2.0
Other	0.5	0.5	0.5	0.75	0.75	0.75	1.0	1.5	1.5	2.0
(c) Credit risk—marketable instruments[4]										
Government	Nil	Nil	Nil	Nil	Nil	Nil	Nil	Nil	Nil	Nil
Other public sector	Nil	Nil	Nil	0.25	0.25	0.25	0.25	0.25	0.25	0.25
Banks etc	0.25	0.25	0.25	0.25	0.25	0.5	0.5	0.5	0.5	1.0
Other	0.25	0.25	0.25	0.5	0.5	0.75	0.75	1.0	1.0	2.0
(d) Credit risk unmarketable exposures										
Government	Nil	Nil	Nil	Nil	Nil	Nil	Nil	Nil	Nil	Nil
Other public sector	0.25	1.25	3	5	5.5	5.5	6	6.5	6.5	n/a
Banks etc	0.5	2	3.5	5.5	7	8	9	10	12	n/a
Other	3.75	6.5	8.5	10	11	13	14	15	16	n/a

[1] All long *and* short positions; an additional weight of 10% will be applied to the *net open position* in each foreign currency. 12% in gold bullion, 15% in silver bullion and 20% in other commodities

[2] All long *and* short positions in *marketable* instruments

[3] In domestic currency only

[4] All gross long positions *only*. Collateral, guarantees and security will in some circumstances be allowed as offsets, and additional weights will be applied to large exposures to individual counterparties or connected groups

its efforts. As it has done the work to produce the business, it is important that some recognition be given. At the same time, the problem is that by adding the extra loading, the overall quotation may be out of line with the competition.

A similar but more complex problem arises in deposit business. For a lending which is linked to some clearly defined rate such as LIBOR (see Chapter 6), the question of transfer pricing is relatively straightforward. The dealers will lend the money to the office making the loan at LIBOR, and the loan-producing office will then add a margin which has previously been agreed upon with the customer in advance. It is then reasonable to say whether the trading room has funded itself successfully or not, by comparing the average funding cost with the LIBOR rates used for on-lending. The issue here is relatively simple, because a rate like LIBOR is defined for set periods such as 1 month, 2 months, 3 months, and so on.

The question becomes more complex when we look at loans which are linked to base or prime rate. In general, such loans are repayable on demand, theoretically at least, although on occasion they may be made available for a fixed period. For theoretically overnight lendings, it seems clear that the right cost-of-funds measure is an overnight interest rate. But these can move very sharply, while the prime or base rate of a bank is normally rather "sticky" in its movements. So the dealing room can experience unexpected profits or losses which have little to do with its own skill in funding the bank's book. They have much more to do with the desire of the bank's management to keep its base or prime rate stable. There is no simple answer to this problem. All one can suggest is that one should consider the overall structure of a bank's book and select the interest rate which seems most appropriate for measuring cost of funds. Then one should stick with it consistently, making due allowances for short-term distortions which may arise as a result of market conditions.

LOAN PRICING

The issue of transfer pricing is closely connected with the overall issue of loan pricing. This is by no means purely a responsibility of the treasurer, since the lending and marketing personnel of a bank will also be concerned. However, since the aim is to ensure a viable overall balance sheet, the treasurer has to be concerned that loan pricing is appropriate. That is, pricing must not be so aggressive that it leads to a rapid expansion of lending and a "ballooning" of the balance sheet to the point where capital and other ratios are breached; equally, it cannot be so conservative that no business is ever done. At least three problems are relevant: average pricing versus marginal pricing, reserve asset costs, and required return on capital.

The average versus marginal cost argument sometimes occurs when lending officers want to adjust the "cost of funds" formula used in loan pricing to reflect the fact that a bank has access to so-called free balances. These will be in the form of current accounts obtained through the branch network, travelers' check float, or other cheap sources of funds. The crucial point is that such free balances are inherently limited in supply. As the bank's balance sheet expands, so they must support a larger and larger volume of business.

Figure 19.2 is based on the assumption that there is a fixed pool of free balances available to a bank, and that additional funds have to be raised in the marketplace at the going interbank rate. This tends to rise against the bank as its bidding for funds increases, because other banks become increasingly less willing to lend to it. As the volume of business expands beyond the crossover point Z, we see that if the bank still prices its loans on the average cost of funds, it is starting to incur a loss. The average cost of funds to it is more than the average yield. For each new loan that it puts on the books, it is increasing its losses, since the yield of the loan is below the cost of the funds.

A second issue is the pricing of reserve asset costs. The issue doesn't really come up if a loan is linked to prime or base rate. These rates generally take into account the average cost of holding reserve assets against lendings. The problem occurs when a bank is making a lending linked to a money market rate, such as LIBOR. In the Euromarkets, reserve costs can

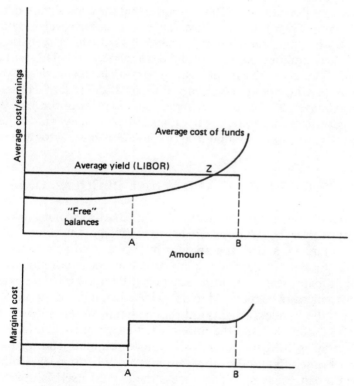

Figure 19.2   Average versus marginal cost of funds.

be ignored. But in domestic markets, they need to be included when pricing a loan of this kind. It may be argued that reserve costs should be borne by the depositor, but this would be hard to justify to the depositor and would create problems in pricing, for the term of the deposit is quite likely to be shorter than that of the loan and possibly shorter than the term of the reserve asset, if this is a government security, for example. Also, and more important, banks compete with many institutions for funds; not all these institutions have reserve costs.

The reason for charging the reserve asset cost to the lendings is as follows. A bank's holding of reserves is usually based on eligible liabilities. Interbank lending in the money market is generally offset (in most countries) against interbank liabilities to work out the total of eligible liabilities. So, in general, interbank lending has no reserve cost while a customer lending creates a need for reserve assets. The exact formula for calculation of reserve asset costs is laid out in Chapter 12.

A related issue is the required return on bank capital. Risk is measured by weighting all assets by a given series of coefficients. A risk asset ratio is then calculated which is defined as the ratio of the adjusted capital base to weighted risk assets. This is defined in accordance with the norms set out by the BIS and other regulators.

Suppose that the ratio were 10%. Suppose that the capital base of the bank were 100 units. Then the capital available will support weighted assets of 1000 units. An expansion of customer lendings (which are weighted at 1.0) of 100 will therefore increase risk weighted assets by 100. This will need an increase of 10 units in the capital base. According to the overall cost of capital, the loan pricing would need to be adjusted. If the cost of capital is 10%, then approximately 1% has to be charged into the price of the loan (less, any assumed earnings on capital). An expansion of money market lendings, though, needs less capital to support it so the capital cost factor will be lower.

BALANCE SHEET RATIOS AND LOCAL REGULATIONS

A third area of concern to the treasurer of a bank is the control of the size and structure of the bank's book. He has to match it to the volume of activity in various markets, and to the amount of capital available to support the total book. In a multi-currency bank, this can cause complications. The bank will probably want a certain ratio of capital to total balance sheet, and will in fact generally be required to do so by law or by custom. For example, in Germany the Bundesaufsichtsamt fur das Kreditwesen (Federal Banking Supervisory Authority) and the Bundesbauk have jointly laid down certain "Basic Principles" which essentially limit a bank's total lending and investments to 18 times capital. But in a multicurrency bank maintaining such a capital ratio can cause problems unless the capital itself is distributed in proportion with the different currencies of the balance sheet.

Suppose a German bank, with a capital denominated purely in deutsche marks, wanted to maintain, say, a 5% capital ratio, but had half of its balance sheet in U.S. dollars because of Eurodollar operations. Then the fall in the deutsche mark exchange rate of about 13% in the year to December 1981 would have forced the bank to raise an extra 6½% of its existing capital (assuming that it had already been at its limits). But the alternative of selecting capital denominated in different currencies according to the proportions which they currently hold in the balance sheet is not entirely satisfactory. It makes it difficult for the bank to switch the composition of its balance sheet from currency to currency according to its business needs.

The treasurer also needs to ensure that his bank complies with the local regulations of the central bank. Typically, these will cover foreign exchange positions, liquidity requirements, and exchange control compliance, where applicable.

20 Measurement and Control of Foreign Exchange Risk

In this chapter we look at the measurement and control of foreign exchange risk. The basis of the risk is common to both banks and corporations, but because foreign exchange trading and position matching is fundamental to a bank and ancillary to the industrialist's business, which may entail quite different operating exposures, the corporate's foreign exchange management may need to be quite different. We start first by looking at it from the bank's point of view, because this is the simplest. Generally, banks do not have to worry, at the trading level, about taxation or about noncash items. Then we go on to think about some of the problems faced by industrial and commercial corporations in foreign exchange. We begin with how its exposure is to be measured. We explain the effect of taxation, and we then look at the U.S. Financial Accounting Standards Board's Statement 52 (also SSAP 20/IAS21) on accounting for foreign exchange rate changes. The following sections look at some of the choices open to the corporation in managing its exposure. We begin with some of the organizational questions: choice of trading philosophy and the question of whether or not to centralize. This leads to multinational netting systems. Then we look at other methods of exposure reduction—nonfinancial and financial. Nonfinancial steps include choices relating to production, pricing, and marketing. Financial steps include choice of borrowing currency, currency swaps, and similar arrangements.

EXCHANGE BOOK AND EXCHANGE LADDER

Let's start with some of the concepts used in the control of a bank treasury. The first is the exchange book. It is the total of all outstanding exchange contracts in any one currency at any one time. The size of the total book is found by adding up all the outstanding contracts in all currencies, in terms of a single common currency—usually the local currency or the U.S. dollar.

The next concept, the foreign exchange ladder, registers every purchase and every sale of a currency in maturity date order. An example is set out in Table 20.1. This bank's book is long overall of DEM 100,000. It has sold DEM 1 million in the 1-month period against a purchase in six months; bought DEM 2 million in the 2-month period against a sale of DEM 2 million in three months; and bought DEM 500,000 in the 1-year against DEM 500,000 sold in the 2-year period. Because its positions do not balance exactly in every period, this bank has a mismatch or gap position. Therefore, it is vulnerable to rate movements against it. If the deutsche mark spot price falls, it will lose on the spot position. And if the forward dollar discount/deutsche mark premium should rise in the 2-year maturity compared with the 1-year, it would lose money on the DEM 500,000 one against 2-years position.

Management will aim to control the risks by setting a mismatch limit for each period. Suppose that the 2-year mismatch limit was only DEM 250,000, but that the spot limit was DEM 2,00υ,000. Then the dealers might have to cut down the 2-year position and might do it by making a swap of DEM 250,000; they would sell spot and buy forward to bring the new 2-year figure back to the limit. Or, if the spot limit were full but they had room in the 6-month band, they might bring part of the position back to the 6-month period.

Table 20.1 Deutsche Mark Ladder

Period	In (+)	Out (−)	Net	Cumulative (from far end)
Spot	+100,000	0	+100,000	+100,000
One month	0	−1,000,000	−1,000,000	0
Two months	+2,000,000	0	+2,000,000	+1,000,000
Three months	0	−2,000,000	−2,000,000	−1,000,000
Six months	+1,000,000	0	+1,000,000	+1,000,000
Twelve months	+500,000	0	+500,000	0
Twenty-four months	0	−500,000	−500,000	−500,000
Total	+3,600,000	−3,500,000		+100,000

REVALUATION

The exchange position ladder is a key tool for management of the bank's position. But of itself, it is only a record of what deals were done. It gives us no information about their current profit. In order to know that, banks will revalue their foreign currency "book" from time to time. The profit or loss is taken to the bank's profit and loss account. Let's look at a U.S. bank which is dealing U.S. dollars against deutsche marks. The way its deutsche mark exchange ladder might look is shown in Table 20.2. This, though, does not tell us if we are making money on the deals. Let's ask ourselves what would happen if the bank were required to go out of business tomorrow. That is, at what prices could we liquidate these contracts? Suppose that we take today's prices for the various periods involved and apply them to the current book. Table 20.3 shows how the position might look.

As we can see, the overall book now shows a loss. There is a small profit in the spot position, since the deutsche mark has strengthened to 1.99. But where the bank had paid a premium of DEM 0.09 for its 6-month against 1-month swap, it would now only earn a premium of 0.02 for reversing the deal. Where

Table 20.2   Deutsche Mark Position Equivalents

Period	DEM Amount	Original Rate	Original US$ Equivalent
Spot	100,000	2.00	50,000.00
One month	1,000,000	2.01	497,512.43
Two months	2,000,000	1.95	−1,025,641.03
Three months	−2,000,000	1.95	1,025,641.03
Six months	1,000,000	1.93	−518,134.72
Twelve months	500,000	1.89	−264,550.26
Two years	−500,000	1.76	284,090.91

Table 20.3   Deutsche Mark Position Revalued

Period	Currency Amount	Original Rate	Original US$ Equivalent	Current Rate	Current Value	Profit Loss
Spot	100,000.00	2.00	−50,000.00	1.99	50,251.26	251.26
One month	−1,000,000.00	2.01	497,512.43	1.98	−505,050.51	−7,538.08
Two months	2,000,000.00	1.95	−1,025,641.03	1.97	1,015,228.40	−10,412.62
Three months	−2,000,000.00	1.95	1,025,641.03	1.96	−1,020,408.16	5,232.87
Six months	1,000,000.00	1.93	−518,134.72	1.96	510,204.08	−7,930.64
Twelve months	500,000.00	1.89	−264,550.26	1.91	261,780.10	2,770.16
Two years	−500,000.00	1.76	284,090.91	1.81	−276,243.09	7,847.82
Totals	100,000.00		−51,081.64		35,762.19	−15,319.45

it had sold 3-month DEM for a nil premium against two months, it would now have to pay a premium of 0.01 to reverse the swap. There is a small profit on the 1- against 2-year deal, since the 2-year was sold at a premium of 0.13 against the 1-year. The bank would have to pay only 0.10 to reverse the swap.

The benefit of the revaluation is that it gives current information about which positions are profitable and which are turning into loss. The example we looked at was simple. It assumed that the various contracts outstanding were for the "standard" maturity dates. A bank will normally have nonstandard forward contracts as well. Assuming that the process is computerized, it will be possible to produce interpolated rates for every single date and to revalue every contract. For practical reasons, it might be easiest to consider contracts to be matched if they fall within the same calendar week, the same semi-monthly period, or even the same month, depending on how close they are to today and on how precise we need to be.

As discussed in the interest rate section, a full picture would include the effect of futures, options, and swaps. Similar considerations apply to the foreign exchange risk of these items as in interest rate risk (the credit risk on currency swaps is different, however, as discussed in Chapters 15 and 21).

MEASUREMENT OF EXPOSURE IN THE CORPORATION

In many ways, the measurement of exposure in the corporation is intrinsically more complex than in a bank. In the banking case, we are concerned with purely monetary assets and liabilities; in the corporation, the asset to be hedged may consist of a trading receivable, or it may consist of a fixed asset such as property which forms part of the corporation's balance sheet. Equally, the bank's trading operations will usually be subject to a fairly uniform tax treatment because its profits and losses on foreign exchange will (normally) be part of its ordinary income. This is often not so for an industrial or commercial corporation.

There are many different measures of exposure which have been applied to corporations. Economic, transaction, translation, and operational exposure are all terms which have been used at various times. The broadest, perhaps, is economic exposure. It has been defined as the impact of exchange rate changes on discounted cash flow of a company at a specified future date.

Two other widely used measures are transaction and translation exposure. They are used by the Financial Accounting Standards Board (FASB) of the United States, which in 1975 published its Statement Number 8, now generally referred to as FASB 8 (see below). In brief, transaction exposure concerns actual transactions in foreign currencies, whereas translation exposure deals with the valuation of overseas assets.

Finally, another measure which is widely used is consolidated after-tax exposure. This, as the name suggests, looks at the translation component and the tax effect of the transaction component of the exposure from a consolidated after-tax viewpoint. This concept of after-tax exposure is often used by corporations with a centralized exposure management function.

The choice of definition is controversial. FASB 8, the first definitive statement of its kind on this subject, in the United States, ran to over 20,000 words, much of it devoted to justifying the Board's decision. But it was subjected to intensive international criticism. After six years of debate, some of the main principles of FASB 8 were abandoned, and a new statement, FASB 52, was published.

There were a number of specific criticisms of FASB 8. But the most widespread concerned the problem of translation losses or profits. The problem was that these had to be reported in current quarterly or annual income statements. This could have very inconvenient and misleading reporting effects. FASB 52 now requires these profits and losses to be taken to an equity account in the balance sheet, rather than being shown in the income statement. FASB 52 also, in general, requires assets and liabilities to be translated at the current exchange rate.

The UK accounting standard SSAP20 varies from FASB52 in the following ways:

1. It allows closing rate conversion for profit and loss calculations as well as allowing average rate.
2. It is not so strict in defining currencies which can be recorded as a hedge for another item.
3. FAS52 only allows a recorded hedge for a subsidiary investment.
4. FAS52 requires the temporal method for hyperinflationary countries. SSAP20 requires inflation-adjusted figures converted at closing rates.
5. FAS52 requires separate profit and loss disclosure of exchange gains and losses. SSAP20 does not.
6. FX adjustments, passed directly through reserves, have to be disclosed separately each year and as a carried forward balance for FAS52. For SSAP20, only the current year's adjustment need be shown separately.
7. For FAS52, if a subsidiary is sold any accumulated exchange differences that were taken direct to reserves, must be passed through the profit and loss account. SSAP20 does not require this.

The international accounting standard IAS21 is similar to SSAP20 and FAS52 but broader than either. Thus anyone complying with SSAP20 or FAS52 will automatically comply with IAS21.

To see how these concepts work in practice, let's take some examples. Let's look at a corporation with a German subsidiary. Assume that the corporation has no foreign exchange exposure of its own. The only foreign exchange exposure of the German subsidiary is an account receivable in U.S. dollars, for $100. At the start of the first period, the exchange rates are US$ 1 = DEM 2 = CHF 2. By period 2, the dollar has depreciated against both the DEM

Table 20.4   Transaction Loss by German Subsidiary

	Period 1	Period 2
	US$ 1 =	US$ 1 =
	DEM 2	1.7778
Exchange Rate	CHF2	1.60
Subsidiary's account receivable:		
in US	$100	100
in DEM	200	177.78
in CHF	200	160.00
Subsidiary's transaction loss:		
in DEM	—	−22.22
in CHF	—	−20.00

and CHF: US$ 1 = DEM 1.7778 = CHF 1.60. These rates mean the deutsche mark has depreciated also against the franc, from a relationship of parity, DEM 1 = CHF 1, to DEM 1 = CHF 0.90. Clearly the subsidiary has an exchange loss by being long of a dollar receivable when the dollar is falling. This transaction loss, measured in deutsche marks, totals DEM 22.22. The franc equivalent of this transaction loss is CHF 20.0. (See Table 20.4.)

So far we've looked at this purely from the point of view of the subsidiary. It has a transaction loss. When it comes to collect the account, it will receive less in deutsche marks than it expected. This loss will have to be shown in

Table 20.5   Swiss Parent's Translation Loss

	Period 1	Period 2
	US$ 1 =	US$ 1 =
	DEM 2	1.7778
Exchange Rate	CHF2	1.60
Subsidiary's account receivable:		
in US	$100	100
in DEM	200	177.78
in CHF	200	160.00
Subsidiary's transaction loss:		
in DEM	—	−22.22
in CHF	—	−20.00
Parent's translation loss: in CHF	—	40.00

the profit and loss statement. But look at it now from the point of view of the parent. The subsidiary's account receivable in dollars was an overseas asset of the parent. So the parent will show a translation loss on the account receivable.

This loss is the difference between the original value in the parent company's currency, namely CHF 200, and the value now, namely CHF 160. That is, the parent company will show a translation loss in francs of CHF 40. As far as the subsidiary is concerned, the transaction loss will show up in cash terms when the account is collected. But from the point of view of the parent company, the loss shows up as a balance sheet adjustment. (See Table 20.5.) The loss at the parent level is greater, because the parent's currency is stronger than the subsidiary's. The subsidiary's loss reflects the DEM's strength. The parent's reflects also the rise of the CHF against the DEM.

TAXATION

We must now look at the impact of taxation. In many countries, exchange transaction losses or profits in the ordinary course of business will be taxed just like other profits and losses. But translation profits or losses often are not taxed. Suppose now that the subsidiary pays tax at 60% on its transaction profits or losses. Then the transaction loss of DEM 22.22 will reduce taxable income and therefore taxes. The tax benefit, of course, is the 60% of DEM 22.22 which would otherwise have been payable in taxes, namely DEM 13.34. So the subsidiary's transaction loss, net of tax, is reduced to DEM 8.88, or CHF 8.00. The parent's overall translation loss (net of the subsidiary's tax credit in CHF terms of CHF 12.00) is reduced to CHF 28.00, as we can see from Table 20.6.

The different effects of transaction and translation losses become clear when we look at the local bookkeeping for intercompany exposures. The translation of intercompany accounts doesn't normally give rise to gains or losses on the consolidated accounts. Intercompany exposure nets out. From a consolidated viewpoint, the two parties involved (the parent and the subsidiary) are long and short in the same currency.

Let's suppose that the only foreign currency exposure of the subsidiary is now an account payable to its parent, denominated in dollars. Assume the same exchange rate changes as before. Then the subsidiary will benefit to the tune of CHF 40 from the depreciation of the dollar. This will show through in translating the subsidiary's accounts. The parent, on the other hand, has a loss of CHF 40 equivalent in the value of its account receivable from the subsidiary. Table 20.7 summarizes the situation.

At the translation level, therefore, the effects of currency changes wash out. But the individual companies will usually keep their books in their own currencies. (In FASB 52 terminology, in their "functional currencies"). In our example, therefore, transaction gains and losses have to be reported at a

Table 20.6   Tax Effect on Transaction and
Translation Loss

	Period 1	Period 2
Exchange rate	US$ 1 = DEM 2 CHF2	US$ 1 = 1.7778 1.60
Tax rate: translation	0.00	0.00
transaction	0.60	0.60
Subsidiary's account receivable		
in US$	100	100
Value in DEM	200	177.78
Value in CHF	200	160
DEM gain/loss	0.00	−22.22
CHF gain/loss	0.00	40.00
Subsidiary's transaction loss		
in DEM	0.00	−22.22
in CHF	0.00	−20.00
Subsidiary's tax credit/charge		
in DEM	0.00	−13.34
in CHF	0.00	−12.00
Subsidiary's transaction loss net of tax:		
DEM	0.00	−8.88
CHF	0.00	−8.00
Parent's translation loss CHF	0.00	−40
Parent's translation loss net of tax CHF	0.00	−40
Subsidiary's tax credit/charge Parent's translation loss after		
net of tax, in CHF	0.00	−28
Parent's transaction loss	0.00	0.00
Parent's transaction loss		
net of tax	0.00	0.00

subsidiary level and at the parent level. The overall effect will depend on the rates of taxation in the two countries. For example, suppose, as before, that the subsidiary is taxed at 60%. Suppose, though, that the parent is taxed at 45%. Then we have the situation shown in Table 20.8.

Here the subsidiary has made a transaction profit, in DEM, of DEM 22.22, which is taxable at 60%. So the tax bill is DEM 13.34, and there is an after-tax profit of DEM 8.88, or CHF 8.00. The parent, on the other hand, has a transaction loss in francs of CHF 40.00. Its tax rate is 45%, so this loss yields a tax credit in francs of CHF 18.00, producing a net after-tax loss of CHF 22.00. In other words, the group as a whole has lost CHF 14.00, purely because the tax rate in the parent company's country has reduced the tax

Table 20.7   Intercompany Exposure

	Period 1	Period 2
	US$ 1 =	US$ 1 =
	DEM 2	1.7778
Exchange Rate	CHF2	1.60
Subsidiary's account payable to parent:		
in US$	100	100
in DEM	200	177.78
in CHF	200	160.00
Parent's account receivable from subsidiary:		
in US$	100	100
in DEM	200	177.78
in CHF	200	160.00

credit obtainable on its transaction loss, compared with the tax cost applied to the subsidiary's transaction profit.

FASB 52

Enough has been said to show that this whole area can be very complex. The problem comes from the difficulty of applying standard monetary methods to corporations which may have different underlying situations. This problem was highlighted by the publication of FASB 8 and its successor FASB 52. As we mentioned earlier, FASB 8 was heavily criticized because the impact of exchange rate changes on the balance sheet was shown up on the income statement, with sometimes misleading results.

As a result of these criticisms, the FASB undertook a review of FASB 8. The revised approach was published as FASB 52, "Foreign Currency Translation" in December 1981. Briefly, FASB 52 has switched away from the approach of FASB 8 toward the so-called "net investment approach." That is, each foreign branch, division, or subsidiary is looked upon as a net investment of the parent. So the parent's exchange risk is related to the business as a whole and not to individual assets and liabilities. FASB 52 lays down:

> The assets, liabilities, and operations of a foreign entity shall he measured using the functional currency of that entity. An entity's functional currency is the currency of the primary economic environment in which the entity operates; normally, that is the currency of the environment in which the entity primarily generates and expends cash. (FASB 52, para. 5)

Table 20.8   Tax Impact on Intercompany Exposure

	Period 1	Period 2
	US$ 1 =	US$ 1 =
	DEM 2	1.7778
Exchange Rate	CHF2	1.60
Subsidiary's account payable		
to parent:		
in US$	100	100
in DEM	200	177.78
in CHF	200	160.00
Parent's account receivable		
from subsidiary:		
in US$	100	100
in DEM	200	177.78
in CHF	200	160
Tax rate on:		
parent	45%	45%
subsidiary	60%	60%
Subsidiary's transaction profit		
in DEM	—	22.22
Subsidiary's tax in DEM	—	13.34
Total in DEM	—	8.88
Total in CHF	—	8.00
Parent transaction loss in CHF	—	40.00
Parent tax credit in CHF	—	18.00
Parent loss net of tax in CHF	—	22.00
Overall effect:		
Parent's after-tax loss +		
subsidiary's after-tax profit		− 14.00

Once the functional currency for a foreign entity is determined, its accounts must be cast in terms of the functional currency. If its accounts are not maintained in the functional currency, remeasurement into the functional currency is required (paragraph 10). The accounts are then translated into the reporting currency of the parent, in the following manner:

All elements of financial statements shall be translated by using a current exchange rate. For assets and liabilities, the exchange rate at the balance sheet date shall be used. For revenues, expenses, gains and losses, the exchange rates at the dates at which those elements are recognized shall be used. (FASB, para. 12)

If an entity's functional currency is a foreign currency, translation adjustments result from the process of translating that entity's financial state-ments into the reporting currency. Translation adjustments shall not he included in determining net income but shall be reported separately and accumulated in a separate component of equity. (FASB 52, para. 13)

FASB 52 has transferred the impact of translation adjustments from the profit and loss account to the balance sheet. It removes erratic fluctuations in income, at the price of erratic fluctuations in the balance sheet. ITT, a corporation which had vehemently criticized FASB 8, switched to FASB 52 in 1982 and showed a swing in the equity adjustment of nearly $500 million between 1980 and 1981(on a stockholder's equity of $6 billion). For companies with critical balance sheet ratios, for example, leverage ratios, the random fluctuations of the balance sheet may cause just as much of a problem as the random fluctuations in income experienced in FASB 8. There are a good many grounds on which one can criticize FASB 52, but on the whole it seems a great deal more sensible than its predecessor.

INVENTORY, FIXED ASSETS, AND LONG-TERM BORROWING

Up to now we have concentrated on transaction and translation exposures only from current assets and liabilities. In the process certain complications have been glossed over. The first of these is inventory. Under FASB 8, FASB 52's predecessor, the U.S. FASB permitted corporations to value inventory in two ways. They could value at current exchange rates if inventory was valued at current cost or historic exchange rates if inventory was valued at historic cost. But the borrowings to finance the inventory were generally valued at current exchange rates. It was possible to get some odd results. Suppose the currency of the country in which the inventory was held began to appreciate. Suppose the inventory were valued at historic cost. The exchange value of the inventory would be held at the old rate while the value of the borrowing rose. The company would seem to lose money.

A similar distortion arose in the case of fixed assets, and this case points up wider issues. Take the case of a U.S. company buying fixed assets in Brazil. Suppose that during that year inflation in Brazil runs at 100%, while there is no inflation in the United States. Suppose that in year 1 US$1 = CR100, and in year 2 US$1 = CR200. In year 1, the U.S. company buys a machine in Brazil costing CR 10,000 that is, US$100. At the end of year 2, the valuation in historic terms is CR10,000 = US$100.

In current terms, the machine's value has fallen to US$50 owing to the fall in the exchange rate. But the Brazilian price of such a machine, owing to the 100% domestic inflation, has doubled from CR10,000 to CR20,000. So if the U.S. company were to replace the machine in year 2, its cost in U.S. dollar terms would be US$100. In this case, measuring the value of the machine at the current exchange rate *understates* its value to the company. The domestic price level change has exactly offset the exchange rate movement.

In the converse case, take a Brazilian company investing in the United States. In year 1 it buys a machine worth US$100 for CR10,000. At the end of year 2 the valuation of the machine is still US$100 as there has been no inflation in the United States. Valued at the historic exchange rate, this produces a value of CR10,000. In current terms, though, the machine's value of US$100 translates to CR20,000. The price arrived at in current terms is the same as that which would apply to the purchase of a new machine. A new machine will also cost US$100, there having been no inflation.

In the case of a U.S. company investing in Brazil—that is, an investment in a soft currency area—the historic rate is the more appropriate measure of the fixed asset. The apparent loss to the company from the exchange rate movement would be fully offset by the domestic price level change. In the reverse case (the Brazilian company investing in the United States, a hard currency area) the exchange rate movement is not offset by any change in the domestic price level, so the current basis of translation gives the more sensible result.

These examples oversimplify the position. If both countries are inflating at different speeds, neither the current nor the historical method will be completely accurate. It will in general tend to be true that *the historic basis will give the more accurate result for investments in weak currencies, while the current basis is better for investments in strong currencies.* (These problems are especially acute in hyperinflationary countries, which FASB 52 essentially treats as if they were being accounted for under the old FASB 8 rules.)

But even this qualified conclusion is subject to further qualifications. Most important, the example above implicitly assumes that the "right" way of valuing the asset at the end of year 2 was by comparing it with a replacement. For most purposes, what matters to the company is not the replacement cost, but how much local currency income the asset can produce. We may be right to assume that a fall in the exchange rate of a country where the asset is held will later be offset by a rise in the domestic price level. This would help the asset to produce future income. Then it would be fair to assume that the value of the asset to the company will remain constant. In this case, the historic measurement will be appropriate. The crucial assumption, though, is the ability of the asset to keep its income generating capacity in "real" terms. If the Brazilian devaluation were accompanied by price controls, the "real" value of the machine in our example would have fallen.

Another area of complication is the question of translation exposures on long-term borrowings. In the case of investment in fixed assets, the exchange risk is a bit unreal. The corporation does not have to put up hard cash if exchange rates move. But in the case of foreign currency borrowings, which have to be repaid, the position is very different. "Cheap" francs borrowed for 10 years in 1965 at CHF4.3730 per dollar would have cost around 80% more to repay in 1975 at CHF2.6200. If these changes were not reflected in the balance sheet of the company, serious distortions would arise in assessing the company's ability to repay its debts.

But suppose the franc borrowing was to finance a franc fixed asset. Revaluing the borrowing at current exchange rates while leaving the franc asset at the historic exchange rate could produce significant distortions as well. Even though the fixed asset in Switzerland might not conveniently be saleable to repay the franc borrowing, it does exist and may provide security for a further franc borrowing with which to refinance the old borrowing, or it may generate a Swiss franc cash flow sufficient to service the borrowing.

CASH VS. INCOME VS. ACCOUNTING

Finally, we need to look at the conflicts among the various types of exposure management strategy. A hedge in the foreign exchange market has an impact on cash flow, net after-tax income, and accounting gains or losses. The cash, income, and accounting impact will vary according to whether the company decides not to hedge, to hedge on a before-tax basis, or to hedge on an after-tax basis. Each of these strategies (if the hedge is properly done) will cut out the impact of exchange rate fluctuations on one of the three variables (cash, net income, or accounting gain/loss).

However, each strategy will also add to the impact on the other two variables. If all other things are equal, we can say that the accounting gain or loss is likely to fluctuate most with no forward cover and least with cover arranged on a before-tax basis. Net after-tax income is most volatile with no cover, and least if the hedge is on an after-tax basis. In contrast, the cash flow effect of translation exposure is nil if it is left completely unhedged, greater if cover is taken on a before-tax basis, and greatest if hedged on an after-tax basis.

A further potential problem is where the hedging should be done. This is linked to the question of centralization discussed next, and also to the existence of exchange controls in the countries involved. For example, a U.S. corporation with an Indian subsidiary would not be able to instruct its Indian subsidiary to hedge against possible translation exposure because of Indian exchange controls. The U.S. company would have to do the hedging operations itself in the U.S. market and accept the consequent cash flow and income implications. Equally, a subsidiary in, say, Switzerland might be able to do the hedge, but might not be able to sustain the possible cash flow or income impact.

IMPLEMENTING EXPOSURE MANAGEMENT

Having discussed how exposure is measured, we come now to the question of what to do about it. This raises a number of issues, but perhaps the most pervasive is the organizational effect of exposure management. The issue surfaces in two particular ways: corporate foreign exchange trading policy and the role of a central treasury. But these in themselves mesh in with many other aspects of a corporation's management style.

Perhaps the most basic question is the corporation's trading aims. In some firms, a high level decision has been taken to lay down general guidelines for foreign exchange trading policies. In others, there is a general style that is clearly understood in the treasury area. In others again, the policy is just to respond to events.

As exchange rates have become more volatile, the risk of large losses has greatly increased. So it would be sensible for a set of formal guidelines to be worked out if this has not yet been done. At least the exercise will help all concerned decide whether the present policies meet the firm's needs. Professional bank dealers deliberately take positions that open up foreign currency exposure, to make a profit from them. Some corporations do the same. At the opposite extreme are those companies who feel that "our business is making widgets, not trading in currency." For each company, the right answer will depend on its size and the scale of its international business.

A conservative view would be that the shareholders are entitled to expect the management of the company to put itself in a position to manage its foreign exchange problems but this does not authorise that management to behave like a bank. This view might see it as acceptable currency management to leave open a foreign exchange exposure that has arisen in the normal course of business. But opening up an exposure deliberately on the other hand, would be speculative and accordingly not acceptable.

Many others take a more aggressive approach. The right answer for each company must lie in its own circumstances and skills. The crucial point is that clear guidelines should be laid down by senior management to those who carry out the company's transactions. To date, relatively few corporations have suffered serious losses from unwise foreign exchange dealings. But the cases of Volkswagen and Allied-Lyons show that large losses can occur.

A second issue which has to be looked at is how far foreign exchange trading should be centralized. The drawback to central control is that it can create a central bureaucracy which is removed from day-to-day problems. A central treasury function can also curb the freedom of the individual profit centers if they lose control over their cash. Also, if the operating divisions no longer have responsibility for their exposure, they may take more risks. (An obvious example is a salesperson pressured to invoice in an undesirable currency.) The group as a whole can suffer because the central treasury has drained foreign exchange skill from the operating units.

But there are arguments in favour of centralization. It helps to justify better facilities. The most obvious is direct telephone lines to foreign exchange dealing rooms in the banks. A direct line gives a much faster response from the banks. It also makes it easier for the corporation to get simultaneous quotes from two or three banks, which is essential for a fair comparison. Second, a centralized treasury can ensure that the firm gets the best rates. It can put together "marketable" amounts. Centralization also makes it easier to match exposures. In general, it is a waste of money if one subsidiary is, say, buying yen while another is selling yen. By the same token, centralization can be a great help to cash management on an international basis. Finally, it helps to concentrate the foreign exchange skills which would otherwise be scattered. This gives scope for full use of the company's information sources and skills.

If the firm decides to centralize, it has to decide how to set the exchange rates within the company. Again, this depends on the volume of foreign currency business done. In some companies, it may be simplest for the central treasury to issue a regular circular telling the units the rates applying for the month or quarter to come. Or it may be best for the central treasury to act like a bank to the rest of the company. When a division has made a commercial contract, the exposure is passed to the central treasury by a "deal" between the division and the center.

Various rates may be used for this deal. First is the rate at which the center later covers in the market. This kills any suspicion by the division that it is being "robbed" by the center. But it will probably cause delay because the center may not cover the deal at once. And it may not be possible to match up the deals exactly.

A second choice is the spot rate on the day that the deal is passed from the division to the center. But if the contract is for a future date, the division may ignore the forward premium or discount on the currency in its pricing. This will harm the group's overall pricing and exposure. A better rate is that for the date that the underlying cash flow will take place. Once the center has bought the currency from, or sold it to, the division, it is the center's job to turn the trade at a profit in the marketplace.

For a multinational treasury, there is an obvious problem in centralizing exposures between countries. Legal, fiscal, and other factors may prevent this. But it is sometimes possible for a corporation's currency (and tax) exposure to be centralized in a reinvoicing vehicle (see below).

Having looked briefly at some of the broader issues, we turn to some of the specifics. In the rest of this chapter, we assume that the corporation is concerned to reduce its exposure, and we look at ways and means to do this. We can divide the major strategies into two broad areas: those which are mainly nonfinancial and organisational, such as decisions on netting, production, input sourcing, and marketing, and those which are more purely financial.

MULTINATIONAL NETTING

A logical step forward from the process of considering exposure on a group basis is the reinvoicing vehicle. This is sometimes referred to as a netting vehicle, or an indirect invoicing approach. Under this system, every company in the group routes all its intragroup transactions and all its external transactions, other than those in its own domestic currency, through a single group company. The central company through which the transactions are routed and which nets out the exposures can be any group company. But often a new subsidiary is set up in a country which is suitable for tax purposes. The latter choice raises tricky considerations, as the tax authorities have to be convinced that no evasion is taking place.

The operation of a reinvoicing company can be complex, but a simple example will show the principles. The case in Table 20.9 assumes a group consisting of three companies. Each has a certain number of intragroup payments to make. We assume payments and receipts are made at the same time of the month. For simplicity, we also assume that all the underlying invoices were booked at the same time. Payments are made at the spot rate on the day of settlement. So each company has a profit or loss according to the difference between the booking rate and the settlement rate.

We see, for example, that the U.S. company had a net sterling exposure. It was long of £150,000. Sterling rose from US$2.0 to US$2.20 between the time of booking and the time of settlement. So the U.S. company made a profit of US$30,000 on its sterling. The profits and losses in the group totaled US$9,333.33.

Suppose now that we set up a reinvoicing vehicle. It buys all exposures from group member companies at the booking rate. So it will buy the U.S. company's £150,000 at the booking rate of US$2.00 per pound. This gives it a receivable from the U.S. company under the sterling exposure heading. At the same time, it must pay the U.S. company the dollar equivalent, namely US$300,000, for this sterling receivable. This opens up a U.S. dollar payable exposure in favour of the U.S. company of US$300,000, which is entered under its U.S. dollar exposure position. Also the sale to the British company of US$100,000 to cover that company's short dollar position of US$100,000 is in

Table 20.9   Intercompany Exposure: Direct Settlement

Company Ownership		Payments	Receipts	Net	Exchange Rates	
					Booking Rate	Settlement Rate
U.S.	DEM	400,000	200,000	−200,000	US$/DEM 2.0	US$/DEM 1.80
	£STG	100,000	250,000	+150,000	£STG/US$ 2.0	£STG/US$ 2.20
German	US$	100,000	300,000	+200,000		
	£STG	300,000	200,000	−100,000		
British	US$	300,000	200,000	−100,000		
	DEM	100,000	180,000	+ 80,000		

		Exposure	Booking Rate	Settlement Rate[a]	Profit/Loss
U.S.	− DEM	200,000	2.0	1.80	− US$11,111.11
	+ £STG	150,000	2.0	2.20	+ US$30,000
German	+ US$	200,000	2.0	1.80	− DEM 40,000
	− £STG	100,000	4.0	3.96	+ DEM 4,000
U.K.	− US$	100,000	2.0	2.2	+ £STG 4,545.46
	+ DEM	80,000	4.0	3.96	+ £STG 202.2
Total profit/loss in US$ (using settlement rates)					US$ 9,333.33

[a] Settlement rate = rate against home currency.

the reinvoicing company's U.S. dollar exposure account. And it creates a sterling receivable of £50,000 from the British company under the sterling exposure heading. The overall result of these operations is shown in Table 20.10.

We can see that when the payments are booked the reinvoicing vehicle acquires a short DEM position of DEM120,000 a long sterling position of £80,000, and a short U.S. dollar position of US$100,000. These positions balance out at the booking rates. The long sterling position is worth US$160,000; the short DEM position is worth US$60,000. But at the settlement date exchange rate movements mean that the short DEM position is equivalent to US$66,666.67 while the long sterling position is equivalent to US$176,000. The US$16,000 profit on the sterling position net of the US$6,666.67 loss on the DEM position produce a net profit of US$9,333.33.

This is exactly the same profit as would have been made under the previous arrangements (see Table 20.9). All that has happened is that the profit has been put in the reinvoicing vehicle. But before, six foreign exchange deals would have been needed two deals per subsidiary. Consolidation means that the reinvoicing vehicle only needs to sell sterling and buy deutsche marks to square its position. The inherent matching abilities of the reinvoicing vehicle have cut down the complexity of the foreign exchange position. Also, centralizing exposures in one company makes it easier to handle exposure and cash management. By leading or lagging a payment, funds can be switched inside the group, within the constraints of exchange control regulations.

Table 20.10 Intercompany Exposure: Use of Reinvoicing Company

	Payable	Receivable	
DEM Exposure with respect to:			
U.S. company	200,000		
British company		80,000	
German company	400,000 (against US$)	400,000 (against £STG)	
	600,000	480,000	Net: − DEM 120,000
£STG Exposure with respect to:			
U.S. company		150,000	
German company	100,000		
British company		50,000 (against US$)	
(against DEM)	20,000		
	120,000	200,000	Net: + £STG 80,000
US$ Exposure with respect to:			
German company		200,000	
British company	100,000		
U.S. company		100,000 (against DEM)	
(against £STG)	300,000		
	400,000	300,000	Net: − US$100,000

Having considered the implications of organization of the foreign exchange function in the corporation, and the extension of centralization to a multinational netting system, we need now to look at other ways of structuring a company's operations to handle exposure. We start by looking at the implications of production, pricing, and marketing.

PRODUCTION, PRICING, AND MARKETING STRATEGIES

The choice of production location implies an exchange exposure. It may not be obvious to a U.S. firm that is exporting, say, 10% of its output that by locating its production in the United States it has made an exchange rate decision. But, in a converse situation, Volkswagen during the 1970s came to realize that by exporting to the United States from Germany it was making itself vulnerable to DEM revaluations. No amount of hedging in the forward market could offset this basic economic exposure. As a result, Volkswagen ultimately decided to locate some of its production in the United States.

It is possible to be exposed to the movement of a currency without producing in that currency's country or selling to that country. For example, sales of jet engines by Rolls-Royce in Britain to India are affected by movements in the dollar. In the world jet engine market, there are effectively only three major players, General Electric, Pratt Whitney, and Rolls-Royce. Since the other two firms are American, the market prices are in dollars. Rolls' profit margins, therefore, are vulnerable to movements in sterling against the dollar, as the company found during the late 1970s.

Another important concern in the area of pricing and marketing is the question of invoicing currency. In the example just mentioned, Rolls-Royce's choice of invoicing currency was fixed by market conditions. In other cases, companies producing in a country with a weak currency have chosen to invoice in a strong currency, such as the deutsche mark or U.S. dollar, to protect the value of their receivables.

In general, therefore, exporters try to use their own currency as currency of invoice. This lets them protect themselves against exchange rate fluctuations. But there have been periods—notably, for example, in the United Kingdom during the prolonged weakness of sterling—when exporters switched their invoices into stronger currencies. That gave them flexibility. They could profit from the devaluation of the domestic currency. Or they could cover forward in the foreign exchange market or alternatively borrow foreign currency against the foreign currency receivable.

The choice of invoice currency is not only dictated by financial considerations. It also depends on what the salesperson can persuade the buyer to accept (or vice versa if the goods are being imported). At this point, exposure management touches the commercial thinking of the firm. The exposure management team needs to know the commercial pressures in the marketplace where the salespeople are working. It is equally important for those selling the company's goods to know the risks they may commit the company to if they accept a change in invoicing currency.

The greatest flexibility, of course, lies in the choice of invoicing currency in trade within a multinational group. If the exporting parent sells in its own domestic currency to its subsidiary, then the subsidiary has the exposure. Alternatively the parent can invoice in the subsidiary's currency and keep the exposure at home. The latter case generally gives more flexibility. Exceptions to this rule would make sense if the parent company's domestic currency were expected to be weak relative to the subsidiary's. Then, provided the subsidiary's profits were taxable at a lower rate than the parent's, invoicing in the parent's currency and shifting profits to the subsidiary might be desirable. A second exception is in the converse case, where the parent's currency is expected to be strong and the parent's tax rate is lower. In this case, parent currency invoicing might be desirable.

The price of this flexibility is complexity at the center. In addition, flexibility could be hampered by exchange controls. Suppose we have a U.S. company with a low domestic tax rate, with a Zambian subsidiary which is paying high taxes. The dollar is expected to appreciate against the Zambian kwacha. The parent decides to invoice its sales to Zambia in dollars. The exposure is passed to the Zambian subsidiary. But Zambian regulations forbid forward cover more than say two months in advance of delivery of the goods. Suppose the goods are shipped on 180 days' credit. Then the Zambian subsidiary is exposed to movements in the franc for four months until they can take cover. The uncertain impact on local profitability may be demoralizing. In this situation, it might be better to invoice in kwacha and to handle the exposure centrally.

CHOICE OF BORROWING CURRENCY

A second obvious method of reducing exposure is to consider the choice of currency for borrowings. Suppose, for example, a U.S. corporation has a British subsidiary that has net assets. It can hedge these through forward sales of sterling in the foreign exchange markets or by borrowing sterling and selling it spot. Or it can instruct the U.K. subsidiary to build up its sterling borrowings and pay down its foreign currency borrowings, or remit the proceeds to the parent, to the point where the net currency asset position is eliminated. Or, if there were a net liability position in sterling (under FASB 8), the U.S. parent might have lent the British subsidiary dollars, letting it pay off some of its sterling borrowings to bring the net position back to zero.

But these operations depend on freedom from exchange controls. And there may be other problems. Funds may not be available from local financial institutions for a sufficiently long maturity. Building up local borrowings, or paying them down, may not be convenient because of balance sheet limitations or loan covenants, as well as possible exchange control problems. Hence various other techniques have been developed to reduce exposure. These are the so-called back-to-back and parallel loans, currency swaps and simulated currency loans. Of these, probably the most widespread are currency swaps, discussed in Chapter 15.

21 Credit and Settlement Risk

Books have been written on the subject of credit risk. This chapter does not show how to analyze the credit quality of a counterparty, rather it briefly explains the controls that have been imposed by regulators in the major countries under the aegis of the BIS. Then we will discuss settlement risk and clearing systems.

MEASUREMENT OF CREDIT RISK

The BIS has set up a two-tier capital standard measured against risk-weighted assets: Tier 1 is defined as fully paid in shareholders' equity and retained earning; Tier 2 includes subordinated debt, loan loss reserves, preferred stock, and certain hybrid instruments. By 1992, banks and bank holding companies will be required to comply fully with these prudential standards, although the guidelines provide for a phased implementation process.

Although a great deal of investment banking ingenuity has been expended upon the creation of Tier 1 or Tier 2 capital, we are concerned here much more with the definition of risk-weighted assets, the denominator of the capital ratio. Precise definitions vary according to the central bank involved, but the following outline is drawn from the Solvency Ratio Directive of the European Communities, which covers a wide range of countries. The procedure used is as follows. All assets (and off-balance-sheet exposures) are allocated a weighting, according to the following categories:

- Zero weighting: Cash; claims on OECD governments and central banks and the European communities, or guaranteed by them; claims on other central governments and central banks denominated and funded in the national currencies of the borrowers, or guaranteed by them; all claims secured by OECD central government or central bank securities or European Community securities, or cash.
- 20% weighting: Claims on or guaranteed by the European Investment Bank or multilateral development banks; claims on OECD regional governments or local authorities, or guaranteed by them; claims on, or guaranteed by, OECD credit institutions, or in the case of non-OECD credit institutions, similar claims with a maturity of one year or less; claims collateralized by securities issued by the EIB or multilateral development banks; cash items in the process of collection.
- 50% weighting: Loans secured on residential mortgages, prepayments and accrued income.
- 100% weighting: All other assets including tangible assets, except for those where provision is made for them to be deducted from own funds.

The treatment of off-balance-sheet items depends on whether or not they are interest rate and foreign exchange risks, or other risks. Interest and foreign exchange risks are treated as follows. Interest rate contracts are defined to include single-currency interest rates swaps, basis swaps (floating/floating swaps), forward rate agreements, interest rate futures, interest rate options purchased, and other contracts of a similar nature. (Interest rate futures are included only if they are not traded on recognized exchanges where they are subject to daily margin requirements.) Foreign exchange contracts include forward foreign exchange contracts (excluding those with an original maturity of 14 calendar days or less) cross currency-interest rate swaps, currency options purchased, currency futures, and other contracts of a similar nature. (Again currency futures are excluded if they are traded on recognized exchanges and subject to daily margin requirements. Interest rate and currency options sold are excluded, since once the premium is paid, the obligation is only one way, from the credit institution to its customer.

Where there is a separate bilateral contract for novation, recognized by the national supervisory authorities, between a credit institution and its counterparty under which any obligations to each other to deliver payments in their common currency on a given date are automatically amalgamated with other similar obligations due on the same date, the single net amount fixed by such a novation is weighted, rather that the gross amounts involved.

Off-balance-sheet items must first be grouped according to the risk categories:

- Full risk: Guarantees having the character of credit substitutes, acceptances, endorsements on bills not bearing the name of another credit institution, transactions with recourse, irrevocable standby letters of credit having the character of credit substitutes, outright forward purchases of assets, asset sale and repurchase agreements where they are treated as off-balance-sheet, forward forward deposits, unpaid portion of partly paid shares and securities, and any other items classified as full risk by the appropriate authority.

- Medium risk: Documentary credits issued and confirmed; warranties and indemnities and guarantees not having the character of credit substitutes (including tender, performance, customs and tax bonds); certain asset sales and repurchase agreements ; irrevocable standby letters of credit not having the character of credit substitutes; undrawn credit facilities with an original maturity of more than one year; note issuance facilities and underwriting facilities; other items classified by the central banks as carrying medium risks.

- Medium/low risk: Documentary credits in which the underlying shipment is collateral, and other self-liquidating transactions. Other items characterized by the central bank as carrying medium/low risk.

- Low risk: Undrawn credit facilities with an original maturity up to an including one year, or which may be canceled unconditionally at any time without notice; other items also classified by the central bank as carrying low risk.

The weightings attached to the full risk items is 100%, medium-risk is 50% and medium/low-risk is 20%, while the value of low-risk items is set at 0%. The off-balance-sheet items are then weighted in accordance with relevant weightings to arrive at a on-balance-sheet equivalent.

For the interest rate and foreign exchange contracts listed, subject to the consent of their supervisory authorities, credit institutions may use one of two methods—the "mark to market approach" or "original exposure" approach.

The mark to market approach proceeds as follows:

1. All outstanding contracts are marked to market with their current replacement cost. The total of all contracts with positive values is obtained. (That is, all of those where the other side of the deal is showing a loss and might walk away from the deal).

2. A figure for potential future credit exposure is added. To obtain this, the notional principal amounts or values underlying the contracts are multiplied by the following percentages:

Residual Maturity	Interest Rate Contracts (%)	Foreign Exchange Contracts (%)
1 year or less	0%	1%
More than 1 year	½%	5%

3. The sum of the current replacement cost and potential future credit exposure is multiplied by the risk weightings allocated to the relevant counterparties (see above).

The "original exposure" approach has two steps:

1. The notional principal amount of each contract is multiplied by the percentages given below:

Original Maturity	Interest Rate Contracts (%)	Foreign Exchange Contracts (%)
1 year or less	½%	2%
Over 1 year, up to 2 years	1%	5%
Each additional year	1%	3%

2. The original exposure is multiplied by the risk weightings allocated to the relevant counterparties as set out above. (In this approach, in the case of interest rate contracts, credit institutions, may, subject to the consent of the supervisory authorities, choose either original or residual maturity.)

SIMULATIONS OF RISK

The methods set out in the previous section are not the only way by which risk can be assessed. In discussing interest rate and foreign exchange risk, we referred to the fact that some institutions now use simulations to test "what if" certain events took place and the impact that would result on their profit and loss or liquidity. For more complex instruments such as swaps and options, such simulation capabilities are very desirable.

Some institutions already use a quite elaborate simulation technique to assess their swap credit risk: the Monte Carlo simulation technique. Monte Carlo simulations were invented by physicists who wanted to model extremely complex systems. They represent a solution using, not intellectual subtlety, but the brute force of the computer. In essence, what we do is

calculate many scenarios using a random number generator. For a sufficiently large number of scenarios, the results can be analyzed statistically
and an accurate assessment of risk made. It is like someone who is playing
dice with loaded dice. He knows they are loaded but not how. If he throws
the dice often enough, and analyzes the outcome, eventually he will be able
to make a very good estimate of the probability of any given face of the dice
turning up on the next throw. Of course, he is still just as uncertain as
before: but now he knows the probabilities. It is the same thing when we have
run all our simulations. We are just as uncertain as before: but we should
have a fairly good idea of the odds against us.

To take a specific example, consider a Monte Carlo simulation applied
to an interest rate swap. (The following discussion is adapted from M.
Ferron and G. Handjinicolau in R. J. Schwartz & C. W. Smith (eds). *The
Handbook of Currency and Interest Rate Risk Management,* New York
Institute of Finance, 1990.) A single interest rate path will be built up over
the life of the transaction. Starting from the level of rates at the time the ·
swap starts, the level of rates at the next period (for example, next year) is
set by the start level plus (or minus) a change. The level of rates two periods
from now is set from the next-period rate plus (or minus) a change. And so
on, until we have created a chain of interest rates for every period in the
swap's life.

Monte Carlo simulation models calculate these interest rate changes by
using an assumed probability distribution function for interest rates, and a
random number generator which kicks the process off randomly. For the
distribution function, most people use the so-called "lognormal" distribution. This implies that changes in the *logarithm* of the interest rate is distributed normally. Using the logarithm implies we assume that percentage
changes in the rate, rather than the rate itself, are normally distributed. That
accords with common sense: if a rate is 20%, it is quite likely to move to 21%
(a 1% change on 20% is a 5% swing); if a rate is at 3%, a 1% rise would be seen
as large (a 1% rise on 3% is a 33.33% swing). The lognormal assumption is
widely used, for example, in the Black & Scholes option pricing model (see
Chapter 16).

Using this lognormal assumption implies several things:

1. There is no underlying trend in interest rates. In each period, rates are
   as likely to rise as to fall.
2. The change in next period's rate is independent of previous changes.
3. The change within a period depends on the assumed standard deviation of the lognormal distribution (that is, the "volatility" of the interest rate). Volatility is an assumption that we have to make before we
   run the model.
4. The scale of interest rate movements over the life of a swap consisting
   of several periods increases with the number of periods. This is a

feature common to most Monte Carlo models and could be called "diffusion."

When we assume a level for volatility, we in effect set global constraints on how far interest rates can move in the future. To be more precise: for the lognormal distribution—the chance of a value lying within one standard deviation of the mean—is roughly 84%. The chance it will be within two standard deviations is 98%.

Suppose rates now are 9% and we guess volatility at 20%. Then one standard deviation will be $9\% \times 20\% = 1.8\%$. So there is an 84% chance that interest rates in the next period will be between 7.2% and 10.8%. Likewise, there is a 98% chance they will be within 5.4% and 12.6%.

Now let's think about the longer term. We said earlier that as the length of the swap grows, so does volatility. More specifically, the "diffusion" (the increase from the starting level of volatility) for a lognormal distribution is a function of the square root of time elapsed since the start of the process. Thus, in our example, at the end of the second period, there is an 84% chance that interest rates will be between 6.5% and 11.5% (one standard deviation two periods from now is equal to $9\% \times 20\% \times \sqrt{2}$) and a 98% chance that interest rates will lie between 2.5% and 30%.

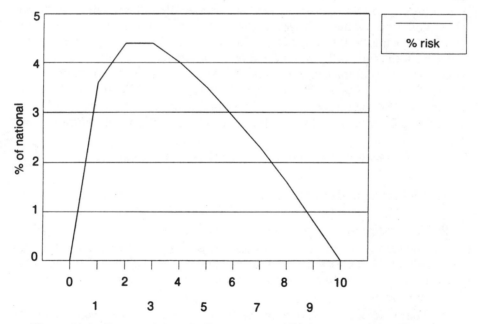

Figure 21.1 Expected swap replacement cost 9% ten-year plain vanilla swap.

In modeling the default risk on an interest rate swap, we shall make the following assumptions:

1. The risk is always positive. That is, the replacement cost is equal to its mark-to-market value, or zero if that value would mean a gain to the other party: i.e. we assume we are always "cherry-picked" by the other party.
2. The timing of default is random: there is equal likelihood of default occurring at any time during the life of the swap.

On these assumptions, the credit risk is equal to the average of the expected replacement costs at each point in the future.

The credit risk will reflect two opposing forces: the "amortization effect" and the "diffusion effect." The amortization effect results from the fact that as time passes and payments are actually exchanged without default, the credit risk on the swap falls towards zero. The diffusion effect is because, as time passes, interest rates have a greater chance of moving from their starting levels.

Figure 21.1 and Table 21.1 show the results of a Monte Carlo simulation for the credit risk of a "plain vanilla" 9% 10-year swap assuming a 20% volatility of interest rates. It will be seen that the profile of the credit risk is humped, with maximum exposure occurring about two years after the start date. On the day of the swap, the credit risk is zero (because it could be replaced immediately with another swap at the same rate) but as interest rates begin to move, the risk rises; against that, the amortization effect kicks in as time moves on.

Table 21.1 Expected Replacement Cost for a 9% Ten-Year "Plain Vanilla" Swap

Year	Expected Replacement Cost (% of Notional Principal)
0	0.0
1	3.6
2	4.4
3	4.4
4	4.0
5	3.5
6	2.9
7	2.3
8	1.6
9	0.8
10	0.0
Average	2.8

Source: Adapted from Ferron & Handjinicolau.

DANGERS OF RISK FORMULAS

There are several ways to assess risk. The risk assessment methods laid down by the BIS are those which have been agreed on by the supervisors. That is not to say that they are perfect; in some ways, they are dangerous. The mechanical application of formulas to credit risk is never appropriate. Each case has to be looked at in the light of the precise structure of the deal to make sure that all cash flows have been properly captured in the credit analysis. The risk on a deal involving forward Saudi riyals where one side settles on Friday and the other on Saturday (see Chapter 8) is very different from a forward dollar/mark deal, for example, where both sides will settle on the same day (but even there, there is a time zone risk).

Another example is the formula applied for swap risk. It needs to be carefully applied with regard to the actual cash flows involved. In some swaps the interest payment varies: that is, interest might be paid by one party quarterly, while the other pays only semi-annually. In this case, the party paying out funds quarterly has a greater risk than the semi-annual payer. Suppose A pays $5 million quarterly to B, in the expectation of being paid six-month Libor by B; if, after a quarterly payment, B defaults, A has paid out $5 million which is lost, in addition to any "replacement cost" of replacing the swap. In this case the BIS factors would need to be adjusted upwards to allow for the cash flow pattern.

In drawing up its regulations, the BIS had to grapple with the fact that the credit risk implied by market activities is fundamentally different from that in normal lending activities. Thus, for example, a bank which lends money to an industrial company will do so in the knowledge that, if its credit analysis has been inadequate or economic conditions turn unfavorable, it will lose 100% of its loan, together with any interest accrued but unpaid thereon. Depending on the strength of its security, and the efforts of any liquidator or administrator, some or all of the loan may be recovered in due course in a "work-out" situation.

But the credit risk implied by market risk is quite different. Unlike a loan to an industrial company, the amount of credit risk is not known for certain on day one. It will depend on market conditions. Suppose a bank contracts to buy forward from company A the sum of £10 million at $1.90. The bank knows that in one year's time, it is contracted to pay out $19 million and to receive £10 million. It will cover its position by a matching deal in the forward exchange market, at say $1.9100. Thus, it is contracted to receive £10 million, paying away $19 million, and pay away £10 million in exchange for $19.1 million, for a clear fixed profit. But suppose that after three months company A goes bankrupt. The sterling that was due to be delivered, now due in nine months time, will no longer be forthcoming. So the bank must go into the market to buy sterling, otherwise it will have an open forward exchange position which could be highly risky. Suppose that sterling is now at $1.70 for delivery in nine months time. Then the bank would have a profit: it now must pay away only $17 million to get the £10 million which it is contracted to hand over in exchange for $19.1 million. Conversely, if sterling were at $2.00, the bank would be on a loss, because to get its hands on the £10 million, it must now pay $20 million, and will still receive only $19.1 million.

Therefore, the credit risk implied by a forward exchange deal with a customer is not "hard," but "soft." That is, bankruptcy of the counterparty could conceivably give a profit to the bank. (In practice, however, this is most unlikely. It is likely that the liquidator or administrator of a failed company would try to insist on retaining the existing forward foreign exchange contract if it were profitable for his company, and try to walk away from it if it were not—the so-called cherry-picking problem.)

Similar problems apply to any of the other interest or foreign exchange contracts that we are discussing, such as interest rate swaps. In every case, the true credit risk cannot be measured in advance. Thus, the BIS formula, like any other possible credit risk measurement method, are essentially a guess at the unknowable. It is critically important for those who are managing the risks involved to be clearly aware that simply because a formula has been laid down by the BIS does not make that formula the best possible, or only method of measuring true counterparty exposure.

SETTLEMENT RISK

In Chapter 18, mention was made of the settlement problems which led to the Bank of New York's urgent need for an overnight overdraft of US$24 billion. No more vivid illustration is, perhaps, required to show how settlement problems have the potential to bring an institution to its knees—though it should be added that the Bank of New York survived "with a little help from its friends."

The authorities are well aware of the risks involved: for example, the Bank of England's risk control procedures treat settlement risk separately. It discusses with individual firms the control systems they have in place to minimize these risks. Moreover, when calculating risk exposure, all unsettled spot transactions will be given a risk weight set at one quarter per cent (a total weight of 0.5% if the asset has been bought and then sold on the same day, and neither part of the deal has settled). This applies both to those deals that would not normally have settled by the reporting date, and to those deals where the settlement date has passed. Where the deal has remained unsettled for an unusually long period, or there are indications that it might fail, the Bank will expect to be informed and may require the transaction to be treated as an open position. Similarly, the Bank of Japan is acutely conscious of the scale of outstanding risks posed to the Japanese system by its settlements and clearing structure (see below) and the Federal Reserve—especially after the experience of October 1987—is very alert to the issue, particularly given the fact that the CHIPS system is effectively the global settlement center for the foreign exchange markets. All foreign exchange market participants will in practice have substantial CHIPS exposure.

In another context, the Group of Thirty produced a report on "Clearance and Settlement Systems in the World's Securities Markets" in March, 1989, as a partial response to the events of the crash of October 1987. The Chairman of the group, Lord Richardson, wrote "the subject of this report . . . cannot claim to be immediately glamorous or eye-catching. Indeed, it has too commonly been thought of as a matter only for the technical experts in back offices. Experience has shown how mistaken, and indeed dangerous, such an attitude is. For the subject is concerned with the core processes that underlie the working of securities market and determine their effectiveness or otherwise . . . At the same time, it is clear that the operational characteristics of these markets . . . are of uneven quality . . . on a global basis this uneven quality in practice inhibits international investment flows while the intersection between local practice and growing volumes and values could, under adverse circumstances, represent a very serious risk to the world's financial network." Therefore it is important to understand something of the way clearing systems work, and we now turn to the question of how money and foreign exchange market dealings are settled.

UNITED STATES CLEARING SYSTEM

The two main clearing and settlement systems relevant to the international markets in the United States are the Fedwire service provided by the Federal Reserve Bank and the Clearing House Interbank Payment System (CHIPS) operated by the New York Clearing House Association. Fedwire is used principally for domestic payments, while over 70 percent of its CHIPS payments are dollar-denominated international payments. Fedwire is normally used for interbank overnight loans, interbank settlement transactions, corporate-to-corporate payments, and settlement of security transactions. In contrast, CHIPS is used to settle foreign exchange transactions and eurodollar placements.

Over 11,000 depository institutions use Fedwire. Approximately 7000 of these are connected to the Federal Reserve via local data communication networks. Fedwire transfers are actually accounting entries effected on the books of the Federal Reserve. The sending bank authorizes the Federal Reserve to debit its account and credit the account of the bank that is to receive the transfer.

Compared with other cashless payments, Fedwires are unique in that the Federal Reserve treats them as final and irrevocable payments. That is, once the Federal Reserve has delivered an advice of credit to the receiving depository institution, it will not reverse the credit. Because of the significant credit exposures implied, the Federal Reserve implemented a program to reduce payment system risk in 1985. The aim was to control daylight overdraft incurred on the books of the Federal Reserve, and to control risks. The program requires banks that incur daylight overdrafts on Fedwire or that participate on private networks to evaluate their creditworthiness, their operational controls, and their credit policies. Based on this self-assessment, each institution selects a "cap" which is a multiple of its capital and serves as a limit on the amount of daylight overdrafts that the institution may incur across all large-dollar funds transfer networks.

Of these networks, CHIPS is the most important. The CHIPS network has over 130 participants. CHIPS participants send payment instructions to the central CHIPS computer, where the instructions are edited and recorded and then transmitted to the receiving institution. During the day, CHIPS maintains running balances of all payment instructions sent and received by each participant. At the close of business the net value of each participant's transfer is computed, and each participant is advised of its balance. Participants in net debit positions send Fedwires to a special account at the Federal Reserve Bank of New York. When the account is fully funded, CHIPS sends Fedwires to each participant in a net credit position. Transfers are considered final payments once all settlement transfers are completed.

The CHIPS system is huge. On an average day it handles over 150,000 transactions. On one day in early 1989 it cleared 260,000 for a total value of $1,260,000,000,000. Looking at that another way, one banker was recently quoted as stating that he turned over the entire capital of his bank every 10 minutes in the CHIPS system. Thus the risks of any system failure or chain default are very substantial. In 1984 the first steps to address this were taken with the introduction of *receivers bilateral net credit limits*. That is, each bank set a limit on how much it was willing to be exposed to each other bank in the system. In 1986, *debit caps* were instituted. Bilateral net credit limits allowed each bank to protect itself against other banks; debit caps allowed the system to protect itself against each bank. Most recently, CHIPS has introduced *settlement finality*. Members have to pledge collateral against their obligations and pledge to make up a pro rata part of any failed member's balances.

CLEARING SYSTEM IN THE UNITED KINGDOM

A payment clearing system has existed in London for some 200 years, and for much of that time was operated through the medium of the Bankers' Clearing House. The Clearing House was for many years owned and controlled by the major retail banks through the Committee of London Clearing Bankers (CLCB). After some discussion and pressure from other banks, in December 1985 a new umbrella body called the Association for Payment Clearing Services (APACS) was established, and three operational clearing companies were set up: Cheque Credit Clearing Company Ltd.—responsible for the bulk paper clearings of checks and credits in England and Wales (the paper clearings in Scotland and Northern Ireland were not included in the new structure); CHAPS and Town Clearing Company Ltd—responsible for the high-value (currently £7,000 and over for CHAPS and £10,000 and over for Town), same-day settlement clearings. CHAPS provides an electronic sterling credit transfer service to its members and is available throughout the United Kingdom. The Town Clearing covers only high-value checks drawn on and paid into member's branches within the designated Town Clearing area of the City of London.

The individual clearing companies are responsible for the day-to-day operation of their clearings and enjoy a high degree of autonomy. All settlements are carried out over accounts maintained at the Bank of England.

In addition to the clearing companies, two other operational groupings have been brought under APACS umbrella to manage certain functions that do not require the same structural approach. These are the Currency Clearings Committee, which operates the London US$ (Retail) Clearing and the London Currency Settlement Scheme; and the Cheque Card Policy Committee, which is responsible for the operation of the domestic cheque guarantee scheme.

For foreign exchange and money market transactions, the relevant systems is CHAPS, which became operational in February 1984. About 200 participants use the system, comprising overseas and domestic banks, of whom 14 Settlement Members communicate directly by means of standard computers and software, known as Gateways, which also provide an interface to each bank's own internal database. There is thus no central installation. Nonsettlement members have access to the CHAPS system through an agreement with one of the Settlement Members and via a terminal operated through that member. Interbank settlement is effected electronically at the end of each day, across the Settlement Member's accounts held at the Bank of England. CHAPS settlement figures are produced shortly after 3 PM each working day.

In 1990, the Bank of England launched a new service to allow settlement of transactions in Sterling money-market bearer securities (Treasury and local authority bills, eligible and ineligible bills, trade bills, bank and building society certificates of deposit, and commercial paper) to be carried out by electronic book-entry transfer. The Central Money Market Office (CMO) operates alongside its sister computerized settlement system in gilt-edged market, the Central Gilt Office (CGO) which the bank has been running since 1986. Until the introduction of this system, the system for transferring Treasury bills and the like was primitive: messengers walked from office to office in the City. The risks were well illustrated when £292 million of treasury bills and certificates of deposit were stolen at knife point from a City messenger in King William Street.

U.K. legislation currently defines money market instruments in terms of pieces of paper or documents, with no provision for the instruments to be issued and traded in purely electronic form. Thus, paper instruments still have to be prepared and brought in for lodgement into CMO. The lodging member guarantees the validity of these paper instruments. Once lodged, they are immobilized in a safe-custody vault at the Bank of England, where provided they are not subsequently sold to a nonparticipant they can remain until maturity.

The system has direct members and indirect members. A direct member has a book-entry account in CMO in its own name. It arranges for a settlement bank to make and receive payments on its behalf for instruments transferred from and to any other direct member. Indirect members conduct settlement through an agent which itself has to be a direct member.

To see how this system works, suppose that the London branch of Salomon Brothers sells some sterling CDs issued by the Royal Bank of Scotland to Nomura Securities. Suppose that Salomon Brothers' agent is Bank of America, and Nomura's is Sumitomo Bank. Salomon Brothers will inform Bank of America. Bank of America will enter the details into their terminal, and the offer of the CDs is transmitted to Sumitomo Bank. Once Sumitomo Bank have accepted the offer, the system will transfer the CDs from Bank of America's to Sumitomo's, and generate the payment instruction for the amount of the sale to the members' payment accounts in CMO. The payment instructions, as shown in the payment accounts, are provided at 16.00 hours each day to the members' respective settlement banks—for example, National Westminster for Bank of America and Midland Bank for Sumitomo Bank. At that time, Midland Bank will pay National Westminster, for account Bank of America, for account Salomon Brothers, the sterling amount required in settlement of the CDs.

A key feature built into the system is that instruments are not allowed to move from one member's account to that of another until both members have authorized the transfer. This ensures that instruments cannot be removed from a member's inventory without his knowledge and approval. The concept of "positive acceptance" ensures that cash and instruments only move between the members. Transfer of instruments to a nonmember has to take place outside the system.

The status of a CMO payment is the same as a banker's payment: an instruction to the buyer's settlement bank to make payment. It is not, however, a guaranteed payment and, in exceptional circumstances, a settlement bank may refuse it.

JAPAN

The Japanese clearing and settlement system is divided into three parts: the bill and check clearing system, the Zengin system (domestic funds transfers) and the Gaitame system (yen transfers arising from foreign exchange and Euro-yen activity).

The bill and check system is a next-day funds system. It provides for the presentation of bills (quite widely used in Japan for payments) and checks on day 1, when they are netted off between the banks, and settlement on day 2. There are 183 officially designated clearing houses and 595 private clearing houses, but the central Tokyo clearing house accounts for 83% of national volume (as of 1988, compared with 66% in 1980).

The Zengin system handles domestic exchange transactions between private financial institutions. It provides same-day settlement between a bank and its customer and next-day settlement between banks. It is an on-line communications network linking financial institutions and the Zengin computer center, which is operated by the Tokyo Banker's Association. Transactions mostly consist of credit transfers, which accounted for 80% by volume and 95% by value. Transactions involving receipts and payments via the Zengin system are calculated in the net balance of each participant and settled by means of transfers across accounts at the Bank of Japan at 1 PM on the next working day. As a result, participants in the system take overnight credit risk on each other; thus the Bank of Japan requires each participant to deposit collateral and requires all participants to assume joint responsibility if the unsettled liabilities of a participant exceed the collateral deposited by a failed bank. A further level of protection was given in March 1987 by the introduction of sender net debit caps.

The Gaitame system for FX and Euro-yen transfers is operated by the Tokyo Bank's Association. It provides same-day settlement between a bank and its customer, and between banks. In March 1989, the system was connected to the Bank of Japan's BOJ-NET, an on-line network linking the Bank of Japan to the major banks participating in the system. Net balances of participating banks are automatically calculated in the Bank of Japan's computer center, and the final settlement conducted according to the results of this calculation. The system includes sender net debit caps.

The BOJ-Net consists of two major parts, namely the funds transfer system and the securities transfer system. The funds transfer system operations began in mid-October 1988, connecting customers financial institutions directly with the computer center at the Bank of Japan through an on-line network. Government bond transfers will also be processed by the BOJ-Net in the future.

Other systems operational in Tokyo include the Tokyo dollar clearing, which provides a local Tokyo clearing system for dollar transactions. Dollar settlements work, in general, as follows. First, settlements are made by transferring funds between the dollar deposit accounts which participants hold with the same Tokyo branch of the U.S. bank, for example Citibank. Second, the net settlement balances in the Tokyo branch are transferred to the New York head office and settled through CHIPS.

An interesting feature of the Japanese system is the concentration on so-called "business settlement days." Japanese business custom tends to concentrate funds transfers on specific days of the month: normally, the 10th, 20th, and last days of the month. Thus CDs and other instruments tend to mature on those dates, as do settlements of government bonds (for example, in April 1987 96% of bond registrations were for value on those three days of the month). The introduction of six days in the month for settlement of government bonds has reduced this effect somewhat, but in April 1988 the ratio of peak activity to the trough in the domestic system was still 8 to 1 (down from 36 to 1 in 1987) compared, for example, with 1.4 to 1 for the U.K. CHAPS system in July 1987. To give an idea of the scale of this problem, an estimate by the Bank of Japan (*Japanese Transfer Systems in the Era of Financial Deregulation and Globalization,* July 1989) for the outstanding level of unsettled trades on an *average* day in Tokyo as JPY183,400,000,000,000,000 (say $1.41 trillion at JPY130 = $1) of which 30% was accounted for by government bond trading and 22% by foreign exchange and Euro-yen trading; so that on peak days in 1987 outstanding system credit exposure was perhaps $40 trillion at its peak and by 1988 was still perhaps $11 trillion.

Another point mentioned by the Bank of Japan in the study referred to was the risk to city banks implied by their inability to forecast which clearing system customers would use: if credits were concentrated in next-day systems but payments away in same-day systems there could be substantial overnight exposure.

FRANCE

There are several levels of settlement systems in France. Sagittaire is a national interbank settlements system designed to complete, in Francs, operations connected with international transfers. The system was set up in 1984, and is managed by the Bank of France, which undertakes the daily clearing of transactions, on completion of which it credits or debits the accounts opened in its books on behalf of the institutions concerned. The system operates from 8 AM to 5.30 PM.

In addition, there is a nationwide network of 104 clearing houses that handle exchanges of paper-based instruments—mainly checks, credit transfers, and commercial bills. There are nine computer clearing centers, operating in Paris, Leon, Strasbourg, Rennes, Nantes, Lille, Marseilles, Bordeaux and Toulouse. The Paris system holds two daily sessions, the first from 8.30 to 10 PM on the preceding settlement day and is called the "anticipated session." The session on settlement day itself, called the "supplementary session," takes places from 11.00 AM to 1.30 PM on the day in question. The "anticipated session" allows non-urgent bulk transactions to be cleared, whereas the "supplementary session" is designed to deal with small quantities of urgent transactions.

Securities clearing is handled via the Saturne and Relit systems. Saturne was launched in September 1988 and mainly handles treasury bills. (Saturne is Systeme Automatise de Traitement Unifie des Reglement de Creances Negociables.) The Saturne computer handles trade matching and effects settlement at the next appropriate clearing session. Clearing takes place four times a day—at 09.30, 11.30, 14.30, and 16.30. The system automatically registers the new ownership details, credit the seller's current account with a price, and debit the buyer's. In due course, the system is expected to handle operations in CDs and commercial paper. The Relit project aims to guarantee the secure execution of stock exchange transactions, carrying out settlement and delivery of securities five days from the date of the trade. The system will match trades between parties and effect clearing of completed transactions before the balances are entered in the books of SICOVAM, the securities depository, and the Bank of France.

GERMANY

Germany has a decentralized system of clearing: banks in the approximately 200 locations in which the Bundesbank has a branch are able to exchange checks, direct debits and other claims as well a credit transfers with one another in the daily local clearing procedure. Money market and foreign exchange dealing transfers are typically handled through the Bundesbank's Frankfurt branch, which accounts for 95% of the overall total cleared. At the close of settlement (2 PM) each Bundesbank branch determines the clearing balance for each bank participating in its clearing, and debits or credits its central bank account with a clearing balance. Until all debit balances have been recovered, the participants in clearing are merely custodians of the clearing instruments delivered to them, and may not finally dispose of the funds received.

The Bundesbank is introducing an electronic clearing system modeled along the lines of CHIPS as an alternative to the conventional paper-based clearing hitherto in operation. It will extend the existing telecommunications links between the Bundesbank's 11 regional clearing centers by allowing all the banks in a Land (province) to connect directly to their regional Bundesbank computing center.

CANADA AND AUSTRALIA

The Canadian Payments Association came into being in December 1980 with the objective of establishing and operating a national clearing and settlement system. The CPA runs its Automated Clearing Settlement System which began in 1984. Membership of the system consists of two levels: Direct Clearers and other members. Direct Clearers represent themselves directly in the clearing and settlement process and act as clearing agents for other deposit-taking institutions. The settlement process begins at approximately 08.30 AM Ottawa time when certain regular transactions affecting Direct Clearers are carried out via the ACSS. These include government payments to and from the Direct Clearers. At 09.30 AM, the preliminary net clearing gain or loss of each Direct Clearer is available to the institution from the ACSS. Until 11.00 AM, bilateral adjustments take place to handle corrections. Shortly after 11.00 AM, the final net gains and losses are available from the ACSS. At 1.30 PM, Ottawa time the Bank of Canada obtains each Direct Clearer's "national standing" and adjusts the balances of the Direct Clearers on its own books. At approximately 4.00 PM, Ottawa time, following any final adjustments and any necessary central bank advances, the bank establishes the closing balances of each Direct Clearer as at the end of the previous day. Final settlement, therefore, takes place retroactively.

The Canadian Depository for Securities was federally incorporated in 1970. It provides services for the clearing and settlement of securities transactions. Principally, these involve equity share transactions. Recently, however, money-market instruments have been included, such as treasury bills, banker's acceptances, bearer deposit notes, commercial paper, provincial and municipal notes, term deposits, and guaranteed investments certificates.

Clearing in Australia is managed by the Clearing House Committee, which consists of representatives of the major trading banks. Funds which have been cleared at the clearing house become eligible for the banks' exchange settlement accounts with the Reserve Bank. By 09.30 AM, the Reserve Bank relays details of banks' exchange-settlement balances to market participants. It also advises the market of its expected activities in open-market bond operations.

Increasingly, money-market clearing is being handled through Austraclear. Austraclear was founded in 1984 to handle trading in money-market securities. It handles bills of exchange, certificates of deposit and promissory notes, public sector bonds, and coupon-bearing corporate bonds and notes. In addition, it handles forward interest rate transactions and in 1988 introduced cash transfer facilities.

ECU CLEARING

The ECU is a special case amongst clearing systems. Alone amongst all currencies, there is no central bank that operates as lender of last resort. This has some fairly critical implications at the operational level. To understand this, we need to understand how the system has developed. In 1982, two banks—Kredietbank in Brussels and Lloyds Bank in London—agreed to open the first Mutual ECU Settlement Accounts (MESA) for the sole purpose of settling daily imbalances which arose from ECU transactions.

Later the MESA banks grow to four, with Credit Lyonnais in Paris and Kredietbank in Luxembourg, followed shortly in 1983 by Generale Brussels. It was agreed that each MESA bank would act in rotation as MESA Settlement Bank (MSB) of the month. This would enable other MESA banks to settle their bilateral clearing imbalances via memorandum accounts with each month's MSB.

The ECU market continued to grow rapidly during 1984, and it became obvious that the existing system was not going to be able to cope. It was agreed that the MESA system should be replaced by a true clearing system, and the Bank for International Settlements was approached and asked if it would fulfill the function of settlement bank for the ECU to replace the MSB. It was agreed that the SWIFT system would be used for handling payments. An ECU Banking Association (EBA) was set up in September 1986, based in Paris. The EBA drew up the rules for the clearing system, which is operated by the BIS under a Clearing Agreement under Swiss law. From May 1987 the clearing system was opened to new member banks of the EBA, which by March 1989 totalled 33, compared with 7 at the outset in 1986.

The ECU clearing system carries two sets of risks: First daylight exposure. A bank could be in a position of having paid out a lot of payments before receiving the corresponding credits. If settlement were aborted due to non-performance by a clearer or clearers, the recipient bank could face heavy losses. Second, much more importantly, after 1 PM Brussels time when the Netting Center notifies clearing members of their positions, the transactions to reduce each clearing account to zero can be effected only with members of the clearing system who have opposite positions. Member banks, therefore, have at present potentially no control over their possible counter parties—a situation which in a crisis could be risky. The absence of lender of last resort forces the other members of the clearing system to fulfill that function.

SWIFT

In 1973, the Society for Worldwide Interbank Financial Telecommmunications (SWIFT) was founded. It first went live on a limited basis in Europe in 1977 and was then extended to North America and the Far East and in 1984 to the Middle East. It is a computerized message switch whose major advantage is that it has a strict format requirement for messages. This allows banks to interconnect it to other computer systems such as CHIPS or Fedwire.

SWIFT's major problem has been success. In 1977, it handled 400,000 messages a month; by 1986, it handled that volume in half a day. It began work in 1982 on SWIFT II, an ambitious project to create more flexibility; but by 1989 the project was seriously delayed and having serious problems. Another problem is that many potential users—such as the securities industry—are currently excluded by the banks, who wish to keep the operating benefit of the network to themselves. As electronic document interchange (EDI) develops worldwide, interfacing SWIFT to customer systems will become an increasingly important issue.

For Further Reading

Part 1. Markets

de Grauw E. and T. Peeters (Eds), *The ECU and European Monetary Integration*, Macmillan, London, 1989.

Dunis, M. and C. Feeny, *Exchange Rate Forecasting*, Woodhead-Faulkner, Cambridge/Simon & Schuster, New York, 1990.

Funabashi, Y., *Managing the Dollar: From the Plaza to the Louvre*, 2nd ed., Institute for International Economics, Washington, DC, 1989.

Japan Securities Research Institute, *Securities Markets in Japan 1990*, Annual publication.

Kaufman, Perry, *The New Commodity Trading Systems & Methods*, John Wiley & Sons, New York, 1987.

Shone, R., "Some Technical Aspects of the European Monetary System," *University of Stirling Discussion Paper No. 73*, July, 1979.

Stigum, M., *The Money Market*, 3rd ed., Dow-Jones Irwin, Homewood, IL, 1990.

"Special Issue on the ECU," *European Affairs*, Elsevier, New York, March, 1988.

"The Exchange Rate Mechanism of the European Monetary System," *Bank of England Quarterly Bulletin*, November, 1990.

"The Exchange Rate Mechanism of the European Monetary System: A review of the literature," *Bank of England Quarterly Bulletin*, February, 1991.

Part 2. Money Market Calculations

Fabozzi, F. J. and I. M. Pollack (Eds), *The Handbook of Fixed Income Securities*, 3rd ed., Business One Irwin, Homewood, IL, 1990.

Fage, P., *Yield Calculations*, CSFB, London, 1986.

Stigum, M., *Money Market Calculations*, Dow-Jones Irwin, Homewood, IL, 1981.

Part 3. Foreign Exchange Calculations

Antony, Steven, *Foreign Exchange in Practice,* IFR Publishing Ltd., London, 1990.

DeRosa, D. F., *Managing Foreign Exchange Risk,* McGraw-Hill, New York, 1991.

Part 4. Derivatives

Bookstaber, R. M., *Option Pricing and Strategies in Investing,* Addison-Wesley, Reading, MA, 1982.

Cavalla, N., *The GNI Handbook of Traded Options,* Macmillan, London, 1989.

Cox, J. & M. Rubinstein, *Options Markets,* Englewood Cliffs, NJ, Prentice Hall, 1990.

Fitzgerald, M.D., *Financial Options,* Euromoney Publications, London, 1987.

Rothstein, N. H. and J. M. Little, *The Handbook of Financial Futures,* McGraw-Hill, New York, 1984.

Schwartz, R. and C. W. Smith (Eds), *Handbook of Currency and Interest Rate Risk Management,* New York Institute of Finance, New York, 1990.

Sutton, William, *The Currency Options Handbook,* Woodhead-Faulkner, Cambridge/Simon & Schuster, New York, 1990.

Walmsley, Julian, *New Financial Instruments,* John Wiley & Sons, New York, 1988.

Part 5. Risk Issues

British Bankers' Association, *The EC Banking Directives of 1989: A Compendium,* London, June, 1990.

Dermine, J., "The BIS Proposal for the Measurement of Interest Rate Risk: Some Pitfalls," *The Journal of International Securities Markets,* Spring, 1991.

Haskins, Deloitte and Sells., *The Securities Association's Capital Adequacy Requirements,* London, 1988.

The Bank for International Settlements, *Payment Systems in Eleven Developed Countries,* Basle, Switzerland, April, 1989.

The Group of Thirty. *Clearance and Settlement Systems in the World's Financial Markets,* New York, March, 1989.

Some other books that may be of general interest:

Walmsley, Julian, *A Dictionary of International Finance*, Macmillan/John Wiley & Sons, New York, 1986.

Walmsley, Julian, *Global Investing*, Macmillan, London, 1991.

Appendixes

Appendix A   EMS and Currency Baskets

The parity grid (see Chapter 4) is simple in bilateral terms. If currency A is at its limit against B, the two central banks must intervene. But the presence of other currencies in the grid means that the apparent 2.25% fluctuation margins are actually less than they seem. Suppose we have three currencies in our system. They declare the following central rates against the ECU.

$$ECU\ 1 = DEM\ 2.5 = FRF\ 6 = BEF\ 40$$

This implies the following parity grid:

	BEF	DEM	FRF
		15.6440	6.5184
BEF	1	16	6.6667
		16.3640	6.8184
	0.06111		0.4074
DEM	0.0625	1	0.41667
	0.06392		0.4261
	0.1467	2.3466	
FRF	0.15	2.4	1
	0.1534	2.4546	

Note that the upper and lower limits calculated here are not exactly 2¼% above or below the parity. The factors are +2.2753% and −2.2247% or, to put it another way, the central parity is multiplied not by 1.0225 and 0.9775 but by 1.022753 and 0.977753, The latter number is the reciprocal of the first, and 0.045 less (that is, the total difference is twice 2¼%, as it would be if 1.0225 and 0.9775 were used). Hence, the DEM/BEF lower limit of 16.3640 multiplied by the BEF/DEM upper limit of 0.06111 produces 1, just as the central rates do when multiplied.

Given this grid, the only way that the deutsche mark can move its full theoretical 4½% range from the bottom of the EMS to the top is if both other currencies were exactly at their central rate, that is, FRF/ BEF 6.6667. In that case, the DEM/BEF rate can move freely between 15.6440 and 16.3640. But suppose the French franc is at its lower limit against the Belgian franc, that is,

FRF/BEF 6.5184. Then the DEM/BEF range is cut in half since long before the deutsche mark has got to its upper limit against the Belgian franc it has reached its upper limit against the French franc. To be exact, the DEM/BEF range is 4½% less the spread between the French franc and Belgian franc; if that spread is at its limit of 2¼%, then the most that DEM/BEF can move is 2¼%.

As a practical point, we should add that if the deutsche mark rose to its upper limit against the French franc, intervention would probably start to pull the French franc up with the deutsche mark, so that it could move more against the Belgian franc. But this applies less is the case of thinly traded currencies. For example, if instead of the deutsche mark, the Danish krona was moving, the volume of DKK/FRF business would be smaller and less likely to pull the French franc up against the Belgian franc.

Another factor which could give greater freedom to "heavy" or important currencies such as the deutsche mark compared with the Danish krona is the technical construction of the ECU. A currency that is pegged against a basket containing the currency has more freedom than if the basket does not contain the currency. To see why, let's look first at a currency that is pegged against a basket not containing itself, let's call it the Home. The Home is pegged against the SDR, say, at SDR 1 = HOME 4. The SDR consists of US$0.54 + DEM0.46 + £STG0.071 + FRF0.74 + Y34. Suppose we have US$/DEM = 2.30, £STG/US$ = 1.80, US$/FRF = 6.0, US$/Y = 220. Then SDR 1 = US$ 1.1456 (see Chapter 13) and the HOME rate will be US$1 = HOME 3.4916. Now suppose that the deutsche mark strengthens by 10% to US$/DEM = 2.07. If all other rates are unchanged, SDR 1 = US$1.1679 and US$ 1 = HOME 3.4249. In other words, the deutsche mark's strength against the U.S. dollar pulls up the SDR against the U.S. dollar. This in turn pulls up the HOME against the dollar. The percentage change in the HOME against the dollar is the same as the change in the SDR, that is, 2% (which is the 10% deutsche mark change weighted by the share of the deutsche mark in the SDR, which is about 20%).

Now let's look at what happens when a currency is pegged against a basket that includes itself. In this case, if the currency moved 10% as before, and the currency's weight were 20% as before, its movement against the basket would be *less than* 10%, because it would pull the basket up with it. Let's look at the deutsche mark in the EMS. Currently, the ECU/DEM parity is ECU 1 = DEM 2.05586. The ECU is defined as DEM0.6242 + GBP0.08784 + FRF1.332 + ITL151.80 + NLG0.2198 + BEF3.301 + LFR0.13 + DKK0.1976 + IEP0.00855 + GRD1.44 + ESP6.885 + PTE1.393. Suppose we have the following rates against the U.S. dollar: US$/DEM = 1.4925, £ = 1.9465, FRF = 5.0700, ITL = 1124.00, NLG = 1.6820, BEF = 30.80, LFR = 30.80, DKK = 5.7500, IEP = 1.7870, GRD = 301.95, ESP = 94.85, PTE = 133.40. These rates give us ECU 1 = US$1.3665 which implies ECU1 = DEM2.0395. Suppose as before the DEM strengthens by 10% against the US$ to 1.3433. This pulls up the ECU to ECU 1 = US$1.4130 which implies ECU1 = DEM1.8980 a swing of 7% instead of 10%.

This technical factor is relevant to the divergence indicator. The divergençe indicator is the movement of a currency from its ECU central rate. The EMS allows a $2^1/4$% movement; within this, there is a "threshold of divergence" at 75% of the permitted movement. As we have seen, a rise in the deutsche mark of 10% against the U.S. dollar would be a rise of only $6^1/2$% against the ECU. For the rising value of its deutsche mark component is pulling the ECU up against the U.S. dollar. But if we assume the same initial rates, and look at a 10% rise of the Danish krona, to DKK 5.175 per US$, we find that the ECU rises only to $1.4373 from $1.3849, instead of rising to $1.4335 as it did when the deutsche mark rose 10%. The reason is that the DKK's weight in the ECU is less: only about 3% compared with more than 30% for the deutsche mark. It follows that a $2^1/4$% move of the deutsche mark against the ECU will allow the deutsche mark to move further against the dollar than would be allowed for the Danish krona, because the deutsche mark would pull the ECU further up than the Danish krona would. To compensate for this, the EC calculates an "adjusted divergence" indicator, which is given by ADI = DI $\times$ (1 – w) where ADI = adjusted divergence indicator, DI = divergence indicator, and w is the official weight for the currency. In the case of the deutsche mark, $w = 0.301$ (that is, 30.1%), whereas for the Danish krona $w = 0.0245$. Hence for the deutsche mark ADI = 0.689 x DI whereas for the Danish krona, ADI = 0.975 $\times$ DI.

There is still one more calculation to be made before we have the finally adjusted divergence indicator. This is to take account of currencies (like sterling and the peseta) which have a wider band than $2^1/4$%, and of currencies (like the drachma) that have no band at all. The problem is that if, say, sterling rises by 6% against the U.S. dollar, pulling the ECU up with it, other currencies would be forced to move up against the dollar to keep their divergence indicator within the threshold. The EC solution is to pretend that sterling, the peseta, and the drachma stay within a $2^1/4$% band. That is, the divergence indicator is adjusted to strip out the effects of movements in sterling, the peseta, and the drachma that exceed $2^1/4$%.

To do this, we start by finding the weakest currency in the EMS. Then we see if it has moved more than $2^1/4$% against sterling. If it has, we calculate an adjustment. This is the percentage change in the currency against sterling from the base date, less $2^1/4$%, multiplied by sterling's weight in the ECU. A parallel factor is calculated for the peseta and the drachma. The three factors are added together to produce a combined adjustment. This is then deducted from the divergence to get the fully adjusted divergence indicator. The results of these calculations are published daily in the *Financial Times* of London and elsewhere. Continuous updates are shown on Reuters Monitor page EMSA. A sample (from the *Financial Times*) is shown in Table A.1.

A final technicality arises in the calculation of new central rates. In the snake, parities were declared against the European Monetary Unit of Account. This was fixed in terms of gold. Its value did not change as exchange rates changed. So if it was agreed to revalue the deutsche mark by 10%. all that was needed was to change the DEM/EMUA rate by 10%. But a deutsche mark revaluation against the ECU pulls up the ECU. Suppose the deutsche mark revalues 10%; it will pull the ECU up by about 3% (as its weight is about 30% of the ECU). So the net deutsche mark movement against the ECU is only 7%, and the deutsche mark and all other currencies will be below their ECU parities, so all EMS currencies would look weak at once. To prevent this, the deutsche mark revaluation has to be combined with devaluations by other countries. A 10% deutsche mark revaluation needs to be achieved by combining a 3% devaluation of all other currencies with a 7% deutsche mark revaluation.

A technical point arises in ECU trading when there is a change in the composition of the unit. (If current discussions on "hardening" the ECU eliminate changes in the ECU this point will no longer matter.) Changes in weight—either because of the entry of new currencies in the system, or because of changes in the relative economic importance of different countries—will change the interest rate payable on the ECU. (They will not change the external value of the ECU on the day of the change, because the recomposition of the ECU is constructed so as to have no net exchange rate effect.)

Table A.1. EMS European Currency Unit Rates

	XEU Central Rates	Currency Amounts against XEU Feb. 13	% Change from Central Rate	% Spread vs. Weakest Currency	Divergence Indicator
Spanish peseta	133.631	128.294	−3.99	5.41	70
Belgian franc	42.4032	42.1267	−0.65	1.87	38
Deutsche mark	2.05586	2.04647	−0.46	1.67	37
Dutch guilder	2.31643	2.30603	−0.45	1.66	28
Italian lira	1538.24	1540.12	0.12	1.08	0
Irish punt	0.767417	0.768956	0.20	1.00	−3
Danish krone	7.84195	7.87615	0.44	0.76	−14
French franc	6.89509	6.97512	1.16	0.04	−57
Sterling	0.696904	0.705285	1.20	0.00	−24

ECU central rates set by the European Commission. Currencies are in descending relative strength. Percentage changes are for ECU; a positive change denotes a weak currency. Divergence shows the ratio between two spread: the percentage difference between the actual market and ECU central rates for a currency, and the maximum permitted percentage deviation of the currency's market rate from its ECU central rate. Adjustment calculated by Financial Times.

Source: Financial Times. 14th February 1991.

As an example, on June 19, 1989, the EC announced that the Spanish peseta and Portuguese escudo would become part of the basket, with effect from September 20, 1989. As just mentioned, those dealing forward ECU for the value date of the change were unaffected because the exchange value of the ECU did not alter. But holders of bonds and ECU deposits were affected because the weighted average ECU rate would reflect the inclusions of two relatively weak, high-interest-rate currencies. The theoretical impact was of the order of 50 basis points; on the day of the announcement, however, the impact was only 4 to 5 basis points because yields were already priced to reflect much of the expected revision. The market started pricing the change in from February.

For those who prefer symbols, the following is a brief summary of the above. We define $W(i)$ as the fixed currency amounts in the ECU; for instance, if the deutsche mark is currency number one, we have $W(1) = 0.6242$. We define $A(i)$ as the current central rates of each currency against the ECU (e.g., $A(1) = 2.05586$ for the deutsche mark), $C(i)$ as the present market exchange rate against the U.S. dollar for each currency. Note that sterling and the Irish pound have to be inverted to make them consistent. We define $G(i)$ as the current percentage weight of each currency in the basket. Then the value of the ECU is give by:

$$ECU = \sum_{i=1}^{12} \frac{W(i)}{C(i)} = E$$

$$\text{Clearly, } G(i) = \frac{W(i)}{A(i)} = \frac{0.6242}{2.05586} = 30.1\% \text{ for the deutsche mark}$$

To calculate the divergence indicator $D(i)$ we first find the current exchange rate for each currency against the ECU, $E \times C(i)$. Then we define:

$$D(i) = 100 - \frac{100 \times E \times C(i)}{A(i)}$$

To allow for the effects of sterling, the peseta, and the escudo we find the weakest currency. K, and calculate (assume sterling is currency two, the peseta currency three, the escudo currency five, and the drachma currency seven):

$$Q(2) = \left[\left(\frac{C(K)}{C(2)} \times \frac{A(2)}{A(K)} \times 100 \right) - 2.25 - 100 \right] \times G(2)$$

$$Q(3) = \left[\left(\frac{C(K)}{C(3)} \times \frac{A(3)}{A(K)} \times 100 \right) - 2.25 - 100 \right] \times G(3)$$

$$Q(5) = \left[\left(\frac{C(K)}{C(5)} \times \frac{A(5)}{A(K)} \times 100 \right) - 2.25 - 100 \right] \times G(5)$$

$$Q(7) = \left[\left(\frac{C(K)}{C(7)} \times \frac{A(7)}{A(K)} \times 100 \right) - 2.25 - 100 \right] \times G(7)$$

The final adjustment $Q = Q(2) + Q(3) + Q(5) + Q(7)$. We then compare $D(I) + Q$ with the permitted threshold.

Appendix B EC Resolution on ECU Composition

Amending Article 1 of Council Regulation (EEC) n. 3180/78 relating to the value of the unit of account used by the European Monetary Cooperation Fund, as amended by Regulation (EEC) n. 2626/84 of 15 September 1984

EXPLANATORY MEMORANDUM

The commission of the European Communities is submitting to the Council a proposal for a Regulation amending Article 1 of Regulation (EEC) n. 3180/78, amended by Regulation (EEC) n. 2626/84 relating to the composition of the ECU.

In accordance with the provisions of the Resolution of The European Council of 5 December 1978, a five-yearly re-examination of the weights of the currencies in the ECU was carried out at the beginning of June 1989, on the basis of analyses and of a proposal presented by the Commission of the European Communities.

Spain and Portugal had each asked for their currencies to be included in the ECU in accordance with the Joint Declaration annexed to the Treaties of Accession. As a result of the re-examination, and taking account of the evolution of the weights of the currencies composing the ECU, the Commission has decided to present to the Council a proposal for a Regulation revising the weights of the component currencies and incorporating the peseta and the escudo into the ECU.

In proposing the new composition of the ECU, the Commission has taken account of the underlying economic criteria; in proposing the inclusion of the peseta and the escudo, it duly notes that the Spanish and Portuguese authorities have taken the appropriate measures to ensure that this will take place in conditions which ensure the smooth functioning of the market.

Lastly, in view of the present importance of the ECU market, of its potential and of the consequent need to ensure that the market is not disrupted, the Commission proposes that the revision procedure should be carried out in two stages:

— the first stage would consist of a Council Decision relating to the inclusion of the peseta and the escudo, the new weights and the date on which these weights are to be translated into new currency amounts;

— the second stage would consist of the determination by the Commission of the new currency amounts composing the ECU.

The Commission proposes to carry out this calculation on 20 September 1989 on the basis of the exchange rates recorded on the European markets at 14.15 h. The new amounts will take effect on 21 September 1989.

The Commission requests the Council to decide on its proposal at its session on 19 June 1989, having received the favourable opinions of the Monetary Committee and the Board of Governors of the European Monetary Cooperation Fund. It furthermore requests that this decision enter into force immediately.

In the light of the above considerations, the Commission of the European Communities requests the Council to adopt the following Regulation.

PROPOSAL FOR A COUNCIL REGULATION (EEC)

Amending Article 1 of Council Regulation (EEC) n. 3180/78 relating to the value of the unit of account used by the European Monetary Cooperation Fund, as amended by Regulation (EEC) n. 2626/84 of 15 September 1984.

The Council of the European Communities,

Having regard . . .

Whereas . . .

Has adopted this regulation:

Article 1

With effect from 21 September 1989, the composition of the ECU as laid down in Article 1 of Council Regulation (EEC) n. 3180/78 of 18 December 1978 will be determined by:

— firstly, the following weights:

	percentages
German mark	30.1
Pound sterling	13.0
French franc	19.0
Italian lira	10.15
Dutch guilder	9.4
Belgian franc	7.6
Luxembourg franc	0.3

	percentages
Danish krone	2.45
Irish pound	1.1
Greek drachma	0.8
Spanish peseta	5.3
Portuguese escudo	0.8

— secondly, the rates for the ECU derived by the Commission from the rates of the dollar recorded by the central banks of the Member States on their respective exchange market, on Wednesday 20 September 1989 at 14.15.

The Commission shall be responsible for carrying out, on 20 September 1989, the calculations required to determine the new national currency amounts corresponding to the weights set out in the present regulation; it shall ensure that the new composition is communicated to the monetary authorities and published in the Official Journal of the European Communities.

Article 2

This Regulation shall enter into force on 20 June 1989. This regulation shall be binding in its entirety and directly applicable in all Member States.

Done at Brussels, 19 June 1989

For the Council,
The President
C. SOLCHAGA

Appendix C Islamic Value Dates

There are a number of complications in value dates for Islamic currencies. They are caused by the different working week and also by Ramadan. Friday is a holiday in Islam. By contrast, Saturday and Sunday are normal working days. A dealing room in a Moslem country dealing a currency such as the Saudi riyal deals the following dates:

Dealing Date	Spot Value
Monday	Wednesday
Tuesday	Thursday
Wednesday	Dollars Friday/Riyals Saturday
Thursday	Monday
Saturday	Wednesday
Sunday	Wednesday

Wednesday deals have split value dates as no Gulf payments can be made on a Friday. The Thursday value date moves to a Monday to enable people to deal against the dollar without making weekend adjustments. Saturday and Sunday deals move the value date to Wednesday to be in line with the rest of world markets when they open on Monday. For money market deals, people try to avoid having maturities on a Sunday or a Tuesday as spot deals are not usually done for these value dates.

Ramadan is another factor. Ramadan is the traditional month of fasting in Moslem countries. As a general rule, economic activity slows somewhat during this period. The problem for dealers is that the holiday at the end of Ramadan (Eid) is determined by the sighting of the moon at the start of Ramadan. Hence, it is difficult to determine in advance. Also, the official holiday is three days, but some banks may close for up to 10 days. The accepted market practice with deals maturing during a holiday is to extend the deal at the existing rate until the first accepted clearing day after the holiday.

Some general remarks may be of help in understanding the Arab calendar. The Arab calendar is a lunar calendar, rather than the solar or Gregorian calendar used in the West. It starts from July 15 or 16 of 622 AD the year of the Hijra (Mohammed's flight to Medina). It is a 354-day year with 12 months. The odd months have 30 days and the even months 29 days. To keep the calculated lunar calendar in line with the new moon, leap years have to be included. There are 11 leap years in every 30 years: the 2nd, 5th, 7th, 10th, 13th, 16th, 18th, 21st, 24th, 26th and 29th. So, to find out if a particular year is a leap year, one has to divide it by 30, take the remainder and see whether it matches one of these years. For instance, 1982 AD is equivalent to 1403 AH. We divide $1403/30 = 46.76 : 46 \times 30 = 1380$, so the remainder is 23. which is not one of the leap years in the cycle. So, 1403 is not a leap year, although 1404 will be since 24 is line of the cyclical leap years.

To convert a Hijra year (AH) into its AD equivalent, we proceed as follows:

1. Find out how far the Hijra calendar is ahead of our calendar by dividing the Hijra year number by 33, since 33 Hijra years are quivalent to 32 years in our calendar.
2. Subtract the quotient (ignoring the remainder) from the Hijra year number. The answer will give the number of solar years since the Hijra.
3. Add 621 to the answer (since 621 is the number of whole years between the base dates of the two calendars). For example, take the Hijra year 1399. $1399/33 = 42.39$; so in 1399 lunar years the Hijra calendar gained 42 years on ours. We subtract 42 from 1399 to find that 1357 solar years have elapsed from the Hijra. Then we add 621 to find that 1399 A.H. = 1978 AD.

The conversion formulas to get from Hijra years to Gregorian years and vice versa are:

$$G = H - \frac{H}{33} + 621$$

$$H = G - 621 + \frac{G - 621}{32}$$

Bear in mind that 33 Hijra years = 32 Gregorian years. These formulas give the Gregorian year in which the Hijra year begins. If we want the year which it ends, we adjust by 622 rather than 621.

Because the two years do not match, Ramadan is continually starting earlier in the Gregorian year.

There may be slight variations from country to country. In particular, the Iranian calendar is different. And there may be a difference of a day or two between eastern and western Islamic countries as the visible new moon differs from the astronomic new moon calculations based on Mecca. There is an interesting general discussion in V. V. Tsybulsky, *Calendars of Middle East Countries,* U.S.S.R. Academy of Sciences Institute of Oriental Studies, Moscow, 1979.

Appendix D Swift and ISO Currency Codes

An alphabetical list of codes for the representation of currencies and funds based on international standard ISO 4217 follows:

Code	Currency	Country
AED	UAE Dirham	United Arab Emirates
AFA	Afghani	Afghanistan
ALL	Lek	Albania
ANG	Netherlands Antillian Guilder	Netherlands Antilles
AOK	Kwanza Angola	Angola
ARS	Peso Argentina	Argentina
ATS	Schilling	Austria
AUD	Australian Dollar	Australia
		Christmas Island
		Cocos (Keeling) Islands
		Gilbert Islands
		Heard and Mcdonald Islands
		Kiribati
		Nauru
		Norfolk Island
		Tuvalu
AWG	Aruban Guilder	Aruba
BBD	Barbados Dollar	Barbados
BDT	Taka	Bangladesh
BEF	Common Belgian Franc	Belgium
BEC	Convertible Belgian Franc	Luxembourg
BGL	Lev	Bulgaria
BHD	Bahraini dinar	Bahrain
BIF	Burundi Franc	Burundi
BMD	Bermudan Dollar	Bermuda
BND	Brunei Dollar	Brunei
BOB	Boliviano	Bolivia
BRE	Cruzeiro	Brazil
BSD	Bahamian Dollar	Bahamas
BTN	Ngultrum	Bhutan
BUK	Kyat	Burma
BWP	Pula	Botswana
BZD	Belize Dollar	Belize
CAD	Canadian Dollar	Canada
CHF	Swiss Franc	Liechtenstein
		Switzerland
CLF	Unidades de formento	Chile
CLP	Chilean Peso	Chile

Code	Currency	Country
CNY	Yuan Renminbi	China
COP	Colombian Peso	Colombia
CRC	Costa Rican Colon	Costa Rica
CSK	Koruna	Czechoslovakia
CUP	Cuban Peso	Cuba
CVE	Cape Verde Escudo	Cape Verde
CYP	Cyprus Pound	Cyprus
DDM	Mark der DDR	German Democratic Republic
DEM	Deutsche Mark	Germany, Federal Republic of
DJF	Djibouti Franc	Djibouti
DKK	Danish Kroner	Denmark
		Faeroe Islands
		Greenland
DOP	Dominican Peso	Dominican Republic
DZD	Algerian Dinar	Algeria
ECS	Sucre	Ecuador
EGP	Egyptian Pound	Egypt
ESP	Spanish Peseta	Andorra
		Spain
ETB	Ethiopian Birr	Ethiopia
FIM	Markka	Finland
FJD	Fiji Dollar	Fiji
FKP	Falkland Islands Pound	Falkland Islands
FRF	French Franc	Andorra
		France
		French Guiana
		French Southern Territories
		Guadeloupe
		Martinique
		Monaco
		Reunion
		St. Pierre and Miquelon
GBP	Pound Sterling	United Kingdom
GHC	Cedi	Ghana
GIP	Gibraltar Pound	Gibraltar
GMD	Dalasi	Gambia
GNF	Guinea Franc	Guinea
GRD	Drachma	Greece
GTQ	Quetzal	Guatemala
GWP	Guinea-Bissau Peso	Guinea-Bissau
GYD	Guyan Dollar	Guyana
HKD	Hong Kong Dollar	Hong Kong
HNL	Lempira	Honduras
HTG	Gourde	Haiti
HUF	Forint	Hungary
IDR	Rupiah	Indonesia
IEP	Irish Pound	Ireland
ILS	Israeli Shekel	Israel
INR	Indian Rupee	Bhutan
		India
IQD	Iraqi Dinar	Iraq
		Neutral Zone (between Saudi Arabia and Iraq)

Code	Currency	Country
IRR	Iranian Rial	Iran
ISK	Iceland Krona	Iceland
ITL	Lira	Italy
		San Marino
		Vatican City State (Holy See)
JMD	Jamaican Dollar	Jamaica
JOD	Jordanian Dinar	Jordan
JPY	Yen	Japan
KES	Kenyan Shilling	Kenya
KHR	Riel	Kampuchea, Democratic
KMF	Comoros Franc	Comoros
KPW	North Korean Won	Korea, Democratic People's Republic of
KRW	Won	Korea, Republic of
KWD	Kuwaiti Dinar	Kuwait
		Neutral Zone (between Saudi Arabia and Iraq)
KYD	Cayman Islands Dollar	Cayman Islands
LAK	Kip	Lao People's Democratic Republic
LBP	Lebanese Pound	Lebanon
LKR	Sri Lanka Rupee	Sri Lanka
LRD	Liberian Dollar	Liberia
LSL	Lotl	Lesotho
LUF	Luxembourg franc	Luxembourg
LYD	Libyan Dinar	Libyan Arab Jamahiriya
MAD	Moroccan Dirham	Morocco
		Western Sahara
MGF	Malagasy Franc	Madagascar
MMK	Kyat	Myanmar
MNT	Tugrik	Mongolia
MOP	Pataca	Macasi
MRO	Ouguiya	Mauritania
		Western Sahara
MTL	Maltese lira	Malta
MUR	Mauritius Rupee	British Indian Ocean Territory
		Mauritius
MVR	Rufiyaa	Maldives
MWK	Malawi Kwacha	Malawi
MXP	Mexican Peso	Mexico
MYR	Malaysian Ringgit	Malaysia
MZM	Metical	Mozambique
NGN	Naira	Nigeria
NHF	New Hebrides Franc	New Herbrides
NIO	Cordoba oro	Nicaragua
NLG	Netherlands Guilder	Netherlands
NOK	Norwegian Krone	Antarctica
		Bouvet Island
		Dronning Maud Land
		Norway
		Svalbard and Jan Mayen Islands
NPR	Nepalese Rupee	Nepal
NZD	New Zealand Dollar	Cook Islands
		Niue Islands

Code	Currency	Country
		New Zealand
		Pitcairn Islands
		Tokelau
OMR	Rial Omani	Oman
PAB	Balboa	Panama
PEN	Nuevo sol	Peru
PGK	Kina	Papua New Guinea
PHP	Philippine Peso	Philippines
PKR	Pakistan Rupee	Pakistan
PLZ	Zloty	Poland
PTE	Portuguese Escudo	Portugal
PYG	Guarani	Paraguay
QAR	Qatari Rial	Qatar
ROL	Leu	Romania
RWF	Rwanda Franc	Rwanda
SAR	Saudi Riyal	Neutral Zone (between Saudi Arabia and Iraq)
		Saudi Arabia
SBD	Solomon Islands Dollar	Solomon Islands
SCR	Seychelles Rupee	British Indian Ocean Territory
		Seychelles
SDP	Sudanese Pound	Sudan
SEK	Swedish Krona	Sweden
SGD	Singapore Dollar	Singapore
SHP	St. Helena Pound	St. Helena
SLL	Leone	Sierra Leone
SOS	Somali Shilling	Somalia
SRG	Surinam Guilder	Surinam
STD	Dobra	Sao Tome and Principe
SUR	Rouble	Byelorussian SSR
		Ukrainian SSR
		Russia
SVC	El Salvador Colon	El Salvador
SYP	Syrian Pound	Syrian Arab Republic
SZL	Lilangeni	Swaziland
THB	Baht	Thailand
TND	Tunisian Dinar	Tunisia
TOP	Pa'anga	Tonga
TPE	Timor Escudo	East Timor
TRL	Turkish Lira	Turkey
TTD	Trinidad and Tobago Dollar	Trinidad and Tobago
TWD	New Taiwan Dollar	Taiwan, Province of
TZS	Tanzanian Shilling	Tanzania, United Republic of
UGX	Uganda Shilling	Uganda
USD	US Dollar Common	
USN	US Dollar next day funds	United States
USD	US Dollar	American Samoa
		British Virgin Islands
		British Indian Ocean Territory
		Guam
		Haiti
		Johnston Island

Code	Currency	Country
		Midway Islands
		Pacific Islands (Trust Territory)
		Panama
		Panama Canal Zone
		Puerto Rico
		Turks and Caicos Islands
		United States Miscellaneous Pacific Islands
		United States Virgin Islands
		Wake Island
UYP	Uruguayan Peso	Uruguay
VEB	Bolivar	Venezuela
VND	Dong	Viet Nam
VUV	Vatu	Vanuatu
WST	Tala	Samoa
XAF	CFA Franc	Cameroon
		Central African Republic
		Chad
		Congo
		Equatorial Guinea
		Gabon
XCD	East Caribbean Dollar	Anguilla
		Antigua and Barbuda
		Dominica
		Grenada
		Montserrat
		St. Kitts-Nevis
		St. Lucia
		St. Vincent and the Grenadines
XEU	European Currency Unit (ECU)	
XOF	CFA Franc	Benin
		Ivory Coast
		Niger
		Senegal
		Togo
		Upper Volta
XPF	CFP Franc	French Polynesia
		New Caledonia
		Walls and Futuna Islands
YER	Yemeni rial	Yemen, Republic of
YUN	Yugoslavian dinar	Yugoslavia
ZAR	Rand	Lesotho
		Namibia
		South Africa
ZMK	Zambian Kwacha	Zambia
ZRZ	Zaire	Zaire
ZWD	Zimbabwe Dollar	Zimbabwe

Appendix E Margin Calculations

The calculation of margin requirements falls into three categories: (1) futures margin; (2) conventional options margins; (3) delta or futures-style option margins. A brief explanation of each category follows.

FUTURES MARGIN CALCULATIONS

Futures margin calculations vary in their details from exchange to exchange and from time to time. Exchanges normally reserve the right to increase margins at times of great market volatility, for example. Margin is of two types: *initial* margin and *variation* margin. Initial margin is put up on the day of the trade. It is usually about 2 to 5% of the total underlying value of the trade. In the following days, the value of the position will vary. As it deteriorates, the trader must put up more margin to keep the amount of margin at some predetermined level, usually about 75% of initial margin. As the position improves and there is excess margin, the margin will be repaid to him in variable amounts called variation margin.

Examples

Suppose I buy a Eurodollar future on the IMM in Chicago. The face amount is $1,000,000 and the initial margin is 2%: I will have to deposit $2000 with my futures broker (who will deposit an equivalent amount with the Exchange). The broker may require customers to deposit more than the Exchange's minimum requirement, but never less. The margin can be deposited in cash or, by prior agreement with the broker, in acceptable securities such as Treasury bonds. I will earn interest on the securities; if I deposit cash, I may be paid interest by the broker, depending on the size of the trade and my arrangements with them.

Suppose I buy the future at 92.75. The implied rate of interest is 7.25%. Next day, interest rates rise by 10 basis points, so that the future is now worth 92.65. I have lost 10 "ticks" on my position. For the Eurodollar contract, each tick is worth $25 ($1,000,000 \times 90/360 \times .01/100$), so I have lost $250. This amount is deducted from my initial margin, so I now have $1750 with the broker. Let us suppose that the variation margin is called at the 80% level: that is, when my margin has fallen from $2000 to $1600. In that case, because my margin remains at $1750, no variation margin is required.

The next day, interest rates rise another 10 basis points, to 7.45%. The futures price is 92.55. I have lost another $250. Now the margin I have at the brokers is reduced to $1500 which is below the threshold at which variation margin is called. The broker telephones me to say that I must put an additional $100 in margin by tomorrow morning. I must either increase the margin or close the position. Suppose I put in the extra $100 to stay in the market.

The next day interest rates drop sharply by 25 basis points. The future is now worth 92.80 and I have a profit: my margin at the brokers increases by the amount of the overnight change of $625 (25 × $25): I now have $1600 + $625 = $2225 on deposit and I could call for the excess margin to be repaid to me. In practice, provided one can negotiate a reasonable rate of interest with the broker, it is often the custom to leave some of the excess with the broker rather than incur the cost of daily movements of small amounts of money.

CONVENTIONAL OPTIONS MARGIN

Conventional options margin follows a pattern similar to futures: an initial margin and a variation margin. There is no margin requirement for the buyer of an option, because once the premium is paid, the buyer has no further risk and thus should not be expected to put up any margin. The size of the margin to be put up by the writer or seller of the option depends on the Exchange. The Chicago Board Options Exchange, for example, requires that for an option written on an equity position, initial margin is 100% of the premium plus 20% of the underlying security value, less any amount by which the option is out of the money. The minimum required by the exchange is the option premium plus 10% of the underlying value.

Example

Suppose I have written an option on a stock at $100, for which I earn a premium of $8.50. The stock today is trading at $95. I have to put up the premium—$8.50—plus $19 (20% of $95) less $5 (amount the option is out of the money) for a net total of $22.50. The minimum in this case is $8.50 + $9.50 = $18, so the required amount is above the minimum. Had the stock been trading at $75, the calculation would have been $8.50 + 20% × $75 − $25 = −$1.50 and the minimum would have come into play: $8.50 + $7.50 = $16.

THE CME SPAN SYSTEM

Delta margining was introduced by LIFFE in 1985 and was followed by the Chicago Mercantile Exchange with its SPAN system in 1989. In 1991, LIFFE introduced its own version of the SPAN system. Since the SPAN system is now so widely used we will confine ourselves to it.

In essence, the CME SPAN system seeks to call margin against the largest loss that a combined portfolio might reasonably suffer. For example, the CME Margin Subcommittee may set the SPAN parameters to cover the largest loss that might occur 95% of the time.

The method by which this is done is that the SPAN system scans futures price changes and volatility changes to find the resulting portfolio gains or losses. It starts at the current futures settlement price and scans up and down three intervals of turues price moves. At each futures price, SPAN also scans up and down a range from the current futures volatility. The ranges are determined by the Margin Subcommittee in the light of market conditions.

Deep out-of-the-money short options pose a special problem. As they come close to expiring, they may not face risk from normal futures price moves. But unusually large moves might cause them to move into the money and then to suffer large losses. To cover this possibility, SPAN also scans up and down twice the normal futures range. Since these unusually large price moves are so rare, SPAN then covers only a fraction of the resulting losses.

In all, SPAN scans 16 different scenarios of futures price changes and volatility changes. As it does so, it calculates the dollar gains and losses from each scenario, which are stored in a Risk Array. The CME transmits these Risk Arrays to member firms so that they can apply them to customers' positions. SPAN then selects the largest portfolio loss for these 16 combinations. This largest reasonable loss is the Scanning Risk Charge, or margin requirement, for each contract.

As an example, one might have the following option risk array for a call DEM option at a strike of $0.60:

Scenario	Profit/Loss	Scenario
1	-$50	Futures unchanged, volatility up
2	$110	Futures unchanged, volatility down
3	-$420	Futures up 1/3 range, volatility up
4	-$250	Futures up 1/3 range, volatility down
5	$260	Futures down 1/3 range, volatility up
6	$420	Futures down 1/3 range, volatility down
7	-$830	Futures up 2/3 range, volatility up
8	-$680	Futures up 2/3 range, volatility down
9	$520	Futures down 2/3 range, volatility up
10	$670	Futures down 2/3 range, volatility down
11	-$1290	Futures up 3/3 range, volatility up
12	-$1150	Futures up 3/3 range, volatility down
13	$730	Futures down 3/3 range, volatility up
14	$860	Futures down 3/3 range, volatility down
15	-$720	Futures up extreme (Cover 35% of loss)
16	$290	Futures down extreme (Cover 35% of loss)

The range might be set at $2000 and the volatility move at 1%. These numbers are for illustration only. The Margin Subcommittee sets the parameter values that fix the actual margin numbers. As an example of the application of the system, suppose we are long one DEM call at a strike of $0.60. The futures scan range is set at the futures maintenance margin level of $2000 per contract. Volatility is 15% and we use a volatility scan range of 1%. Then we have:

Futures settle at:	57	58	59	60	61	62	63
SPAN margin($)	0	10	120	520	1230	1800	1980
Premium		1	13	118	525	1372	2513	3747

As the Premium line shows, the SPAN system allows the option buyer to get into the position for substantially less cash outlay than would be needed if the premium were paid up front.

For ease of processing, the SPAN system uses a single composite delta for each risk array. This composite delta is a weighted average of deltas from across the futures scanning range. The deltas corresponding to likely price moves get more weight in the average; deltas corresponding to unlikely moves get less weight. The SPAN system adds an intermonth spread charge to portfolios holding contracts in different months.

Index

Index of Formulas